Programming Firefox

Other resources from O'Reilly

Related titles

- Ajax Design Patterns
- Ajax Hacks™
- Creating Applications with Mozilla
- CSS: The Definitive Guide
- Greasemonkey Hacks™
- JavaScript: The Definitive Guide
- Learning JavaScript
- Practical RDF
- XML Hacks™
- XML in a Nutshell

oreilly.com

oreilly.com is more than a complete catalog of O'Reilly books. You'll also find links to news, events, articles, weblogs, sample chapters, and code examples.

oreillynet.com is the essential portal for developers interested in open and emerging technologies, including new platforms, programming languages, and operating systems.

Conferences

O'Reilly brings diverse innovators together to nurture the ideas that spark revolutionary industries. We specialize in documenting the latest tools and systems, translating the innovator's knowledge into useful skills for those in the trenches. Visit *conferences.oreilly.com* for our upcoming events.

Safari Bookshelf (*safari.oreilly.com*) is the premier online reference library for programmers and IT professionals. Conduct searches across more than 1,000 books. Subscribers can zero in on answers to time-critical questions in a matter of seconds. Read the books on your Bookshelf from cover to cover or simply flip to the page you need. Try it today for free.

Programming Firefox

Kenneth C. Feldt

O'REILLY®

Beijing • Cambridge • Farnham • Köln • Paris • Sebastopol • Taipei • Tokyo

Programming Firefox
by Kenneth C. Feldt

Printed in the United States of America.

Published by O'Reilly Media, Inc., 1005 Gravenstein Highway North, Sebastopol, CA 95472.

O'Reilly books may be purchased for educational, business, or sales promotional use. Online editions are also available for most titles (*safari.oreilly.com*). For more information, contact our corporate/institutional sales department: (800) 998-9938 or *corporate@oreilly.com*.

Editor: Simon St.Laurent
Production Editor: Rachel Monaghan
Copyeditor: Audrey Doyle
Proofreader: Rachel Monaghan
Indexer: Reg Aubry
Cover Designer: Karen Montgomery
Interior Designer: David Futato
Illustrators: Robert Romano and Jessamyn Read

Printing History:

April 2007: First Edition.

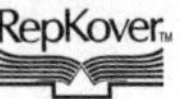

This book uses RepKover™, a durable and flexible lay-flat binding.

ISBN-10: 0-596-10243-7
ISBN-13: 978-0-596-10243-2
[M]

Table of Contents

Preface

A technology is only a tool.

No matter how creative its design, innovative its approach, or impressive its performance, a technology is still defined (according to Webster) as "a manner of accomplishing a task."

The successful adoption of a technology into the community of those who rely on it to conduct business is a complicated journey—one that starts with the unyielding work of designers who see something that others don't. But without the efforts of those who believe in its value and are willing to promote (evangelize), to educate, and to adapt the tool to the needs of the community, the technology remains little more than a subject of academic interest.

The Mozilla component framework, and its implementation in a form more commonly known as the Firefox browser, represents one technology that aspires to be a useful tool for the community that relies on the Internet to communicate, learn, and express (we often coldly refer to these people as "users").

The evangelists of the Mozilla framework promote its technology as a premier contribution of the open source community, a team of developers whose mission is to develop the best possible software for browsing the Internet (Firefox) and exchanging messages (Thunderbird). This community is also strongly committed to demonstrating how applying the most current standards in electronic document rendition and data exchange can make possible new techniques that improve the richness of expression and the ability to move those rich ideas throughout the community.

But to evangelize is not enough. I hope this text will play a modest role in helping to educate application developers in how to use Mozilla technology—not for the sake of using a different technical platform, but to demonstrate what is possible when the collective knowledge of the international standards community finds its voice in the marketplace. With such a diverse and creative pool of contributors, new Internet applications are possible that feature improvements in responsiveness, greater flexibility of interface design, and more expressive graphics.

The goal of this book has little to do with searching for a victor in the browser wars. Rather, this book is intended to discuss, through example, the application of international standards in helping to launch the "next generation" of Internet applications. The Mozilla technology is one of the best technologies, and one of the best tools available, to make such a discussion possible.

Intended Audience

This book is intended for designers and developers charged with delivering innovative standards-based Internet applications. This includes those responsible for server applications or for the development of Internet-enabled desktop applications.

This book is designed to cover many of the practical issues related to the nuances of XML User Interface (XUL)-based design. Rather than trying to be the authoritative resource on browser internals, it focuses on the nuts and bolts of using the existing tools to take advantage of the Firefox framework.

The development setting for this audience may involve any number of tools—the Personal Hypertext Processor (PHP) or Java on the server side, and the Firefox browser engine on the client side. The dominant language for the client platform is most likely to be JavaScript, and developers should have a good understanding of HTML and, hopefully, some exposure to eXtensible Markup Language (XML)-based documents such as XHTML.

Members of the target audience could be developers of commercial applications, extensions to the Firefox browser, or corporate applications. Some knowledge of JavaScript will be very helpful, although most developers can pick up the language quickly enough to learn it on the fly.

Most importantly, this book is targeted to those developers who are interested in (and maybe committed to) using this technology to see what the next generation of Internet applications will look like.

Why Buy This Book?

There is no doubt that online documentation, Wikis, and newsgroups provide the lion's share of information to developers using technologies such as XUL (pronounced "zool"). A precious element of constant availability characterizes the web-centric support community—you need not carry around a 500-page book to guarantee access to important information.

But web access to online documentation can go only so far. Online documents are best designed for quick searches and linked references that point to pages that, generally speaking, are read for only a few minutes at a time. Such spontaneous access works well for reference lookups or quick reminders, but thoroughly covering a topic from start to finish (as in the case of building XUL applications) requires a more comprehensive approach that involves text, illustrations, and code.

The Web is also at a crossroads. Browser technologies are now stabilizing to the point where security and reliability are a given. Growing use of web standards to encode page content is also helping to improve the consistent look of content across rendering engines.

The time is now ripe for the browser community to explore the next generation of web standards, and to initiate a wider range of support for new document models to render graphics, deliver music, and audit user input without needlessly imposing simple tasks on tomorrow's web servers.

This book doesn't serve as just a reference source; it is a practical, hands-on introduction to some of these evolving standards that allow developers to combine creativity with technology. *Programming Firefox* is less of a how-to book and more of a *what-if* exploration that encourages developers to push the envelope of the Internet experience.

Conventions Used in This Book

The following conventions are used throughout this book:

`Constant width`
: Used in code segments, or in terms and phrases in the text that represent code entries.

`Constant width bold`
: Code that is being referenced in the text.

`Constant width italic`
: Used in code segments meant to be customized by the reader.

Italic
: Used to introduce new technical terms, to emphasize certain terms, and to refer to filenames or pathnames.

Menu items
: Used with arrows to illustrate a menu hierarchy, such as File → Open.

This icon signifies a tip, suggestion, or general note.

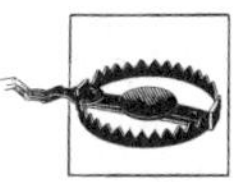

This icon signifies a warning or caution.

Terms and Usage

This book discusses applications of a software engine consisting of a collection of cross-platform libraries written in C++. This collection of libraries was first wrapped together as a browser named Mozilla.

Technically, I should call this book's main topic the Mozilla Cross-Platform Component Model (XPCOM) framework. Not all XPCOM libraries are used in the Firefox browser, however, so I use the term *Firefox framework*—those libraries that are distributed as part of the browser-only components supported by the Mozilla Foundation.

A Tag or an Element?

This book is about interface elements, document elements, and technologies, each having its own terminology. Several terms are used repeatedly throughout this book and should be clarified here:

Widget
: The actual physical representation of an interface element. The term *widget* is most often used when discussing the physical appearance of a document. Widgets include buttons, listboxes, and checkboxes.

Element
: The basic unit that composes XHTML documents. `Tables` and `divs` are examples of elements.

Tag
: The XML encoding of a document element. Examples of tags are `<table>`, `<div>`, and `<button>`.

How This Book Is Organized

This book comprises a number of chapters designed to demonstrate the combination of the XUL interface and emerging Internet standards.

Developing a working application is one of the best ways to illustrate how to use a new feature. Chapters 4 through 7 of this book focus on an embedded annotation tool for citing and storing references to visited web sites. This project (dubbed *NewsSearch*) is designed to demonstrate a progression of tasks and feature enhancements for a real-world project. When added to the balance of the text, each chapter can stand on its own to demonstrate a particular topic:

Chapter 1, *Firefox and Friends*
: Provides an overview of Firefox technology and its history, and a review of the technologies that are the focus of this book.

Chapter 2, *XUL Basics*
: Gives an introduction to the graphical elements that compose a XUL application.

Chapter 3, *Coding and Testing for the Real World*
: Explains how to use the tools for development, including the JavaScript debugger and Document Object Model (DOM) inspector. This chapter is a good foundation for understanding the Firefox development tools and the process used to design and build applications.

Chapter 4, *Configuring for Chrome and a Server*
: Sketches out the first NewsSearch application—understanding the chrome URL and how Firefox applications can communicate with a server using the asynchronous HTTP Request protocol.

Chapter 5, *Multiframe XUL*
: Covers managing an application with multiple content areas, and moving content selections between windows. This section deals somewhat with accessing DOM data structures, and dealing with the sometimes thorny issue of managing multiple frames of content.

Chapter 6, *Trees, Templates, and Datasources*
: Describes connecting interface elements to the server-based Resource Description Framework (RDF). Here you'll find a good introduction to RDF and how the Firefox interface renders RDF content with trees, as well as how a JavaScript program can manipulate RDF content.

Chapter 7, *DOM Manipulation and Input/Output*
: Discusses altering document content and appearance using the DOM. This is a more extensive discussion than that in Chapter 5, including steps to insert content and dynamically modify display styles.

Chapter 8, *Graphics*
: Covers displaying graphics-rich documents using the Scalable Vector Graphics (SVG) standard, and painting document regions using the drawing features of the HTML `Canvas` element.

Chapter 9, *Extending the Interface*
: Explains how to make the most of the Firefox framework by extending the functionality of existing graphics elements as well as the Firefox interface.

Chapter 10, *XForms*
: Discusses implementing the next-generation Forms interface through XForms, a technology designed to increase validation features while reducing the overhead on server logic.

Chapter 11, *Installation and Deployment*
: Outlines developing for different languages and different deployment options.

Chapter 12, *XUL Widget Reference*
: Gives an overview of the XUL widgets.

Glossary, *XUL Widgets: Attributes, Properties, and Methods*
: Provides a list of attribute names used within the Firefox framework.

Demonstration Platforms

Throughout this book are numerous screenshots of example sessions using code samples. Many of the images are from an OS X implementation; I've also included several images from the Windows XP platform. There is no (intentional) emphasis on one operating system's implementation over another—only a reasonable effort to show a good mix of cross-platform support.

Using Code Examples

This book is here to help you get your job done. In general, you may use the code in this book in your programs and documentation. You do not need to contact us for permission unless you're reproducing a significant portion of the code. For example, writing a program that uses several chunks of code from this book does not require permission. Selling or distributing a CD-ROM of examples from O'Reilly books *does* require permission. Answering a question by citing this book and quoting example code does not require permission. Incorporating a significant amount of example code from this book into your product's documentation *does* require permission.

We appreciate, but do not require, attribution. An attribution usually includes the title, author, publisher, and ISBN. For example: *Programming Firefox* by Kenneth C. Feldt. Copyright 2007 O'Reilly Media, Inc., 978-0-596-10243-2."

If you feel your use of code examples falls outside fair use or the permission given above, feel free to contact us at *permissions@oreilly.com*.

Comments and Questions

Please address comments and questions concerning this book to the publisher:

O'Reilly Media, Inc.
1005 Gravenstein Highway North
Sebastopol, CA 95472
800-998-9938 (in the United States or Canada)
707-829-0515 (international or local)
707-829-0104 (fax)

We have a web page for this book, where we list errata, examples, and any additional information. You can access this page at:

http://www.oreilly.com/catalog/9780596102432

To comment or ask technical questions about this book, send email to:

bookquestions@oreilly.com

For more information about our books, conferences, Resource Centers, and the O'Reilly Network, see our web site at:

http://www.oreilly.com

Safari® Enabled

When you see a Safari® Enabled icon on the cover of your favorite technology book, that means the book is available online through the O'Reilly Network Safari Bookshelf.

Safari offers a solution that's better than e-books. It's a virtual library that lets you easily search thousands of top tech books, cut and paste code samples, download chapters, and find quick answers when you need the most accurate, current information. Try it for free at *http://safari.oreilly.com*.

Acknowledgments

Designing reusable frameworks and writing the implementation code is grueling, exhausting work.

Making that effort pay off requires patient, persistent work to promote it and educate users about how such a new product can be used, what benefits it provides, and yes, even what shortcomings exist.

This book would not be possible if it weren't for those developers and designers who took the time to explain the technology through newsgroups, emails, and online documentation.

Particularly critical was the work done at XULPlanet.com (Aaron Anderson and Neil Deakin). Their original documentation and examples gave me the confidence that a sufficient foundation of information was available to take the "next step" in presenting an updated overview of XUL technology.

Also helpful were the contributors at mozilla.dev.tech.xul on *news.mozilla.org* who responded to my questions with patience and grace. The work being done there by Christian Biesinger and the other "regulars" has resulted in an invaluable tool available to the online community in supporting Mozilla/Firefox technology.

I also extend thanks to my editor, Simon St.Laurent, who provided positive feedback when I needed it most. Sincere thanks also goes to those who provided technical and editorial review—those who took the time to point out that even in technical books, readers expect to be able to read and understand sentences.

I would also be remiss if I did not extend a thank you to the pioneering companies and businesses that risk much to integrate Mozilla and forward-looking Internet technologies into their operations. No single event is more important to a new technology than the choice to use it in the affairs of business. The decision to tie one's economic future to an evolving family of technologies is the ultimate commitment to "just make it work." And without that commitment, there would be no need for bug fixes, new revisions, conferences...or this book.

Finally, my thanks goes to the family members who sacrificed much in companionship and demeanor during the difficult weeks that accompany such a project. I am especially grateful to my mom, who gave me passion for the written word, and to Betsy, whose interest and pride helped sustain my effort.

CHAPTER 1

Firefox and Friends

The Firefox browser is a collection of C++ libraries designed to be assembled into any number of applications that you can run on machines with any of the major desktop operating systems (Windows, OS X, Linux, etc.).

A browser's functionality combines what the user sees—through web content—and underlying technologies used to access information and to decode, render, and stylize content. Although much of this book focuses on the XUL interface language to build application interfaces, it also touches on the evolving Internet standards that extend the breadth and depth of information available through the Web.

Mozilla to Firefox and Thunderbird

Most people say the World Wide Web was "born" in the spring of 1993, when Jon Mittelhauser and Marc Andreesen, working out of the University of Illinois, developed what would become the first widely acceptable graphical interface to the Internet.

The software was known as Mosaic, and its widespread acceptance provided the first indication that the Internet was something that could interest (and provide value to) business users and the public.

Marc Andreesen went on to start Netscape Communications Corporation, a company that focused on the commercialization of the Netscape Navigator browser. In 1998, Netscape turned development of the browser over to the open source community in the form of the Mozilla Organization. The Mozilla community rewrote the Netscape code base and released the first commercial product in the form of Netscape 6.

The browser was, unfortunately for Netscape, technically and commercially disappointing. Netscape continued to support Mozilla-based browsers through 2003, when America Online (which owned Netscape) shut down operations, leaving the Mozilla organization on its own to continue development and commercialization of the browser code.

The Mozilla browser was actually a suite of applications that incorporated both a browser and an email and newsreader client. To reduce the perceived "bloat" of the suite, Mozilla decided to break the browser portion out of the suite.

The initial browser was referred to as Phoenix, was renamed Firebird, and finally was released as Firefox version 1.0 in November 2004.

Today the Mozilla Foundation operates as a nonprofit organization to manage the open source development aspects of the program. The foundation owns the for-profit Mozilla Corporation, which focuses on browser support for end users and commercialization programs.

The Mozilla code base now supports the Firefox browser, the Thunderbird email client (Figure 1-1), and the Camino browser for OS X. The complete application suite (formerly the Mozilla suite) is now branded as the SeaMonkey Internet application suite. All the browser engines implement the same rendering logic (the code that paints the screen web content), known as the Gecko rendering engine. The Mozilla suite offers tools to allow developers to embed the Gecko engine alone in customized applications.

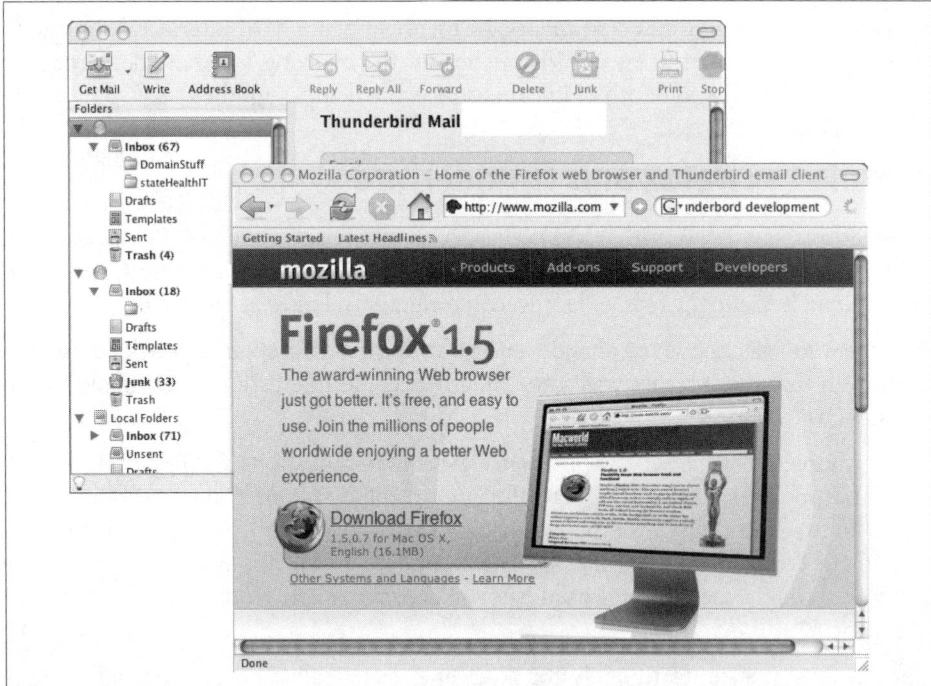

Figure 1-1. Firefox browser and Thunderbird email client

At its inception, much of the "buzz" around the original Mozilla browser concerned the ability to extend the functionality of the Cross-Platform Component Model (XPCOM) libraries on which it is built. Using XPCOM services and interfaces, a C++ (or JavaScript) programmer could build new components and add new logic to the underlying Mozilla engine.

Although many developers still build on and extend the XPCOM library, the lion's share of developers' work focuses on extending the interface and functionality using "higher-level" services, such as the XML Bindings Language (XBL). Regardless of the specific underlying technologies, the interfaces of all Mozilla applications are represented as XML User Interface Language (XUL) files.

XML Technologies

As I just mentioned, XUL stands for XML User Interface Language. In fact, many of the key technologies discussed here are based on XML, or the Extensible Markup Language. As the XML form so dominates both the interface design and the structure of displayed documents, it makes sense to consider what XML is, why it is so important, and what impact it has on electronic document structure.

XML History

XML has its roots in the Standard Generalized Markup Language (SGML). SGML was developed out of a 1960s IBM project to develop documents whose content could be machine-readable. SGML was a metalanguage, a self-describing form that allowed document contents to describe how it was encoded, facilitating machine-driven typographic processes and, eventually, decoding and cataloging.

But SGML was very complex, and with the advent of the "GUI-friendly" Web, work was initiated to carry over some of SGML's advantages of portability to Internet-rendered documents.

In 1995, work began under the auspices of the World Wide Web Consortium (W3C), and XML version 1.0 became a consortium recommendation in February 1998.

XML's power lies in a simple tree structure of text fields, and the capability to define document types that enable decoders to interpret text fields in different ways. The *tree structure* means that any software accessing a well-formed XML file "knows" how to traverse the contents, which themselves are a feature of some utility.

But more exciting is the capability of an XML document to include a document type reference that adds a context to the tree elements, giving meaning to the document's content. For example, an XML document type can define a row as a horizontal alignment of text, but a different document type can define a row as a portion of a mathematical formula. That context can be used to direct the document renderer to display graphics tables or math formulas.

XUL ("zool") files are themselves XML documents. A document namespace field instructs the browser logic that the XUL content is to be interpreted and painted according to a XUL document type. The Firefox framework is "smart" enough so that if other portions of the document need to be drawn as HTML elements, a namespace prefix can be attached to those elements to "switch" the rendering into HTML mode. Designers no longer need to build one monolithic GUI file structure—different display types can now be constructed and mixed together to extend the widget vocabulary.

XSLT and XPath

The design of XML as a well-defined structure of trees certainly makes it easier to develop software that programmatically parses XML content for some purpose.

Because the word *document* generally implies some form of static data, it becomes practical to develop *declarative* processes that can just as easily decode XML files. Two companion standards have now stepped into the fray.

The Extensible Stylesheet Language (XSL) was designed to provide a broader range of tools to modify the style of XML documents. Where Cascading Style Sheets (CSS) were designed to alter the appearance of documents, XSL allowed structural changes in the document (e.g., changing the order of content, removing content, etc.). The use of XSL to transform document content became known as XSL Transformations, or XSLT.

XSL needed a robust tool to reference the treelike content of the XML files it was to transform. XPath is (yet another) standard that provides a straightforward method to reference the nodes of the XML input document. XSL uses XPath to find elements in an XML file that are output to a browser (or to an external file).

Today you can apply all three of these standards in the form of declarative XSLT files or through plug-ins to languages such as Java and PHP.

Here's what this means for the Firefox environment:

- As an XML file, the XUL file is subject to use of CSS to modify the appearance of its widgets; one interface file can be given a completely different look (color, graphical look) with stylesheets. (Much of the concept of different Firefox "skins" is based on XUL and stylesheets.)
- As a rendering engine, the Firefox framework was designed to handle a number of different XML-based display standards. (Chapter 8 covers one such transformation of tabular data into graphical renderings.)

RDF

Most developers have heard of the *Semantic Web*, a term used to describe how information and data can be interconnected for computer access. The Semantic Web for *computer access* is not the same as the World Wide Web and *browser access*.

Browsers know how to interpret and render content by decoding web pages. Internet sites organize information for the purpose of communicating information to a user. Neither the browser nor individual web sites make it their business to connect the information behind the web page—to interpret the biography of the person whose image is displayed and to associate it with the subject's technical expertise for connection to career search engines. Such connections are the domain of the Semantic Web initiative, a program built on common formats with the aim of integrating and combining data from diverse sources. To succeed at this task, computers need access to *information about the information* being sent to browsers and sites.

The method to encode such required *metadata* (information about information) is the Resource Description Framework (RDF), a W3C standard for encoding knowledge.

RDF is often implemented through XML-formatted files that encode a graph of relationships—nodes containing names and values that a computer can process to interpret the nature of the information store. RDF is used in the Firefox framework to manage a number of internal data structures, such as its internal bookmark references. Commercial implementations include applications in online publishing and information distribution (Really Simple Syndication [RSS]).

The Firefox framework has specialized template processing logic designed to access and display RDF content with little procedural code (see Chapter 6).

CSS

CSS is a mechanism to add style (color, font types, dimensions) to elements on web documents.

Early web documents included styling information as attributes attached to HTML elements. This approach embedded the structure of an interface with its appearance; changing the look of a web page required a rewrite of the web page to change the values of the style attributes. Developers looked for an alternative method to attach appearance characteristics to elements without complicating the relatively simple HTML syntax. The idea was to develop a syntax in which a designer could generalize the appearance of all the elements of the same type on a page, such as a declaration to set the font for all `<P>` tags: `P:font.family=Helvetica`.

Formal development of CSS began with a draft specification in 1995, with the W3C drafting a recommendation in 1996. Today's stylesheets also cascade—declarations can accumulate the details of an appearance through a sequential layering of styles (e.g., a paragraph within a `<div>` of one class type can look different from a paragraph enclosed by a `<div>` of another class type).

CSS made possible improved separation of form from function—you could change almost any physical attribute of a web element with a simple change to the text of a stylesheet defined outside the traditional HTML declarations, or defined in CSS files external to the web page.

In Firefox, CSS not only provides the link between the elements of a XUL page and their appearance, but it also provides the linkage to complex widget behaviors. Firefox makes possible an extension of user interface widgets by using CSS to reference binding files that extend a widget's function as well as its "look and feel."

At the Top of It All: The DOM

The Document Object Model (DOM) represents a programmatic interface to web page content. The DOM model is used to define how any XML document may be accessed and manipulated by software.

Early HTML allowed scripting languages limited access to page elements. Scripts could access HTML elements by name or by an element's position within an HTML form. Programmers used this access to manipulate the interface on the basis of the correctness of an entry or to otherwise manipulate the interface based on the input values.

In 1998, the development community recast the HTML 4.0 specification into an XML syntax. This combination of HTML and XML, in the form of XHTML, meant that web documents could now be accessed through the DOM interface. This XHTML document model goes far beyond simple access to basic forms or HTML elements by name. The XHTML DOM makes public a document interface to allow scripts to access the entire document content as a tree of nodes, each node representing a part of the document. Developers use the DOM specification to traverse the document tree, to access and modify element attributes, and to dynamically modify element styles.

Scripts can also dissect the entire document structure, adding event listeners to all elements of a given class, inserting interface widgets as a specific position in the interface tree, moving elements around the tree, accessing document content, and even removing page elements under program control.

DOM access is the lynchpin to most modern web applications that employ JavaScript to manipulate the user interface. Many of the functions behind Firefox's more complicated XUL widgets use JavaScript that accesses elements through DOM methods.

Mixing Document Types

One of the most underutilized features of the Firefox framework is the ability to render XML documents of different types—that is, XML documents that may represent HTML along with content representing mathematics (MathML) and Scalable Vector Graphics (SVG).

The preceding section described how you can define different document types. The Firefox framework can render most of those types without the need for an external plug-in. Figure 1-2 shows an example of MathML (the XML rendering of mathematics).

The capability of Firefox to render such content without the need for plug-ins should not be understated. Once a plug-in is used to render specialized content, additional scripting complexity is added if the designer wishes to "connect" the logic of a web page with the specialized content (e.g., a page that includes an XHTML table full of data and an SVG graphic controlled by the same code). The capability to manage such content makes the Firefox engine a good candidate for simpler, cleaner code to extend interface interactivity.

A number of XML document types exist that promise to bring additional innovation to the Web. Time will tell whether the content development community can take advantage of the delivery platform that Firefox offers:

- XHTML
- SVG
- Geography Markup Language (GML)
- MusicXML
- RSS
- Chemical Markup Language (CML)

Getting Started

The development tools required for XUL development (and to experiment with the examples in this book) are relatively modest.

A good text editor is essential—the editor included with most development systems is more than adequate. If you don't want to shell out the cash for a full-fledged development system, you still have inexpensive options.

OS X platforms use the XCode developer tools that come with the Mac OS X distributions; users can also subscribe to the Apple Developer Connection to get a copy of the tools.

For the Windows platform, plenty of options are available. One of the most serviceable of such tools is the Notepad++ application from the SourceForge project.

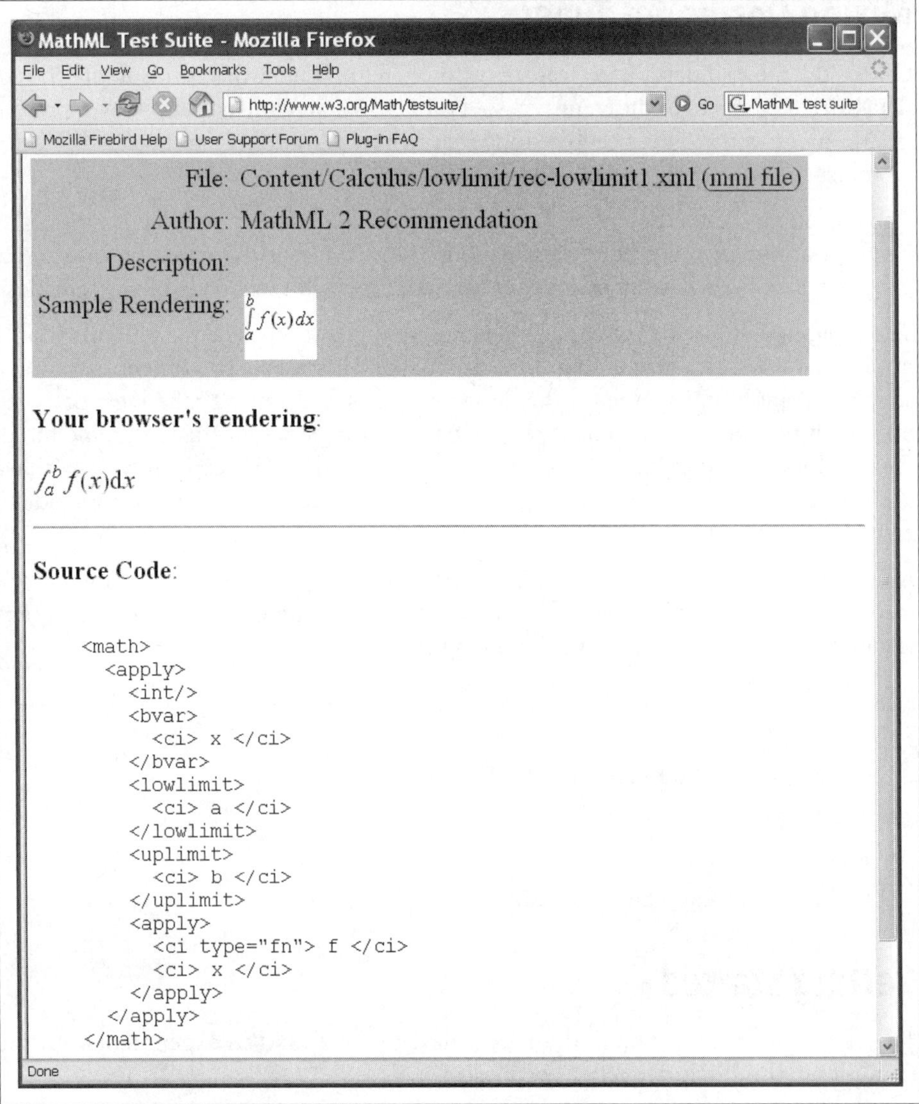

Figure 1-2. Firefox and W3C MathML test page

Regardless of your preferences, all you really need is an editor with syntax highlighting and syntax folding, the features that allow highlighting of keywords and of code segments bracketed by braces and parentheses, as shown in Figure 1-3.

On Unix platforms, you have a wide range of usable editors from which to choose—from `vim` and `emacs` to more user-friendly tools such as Anjuta and KDevelop. It is also possible to use the Eclipse cross-platform development environment for the exercises in this book.

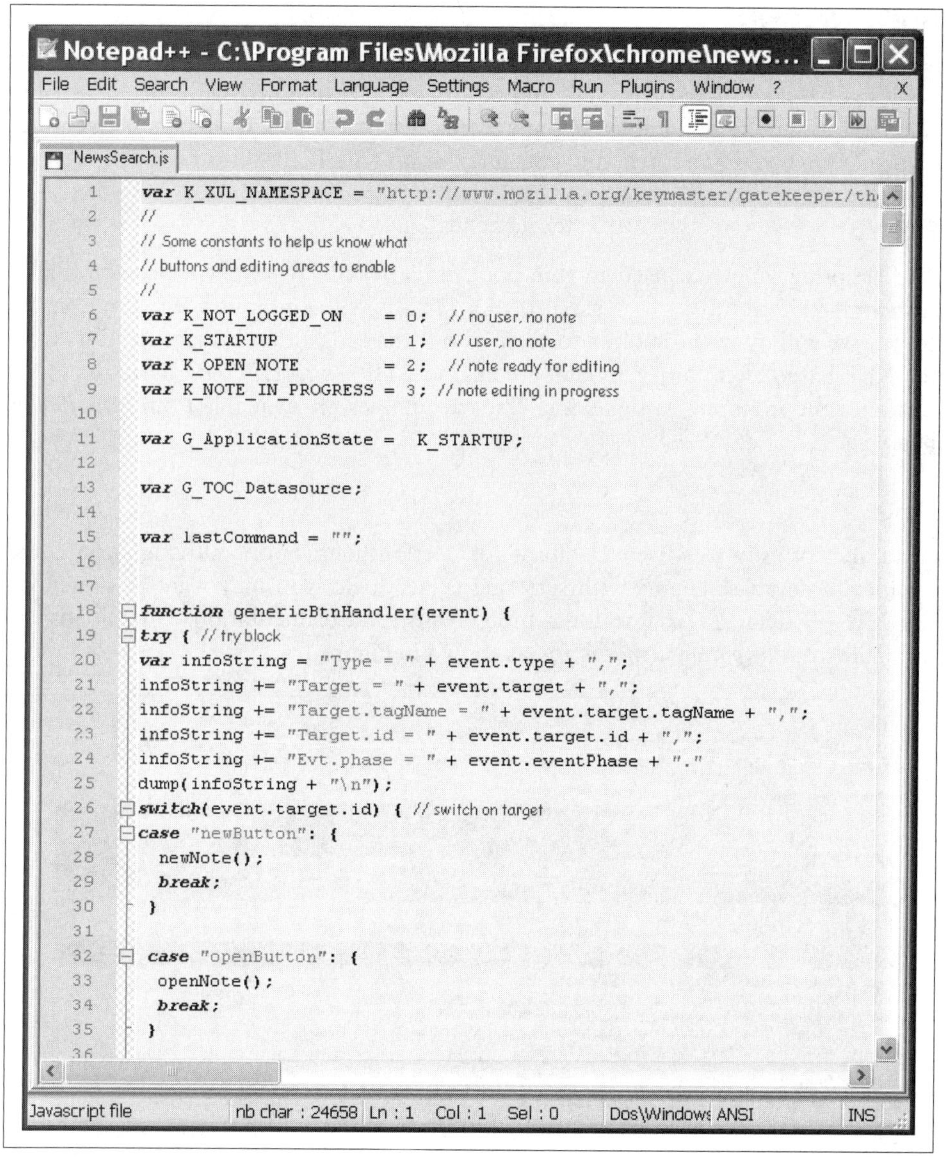

Figure 1-3. Notepad++

Supporting Tools

A number of chapters demonstrate how to integrate XUL applications with server code. Developers may want to implement similar functionality on their machines by installing their own servers.

Apache web server

The web server of choice is the Apache web server (*http://www.apache.org*). This book uses Apache 2.0 for the PC and Apache 1.3 as bundled with OS X distributions. You should not encounter any compatibility issues with later versions of Apache, the only requirement being its integration with PHP.

PHP

The scripting language used in this book is Personal Hypertext Processor (PHP). Although PHP is most often used to mix HTML with programmatic logic on the server, we will use it more often to serve as frontend logic that bridges requests from the XUL-based client and the database engine. PHP 4 or PHP 5 are more than adequate for the examples in this book. The executables are available from *http://www.php.net*.

MySQL

A number of examples use a database for user authentication. Although you could simulate a database engine with scripting (PHP) logic, you may want to download the MySQL database engine for a more realistic implementation. Downloads are available from *http://www.mysql.org*, as shown in Figure 1-4.

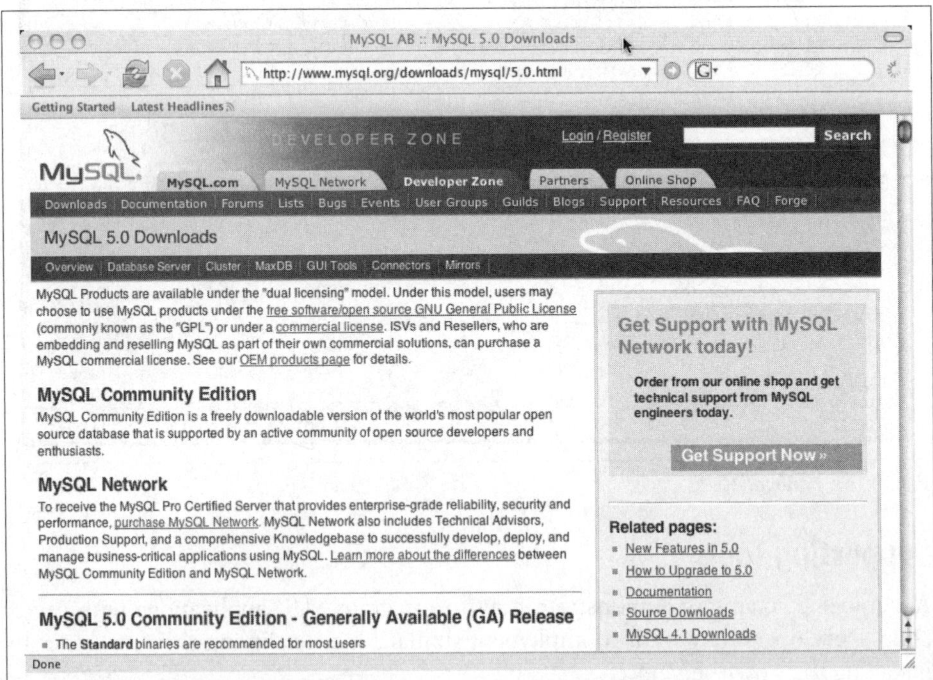

Figure 1-4. MySQL Downloads site

Getting the Browser

With a good development editor in hand, the development process requires use of the Firefox browser. The latest version is available from *http://www.mozilla.com*. When downloading the Firefox browser, you should check the Developer Tools option during the installation process (it often appears as a checkbox on the installation panel). Once the browser is installed, it will automatically be configured to receive any additional updates that the Mozilla.com team makes available.

With the development tools online and the latest version of Firefox on hand, we can start to look at the basic components of the XUL interface.

CHAPTER 2

XUL Basics

The XML User Interface language, XUL, is a document format and vocabulary used to describe cross-platform user interfaces that the Firefox engine renders.

HTML and XHTML (HTML's XML-compliant kin) are used to build web pages—combinations of text, images, and multimedia, with interactivity built in by adding JavaScript event handlers to interface elements or server scripts acting on client-provided forms. XUL interface elements, or widgets, are designed to wrap interactivity around web pages. The Firefox browser itself is a collection of XUL buttons, frames, and menus defined by XUL source. The Gecko rendering engine is the drawing logic that displays all XUL interfaces.

This chapter provides an introduction and basic overview of XUL interfaces (most of these elements will be discussed in greater detail later in this book), including:

- The structure of a XUL file
- Introduction to the box model
- Setting dimensions and positioning
- Simple interface elements (buttons, labels, text)
- Menus and toolbar buttons
- Containers (group boxes, tab boxes)
- Content display
- Utility widgets

File Structure

XML files may include the XML preamble that identifies the file type:

```
<?xml version="1.0"?>
```

As XML files, XUL interfaces must be *well formed*—that is, the *elements* must have opening and closing tags.

In the case of XUL windows, the root element must be a `window`:

```
<window>
    ... some children
</window>
```

The term *element* refers to the basic unit of a XUL document. Elements are represented via their *tags*, or terms surrounded by angle brackets (<>). Each opening tag (`<tag>`) must include a closing or terminating tag (`</tag>`). Elements enclosed by an opening and closing tag are said to be *children* of the tag.

XML elements often have *attributes* that are of the form *attributeName=attributeValue* and are declared within the element's opening tag. In the case of a XUL window, attributes must be defined to set the window's height and width:

```
height="heightInPixels"
width="widthInPixels"
```

Other common attributes for the window include an `id` (used when JavaScript scripts need to get a reference to the window), `title` (for interface display), and `orient` (to set the initial layout direction of children).

The final critical attribute for the topmost node is the `xmlns` attribute, which defines the namespace to be used within the document.

XML documents are meant to be extensible, or able to incorporate different types of elements depending on what information is to be encoded in the document. XHTML documents have elements that represent HTML document elements such as `body`, `head`, `div`, and others.

But as mentioned in Chapter 1, you can use different types of documents to represent mathematical relationships, graphics, or chemical structures. It is quite possible that these different document types may use an element tag that another document type uses as well. The `xmlns` namespace declaration is a mechanism for defining what namespace a specific element belongs to, providing the browser engine with a pointer or reference to a dictionary that describes the required structure of a tag.

As an example, the following code sets the default namespace for all tags that are not prefixed:

```
xmlns="http://www.mozilla.org/keymaster/
      gatekeeper/there.is.only.xul"
```

Firefox allows for mixed-mode documents, meaning that we could add additional namespaces to the file. Adding a second `xmlns` attribute to the topmost node formed as:

```
xmlns:html=http://www.w3.org/1999/xhtml
```

tells the browser that elements with the `html` prefix (e.g., `<html:`*`someElement`*`>`) can be included in this document. If the designer should mix elements that have the same tag, he would use a namespace prefix to tell the browser what rules are to be followed in determining document correctness. If, for example, XUL files supported a table element, and the designer wanted to include an HTML table, the source file would include declarations such as:

```
<html:table>
 ... some stuff
</html:table>
<table>
.... some other stuff
</table>
```

Any XML syntax checking would use the rules for HTML tables to validate the first table, and the rules for XUL tables to validate the second table.

Now that we've discussed the basics of XML formatting, we can use our text editor or development tool to create *theWindow.xul*, which looks like this:

```
<?xml version="1.0"?>
<?xml-stylesheet href="chrome://global/skin/" type="text/css"?>
<window
    id="theWindow"
    title="The Window"
    orient="horizontal"
    width = "400"
    height = "300"
    xmlns="http://www.mozilla.org/keymaster/gatekeeper/there.is.only.xul">

</window>
```

If we were to open this file with the Firefox browser, we would be disappointed to see a blank window, which almost gives the impression that something is wrong with the source file. But using the Firefox tool to view the source file (View → Page Source) displays the source code of our file. The colorized formatting (the standard display mode for XML files) shows that the file is correctly formed, as shown in Figure 2-1.

```
<?xml version="1.0"?>
<?xml-stylesheet href="chrome://global/skin/" type="text/css"?>
<window
    id="theWindow"
    title="The Window"
    orient="horizontal"
        width="400"
        height="300"
    xmlns="http://www.mozilla.org/keymaster/gatekeeper/there.is.only.xul">

</window>
```

Figure 2-1. Firefox view page source window

We see nothing in our browser window because our window has no content.

XUL Widgets

XUL widgets are at the heart of building Firefox applications.

Boxes

The XUL layout hierarchy is based on a primitive <box> container—all XUL interfaces are a collection of nested boxes that contain any number of other boxes. Most developers will use two box subclasses: a <vbox> that lays out child elements in a vertical alignment, and an <hbox> that presents children in a horizontal alignment.

A designer can control how a box positions child content by using the `orient` attribute: a value of `horizontal` will result in a box's children being placed along a horizontal axis and a value of `vertical` will result in content being placed along the vertical axis. The Firefox framework supports <vbox> and <hbox> elements as a shortcut alternative to using the `orient` attribute.

For our first test, we will combine our boxes with the simple XUL `label` element. Adding child elements to the different forms of boxes illustrates the difference in how vboxes and hboxes work:

```
<?xml version="1.0"?>
<?xml-stylesheet href="chrome://global/skin/" type="text/css"?>
<window
    id="theWindow"
    title="The Window"
    orient="horizontal"
    width = "400"
    height = "300"
    xmlns="http://www.mozilla.org/keymaster/gatekeeper/there.is.only.xul"
    xmlns:html="http://www.w3.org/1999/xhtml"
    >

  <hbox>
   <label value="label 1"/>
    <label value="label 2"/>
     <label value="label 3"/>
  </hbox>
   <vbox>
   <label value="label 4"/>
    <label value="label 5"/>
     <label value="label 6"/>
  </vbox>
</window>
```

The resulting window now illustrates the difference, as shown in Figure 2-2.

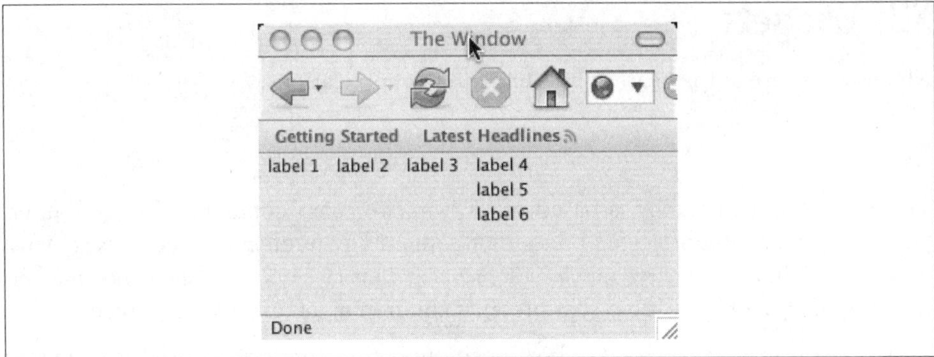

Figure 2-2. hbox and vbox layouts

Adding Styling

One technique to use when learning (and when debugging advanced designs) is to create a specialized appearance, or style, that is associated with a class of elements being tested. By setting distinctive colors and borders, it is sometimes easier to spot problems with a design.

The style assignment follows the CSS style:

```
style="stylePropery:propertyValue"
```

One `style` attribute can include several property assignments in one statement:

```
style="background-color:blue; border-style:solid;"
```

(You can find the specific format of properties supported by the CSS Level 2 specification at *http://www.w3.org/TR/REC-CSS2*.)

Rather than assigning this distinctive style *inline*, by attaching a `style` attribute to an element as:

```
<hbox style="background-color:yellow;"/>
```

we will use an *internal* CSS declaration to provide a style to a class name that we can move to any element being tested (later in this book, we will migrate to using an *externally linked* stylesheet).

We make some changes to our source file to see how such styling can help clarify the details of our XUL elements:

```
<?xml version="1.0"?>
<?xml-stylesheet href="chrome://global/skin/" type="text/css"?>

<?xml-stylesheet href="data:text/css,
        .test_a {
          background-color:#808080;
          border-color:black;
```

```
        border-style:dashed;
        border-width: thin;
        }

"?>

<window
    id="theWindow"
    title="The Window"
    orient="horizontal"
    width = "400"
    height = "300"
    xmlns="http://www.mozilla.org/keymaster/gatekeeper/there.is.only.xul"
    xmlns:html="http://www.w3.org/1999/xhtml"
    >
.
.
.
```

The highlighted text shows how stylesheets are attached to XML files; the reference uses a class selector to bind a gray box with a dashed outline to any element with a class attribute of test_a. Changing one of the box references to add the class attribute:

```
<hbox class="test_a">
   <label value="label 1"/>
    <label value="label 2"/>
     <label value="label 3"/>
```

results in a display that gives us a better idea of what is happening behind the interface, as shown in Figure 2-3.

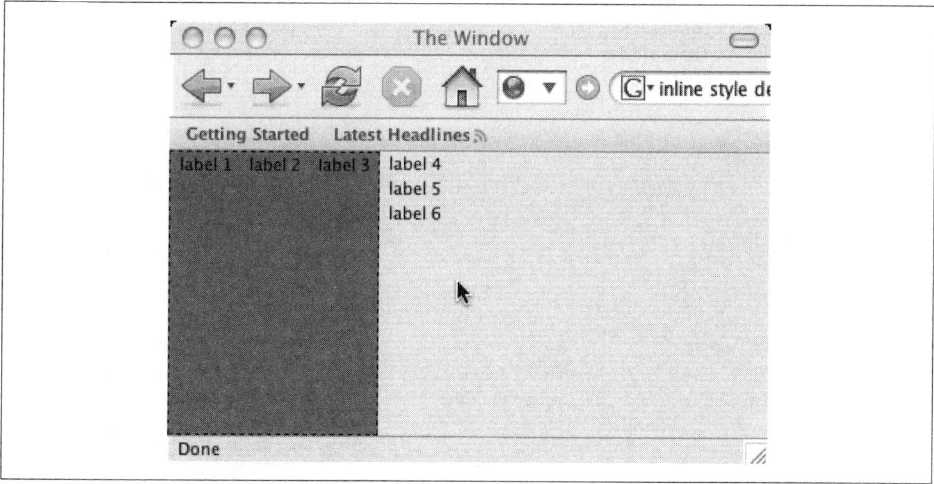

Figure 2-3. Using styles as a debugging aid

Box Sizes

XUL boxes support setting height and width dimensions through the use of both attributes and style properties. But setting fixed values on the outermost containers can be problematic.

When the Firefox framework displays a window, a topmost container box fills the entire space made available by the window, regardless of any explicit values set for height and width. In addition, *topmost* horizontal boxes will stretch to fill the entire vertical space available, and topmost vertical boxes will stretch to fill the available horizontal space. For example, setting the `height` attribute of the `hbox` in the original file has no effect on the visual appearance of the elements. As one of the outermost containers (that is, a direct descendant of the topmost window), the size of the box is automatically expanded (or "flexed") to fill the available vertical space.

To see the effect of an explicitly set dimension, you must place the box in question inside one of the top-level boxes. We can see the effect by modifying the source to add a second test class that styles our outermost box, and adding a `height` and `width` attribute to the first enclosed `hbox`:

```
<?xml-stylesheet href="data:text/css,
      .test_a {
        background-color: #808080;
        border-color:black;
        border-style:dashed;
        border-width: thin;
        }

    .test_b {
        background-color: #c0c0c0;
        border-color:black;
        border-style:solid;
        border-width: thin;
        }

 "?>

<window
    id="theWindow"
    title="The Window"
    orient="horizontal"
    width = "400"
    height = "300"
    xmlns="http://www.mozilla.org/keymaster/gatekeeper/there.is.only.xul"
    xmlns:html="http://www.w3.org/1999/xhtml"
    >


  <vbox height="155" class="test_b" >
  <hbox height="150" width="150" class="test_a">
```

```
    <label value="label 1"/>
     <label value="label 2"/>
      <label value="label 3"/>
  </hbox>
  </vbox>

   <vbox>
   <label value="label 4"/>
    <label value="label 5"/>
     <label value="label 6"/>
  </vbox>

</window>
```

Figure 2-4 shows the results.

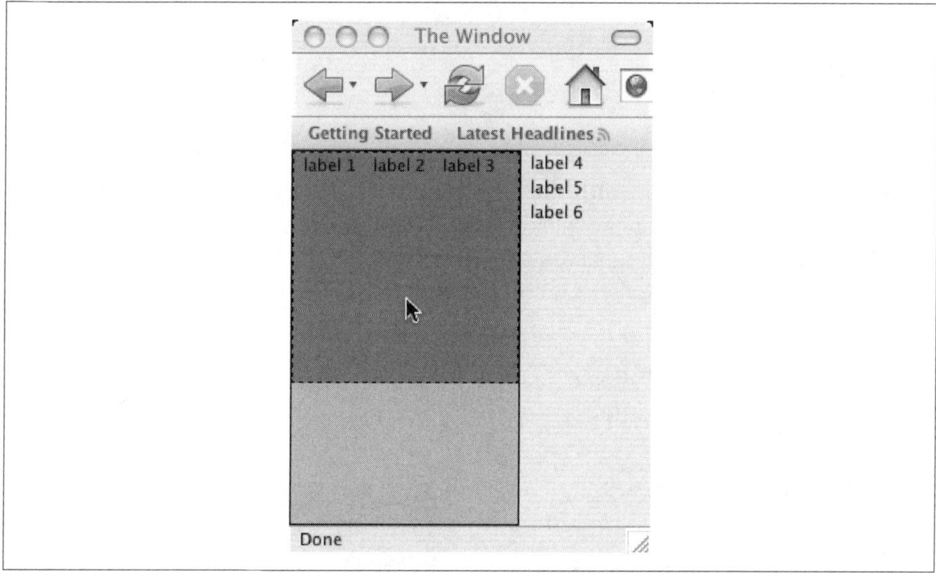

Figure 2-4. Outermost boxes "flexing" to fill the window

In this case, the outermost vbox (the lighter gray with the solid border) flexes to fill in the entire vertical area, even though its height attribute was set to only five pixels greater than the height of the box that it encloses. The size dimensions for the enclosed vbox (test_a) take effect because the vbox parent container takes care of filling in the available window space.

Although topmost boxes stretch to fill available space, *inner boxes with content shrink to the smallest size required to display their contents*. This can sometimes cause problems during initial layout design—omitting content in a box can result in an invisible area that may confuse developers.

The following code demonstrates that behavior:

```
<window
    id="theWindow"
    title="The Window"
    orient="horizontal"
    width = "400"
    height = "300"
    xmlns="http://www.mozilla.org/keymaster/gatekeeper/there.is.only.xul">

<vbox height="155"  >
  <hbox height="150" width="150" class="test_a">
   <label value="label 1"/>
    <label value="label 2"/>
     <label value="label 3"/>
  </hbox>
  </vbox>

   <vbox class="test_b" >
    <label value="Box class='test b'"/>
  </vbox>
</window>
```

Displaying the test file first, with the label within the second vbox, and conducting a second run after removing the vbox's label, shows how the box shrinks to nearly invisible. If the border styling weren't set as a thin line, the box would almost appear to be omitted from the interface, as shown in Figure 2-5.

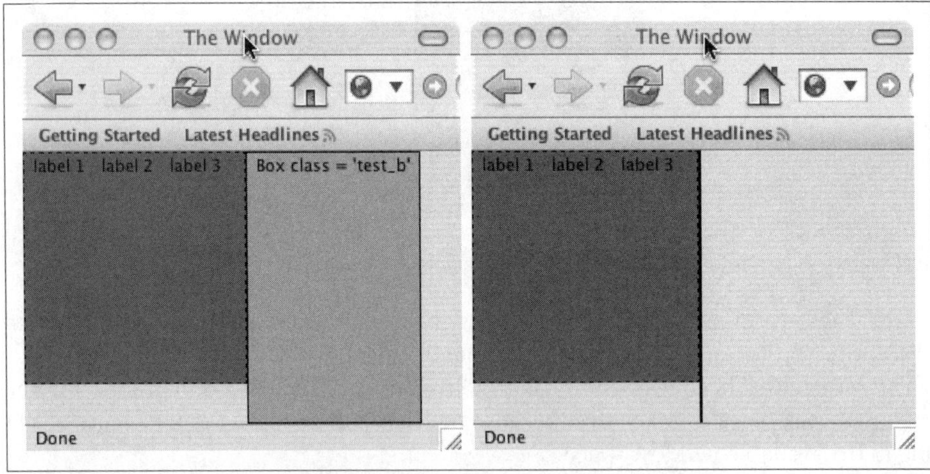

Figure 2-5. Effect of removing box content

One alternative method to alert the designer to such problems is to set the minimum dimensions of boxes in a style declaration:

```
vbox {
    min-width:20px;
    min-height:20px;
    }
```

This CSS style declaration is an alternative to using a test style. It has the advantage of applying to all vboxes in the window and can sometimes save a designer time in tracking down positioning or content problems.

The Flex, Pack, and Align Attributes

In practice, the use of explicit dimensions in element declarations is often replaced by the use of attributes that define how a widget is to expand, and how the widget orients its enclosed elements.

Flex

As mentioned earlier, a box will normally shrink to the minimum size needed to display its children along its specific axis (e.g., the minimum possible vertical space for vboxes, and the minimum possible horizontal space for hboxes). By default, the space orthogonal to the layout axis *stretches* to fill the total space available from the parent container.

The flex attribute instructs the Firefox framework about how a parent container should allocate the space among its child containers along the axes of their orientation. The amount of space allocated to child containers is assigned according to the ratio of the respective flex values. *How* the flex attribute of an element is applied depends on the orientation of the parent container.

A vbox container with one child container holding a flex value of 1 and a second child container with a flex value of 2 will allocate twice as much *surplus* vertical space to the second child. An hbox parent would allocate the same proportion or surplus along the horizontal axis.

The flex algorithm first determines how much space is required by a child container, and then allocates the *remaining* free space according to the flex ratios.

The following changes to our source XUL file show how you can use the flex attribute:

```
<vbox flex="1">

  <hbox flex="1" class="test_a">
   <label value="label 1"/>
    <label value="label 2"/>
     <label value="label 3"/>
  </hbox>

   <vbox flex="3" class="test_b" >
     <label  value="label 4"/>
    <label value="label 5"/>
     <label value="label 6"/>
  </vbox>

  </vbox>
```

The two child containers have been assigned relative `flex` values of `1` and `3`, and the parent `vbox` has been assigned a `flex` value of `1` to fill the entire available space.

Figure 2-6 illustrates the effects of changing the type of containers while keeping the flex assignments fixed.

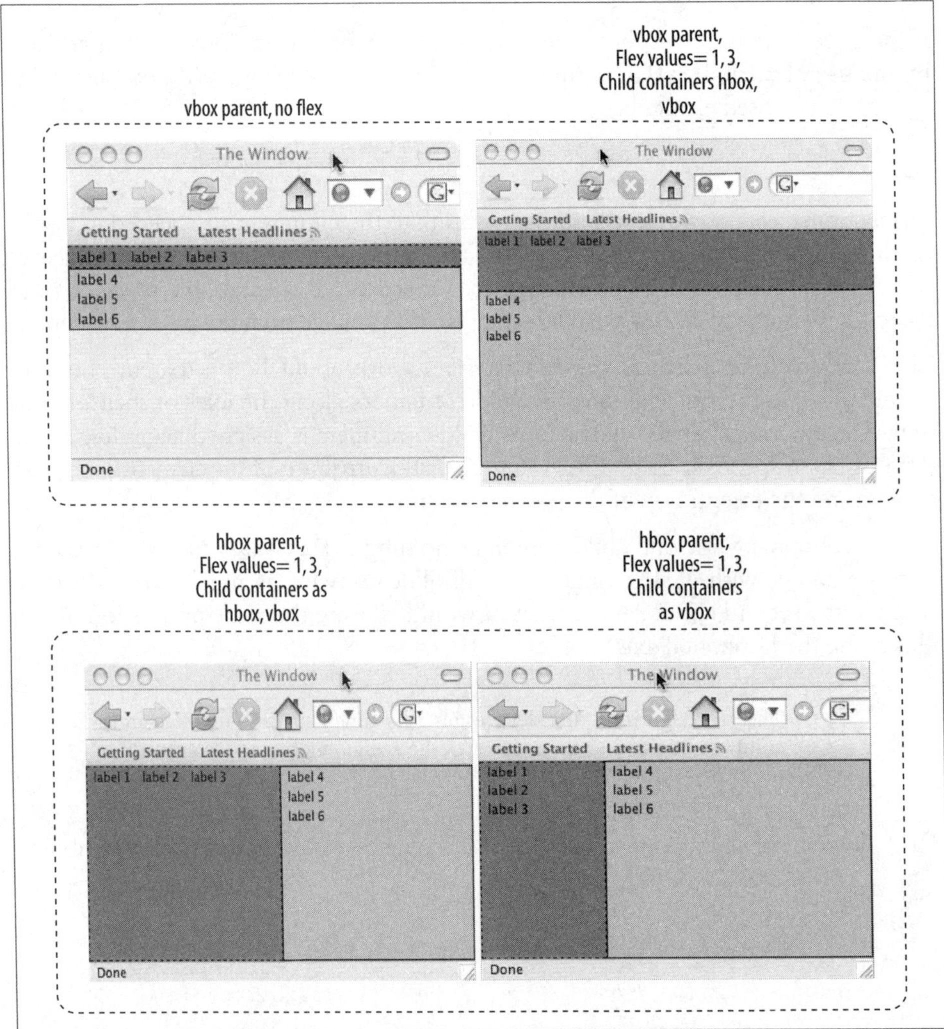

Figure 2-6. Box orientation and flex attributes

Pack

The `flex` attribute defines how to allocate surplus space to a container's children; the `pack` attribute tells the Firefox framework how to position child elements along the container's axis of orientation within the surplus space. If a `vbox` has more space than it needs to position its child elements, the pack attribute directs the framework on where to place children within the total space available. The values for the pack attribute are as follows:

start *(default)*
: The child elements are placed at the top of vboxes or at the leftmost point of hboxes.

center
: The child elements are centered within the parent.

end
: The child elements are placed at the bottom of vboxes or along the right edge of hboxes.

Figure 2-7 illustrates the effects of different packing attributes for a collection of three vboxes.

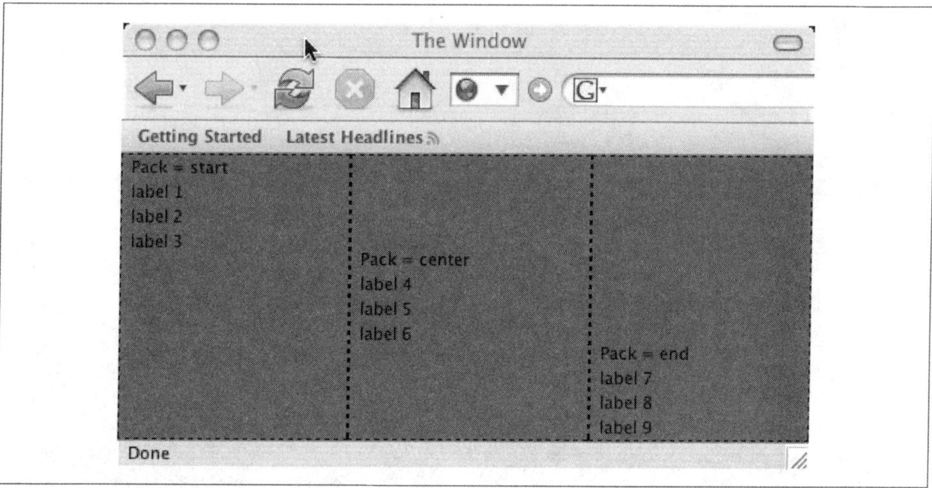

Figure 2-7. Packing

Align

The align attribute defines the position of child elements orthogonal to a container's orientation. The values for the align attribute are as follows:

start
: Elements are placed at the leftmost edge for vboxes and at the topmost point for hboxes.

center
: Elements are centered.

end
: Elements are placed along the right edge for vboxes and along the bottom edge for hboxes.

`baseline`
: For `hboxes`, elements are positioned so that they align with the baseline of text labels.

`stretch` *(default)*
: Child elements are stretched to fill all available space.

Figure 2-8 illustrates the difference between the `stretch` and `start` values. Different background color styles were applied to the labels to show how the child labels are sized to the minimum required for the `start` value, while expanding to the maximum space available when assigned a value of `stretch`. (All the containers except the baseline example are `vboxes` with the `pack` attribute set to `start`.)

Figure 2-8 also illustrates how the `baseline` value aligns children so that the text labels are aligned. We will cover the group box widget in this example later in this chapter.

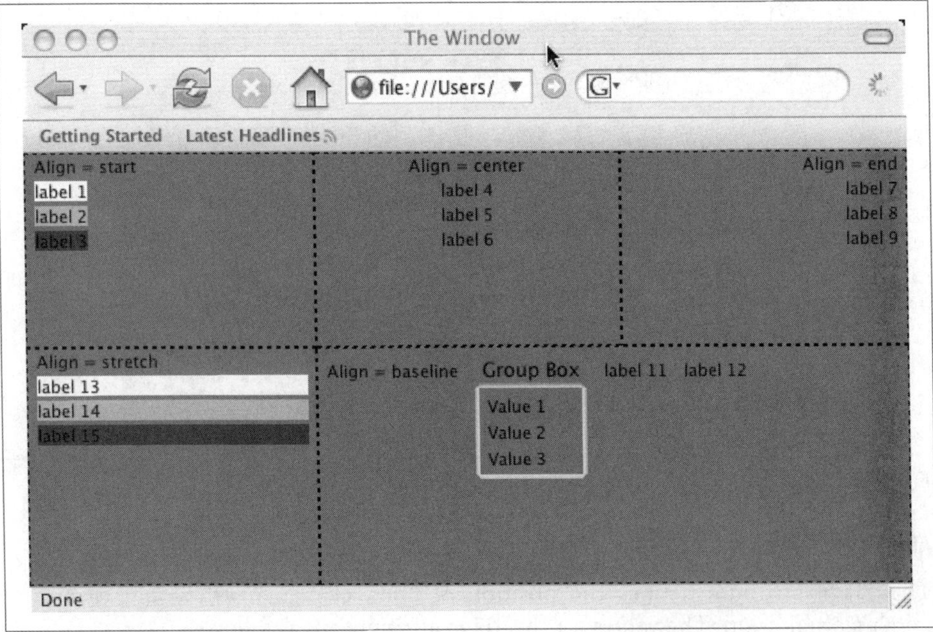

Figure 2-8. Align values

Introducing Input Controls

Controls represent the user interface widgets responsible for fielding interaction with the user. Buttons, text fields, text areas, and various forms of menus provide the lion's share of control logic.

Labels and Buttons

Labels provide the designer with the simplest of all interface elements—a string of displayed text:

```
<label value="My Label"/>
```

Buttons represent the basic interaction tool. Buttons are painted using the native operating system's GUI, resulting in an interface that looks much more like a desktop application than a browser.

Buttons allow you to add an image icon, using attributes that enable you to control the button's appearance:

`label`
: The text appearing on the button.

`image`
: The URI of an image to appear as an icon on the button.

`dir`
: Sets the position of the icon relative to the label:

  `normal` *(default)*
  : The icon appears to the left of or above the button label.

  `reverse`
  : The icon appears to the right of or below the button label.

`orient`
: Determines the layout of the label and the icon:

  `horizontal` *(default)*
  : The icon and label are oriented horizontally.

  `vertical`
  : The icon and label are oriented vertically.

Figure 2-9 illustrates the effects of altering the attributes for a button.

Figure 2-9. Buttons with an icon

Text Entry

All text entry is conducted through the `textbox` element. The default nature of a textbox is to support a one-line entry, but several attributes affect the nature of the entry area:

`maxlength`
: The maximum number of characters allowed in the text box for single-line text entry.

`multiline`
: If `true`, pressing Enter during text entry forces a new line entry; otherwise, all text is combined in a single text line.

`rows`
: The number of rows displayed for a multiline text entry area.

`size`
: The total number of characters displayed within a single-line text entry box.

`wrap`
: Turns word wrapping on or off; a value of `off` disables word wrapping.

Developers use a single-line text area when the size of text will be limited for data fields, and they use a multiline text area for a general-purpose "narrative" entry. The actual number of vertical and horizontal rows visible in the text box may also depend on the `flex` attributes of the parent container and the value of the `wrap` attribute. The `rows` and `size` attributes also presume the appearance of scrollbars: if the `rows` attribute is `3` but no horizontal scrollbar exists, four rows will be displayed.

For example, given the following code snippet:

```
<vbox>
  <hbox flex="1">
  <vbox>
  <textbox  rows="3"  multiline="true" size="20" wrap="on"/>
  </vbox>
  <textbox  rows="3"  multiline="true" size="20" wrap="off" />
  </hbox>
  </vbox>
```

the interface would appear as shown in Figure 2-10.

Figure 2-10. Text element appearance

Both text elements define three rows, but the right box expands to fill the available vertical space (the left text box is enclosed by a vbox that shrinks to the minimum size required). The text on the left sets wrap to on, meaning that the text line will automatically break at a space. As a result, no horizontal scrollbar will be created and four rows will appear. In the case of the right box, the wrap has been turned off, so as the user continues to type text (without pressing Enter), the text remains on the first line with a horizontal scrollbar. The number of rows visible depends on the total vertical space available.

This illustration demonstrates that if precise control is required for the number of visible rows and columns, you may need to experiment with various container flexing strategies and wrap attributes to get the desired results.

Menus and Toolboxes

Most applications use *menus*, collections of text fields, buttons, or icons that appear in hierarchical structures.

The menu structure begins with a *menu bar*, a horizontal container for menu elements. You can place menu bars anywhere on the interface, but they are generally placed within a toolbar element. (If you do not place the menubar within some container, it will expand to fit the available space.)

A menu element is little more than a named container for a menupopup, the container that appears when a menu is accessed. Menupopups contain menuitems, the actual buttons that interact with the user.

A similar structure is a toolbar and its topmost container, a toolbox.

Toolbars are useful for situations where a row or column of controls needs to be present, but they do not require any hierarchical containment for the individual toolbarbuttons that are children of the toolbar. Toolbarbuttons are functionally identical to buttons, but rather than being rendered as the native GUI's button, they are designed to contain an image icon.

The following source illustrates one implementation of menu bars and toolbars:

```
<hbox flex="1">
  <hbox flex="1" class="test_a">
  <toolbox >
  <toolbar orient="vertical" id="theToolbar">
    <toolbarbutton label="TB 1" image="buttonIcon.png"/>
    <toolbarbutton label="TB 2" image="buttonIcon.png"/>
    <toolbarbutton label="TB 3" image="buttonIcon.png"/>
    <toolbarbutton label="TB 4" image="buttonIcon.png"/>
    <toolbarbutton label="TB 5" image="buttonIcon.png"/>
   </toolbar>
  </toolbox>
  </hbox>
```

```
<hbox flex="1"  class="test_b">
<toolbox>
 <menubar id="theMenubar">
    <menu id="menu1" label="Menu 1">
      <menupopup id="m1-popup">
        <menuitem label="Menu item 1-1"/>
        <menuitem label="Menu item 1-2"/>
        <menuitem label="Menu item 1-3"/>
        <menuseparator/>
        <menuitem label="Extra menu item 1"/>
      </menupopup>
    </menu>
    <menu id="menu2" label="Menu 2">
      <menupopup id="m2-popup">
        <menuitem label="Menu item 2-1"/>
        <menuitem label="Menu item 2-2"/>
      </menupopup>
    </menu>
  </menubar>
 </toolbox>
  </hbox>
```

Figure 2-11 demonstrates the result.

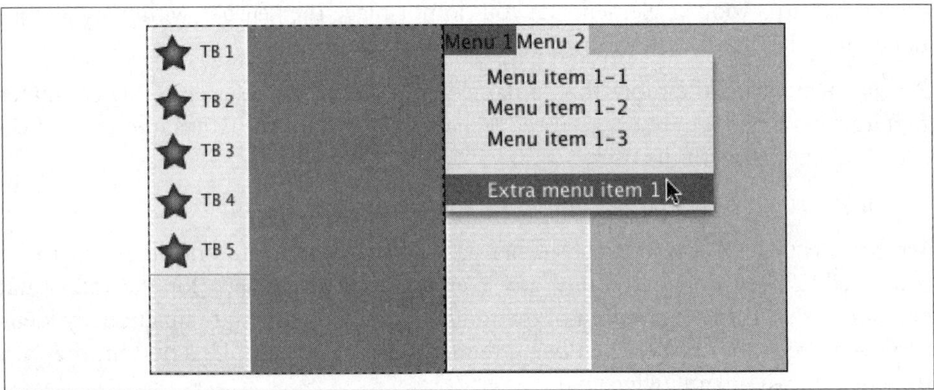

Figure 2-11. Toolbars and menus

More Complex Containers

Vertical presentations of selection options are made possible by lists (for simple collections) and trees (for hierarchical relationships).

Lists

In its simplest form, a list is merely a `listbox` container with `listitem` children. `Listitems` display the contents of the `label` attribute, but they also support a `value` attribute that scripts use to obtain some data that the designer chooses not to be rendered in the interface.

You also can divide listboxes into multiple columns in a fashion very similar to that of the HTML table element. For multiple-column lists, the first child of a listbox is a <listhead> element that contains one <listheader> child for each column to be displayed with a header. Following the <listheader> child is the <listcols> entry with one child for each column to be displayed.

Finally come the <listitem> children, but unlike the simplest single-column implementation (and similar to the table layout), multicolumn list items contain <listcell> children that are rendered in the columns. An example of multicolumn lists is shown in the following code fragment and in Figure 2-12:

```
<hbox flex="1"  class="test_b">
<listbox>
  <listhead>
    <listheader label="Column 1"/>
    <listheader label="Column 2"/>
    <listheader label="Column 3"/>

  </listhead>

  <listcols>
    <listcol/>
    <listcol/>
    <listcol flex="1"/>
  </listcols>
  <listitem>
    <listcell label="R1C1"/>
    <listcell label="R1C2"/>
     <listcell label="R1C3"/>
  </listitem>
  <listitem>
    <listcell label="R2C1"/>
    <listcell label="R2C2"/>
      <listcell label="R2C3"/>

  </listitem>
  <listitem>
    <listcell label="R3C1"/>
    <listcell label="R3C2"/>
    <listcell label="R2C3"/>

  </listitem>
   <listitem>
    <listcell label="R4C1"/>
    <listcell label="R4C2"/>
    <listcell label="R4C3"/>

  </listitem>
</listbox>
</hbox>
```

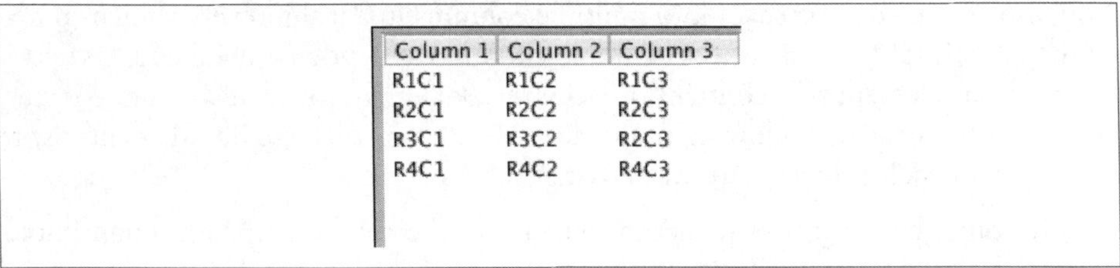

Figure 2-12. Multicolumn list

Trees

A more complicated interface that makes possible a hierarchical representation is the *tree*.

The logic that constructs trees can be quite complex (we will visit tree logic at greater length in Chapter 6). In its simplest form, a tree resembles listbox content in that a header area (in this case, `<treecols>`) is used to contain labels for column headings.

The `<treechildren>` element contains all the children of one tree node—`<treeitem>` elements represent all the items that are enclosed as children from any given node of branches. One may think of a `treeitem` as the root node to which all nested children are attached. The displayed elements themselves are `<treecell>` elements wrapped by `<treerows>`. The following code shows how trees are constructed (XML comments are used to help identify the binding between `treeitems` and their parents):

```
<hbox flex="1"  class="test_b">
<tree flex="1" rows="6">
  <treecols>
      <treecol  label="Tree column 1" primary="true" flex="2"/>
      <treecol  label="Tree column 2" flex="1"/>
  </treecols>

  <treechildren>

    <!-- tree item for cat 1 node -->
    <treeitem container="true" open="true">
      <treerow>
        <treecell label="Category 1"/>
      </treerow>

      <!-- tree children for first category -->
      <treechildren>
        <treeitem>
          <treerow>
            <treecell label="Cat 1 - Sub cat 1"/>
            <treecell label="Value 1"/>
          </treerow>
        </treeitem>
```

```
            <treeitem>
              <treerow>
                <treecell label="Cat 1 - Sub cat 2"/>
                <treecell label="Value 2"/>
              </treerow>
            </treeitem>
          </treechildren>
          <!-- end tree children for first category -->

        </treeitem>
        <!-- tree item for cat 1 node -->

        <!-- tree item for cat 2 node -->
         <treeitem container="true" open="true">
          <treerow>
            <treecell label="Category 2"/>
          </treerow>

            <!-- tree children for second category -->
          <treechildren>
            <treeitem>
              <treerow>
                <treecell label="Cat 2 - Sub cat 1"/>
                <treecell label="Value 3"/>
              </treerow>
            </treeitem>
            <treeitem>
              <treerow>
                <treecell label="Cat 2 - Sub cat 2"/>
                <treecell label="Value 4"/>
              </treerow>
            </treeitem>
          </treechildren>
          <!-- end tree children for second category -->


          </treeitem>
        <!-- end tree item for cat 2 node -->


      </treechildren>
    </tree>
     </hbox>
```

Figure 2-13 shows the results of this tree.

For simple trees that may involve only a couple of levels of nesting, "hardcoding" the structure in the XUL file, as shown earlier, may suffice. More complex trees are made possible through templates and remote data sources, which we will cover in Chapter 6.

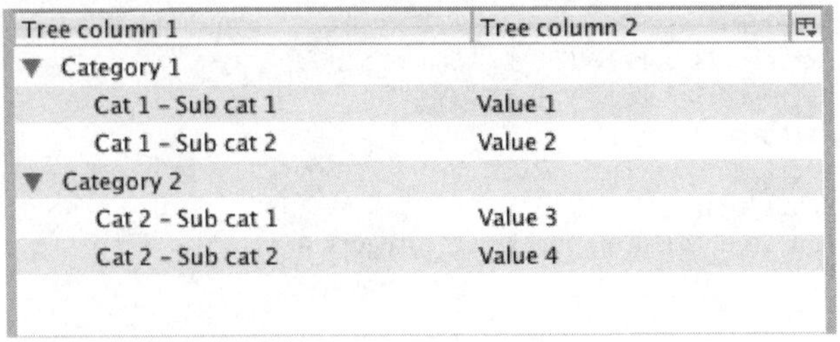

Tree column 1	Tree column 2
▼ Category 1	
Cat 1 - Sub cat 1	Value 1
Cat 1 - Sub cat 2	Value 2
▼ Category 2	
Cat 2 - Sub cat 1	Value 3
Cat 2 - Sub cat 2	Value 4

Figure 2-13. Simple trees

Grids

Lists and trees provide a structural layout tool for text-based widgets, and *grids* provide a convenient tool for organizing a table-like representation of any type of content, making them ideal to structure panels of buttons and text entry fields.

Grids support `<rows>` and `<columns>` children, which in turn contain `<row>` and `<column>` elements. When the Firefox framework encounters a `<rows>` element, all children are stacked vertically and `<row>` elements have their content divided among the number of columns in the grid. For `<columns>`, Firefox stacks children horizontally and breaks the children of `<column>` elements vertically among the number of rows in the grid.

A designer may choose to place the tabular content in either of two ways: by specifying a collection of columns, with each entry in the column being placed in a corresponding row cell; or by specifying a collection of rows, with each row entry being placed in a corresponding column cell as follows:

```
<hbox flex="1"  >
<grid class="test_b" flex="1">
<columns>
    <column>
      <label value="Name:"/>
      <label value="Address:"/>
      <label value="Phone:"/>
    </column>
    <column flex="1">
      <textbox id="Nm"/>
      <textbox id="Addr"/>
      <textbox id="Ph"/>
    </column>
  </columns>
</grid>
</hbox>
```

This simple grid will display a table of labels and text entry fields.

How a designer organizes a grid may depend on what mix of controls is desired and whether there is the need for one cell to span multiple columns or rows.

Although grids do not support the colspan or rowspan attributes available in HTML tables, a designer may span the width or height of a grid by placing elements inline with rows (or columns), but not inside a row (or column) element.

If, for example, the designer wants to add a button at the bottom of our field entry, she may redesign the grid as a series of rows. The last element within the <rows> tag is a simple button (wrapped in a box for centering):

```
<hbox flex="1"  >
<grid class="test_b" flex="1">
<columns>
 <column/>
 <column flex="1"/>
</columns>

  <rows>
    <row>
     <label value="Name:"/>
     <textbox id="Nm"/>
    </row>

     <row>
     <label value="Address:"/>
     <textbox id="Addr"/>
    </row>

     <row>
     <label value="Phone:"/>
     <textbox id="Ph"/>
    </row>

     <hbox pack="center">
     <button label="Send"/>
     </hbox>

   </rows>
</grid>
</hbox>
```

Figure 2-14 shows the results.

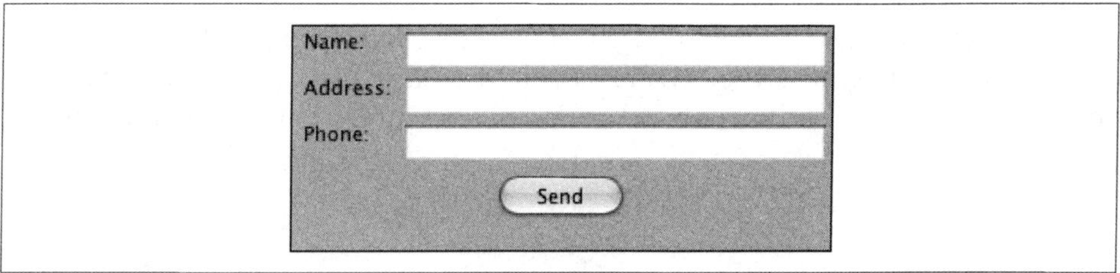

Figure 2-14. Grid with button outside of <row> element

Group Boxes

Similar to a grid is the groupbox, which is a container that provides borders and captions for collections of interface widgets. Aside from the default border around the contents and a caption area, the layout of a groupbox is straightforward:

```
<groupbox  flex="1">
  <caption>
   <label value="Please send me info:"/>
  </caption>
  <hbox>
    <label value="Comments:"/>
    <textbox flex="1"/>
  </hbox>
  <checkbox label="Touring in the British Isles"/>
   <checkbox label="Cycling in France"/>
    <checkbox label="Skiing in Switzerland"/>
 </groupbox>
```

Figure 2-15 shows the result.

Figure 2-15. Group box with caption

Our demonstration of the checkboxes naturally leads to a description of the radio group—a type of group box that imposes certain rules on the content elements:

```
<radiogroup  class="test_b">
 <radio label="Option 1"/>
 <radio label="Option 2"/>
 <radio label="Option 3"/>
</radiogroup>
```

Radio groups don't have captions and default borders (which you could easily add with the proper box elements). They enforce a behavior on the grouped <radio> elements such that only one of the elements can be selected at a time, as shown in Figure 2-16.

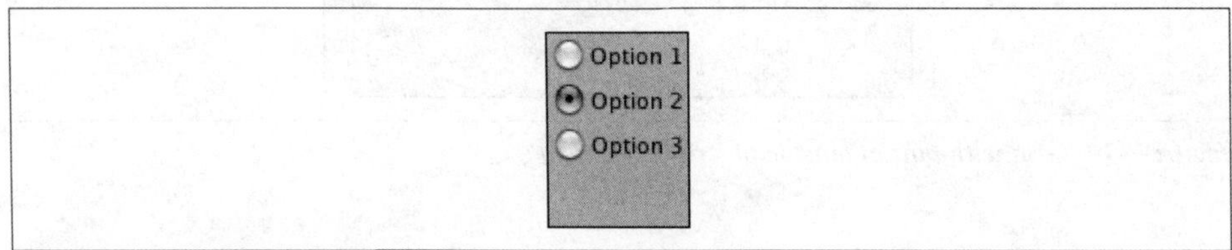

Figure 2-16. Radio group

Managing the Display Space

Firefox includes a number of widgets that help organize controls and labels as they appear in a window.

Tab Boxes

Most applications require some interface element to set a context for a collection of commands. The XUL <tabbox> element provides a family of containers that represent the tabbed-index collection of panels.

Each <tabbox> element starts with a <tabs> element, whose <tab> children represent the buttons attached to their respective content panels.

The main content of a tab box is wrapped by the <tabpanels> element, which contains <tabpanel> children. The tab panels are the topmost container for the interface widgets bound to the tab. The following code and Figure 2-17 illustrate the use of a tab box:

```
<tabbox flex="1">
  <tabs>
    <tab label="Sports"/>
    <tab label="News"/>
     <tab label="Weather"/>
      <tab label="Entertainment"/>
  </tabs>

  <tabpanels flex="1">
    <tabpanel id="sports">
     <vbox flex="1">
      <label value="Sports"/>
     </vbox>
    </tabpanel>
     <tabpanel id="news">
     <vbox flex="1">
      <label value="News"/>
     </vbox>
    </tabpanel>
     <tabpanel id="Weather">
     <vbox flex="1">
      <label value="Weather"/>
     </vbox>
    </tabpanel>
     <tabpanel id="Entertainment">
     <vbox flex="1">
      <label value="Entertainment"/>
     </vbox>
    </tabpanel>
  </tabpanels>

</tabbox>
```

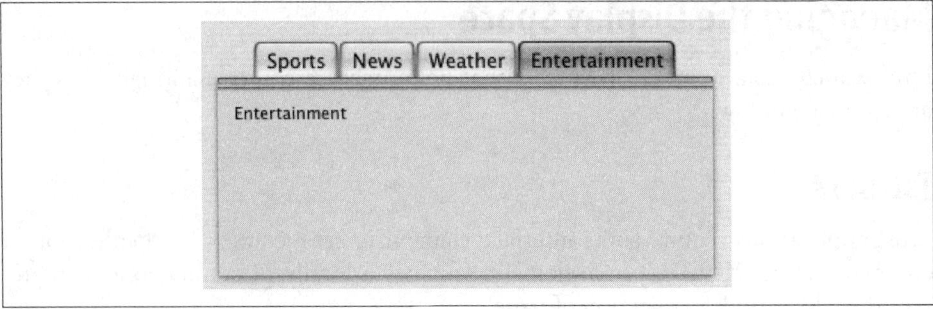

Figure 2-17. Tab box

The use of the flex attribute can significantly affect the appearance of tab boxes.

Adjusting the flex attribute on the <tabbox> affects the amount of horizontal space the tab box occupies; setting the flex attribute on the <tabpanels> element changes the amount of vertical space the entire box occupies.

Splitters

Now that we've discussed flexing, it's time to discuss the widget used to reallocate space, or *split* the content area into different sections. Splitters placed in <hbox> elements divide the area into vertical segments. Splitters in <vbox> elements create segmented horizontal areas. The following code fragment and Figure 2-18 illustrate how to add a splitter to our existing window:

```
.
.
.
<vbox align="end" flex="1"  >
     <label value="Align = end"/>
     <label  value="label 7"/>
     <label value="label 8"/>
     <label value="label 9"/>
  </vbox>
  </hbox>

    <splitter collapse="before" class="test_b" resizeafter="farthest"/>

 <hbox flex="1">

   <vbox align="stretch" flex="1"  >
    <label value="Align = stretch"/>
     <label style="background-color:white;" value="label 13"/>
    <label  style="background-color:#c0c0c0;" value="label 14"/>
     <label style="background-color:#404040;" value="label 15"/>
  </vbox>
.
.
.
```

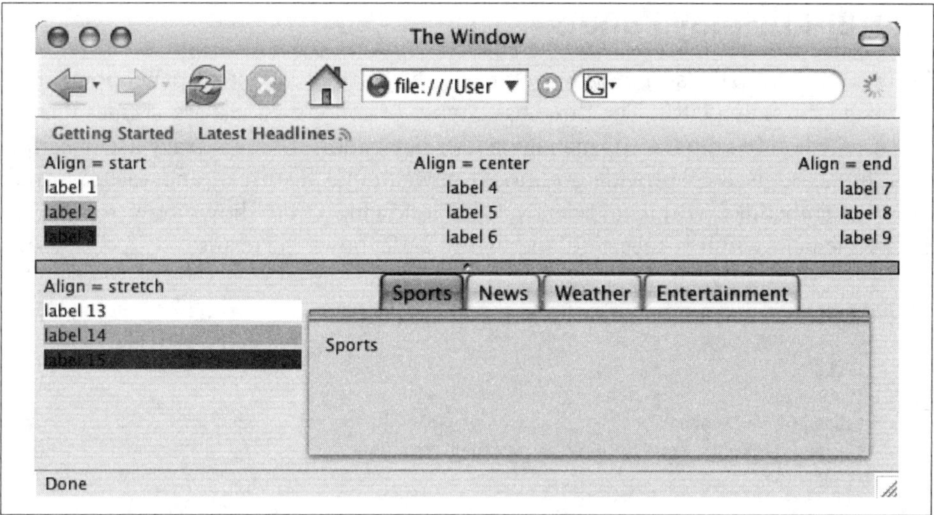

Figure 2-18. Horizontal splitter

Splitters have a number of attributes that tell the Firefox framework how to adjust the views in the areas being split:

`resizebefore`
: This attribute tells the Firefox framework to resize the elements in the panel to the left of vertical splitters or above horizontal splitters:

  `closest` *(default)*
  : Elements immediately to the left or above the splitter are resized.

  `farthest`
  : Elements farthest to the left or farthest above the splitter are resized.

`resizeafter`
: This attribute tells the Firefox framework to resize the elements to the right (for vertical splitters) or below (for horizontal splitters):

  `closest` *(default)*
  : Elements immediately to the right or below the splitter are resized.

  `farthest`
  : Elements farthest to the right or above the splitter are resized.

Readers referring to online resources may find XUL references to a *grippy*, which is a button designed to be attached to splitters and toolboxes that "snaps" an area open or closed. The grippy is a part of the core Mozilla Cross-Platform Component Model (XPCOM) library, and is not included in the Firefox framework.

Content Display Panels

You use content panels to display web pages. The `src` of a content panel points to a web page through a URL. The three basic types of content panels are `iframes` (generally used when the interface is managing user navigation through heavy use of scripting), `browser` (used to provide additional navigational features), and `tabbrowser` (a browser embedded within a `tabbox`). The following code shows how to add an `iframe` element within a `tabpanel`, and Figure 2-19 shows the result:

```
<tabpanel class="test_a" id="news">
 <vbox  >
   <label value="News"/>
 </vbox>
</tabpanel>
<tabpanel id="Weather">
 <iframe flex="1" src="http://www.weather.com/"/>
</tabpanel>
<tabpanel id="Entertainment">
 <vbox flex="1">
  <label value="Entertainment"/>
 </vbox>
</tabpanel>
```

Figure 2-19. Addition of an iframe

Remember to set the `flex` attribute on the `iframe` element. Omitting this step can result in very tiny slices of a web page being displayed.

Miscellaneous Widgets

In addition to simple container boxes and controls, most XUL programmers enhance their applications by using a number of widgets that provide both layout services and useful programming interfaces. Here are some examples:

<spacer>
: Sometimes it's not enough to use the flex and pack attributes to organize widgets in the manner desired. Spacer widgets act as invisible "springs." Setting the flex attribute of a spacer allows the designer to push elements to one side of a parent container.

<statusbar>
: A status bar is placed along the bottom of a window. A <statusbar> contains a <statuspanel> child, which includes label attributes. Developers can access the label property of a statuspanel to provide feedback to the user:

```
<statusbar pack="end">
  <statusbarpanel label="Still waiting...."/>
</statusbar>
```

<progressmeter>
: This widget displays an operating-system-specific progress meter. A value attribute represents an integer percentage of completion. When the mode attribute is set to determined, the meter changes to show the percentage of completion. When the mode attribute is set to undetermined, the meter displays a graphic to indicate ongoing activity. Developers use the determined mode when an activity consists of known steps of completion and they want to indicate task progression. They use the undetermined mode to indicate an ongoing task.

<description>
: Whereas you can use label fields to display short lines of text, you can use a <description> element to display longer segments of text. The contents will wrap as the enclosing box changes size.

Here is an example of code that displays information and the status of an activity at the bottom of our window:

```
<description style="color:gray;">
We are currently processing your order. Please do not press
  any buttons unless you are really tired of waiting.
</description>

<statusbar >
  <progressmeter mode="undetermined" />
  <spacer flex="1"/>
  <statusbarpanel label="Still waiting...."/>
</statusbar>
...
```

Figure 2-20 shows the results.

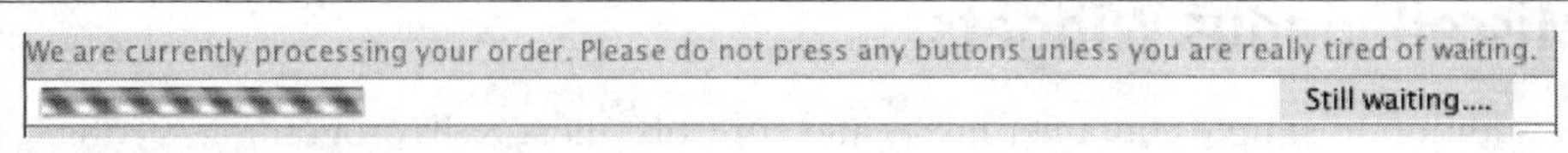
We are currently processing your order. Please do not press any buttons unless you are really tired of waiting.
Still waiting....

Figure 2-20. Status bar with progress meter

Helper Features

A number of additional features help designers deliver flexible interfaces that are more intuitive and user-friendly.

XUL `labels` provide a `control` attribute that supports a binding to GUI controls to specify which control receives focus when the label is clicked. Setting the value of the `control` attribute of a label will result in shifting input focus to the control with the matching `id` attribute.

The `tabindex` provides the same functionality available in most interface models that allow the user to quickly traverse through a series of text entry and control fields:

```
tabindex="someIndex"
```

Higher indices define the order of the next focused text entry area when the Tab key is pressed. Radio box elements should have a `tabindex` set to the first element of the box.

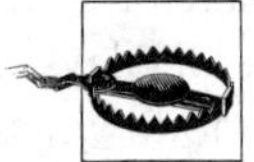

Implementation of `tabindex` is operating-system-specific. Windows platforms traverse focus to include buttons and checkboxes; OS X implementations may send focus only to text entry fields depending on a control panel setting.

The following source file illustrates the addition of the `control` attribute and `tabindex` to several fields. Figures 2-21 and 2-22 illustrate the differences between Windows and OS X implementations.

```
<?xml version="1.0"?>
<?xml-stylesheet href="chrome://global/skin/" type="text/css"?>

<?xml-stylesheet href="data:text/css,
      .test_a {
        background-color: #808080;
        border-color:black;
        border-style:dashed;
        border-width: thin;
        }

     .test_b {
        background-color: #c0c0c0;
        border-color:black;
        border-style:solid;
        border-width: thin;
        }
```

```
 type="text/css"?>

<window
    id="theWindow"
    title="The Window"
    orient="horizontal"
    width = "400"
    height = "300"
    xmlns="http://www.mozilla.org/keymaster/gatekeeper/there.is.only.xul"
    xmlns:html="http://www.w3.org/1999/xhtml"
    >

 <vbox flex="1">

<vbox>
<hbox>
<groupbox  flex="1">
  <caption>
   <label value="Please send me info:"/>
  </caption>
 <hbox>
    <label control="cmt" value="Comments:"/>
    <textbox tabindex="1" id="cmt" flex="1"/>
 </hbox>
  <checkbox   tabindex="2" label="Touring in the British Isles"/>
   <checkbox   tabindex="3"  label="Cycling in France"/>
    <checkbox   tabindex="4" label="Skiing in Switzerland"/>
 </groupbox>

<radiogroup pack="center" >
 <radio  tabindex="5"  label="Option 1"/>
 <radio  label="Option 2"/>
 <radio  label="Option 3"/>
</radiogroup>
</hbox>

<grid class="test_b" flex="1">
<columns>
 <column/>
 <column flex="1"/>
</columns>

  <rows>
    <row>
     <label control="Nm" value="Name:"/>
     <textbox tabindex="6" id="Nm"/>
    </row>

     <row>
     <label control="Addr" value="Address:"/>
     <textbox tabindex="7" id="Addr" />
    </row>
```

```
      <row>
      <label control="Ph" value="Phone:"/>
      <textbox tabindex="8"  id="Ph" />
     </row>

      <hbox pack="center">
      <button  tabindex="9" label="Send" />
     </hbox>
   </rows>
 </grid>
  </vbox>
 </vbox>

 </window>
```

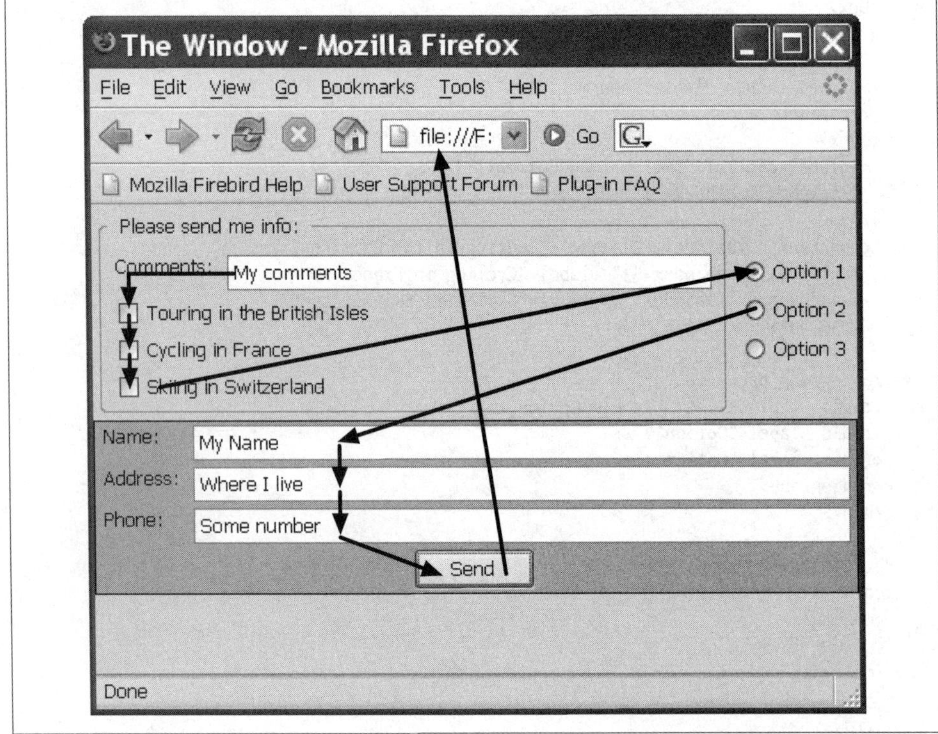

Figure 2-21. Windows tab index

Mozilla Style Declarations

The Firefox framework extends the CSS specification to support the enhanced styling of elements. (We will provide a more thorough discussion of CSS pseudoclasses and properties in Chapters 9 and 10.)

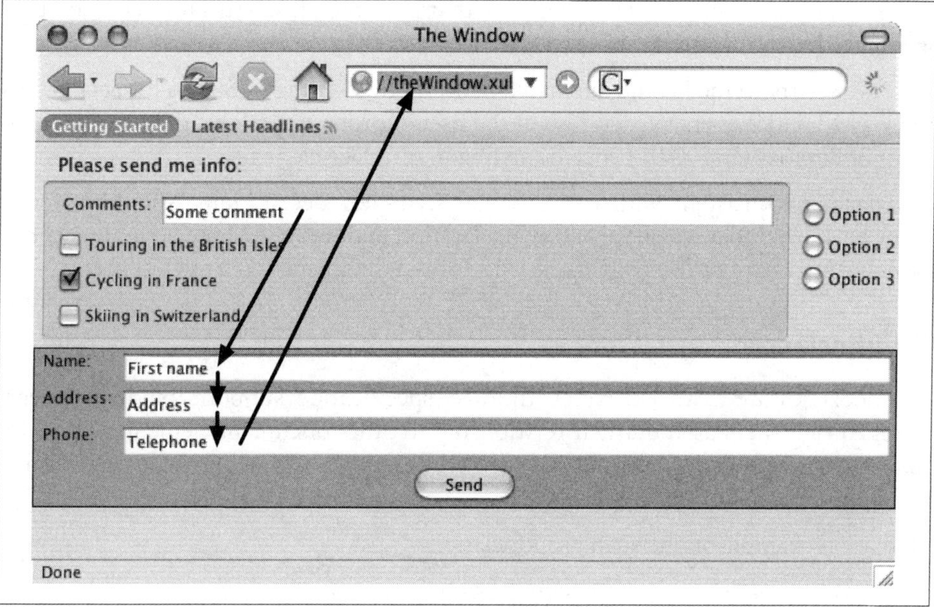

Figure 2-22. OS X tab index

Familiar CSS notation to style a class of HTML elements looks like this:

```
tagName : {
 someStyleAttribute: someValue;
someOtherStyleAttribute: someOtherValue;
....
}
```

This statement directs the rendering engine to assign styling characteristics to document elements that match the `tagName` (e.g., `div` elements).

Developers can design an interface that is much richer than those available only through HTML's styling specifications. Not only is there now a richer portfolio of style properties, but the variety of GUI widgets added by the XUL framework also calls for adding functionality to the CSS specification.

The Firefox framework supports Mozilla-enhanced CSS *pseudoproperties* that allow creation of new styling directives, and *pseudoelements* that enable the application of "standard" style declarations to customized element declarations.

Pseudoproperties

The use of an extended pseudoproperty looks like this:

```
hbox.myClass {
 -moz-box-pack:center;
}
```

In this case, any document `hbox` elements that have the `class` attribute set to `myClass` will have the `pack` property set to `end`.

Here we see the value behind such an extension; no existing CSS style for `pack` works the way XUL designers expect. Use of the pseudoproperties allows the broad assignment of Firefox- (and XUL-) specific styling to interface elements.

In a fashion consistent with conventional stylesheet declarations, should any element be subject to a pseudoproperty declaration and have attribute assignments referencing attributes of the same name, the inline assignment takes precedence.

Pseudoclasses

Pseudoclasses are a way in which the CSS specification supports binding appearances to elements based on their relationship to other document elements. The Firefox framework includes a number of such classes, most of which involve customizing tree appearances.

Here is an example of one such pseudoclass:

```
treechildren::-moz-tree-row { color:blue; }
```

This will set the text color to blue for any tree row elements that are children of the `treechildren` element.

Summary

The XUL framework provides a family of interface widgets that look similar to other GUI toolkits.

XUL interfaces are distinct in their use of the XML structure to represent the interface. Using XML to describe interfaces in turn allows the use of industry-standard stylesheets to add a distinctive look and to extend the interface appearance.

The box model used by Firefox generally discourages the use of absolute numbers for positioning or sizing, relying instead on attributes that describe how a box fills its available space and how child elements are to be positioned.

Now that we've covered the basics of how interface files are structured and you've been introduced to the core widget set, we have the tools we need to build XUL applications.

CHAPTER 3

Coding and Testing for the Real World

I'll start this chapter with an overview of using JavaScript with a specific XUL application—in particular, I'll discuss how JavaScript objects and the XUL document structure interact to put some machinery behind the interface widgets. I will follow up the development topics with an overview of debugging techniques and services offered by Mozilla.

Defining a Target Application

One effective technique for exploring different elements of an interface is to define a target application that exercises topics of interest. With that in mind, in the next few chapters we'll design an Internet application that allows the user to select portions of a web page and create a text note that cites the page (and selected text).

The application will allow users to do the following:

- Manually enter a web page for viewing
- Save the viewed web page into a category of bookmarks
- Create a note that captures their comments about a topic
- Cite in a note the text they've selected in the viewed web page
- Change the font style and size attributes of the note text
- Export the note text as an HTML document

We will also use custom code to "bookmark" viewed pages, and we will build the application to run as a standalone application. Figure 3-1 shows a rough sketch of what we will be designing.

With this sketch, we can start by building a simple source file that contains our boxes for content.

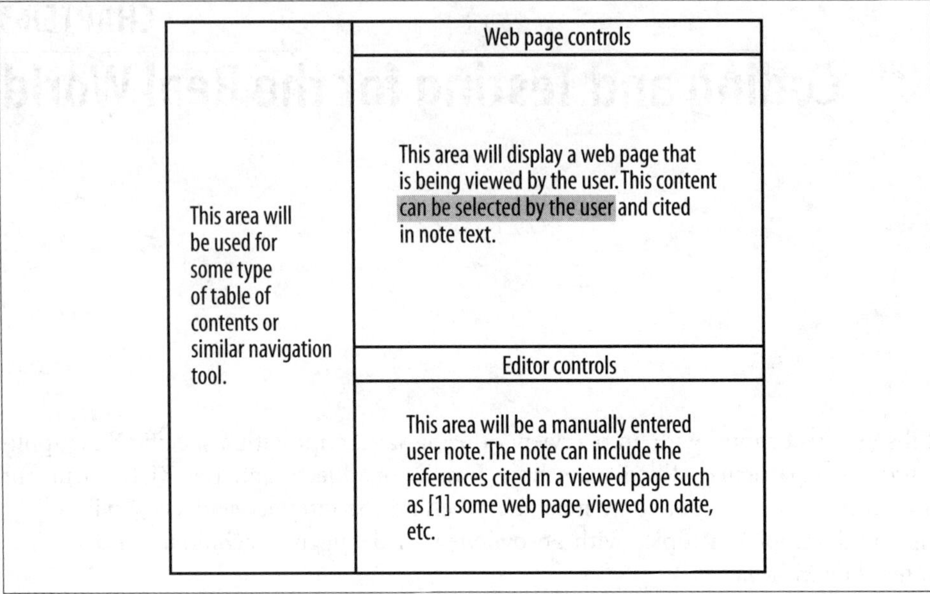
Web page controls
This area will display a web page that is being viewed by the user. This content can be selected by the user and cited in note text.
This area will be used for some type of table of contents or similar navigation tool.
Editor controls
This area will be a manually entered user note. The note can include the references cited in a viewed page such as [1] some web page, viewed on date, etc.

Figure 3-1. NewsSearch interface sketch

A first cut at the source file *newssearch.xul* follows:

```
<?xml version="1.0"?>
<?xml-stylesheet href="testStyles.css" type="text/css"?>

<window
  id="theMainWindow"
  title="Test Window"
  orient="horizontal"
  xmlns:xlink="http://www.w3.org/1999/xlink"
  xmlns="http://www.mozilla.org/keymaster/gatekeeper/there.is.only.xul">

 <!-- main top level container -->
 <hbox flex="1" >

 <!-- a container for some kind of list -->
 <vbox style="background-color:yellow;" flex="2" >
  <description id="tocDescription">
   Table of contents
  </description>
 </vbox>

 <!-- container for content and tool areas -->
 <vbox flex="2" >

 <!-- used to display content -->
 <hbox  style="background-color:green;" flex="3" >
  <description id="msgDescription">
```

```
    Content to be displayed
   </description>
  </hbox>

   <!-- used to display typing area  -->
  <hbox style="background-color:blue;" flex="3" >
  <description id="noteDescription">
    Note area
   </description>
  </hbox>

   <!-- used to display tool area-->
  <hbox flex="1" >

   <spacer flex="1"/>

     <vbox>
      <spacer flex="1"/>
       <hbox>
        <button id="B1" label="B1" />
        <button id="B2" label="B2"/>
        <button id="B3" label="B3"/>
        <button label="B4"/>
       </hbox>
       <spacer flex="1"/>
     </vbox>

   <spacer flex="1"/>

  </hbox>

  </vbox>
  <!-- container for messages and tool areas -->

  </hbox>
  <!-- main container -->

</window>
```

This sample includes some style attributes to help us visualize the boundaries of the various boxes. It also uses description elements to add some text identifying the main display areas. Opening the file in Firefox renders a collection of boxes, as shown in Figure 3-2.

Adding Logic

So far, we have a main window with a few boxes and buttons. The next step is to attach some type of trigger to an interface widget, and then some software to execute the logic the user expects. To start off, let's assume that our NewsSearch application will require a button to launch a server-based login process. To do that, we will attach a login script to one of our buttons. That script will conduct an initial

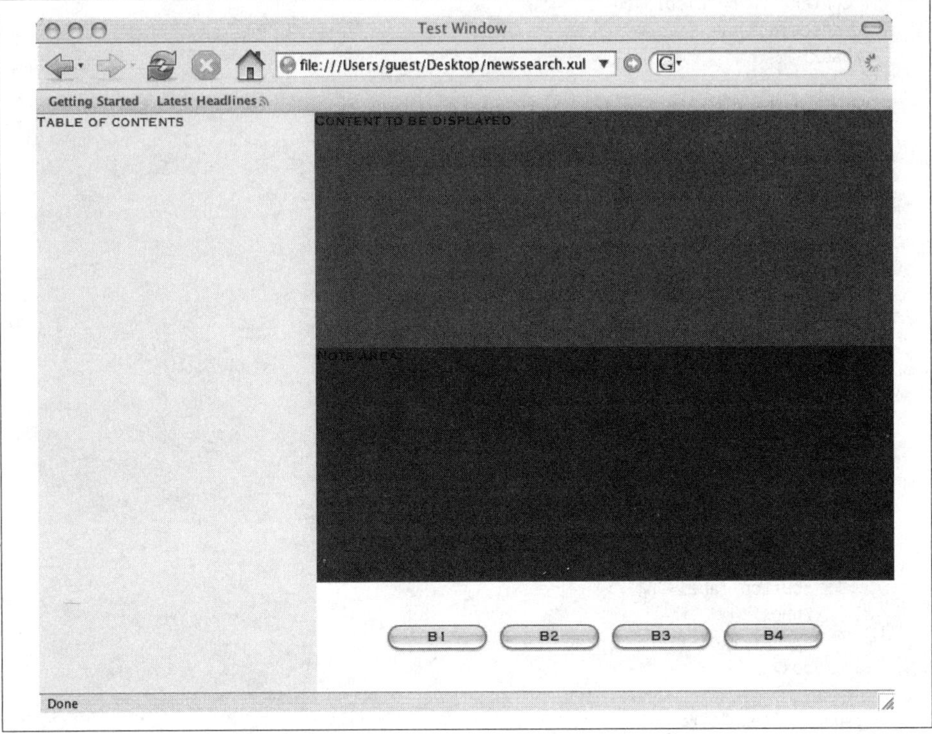

Figure 3-2. Application content areas

connection with a server (which we will only simulate in this chapter) to verify a user account. The completion of the process will allow us to display a list of news items that are available for viewing. These requirements lead us to explore the following topics:

- Attaching logic to widgets that execute some function as a result of user input
- Developing a script to authenticate a user and modify the interface by changing the contents and appearance of document elements
- Using the debugger when things don't work

All of these stages in one way or another require an understanding of how XUL, JavaScript, and the Document Object Model (DOM) interact. Although I will provide detailed information about JavaScript, DOM, and XUL in Chapter 7, we need to at least lay the foundation for some basic concepts before we continue.

JavaScript, Events, and DOM Nodes

JavaScript is a language that a browser engine interprets at runtime. There are two broad areas you must understand to use the language effectively: the syntax of the language itself (not a subject of this book), and the interaction of the language with the DOM to which XUL documents adhere.

The Document Object Model

Any manipulation of an XML structured document relies on the DOM as defined by the World Wide Web Consortium (W3C). The W3C defines several layers of DOM specifications that build upon one another:

DOM Level 1
: Level 1 defines the structure of XML documents, including XML-formatted HTML documents (technically referred to as XHTML documents). The *core* DOM 1 specification provides the initial description of document nodes, how to access them, and how to change the structure of a document by adding and removing nodes from the DOM document tree. Also part of DOM Level 1 is the description of *HTML Elements*, including the methods to access and manipulate structural aspects of the document tree representing an HTML document.

DOM Level 2
: The Level 2 core specifications add namespaces and the concept of document views, and fully specify the event model, stylesheet manipulation, and document traversal interfaces. The Level 2 HTML Element specification adds a number of interfaces that provide additional utility methods to process HTML-specific elements.

DOM Level 3
: The Level 3 specification adds features for managing document state and supporting document validation.

Although most of the topics relevant to our discussion involve DOM Level 2 and earlier, there is no substantive difference in functionality among the different levels, only extensions or enhancements in functionality.

Interfaces

Throughout this book, we will refer to objects that implement interfaces. Whereas an *object* represents a collection of methods (functions) and properties (data members) that model an entity, an *interface* represents a collection of methods and properties that are bound by related characteristics.

Consider a nonsoftware example:

A Subaru Outback may represent an object of a class named "all-wheel-drive cars." We could also describe the class of "all-wheel-drive cars" as implementing several interfaces:

- The rolling interface for vehicles that have four wheels, tires, and brakes
- The gasoline-fueled interface that provides methods for fueling and combustion
- The passenger-carrier interface for the characteristics of cabin size, interior climate control, and safety features

A delivery truck, on the other hand, would implement a rolling interface, but would probably also implement a cargo-carrier and diesel-fueled interface.

Rolling, gasoline-fueled, and passenger-carrier collections don't, by themselves, provide sufficient information to create a meaningful object. An object that implements an interface, however, can use the interface's methods and properties to provide a type of needed functionality.

As an example relevant to XUL and DOM, I will describe references that implement a *node* interface which, in turn, also implements an *element* interface. This means that the object referenced will implement functions that are related both to the document structure (node characteristics), and to information such as style, tag name, and attributes (element characteristics).

In summary, *interface* is best thought of as a well-defined characteristic of an object implemented through a set of related functions and properties.

Moving from widgets to document nodes

A XUL interface document is an XML file that is structured according to the rules of the DOM. In its simplest form, the DOM describes a tree of nodes, each node serving as either a point where multiple branches sprout, or the endpoint of a branch.

Looking at the source code in our XUL file, you can easily see a structure of document tags that contain other tags. The interface file of containers maps to a logical document model where each tag maps to a node in a document tree. A simple snippet of our interface illustrates a mapping of interface elements to document nodes, as shown in Figure 3-3.

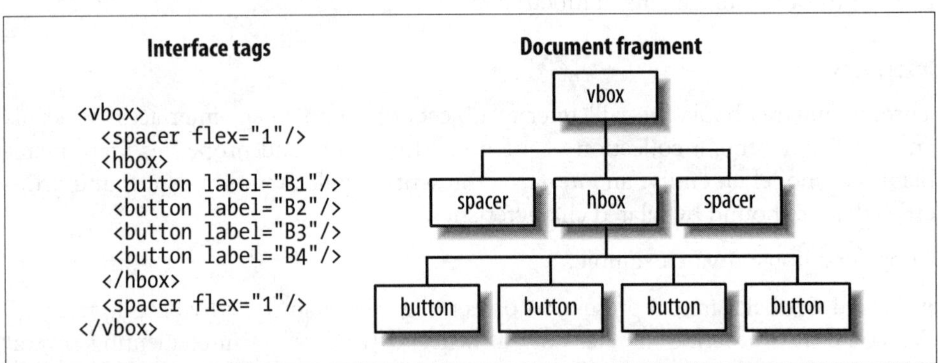

Figure 3-3. DOM tags and nodes

The nodes of a document are the basic objects with which JavaScript code most often interacts during DOM-based applications that manipulate the user's interface.

Each element's *node* encodes the information of a document's element *tag*, and all the information appearing in a tag in a source file is available to JavaScript through methods associated with the node interface.

Consider a simple hierarchy of the XUL `<description>` tag used to display long lines of text within a box. We could use a `description` to add a simple label to one of our boxes:

```
<hbox  flex="3" >
  <description id="msgDescription">
   Messages to be displayed
  </description>
 </hbox>
```

Here we add an attribute named `id` that will make our JavaScript code easy to write.

A detailed relationship of the XML tags represented as DOM element nodes would look something like Figure 3-4.

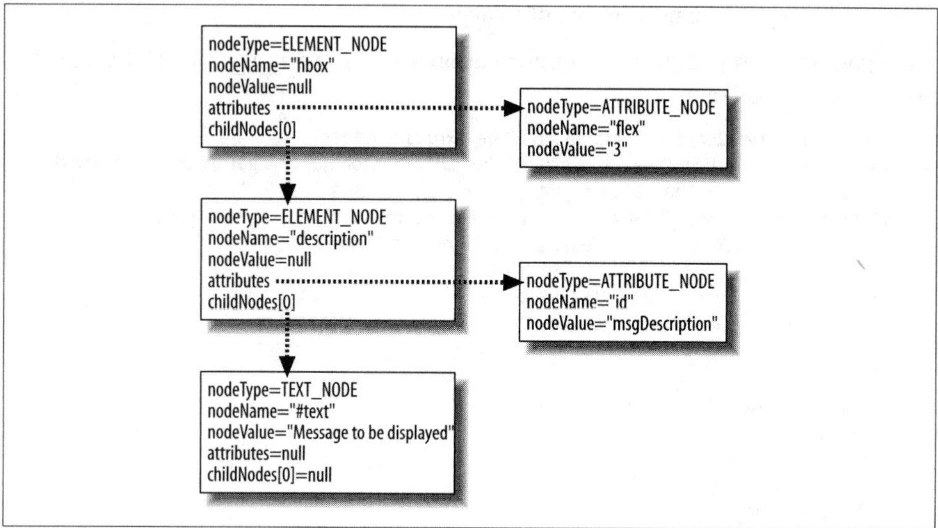

Figure 3-4. Node elements and attributes

A number of frequently used JavaScript methods and properties are supported by either the *document interface* or the *node interface* to obtain information about a node, as shown in Table 3-1.

Table 3-1. Frequently used JavaScript methods and properties

Method( ) or property	Returns
`Document.getElementById("`*`idValue`*`")`	A reference to a node with an `id` attribute of *`idValue`*.
`Node.getAttribute("`*`attributeName`*`")`	A string representing the value of the attribute identified by *`attributeName`*.

Table 3-1. Frequently used JavaScript methods and properties (continued)

Method( ) or property	Returns
`Node.nodeName`	A string representing the name of the node, most often reflecting the tag name.
`Node.nodeType`	An enumerated integer identifying the type of node.
`Node.childNodes`	`NodeList`: an array of all the immediate descendants of a node.
`Node.nodeValue`	Dependent on the node type. If the node is a `TEXT_NODE`, it returns the string value of the node. If the node is an `ATTRIBUTE_NODE`, it returns the value of the attribute. It returns null for `ELEMENT_NODES`.

Developers who want to use the `Document` interface can use the global JavaScript `document` object in their scripts to obtain a reference to the object that implements the methods of a `Document` interface. Functions that illustrate implementations of the `Node` interface will use a reference returned by some document function that provides a reference to the node we want to access.

So, a JavaScript snippet to obtain information about the text from our "description" node would look like this:

```
try {   // try block: exceptions will be explained later
var theNode = document.getElementById("msgDescription");  // get node of interest
var theNodeValue = "no value found";
if (theNode.childNodes.length > 0) { // assume child 0 is the text node
 var tNode = theNode.childNodes[0];        // check node 0 type

 if (tNode.nodeType == Node.TEXT_NODE) {
   theNodeValue = tNode.nodeValue;
  }
 }
alert("My value is " + theNodeValue);
} // try block
catch (e) { // exception
 alert("Some exception: " + e);
} // exception
```

Now that you have an understanding of the tools to use to access a node, we can look at what it takes to get an interface widget to respond to user input by using these functions and properties to associate nodes, user interactions, and scripts. This requires an understanding of DOM events, and how to attach a script that responds to the user.

Events

The DOM specifies the details of *events*, information that reflects some user-initiated interaction with an interface widget. To respond to those events, a developer attaches an *event handler* script to an interface widget.

Inline event handlers

The most straightforward manner to attach a script to a user interface widget is through the *inline* assignment method, in which a text script is set as an attribute to an element in the XUL document.

```
<hbox  onclick="alert('hello');">
```

In this case, the event to which we are responding is the "click" event, defined as the occurrence of a mouse-down and mouse-up over the same location on the screen. Event handler attributes always consist of the name of the event prefaced with the word *on*. Notice that all characters in the attribute name (`onclick`) are lowercase. As we are using XML, all strings are case-sensitive (HTML is case-insensitive, so developers often mix cases of attribute names for readability). Were we to code up this attribute to any of the boxes in our interface, we would see the friendly hello message pop up with a mouse click on the box whose attribute was modified.

The XUL designers have also added a convenience *command* event that goes one step beyond simple mouse clicks: it is fired when an interface element is activated. In the case of simple buttons, this means firing when the mouse is clicked on top of the element, but command events can also be fired when the interface widget has focus and the Enter key is pressed. The same goes for scrolled lists or menu items. Without the command event, developers would not only have to code up responses to click events, but also write special handlers to process keyboard entry input while the interface widget has focus. The command event makes all of this unnecessary. As a result, we could attach the following to any of our buttons:

```
<button label="B1" oncommand="alert('B1 received command');"/>
```

Take some care in assigning `oncommand` handlers to widgets where the nature of a command is not clear. For example, assigning an `oncommand` attribute to a simple `<vbox>` wouldn't work, because the nature of the commands to which a box would respond is ambiguous. A good rule of thumb is to consider whether a widget can get actuated through a number of different interactions with the user. If so, you can use the `oncommand` handler. If not, use a more primitive handler, such as `onclick`.

Dynamic assignment of attributes

A second way to add a behavior to an interface element is *dynamically* (as JavaScript is parsed and executed), either by assigning an event handler as a property to an element, or by adding an event-listener function reference to the element's DOM node. When using either approach, you should place the code for such assignments in an external script file, thus keeping complex logic outside the interface file and making the source XUL file cleaner and more readable.

The property assignment method discussed here became popular as Dynamic HTML (DHTML) techniques developed to move the Web beyond static web pages. This statement simply assigns a function to an element's event handler property:

```
element.onclick=theOnclickFunction;
```

The entire function will be copied into the element's `onclick` property. It is important to note, however, that this approach works only for events that the W3C has defined as part of the HTML 4.0 set of intrinsic events (described, among other places, at *http://www.w3.org/TR/REC-html40/interact/scripts.html*). If we wanted to use this form to add an event handler to one of our buttons, we would use the HTML standard `onclick` attribute.

If we want to use the XUL event `oncommand`, we will need to follow the XUL specification to provide additional guidance for XUL nodes. That specification (available at *http://www.xulplanet.com*) requires that an event handler for a XUL widget be assigned in one of only two ways: either as an attribute assigned to an element tag (as previously discussed), or as an *event listener* attached to the element's DOM node.

Dynamic addition of event listeners

If we want our application to adhere to the latest DOM standard, we would use the `AddEventListener` function to add an event handler to the node representing the element's tag. This method takes three arguments: the name of the event, the function name, and a parameter called `cancel` that controls the propagation of the event (more on event propagation later). The JavaScript to use this approach to set an event handler function named `button3Command` to our third button would look like this:

```
var b3 = document.getElementById("B3");
 b3.addEventListener("command",button3Command,true);
```

Now it's time to see how these different approaches work in attaching handlers to our interface buttons. We'll first try to use these techniques on our interface; we'll place the two latter approaches in an external script file.

External script files

Although you can include event handlers directly between script tags in the source XUL file, the preferred method is to include a script file reference to a JavaScript file. We can then use an `onload` attribute of the `<window>` element to call an event handler to assign event handlers to the window's interface widgets. To be thorough, we will use different forms to illustrate the variations in event handler assignment. Button 1 uses inline assignment, button 2 uses the form that assigns a function reference to the element's `onclick` property, and button 3 uses the DOM-preferred `addEventListener` function. We will put the JavaScript in a file named *newssearch.js* that exists in the same directory.

We remove the colorful styling information and some of the extraneous `description` tags while adding event listeners to the XUL source:

```
<?xml version="1.0"?>
<?xml-stylesheet href="testStyles.css" type="text/css"?>

<window
  id="theMainWindow"
  onload="initialize();"
  title="Test Window"
  orient="horizontal"
  xmlns:xlink="http://www.w3.org/1999/xlink"
  xmlns="http://www.mozilla.org/keymaster/gatekeeper/there.is.only.xul">

<script src="newssearch.js"/>
 <!-- main top level container -->
 <hbox flex="1" >

 <!-- a container for some kind of list -->
 <vbox flex="1" >
 </vbox>

 <!-- container for content and tool areas -->
 <vbox flex="2" >

 <!-- used to display content -->
 <hbox   flex="3" >
  <description id="msgDescription">
   Content to be displayed
  </description>
 </hbox>

  <!-- used to display typing area  -->
 <hbox flex="3" >
 </hbox>

  <!-- used to display tool area-->
 <hbox flex="1" >

  <spacer flex="1"/>

    <vbox>
     <spacer flex="1"/>
      <hbox>
       <button id="B1" label="B1" oncommand="alert('B1 received command');"/>
       <button id="B2" label="B2"/>
       <button id="B3" label="B3"/>
       <button label="B4"/>
      </hbox>
      <spacer flex="1"/>
    </vbox>

  <spacer flex="1"/>

 </hbox>

 </vbox>
```

```
<!-- container for messages and tool areas -->


</hbox>
<!-- main container -->

</window>
```

For our JavaScript file, *newssearch.js*, our code would look like this:

```
function button2Command(event) {
 alert("button 2 command " + event);
}

function button3Command(event) {
 alert("button 3 command " + event);
}

//
// Dynamically assign our event handler properties
//
function initialize() {
 var b2 = document.getElementById("B2");
 b2.onclick = button2Command;  // property assignment works best
// with HTML 4.0 events like onclick
 var b3 = document.getElementById("B3");
 b3.addEventListener("command",button3Command,true); // use XUL command
                                                    // event here
}
```

You will notice that the event handlers call out an event parameter. The event is an *implied parameter* for all event handlers, meaning we don't have to include it in any forms of our event handler assignment.

By launching Firefox and opening the *newssearch.xul* file, we see our "shades of gray" interface. We should now see an alert screen pop up for each of our buttons. Before we continue with our code to display (and change) node attributes, let's try to streamline our application by using the event parameter.

The event parameter

The two event handler functions display the implied event parameter in an alert box. This parameter gives us enough information so that we could move all our different event handlers into one function, and then parse the event parameter to take a specific course of action.

We can start by changing the code to dynamically assign event handlers to use the same form and the same function to handle button commands. So, we remove the inline event handler assignment from B1 in the source XUL file, and change both the button 1 and button 2 event handler assignments to use the same form as button 3:

```
function genericBtnHandler(event) {
 alert("button command " + event);
}

//
// Dynamically assign our event handler properties
//
function initialize() {
try {
 document.getElementById("B1").addEventListener("command",genericBtnHandler,true);
 document.getElementById("B2").addEventListener("command",genericBtnHandler,true);
 document.getElementById("B3").addEventListener("command",genericBtnHandler,true);
 }
 catch (e) {
  alert ("Exception: " + e)
  }
}
```

The snippet from the XUL file with our buttons now looks like this:

```
<hbox>
  <button id="B1" label="B1" />
  <button id="B2" label="B2"/>
  <button id="B3" label="B3"/>
  <button label="B4"/>
</hbox>
```

Now, pressing all the buttons calls the same function that displays a message, along with the event object.

Frequently used properties of the event are the `event.type` property, which provides a string with the event name, and the `event.target` property, which returns a reference to the object that is the target of the event (e.g., the button that was clicked). Once we have the object reference, we can access the object's `tagName` property, as well as the object's attributes—for example, its `id` and `label` attributes. Table 3-2 shows a summary of some of the most commonly used event and target properties used for building event decoding.

Table 3-2. Commonly used event and target properties for building event decoding

Property	Description
`event.type`	A string representation of the name, such as `click`, `mouseover`, etc.
`event.target`	The object from which the event originated.
`event.target.tagName`	The XML tag of the target.
`event.target.id`	Property reference shorthand for the `id` attribute (could also use `event.target.getAttribute("id")`).

We can now add some of these functions to our event handler to display this information:

```
function genericBtnHandler(event) {

var infoString = "Type = " + event.type + "\n";
infoString += "Target = " + event.target + "\n";
infoString += "Target.tagName = " + event.target.tagName + "\n";
infoString += "Target.id = " + event.target.id + "\n";
alert("button command \n" + infoString);
}
```

Pressing any of the buttons now presents a good summary statement that could allow us to continue button-specific decoding, as shown in Figure 3-5.

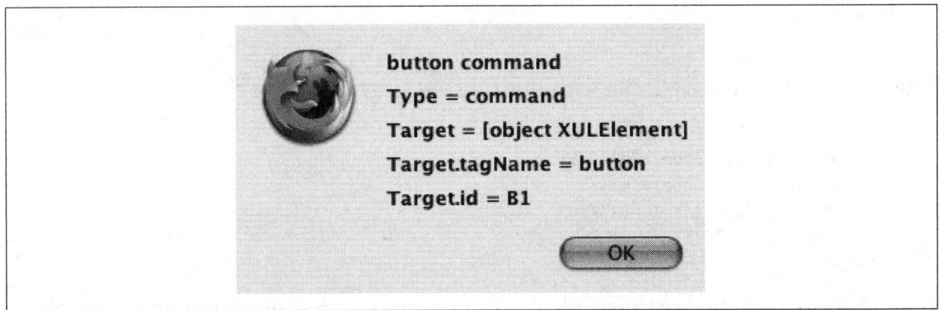

Figure 3-5. Event summary dialog

Now that we've covered the basics of attaching event handlers to nodes, we can take the next step by writing code that interacts with the node *contents* and node *attributes*.

Modifying Node Contents

We often need to modify the user interface in response to events or programmatic operations. We do so by calling functions that set node attributes.

We can start by reviewing our `<description>` tag used to display lengthy strings of text. Figure 3-2 showed how a simple tag is represented in the DOM tree as an element node with a child text node whose value is the text bracketed by the `<description>` tag.

We can get to the array of a node's children through the `node.childNodes` property. As with any JavaScript array, we can determine how many children a node has by the JavaScript `node.childNodes.length` statement.

In the case of our `<description>` node, we can access the text through its first child's `nodeValue` property:

```
var descTextNode = document.getElementById("msgDescription").childNodes[0];
var theDescription = descTextNode.nodeValue;
```

Text nodes are a special case. Although many properties are intended to be read-only, you can set text node contents by modifying the `nodeValue` property:

```
document.getElementById("msgDescription").nodeValue="some new value";
```

For this simple example, if we wanted to change the text in our description node to reflect our node information, we would change the button handler in our *newssearch.js* file accordingly:

```
function genericBtnHandler(event) {
try { // try block
var infoString = "Type = " + event.type + ",";
infoString += "Target = " + event.target + ",";
infoString += "Target.tagName = " + event.target.tagName + ",";
infoString += "Target.id = " + event.target.id + ".";
document.getElementById("msgDescription").childNodes[0].nodeValue = infoString;
} // try block
catch (e) {
 alert("genericBtnHandler exception: " + e);
 }
}
```

(Note that we replaced the newline characters in the `infoString` variable with commas.)

Pressing any of our buttons now results in the description text reflecting the information we previously saw in our alert dialog, as shown in Figure 3-6.

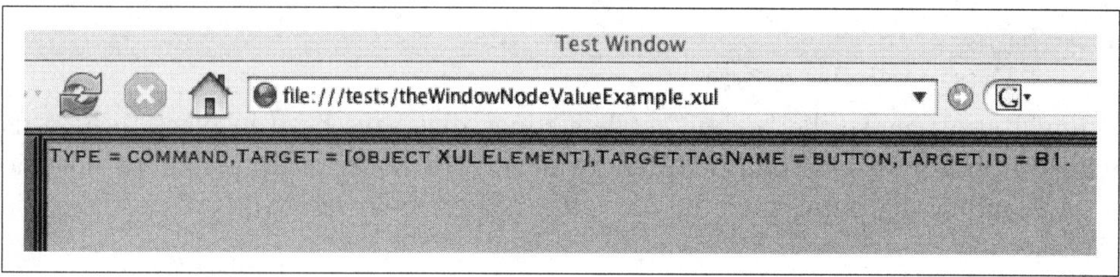

Figure 3-6. Event description

Simple Authentication Script

Because we will probably want to provide our NewsSearch service to a limited clientele, we will have to log in and authenticate users.

Our "real" application will involve a server authentication process that passes data from XUL text widgets and is triggered by XUL buttons, but for now, let's just hard-code some fictitious names into the application. We'll focus on the use of some XUL input widgets, and then modify our application to display a nice startup screen welcoming the user. To accomplish those tasks, we will break our work into two phases:

- Read a username and password from a XUL input field
- Change one of our display areas to remove the login buttons and generate a new welcome message

XUL Input Widgets

We accomplish single-line input through the XUL <textbox> element. Textboxes also have attributes to define password entries and a maximum length attribute.

Now we'll add a couple of text entry areas to the center area of our interface and a few spacers to line things up. The resulting changes in our source file follow:

```
<!-- used to display message -->
 <hbox   flex="3" >

  <spacer flex="1"/>
  <vbox>  <!-- stack message and login controls vertically -->

    <spacer flex="1"/>
      <description id="msgDescription">
       Waiting for login.
      </description>
      <label value="User Name:" control="userName"/>
      <textbox id="userName"/>
      <label value="Password:" control="userName"/>
      <textbox id="password"  type="password" maxlength="8"/>
      <button id="loginButton " label="Logon"/>
     <spacer flex="1"/>
  </vbox>
  <spacer flex="1"/>

 </hbox>
 <!-- used to display message -->
```

We will also remove the "debug" style settings that have been in place to help us with our box positions and settings. And we will temporarily comment out the groove and background color of our styles specified in *testStyles.css* to make the interface look a little more realistic:

```
vbox {
/*
  border-style:groove;
  background-color:#888888;
  */
  }

 hbox {
 /*
  border-style:groove;
  background-color:#cccccc;
  */
  }
```

Our changes yield something that looks a little more like a real application, as in Figure 3-7.

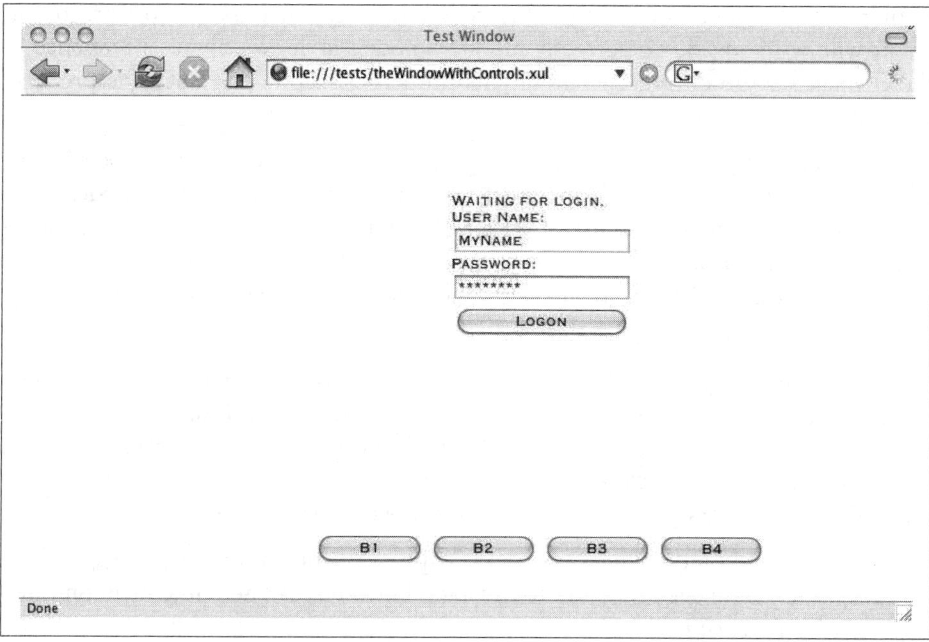

Figure 3-7. Simple login window

Next we will write some code to check the username and password against some known values, and if the results match, we will provide some visual feedback to indicate that the user has logged in. If the entry is invalid, we'll change the content of the `<description>` node to issue an appropriate message, and change its color to draw the user's attention.

Modifying node styles

If the user enters an invalid username/password combination, we will change the "Waiting for Login" message to "Unregistered user," and change the appearance of the text to provide a visual clue of what happened. To do this, we will need to modify the style attribute of the document node we want to change. In this case, the node of interest will be the `<description>` node.

One way to access node attributes is to get a reference to the description, look through all the `childNodes`, find an attribute node whose name matches what we are looking for, and change that node's value.

The DOM's `Element` interface provides us with a convenience function that makes things much easier:

```
messageNode.setAttribute("style","background-color:red");
```

Although this function will yield a red background for our node, it also removes any other style values that may have been set, resulting in a node that has only one style setting: a background color. Any other style attributes, such as font or foreground color, will be removed. To correctly modify a node's style, we obtain a reference to the element's `style` object, and modify its properties. Modifying one style property leaves all other style properties unchanged.

XUL elements implement a number of interfaces, one of which is the `DomElement` interface used to collect the characteristics of XUL and HTML element nodes. As a result, XUL elements behave just as HTML element nodes in terms of the style property object. The JavaScript used to set the background color of a XUL element is identical to the code that sets the background color of any HTML element:

```
messageNode.style.backgroundColor="red";
```

Note that when using the `style` object's properties, the property name takes the inline form, capitalizes every word except the first, and removes all dashes. This transformation provides a reference that is compatible with the JavaScript language. Hence, we would access the inline `background-color` attribute of our message node by using JavaScript through the `backgroundColor` property of the message's style node.

Now we'll make some changes to begin to phase in our authentication interface. First, we will add an event handler to the login button to call an authentication function in our *newsearch.js* file:

```
function initialize( ) {
try {
 document.getElementById("B1").addEventListener("command",genericBtnHandler,true);
 document.getElementById("B2").addEventListener("command",genericBtnHandler,true);
 document.getElementById("B3").addEventListener("command",genericBtnHandler,true);
 //
 // Add a login script
 document.getElementById("loginButton").addEventListener("command",doLogin,true);
 }
 catch (e) {
  alert ("Exception: " + e);
  }
}
```

In the `doLogin` function, we will stub out a test that services properly authenticated users, and force an unconditional branch to the failure case that sets the background of the message to red and the text color to white. We will also add the call to change the text in our description field to provide some needed information. We add the following script:

```
function doLogin(event) {
try { // try
 if (0) { // we'll add code here later
 }
 else { // login failure
  document.getElementById("msgDescription").style.backgroundColor="red";
  document.getElementById("msgDescription").style.color="white";
  document.getElementById("msgDescription").childNodes[0].nodeValue =
    "User not authenticated.";
```

```
      } // login failure

      } // try
      catch (e) { //
       alert("doLogin exception: " + e);
      }//
    }
```

The code will result in the description area always being highlighted with reversed text, as shown in Figure 3-8.

Figure 3-8. Authentication window

Removing and adding document nodes

We have covered examples of what to do to change a node's content and appearance, but what about the cases when we want to remove content completely (or add new content) to the document tree? In this simple example, if the user is authenticated, we want to remove all the login buttons and entry areas, and add a new description widget to welcome her.

To accomplish this task, we will look at some useful functions that come from the `Document` and `Element` interfaces, as outlined in Table 3-3.

Table 3-3. Useful functions that derive from the Document and Element interfaces

Property or function	Description
`Element.childNodes`	Returns the array of node children
`Element.removeChild(childNode)`	Removes a child from a parent
`Document.createElement("tagName")`	Creates a new node with the specified tag
`Element.appendChild(newChildNode)`	Adds a node to a parent's array of children

Because each element is a node in a tree, the DOM `Element` interface provides a `childNodes` property that returns a JavaScript array of all the first-generation children of the node. With that array reference, we can use the `Element` interface's `removeChild` function to delete all of the node's children (and descendants).

We change the main container of our login area to add an `id` attribute:

```
<hbox id="contentArea" flex="3" >

  <spacer flex="1"/>
```

```
<vbox >  <!-- stack message and login controls vertically -->
  <spacer flex="1"/>
    <description id="msgDescription">
     Waiting for login.
    </description>
    <label value="User Name:" control="userName"/>
    <textbox id="userName"/>
    <label value="Password:" control="userName"/>
    <textbox id="password"  type="password" maxlength="8"/>
    <button id="loginButton" label="Logon"/>
   <spacer flex="1"/>
</vbox>
<spacer flex="1"/>
```

This allows us to modify our `doLogin` script to easily obtain a reference to the login pane from the content area and remove all of its children if we get a successful login:

```
var theParent = document.getElementById("contentArea");

  while(theParent.childNodes.length != 0)
   theParent.removeChild(theParent.childNodes[0]);
```

With code to remove all our unused interface widgets, we need to create something new for our welcome message.

The `Document` interface provides a function, `createElement("tagName")`, to allow for the creation of a node of a given tag. Once a node is created, it must be appended to a parent node to be inserted in the document tree.

To create a description interface element, we need to create an element node with a `description` tag, and a text node for the text to be displayed. For the creation of simple text nodes, the `Document` interface implements a convenience function, `createTextNode("theTextValue")`. The text node is appended to the description node, which in turn is appended to the node that parented the previous login panel:

```
var newDescription = document.createElement("description");
var newDescriptionText = document.createTextNode("Welcome");
newDescription.appendChild(newDescriptionText);
theParent.appendChild(newDescription);
```

Developers should familiarize themselves with the method `createElementNS`, which is a more robust way to create elements that are bound to a specific XML namespace and vocabulary. For the sake of this introductory exercise, we can use the simpler `createElement` method.

The final piece to our simulated login is to compare the data in the text entry fields to some hardcoded strings that we'll interpret as an authentic user. To obtain the value of a XUL text field, we use the `value` property; using the function `getAttribute("value")` would return only the default value that was specified as an inline attribute. Rather, we get the dynamic content by accessing the widget's `value` property:

```
var loginName = document.getElementById("userName").value;
var password = document.getElementById("password").value;
```

When we add all these changes, and make a few modifications to the content area's style to add some graphical interest, *newssearch.js* looks like this:

```
function genericBtnHandler(event) {
try { // try block
var infoString = "Type = " + event.type + ",";
infoString += "Target = " + event.target + ",";
infoString += "Target.tagName = " + event.target.tagName + ",";
infoString += "Target.id = " + event.target.id + ".";
document.getElementById("msgDescription").childNodes[0].nodeValue = infoString;
} // try block
catch (e) {
 alert("genericBtnHandler exception: " + e);
 }
}

function doLogin(event) {
var loginName = document.getElementById("userName").value;
var password = document.getElementById("password").value;
try { // try
 if ( (loginName == "XULuser") &&
      (password == "XULpass")) { // we'll add code here later

 // Remove all the old login widgets
 var theParent = document.getElementById("contentArea");

  while(theParent.childNodes.length != 0)
   theParent.removeChild(theParent.childNodes[0]);

// Now re-create a welcome area
 theParent.style.backgroundColor = "LightSeaGreen";
 theParent.style.borderColor = "gray";
 theParent.style.borderStyle = "ridge";
 var leftSpacer = document.createElement("spacer");
 leftSpacer.setAttribute("flex","1");
 theParent.appendChild(leftSpacer);
 var newDescription = document.createElement("description");
 var newDescriptionText = document.createTextNode("Welcome " + loginName);
 newDescription.appendChild(newDescriptionText);
 theParent.appendChild(newDescription);
 var rightSpacer = document.createElement("spacer");
 rightSpacer.setAttribute("flex","1");
 theParent.appendChild(rightSpacer);
 }
 else { // login failure
  document.getElementById("msgDescription").style.backgroundColor="red";
  document.getElementById("msgDescription").style.color="white";
  document.getElementById("msgDescription").childNodes[0].nodeValue =
    "User not authenticated.";

 } // login failure
```

```
} // try
 catch (e) { //
  alert("doLogin exception: " + e);
 }//
}
//
// Dynamically assign our event handler properties
//
function initialize( ) {
try {
 document.getElementById("B1").addEventListener("command",genericBtnHandler,true);
 document.getElementById("B2").addEventListener("command",genericBtnHandler,true);
 document.getElementById("B3").addEventListener("command",genericBtnHandler,true);
 //
 // Add a login script
 document.getElementById("loginButton").addEventListener("command",doLogin,true);
 }
 catch (e) {
  alert ("Exception: " + e);
  }
}
```

Saving our working XUL file as *theWindowWithLogin.xul*, the listing is now as follows:

```
<?xml version="1.0"?>
<?xml-stylesheet href="testStyles.css" type="text/css"?>

<window
  id="theMainWindow"
  onload="initialize( );"
  title="Test Window"
  orient="horizontal"
  xmlns:xlink="http://www.w3.org/1999/xlink"
  xmlns="http://www.mozilla.org/keymaster/gatekeeper/there.is.only.xul">

<script src="newssearch.js"/>
 <!-- main top level container -->
 <hbox flex="1" >

 <!-- a container for some kind of list -->
 <vbox flex="1" >
 </vbox>

 <!-- container for messages and tool areas -->
 <vbox flex="2" >

 <!-- used to display message -->
 <hbox  id="contentArea"  flex="3" >
```

```
  <spacer flex="1"/>
  <vbox >  <!-- stack message and login controls vertically -->
    <spacer flex="1"/>
      <description id="msgDescription">
       Waiting for login.
      </description>
      <label value="User Name:" control="userName"/>
      <textbox id="userName"/>
      <label value="Password:" control="userName"/>
      <textbox id="password"  type="password" maxlength="8"/>
      <button id="loginButton" label="Logon"/>
     <spacer flex="1"/>
  </vbox>
  <spacer flex="1"/>

 </hbox>
 <!-- used to display message -->


  <!-- used to display typing area  -->
 <hbox flex="3" >
 </hbox>

  <!-- used to display tool area-->
 <hbox flex="1" >

  <spacer flex="1"/>

    <vbox>
     <spacer flex="1"/>
      <hbox>
       <button id="B1" label="B1" />
       <button id="B2" label="B2"/>
       <button id="B3" label="B3"/>
       <button label="B4"/>
      </hbox>
      <spacer flex="1"/>
    </vbox>
  <spacer flex="1"/>
 </hbox>

 </vbox>
 <!-- container for messages and tool areas -->
 </hbox>
 <!-- main container -->
</window>
```

When we now log in with the hardcoded values for username and password, we see our welcome message, as shown in Figure 3-9.

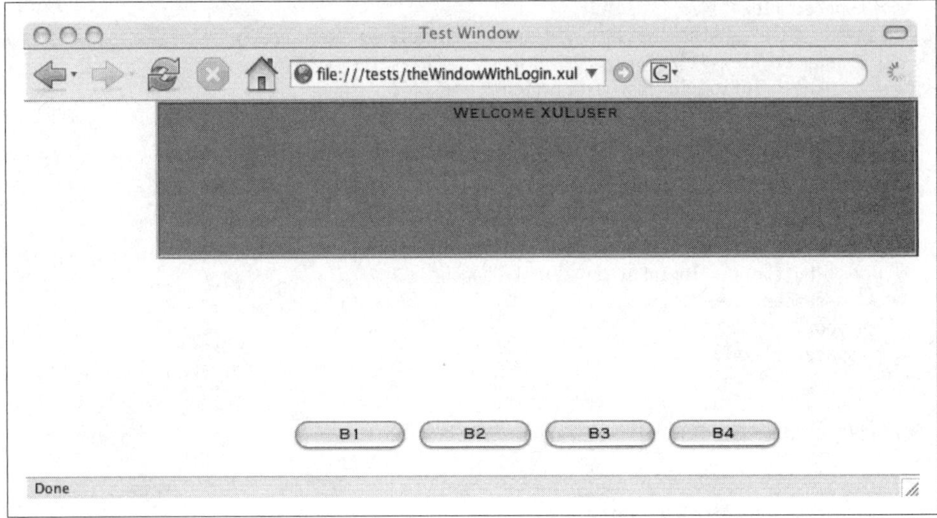

Figure 3-9. Simple welcome message

When Things Don't Work

Mistakes happen—there always exists the possibility that this program, as simple as it is, may not work. We will take a brief side trip to look at the simplest (though often most common) errors, and how to quickly find them.

Developers often find themselves confronting problems that fall into three categories:

- Typographical errors that prevent a script from being parsed and interpreted
- Programming errors in which the mistake consists of an improper implementation of logic that is otherwise sound
- Logic errors that represent a flawed design

In terms of XUL development, the designer can rely on the *JavaScript console* to help report coding and logic errors, the *DOM inspector* to view a XUL interface tree, the *JavaScript debugger* to help trace programming and logic errors, and the *operating system console* to report the output of `TRACE` statements during program execution.

To show how you can use these tools, we'll look at the basic types of errors and how to identify them.

Looking for the Obvious: Bad Typing

Because this is a simple application, let's purposely break the file and see what happens.

In the case of typographical errors that result in a corrupted XUL file, most mistakes are caught rather quickly. For example, removing one of the double quotes for an attribute assignment:

```
<!-- a container for some kind of list -->
<vbox flex="1 > <!-- quote intentionally left out -->
</vbox>
```

yields an immediate response when we try to open the source XUL file, as shown in Figure 3-10.

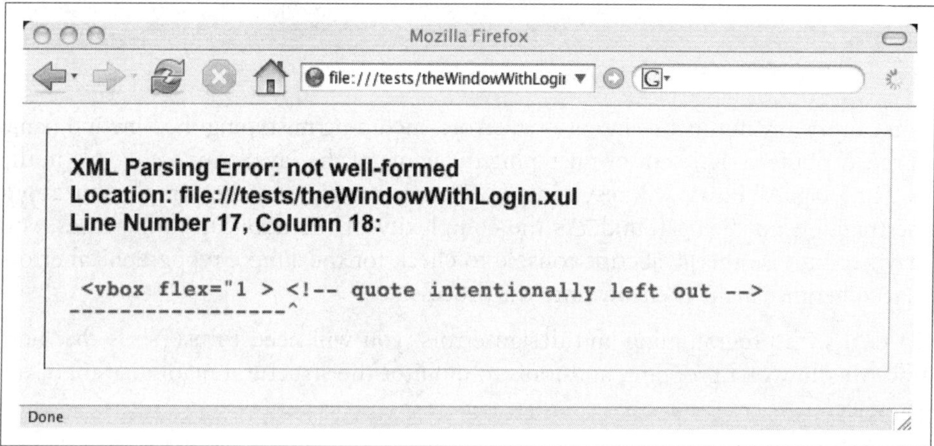

Figure 3-10. XUL file parsing error

Less obvious is how to detect a problem with a source JavaScript file.

For example, if we intentionally leave out one of the closing parentheses in our `initialize` function:

```
function initialize() {
try {
  document.getElementById("B1").addEventListener("command",
   genericBtnHandler,true; // Oops no closing paren
```

when we open the corrupt source file with Firefox, the interface looks fine, but pressing button 1 does nothing. How do we find out what is wrong?

The JavaScript console

One of the fastest and easiest tools for identifying the source of many types of errors is the JavaScript console. To access the JavaScript console, follow these steps:

1. From the Firefox browser, select Tools → JavaScript Console.
2. Press the Clear button on the JavaScript console tool panel to remove any residual messages.
3. Press the Reload Source button on the browser to reload the source file.

Looking at the JavaScript console, you see a list of statements that provide a clue of where to look, as shown in Figure 3-11.

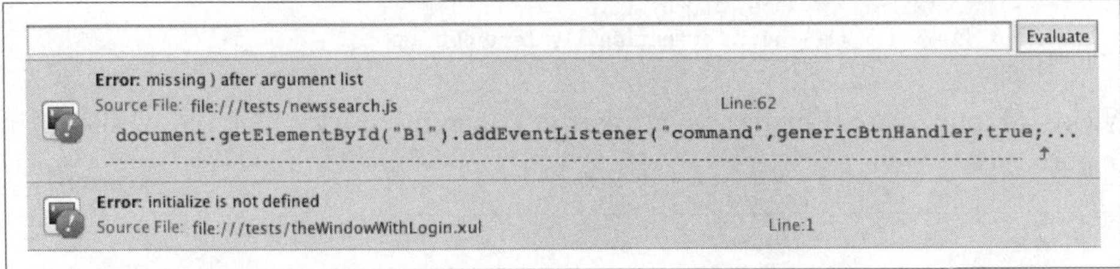

Figure 3-11. JavaScript console flagging source code error

You can try any number of intentional errors, including mistyping the function name in the attribute assignment or mistyping the name of the JavaScript source file in the `<script>` tag. All errors will result in a JavaScript console message complaining about the function not being found. As the complexity of the application increases, you may need to use the JavaScript console to check for the simple typographical errors that sometimes make their way into the process.

To deal with programming and design errors, you will need to use tools that help trace the flow of a program, and tools to monitor the structural manipulation of the interface.

Programming and Design Errors

Once the developer has his code properly parsed and running within the Firefox browser, the testing and debugging task turns to tracking code functions to verify that the intended tasks are being carried out. This runtime form of debugging requires a number of tools and techniques that monitor code execution.

The console dump( ) command

Although we could seed JavaScript `alert` statements throughout the code, they can become annoying as you add the pop ups to initially track down a problem and then remove them once a problem is resolved. (Later, we often add the same statements back in to conduct a form of regression testing to track down the latest bug.)

To provide a display of variables as well as simple debugging messages, we can use the `dump(`*`someValues`*`)` command. This will send whatever you specify to a system console. There are two steps to follow before using the `dump` command: enable the Cross-Platform Component Model (XPCOM) framework to access the console, and then launch the browser from the command line.

To enable the XPCOM framework to utilize a system console for the `dump` command, launch the browser and type **`about:config`** in the URL bar. We see a complete list of preferences that we can modify.

Use the right mouse button (or Ctrl-Click for Macs) to bring up a panel to add a new Boolean setting. In the window for the setting name, type **browser.dom.window.dump.enabled** and set the value to true (see Figure 3-12).

Figure 3-12. Enabling browser dump preference

Next, we'll change some of our JavaScript source code to use the dump command. We will alter the button event handler to dump the event information to the console rather than modify the description node:

```
function genericBtnHandler(event) {
try { // try block
var infoString = "Type = " + event.type + ",";
infoString += "Target = " + event.target + ",";
infoString += "Target.tagName = " + event.target.tagName + ",";
infoString += "Target.id = " + event.target.id + ".";
//document.getElementById("msgDescription").childNodes[0].nodeValue = infoString;
dump(infoString + "\n");
} // try block
```

Finally, we need to launch the browser from a console session and use the -console flag. Launching the browser and pressing the bottom row of buttons should pass the following information to the console:

```
./firefox -console&
[1] 544
Type = command,Target = [object XULElement],Target.tagName = button,Target.id = B1.
Type = command,Target = [object XULElement],Target.tagName = button,Target.id = B2.
Type = command,Target = [object XULElement],Target.tagName = button,Target.id = B3.
```

The dump command ends up being much more useful than scattering alert messages through an application, especially when the introduction of a pop-up window may interfere with some other user interaction being tested.

The Venkman debugger

Serious debugging involves the ability to freeze a program as it executes, view variables, and step through execution while observing the variable as it changes.

The Venkman JavaScript debugger is available to all Mozilla-based browsers. You launch it from the browser's menu bar by selecting Tools → JavaScript Debugger.

> If JavaScript Debugger does not show up on your menu, you have not installed the developer options with your browser. To install the debugger separately, select Tools → Extensions and use the browser window to find and download the Venkman debugger.

Once the debugger is launched, we see a variety of windows, most of which are self-explanatory. If we use the browser to open our source XUL file, the Loaded Scripts window is filled in with a number of files, including the *newssearch.js* source file. If we open the source file and click on the doLogin function, the Source Code window scrolls to that function. Breakpoints are set by clicking the mouse in the column to the left of the source code line number. If we set a breakpoint in the doLogin function (we should see a red *B* next to the source line) and execute our application, the debugger will stop execution after we attempt to log in. Figure 3-13 shows the display.

All variables are available for inspection, and selecting a variable provides us with a host of information regarding the nature of the JavaScript object, function definitions, and variable values. The entry area under the Interactive Session window even allows us to type in JavaScript expressions that we can use to explore other variables or code settings that may not be built into the source code. When it comes to debugging an interactive XUL application, the Venkman debugger will carry the lion's share of work.

The DOM Inspector tool

Sometimes the code seems to work, but the interface doesn't look as we expected. The DOM Inspector tool provides us with a graphical representation of the document tree.

To see the DOM Inspector at work, launch Firefox and open the source XUL file. Then select Tools → DOM Inspector. By using the main tree display, we can open all the document nodes. Selecting a node will also display a blinking red outline around the interface widget that the node represents.

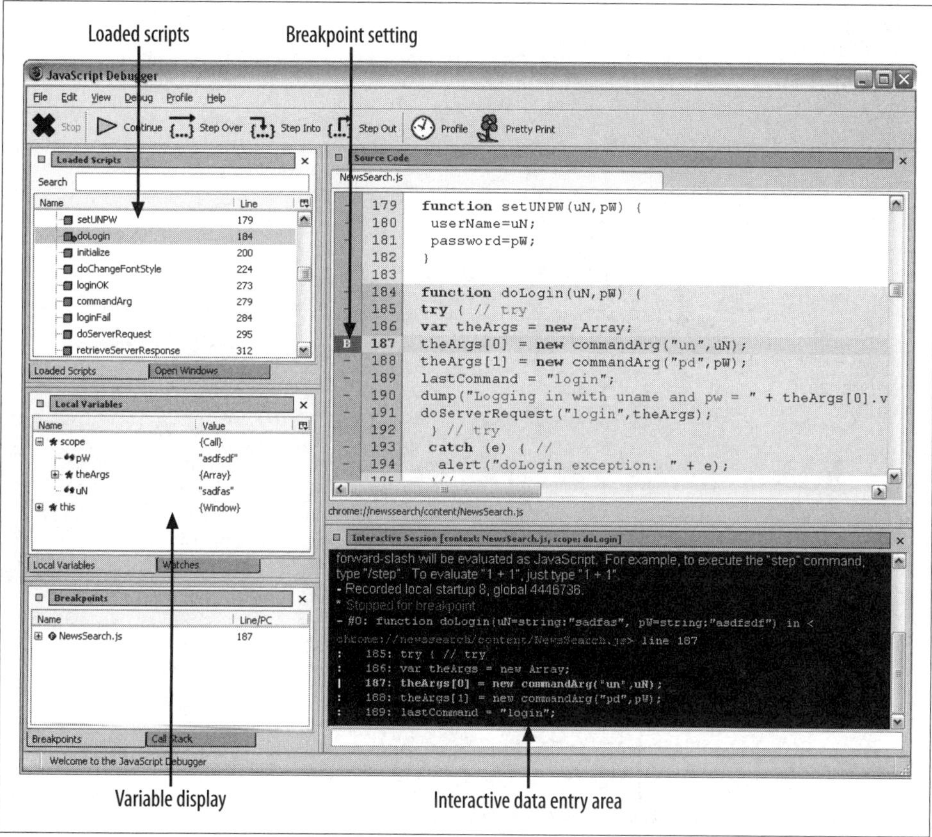

Figure 3-13. Venkman debugger with breakpoints

The DOM Inspector provides the developer with a view of the interface, just as the DOM interface sees it. Notice in particular how the tree changes by examining the portion of the tree that encompasses the content and login areas.

Figure 3-14 shows the display before we log in.

After we conduct a successful login, the tree shows us what our script did to the interface, as shown in Figure 3-15.

Summary

This chapter introduced the basics of using JavaScript to interact with a XUL interface through the DOM. The basics of accessing the DOM tree, looking up element nodes, and modifying their style and content provide developers with the fundamental skills to build a XUL application.

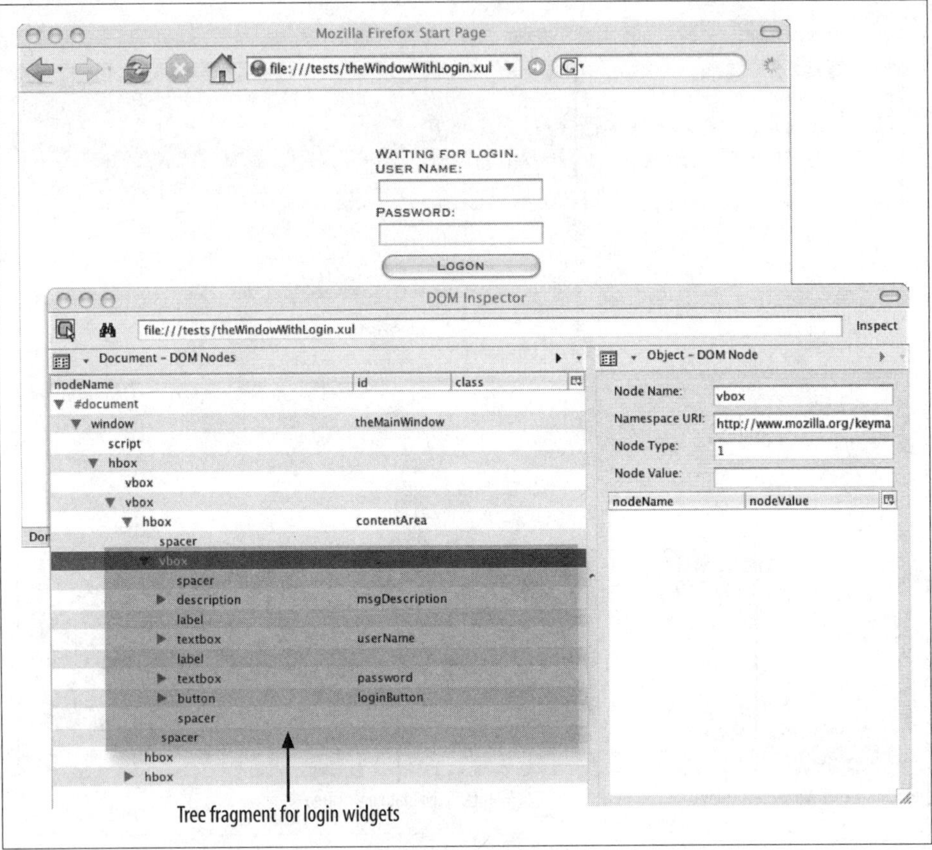

Figure 3-14. DOM Inspector: Before login

We also covered the main debugging techniques and tools that we will use for the rest of this project, including the JavaScript console for reporting execution errors and viewing diagnostic information, the Venkman debugger for interactive debugging, and the DOM Inspector for viewing the DOM tree as the user and our code interact with the interface.

Next, we move our application that runs as a XUL file in a local directory to one that more closely resembles a commercial implementation.

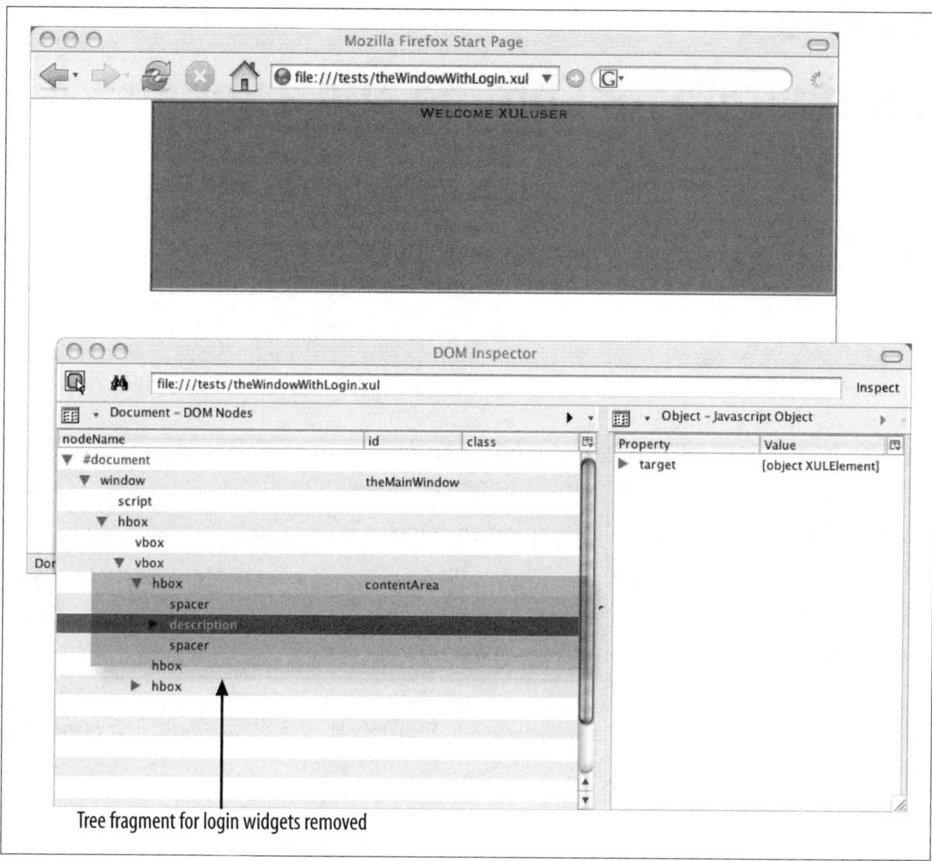

Figure 3-15. DOM tree after modification

CHAPTER 4

Configuring for Chrome and a Server

In this chapter, we will move our application from its home in a test directory to a setting that is more consistent with commercial implementations.

We will create two key pieces for implementing our application:

- A local XUL application communicating with a Personal Hypertext Processor (PHP) server
- A remote XUL application being served by PHP scripts

Both implementations will use an SQL database to hold user and password information to conduct the authentication process. Figure 4-1 shows a block diagram illustrating the relationship of the main elements of our design.

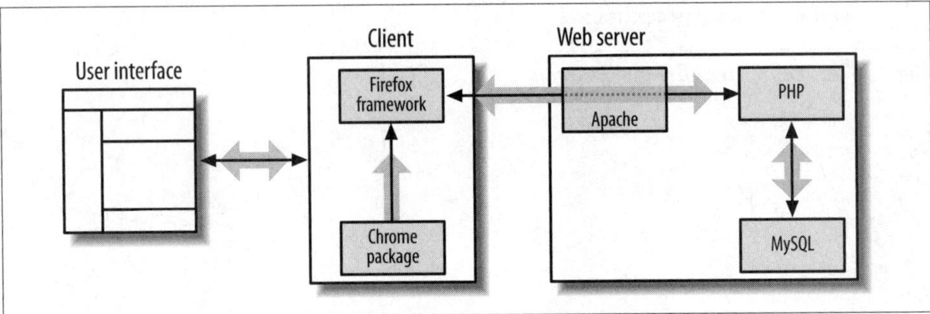

Figure 4-1. NewsSearch information flow

Chrome Overview

This book uses the term *XUL application* to describe our NewsSearch project. This differs from conventional web applications that are designed to be served web pages that are rendered by web browsers. A XUL application, however, can be implemented as a page served to a XUL-capable browser, or it can be configured to run as an application local to the user's machine. In the case of the latter, the files that comprise the application (JavaScript source, stylesheets, datafiles) are installed in a *chrome* directory and run as a chrome URL.

To date, the most popular XUL applications, such as the Firefox browser, Thunderbird mailer, and Sunbird calendar, are implemented as bundled applications running from the user's *chrome* directory.

Web developers refer to traditional web applications as being subject to the rules of a security *sandbox*. Originating from the Java language's security policy, the sandbox philosophy limits the reach of executable code to a certain area. For browsers, this means that unprivileged JavaScript can access data from a served document and from documents sharing its URL, but the browser infrastructure allows no access to the local filesystem or to potentially destructive operating system and network services.

There are cases when the local browser needs to store information on a user's computer. This information may include bookmarks, runtime preferences, or other saved settings that would impair the user experience if not kept locally accessible; the sandbox is therefore expanded to include a controlled portion of the local filesystem. Applications that are registered within Firefox's chrome are granted an area on the local disk to which full read/write access is granted.

In addition to meeting the security requirements imposed by the Firefox framework, a chrome application has a different look to it.

Before launching our code as a chrome application, we should change the *testStyles.css* stylesheet to provide a default background color for our window:

```
window {
 background-color:white;
}
```

(The default window color is needed when launching a chrome application from the command line.)

To see what our test application would look like as a chrome application, open a command window and launch Firefox from the command line, specifying the `-chrome` option along with the pathname to the source file. The `-chrome` option directs the framework to display the source as a chrome window, not as a browser window.

On an OS X machine, the code would look like this:

```
theUser% pwd
theUser% /Applications/Firefox.app/Contents/MacOS
theUser% ./firefox -chrome "file:Macintosh HD:tests:theWindowWithLogin.xul"
```

Our NewsSearch application now appears as a chrome window with none of the controls we associate with a browser (see Figure 4-2).

Simply launching an application with the `-chrome` option and a file URL will give us a chrome appearance, but to run it as a client/server chrome application, we will need to install the application as a *chrome package*, or serve the interface as a XUL page.

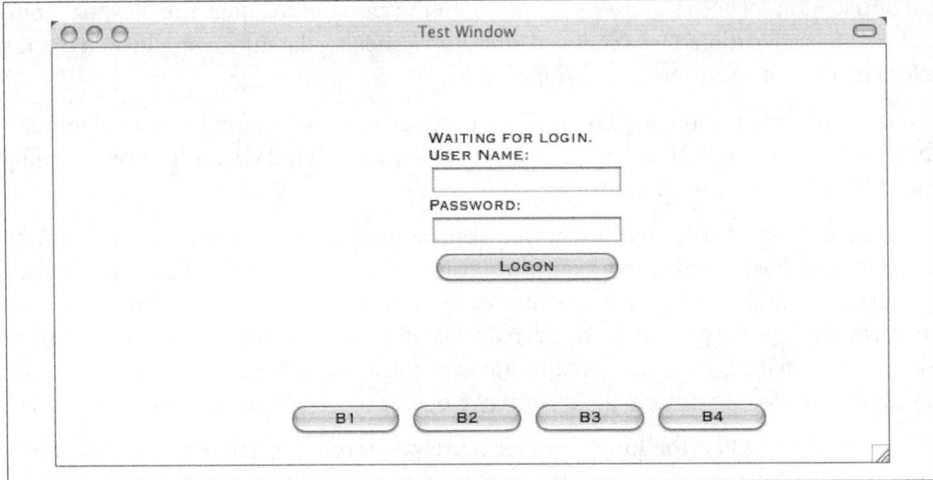

Figure 4-2. Application launched as a chrome window

Running as a Local Installation

We will first look at what we need to install the application on the local machine and to communicate with a server through a form of HTTP request. For both versions, we must have an Apache web server running, PHP installed, and an SQL database up and running.

Chrome Directory Structure

An application registered as a chrome package is not required to be located in a specific directory; convention, however, has placed most chrome applications within Firefox's *chrome* directory. The *chrome* directory is located in the same directory as the binary executable for Firefox. Most of the files in the *chrome* directory are *.jar* files, or Java archive files.

Although XUL applications use the Java archive as a preferred distribution medium, the source code files are not written in Java. XUL applications are developed as JavaScript and XUL source files.

To see the content of any of the archives, use the `jar -tf` command. For example, to view the contents of the *inspector.jar* file, change to the *chrome* directory and type the following:

```
jar -tf inspector.jar
```

If we were to do the same for all the archive files, we would see that they share a common directory structure:

Content
: For user interface (XUL) files, stylesheets, and scripts

Skin
: Stylesheets and images that collectively provide a theme to an appearance

Locale
: To provide multiple-language support for interface widgets

For our application, we will work with only the `content` root.

Before we continue installing our application in the Firefox *chrome* directory, we need to understand that such an application is referred to through a special chrome URL. The form of this URL is:

```
chrome://<package>/<part>/<fileName>
```

The *package* and *part* names are consistent with conventions used for *.jar* files. This URL instructs the Firefox framework to scan its installed packages to access a filename located as part of a specific package. Once our application is registered, we would use a command line with the `-chrome` option (to open the file in a chrome window) or specify a chrome URL (to launch the application with chrome privileges):

```
firefox -chrome chrome://<package>/<part>/<filename>
```

Figure 4-3 illustrates an example directory structure.

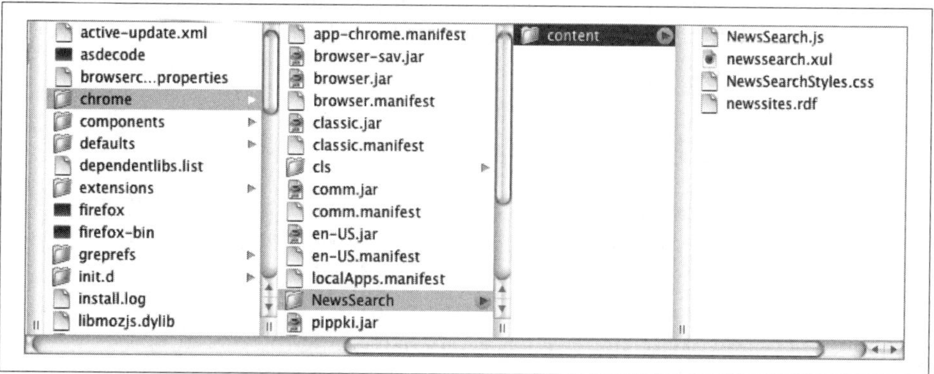

Figure 4-3. Chrome directory structure

Package Registration

Every time the Firefox browser launches, its framework looks for any file with an extension of *.manifest* to inform it of the chrome content packages, skins, or locales that need to be loaded. To inform Firefox of our NewsSearch application, we will use a text editor to create a line for a file named *localApps.manifest* (any unique filename with a *.manifest* extension will do) and save it in Firefox's *chrome* directory:

```
content newssearch NewsSearch/content/newssearch.xul
```

The format of this line consists of space-delimited entries as follows:

- The first field, `content`, declares the installation to be a content package. Other options include `skin` and `locale`.
- The `newssearch` entry names the package.
- The last entry is the source file location relative to the *chrome* directory.

We can now launch Firefox and type the chrome URL directly in the locator window to launch the same application, but within a browser window (see Figure 4-4).

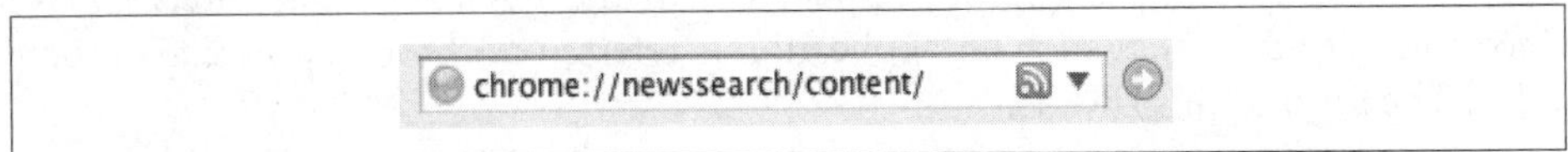

Figure 4-4. Specifying the package name, and specifying the package type as a chrome URL

Once we make this entry in the URL bar, Firefox will autocomplete the line to add the filename that matches the package name—in this case, our *newssearch.xul* file.

Alternatively, we could launch our application directly from the command line, using the `-chrome` option and a chrome URL that specifies our package name and package type:

```
firefox -chrome chrome://newssearch/content/
```

Figure 4-5 illustrates the results of launching our chrome application from the command line and entering correct login information, for both a Windows and an OS X implementation of the same code.

XUL-to-Server Communications

A user can communicate to a server using several models, including a XUL application that runs locally while obtaining needed server information through asynchronous HTTP requests. Using this approach, the local application is in complete control of the user interface, with the server providing only textual information in response to requests. Here are the steps for implementing this model:

1. Configure a web server.
2. Install a scripting language to provide logic that manages communications with a client application.
3. Implement the communication connection between the application and the server.
4. Add a database on the server to communicate with the scripting language.

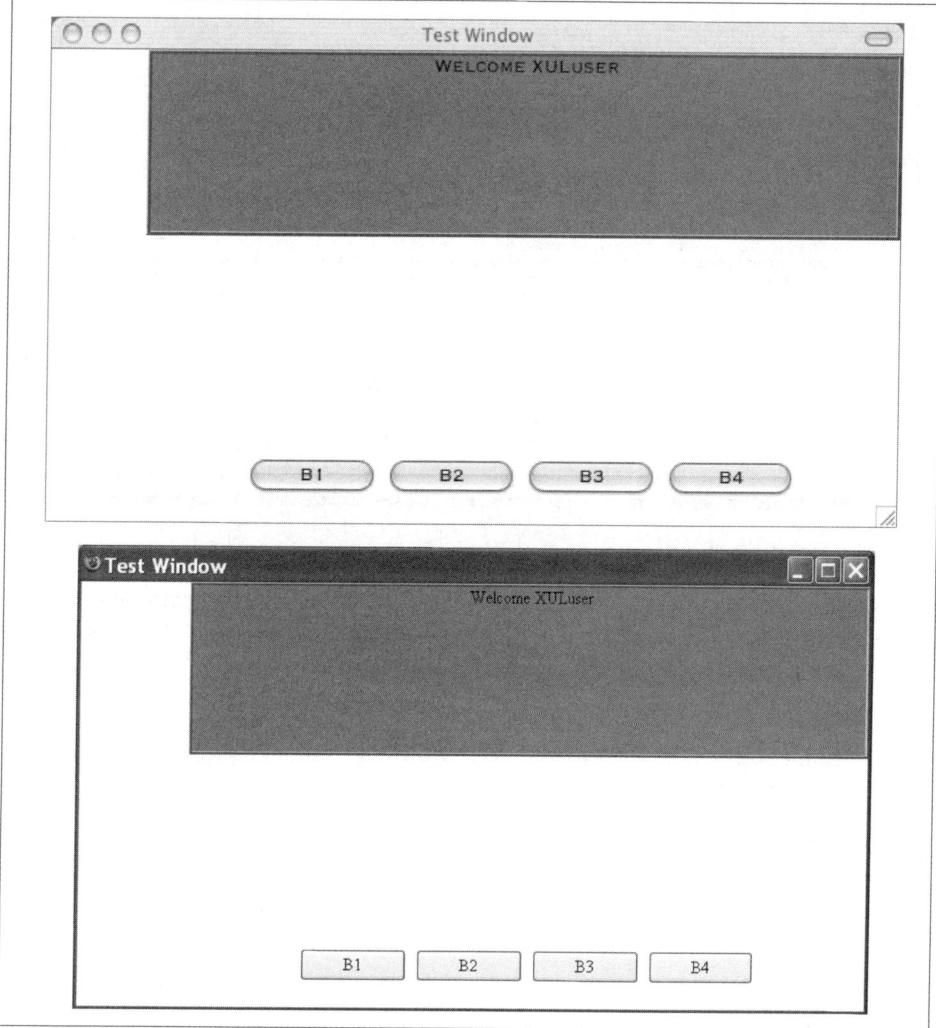

Figure 4-5. OS X and Windows presentation of newssearch.xul (after simulated login)

Configuring the Server

We first must install a web server on our local machine; for this application we install Apache. Once the web server is installed and running, we should see the startup page shown in Figure 4-6 when we enter **`http://localhost/`** in a browser's URL field.

Apache is managed through the text file *httpd.conf*. On Unix systems, this is located in the */etc/http/* directory, whereas Windows systems will put this file in Apache's *conf* directory. You can edit the file using a text editor.

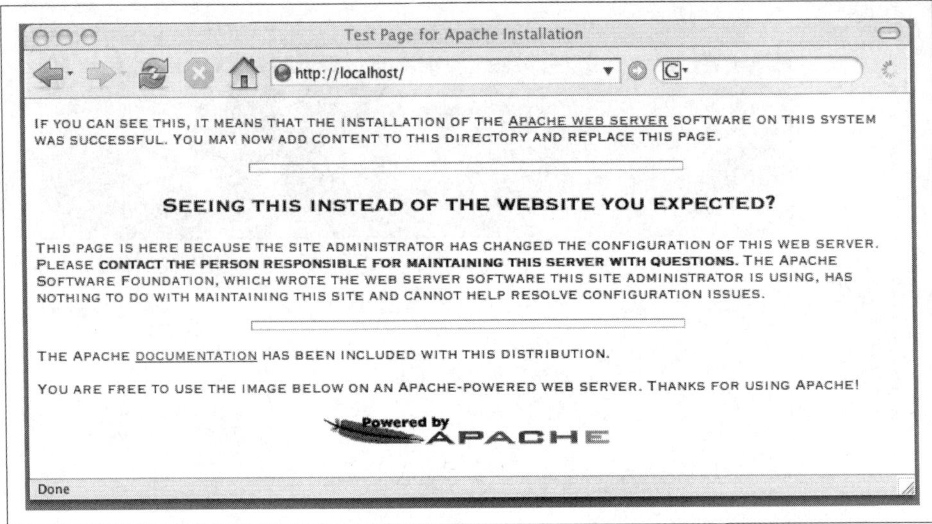

Figure 4-6. Apache startup page

The *DocumentRoot* directory is used to select the home directory for serving web pages. That entry, in *httpd.conf*, is operating-system-specific, and depends on the options we have specified during the installation:

```
DocumentRoot "<YourApacheDocumentRoot>"
```

If the installation was performed correctly, an entry should provide Apache with information about the directories served:

```
<Directory "YourApacheDocumentRoot">
```

Although we don't need to make any changes to the *httpd.conf* file, we must note what these entries are in order to place our Common Gateway Interface (CGI) scripts in the correct directory. We will use the PHP scripting engine to provide the logic for our CGI.

We can install the PHP binaries into any directory. In a Windows environment, an example would be *C:\php*, whereas a Unix install may be in */usr/local/php/*. Regardless, we must make changes to Apache's *httpd.conf* to properly serve PHP-generated output.

Depending on the version of PHP installed, entries in Apache's configuration file will take one of two forms. In the first:

```
LoadModule phpn_module " <YourPHPInstallDirectory> "
```

n may be the version of PHP being installed.

The second form would instruct Apache to use an external configuration file to load the PHP libraries:

```
Include <YourPHPInstallDirectory>/httpd.conf.php
```

Regardless of the particular PHP version and operating system, we can check the installation by using a text editor to write a simple PHP script to echo version information:

```
<?php
phpinfo( );
?>
```

Save the preceding text as *test.php* in your Apache document root directory:

```
<YourApacheDocumentRoot>/test.php
```

Now type the URL into a browser to yield a page that looks like Figure 4-7.

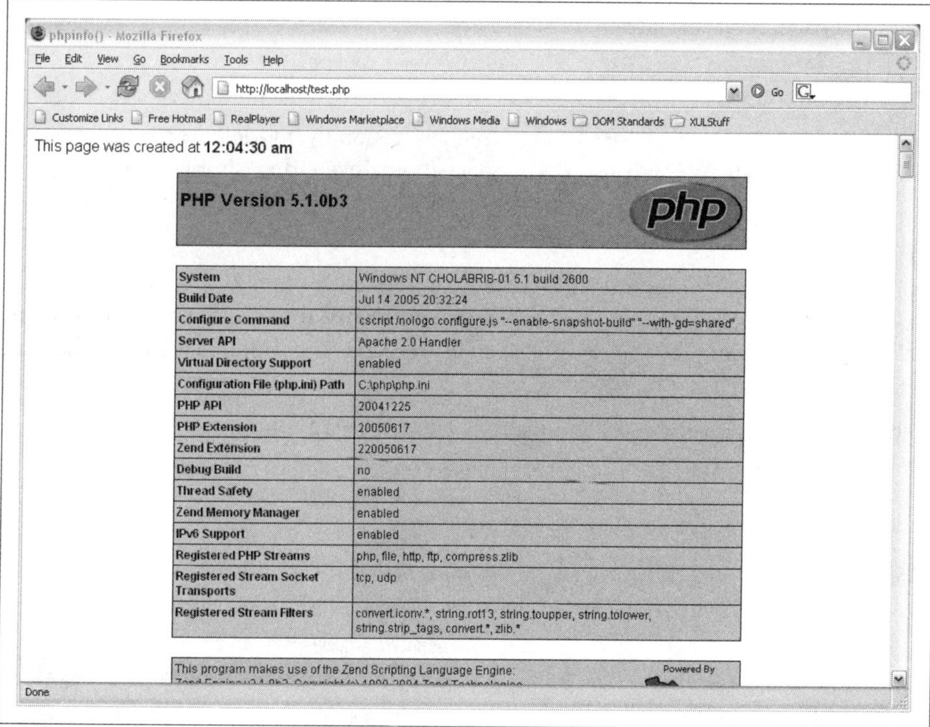

Figure 4-7. Testing PHP installation

With a PHP engine running on our server, we can now conduct some simple connection tests between our application and the server.

The Client/Server Protocol

This approach will use the `XMLHttpRequest` object to send inquiries to our PHP server, and PHP scripts to return textual responses to the client.

Conventional `POST` messages from a browser to a server result in the server generating an entire page to be displayed by the browser. This process is what causes many web applications to "freeze up" after the user presses a form submission button and waits for a response.

We will first use a simpler protocol to issue a request for data resembling "classic" client/server operations. The server provides only data; the client determines what to do with the data and how to render the interface.

We can write a JavaScript function to receive the server data and format HTML table data with responses, populate text areas, or otherwise modify the GUI without forcing a complete redraw of the page. For many applications that require only a partial update of the screen, this asynchronous approach reduces the waste incurred by conventional page-based updates.

The client-side request

Firefox supports the `XMLHttpRequest`, which is generally modeled after Microsoft's `IXMLRequest` design. We can use the request to retrieve either simple text strings, or XML fragments that may be parsed and passed to the interface document's Document Object Model (DOM) structure.

To use the request, JavaScript scripts create an instance of an `XMLHttpRequest` object to be sent to the server, passing the object a reference to a callback function to be invoked once the request is completed. The callback function then takes whatever action is determined by the response.

Table 4-1 summarizes the functions and properties of the `XMLHttpRequest` object most relevant to us for the upcoming exercise.

Table 4-1. XMLHttpRequest methods and properties

Method/Property	Description
`open(sendMethod, sendURL, doAsync)`	*sendMethod* = `POST` | `GET`. *sendURL* = query string. *doAsync* = if `TRUE`, return upon transmission of request.
`.onreadystatechange`	Function called when the request's "ready" state changes.
`send(null)`	Sends the request to the server.
`.readyState`	Monitored within the callback; `code == 4` signals that the request is completed.
`.status`	Monitored within the callback; `code == 200` signals that the server was successful in executing the request.
`.responseText`	Accesses the text returned by the server to be parsed and processed in an application-specific format.
`.responseXML`	Accesses the text returned by the server when the text is presumed to consist of an XML document.

Before we start to code, we need to decide on a send/receive protocol between our client application and the server. We will use a very simple URL string to send commands to our server:

```
command=someCommand&param1=val1&param2=val2...
```

From our server, we will expect a comma-delimited string for a response:

```
RetCode=ReturnCode,retKey1=retVal1...
```

We will expect the first value token to be a case-insensitive `true|false` value to indicate the success of the command.

We will now change our *newssearch.js* file to implement a few modifications for our client/server model:

- We will build a generic `doServerRequest` function to build an `XMLHttpRequest` object and send it to the server. To support that function, we will also create a `commandArg` object to hold name-value pairs of arguments that can be used to populate an array of arguments. The function will set the `async` flag in the `open` function to `TRUE`, meaning that control will immediately return to the application once the request is sent.
- We will change our login-button command handler to call the newly created `doServerRequest` function.
- We will change the logic to move successful and failed paths for login into separate functions.
- We will write some JavaScript to add a callback function to interpret the response from the server and call the successful or failed login functions:

```
function genericBtnHandler(event) {
try { // try block
var infoString = "Type = " + event.type + ",";
infoString += "Target = " + event.target + ",";
infoString += "Target.tagName = " + event.target.tagName + ",";
infoString += "Target.id = " + event.target.id + ".";
dump(infoString + "\n");
} // try block
catch (e) {
 alert("genericBtnHandler exception: " + e);
 }
}

function doLogin(event) {

try { // try
var theArgs = new Array;
theArgs[0] = new commandArg("un",document.getElementById("userName").value);
theArgs[1] = new commandArg("pd",document.getElementById("password").value);
doServerRequest("login",theArgs);
 } // try
 catch (e) { //
  alert("doLogin exception: " + e);
 }//
}
//
// Dynamically assign our event handler properties
//
```

```
function initialize( ) {
try {
 document.getElementById("B1").addEventListener("command",genericBtnHandler,true);
 document.getElementById("B2").addEventListener("command",genericBtnHandler,true);
 document.getElementById("B3").addEventListener("command",genericBtnHandler,true);
 //
 // Add a login script
 document.getElementById("loginButton").addEventListener("command",doLogin,true);
 }
 catch (e) {
  alert ("Exception: " + e);
  }
}


function loginOK( ) {
 var theParent = document.getElementById("contentArea");

  while(theParent.childNodes.length != 0)
   theParent.removeChild(theParent.childNodes[0]);

// Now re-create a welcome area
 theParent.style.backgroundColor = "LightSeaGreen";
 theParent.style.borderColor = "gray";
 theParent.style.borderStyle = "ridge";
 var leftSpacer = document.createElement("spacer");
 leftSpacer.setAttribute("flex","1");
 theParent.appendChild(leftSpacer);
 var newDescription = document.createElement("description");
 var newDescriptionText = document.createTextNode("Welcome!");
 newDescription.appendChild(newDescriptionText);
 theParent.appendChild(newDescription);
 var rightSpacer = document.createElement("spacer");
 rightSpacer.setAttribute("flex","1");
 theParent.appendChild(rightSpacer);
 }

 function commandArg(argKey,argValue) {
  this.key = argKey;
  this.value = argValue;
 }

 function loginFail( ) {
  document.getElementById("msgDescription").style.backgroundColor="red";
  document.getElementById("msgDescription").style.color="white";
  document.getElementById("msgDescription").childNodes[0].nodeValue =
 "User not authenticated.";
  document.getElementById("userName").value = "";
  document.getElementById("password").value = "";
```

```
}

//
//  CreateServerRequest
//
var theServerRequest;
//
// commandArgs is an array of arguments, each element
// is converted into a PHP GET URL field
function doServerRequest(commandString,commandArgs) {

 theServerRequest = new XMLHttpRequest( );
 var theString ="http://localhost/doCommand.php?"+"&command="+commandString+"&";
 for (var i = 0; i < commandArgs.length; i++) { // build remaining parameters
   theString += commandArgs[i].key + "=" + commandArgs[i].value ;
  if (i != (commandArgs.length-1)) theString += "&";
 } // build remaining parameters
 theServerRequest.onreadystatechange = retrieveServerResponse;
 theServerRequest.open("GET",theString,true);
 theServerRequest.send(null);
}



function retrieveServerResponse( ) {
 if (theServerRequest.readyState == 4) { // all done
  // Check return code
   if (theServerRequest.status == 200) { // request terminated OK
    alert("Response is " + theServerRequest.responseText);
    if (theServerRequest.responseText == "retcode=true") { // all OK
     loginOK( );
    } // all OK
    else loginFail( );
   } // request terminated OK
   else { // something is wrong
    alert("Response failed.");
   } // something is wrong
  } // all done
}
```

We wrote the `doServerRequest` function to take an array of input arguments. The code then steps through the array to build a URL containing our complete `GET` request URL.

The request object calls the `retrieveServerResponse` function each time the state changes, and once it reaches `"4"` (a code that means the server has completed the request), it checks for a status of `200` (meaning the server successfully completed the request) and finally parses the text returned by the server to see whether the user is authenticated.

The server-side response

PHP scripts result in text being returned to a browser in one of two ways:

- Any text not bracketed by the PHP directives `<?php` and `?>` is passed directly to the browser.
- PHP statements within the PHP tags send text to the browser through a function such as `echo( )`.

The parameters sent to a script from a browser's `GET` request arrive as values in an associative array named `$_GET`. To assign a PHP variable (a token that begins with $) a parameter from a `GET` request, we would write:

```
$myValue = $_GET['keyString']
```

For now, our command processor script will presume only valid commands, and compare the command against our temporarily hardcoded strings to return a `true` or `false` response to the client. We can use any text editor to create the *doCommand.php* file:

```
<?php
$cmd   = trim($_GET['command']);
$uName = trim($_GET['un']);
$uPass = trim($_GET['pd']);

echo check_user($uName,$uPass);

function check_user($name,$pass) {
   if (($name == 'XULuser') &&
       ($pass == 'XULpass'))
       return 'retcode=true';
       else return 'retcode=false';
  }

?>
```

Save this file in the Apache document root directory.

The code illustrates assignment of the `GET` parameters to global variables. The `trim` function takes care of any leading or trailing spaces that may have been entered. The script then passes the username and password to a comparison function that returns `true` or `false`, which is echoed back to the client.

Repeating the same launch of our `newssearch` chrome package will yield the same results with our client-only code, but we are now operating in client/server mode.

When Things Go Wrong

If things don't work out, we can take a few steps to quickly isolate the cause of the problem. We can use either JavaScript `alert` or `dump` commands to see what we are sending and what we are retrieving. We can also use simplified PHP scripts to return a known value to make certain the script is doing what we think.

Assuming we want to dump information to the screen, we could make the following changes to the doServerRequest function in our *newssearch.js* code:

```
theServerRequest.onreadystatechange = retrieveServerResponse;
 theServerRequest.open("GET",theString,true);
 dump("About to send " + theString + "\n");
 theServerRequest.send(null);
```

And we could report the entire string returned in our retrieveServerResponse function:

```
if (theServerRequest.status == 200) { // request terminated OK
    dump("Received from server: " + theServerRequest.responseText + "\n");
    if (theServerRequest.responseText == "true") { // all OK
```

We can also stub out our login check in *doCommand.php* just to return the parameters we received from the client:

```
/* echo check_user($uName,$uPass); */
echo 'Script has received: '."$cmd".','."$uName".','."$uPass";
```

We have removed the call to check_user in favor of a change to echo a string that concatenates (using the . operator in PHP) a simple message with the values for command, username, and password.

When we launch Firefox from the command line with the -console option, we will see our sent and retrieved strings displayed on the console:

```
About to send http://localhost/doCommand.php?&command=
  login&un=SomeUser&pd=SomePass
Received from server: Script has received: login,SomeUser,SomePass
```

For developers just beginning to work with PHP, including echo statements to use the browser to display variable values is often the best way to identify many of the most common PHP coding errors. Displaying variable values is one sure way to quickly identify problems related to misuse of the single quote (used to form strings with special characters), double quote (used to assemble strings that include the evaluation of variables), and terminating semicolons. Echoing variables is also a good tool to find misspelled variable names and the occasionally misplaced $ variable prefix.

We change our command parser to remove the debug echo statement and uncomment the call to check_user that will now be used with a database of valid user identifiers.

Adding a Database

Using hardcoded information in a script file may be appropriate for some limited applications, but the designer can improve the reliability of server code by allowing access to a dynamic information store without having to change any script files. Such a store can be maintained and updated to reflect the changing nature of business operations without risking any side effects caused by changes in server or client code.

Using a relational database is not a required element for this book's sample application. If database use is inappropriate for some reason, we could write PHP "stub code" to mimic our database. The use of MySQL is included here as an example of an implementation that models true commercial applications.

The use of a relational database is the most commonly accepted technique to provide a secure and maintainable information store that server scripts can access in response to a client request. We will use the open source MySQL database engine to provide the store for our username and password information. The steps for this task are as follows:

1. Create the NewsSearch database.
2. Create a database user account to act as administrator.
3. Create the tables for our account name and password.
4. Create a database user account to act as a "guest" with read-only access to database information.
5. Configure PHP to use libraries to access the database.
6. Write the PHP scripts to communicate with the database in response to a client request.

Creating the database

Once we have installed MySQL, we create the database for our project.

Upon initial installation, MySQL has a `root` account that we can use to create a new table (refer to the glossary to set up a root password if you have not already done so). We log into the database with the following command:

```
mysql -u root -p
```

You will now be prompted for the root password. When you're successfully logged in, you will see a welcome message that looks like this:

```
Welcome to the MySQL monitor.  Commands end with ; or \g.
Your MySQL connection id is 4 to server version: Version specific information
mysql>
```

We create a database with this command:

```
mysql> create database newssearch;
Query OK, 1 row affected (0.59 sec)
```

Creating account tables

Rather than having the PHP script compare usernames and passwords that are kept in the script, we can write code to access the database and compare its entries with the fields entered in the XUL interface.

Databases are organized as tables of information rows. Users can access row information through SQL `SELECT` statements that include qualifiers to help identify the information being sought. We can embed the `SELECT` statement in our PHP scripts that support the SQL access libraries.

The database administrator creates the database table, specifies its structure, and assigns privileges to restrict a user account's ability to access and modify table data.

For our simple application, we will create a table named `accounts` to hold the username and password information. We will also add information to indicate a user's status (e.g., active or inactive), and the time and date of the last login. The initial assumptions of the format for the row data are:

Username
: Up to 40 characters (arbitrary)

Password
: Up to 40 characters

Status
: A string of up to 16 characters to support entries such as active, suspended, provisional (for temporary accounts), and terminated

Date
: A string that describes the date and time of the last successful login session

The SQL statement to create such a table consists of a `CREATE` statement:

```
mysql> create table account (
    -> username char(40) not null primary key,
    -> password char(40) not null,
    -> last_session datetime,
    -> status char(32) not null);
Query OK, 0 rows affected (0.47 sec)
```

This statement creates our tables with rows named `username`, `password`, `last_session`, and `status`. The data types include character strings and a timestamp (an SQL-formatted statement for time of day). Additional qualifiers allow us to specify that the username will be unique (as a primary key), and which fields must have values specified when a table row is created.

We can see the results of our work through the `describe` command:

```
mysql> describe account;
+-------------+---+-----+------------------+----------+
| Field       | Type      | Null | Key | Default     | Extra
+-------------+---------+------------------+----------+
| username    | char(40)  |      | PRI |                 |
| password    | char(40)  |      |     |                 |
|last_session| datetime   | YES  |     |CURRENT_TIMESTAMP|
| status      | char(32)  |      |     |                 |
+-------------+----------+------+-----+----------------
4 rows in set (0.00 sec)
mysql>
```

We can now create the accounts for the application users—individuals who will be using our NewsSearch service.

Rather than storing the passwords for our users in plain text, we will add some security by using MySQL's one-way encryption.

A *one-way encryption scheme* applies a function to input text to render an encrypted form of it in the database. The programmer or application scripts do not need to know what the encrypted output is, only that the encryption function is used consistently for comparison purposes. Should the database be compromised, there is no way for the intruder to reverse the encrypted data into the user-provided passwords.

A number of encryption functions are available for both PHP and MySQL. For this application, we will use MySQL's function for the Secure Hash Algorithm (SHA): `sha1('someEntry')`. We can now create a couple of application users who will be in our authentication database.

Although we could use the MySQL command-line interpreter to do this, it is often easier to create a text file with the commands we need to manipulate the database. A *createUser.sql* file to create two users would look like this:

```
use newssearch;
insert into account values ('bugsbunny',sha1('wabbit'),'','active');
insert into account values ('elmerfudd',sha1('scwewy'),'','active');
```

We could read in this script file directly from the operating system command prompt:

```
%mysql -u root -p < createUsers.sql;
>password: 'sqlRootPassword'
%
```

We could also use the source command (`\.`) to enter the script name while within the MySQL interpreter. The following command shows how to load the script from the current working directory:

```
mysql> \. createUsers.sql
```

We can view the results of our script files by issuing a `SELECT` command:

```
mysql> select * from account;
```

The results will show the account information created by the script file, along with the encrypted passwords. The `last_session` entries will be initialized to 0, as no entry was entered in the `INSERT` statement.

Creating database user accounts

When the server software requests information from a database, the software will have to make its request through a MySQL account. We should set this account so that it has only the minimum privileges necessary for the task at hand. That means we limit a user's read and write authorization to specific tables in the database.

The commands to manage account privileges involve specifying the account or user name, setting a boundary to a limited set of objects that are affected, and setting the privilege itself that describes what degree of access and modification is granted. The minimal, general form of a command to assign a privilege is as follows:

```
GRANT priv_type [(column_list)] [, priv_type [(column_list)]] ...
    ON [object_type] {tbl_name | * | *.* | db_name.*}
    TO user [IDENTIFIED BY [PASSWORD] 'password']
        [, user [IDENTIFIED BY [PASSWORD] 'password']] ...
    [REQUIRE
        NONE |
        [{SSL| X509}]
        [CIPHER 'cipher' [AND]]
        [ISSUER 'issuer' [AND]]
        [SUBJECT 'subject']]
    [WITH with_option [with_option] ...]

object_type =
    TABLE
  | FUNCTION
  | PROCEDURE
```

The *priv_type* parameter is one of a fairly substantial number of tokens that define the privilege being granted. The most familiar of these types includes SELECT (to select information from tables), INSERT (to insert new rows into tables), UPDATE (to modify table entries), and DELETE (to remove rows from a table).

The *object_type* parameter sets a boundary on the privilege being granted. The object type can range from * (all tables on all databases), to an entry of the form *databaseName.tableName* to further qualify the objects to which the GRANT statement applies.

To create a newssearch_guest account that can read any data from the table, you could specify the following script file to create the account:

```
use newssearch;
grant select on newssearch.account to
    newssearch_guest identified by 'nsgst';
grant update (last_session) on account to newssearch_guest;
```

Reading this script file (or typing it into the MySQL interpreter) will create a database user account, newssearch_guest, that can SELECT data only from the accounts table. The second statement adds UPDATE privileges to the database account to allow scripts to update the session information in the database. We now have enough information to turn our attention to the PHP script that accesses the database.

Connecting PHP to MySQL

To configure PHP to use the MySQL programming interface, we must modify PHP's configuration file to load the MySQL libraries. The configuration file, *php.ini*, is located in the user's PHP installation directory.

The specific switches to set depend on the versions of MySQL and PHP in use (check the most recent content of the MySQL and PHP web sites for specific entries). We will be using the MySQL Improved extension from our PHP scripts. The settings to enable the MySQL Improved extension are:

```
mysqli.max_links          "-1"
mysqli.default_port       "3306"
mysqli.default_socket     NULL
mysqli.default_host       NULL
mysqli.default_user       NULL
mysqli.default_pw         NULL
```

Once we have the correct settings, we can verify that Apache, PHP, and MySQL are up and running by using Firefox to open *http://localhost/test.php*. Scrolling down the window, we see the entries confirming a successful configuration (see Figure 4-8).

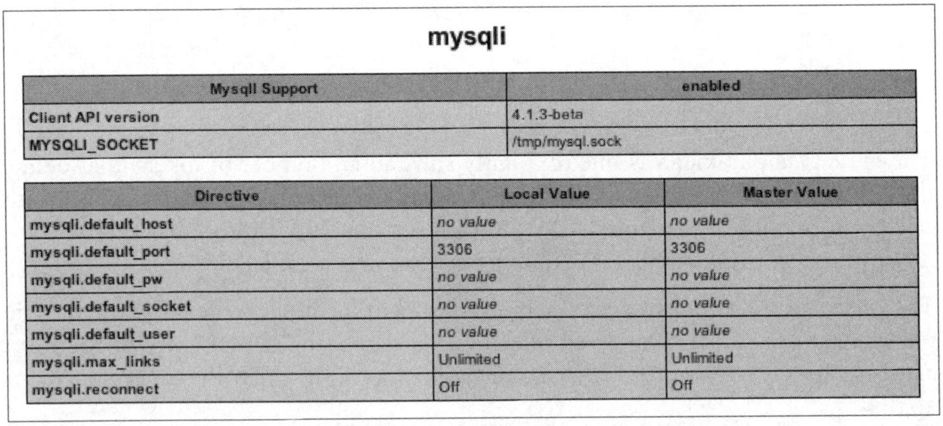

mysqli

Mysqli Support	enabled
Client API version	4.1.3-beta
MYSQLI_SOCKET	/tmp/mysql.sock

Directive	Local Value	Master Value
mysqli.default_host	*no value*	*no value*
mysqli.default_port	3306	3306
mysqli.default_pw	*no value*	*no value*
mysqli.default_socket	*no value*	*no value*
mysqli.default_user	*no value*	*no value*
mysqli.max_links	Unlimited	Unlimited
mysqli.reconnect	Off	Off

Figure 4-8. Successful configuration of MySQL Improved (mysqli) extension

Calling the MySQLi API

We will use functions for the MySQLi library to compare the user input login and password against the entries in the `accounts` table.

Using the object-oriented approach to the MySQLi library, we create a database connection object and use that object reference to execute an SQL `SELECT` statement against the database.

The results of this statement are contained in a variable pointing to a *result object*. The result object will contain a collection of all the database rows that were selected. Table 4-2 shows a summary of the `mysqli` PHP calls that we will be using.

Table 4-2. MySQLi objects and methods

Object/Function	Use
`$database = new mysqli('hostname','username', 'password','databaseName');`	Creates a database object reference by connecting to the database with the username and password specified. The database is identified by `databaseName`.
`mysqli_connect_errno( )` `mysqli_connect_error( )`	If the database object creation fails, these functions are used to audit an error code, and to extract the `connect_error` text for reporting.
`$searchResults = $database->query('queryString')`	Executes an SQL query, returning the result in a `mysqli_result` object.
`$searchResults->num_rows`	Returns the number of rows selected from the database as a result of the query.
`$row = $searchResults->fetch_assoc( )`	Fetches the next row from the result object, returning the results as an associative array in which the keys to the array match the names of the row's columns (e.g., to return the contents of a row's "status" column, the PHP script would read `$row["status"];`).
`$searchResults->close( )`	Search results must be closed before attempting any additional queries.
`$database->close( )`	Scripts must close the database prior to exiting.

We will rewrite the PHP scripts to use the database to select the rows for the username and password supplied by the interface. If there is a match (if one row is returned), we will return the proper flag, along with the last time the user logged in.

On the interface, if the user is authenticated, we will display the last login time in the application's status bar.

The PHP *doCommand.php* file now has a checkUser function that looks like this:

```
function check_user($name,$pass) {
   $database = new mysqli('localhost','newssearch_guest','nsgst','newssearch');
   if (mysqli_connect_errno()) { // failing case
      $retString = 'retcode=false,message='.mysqli_connect_error( );
      return $retString;
      } // failing case

    $encryptPass = sha1($pass);

    $query = "select status,last_session from account where
        username = '$name' and password = '$encryptPass'";

    if ($theResult = $database->query("$query")) { // we have some kind of result

    if ($theResult->num_rows == 1) { // we have our user

       $theRow = $theResult->fetch_assoc( ); // get the only row that exists
       $lastLogin = $theRow["last_session"];
```

```
        if ($theRow['status'] == 'active') { // all OK
         $retString='retcode=true,last_login='.$theRow['last_session'];
    //    update the session info
         $theResult->close( );
         $curTime = date('c');
         $update = "update account set last_session = '$curTime' where
                            username = '$name'";
         $theResult = $database->query("$update");
         } // account is active

         else { // account not active
         $theResult->close( );
         $retString = 'retcode=false,message=user account not active';
          } // account not active

        } // we have our user
        else { // user not found
         $theResult->close( );
         $retString = 'retcode=false,message=user not found';
         } // user not cound


        } // we have some kind of result

        else { // no result returned
         $retString = 'retcode=false,message=invalid query';
        } // no results returned

      $database->close( );
      return $retString;

  }
```

Before building the command string, we see the call to encrypt the password prior to its comparison with the database. Our query statement returns columns for `last_session` and `status`. If one row is returned, there are statements to verify that the user has an "active" account before building a successful return code. We also call an `UPDATE` command on the database to set the `last_session` entry to the current date and time.

We can change the XUL interface slightly to add a horizontal box with a status area to show the time of the user's last login. The file *newssearch.xul* now looks like this:

```
<?xml version="1.0"?>
<?xml-stylesheet href="testStyles.css" type="text/css"?>
<window
  id="theMainWindow"
  onload="initialize( );"
  title="Test Window"
  orient="horizontal"
  xmlns:xlink="http://www.w3.org/1999/xlink"
  xmlns="http://www.mozilla.org/keymaster/gatekeeper/there.is.only.xul">
```

```
<script  src="newssearch.js"/>
 <!-- main top level container -->
 <vbox flex="1">

 <hbox flex="1" >

 <!-- a container for some kind of list -->
 <vbox flex="1" >
 </vbox>

 <!-- container for messages and tool areas -->
 <vbox flex="2" >

 <!-- used to display message -->
 <hbox  id="contentArea"  flex="3" >

  <spacer flex="1"/>
  <vbox >  <!-- stack message and login controls vertically -->
    <spacer flex="1"/>
      <description id="msgDescription">
       Waiting for login.
      </description>
      <label value="User Name:" control="userName"/>
      <textbox id="userName"/>
      <label value="Password:" control="userName"/>
      <textbox id="password"  type="password" maxlength="8"/>
      <button id="loginButton" label="Logon"/>
     <spacer flex="1"/>
  </vbox>
  <spacer flex="1"/>

</hbox>
<!-- used to display message -->


 <!-- used to display typing area  -->
<hbox flex="3" >
</hbox>

 <!-- used to display tool area-->
<hbox flex="1" >

 <spacer flex="1"/>

   <vbox>
    <spacer flex="1"/>
     <hbox>
      <button id="B1" label="B1" />
      <button id="B2" label="B2"/>
      <button id="B3" label="B3"/>
      <button label="B4"/>
     </hbox>
     <spacer flex="1"/>
   </vbox>
```

```
<spacer flex="1"/>

</hbox>

</vbox>
<!-- container for messages and tool areas -->

</hbox>
<!-- horizontal container for all content (except status info) -->


<hbox >
  <!-- stack info and resizer horizontally -->
  <!-- right align our status bar -->
    <statusbar id="status-bar" class="chromeclass-status">
    <statusbarpanel id="status-text" />
  </statusbar>
 <spacer flex="1"/>
</hbox>

 <!-- main container -->
</vbox>
</window>
```

Within the JavaScript code, first we need to make certain we are responding to the correct command, so we add a global variable at the top of the source file to hold the last command issued:

```
var K_XUL_NAMESPACE = "http://www.mozilla.org/keymaster/
    gatekeeper/there.is.only.xul";

var USER_LOGGED_IN = 0;

var lastCommand = "";
```

and modify the doLogin function to save the last command sent:

```
function doLogin(event) {

try { // try
var theArgs = new Array;
theArgs[0] = new commandArg("un",document.getElementById("userName").value);
theArgs[1] = new commandArg("pd",document.getElementById("password").value);
lastCommand = "login";
doServerRequest("login",theArgs);
 } // try
 catch (e) { //
  alert("doLogin exception: " + e);
 }//
}
```

When processing the server response, we use the JavaScript split() function to break our comma-delimited responses into an array of name-value pairs. We then compare the value of the first entry to "true" before extracting the second returned value and setting the status text:

```
function retrieveServerResponse( ) {
 if (theServerRequest.readyState == 4) { // all done
  // Check return code
   if (theServerRequest.status == 200) { // request terminated OK
    dump("Received from server: " + theServerRequest.responseText + "\n");

    //
    var theResults = theServerRequest.responseText.split(",");
    //

    var rCode = (theResults[0].substring((theResults[0].indexOf("=")+1),
                                          theResults[0].length)).toLowerCase( );

    if (lastCommand == "login") { // process login command

     if (rCode == "true") { // everything OK, we know next parameter is
                            // session info
      var lastSession = "Last login was ";
      lastSession += (theResults[1].substring((theResults[1].indexOf("=")+1),
                                          theResults[1].length)).toLowerCase( );
      loginOK( );
      setStatusText(lastSession);

     } // everthing OK
     else { // user NG
      loginFail( );
      setStatusText("No user logged in");
     } // user NG

    } // process login command


   } // request terminated OK
   else { // something is wrong
    alert("Response failed.");
   } // something is wrong
  } // all done
}
```

This version of the program will now log into the database, and if the username and password match (and the account is active), the welcome screen will include a status line along the bottom of the display reporting the last date and time of the user's login:

```
Last login was 0000-00-00 00:00:00
```

All zeros appear because our initial script to create the database tables did not set an initial date in the database. Once we log in under a valid account name, the next login will yield a more welcoming message.

When Things Go Wrong

There are many "moving parts" to this integration involving XUL source, PHP statements, and SQL statements. Most of the problems at this stage will involve either syntax or logic errors with PHP, or problems with the structured SQL statements. These errors can be difficult to track down, but these suggestions may help:

- Errors in PHP scripts often result in nothing being displayed on the browser screen. Try using the JavaScript `dump` function to unconditionally display the results of the `XMLHttpRequest`. Then change the PHP script to set a variable such as `$returnString` to some suspect variable and `echo` the variable. If nothing is returned to the JavaScript function, the syntax error occurs prior to the `echo` statement. Otherwise, we can use the variable to help identify any other syntax errors.
- Errors with the SQL statements often involve syntax or an error in setting user privileges. When suspecting such problems, try using the MySQL command-line interface to type in a statement identical to the script-generated code to verify the expected results.
- When all else fails, continue to simplify the code (e.g., use `SELECT * from tableName`) or use PHP stubs to build a string of `debug trace` statements that end up returned to the JavaScript function.

Serving XUL Files

Sometimes we may want to use a web server to deliver the XUL files. To implement our login user interface by placing the XUL file on our web server, do the following:

1. Write a source XUL file that will be delivered upon a successful login and place that file along with stylesheets and JavaScript source files on the server.
2. Configure the server to properly serve a XUL MIME type.
3. Change the XUL file to a PHP script file.
4. Add an HTML screen to read the user login and password.
5. Modify our PHP `doCommand` function to call the PHP script that delivers the XUL source.

Creating a XUL File to Be Served

The XUL source to be served will actually be sent by a PHP script—but a good first step is to develop a XUL file that we will convert into PHP.

We copy the *newssearch.js* and *NewsSearchStyle.css* files into the Apache root directory.

We will copy the *newssearch.xul* file but rename it to *startupScreen.xul*. We also change the source file to remove the login areas, replacing them with the graphics that render a successful login screen:

```
<hbox  id="contentArea"
   style="borderColor:gray;
    border-style:ridge;background-color:LightSeaGreen;
    border-color:gray;" flex="3" >

  <spacer flex="1"/>
  <vbox >  <!-- stack message and login controls vertically -->
    <spacer flex="1"/>
      <description id="msgDescription">
       Welcome.
      </description>
      <spacer flex="1"/>
  </vbox>
  <spacer flex="1"/>

</hbox>
```

Configuring the Server

Without "understanding" what to do with a XUL file, the Apache web server would deliver a XUL file to a browser as an XML text file. A browser receiving such a file most often just presents the source to the user of the browser.

We must add an entry to either the *mime.types* or the *httpd.conf* file for Apache:

```
application/vnd.mozilla.xul+xml          xul
```

After making this change, restarting the web server will allow us to enter the XUL file reference URL:

```
http://localhost/startupScreen.xul
```

The browser will now render the XUL interface shown earlier in our client/server implementation.

PHP Serving XUL

We will modify our code to read username and password information from the user, and if we have a valid user, we will render our XUL success screen. The first step to that process is to build an HTML interface to read our entries, and modify the PHP login script to return the XUL source rather than the simple text response.

The PHP interpreter processes any text between the PHP tags (`<?php... ?>`). All other text outside of the PHP tags is returned directly to the browser. PHP scripts build an HTML interface when a designer builds an HTML page and places PHP scripts where conditional processing will change the text returned to the browser.

Our first step to cut over to a served XUL file is to modify our original PHP script to output a standard FORM to read in the username and password. The POST action will send the data to the same script file (we will add logic to check for input values that will help flag different entry points to the script).

Once the script obtains the username and password, we will use the same logic to determine success or failure. Although our finished version will then serve a XUL interface, for now we will simply send our previous return code string to the browser.

The changes from the previous *doCommand.php* file to a *doCommandXUL.php* file are summarized as follows:

- The variables that were obtained through $_GET variables are now obtained through $_POST variables (we will be using an HTML form that uses the POST method for input).
- A check will be added to read the username and password variables. If they are blank, we will issue a login screen; if they are not blank, we will check the input information to see whether the user is authorized.
- The login screen is designed to be a simple HTML table with input fields.
- If the user is authorized, the script echoes the return code to the browser for display.

The PHP script file *doCommandXUL.php* now looks like this:

```
<?php

$uName = trim($_POST['un']);
$uPass = trim($_POST['pd']);

if (empty($uName) || empty($uPass))

{ // build our HTML login stuff

?>

<h1>REGISTERED NEWSSEARCH USERS ONLY!</h1>
<form method="post" action="doCommandXUL.php">
<table>
 <tr>
  <td>User name:</td>
  <td> <input type="text" name="un"/></td>
 </tr>
 <tr>
  <td>Password:</td>
  <td> <input type="password" name="pd"/></td>
 </tr>
  <tr>
  <td colspan="2" align="center"> <input type="submit" value="LOG IN"/></td>
 </tr>
```

```
</table>
</form>

<?php
}

else {
  echo check_user($uName,$uPass);
 }

?>

<?php

// Check user will make certain the user exists, and return
// true with the last login date in the command string
//
// Error conditions return false with a 'message' parameter
// set to the string returned by mysql
//
function check_user($name,$pass) {

   $database = new mysqli('localhost','newssearch_guest','nsgst','newssearch');
   if (mysqli_connect_errno( )) { // failing case
      $retString = 'retcode=false,message='.mysqli_connect_error( );
      return $retString;
      } // failing case

    $encryptPass = sha1($pass);

    $query = "select status,last_session from
      account where username = '$name' and
         password = '$encryptPass'";

    if ($theResult = $database->query("$query")) {
     // we have some kind of result

    if ($theResult->num_rows == 1) { // we have our user

       $theRow = $theResult->fetch_assoc( );
       // get the only row that exists
       $lastLogin = $theRow["last_session"];

       if ($theRow['status'] == 'active') { // all OK
        $retString='retcode=true,last_login='.$theRow['last_session'];
   //     update the session info
        $theResult->close( );
        $curTime = date('c');
        $update = "update account set last_session =
          '$curTime' where username = '$name'";
        $theResult = $database->query("$update");
        } // account is active

       else { // account not active
```

```
        $theResult->close( );
        $retString = 'retcode=false,message=user account not active';
        } // account not active

      } // we have our user
      else { // user not found
       $theResult->close( );
       $retString = 'retcode=false,message=user not found';
       } // user not found


      } // we have some kind of result

      else { // no result returned
       $retString = 'retcode=false,message=invalid query';
      } // no results returned

    $database->close( );
    return $retString;

}

?>
```

When we enter the URL for this file into a Firefox browser, and enter a valid username and password into the fields, we get a browser's rendering of the return code generated by the check_user function, as shown in Figure 4-9.

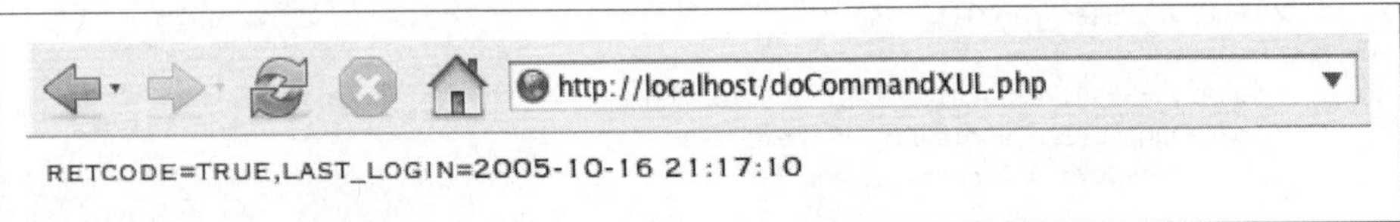

Figure 4-9. PHP-served return code as HTML text

The remaining step to this transition is to serve the XUL source to the user. By renaming our *startupScreen.xul* file to *startupScreen.php*, we can merge PHP statements into the XUL source to accomplish the required tasks to report the last login time for a registered user.

Using PHP require( )

This test application will use a PHP `require` function to insert the XUL source file into the output stream being returned to the user. The code will execute the same user test, and if the user is registered, a PHP variable will be set to the login time, and a require statement will be set to merge the XUL source file into the output stream. The XUL source file will be changed to pass the login time to the status label. Figure 4-10 illustrates the logic.

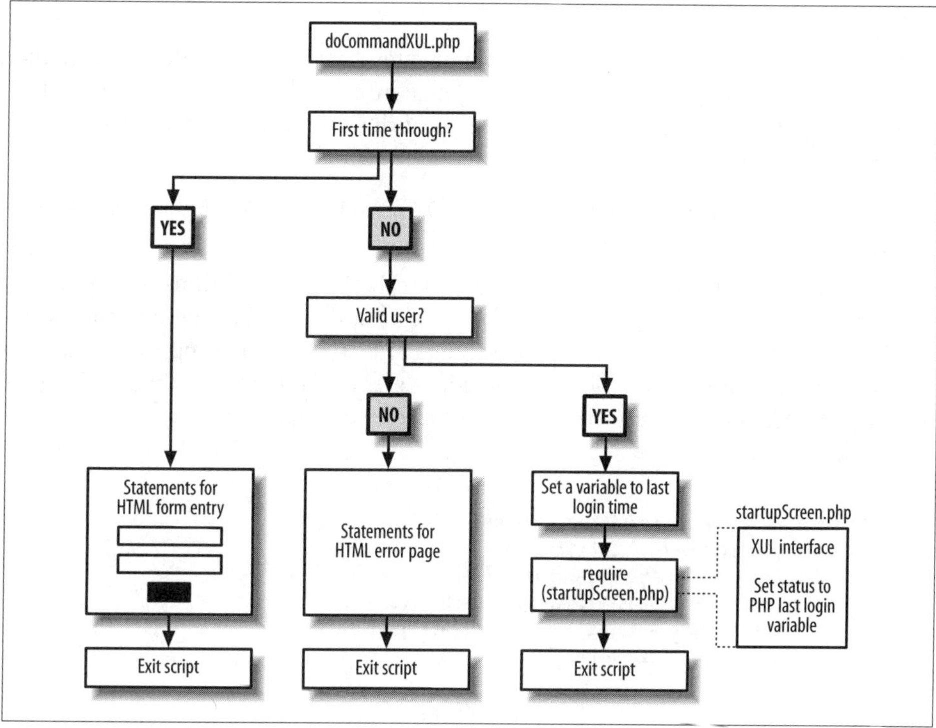

Figure 4-10. PHP login sequence

PHP serving XUL files

If we were to use only a require script to serve a XUL file, we would not be able to merge PHP statements to set the status field of our interface. But by renaming only the *startupScreen.xul* file to *startupScreen.php*, the PHP interpreter would send the XUL source file to the web server without sufficient information to instruct the browser of the required media type.

To allow PHP to properly serve the XUL file, we must make a change to our *php.ini* file:

```
short_open_tag  =  Off
```

This tells the PHP interpreter to ignore parsing the tags <? and ?>, except for those that include the PHP token. Otherwise, PHP would attempt to interpret the XML-structured XUL content.

Our renamed *startupScreen.php* file must also include a PHP directive to set the content type of the text being sent to the browser. The first line in our *startupScreen.php* file must be changed to:

```
<?php header("Content-type: application/vnd.mozilla.xul+xml"); ?>
   <?xml version="1.0"?>
   <?xml-stylesheet href="NewsSearchStyles.css" type="text/css"?>
```

Logic changes

Next, we change our *doCommandXUL.php* frontend script to execute the logic that decides what interface to serve. The only change from the last iteration of the code is to alter the path that actually checks the result if the user entered data into the name and password fields.

The code takes advantage of the PHP `explode` function to break up the returned string into an array of name-value pairs.

We use the PHP `subst(inString,startingChar,lastChar)` functions to break the result array's strings into values, given the fact that we know the length of the names being used as tags. If the first returned value is `true`, we save a string that holds session information into a variable, and include the PHP file that holds the XUL interface content. If the first returned value is `false`, we build a message that flags an unregistered user:

```
else {
  $retString = check_user($uName,$uPass);
  $resArray = explode(',',$retString);
  if ($resArray[0] == 'retcode=true') {
     $lastLoginTime = 'Last login was '.substr($resArray[1],
        11,strlen($resArray[1]));  // extract last session
     require('startupScreen.php');
     }
    else { // invalid user, send rejection page
    echo '<h1>Sorry!</h1>';
    echo '<h2>You are not registered to use this service.</h2>';
    } // invalid user
  }

?>
```

We need to insert another subtle change into the *newssearch.js* file. Because the login button is no longer on our startup screen (the *doCommandXUL.php* file is generating it), we can no longer try to attach a login script upon initialization. We could edit the code to remove all initialization references, or (if we wanted to use the same file for both local and served versions) we could add a test to make certain the button exists before attaching an event listener:

```
function initialize() {
try {
 document.getElementById("B1").
   addEventListener("command",genericBtnHandler,true);
 document.getElementById("B2").
   addEventListener("command",genericBtnHandler,true);
 document.getElementById("B3").
   addEventListener("command",genericBtnHandler,true);
 //
 // Add a login script
```

```
    if (document.getElementById("loginButton")) {
      document.getElementById("loginButton").
          addEventListener("command",doLogin,true);
      }

    }
    catch (e) {
     alert ("Exception: " + e);
     }
  }
```

Finally, we change the segment of the XUL source in our *startupScreen.php* file that manages the status label to include the PHP directives to substitute the `$lastLoginTime` variable into the `label` attribute of the status display:

```
<hbox >
   <!-- stack info and resize horizontally -->
   <!-- right align our status bar -->
     <statusbar id="status-bar" class="chromeclass-status">
     <statusbarpanel id="status-text"
     <?php
      echo('label=\''."$lastLoginTime".'\'/>');
      ?>
   </statusbar>
  <spacer flex="1"/>
 </hbox>
```

Now referencing the *doCommandXUL.php* file from the Firefox URL will present the same interaction with the user, except with the interface delivered from the web server. Figure 4-11 shows our XUL-served page for a successful login and a failed login.

Summary

We have now completed a number of exercises that demonstrate two of the most common implementations of a XUL application. These examples included:

- Moving the application into a chrome package
- Connecting the application to a server running PHP scripts
- Using a relational database engine to store user account information
- Implementing the same interface using XUL source served by PHP scripts

Although we can use any of these forms of implementation for our application, we will continue to focus on the client/server form. The use of the server to provide only textual information lends itself well to our design, in which the Firefox framework accepts the lion's share of interface rendering, and leaves the server to focus on protocol, security, and content.

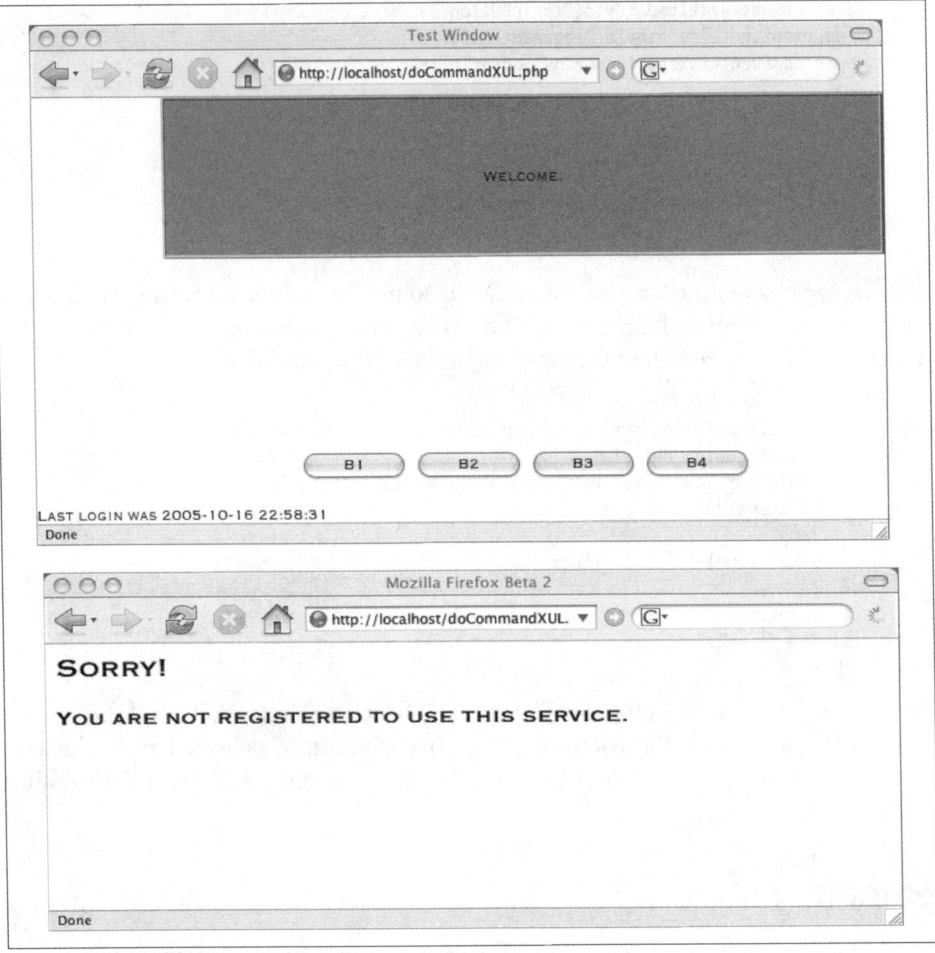

Figure 4-11. Successful and failed logins from a XUL-served interface

CHAPTER 5
Multiframe XUL

This chapter focuses on the design considerations behind a multiframe XUL application. These types of applications involve one or more "content" documents with which the user interacts. We will look at the following topics to help us understand the graphical and programmatic challenges of keeping application logic "in sync" with user interactions in different frames:

- The use of `<iframe>` and `<splitter>` tags to divide content display areas
- Adding a document editor and supporting controls
- The relationship between windows, documents, and content
- Event bubbling and handling
- Keeping interface widgets in sync with the content of different frames
- Adding drop-down menus to manage frame contents
- Adding dialog windows

Dividing the Display Area

Our design objective for the next few chapters is to assemble the main interface for an application that displays web pages, to cite references to web pages, and to keep references to viewed pages in some type of scratchpad.

The first step in making our NewsSearch application look like a real web utility to annotate news articles is to add some substance to the document display and control areas. Because we will be using scripts to modify the interface document (e.g., to change the document source, modify lists, and enable and disable buttons), a good practice is to stage the development by first coding up a static interface file to illustrate what the user will see. We will then incrementally code up the scripts to build the same interface dynamically. Figure 5-1 is a rough sketch of what the interface will look like.

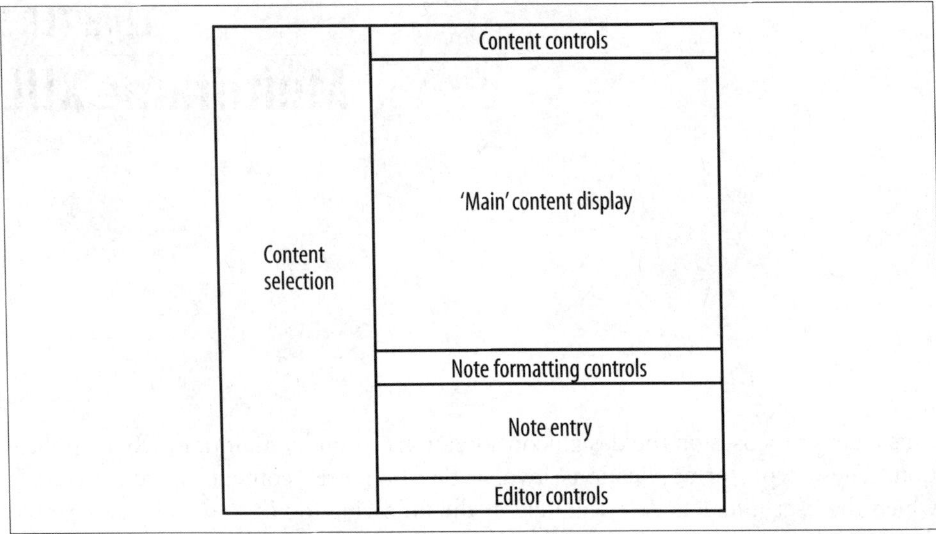

Figure 5-1. Updated frame layout

We will save the *newssearch.xul* file under a new filename, *saved-newssearch.xul*, to keep the login logic interface intact, and we will "hack" at the existing file to experiment with the interface.

We will change the *newssearch.xul* file to replace the login area with a single `<iframe>`. We will also give button 4 our login ID to keep the `initialize( )` script happy:

```
<?xml version="1.0"?>
<?xml-stylesheet href="NewsSearchStyles.css" type="text/css"?>

<window
  id="theMainWindow"
  title="Test Window"
  onload="initialize( );"
  orient="horizontal"
  xmlns:html="http://www.w3.org/1999/xhtml"
  xmlns:xlink="http://www.w3.org/1999/xlink"
  xmlns="http://www.mozilla.org/keymaster/gatekeeper/there.is.only.xul">

<script src="NewsSearch.js"/>
 <!-- main top level container -->
<vbox flex="1">

 <!-- horizontal container for all content (except status info) -->
 <hbox flex="1" >

  <!-- a container for some kind of list -->
  <vbox flex="1" >
  </vbox>

  <!-- container for messages and tool areas -->
  <vbox>
```

```
<!-- used to display message -->
<iframe id="contentIFrame" src="http://www.mozilla.org"
   flex="4" type="content-primary" >
</iframe>

 <!-- used to display typing area  -->

<hbox flex="2" class="typingArea" >
</hbox>

 <!-- used to display tool area-->
<hbox flex="1" class="buttonArea">

 <spacer flex="1"/>

   <vbox>
    <spacer flex="1"/>
     <hbox>
      <button id="B1" label="B1" />
      <button id="B2" label="B2"/>
      <button id="B3" label="B3"/>
      <button id="loginButton" label="LOGIN"/>
     </hbox>
     <spacer flex="1"/>
   </vbox>

 <spacer flex="1"/>

</hbox>

</vbox>
<!-- container for messages and tool areas -->

</hbox>
<!-- horizontal container for all content (except status info) -->


 <hbox >
  <!-- stack info and resizer horizontally -->
  <!-- right align our status bar -->
    <statusbar id="status-bar" class="chromeclass-status">
    <statusbarpanel id="status-text" label="Waiting for login."/>
  </statusbar>
 <spacer flex="1"/>
</hbox>

 <!-- main container -->
</vbox>
</window>
```

An <iframe> element adds an inline frame that we can set to any URL. The "main" content area will hold an iframe with an src attribute set to the URL of the document that we want to view and reference in our note. The attributes of an iframe that are of interest to us include:

`src`
: The URL of the document to be displayed in the frame.

`content-type`
: An attribute that defines rules for scope and user interaction events as content selection. `content-type` is an optional attribute that may be `content` or `content-primary`. (We will discuss `content-type` in greater detail in the section "HTML Documents, Windows, and iframes.")

The results of the interface with the previously listed changes will render the Mozilla.org URL in the top-right area of the interface. To give the user some control over the size of the display areas, we will add a couple of *splitters*.

Splitter widgets consist of a divider that the user can slide along to change the size of the display areas it separates. Splitters include the attributes shown in Table 5-1.

Table 5-1. Splitter attributes

Attribute	Description
`resizebefore`	`Closest`: The size of the element closest to the left (or top) of the splitter changes size.
	`Farthest`: The size of the element farthest to the left (or top) of the splitter changes size.
`resizeafter`	`Closest`: The size of the element closest to the right (or bottom) of the splitter changes size.
	`Farthest`: The size of the element farthest to the right (or bottom) of the splitter changes size.
	`Grow`: No elements change size; the entire container changes size.
`collapse`	`None`: No collapsing is allowed.
	`Before`: When clicked, the splitter reduces the width (height) of the element to the left (top) of the splitter to 0.
	`After`: When clicked, the splitter reduces the width (height) of the element to the right (bottom) of the splitter to 0.
`state`	`Open`: The content before or after the splitter is displayed.
	`Closed`: The content before or after the splitter is hidden.
	`Dragging`: The splitter is currently being dragged by the user's mouse actuation.

Two splitters are added to the interface: one to divide the interface horizontally, between the area that will hold the content selection list and the content, editing, and control areas; and a second splitter to separate the content display from the typing area. Once the splitters are added, it is a good practice to change the interface to prevent objects from stretching too big or shrinking too small. We set the `height` attribute of the control area, and the `minwidth` and `minheight` attributes to keep the type area from completely disappearing:

```
<splitter resizebefore="closest" resizeafter="closest" state="open"/>
<!-- container for messages and tool areas -->
<vbox>

<!-- used to display message -->
```

```
<iframe id="contentIFrame" src="http://www.mozilla.org"
 flex="4" type="content-primary" >
</iframe>

 <splitter resizebefore="closest" resizeafter="closest" state="open"/>
 <!-- used to display typing area  -->
<hbox flex="2" minheight="75" minwidth="100" class="typingArea" >
</hbox>

 <!-- used to display tool area-->
<hbox height="50" class="buttonArea">

 <spacer flex="1"/>
```

To add visual clarity to the interface, we make changes to the stylesheet *NewsSearchStyles.css* to give some definition to the areas with the `typingArea` and `buttonArea` classes, and the `splitter` tag:

```
splitter {
 background-color:#c0c0c0;
}

 .typingArea {
  background-color:#ffff66;
 }

 .buttonArea {
  border-style:groove;
  border-color:gray;
 }
```

These changes produce an interface that starts to look more user-friendly, as shown in Figure 5-2.

Editing Documents

Before we add code to respond to user input and text entry, we will take a closer look at the relationship between the main XUL document and documents contained within nested frames.

HTML Documents, Windows, and iframes

In scripting HTML documents, JavaScript scripts have access to a `window` property that represents the topmost container of a visual hierarchy. The properties of a window (with the exception of the `location` and `document` properties) reflect:

- The physical attributes of the interface, such as width and height attributes of areas hidden by scrolling, screen characteristics, and status bar information
- Information pertaining to the software that manages the interface, such as the vendor name, version identifiers, supported MIME types, and user agent information

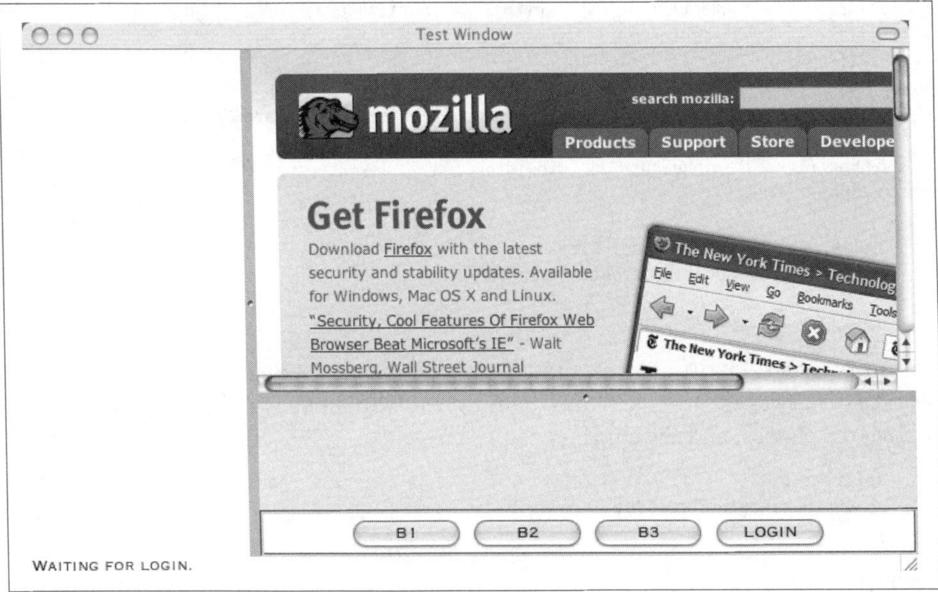

Figure 5-2. iframe with splitters

Such `window` properties are independent of the web page being displayed. The `location` property provides the URL of the document being displayed. A window's document represents the information that specifies what the interface looks like. The document contains all the HTML elements that encode an interface, and the window provides the management logic to physically display the interface described by the following HTML document, as shown in Figure 5-3.

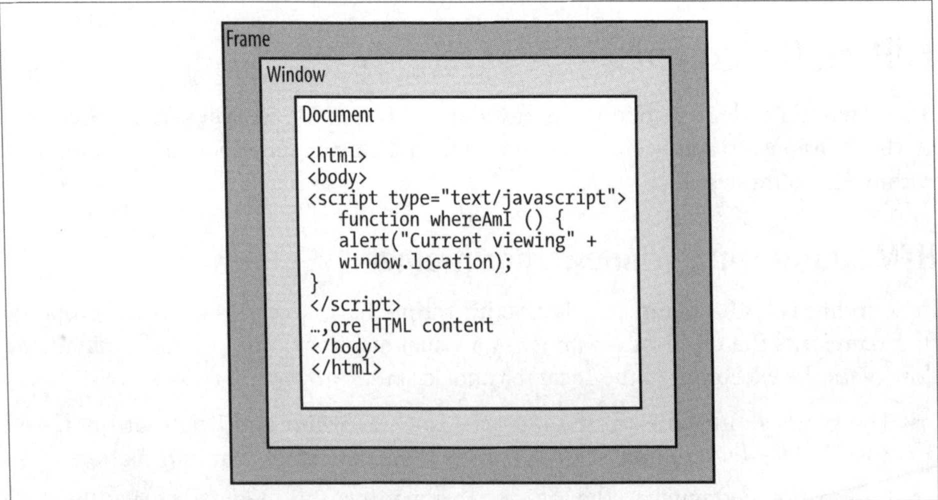

Figure 5-3. Visual hierarchy

When an application is designed to display multiple content areas, such as a navigation area along with a primary web page, you may divide the interface into a *frameset* (a collection of frames), each frame having a `src` attribute that specifies the URL from which content is loaded.

XUL Documents, Windows, and iframes

XUL interfaces consist of a hierarchy that you access using many of the same properties previously described for HTML interfaces. The visual hierarchy is also the same:

- The `<window>` tag of a XUL file defines the topmost container for all visual elements of an interface.
- In JavaScript, the `window.document` property returns the document that provides access to content nodes and document properties.
- XUL documents may include XUL *view* tags, such as `<iframe>`, `<editor>`, and `<browser>`, to divide an interface into separate display areas.

In addition to these elements, the XUL interface makes available additional attributes and properties to allow easier programmatic access to windows and documents deeply nested in the visual hierarchy.

XUL Windows and Content Type

The XUL interface considers a view element such as an `iframe` to be *a content panel*, which is an area used to display its own content information. The content panels allow a `type` attribute that associates a number of privileges and properties with each type of content:

`content`
: `type=content` implies that the panel will have `contentWindow` and `contentDocument` properties that facilitate access to scripts attached to parent containers. Scripts attached to the documents displayed in these types of content panels have access rights that are bounded by the content panel's window.

`content-primary`
: Panels with `type=content-primary` impose the same security rules as content panels (scripts attached to documents in such panels cannot access any elements outside the containing window). In addition, this attribute flags the content pane as the one presenting the main content of the interface; the application's main `window.content` property will return a reference to the window wrapped by an `iframe` with a `content-primary` type attribute.

`none`
: Content panels with no `type` attribute are presumed to be logically integrated with the interface. Scripts attached to documents in such panels have access to any interface element (e.g., the "top" reference will return the topmost XUL window containing all interface elements).

Figure 5-4 illustrates these differences.

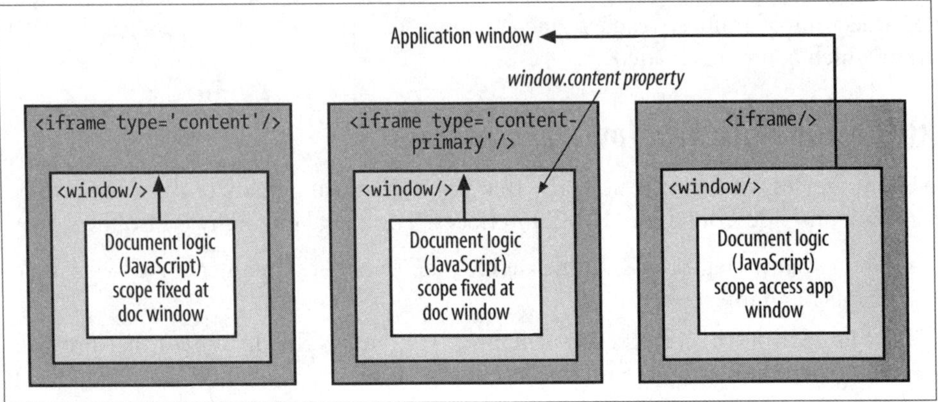

Figure 5-4. Frames and content types

We can programmatically observe the differences in security restrictions by creating a content document with a script that tries to access the "top" window.

A *test.html* file created in the home directory illustrates this:

```
<html>
<body onclick="dump('my top  and location are' + top + ',' +
  top.location + '\n');">
test
</body>
</html>
```

Temporarily change the `<iframe>` declaration in the *newssearch.xul* file to load the test source file:

```
<iframe id="contentIFrame"  type="content-primary" src="test.html"
  flex="4">
</iframe>
```

When we launch the application from the command line as a chrome application and click in the body area, we see the message that identifies `top.location` as the test file, not the URL of the application's main chrome window:

```
% ./firefox -console -chrome chrome://newssearch/content/
my top  and location are[object Window],
  chrome://newssearch/content/test.html
```

The script in the document has a scope that is limited by the boundaries set by the `iframe`'s window. When we remove the `content-type` in the `<iframe>` declaration:

```
<iframe id="contentIFrame"  src="test.html" flex="4">
</iframe>
```

the same command-line launch of the chrome application yields a reference to the application's main chrome window and URL:

```
% ./firefox -console -chrome chrome://newssearch/content/
my top  and location are[object
 ChromeWindow],chrome://newssearch/content/newssearch.xul
```

Scripts that run in the editor's document space cannot access any information outside that of the enclosing `iframe`.

We can easily demonstrate the difference between `content-primary` and `content` types by adding a diagnostic statement to the button handler that displays the *application* window's `content` property:

```
dump("main content location is " + window.content.location + "\n");
```

This statement will display the `window.location` for the `iframe` with the `content-primary` attribute; if no `iframes` have the `content-primary` attribute, `window.content` returns `undefined`. This feature allows developers to write code that can determine the main viewing window if an application includes multiple frames for content, navigation, and controls.

Other Content Panels

The other primary content panels Firefox supports include the `<editor>` element and the `<browser>` element.

<editor>

An editor panel, in its simplest form, can serve as a text entry area or as a typing area for any HTML-styled text. When editors have a `type=html` attribute, either by the tag declaration or through the `makeEditable` method, we can use the `getHTMLEditor()` method to obtain a reference to an interface with a number of styling and formatting methods. (Editors with a `type=text` attribute will make an editing interface available through the `getEditor()` method, which has a more limited set of text manipulation functions.)

The typing area for our application needs to support text entry. The `textbox` widget allows multiline text entry; more sophisticated interfaces should support the various styling options made available by the `editor` widget.

The attributes and methods of the editor that I will demonstrate include those listed in Table 5-2.

Table 5-2. Editor attributes and methods

Attribute/Method	Description
`src`	The URL of the content being edited
`type`	The type of content panel: `"content-primary"` | `"content"` | none
`makeEditable(editorType,waitForLoad)`	Makes the editor area responsive to user entry; sets the editor type to `"html"` | `"text"`
`getHTMLEditor(theEditorWindow)`	Returns a reference to an `htmlEditor` interface that supports styling and formatting methods

We now add an editor to serve as the main user data entry typing area:

```
<!-- used to display typing area  -->
 <hbox flex="2" minheight="75" minwidth="100" >
 <editor id="memoEditor" src="about:blank" flex="1"  class="typingArea" >
 </editor>
 </hbox>
```

When an application requires some form of initialization logic (JavaScript) that accesses document properties, the application must make certain that the document has been completely loaded into a window before content-specific initialization can take place.

Web developers writing code that loads and manipulates content in HTML or XUL iframes must take into account an inherent lag between setting a frame's source and having the document loaded. Without some form of event handling to be triggered off a load event, developers may easily lose track of which content is being accessed.

To add JavaScript that provides our editor and its controls with initialization logic, we must call the makeEditable(editorType,waitForLoad) method *after* the window has been loaded. We set the editorType parameter to html to enable us to add HTML styling directives to the document. We add the method call to the initialize function in the file *newssearch.js*. We call initialize after the application's main window has been loaded:

```
function initialize() {
try {
 document.getElementById("B1").
  addEventListener("command",genericBtnHandler,true);
 document.getElementById("B2").
  addEventListener("command",genericBtnHandler,true);
 document.getElementById("B3").
    addEventListener("command",genericBtnHandler,true);
 //
 // Add a login script
 document.getElementById("loginButton").
  addEventListener("command",doLogin,true);
 //
// Make the memo area editable
 document.getElementById("memoEditor").makeEditable("html",false);
 }
 catch (e) {
  alert ("Exception: " + e);
  }
}
```

Launching the application gives the same layout, but we can now type information in the memo typing area, as shown in Figure 5-5.

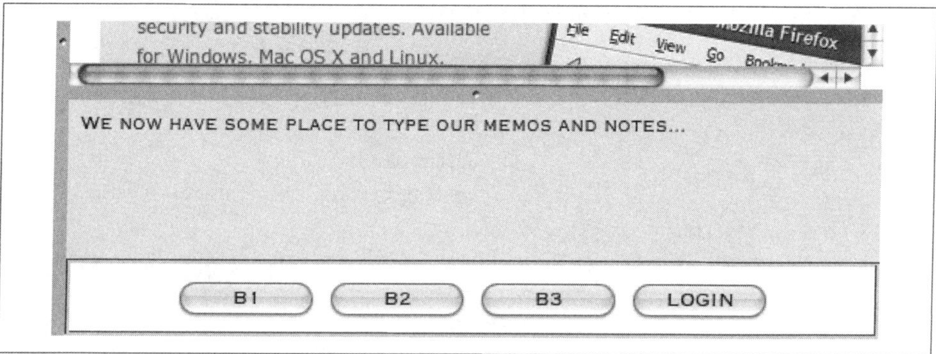

Figure 5-5. XUL editor widget

We can quickly test some of the extended features of the `HTMLEditor` interface returned by the `getHTMLEditor( )` method by attaching a method to increase the editor's font size when one of the control buttons is pressed.

We change the `genericButtonHandler` function to demonstrate this one feature of the `HTMLEditor` interface:

```
function genericBtnHandler(event) {
try { // try block
var infoString = "Type = " + event.type + ",";
infoString += "Target = " + event.target + ",";
infoString += "Target.tagName = " + event.target.tagName + ",";
infoString += "Target.id = " + event.target.id + ".";
dump(infoString + "\n");
var theEditor = document.getElementById("memoEditor").
  getHTMLEditor
  (document.getElementById("memoEditor").contentWindow);
theEditor.increaseFontSize( );
} // try block
catch (e) {
 alert("genericBtnHandler exception: " + e);
 }
}
```

Once we launch the application and begin typing in the note area, pressing any of the control buttons will increase the text size. We will later move these styling features into pull-down menus.

<browser>

A browser content area provides a full-fledged URL viewer in a section of a user interface.

Whereas an `<iframe>` can display any URL by virtue of the `src` attribute, a `<browser>` element includes methods to advance or return to previous pages, to set a home page, and to support various methods that deal with security features. Table 5-3 shows some of the attributes and methods of a `<browser>`.

Table 5-3. Selected <browser> attributes and methods

Attribute/Method	Description
`src`	The URI of the browser (this attribute's use is generally replaced by the `loadURI` method).
`type`	The type of content panel: `"content-primary" | " content " | none`

`loadURI(theURI, referrer, charset)`	Load the URI:
	`theURI`
	URI to load
	`referrer`
	The referring site | none
	`charset`
	The desired character set | none

`goBack( )`	Go back one page in the browser history.
`goForward( )`	Go forward one page in the browser history.

We change the source file *newssearch.xul* to replace the main content area with a `<browser>` tag, along with some optional controls to demonstrate browser features:

```
<!-- some simple controls to manage display pages -->
<hbox class="buttonArea">
 <button id="stepBackward" label="BACK"
  oncommand="stepPage(event);"/>
 <button id="stepForward" label="FORWARD"
   oncommand="stepPage(event);"/>
 <hbox>
  <vbox pack="center">
  <label control="theURL" value="URL:"/>
  </vbox>
  <textbox id="theURL" size="32" type="autocomplete" autocompletesearch="history"/>
  <button id="loadURL" label="GO" oncommand="loadURL( );"/>
  </hbox>

</hbox>
<!-- used to display message -->
<browser id="contentIFrame"  type="content-primary"
   src="http://www.mozilla.org" flex="4">
</browser>

 <splitter resizebefore="closest" resizeafter="closest"
   state="open"/>
 <!-- used to display typing area  -->
 <hbox flex="2" minheight="75" minwidth="100" >
 <editor id="memoEditor" flex="1"  type="content"
   class="typingArea">

</editor>
```

We create a horizontal box with a class of buttonArea (to provide the styled border through the existing Cascading Style Sheet [CSS] declaration) to contain some control buttons and a text area to allow the user to type in URLs. The <vbox> wrapping the label for the text area exists to provide vertical centering (pack="center") for the text labels alongside the text area.

The <textbox> itself has a couple of unfamiliar attributes:

type
: For text boxes, type=autocomplete will result in the Firefox framework completing partially entered text.

autocompletesearch
: This attribute tells Firefox on what basis to carry out the autocompletion. A value of history will autocomplete the text field with entries from the history of previous entries.

Event listeners are attached to the control buttons in the XUL file. For the Back/Forward buttons, we use the same handler that audits the label attached to the event target. The Go button calls the loadURL function that passes the value in the text box to the browser, and the button handler is modified to call a "stepPage" function that decodes the button's ID to advance or return through the browser's navgation hierarchy, as shown in the changes to the source file, *newssearch.js*:

```
function loadURL() {
try{
var newURL = document.getElementById("theURL").value;
document.getElementById("contentIFrame").loadURI(newURL);
 }
 catch (e) {
 alert("Exception loading URL " + e);
 };
};

function stepPage(event) {
 try {
  if (event.target.id == "stepBackward")
    document.getElementById("contentIFrame").goBack();
  else
    document.getElementById("contentIFrame").goForward();
 }
 catch (e) {
  alert("exception in stepPage " + e);
  }
}
```

The result is an application with an editor for note entry, and a content window that displays whatever URL the user typed in, as shown in Figure 5-6.

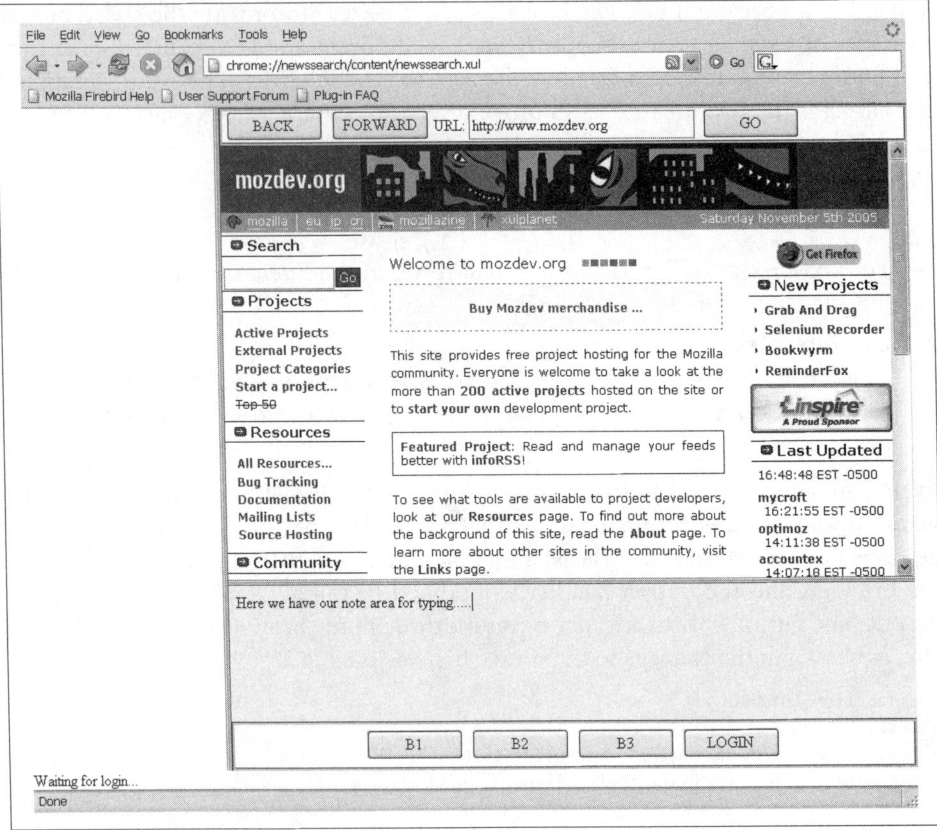

Figure 5-6. The results of creating a <browser> tag with page controls

Dealing with Events

The execution of functions and the manipulation of interface widgets are managed by programmatic events representing a change in a system's state, or more often, as a result of some user interaction with the system. In either case, scripts and interface elements must respond to events that reflect a state change.

The next section discusses the implications of attaching event listeners to respond to events as the event traverses the Document Object Model (DOM) tree, as well as the effect of attaching event handlers to different members of the visual hierarchy.

Event phases

User interface events propagate through the interface in two phases.

The *capture* phase of an event refers to its traversal from the topmost container of the visual hierarchy (the window), to the window's document, and through descendant containers toward the widget that represents its source. The *bubble* phase represents a return trip during which the event travels upward from the source through all the ancestors of the interface hierarchy.

Figure 5-7 shows the phases of event traversal for our button area and its enclosing vbox.

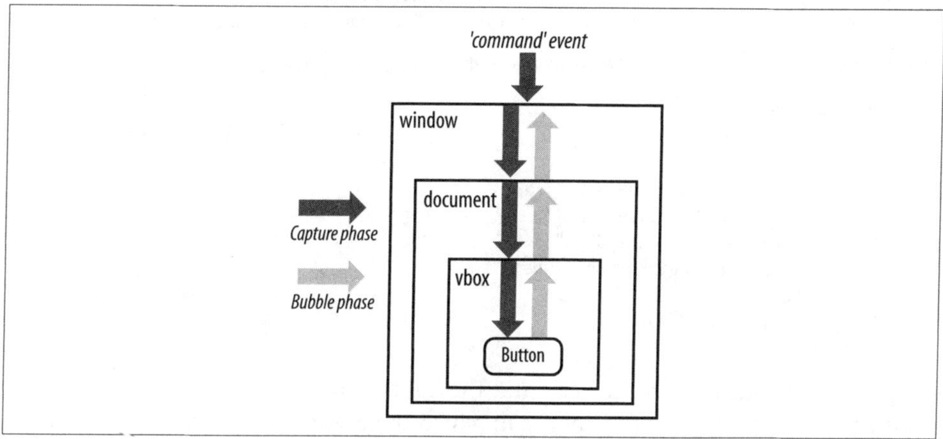

Figure 5-7. Event phases

A DOM function allows the designer to specify whether an event listener should respond to an event during either the capture or the bubble phase:

```
addEventListener(eventType, listenerFunction, useCapture)
```

The `useCapture` parameter, if `true`, will result in the listener function being triggered during the event's capture phase, traversing down the interface hierarchy toward the event's source. When `false`, the function is triggered after the event has reached the source and is "bubbling" back up the interface tree.

Within the event listener, we can also audit the `eventPhase` property of the event to determine the event's direction at the time the function was called:

```
1: event is in capturing phase
2: event is at target
3: event is in bubbling phase
```

We can see these effects by making some simple changes to our *newssearch.js* file to illustrate the interactions between event targets and phases.

We add an event listener function to report when our control button's `vbox` is handling a `command` event:

```
func1 = function (evt) { dump("vbox command with event phase =
" + evt.eventPhase + "\n"); }
```

We make a subtle change to the `genericButtonHandler` to display the event phase to the console:

```
infoString += "Target.id = " + event.target.id + ",";
infoString += "Evt.phase = " + event.eventPhase + "."
dump(infoString + "\n");
```

Now we change the statements that assign the event handlers to the buttons, adding an event handler to the enclosing <vbox>, which is "higher" in the visual hierarchy than the button:

```
document.getElementById("vbox").addEventListener("command",func1,true);
document.getElementById("B1").addEventListener("command",genericButtonHandler,true);
```

And finally we add an id attribute to the <vbox> enclosing the button:

```
<vbox id="vbox">
     <spacer flex="1"/>
      <hbox>
       <button id="B1" label="B1" />
       <button id="B2" label="B2"/>
       <button id="B3" label="B3"/>
       <button id="loginButton" label="LOGIN"/>
      </hbox>
      <spacer flex="1"/>
    </vbox>
```

As currently defined, both the vbox and the button are set to fire the event listener during the "capture" phase, the phase in which the event is working down the visual hierarchy toward the end node of the interface tree (the button). We see the intended results—func1 displays the vbox listener function followed by the output of the generic button handler:

```
vbox command with event phase = 1
Type = command,Target = [object XULElement],Target.tagName =
  button,Target.id = B1,Evt.phase = 2.
```

If we change the useCapture parameter on the vbox to false:

```
document.getElementById("vbox").addEventListener("command",func1,false);
```

the vbox's event listener will be triggered during the bubble phase—after the event reaches the button and begins to "bubble" back up the visual hierarchy. The console output identifies the button first responding to the command event, followed by the vbox:

```
Type = command,Target = [object XULElement],Target.tagName =
  button,Target.id = B1,Evt.phase = 2.
vbox command with event phase = 3
```

Predictably, the genericButtonHandler is fired with an event phase of 2, because the function was attached to the object acting as the origin of the event.

Sometimes a designer may want to stop the event from propagating through the interface tree. Scripts calling event.stopPropagation( ) will result in the event being "swallowed" by the script—the event stops within such a handler, regardless of its phase.

In many situations, the phase of an event is significant to developers:

- Designers may choose to respond to events by allowing a "primitive" interface widget (e.g., a button) to conduct some initialization prior to passing the event "up" the visual hierarchy, letting a more complex structure (a window) handle the event. In such a case, the window's event listener must be set to respond when the event is bubbling up from the button, guaranteeing that the button's preparation code was executed prior to the window's event handler.
- If the interface includes a complex drawing space on which graphical items may be dropped, dragged, or selected, such a service will likely have listeners for mouse-move, mouse-down, and mouse-up events. Objects being dragged or dropped on the service are also likely to have such handlers. Proper use of the event's capture phase will allow the designer to simplify the algorithms for distinguishing between dynamic repositioning (dragging) of an object versus dragging and dropping onto select objects.
- Applications that display multiple documents may need to carefully manage the flow of "close" or "open" events, such as saving the view to preserve state information.

Synchronizing Interface Widgets and Frames

Conventional HTML multiframe sites often implement a content selection frame through the HTML hyperlink anchor (`<a>` element), with a target attribute controlling the content displayed in another frame, such as `<a target="nameOfDestinationFrame" href="some URL"/>`.

In the case of our application, the management of the interface is more complicated.

Assuming that our button area will have controls to create new notes and save/send notes, we impose a number of interface requirements to develop a user-friendly interface:

- A "not logged" state during which only the login button is enabled
- A successful "startup" state after a user has logged in, but before she has requested any activity from the interface
- An "open-note" state during which the user is able to type in the editor area
- A "note-in-progress" state during which the note disposal buttons are enabled

The simplified diagram in Figure 5-8 illustrates the transitions.

These requirements mandate logic that is sensitive to how the user interacts with the control buttons and the editor area. For that, we will add an `updateInterface` function that manages the application states. Event listener functions attached to our state buttons will be enabled or disabled based on the current state, and the state transition logic will take care of calling functions to conduct state-specific logic.

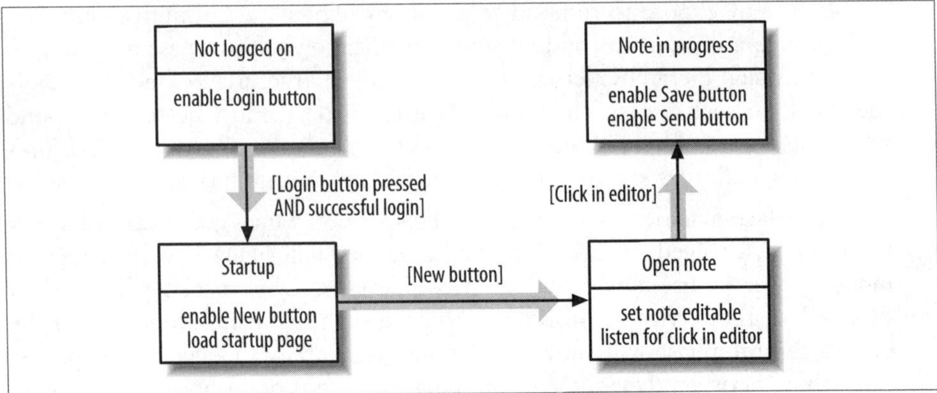

Figure 5-8. Interface state transitions

Adding state transitions

First we rename the interface buttons and relabel them in the *newssearch.xul* file; we also add a button to cancel operations:

```
<vbox id="vbox">
     <spacer flex="1"/>
      <hbox>
       <button id="newButton" label="New" />
       <button id="saveButton" label="Save"/>
       <button id="sendButton" label="Send"/>
       <button id="cancelButton" label="Cancel"/>
       <button id="loginButton" label="LOGIN"/>
      </hbox>
      <spacer flex="1"/>
    </vbox>
```

We add to *newssearch.js* a global variable to define the state of the application as users log in and create and edit notes:

```
//
// Some constants to help us know what
// buttons and editing areas to enable
//
var K_NOT_LOGGED_ON   = 0;  // no user, no note
var K_STARTUP         = 1;  // user, no note
var K_OPEN_NOTE       = 2;  // note ready for editing
var K_NOTE_IN_PROGRESS = 3; // note editing in progress
```

We change the initialize function to reflect the new button names, direct the login button listener to the generic button handler, remove the statements that enabled the editor (to be moved to updateInterface), and set an initialized state:

```
function initialize(event) {
try {
 dump("initialize: Event target, current target and phase
   are: " + event.target + "," + event.currentTarget + "," +
    event.eventPhase + "\n");
```

```
document.getElementById("newButton").addEventListener
  ("command", genericButtonHandler,true);
document.getElementById("saveButton").addEventListener
  ("command", genericBtnHandler,true);
document.getElementById("sendButton").addEventListener
  ("command", genericBtnHandler,true);
document.getElementById("cancelButton").addEventListener
  ("command",genericBtnHandler,true);
document.getElementById("loginButton").addEventListener
  ("command",genericBtnHandler,true);
G_ApplicationState = K_NOT_LOGGED_ON;
updateInterface( );

 }
 catch (e) {
  alert ("Exception: " + e);
  }
};
```

We upgrade our generic button handler to execute a case jump that switches on the target (button) IDs and manages the actual state transitions:

```
function genericBtnHandler(event) {
try { // try block
var infoString = "Type = " + event.type + ",";
infoString += "Target = " + event.target + ",";
infoString += "Target.tagName = " + event.target.tagName + ",";
infoString += "Target.id = " + event.target.id + ",";
infoString += "Evt.phase = " + event.eventPhase + "."
dump(infoString + "\n");
switch(event.target.id) { // switch on target
case "newButton": {
  newNote( );
  break;
 }
 case "saveButton": {
 // TBD
  break;
 }
case "sendButton": {
// TBD
  break;
 }
case "cancelButton": {
  cancelNote( );
  break;
 }
case "loginButton": {
  doLogin( );
  break;
 }
} // switch on target
} // try block
catch (e) {
```

```
alert("genericBtnHandler exception: " + e);
}
}
```

We change the function that responds to the login button to a stub that presumes a valid login and sets a state to K_STARTUP (we will move the login interface to a pop-up dialog later in this chapter):

```
function doLogin( ) {

try { // try
// !!!!! STUB FOR NOW
G_ApplicationState = K_STARTUP;
updateInterface( );
return;
// !!!!!! STUB FOR NOW

var theArgs = new Array;
theArgs[0] = new commandArg("un",document.
  getElementById("userName").value);
theArgs[1] = new commandArg("pd",document.
  getElementById("password").value);
lastCommand = "login";

doServerRequest("login",theArgs);
 } // try
 catch (e) { //
  alert("doLogin exception: " + e);
 }//
}
```

We add two functions to manage the interface widgets. The disableEverything function acts as a utility to disable all buttons on the interface. Soon we will add simplified logic to the updateInterface function that will turn on only the buttons we need for each state. We also add functions to take care of button actuations:

```
// function turns off all buttons, disables
// note typing area
function disableEverything( ) {
document.getElementById("newButton").disabled=true;
document.getElementById("saveButton").disabled=true;
document.getElementById("sendButton").disabled=true;
document.getElementById("cancelButton").disabled=true;
document.getElementById("loginButton").disabled=true;
}

function cancelNote( ) {
 G_ApplicationState = K_STARTUP;
 updateInterface( );
}

function newNote( ) {
G_ApplicationState = K_OPEN_NOTE;
updateInterface( );
}
```

```
function editorClicked(event) {
dump("Click event " + event.target + " window is " +
  window + " location = " + window.location.toString( ) +  "\n");
event.target.removeEventListener("click",editorClicked,true);
G_ApplicationState = K_NOTE_IN_PROGRESS;
updateInterface( );
};
```

The updateInterface function modifies the interface widgets to reflect our application's state transitions. Each application state enables or disables buttons and typing areas to prepare for the next transition:

```
// Takes care of buttons and editing areas
// based on global variable
function updateInterface( ) {
try{
dump("In update interface with state = " +
 G_ApplicationState + "\n");
 disableEverything( );
 switch(G_ApplicationState) { // switch on state
  case (K_NOT_LOGGED_ON): { // not logged on
  document.getElementById("loginButton").disabled=false;
  break;
  } // not logged on
  case (K_STARTUP): { // startup
  // enable only the new button
  document.getElementById("newButton").disabled=false;
  document.getElementById("contentIFrame").setAttribute
    ("src","http://www.mozdev.org");
  break;
  } // startup
  case (K_OPEN_NOTE): { // note ready for editing
  // Make the memo area editable, and enable the cancel button
  // to give the user a way out
  var theEditor = document.getElementById("memoEditor");
  theEditor.makeEditable("html",false);
  theEditor.addEventListener("click",editorClicked,true);

  break;
  } // note ready for editing

  case (K_NOTE_IN_PROGRESS): { // note is/has been edited
  document.getElementById("saveButton").disabled=false;
  document.getElementById("sendButton").disabled=false;
  break;
  } // note is/has been edited

 } // switch on state
 }
catch(e) { //
alert("update interface exception " + e);
}//
}
```

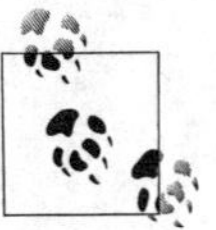

Note that all functions include `dump` statements liberally scattered about to help in debugging.

The last point to consider involves differences between the event-handling process in chrome applications and in browser windows.

An event handler too many

If we open Firefox and enter the chrome URL in the browser's URL window, pressing the login button results in a "flash" of the New note button being enabled but a return to the initial login state with only the Login button enabled. The console reports some unexpected calls to `initialize`:

```
Event target, current target and phase are: null,
 [object XPCNativeWrapper [object Window]],3
In update interface with state = 0
initialize: Event target, current target and phase are:
  null,[object XPCNativeWrapper [object Window]],3
In update interface with state = 0
initialize: Event target, current target and phase are:
 [object XULDocument],[object XPCNativeWrapper [object Window]],2
In update interface with state = 0
Type = command,Target = [object XULElement],Target.tagName =
  button,Target.id = loginButton,Evt.phase = 2.
In update interface with state = 1
initialize: Event target, current target and phase are: null,
 [object XPCNativeWrapper [object Window]],3
In update interface with state = 0
```

Although the state transition from `0` to `1` (`K_STARTUP` to `K_USER_LOGGED_ON`) looks fine, there are a number of unexpected calls to `initialize`, as indicated by the dump of the event target.

We can obtain the desired results if we launch the application from the command line as a chrome URL:

```
./firefox -chrome chrome://newssearch/content
initialize: Event target, current target and phase are:
 [object XULDocument],[object ChromeWindow],2
In update interface with state = 0
Type = command,Target = [object XULElement],Target.
  tagName = button,Target.id = loginButton,Evt.phase = 2.
In update interface with state = 1
```

The interface now looks as we expected, with the New button enabled. To determine why the application does not perform as expected when it is launched within a browser, we need to revisit the topic of event propagation.

Event generation: XUL events and HTML events

When the application is launched as part of a browser window, the initialize function is being called more often than expected. The display of the event phase indicates that when the login button is pressed, initialize is being called with a null target:

```
Event target, current target and phase are: null,[object
 XPCNativeWrapper [object Window]],3
```

Our dump traces indicate the interface is being updated to state 1 (K_USER_LOGGED_ON), but then the initialize function is called again, resetting our application state to K_STARTUP. Some portions of the dump statements make sense: the statements with event.currentTarget pointing to an XPCNativeWrapper [object Window] reference indicate that the particular function call is due to the XUL window's assignment as the event listener for the load event. The calls with the null reference as the event target need to be explained.

The problem lies with the assignment of the initialize function as the onload handler for the top XUL window; the initialize function is called *any* time our XUL window is in the path of a load event as it passes down from the main window to whatever target fired the event.

When the application is loaded within the Firefox browser, HTML load events are fired when a document, frameset, or object is completely transferred from a server into the browser (the World Wide Web Consortium [W3C] web site, *http://www.w3.org/TR/2000/REC-DOM-Level-2-Events-20001113*, fully describes the circumstances behind each event creation). When we run the application in a browser window, we can expect load events not only when the main XUL interface document is loaded, but also when iframe elements have src attributes assigned, and editor documents are loaded.

If we run the application only as a standalone XUL (chrome) application, the XUL specification states that load events are fired *only* for window and image elements, or elements that accept an image attribute. In a chrome-only window, for example, the editor element does not generate a load event as it is loaded, nor does the main content iframe. We have a situation in which the number of load events is different depending on whether we run the application in a browser window or as a standalone XUL chrome application. Our scripts must be able to determine which instance will trigger the intended response.

Responding to the "right" event target

One technique to determine whether our function is responding to the correct occurrence of an event is to audit the properties of the event.

The event.target property identifies the element that caused the event to be fired. The event.currentTarget property references the element whose event handler is currently being called; it changes as the event propagates down through the interface hierarchy toward the event.target element.

If we modify the initialize function to execute only when event.target is the document for the main interface window (the main XUL interface window), we guarantee that the function's main logic will be executed only when the window's load event is fired:

```
function initialize(event) {
try {
dump("initialize: Event target, current target and phase are: " + event.target + ","
+ event.currentTarget + "," + event.eventPhase + "\n");
if (event.target == document) { // target is the main window
 document.getElementById("newButton").addEventListener
  ("command",genericBtnHandler,true);
 document.getElementById("saveButton").addEventListener
     ("command",genericBtnHandler,true);
 document.getElementById("sendButton").addEventListener
    ("command",genericBtnHandler,true);
 document.getElementById("cancelButton").addEventListener
    ("command",genericBtnHandler,true);
 document.getElementById("loginButton").addEventListener
    ("command",genericBtnHandler,true);
 //

G_ApplicationState = K_NOT_LOGGED_ON;
   // will change to NOT LOGGED ON LATER
updateInterface( );
  } // target is the main window
 } // try
 catch (e) {
  alert ("Exception: " + e);
   }
};
```

This change fixes our first transition after the login button is pressed. The next enhancement involves managing events from the editor window.

Managing events in iframes

The application is currently designed to enable the send and save buttons once the user begins typing in the editor area. But the event generation's scope for the content panes (iframe, editor, and browser elements) is upward-bounded by their respective windows. Scripts attached to the main application document or application window will never see events that the editor triggers.

To properly register an event listener in our application that is in the scope of the editor element, we must attach the function to the editor's contentDocument property:

```
case (K_OPEN_NOTE): { // note ready for editing
  // Make the memo area editable, and enable the cancel button
  // to give the user a way out
```

```
var theEditor = document.getElementById("memoEditor");
theEditor.makeEditable("html",false);
theEditor.contentDocument.addEventListener("click",editorClicked,true);
break;
} // note ready for editing
```

We now have a version that runs on both browser and standalone windows, and we can complete the updateInterface function to manage our interface widgets.

This last addition will enable the note disposal buttons only when text has been entered in the window.

Adding Pull-Down Menus

Most users are accustomed to being able to change the style of text as they are typing. The <editor> content area supports the relevant commands to do this. We will now add some drop-down menus to give users some simple styling controls.

We can obtain an HTMLEditor interface from the editor element through the getHTMLEditor( ) method. The HTMLEditor interface provides us with methods to style and format text, as listed in Table 5-4.

Table 5-4. HTMLEditor text formatting methods

Method	Description
decreaseFontSize( ) increaseFontSize( )	Changes the size of the font for newly typed characters in the editor area
setCSSInlineProperty(propertyAtom, attributeName, attributeValue);	Sets the value of the property's attribute at the current insertion point

The setCSSInlineProperty function requires a propertyAtom parameter.

To obtain a property atom, the script must acquire a Cross-Platform Component Model (XPCOM) service interface that converts a string into the nsIAtom interface:

```
var atomService = Components.classes["@mozilla.org/atom-service;1"].
    getService(Components.interfaces.nsIAtomService);
```

When the editor's setCSSInlineProperty function is called, the first parameter is used to create a new inline HTML element at the editor's insertion point. The attributeName and attributeValue are inserted as inline attributes. To create a newly styled segment of text through the insertion of a <span> tag, the function is:

```
setCSSInlineProperty(atomService.getAtom("span"), "style", "style-property:value")
```

To construct the interface for the user to change the appearance of text in the editor's typing area, we will add a series of menu items, menu pop ups, menus, and menu bars organized in a hierarchy:

Menu item
: The lowest widget on the menu hierarchy. A menu item is the "last" button available for a user to actuate that results in an action or command being executed.

Menu pop up
: The container for a collection of menu items that "pops up" when a menu is selected.

Menu
: A visual representation of the topmost button that opens a menu pop up.

Menu bar
: A spatially linear collection of menus.

These elements are often collected in a `<menubar>` element to provide a horizontal or vertical orientation for menus, but `<menu>` elements can also exist within `<menupopup>` to provide cascading menus. Figure 5-9 illustrates various arrangements of menus and pop ups.

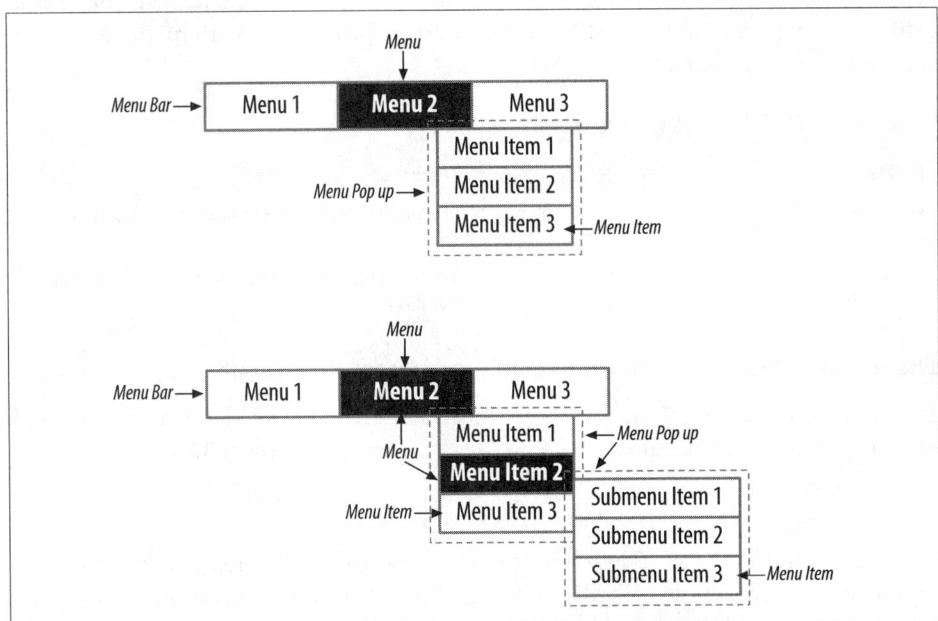

Figure 5-9. XUL menus

We will add menus to the XUL interface to allow the user to change the font family, typeface, font size, and text color in the typing area. The file *newssearch.xul* adds a menu bar with two top-level menus and two cascading submenus in the pop ups:

```
<splitter resizebefore="closest" resizeafter="closest" state="open"/>
  <!-- used to display typing area  -->
  <vbox flex="2" minheight="75" minwidth="100" >
```

```
  <menubar id="editor-menubar" oncommand="doChangeFontStyle(event);">

<menu id="font-menu" label="Font">
      <menupopup id="font-popup">

         <menu label="Family">
          <menupopup id="font-family-popup">
            <menuitem label="serif"/>
            <menuitem label="sans-serif"/>
            <menuitem label="monospace"/>
          </menupopup>
        </menu>

        <menu label="Size">
         <menupopup id="font-size-popup">
         <menuitem label="Bigger"/>
         <menuitem label="Smaller"/>
         </menupopup>
        </menu>

      </menupopup>
    </menu>

    <menuseparator/>
      <menu id="style-menu" label="Color">
           <menupopup id="font-color-popup">
           <menuitem label="Black"/>
           <menuitem label="Red"/>
           <menuitem label="Green"/>
           <menuitem label="Blue"/>
          </menupopup>
        </menu>

     <menuseparator/>

      <menu label="Style">

       <menupopup id="font-style-popup">

        <menu label="Face">
         <menupopup id="font-face-popup">
           <menuitem label="Normal"/>
           <menuitem label="Italic"/>
         </menupopup>
         </menu>

         <menu label="Weight">
           <menupopup id="font-weight-popup">
           <menuitem label="Normal"/>
           <menuitem label="Bold"/>
         </menupopup>
        </menu>
```

```
        </menupopup>

      </menu>

    </menubar>

    <editor id="memoEditor" flex="1"  type="content" class="typingArea">

    </editor>
```

Notice that we've added one command handler to the <menubar> element—any menu item that is pressed will pass its event up the visual hierarchy, a feature that allows us to specify one handler to field commands from any interface widget.

The command handler for the menu bar interrogates the `event.target` property—the target in this case will be the `menuitem` the user presses.

The `doChangeFontStyle` command handler audits the ID of the parent node to decode the nature of the font manipulation. The `event.target.label` is converted to all lowercase and is used to form the style attribute to be attached to a newly inserted <span> tag:

```
function doChangeFontStyle(event) {
try {

 var atomService = Components.classes["@mozilla.org/atom-service;1"].
    getService(Components.interfaces.nsIAtomService);

 var theEditor = document.getElementById("memoEditor").
     getHTMLEditor(document.getElementById("memoEditor").
       contentWindow);


 var newValue = event.target.label.toLowerCase( );

 switch(event.target.parentNode.id) { // switch on the menu

  case "font-size-popup": {
  if (event.target.label == "Bigger")
    theEditor.increaseFontSize( );
    else theEditor.decreaseFontSize( );
  break;
  }
  case "font-family-popup": {
   theEditor.setCSSInlineProperty(atomService.getAtom("span"),
   "style","font-family:" + newValue);
   break;
  }
   case "font-color-popup": {
   theEditor.setCSSInlineProperty(atomService.getAtom("span"),
    "style","color:" + newValue);
   break;
   }
```

```
        case "font-face-popup": {
         theEditor.setCSSInlineProperty(atomService.getAtom("span"),
           "style","font-style:" + newValue);
         break;
         }

         case "font-weight-popup": {
         theEditor.setCSSInlineProperty(atomService.getAtom("span"),
            "style","font-weight:" + newValue);
         break;
         }

       } // switch on the menu
     }
     catch (e) {
     dump("doChangeFontStyle exception " + e );
     }
   }
```

The result is an interface that allows the user to change most of the major attributes of the text entered in the note area, as shown in Figure 5-10.

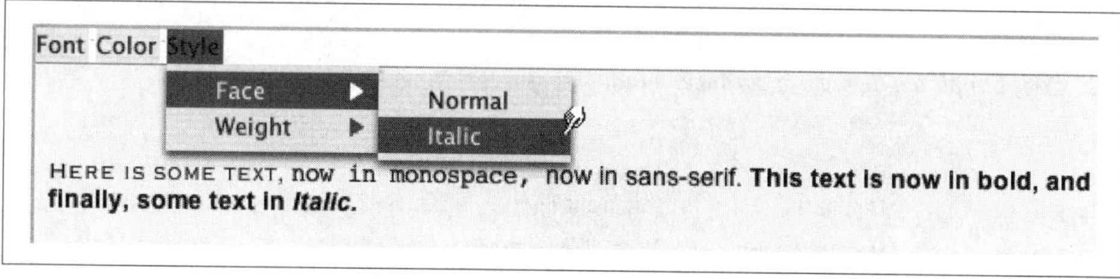

Figure 5-10. <editor> with menus

Operating system caveats

Menu management is the domain of the operating system that provides all of Firefox's services. The display and management of menu bars is one of those instances where there are operating system variations for a XUL application.

When running an application on a Windows platform, the attachment of a menu bar is consistent for cases where the application is launched from within a browser as a chrome URL, or from the command line as a chrome application.

OS X's window manager behaves differently. When the application is launched within a browser as a chrome URL, the menu bar is placed at the topmost window; if launched as a chrome application, our menu bar appears where the XUL file is specified (above the editor area). Functionally, the two presentations perform identically.

Adding Dialog Windows

The original application included a login area built into the display panel. A more familiar interaction would involve a pop-up login window that results in the main window being populated upon a successful login.

We can accomplish this by using a script to open a XUL dialog window. We open dialogs and windows using the same general form:

```
window.open | window.openDialog (
 URL [, windowTitle [, windowFeatures ]])
```

where *`windowFeatures`* represents a combination of parameters that set the appearance of the window.

Depending on the operating system, the window or dialog may have subtly different behaviors: modal dialogs on OS X Firefox appear attached to the main browser window, and Windows displays dialogs as simple pop ups. Border styles may also differ slightly between platforms. Functional performance, however, is identical. Table 5-5 provides a simplified summary of *`windowFeatures`* values to use for various implementations of dialogs.

Table 5-5. Simplified dialog appearance: windowFeatures settings

Window features	OS X: Chrome URL	OS X: Chrome app (command line)	Win: Chrome URL	Win: Chrome app (command line)
`"chrome"`	Modal dialog with no frame	Modal dialog with no frame	Nonmodal dialog with title bar	Nonmodal dialog with title bar
`"chrome titleBar"`	Nonmodal dialog with title bar	Nonmodal dialog with title bar	Nonmodal dialog with title bar	Nonmodal dialog with title bar
`"modal"`	Modal dialog attached to the top of the chrome app frame	Modal dialog attached to the browser frame	Modal dialog with title bar	Modal dialog with title bar

Dialogs are different from windows in two key areas:

- By default, using `openWindow` on a XUL file with a top-level `dialog` element (rather than a `window` element) will include buttons to cancel or accept the user input. Each button has a prebuilt event listener that must return `true` in order for the dialog to be dismissed.
- Dialogs can accept any number of arguments concatenated onto the list of *`windowFeatures`*; the arguments are available to the dialog window as entries in an `arguments` array.

In our case, we will cut the login panel of our interface developed in Chapter 4, and paste it into a new XUL window named *login.xul* (note the `dialog` element as the topmost element):

```
<?xml version="1.0"?>
<?xml-stylesheet href="NewsSearchStyles.css" type="text/css"?>
<dialog
  id="loginWindow"
  title="LOGIN"
  orient="vertical"
  ondialogaccept="return doOK( );"
  ondialogcancel="return doCancel( );"
  xmlns=
   "http://www.mozilla.org/keymaster/gatekeeper/there.is.only.xul">

 <script >
 <![CDATA[
  function doOK( ) {
  try {
  if (!fieldsFilledIn( )) { // set ask for fields to be entered
   document.getElementById("msgDescription").setAttribute("value",
      "Please fill in both fields");
   return false;
   } // ask for fields to be filled in

   // Pass info to logic that knows what to do...
   window.arguments[0](document.getElementById("userName").
      value,document.getElementById("password").value);
   return true;
  }
  catch(e) {
   alert("doOK exception " + e);
  }
  };

  function doCancel( ) {
   return true;
  };

  function fieldsFilledIn( ) {
   return  ((document.getElementById("userName").value != "")
            && (document.getElementById("password").value != ""));
  };
  ]]>
</script>

  <vbox >
    <spacer flex="1"/>
      <description id="msgDescription">
       Waiting for login.
      </description>
      <label value="User Name:" control="userName"/>
      <textbox id="userName"/>
      <label value="Password:" control="userName"/>
      <textbox id="password"  type="password" maxlength="8"/>

     <spacer flex="1"/>
  </vbox>
</dialog>
```

This file includes scripts to audit the user and password fields before passing the values to the function passed as the first parameter after the *windowFeatures* entry in the openDialog statement:

```
window.arguments[0](document.getElementById("userName").value,document.
    getElementById("password").value);
```

As with windows, a chrome dialog needs to have a default background color in *NewsSearchStyles.css*:

```
window {
 background-color:white;
 }

 dialog {
  background-color:white;
  }

vbox {
/*
  border-style:groove;
  background-color:#888888;
  */
  }

 hbox {
 /*
  border-style:groove;
  background-color:#cccccc;
  */
```

The original *newssearch.js* file has a number of changes for the new version.

For instance, openLoginWindow passes a function to save the values for username and password in the global variable space. The doLogin function is called after the dialog returns to send the request to the server:

```
var userName;
var password;

function openLoginWindow( ) {
 var lWindow =
   window.openDialog("chrome://newssearch/content/login.xul",
     "LOGON","chrome,modal",setUNPW);
 if ((userName != null) && (password != null))
  doLogin(userName,password);
  userName = null;
  password = null;

}

function setUNPW(uN,pW) {
 userName=uN;
 password=pW;
}
```

```
function doLogin(uN,pW) {
try { // try
var theArgs = new Array;
theArgs[0] = new commandArg("un",uN);
theArgs[1] = new commandArg("pd",pW);
lastCommand = "login";
dump("Logging in with uname and pw = " + theArgs[0].value +
    "," + theArgs[1].value + "\n");
doServerRequest("login",theArgs);
 } // try
 catch (e) { //
  alert("doLogin exception: " + e);
 }//
}
```

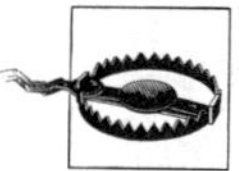

We do not pass a function to the modal dialog that directly accesses the `XMLHttpRequest` object. Bug 317600 currently results in an exception while processing an `XMLHttpRequest` sent from a pop-up or modal dialog window.

The generic button handler case that serves the login button calls a function to open the login window as a modal dialog:

```
case "loginButton": {
  openLoginWindow()
//  doLogin();
  break;
 }
```

Now launching the application results in a pop-up dialog to prompt the user for her login name and password, as shown in Figure 5-11.

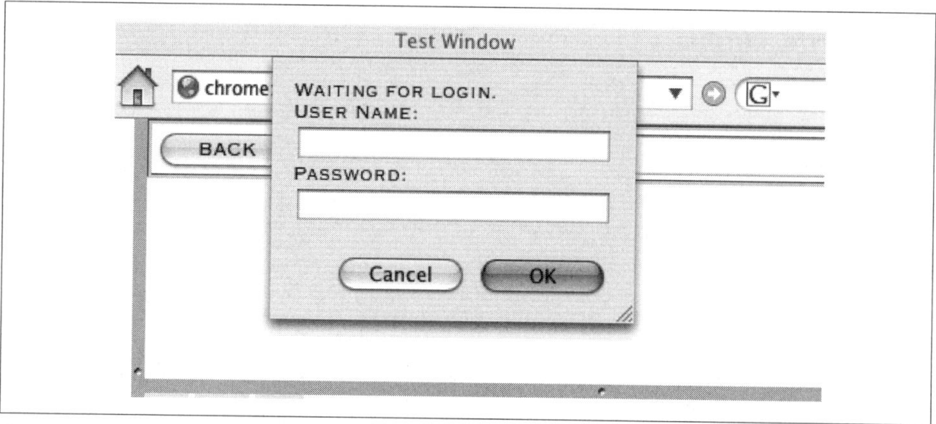

Figure 5-11. Login pop-up dialog

The file *newssearch.js* now looks like this:

```
var K_XUL_NAMESPACE =
 "http://www.mozilla.org/keymaster/gatekeeper/there.is.only.xul";
//
// Some constants to help us know what
// buttons and editing areas to enable
//
var K_NOT_LOGGED_ON    = 0;  // no user, no note
var K_STARTUP          = 1;  // user, no note
var K_OPEN_NOTE        = 2;  // note ready for editing
var K_NOTE_IN_PROGRESS = 3; // note editing in progress

var G_ApplicationState = K_NOT_LOGGED_ON;

var lastCommand = "";

function genericBtnHandler(event) {
try { // try block
var infoString = "Type = " + event.type + ",";
infoString += "Target = " + event.target + ",";
infoString += "Target.tagName = " + event.target.tagName + ",";
infoString += "Target.id = " + event.target.id + ",";
infoString += "Evt.phase = " + event.eventPhase + "."
dump(infoString + "\n");
switch(event.target.id) { // switch on target
case "newButton": {
  newNote();
  break;
 }
 case "saveButton": {
 // TBD
  break;
 }
case "sendButton": {
// TBD
  break;
 }
case "cancelButton": {
  cancelNote();
  break;
 }
case "loginButton": {
  openLoginWindow()
//  doLogin();
  break;
 }
} // switch on target
} // try block
catch (e) {
 alert("genericBtnHandler exception: " + e);
 }
}
```

```
function loadURL() {
try{
var newURL = document.getElementById("theURL").value;
document.getElementById("contentIFrame").loadURI(newURL);
 }
 catch (e) {
 alert("Exception loading URL " + e);
 };
};

// Takes care of buttons and editing areas
// based on global variable
function updateInterface() {
try{
dump("In update interface with state = " + G_ApplicationState + "\n");
 disableEverything();
 switch(G_ApplicationState) { // switch on state
  case (K_NOT_LOGGED_ON): { // not logged on
  document.getElementById("loginButton").disabled=false;
  break;
  } // not logged on
  case (K_STARTUP): { // startup
  // enable only the new button
  document.getElementById("newButton").disabled=false;
  document.getElementById("contentIFrame").
       setAttribute("src","http://www.mozillazine.org");
  break;
  } // startup
  case (K_OPEN_NOTE): { // note ready for editing
  // Make the memo area editable, and enable the cancel button
  // to give the user a way out
  var theEditor = document.getElementById("memoEditor");
  theEditor.makeEditable("html",false);
  theEditor.contentDocument.addEventListener("click",
    editorClicked,true);
  break;
  } // note ready for editing

  case (K_NOTE_IN_PROGRESS): { // note is/has been edited
  document.getElementById("saveButton").disabled=false;
  document.getElementById("sendButton").disabled=false;
  break;
  } // note is/has been edited

 } // switch on state
 }
 catch(e) { //
 alert("update interface exception " + e);
 }//
}

// function turns off all buttons, disables
// note typing area
function disableEverything() {
```

```
document.getElementById("newButton").disabled=true;
document.getElementById("saveButton").disabled=true;
document.getElementById("sendButton").disabled=true;
document.getElementById("cancelButton").disabled=true;
document.getElementById("loginButton").disabled=true;
}

function cancelNote( ) {
 G_ApplicationState = K_STARTUP;
 updateInterface( );
}

function newNote( ) {
G_ApplicationState = K_OPEN_NOTE;
updateInterface( );
}


function editorClicked(event) {
dump("Click event " + event.target + " window is " + window +
   " location = " + window.location.toString( ) +  "\n");
event.target.removeEventListener("click",editorClicked,true);
G_ApplicationState = K_NOTE_IN_PROGRESS;
updateInterface( );
};

function stepPage(event) {
 try {
  if (event.target.id == "stepBackward")
    document.getElementById("contentIFrame").goBack( );
  else
    document.getElementById("contentIFrame").goForward( );
 }
 catch (e) {
  alert("exception in stepPage " + e);
  }
}

var userName;
var password;

function openLoginWindow( ) {
 var lWindow = window.
    openDialog("chrome://newssearch/content/login.xul",
      "LOGON","chrome,modal",setUNPW);
 if ((userName != null) && (password != null))
  doLogin(userName,password);
  userName = null;
  password = null;
// doLogin('bugsbunny','wabbit');
 }
```

```
function setUNPW(uN,pW) {
 userName=uN;
 password=pW;
}

function doLogin(uN,pW) {
try { // try
var theArgs = new Array;
theArgs[0] = new commandArg("un",uN);
theArgs[1] = new commandArg("pd",pW);
lastCommand = "login";
dump("Logging in with uname and pw = " + theArgs[0].value +
    "," + theArgs[1].value + "\n");
doServerRequest("login",theArgs);
 } // try
 catch (e) { //
  alert("doLogin exception: " + e);
 }//
}
//
// Dynamically assign our event handler properties
//
function initialize(event) {
try {
dump("initialize: Event target, current target and phase are: " +
   event.target + "," + event.currentTarget + "," +
    event.eventPhase + "\n");
if (event.target == document) { // target is the main window

 document.getElementById("newButton").addEventListener
   ("command",genericBtnHandler,true);
 document.getElementById("saveButton").addEventListener
   ("command",genericBtnHandler,true);
 document.getElementById("sendButton").addEventListener
   ("command",genericBtnHandler,true);
 document.getElementById("cancelButton").addEventListener
   ("command",genericBtnHandler,true);
 document.getElementById("loginButton").addEventListener
   ("command",genericBtnHandler,true);
 //

G_ApplicationState = K_NOT_LOGGED_ON;
 // will change to NOT LOGGED ON LATER
updateInterface();
  }  // target is the main window
 } // try
 catch (e) {
  alert ("Exception: " + e);
   }
};
function doChangeFontStyle(event) {
try {
```

```
var atomService = Components.classes["@mozilla.org/atom-service;1"].
   getService(Components.interfaces.nsIAtomService);

var theEditor = document.getElementById("memoEditor").
    getHTMLEditor(document.getElementById("memoEditor").
      contentWindow);

var newValue = event.target.label.toLowerCase( );
switch(event.target.parentNode.id) { // switch on the menu

 case "font-size-popup": {
 if (event.target.label == "Bigger")
   theEditor.increaseFontSize( );
   else theEditor.decreaseFontSize( );
 break;
 }
 case "font-family-popup": {
  theEditor.setCSSInlineProperty(atomService.getAtom("span"),
   "style","font-family:" + newValue);
  break;
 }
  case "font-color-popup": {
  theEditor.setCSSInlineProperty(atomService.getAtom("span"),
    "style","color:" + newValue);
  break;
  }
 case "font-face-popup": {
  theEditor.setCSSInlineProperty(atomService.getAtom("span"),
    "style","font-style:" + newValue);
  break;
  }
  case "font-weight-popup": {
  theEditor.setCSSInlineProperty(atomService.getAtom("span"),
    "style","font-weight:" + newValue);
  break;
  }
 } // switch on the menu
}
catch (e) {
dump("doChangeFontStyle exception " + e );
}
}

function loginOK( ) {
 G_ApplicationState = K_STARTUP;
 updateInterface( );
}
function commandArg(argKey,argValue) {
 this.key = argKey;
 this.value = argValue;
}
function loginFail( ) {
 alert("Sorry, user not authenticated.");
 }
```

```
//
//  CreateServerRequest
//
var theServerRequest;
//
// commandArgs is an array of arguments, each element
// is converted into a PHP POST field
function doServerRequest(commandString,commandArgs) {

 theServerRequest = new XMLHttpRequest( );

 var theString ="http://localhost/doCommand.php?" + "&command="
   + commandString + "&";
 for (var i = 0; i < commandArgs.length; i++)
 { // build remaining parameters
   theString += commandArgs[i].key + "=" + commandArgs[i].value ;
  if (i != (commandArgs.length-1)) theString += "&";
 } // build remaining parameters
 theServerRequest.onreadystatechange = retrieveServerResponse;
 theServerRequest.open("GET",theString,true);
 dump("About to send " + theString + "\n");
 theServerRequest.send(null);
}



function retrieveServerResponse( ) {

try {

dump("server response ready state = " +
 theServerRequest.readyState + "\n");

if (theServerRequest.readyState == 4) { // all done

dump("Server request status =" +
  theServerRequest.status + "\n");
// Check return code
if (theServerRequest.status == 200) { // request terminated OK
dump("Received from server: " +
  theServerRequest.responseText + "\n");
//
var theResults = theServerRequest.responseText.split(",");
//

var rCode = (theResults[0].substring((theResults[0].indexOf("=")+1),
  theResults[0].length)).toLowerCase( );

if (lastCommand == "login") { // process login command

 if (rCode == "true") { // everything OK, we know next parameter is
                                       // session info
 var lastSession = "Last login was ";
 lastSession += (theResults[1].substring((theResults[1].
```

```
    indexOf("=")+1),
     theResults[1].length)).toLowerCase();
     loginOK();
     setStatusText(lastSession);

  } // everthing OK
 else { // user NG
  loginFail();
  setStatusText("No user logged in");
 } // user NG

 } // process login command

 } // request terminated OK
 else { // something is wrong
  alert("Response failed.");
  } // something is wrong
 } // all done
   } // try
 catch (e) {
 alert("Retrieve response exception: " + e);
 dump (e);
 }
 }

 function setStatusText(theText) {
 document.getElementById("status-text").
   setAttribute("label",theText);
 };
```

The main interface file, *newsearch.xul*, is now this:

```
<?xml-stylesheet href="NewsSearchStyles.css" type="text/css"?>

<window
  id="theMainWindow"
  title="Test Window"
  width="800"
  height="700"
  onload="initialize(event);"
  orient="horizontal"
  xmlns:html="http://www.w3.org/1999/xhtml"
  xmlns:xlink="http://www.w3.org/1999/xlink"
  xmlns=
  "http://www.mozilla.org/keymaster/gatekeeper/there.is.only.xul">

 <script src="NewsSearch.js"/>
 <script>
 editorLoaded = function(event) {
  dump("Ed loaded Event target, current target and phase are: " +
    event.target + "," + event.currentTarget + "," +
     event.eventPhase + "\n");
  };
 </script>
```

```
 <!-- main top level container -->
<vbox flex="1" >

 <!-- horizontal container for all content (except status info) -->
 <hbox flex="1" >

 <!-- a container for some kind of list -->
 <vbox flex="1" >
 </vbox>

  <splitter resizebefore="closest" resizeafter="closest" state="open"/>
 <!-- container for messages and tool areas -->
 <vbox>

 <!-- some simple controls to manage display pages -->
 <hbox class="buttonArea">
  <button id="stepBackward" label="BACK"
   oncommand="stepPage(event);"/>
  <button id="stepForward" label="FORWARD"
   oncommand="stepPage(event);"/>
  <hbox >
   <vbox pack="center">
   <label control="theURL" value="URL:"/>
   </vbox>
   <textbox id="theURL" size="32" type="autocomplete"
        autocompletesearch="history"/>
   <button id="loadURL" label="GO" oncommand="loadURL( );"/>
   </hbox>

</hbox>
<!-- used to display message -->
<browser id="contentIFrame"  type="content-primary"
 src="about:blank" flex="4">
</browser>

 <splitter resizebefore="closest" resizeafter="closest"
  state="open"/>
 <!-- used to display typing area  -->
 <vbox flex="2" minheight="75" minwidth="100" >


 <menubar id="editor-menubar"
  oncommand="doChangeFontStyle(event);">

   <menu id="font-menu" label="Font">
     <menupopup id="font-popup">

        <menu label="Family">
         <menupopup id="font-family-popup">
           <menuitem label="serif"/>
           <menuitem label="sans-serif"/>
           <menuitem label="monospace"/>
         </menupopup>
       </menu>
```

```
     <menu label="Size">
      <menupopup id="font-size-popup">
      <menuitem label="Bigger"/>
      <menuitem label="Smaller"/>
      </menupopup>
     </menu>

   </menupopup>
 </menu>

 <menuseparator/>
   <menu id="style-menu" label="Color">
        <menupopup id="font-color-popup">
        <menuitem label="Black"/>
        <menuitem label="Red"/>
        <menuitem label="Green"/>
        <menuitem label="Blue"/>
       </menupopup>
     </menu>

  <menuseparator/>

   <menu label="Style">

    <menupopup id="font-style-popup">

     <menu label="Face">
      <menupopup id="font-face-popup">
        <menuitem label="Normal"/>
        <menuitem label="Italic"/>
      </menupopup>
      </menu>

      <menu label="Weight">
        <menupopup id="font-weight-popup">
        <menuitem label="Normal"/>
        <menuitem label="Bold"/>
      </menupopup>
     </menu>

   </menupopup>

  </menu>

 </menubar>

 <editor id="memoEditor" flex="1" type="content"
  src="about:blank"
   class="typingArea">

</editor>
</vbox>

 <!-- used to display tool area-->
```

```
<hbox height="50" class="buttonArea">

 <spacer flex="1"/>

   <vbox id="vbox">
    <spacer flex="1"/>
     <hbox>
      <button id="newButton" label="New" />
      <button id="saveButton" label="Save"/>
      <button id="sendButton" label="Send"/>
      <button id="cancelButton" label="Cancel"/>
      <button id="loginButton" label="LOGIN"/>
     </hbox>
     <spacer flex="1"/>
   </vbox>

 <spacer flex="1"/>

</hbox>

</vbox>
<!-- container for messages and tool areas -->

</hbox>
<!-- horizontal container for all content (except status info) -->


 <hbox>
   <statusbar id="status-bar" >
     <statusbarpanel id="status-text" label="Waiting for login.">

   </statusbarpanel>
  </statusbar>

</hbox>  <!-- main container -->
</vbox>
</window>
```

And the login interface, *login.xul*, is as follows:

```
<?xml version="1.0"?>
<?xml-stylesheet href="NewsSearchStyles.css" type="text/css"?>
<dialog
  id="loginWindow"
  title="LOGIN"
  orient="vertical"
  ondialogaccept="return doOK( );"
  ondialogcancel="return doCancel( );"
  xmlns=
  "http://www.mozilla.org/keymaster/gatekeeper/there.is.only.xul">

<script >
<![CDATA[
 function doOK( ) {
```

```
try {
if (!fieldsFilledIn( )) { // ask for fields to be entered
 document.getElementById("msgDescription").setAttribute("value",
    "Please fill in both fields");
 return false;
 } // ask for fields to be filled in

 // Pass info to logic that knows what to do...
 window.arguments[0](document.getElementById("userName").
     value,document.getElementById("password").value);
 return true;
}
catch(e) {
 alert("doOK exception " + e);
}
};

function doCancel( ) {
 return true;
};

function fieldsFilledIn( ) {
 return  ((document.getElementById("userName").value != "")
          && (document.getElementById("password").value != ""));
};
]]>
</script>

  <vbox >
    <spacer flex="1"/>
      <description id="msgDescription">
       Waiting for login.
      </description>
      <label value="User Name:" control="userName"/>
      <textbox id="userName"/>
      <label value="Password:" control="userName"/>
      <textbox id="password"  type="password" maxlength="8"/>

     <spacer flex="1"/>
  </vbox>
</dialog>
```

Summary

Multiframe XUL interfaces can provide a rich user interface experience that renders web pages, editors, and other HTML content within the same interface. Using splitters while providing subtle style changes to various content panels can provide the user with the controls necessary to alter the layout as needed, along with the "hints" of where text entry or button actuation are expected.

The `editor` element provides a text entry field that supports the styling features most users expect from a modern data interface.

Multiframe designs do carry complexities in terms of synchronizing different windows, events, and logic spaces into one application. Particular care must be taken when considering the following design issues:

- The designers of the Firefox framework had to design the XUL interface to accommodate both standalone (chrome) and in-browser displays. As a result, certain rules, particularly those involving `load` events, may yield different event scenarios for chrome and browser implementations.
- Event handling should avoid reliance on the `this` reference, and instead use the `target` and `currentTarget` properties of the `event` interface to ascertain where in the event chain a function is being called.
- Content panels such as `iframes`, editors, and browsers must be approached as separate window and application spaces; linkage can be handled by attaching event listeners to the `contentWindow` property.
- Setting the `type` attribute on content panels can have a significant impact on the design of the application. Panels without this attribute can render content (and scripts) that have access to the "top" window reference for the application's main window; adding a `type` that specifies a form of `content` adds a security restriction to the frame and yields a "top" reference that is bound by the enclosing frame.

Now that we have covered the basic structure for the major content area, we can turn our attention to designing the interface to allow content selection.

CHAPTER 6
Trees, Templates, and Datasources

The previous chapters covered some of the basic user interface widgets that are common to most applications. This chapter explores special-purpose widgets used to display hierarchies of topics. Specifically, we will cover:

- The use of tree widgets to present categories of information to the user
- The use of templates to ease the creation of trees when the source data is of a well-understood format
- The role of datasources and the Resource Description Framework (RDF) in providing the developer with a framework to organize and present categories of information to the user

Trees

User interfaces that require a selection from a collection of options must often rely on some form of a list. The conventional approach in HTML is to present the options in the form of a `<select>` element that encloses all the options available to the user. But for an interface to present options that reflect some type of organizational structure or categories of selections—such as selections from a list of categorized bookmarks, or topic selection—a more flexible widget is required. For such cases, the XUL framework provides developers with the *tree* widget.

Tree Structure

In its simplest form, a tree widget consists of a collection of *cells* that can hold the displayed content, *rows* that contain a horizontal collection of cells, and *columns* that bind cells vertically. Figure 6-1 illustrates this simplest overview of the tree structure for a series of topic selections and descriptions. Here are a few of the basic elements used in this construction:

Tree columns
: Elements that provide for vertical organization of trees

Tree cell
: The portion of a tree that displays text

Tree row
: A horizontal collection of tree cells

Tree items
: Selectable portions of a tree

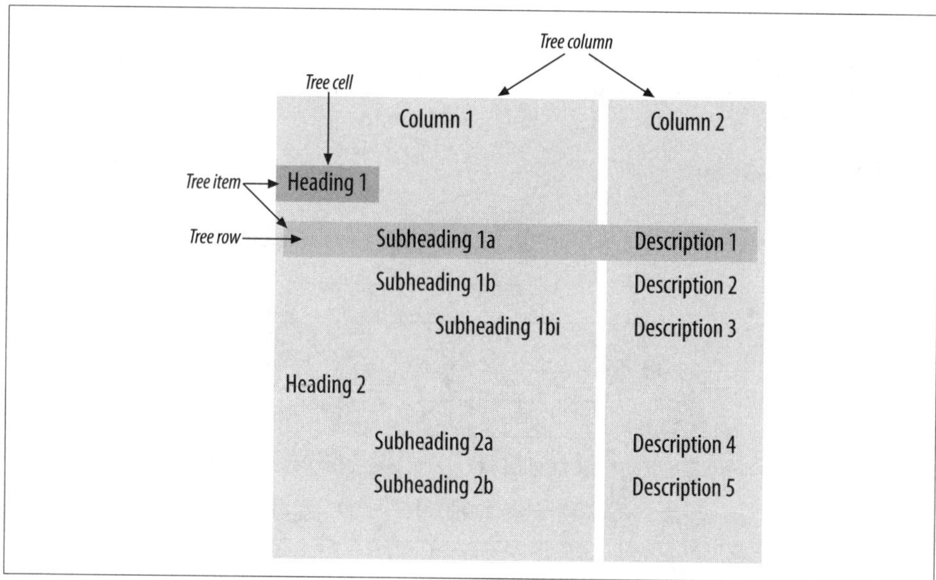

Figure 6-1. Basic tree elements

We can see that Column 1 in this case holds all the nested cells that provide the hierarchical structure, and Column 2 holds only the single cells that intersect tree columns and rows. Programmatically, Column 1 will have the attribute `primary="true"` to indicate its designation as the column to manage nested rows.

The containment hierarchy, in its simplest form, consists of a *tree item* tag. Tree items represent the portion of a tree that is selectable by the user. Following is a tree item that encloses a tree row, which in turn contains the displayed cells:

```
<treeitem>
 <treerow>
  <treecell label="Subheading 1a"/>
  <treecell label="Description 1"/>
  </treerow>
</treeitem>
```

When a row contains a subordinate row, a *tree children* tag follows the tree row and wraps the subordinate rows. The `<treeitem>` containing the children must have a `container="true"` attribute to flag the XUL framework to support the item with a "twisty" that we can use to hide or display the subordinate rows:

```
<treeitem container="true" open="true">
 <treerow>
  <treecell label="Subheading 1b"/>
  <treecell label="Description 2"/>
 </treerow>
<treechildren>
 <treeitem open="true">
  <treerow>
   <treecell label="Section 1Bi"/>
   <treecell label="Description 3"/>
  </treerow>
 </treeitem>
</treechildren>
</treeitem>
```

Figure 6-2 illustrates a more detailed hierarchy that adds tree children references.

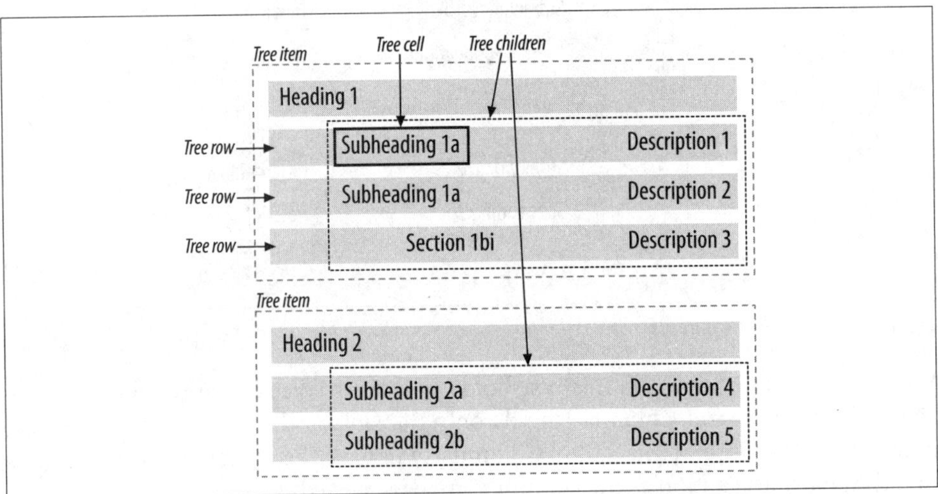

Figure 6-2. Tree container hierarchy

To build any number of nested rows, `<treeitem>` elements must contain the `<treerow>` to serve as the top container, followed by a `<treechildren>` container that holds the subordinate `<treeitem>` elements. We can continue that sequence as often as needed with the cells for all the nested rows placed in the primary tree column.

To see what a real exercise would look like, we can create a *tree.xul* file:

```
<?xml-stylesheet href="NewsSearchStyles.css" type="text/css"?>

<window
  id="treeWindow"
```

```
    title="Trees"
    width="800"
    height="700"
    orient="horizontal"
    xmlns:html="http://www.w3.org/1999/xhtml"
    xmlns:xlink="http://www.w3.org/1999/xlink"
    xmlns="http://www.mozilla.org/keymaster/
        gatekeeper/there.is.only.xul">

  <vbox flex="1" >
  <tree flex="1">
    <treecols>
      <treecol  primary="true" label="Column 1" flex="1"/>
      <treecol  label="Column 2" flex="2"/>
    </treecols>

    <treechildren>
     <treeitem container="true" open="true">
      <treerow>
       <treecell label="Heading 1"/>
      </treerow>

      <treechildren>
       <treeitem>
        <treerow>
         <treecell label="Subheading 1a"/>
         <treecell label="Description 1"/>
        </treerow>
       </treeitem>

        <treeitem container="true" open="true">
        <treerow>
         <treecell label="Subheading 1b"/>
         <treecell label="Description 2"/>
        </treerow>
          <treechildren>
            <treeitem >
             <treerow>
             <treecell label="Section 1Bi"/>
             <treecell label="Description 3"/>
            </treerow>
            </treeitem>
          </treechildren>
       </treeitem>
     </treechildren>

    </treeitem>


    <treeitem container="true" open="true">
     <treerow>
      <treecell label="Heading 2"/>
     </treerow>
```

```
      <treechildren>
       <treeitem>
        <treerow>
         <treecell label="Subheading 2a"/>
         <treecell label="Description 4"/>
        </treerow>
       </treeitem>
        <treeitem>
        <treerow>
         <treecell label="Subheading 2b"/>
         <treecell label="Description 5"/>
        </treerow>
       </treeitem>
      </treechildren>

     </treeitem>

   </treechildren>
   </tree>
   </vbox>
   </window>
```

Figure 6-3 shows the resulting tree.

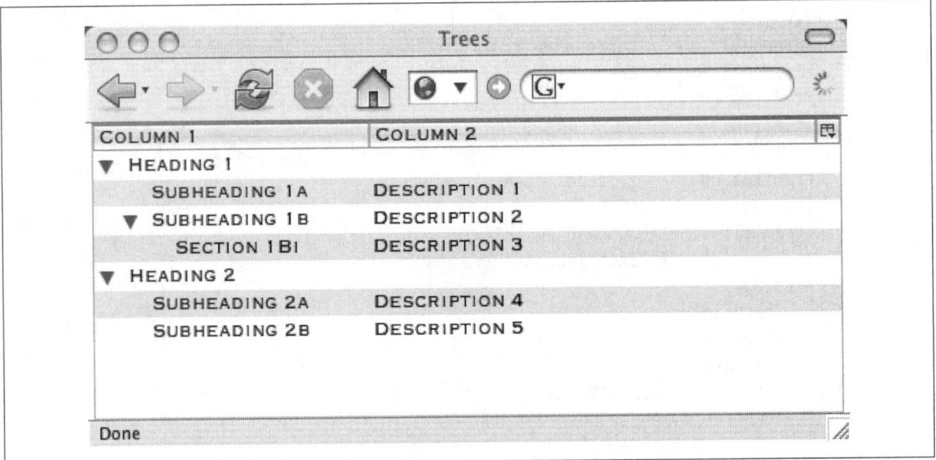

Figure 6-3. XUL tree example

Table 6-1 summarizes the key elements and attributes associated with XUL trees (only the attributes for basic tree display and management are included here).

Table 6-1. Basic tree elements and attributes

Element	Attributes	Description
tree	N/A	Topmost container for a tree widget.
treecols	N/A	Topmost container for tree columns.

Table 6-1. Basic tree elements and attributes (continued)

<table>
<tr><th>Element</th><th>Attributes</th><th>Description</th></tr>
<tr><td>treecol</td><td>Primary = true | false.
If true, column is used to organize the tree hierarchy.
Label = columnHeading. Label attributes are used to set the column headings.</td><td>Container for a vertical collection of tree cells.</td></tr>
<tr><td>treeitem</td><td>Container = true.
If true, XUL tree builder logic will manage widgets to hide and display hierarchy.
Open = true | false.
If open, initial state of the tree displays hierarchy.</td><td>Any element that is user-selectable is a tree item. Tree items can wrap tree rows, or tree rows with additional children.</td></tr>
<tr><td>treerow</td><td>N/A</td><td>A container for tree cells.</td></tr>
<tr><td>treechildren</td><td>N/A</td><td>The topmost container within a tree; also the topmost container for subordinate branches of a tree row. For most applications, the first child of a treechildren element should be a treeitem element.</td></tr>
<tr><td>treecell</td><td>Label = cellText. The label is the text displayed in the tree.</td><td>The container for the displayed tree content.</td></tr>
</table>

Different Types of Tree Content

Although the tree illustrated to this point displays the text strings so often associated with views of outlines or lists, tree cells also have an src attribute to allow reference to an image URI that may also be inserted into the cell.

We can also use trees to quickly provide a bar graph representation of some sort of proportion or magnitude.

With a tree column attribute of type="progressmeter", a tree cell with a mode="normal" turns into a progress meter with the value attribute specifying a percentage to display.

The following tree cell illustrates a combination of the ubiquitous *smiley.gif* and a simple progress meter:

```
<tree flex="1">
  <treecols>
    <treecol  primary="true" label="Column 1" flex="1"/>
    <treecol  label="Column 2" flex="2" type="progressmeter"/>
  </treecols>

  <treechildren>


   <treeitem container="true" open="true">
    <treerow>
     <treecell label="Heading 1"/>
    </treerow>
```

```
    <treechildren>
     <treeitem>
      <treerow>
       <treecell label="Subheading 1a"/>
       <treecell src="smiley.gif" value="65" mode="normal" />
      </treerow>
     </treeitem>
```

These changes would result in the row illustrated in Figure 6-4.

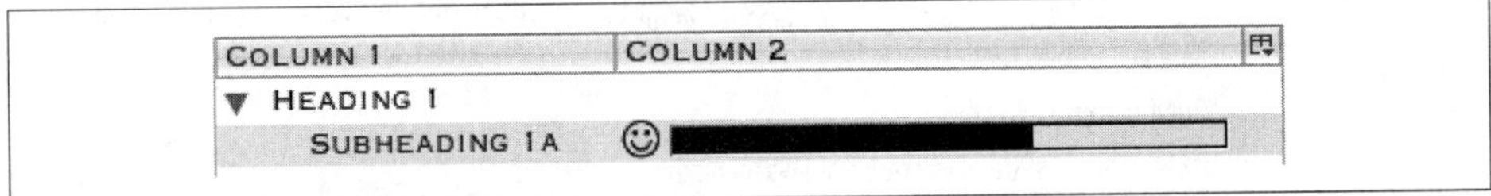

Figure 6-4. Tree cells as progress meter

Selecting Tree Items

Trees are designed to support complex hierarchies that can be dynamically created by builder logic that manages the creation and display of the tree items. Managing events most often involves manipulating tree attributes rather than attaching handlers to individual cells or rows.

Event handling starts by attaching a function to a tree's `onselect` attribute. Trees allow for single or multiple selection; when in single-selection mode (through use of the `seltype` attribute), a `currentIndex` property provides a zero-based index of the currently focused row.

Here we have modified our original *tree.xul* file to add an event handler and display the index of the selected item:

```
<window
  id="treeWindow"
  title="Trees"
  width="800"
  height="700"
  orient="horizontal"
  xmlns:html="http://www.w3.org/1999/xhtml"
  xmlns="http://www.mozilla.org/keymaster/gatekeeper/there.is.only.xul">

<script>
   function somethingSelected(event) {
   alert(event.target.currentIndex);
   }
  </script>

<vbox flex="1" >
<tree flex="1" onselect="somethingSelected(event);">
```

```
<treecols>
  <treecol  primary="true" label="Column 1" flex="1"/>
  <treecol  label="Column 2" flex="2"/>
</treecols>
.
.
```

Because we attached the event handler to the tree element, we know the event.target property will reference that tree in the event handler.

Most applications will need to get more information than simply an index of a row. To get access to more detailed information about the item that has been selected, we will need to access the tree's `view` property.

A tree `view` represents the data and logic encompassing the physical appearance of the tree. The tree property will implement a number of different interfaces, depending on how the tree was built and where the tree obtains its source data. Simple trees—XUL trees with data explicitly set in the source file—implement a tree interface and a *content builder* interface. Trees obtaining data from datasource resources (e.g., RDF files) implement a tree interface and a *XUL tree builder* interface.

For this simple tree, the `view` property implements the tree and content view interface; a `getItemAtIndex` method is available that returns a `treeitem` at the specified index. If we embedded some attribute to include data to be acted upon, we would use a simple Document Object Model (DOM) function to access the attribute and carry out any item-specific logic:

```
<script>
   function somethingSelected(event) {
   var tI = event.target.currentIndex;
   alert(event.target.view.getItemAtIndex(tI).getAttribute("hiddenAttribute"));
   }
  </script>
.
.
.
<treeitem hiddenAttribute="myAttribute" container="true" open="true">
    <treerow>
     <treecell label="Heading 1"/>
    </treerow>
```

The `getItemAtIndex` returns only `treeitem` objects, so any attributes that we want to pass to an event handler must be bound to `treeitem` tags, not rows or cells.

Multiple Selections

We can configure a tree to support multiple selections by setting its seltype attribute to "multiple". Selecting items with the Shift key will select contiguous rows of the tree, and holding down the Command/Ctrl key will now select any number of individual rows.

To get access to the selection, the developer must access the view's selection property and parse a range object.

Parsing ranges

The XUL framework uses selection and range objects to represent a user selection that may contain either an adjacent or a noncontiguous collection of document nodes. Selection objects that include a noncontiguous collection of nodes will have multiple ranges; if the selection includes a collection of adjacent nodes, there will be only one range. For tree selections, each range will consist of the index of the tree item that starts the range, and the index of the last tree item selected.

To access the selected items, first we need to get the number of ranges selected:

```
var rC = event.target.view.selection.getRangeCount( );
```

We then can parse each range using the getRangeAt method, which takes objects as two output parameters. The object's value property will be filled in with the indices of the contiguous items selected. By setting the seltype attribute to multiple:

```
<vbox flex="1" >
<tree id="mainTree" seltype="multiple" flex="1" onselect="somethingSelected(event);">
  <treecols>
    <treecol  primary="true" label="Column 1" flex="1"/>
    <treecol  label="Column 2" flex="2"/>
  </treecols>
```

and adding the appropriate changes to the selection script (note the addition of the CDATA directive to manage the < sign in the for loop), we can now display the indices of the selected tree items:

```
<script>
  <![CDATA[
   function somethingSelected(event) {
   var tI = event.target.currentIndex;
   var rC = event.target.view.selection.getRangeCount( );
   var startIndex = new Object( );
   var endIndex = new Object( );
   for (var i = 0; i < rC; i++) {
    event.target.view.selection.getRangeAt(i,startIndex,endIndex);
    alert("First and last items are " + startIndex.value + "," + endIndex.value);
   }
   }
   ]]>
  </script>
```

Selecting multiple noncontiguous rows will cause multiple passes through the `alert` statement, each pass displaying the index of the first and last rows of a range.

Table 6-2 lists the most common properties and methods used to access tree selections.

Table 6-2. Common tree selection properties and methods

Property/Method	Description
`tree.onselect`	The script to respond to user selection of tree items
`tree.selType`	`multiple` to support multiple selections; default is `single` selection
`tree.currentIndex`	Index of selected tree item (when `seltype` is `single`)
`tree.view`	View property that exposes methods to access viewed cells, rows, and tree items
`tree.view.getItemAt(`*`someIndex`*`)`	Method to return the selected `treeitem` object
`tree.view.selection`	A view's `selection` property that returns the selected ranges for trees supporting multiple selections
`tree.view.selection.getRangeCount( )`	Method to obtain the number of ranges selected
`tree.view.selection.getRangeAt (someIndex, startObject,endObject)`	Method to obtain the starting and ending indices of tree items in a given range

Templates and RDF (Simple View)

XUL provides a `template` tag to allow for the automated generation of interface content that originates from a file specially structured to describe web content. This RDF structure is a data model that (in the context of this book) is represented using XML syntax. The RDF/XML data provides a consistent form to access information about Internet resources (URIs) and information that describes those resources (metadata).

Because a discussion about RDF can quickly become complicated, we will start with a discussion of RDF files from a tag and attribute perspective, and look at a simple template that can automate the generation of interface widgets.

RDF tags and attributes

The basic element of an RDF file is a *resource*. In XML syntax, we describe this basic element with the `RDF:Description` tag that includes an attribute identifying the resource that the description is about:

```
<RDF:Description about="Some Resource Identifier">
</RDF:Description>
```

Children of an RDF description represent the metadata about the resource, or properties of the resource, as well as the values of the property:

```
<RDF:Description about="Some Resource Identifier" >
<numberOfVisits>234</numberOfVisits>
<rating>general audience</rating>
</RDF:Description>
```

In this case, a complete RDF *statement* provides a description about a resource named "Some Resource Identifier." The description includes a property, `numberOfVisits`, with a value of `234`, and a property `rating` with a value of `general audience`.

Let's assume that we want to use an RDF file to collect a description of resources for web sites that are to be included in our NewsSearch application. Our description will include properties such as a textual nickname to act as a display label, the real URL for the site, and a count for the number of times we have visited the site (hits). A complete RDF file named *simple.rdf* would look like this:

```
<?xml version="1.0"?>
<RDF:RDF xmlns:RDF="http://www.w3.org/1999/02/22-rdf-syntax-ns#"
  xmlns:nssrch="http://www.mySites.com/rdf#">

<RDF:Seq RDF:about="http://www.mySites.com/all-sites">
<!-- Resources for technology-->
<RDF:li>
<RDF:Description RDF:about="http://www.mySites.com/php" >
 <nssrch:nickname>PHP.net</nssrch:nickname>
 <nssrch:hits>34</nssrch:hits>
 <nssrch:url>http://www.php.net</nssrch:url>
</RDF:Description>
</RDF:li>
<RDF:li>
<RDF:Description RDF:about="http://www.mySites.com/w3c" >
 <nssrch:nickname>W3C</nssrch:nickname>
 <nssrch:hits>29</nssrch:hits>
 <nssrch:url>http://www.w3c.org</nssrch:url>
</RDF:Description>
</RDF:li>
<RDF:li>
<RDF:Description RDF:about="http://www.mySites.com/apache" >
 <nssrch:nickname>Apache</nssrch:nickname>
 <nssrch:hits>117</nssrch:hits>
 <nssrch:url>http://www.apache.org</nssrch:url>
</RDF:Description>
</RDF:li>

<!-- Resources for news-->
<RDF:li>
<RDF:Description RDF:about="http://www.mySites.com/cnn" >
 <nssrch:nickname>CNN</nssrch:nickname>
 <nssrch:hits>23</nssrch:hits>
 <nssrch:url>http://www.cnn.com</nssrch:url>
</RDF:Description>
</RDF:li>
<RDF:li>
<RDF:Description RDF:about="http://www.mySites.com/bbc" >
 <nssrch:nickname>BBC</nssrch:nickname>
 <nssrch:hits>9</nssrch:hits>
 <nssrch:url>http://news.bbc.co.uk</nssrch:url>
</RDF:Description>
</RDF:li>
```

```
<RDF:li>
<RDF:Description RDF:about="http://www.mySites.com/washingtonpost" >
 <nssrch:nickname>Washington Post</nssrch:nickname>
 <nssrch:hits>13</nssrch:hits>
 <nssrch:url>http://www.washingtonpost.com</nssrch:url>
</RDF:Description>
</RDF:li>

<!-- Resources for sports -->
<RDF:li>
<RDF:Description RDF:about="http://www.mySites.com/fifa" >
 <nssrch:nickname>FIFA Home</nssrch:nickname>
 <nssrch:hits>7</nssrch:hits>
 <nssrch:url>http://www.fifa.com/en/index.html</nssrch:url>
</RDF:Description>
</RDF:li>
<RDF:li>
<RDF:Description RDF:about="http://www.mySites.com/espn">
 <nssrch:nickname>ESPN</nssrch:nickname>
 <nssrch:hits>20</nssrch:hits>
 <nssrch:url>http://www.espn.com</nssrch:url>
</RDF:Description>
</RDF:li>
<RDF:li>
<RDF:Description RDF:about="http://www.mySites.com/leafs">
 <nssrch:nickname>Toronto Maple Leafs</nssrch:nickname>
 <nssrch:hits>10</nssrch:hits>
 <nssrch:url>http://www.mapleleafs.com</nssrch:url>
</RDF:Description>
</RDF:li>
</RDF:Seq>

</RDF:RDF>
```

Here we see that the file is organized as a *list* (`RDF:li` tags) of descriptions in a *sequence* (`RDF:Seq` tag). Most RDF elements are organized within some type of RDF container:

Sequences (`RDF:Seq`)
: Contain ordered lists of elements

Bags (`RDF:Bag`)
: Contain unordered lists

Alternatives (`RDF:Alt`)
: Contain a list of alternative selections, only one of which is to be selected or active at a time

We have also added a namespace for our NewsSearch application; this will allow us to add any classes or attributes to our RDF structure without worrying about conflicts with other RDF files or any other XML sources.

Templates (simple form)

We use the term *template* to refer to structures or rules that are used as a pattern to facilitate replication of output. A template uses a set of rules to determine how to output data from an RDF *datasource*. These rules need to tell the template:

- Where to start looking in the datasource
- What pattern to look for
- What output to produce when a match is found

We define a starting point for a template search using a XUL element's `datasource` attribute. Setting this attribute informs Firefox that the included URIs are to be considered the datasources for an upcoming template. A `ref` attribute on the same elements sets the starting point within the RDF datasources for the template logic to begin its matching search. The `ref` attribute is most often set to a string that matches the `about` attribute of an RDF *container*.

The difference between a URI (Uniform Resource Identifier) and a URL (Uniform Resource Locator) is subtle. A URI can identify any resource on the Internet, and can include identifiers to portions of documents. As we will see, the RDF accessing mechanism uses URIs to reference properties within an RDF file. URLs are generally used to reference web pages. The term *URL* is appropriate for this example's `<nssrch:url>` property, which points our application's browser to specific web pages.

The `datasource` and `ref` attributes are attached to the visual container closest to where we want a template to begin replication. If we were building a menu that included a dynamically created list of menu items, we would attach the attributes to the enclosing `menupopup` element:

```
<menupopup  datasources="simple.rdf"
    ref="http://www.mySites.com/all-sites">
```

We want the XUL template search to begin with the topmost container that has its `about` attribute set to `http://www.mySites.com/all-sites`.

One of the immediate children of the element containing the `datasources` attribute must be a template element. Template elements enclose the XUL widgets that are to be parsed for the RDF namespace to trigger replication and value substitution logic. In this simple form of a template, the first child is a `rule` element that contains the rules for selection and substitution.

The first XUL element within the template that includes the `uri="rdf:*"` attribute is the trigger that instructs Firefox logic to begin the replication process. That element and its child elements are replicated for each RDF element within the container. XUL elements within a template that occur before the element containing the `uri` attribute are created only once.

We can move values from the RDF datasource into the XUL interface by specifying an attribute that concatenates the `rdf` namespace specifier, or the namespace URL used in the RDF file, and appending the property name whose value we want to insert into the interface, as shown in Figure 6-5.

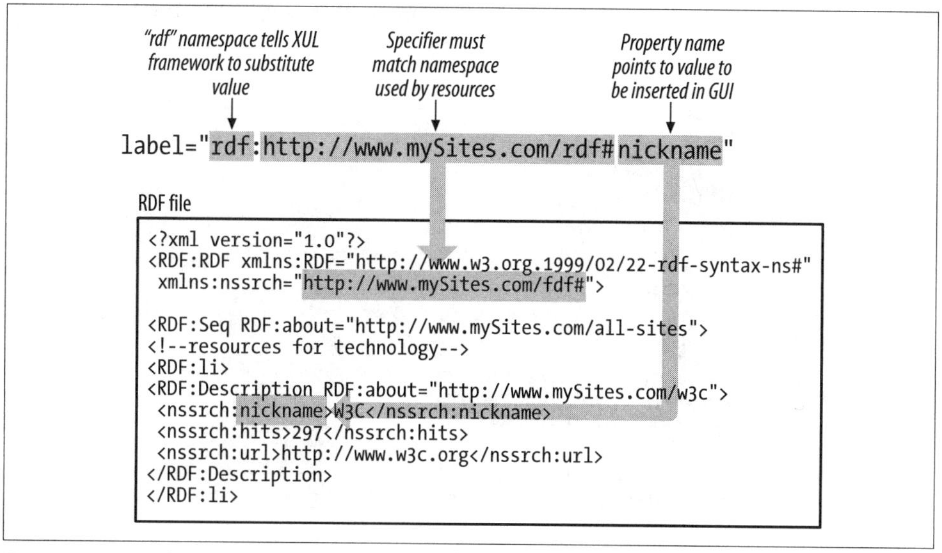

"rdf" namespace tells XUL framework to substitute value

Specifier must match namespace used by resources

Property name points to value to be inserted in GUI

```
label="rdf:http://www.mySites.com/rdf#nickname"
```

RDF file

```
<?xml version="1.0"?>
<RDF:RDF xmlns:RDF="http://www.w3.org.1999/02/22-rdf-syntax-ns#"
 xmlns:nssrch="http://www.mySites.com/fdf#">

<RDF:Seq RDF:about="http://www.mySites.com/all-sites">
<!--resources for technology-->
<RDF:li>
<RDF:Description RDF:about="http://www.mySites.com/w3c">
 <nssrch:nickname>W3C</nssrch:nickname>
 <nssrch:hits>297</nssrch:hits>
 <nssrch:url>http://www.w3c.org</nssrch:url>
</RDF:Description>
</RDF:li>
```

Figure 6-5. Templates and RDF processing

We can now create a simple XUL file named *simpleTemplate.xul* (placed in the same directory as the *simple.rdf* file):

```
<?xml-stylesheet href="NewsSearchStyles.css" type="text/css"?>

<window
  id="treeWindow"
  title="Template"
  width="800"
  height="700"
  orient="horizontal"
  xmlns:html="http://www.w3.org/1999/xhtml"
  xmlns="http://www.mozilla.org/keymaster/gatekeeper/there.is.only.xul">

 <toolbox flex="1">
  <menubar id="a-menubar">
    <menu id="a-menu" label="Select">
      <menupopup  datasources="simple.rdf"
                  ref="http://www.mySites.com/all-sites">
        <template>
         <rule>
          <menuitem uri="rdf:*" label="rdf:http://www.mySites.com/rdf#nickname"/>
         </rule>
        </template>
      </menupopup>
```

```
        </menu>
      </menubar>
    </toolbox>

    </window>
```

Executing the file provides a menu that is dynamically created from the RDF list, as shown in Figure 6-6.

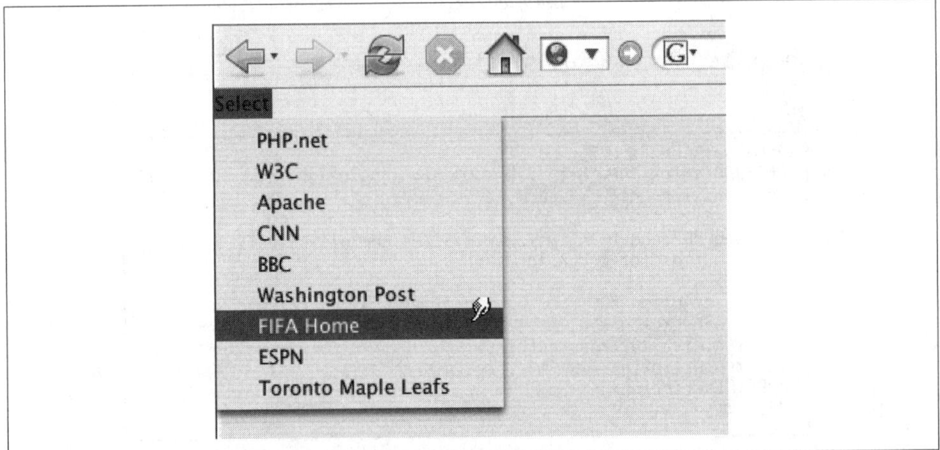

Figure 6-6. Template-driven menu

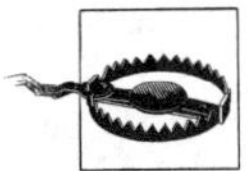

Firefox caching of datasources can sometimes cause problems when debugging RDF files. If you try to interactively change the content of an RDF file that has already been loaded, you may not see the results of your editing until you relaunch Firefox.

Hierarchical output

In this simple template, all the children contained by the RDF container *http://www.mySites.com/all-sites* were processed. One interesting aspect of the default template processing is that if any of the processed RDF nodes had child nodes, the template output would have been replicated with the resulting nodes also as children.

Although this may not make sense for output that includes a list of buttons, it certainly makes sense if the RDF source includes resources organized within categories, in which case a template-driven tree makes perfect sense.

Let's start by copying the original RDF file (or modifying it) to a new *newssites.rdf* file. This time, we will build a hierarchy of containers to organize our sites by news, sports, and technology:

```
<?xml version="1.0"?>
<RDF:RDF xmlns:RDF="http://www.w3.org/1999/02/22-rdf-syntax-ns#"
  xmlns:nssrch="http://www.mySites.com/rdf#">


<RDF:Seq heading="CONTENTS" RDF:about="http://www.mySites.com/all-sites" >
<!-- Resources for technology-->
 <RDF:li>
  <RDF:Description RDF:about="http://www.mySites.com/php" >
  <nssrch:nickname>PHP.net</nssrch:nickname>
  <nssrch:hits>34</nssrch:hits>
  <nssrch:url>http://www.php.net</nssrch:url>
  </RDF:Description>
  </RDF:li>

 <RDF:li>
  <RDF:Description RDF:about="http://www.mySites.com/w3c" >
  <nssrch:nickname>W3C</nssrch:nickname>
  <nssrch:hits>29</nssrch:hits>
  <nssrch:url>http://www.w3c.org</nssrch:url>
  </RDF:Description>
  </RDF:li>

<RDF:li>
  <RDF:Description RDF:about="http://www.mySites.com/apache" >
  <nssrch:nickname>Apache</nssrch:nickname>
  <nssrch:hits>11</nssrch:hits>
    <nssrch:url>http://www.apache.org</nssrch:url>
  </RDF:Description>
  </RDF:li>

<!-- Resources for news-->

<RDF:li>
 <RDF:Description RDF:about="http://www.mySites.com/cnn" >
   <nssrch:nickname>CNN</nssrch:nickname>
   <nssrch:hits>23</nssrch:hits>
   <nssrch:url>http://www.cnn.com</nssrch:url>
  </RDF:Description>
  </RDF:li>

 <RDF:li>
  <RDF:Description RDF:about="http://www.mySites.com/bbc" >
  <nssrch:nickname>BBC</nssrch:nickname>
  <nssrch:hits>9</nssrch:hits>
  <nssrch:url>http://news.bbc.co.uk</nssrch:url>
  </RDF:Description>
  </RDF:li>

 <RDF:li>
  <RDF:Description RDF:about="http://www.mySites.com/washingtonpost" >
  <nssrch:nickname>Washington Post</nssrch:nickname>
```

```
   <nssrch:hits>13</nssrch:hits>
   <nssrch:url>http://www.washingtonpost.com</nssrch:url>
  </RDF:Description>
 </RDF:li>

<!-- Resources for sports -->

<RDF:li>
<RDF:Description RDF:about="http://www.mySites.com/fifa" >
  <nssrch:nickname>FIFA Home</nssrch:nickname>
  <nssrch:hits>7</nssrch:hits>
  <nssrch:url>http://www.fifa.com/en/index.html</nssrch:url>
 </RDF:Description>
</RDF:li>

<RDF:li>
<RDF:Description RDF:about="http://www.mySites.com/espn">
  <nssrch:nickname>ESPN</nssrch:nickname>
  <nssrch:hits>20</nssrch:hits>
  <nssrch:url>http://www.espn.com</nssrch:url>
 </RDF:Description>
 </RDF:li>

<RDF:li>
<RDF:Description RDF:about="http://www.mySites.com/leafs">
  <nssrch:nickname>Toronto Maple Leafs</nssrch:nickname>
  <nssrch:hits>10</nssrch:hits>
  <nssrch:url>http://www.mapleleafs.com</nssrch:url>
 </RDF:Description>
 </RDF:li>

</RDF:Seq>

<RDF:Description RDF:about="http://www.mySites.com/technology">
     <nssrch:nickname>Bits and bytes</nssrch:nickname>
</RDF:Description>

<RDF:Description RDF:about="http://www.mySites.com/news">
     <nssrch:nickname>In the world</nssrch:nickname>
</RDF:Description>

<RDF:Description RDF:about="http://www.mySites.com/sports">
     <nssrch:nickname>Games and scores</nssrch:nickname>
</RDF:Description>

<!-- The main table of contents -->

<RDF:Seq RDF:about="http://www.mySites.com/TOC" >

<RDF:li>
<RDF:Seq  RDF:about="http://www.mySites.com/technology">
 <RDF:li RDF:resource="http://www.mySites.com/php"/>
 <RDF:li RDF:resource="http://www.mySites.com/w3c"/>
 <RDF:li RDF:resource="http://www.mySites.com/apache"/>
```

```
</RDF:Seq>
</RDF:li>

<RDF:li>
<RDF:Seq RDF:about="http://www.mySites.com/news">
 <RDF:li RDF:resource="http://www.mySites.com/cnn"/>
 <RDF:li RDF:resource="http://www.mySites.com/bbc"/>
 <RDF:li RDF:resource="http://www.mySites.com/washingtonpost"/>
</RDF:Seq>
</RDF:li>

<RDF:li>
<RDF:Seq  RDF:about="http://www.mySites.com/sports">
 <RDF:li RDF:resource="http://www.mySites.com/fifa"/>
 <RDF:li RDF:resource="http://www.mySites.com/espn"/>
 <RDF:li RDF:resource="http://www.mySites.com/leafs"/>
</RDF:Seq>
</RDF:li>

</RDF:Seq> <!-- TOC -->

</RDF:RDF>
```

We now edit our previous tree example or create a new *treeWithTemplate.xul* file. Here, we set the template to start replication with a `treeitem` element, and set the starting point for the template creation at the RDF resource for the table of contents resource (*http://mySites.com/TOC*):

```
<?xml-stylesheet href="NewsSearchStyles.css" type="text/css"?>

<window
  id="treeWindow"
  title="Trees from a template"
  width="800"
  height="700"
  orient="horizontal"
  xmlns:html="http://www.w3.org/1999/xhtml"
  xmlns="http://www.mozilla.org/keymaster/gatekeeper/there.is.only.xul">

<vbox flex="1" >
<tree datasources="newssites.rdf"
      ref="http://www.mySites.com/TOC"
      id="mainTree"  seltype="single" flex="1" >

  <treecols>
    <treecol  primary="true" label="Column 1" flex="1"/>
    <treecol  label="Column 2" flex="2"/>
  </treecols>

<template>
 <rule>
  <treechildren >
```

```
      <treeitem container="true" open="true" uri="rdf:*">
       <treerow>
        <treecell label="rdf:http://www.mySites.com/rdf#nickname"/>
        <treecell label="rdf:http://www.mySites.com/rdf#url"/>
       </treerow>
       </treeitem>

    </treechildren>
   </rule>
  </template>
  </tree>
  </vbox>
  </window>
```

The results show the hierarchy of the RDF file in Figure 6-7.

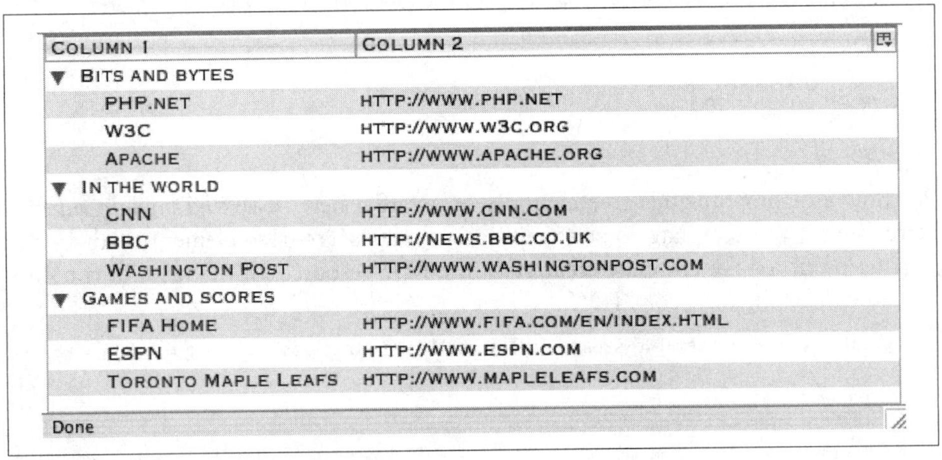

COLUMN 1	COLUMN 2
▼ BITS AND BYTES	
PHP.NET	HTTP://WWW.PHP.NET
W3C	HTTP://WWW.W3C.ORG
APACHE	HTTP://WWW.APACHE.ORG
▼ IN THE WORLD	
CNN	HTTP://WWW.CNN.COM
BBC	HTTP://NEWS.BBC.CO.UK
WASHINGTON POST	HTTP://WWW.WASHINGTONPOST.COM
▼ GAMES AND SCORES	
FIFA HOME	HTTP://WWW.FIFA.COM/EN/INDEX.HTML
ESPN	HTTP://WWW.ESPN.COM
TORONTO MAPLE LEAFS	HTTP://WWW.MAPLELEAFS.COM

Done

Figure 6-7. Tree constructed from template

Adding rules

The simple template syntax allows us to use multiple rules within a tag. This allows the designer a limited set of tools for conditional processing without requiring use of a complex syntax.

Rule elements can have a number of attributes that the template logic uses to determine whether the rule is true; if so, the XUL elements within the rule are generated. If the rule is not true, the enclosed XUL elements are ignored.

The attributes available to the rule element are:

`iscontainer`
: If `true`, the rule is true only if the current node is an RDF container. If `false`, the rule is true only if the node is not a container.

`isempty`
: If `true`, the rule is true only if the current node has no children.

`parent`
: Set to the element tag name for the node's parent that is required for the rule to be true. We use this when the RDF graph may have distinct container types for nodes that require special processing.

`parsetype`
: When set to `integer`, returns `true` only when RDF nodes parse to a type of integer.

Let's assume that we want the tree rows to have a special type of style applied to headings. We will set a conditional rule that assigns a special `tree` attribute used for style changes based on a test of whether the node is a container.

Unfortunately, individual tree rows do not have a `style` attribute to control only a particular row. Rather, the highly specialized tree builder logic uses a `properties` attribute that maps to a Cascading Style Sheet (CSS) `style` property.

For example, if we add a property called `siteHeading` for a tree style, we must add the following code to our *NewsSearchStyles.css* file:

```
treechildren::-moz-tree-row(siteHeading)
 {
   background-color: #008080;
 }
```

We change the source code for our *treesWithTemplate.xul* file to add two rules for our tree item. The first rule will be true if the node is a container, in which case the property for a site heading is set. We also remove the cell label assignment when a URL is not a section heading. The second rule is in place to generate the widgets for nonheadings:

```
<?xml-stylesheet href="NewsSearchStyles.css" type="text/css"?>

<window
  id="treeWindow"
  title="Trees from a template"
  width="800"
  height="700"
  orient="horizontal"
  xmlns:html="http://www.w3.org/1999/xhtml"
  xmlns="http://www.mozilla.org/keymaster/gatekeeper/there.is.only.xul">

<vbox flex="1" >
<tree datasources="newssites.rdf"
      ref="http://www.mySites.com/TOC"
      id="mainTree"  seltype="single" flex="1" >

  <treecols>
    <treecol  primary="true" label="Column 1" flex="1"/>
    <treecol  label="Column 2" flex="2"/>
  </treecols>

<template>
 <rule iscontainer="true">
  <treechildren >
```

```
    <treeitem  container="true" open="true" uri="rdf:*">
     <treerow properties="siteHeading">
      <treecell label="rdf:http://www.mySites.com/rdf#nickname"/>
     </treerow>
     </treeitem>

   </treechildren>
  </rule>

  <rule iscontainer="false">
   <treechildren >

    <treeitem   uri="rdf:*">
     <treerow >
      <treecell label="rdf:http://www.mySites.com/rdf#nickname"/>
      <treecell label="rdf:http://www.mySites.com/rdf#url"/>
     </treerow>
     </treeitem>

   </treechildren>
  </rule>

  </template>
  </tree>
  </vbox>
  </window>
```

The tree now shows the results of our conditional GUI generation by applying rule attributes to the simple template form, as shown in Figure 6-8.

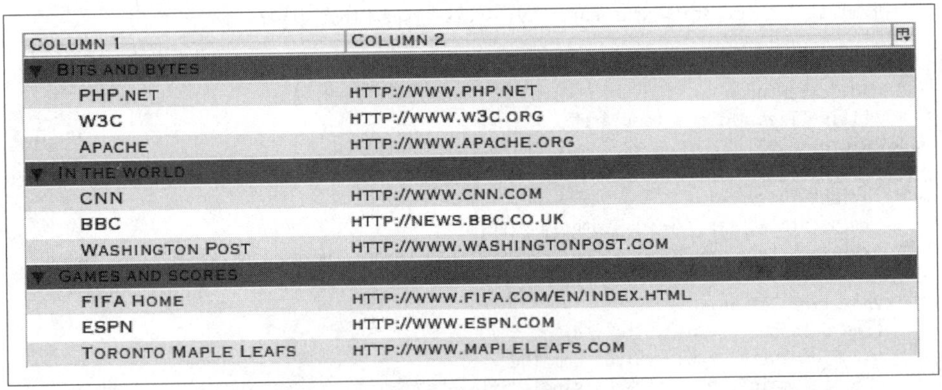

Column 1	Column 2
▼ Bits and Bytes	
PHP.net	http://www.php.net
W3C	http://www.w3c.org
Apache	http://www.apache.org
▼ In the World	
CNN	http://www.cnn.com
BBC	http://news.bbc.co.uk
Washington Post	http://www.washingtonpost.com
▼ Games and Scores	
FIFA Home	http://www.fifa.com/en/index.html
ESPN	http://www.espn.com
Toronto Maple Leafs	http://www.mapleleafs.com

Figure 6-8. Template with conditional processing of headings

The addition of conditional attributes to a rule allows for some simple modification of the GUI based on the characteristics of a node or its parent. There are, however, cases where more ambitious manipulation of the output tree requires the advanced syntax for templates.

More Complex Templates

The previous examples illustrated the simple syntax of templates, which is useful for basic RDF processing. When designers want to use templates to access RDF datasources that are more complex, such as publicly available resources used in research and business sites, a more robust form of template syntax is available.

Let's say we want to specially mark category headings through a style change. The declaration of a CSS class with the appropriate style information is straightforward enough, but we need to know when to assign the appropriate class attribute to the widget. In this case, we can use the more complete template syntax to detect RDF containers and assign the proper style information.

Formal RDF terminology

The formal term for a resource element in an RDF file is an RDF *statement*. Statements consist of a subject identifier, properties, and the literal value of the object. We can also look at a statement from a logical perspective in which the resource is the *subject*, the properties state what is *predicated* of the subject, and an *object* expresses the literal value of the property.

Consider one of the statements from our RDF file:

```
<RDF:Description RDF:about="http://www.mySites.com/apache" >
  <nssrch:nickname>Apache</nssrch:nickname>
  <nssrch:hits>117</nssrch:hits>
    <nssrch:url>http://www.apache.org</nssrch:url>
  </RDF:Description>
```

We can break the statement into its constituent parts (see Table 6-3).

Table 6-3. RDF statement components

Subject	*http://www.mySites.com/apache*	The resource description's `about` attribute is considered the subject of a statement.
Predicate	Nickname Hits URL	The statement predicates the existence of a nickname, hits, and a URL of the subject.

Object	`Apache`
	`117`
	`http://www.apache.org`
		Property values are the statement's objects.

Conditions. Firefox's template processor allows the designer to set rules for conditional processing of RDF statements matching conditions that we can express in more detail than the previously discussed form.

Under the hood of the simple syntax, templates consist of *rules* to follow for replication; rules in turn consist of *conditions* to satisfy, and *actions* to execute upon the match of a condition:

```
<rule>
  <conditions/>
  <action/>
</rule>
```

The conditions element itself consists of a content element to specify where RDF content is initially obtained, a member element to define how resources and properties are assigned to template variables, and a triple element that sets a required test condition or assertion that must be met to trigger content generation:

```
<conditions>
 <content/>
  <member/>
  <triple/>
</conditions>
```

The content element includes an attribute that acts as an assignment statement to select the initial RDF node being processed throughout the condition. The template syntax allows the assignment of the current RDF node being tested to a template variable. *Template variables* are text tokens preceded by a ?, and are used to pass information to other elements in the rule for conditional testing and assignment to the elements that generate the widgets:

```
<content uri="?currentContainer"/>
```

When XUL logic encounters the datasources attribute, it begins template processing with the first rule it discovers within a template element. The process starts by assigning the value in the ref attribute (of the element with the datasources attribute) as the RDF node for the initial test and code generation. Once an RDF node is matched and template code is generated, the template logic continues by descending to each child of the preceding search node until all remaining nodes in the RDF tree have been traversed. As each step of descent occurs, the uri attribute of the content element is set to the resource being tested. The variable assignment provides a reference that we can use to get information about the tested node. In this case, if we were to set the tree's datasources attribute to newssites.rdf and the ref attribute to http://www.mySites.com/TOC, the first pass through the template would assign the TOC resource to the template variable ?theHeading, and the next pass would assign the resource for the technology heading, news heading, and finally, sports heading.

The conditions child member provides a template variable referencing a resource of the container's child.

RDF datasources often include container elements such as an RDF sequence, bag, or alternatives. The template logic uses the member element to set template variables that reference the current container and its children. The variables are then used within the action element to control the generation of widgets:

```
<member container="?currentContainer" child="?heading"/>
```

The container attribute is set to the resource specified by the ?currentContainer variable. The template logic will scan the RDF graph for the container resource that matches the template variable, and set the child attribute to the set representing the container's children. The previous statement assigns the set of references to the ?heading template variable, which will be used in the remainder of the conditions element and the actions element as the template generator steps through all RDF container nodes and children.

On first glance at these examples, it may seem unclear what the difference is between the content and member elements. The significance lies in the fact that the content element sets the first search point for the template; without a content element assigning the uri attribute to the template variable, the template logic would not have sufficient information about where to start the RDF search. The member element is used to set the starting point for iterating over a container's children. We can position member elements anywhere within a condition to set the variables that reflect each RDF child being processed.

The triple element of a condition sets the rules for conditional generation of interface widgets. A triple's attributes specify the *subject*, *predicate*, and *object* that must exist for the condition to be satisfied. If the triple is asserted, the condition is true and ensuing action elements will be used to generate widgets. If the triple is not asserted, no actions are taken.

For example:

```
<triple subject="?heading"
 predicate="http://www.mySites.com/rdf#nickname"
 object="?nickname"/>
```

This triple tests the current RDF node. If the subject (resource) is the same one specified by the ?heading template variable, and it predicates the existence of a nickname property, a template variable is assigned the property's value, and the condition is considered to be true. We can include any number of triples in the condition; if no triples exist in a condition, it is presumed to be asserted (true), and any following actions will be invoked. If more than one triple exists in a condition, all triples must be asserted for the condition to be satisfied.

One last optional tag provides the developer with a tool to assign a resource property to a template variable, regardless of whether the property exists. This binding element looks just like a triple element:

```
<bindings>
  <binding subject="?someObject"
           predicate="http://www.mySites.com/rdf#someProperty"
           object="?someValue"/>
</bindings>
```

The difference between the binding and triple elements is that if the property does not exist in the RDF datasource, the variable ?someValue would simply be assigned a NULL value. *It has no effect on the assertion of the condition.* If we used the same RDF statement (subject, predicate, and object) within a triple element, the condition would fail if the property did not exist. We use binding elements where optional widgets (labels, text) may be displayed, but the structure of interface widgets is not to be affected.

Actions. The action element specifies the XUL elements to generate when the previous conditions are true. Action elements have access to any of the template variables assigned within the conditions of the rule.

The element:

```
<action>
 <treechildren>
  <treeitem uri="?heading">
   <treerow>
     <treecell label="?nickname"/>
   </treerow>
  </treeitem>
 </treechildren>
</action>
```

will generate a tree cell filled with the template variable ?nickname that was set by elements within the conditions tag.

We can illustrate how to use the extended template syntax by modifying our *treesWithTemplate.xul* file to create a new *treesWithExtendedTemplate.xul* file. As part of the exercise, we will use tree cells to display the container and child template variables as they are processed. We will also add column headings and tree column splitters that allow us to adjust the size of the columns displayed:

```
<?xml-stylesheet href="NewsSearchStyles.css" type="text/css"?>

<window
  id="treeWindow"
  title="Trees from a template"
  width="800"
  height="700"
  orient="horizontal"
  xmlns:html="http://www.w3.org/1999/xhtml"
  xmlns="http://www.mozilla.org/keymaster/gatekeeper/there.is.only.xul">

<vbox flex="1" >
<tree datasources="newssites.rdf"
      ref="http://www.mySites.com/TOC"
      id="mainTree"  seltype="single" flex="1">
```

```
  <treecols>
    <treecol  primary="true" label="Nickname" flex="1"/>
    <splitter class="tree-splitter"/>
    <treecol  label="Current Container" flex="2"/>
    <splitter class="tree-splitter"/>
    <treecol  label="Heading" flex="2"/>
  </treecols>

 <template>
    <rule>
      <conditions>
        <content uri="?currentContainer"/>
        <member container="?currentContainer" child="?heading"/>
        <triple subject="?heading"
                predicate="http://www.mySites.com/rdf#nickname"
                object="?nickname"/>
      </conditions>
      <action>
        <treechildren>
          <treeitem uri="?heading">
            <treerow>
              <treecell label="?nickname"/>
              <treecell label="?currentContainer"/>
              <treecell label="?heading"/>
            </treerow>
          </treeitem>
        </treechildren>
      </action>
    </rule>
  </template></tree>
</vbox>
</window>
```

The resulting tree shows us how this template parsed the RDF data sources (see Figure 6-9).

NICKNAME	CURRENT CONTAINER	HEADING
▼ BITS AND BYTES	HTTP://WWW.MYSITES.COM/TOC	HTTP://WWW.MYSITES.COM/TECHNOLOGY
PHP.NET	HTTP://WWW.MYSITES.COM/TECHNOLO...	HTTP://WWW.MYSITES.COM/PHP
W3C	HTTP://WWW.MYSITES.COM/TECHNOLO...	HTTP://WWW.MYSITES.COM/W3C
APACHE	HTTP://WWW.MYSITES.COM/TECHNOLO...	HTTP://WWW.MYSITES.COM/APACHE
▼ IN THE WORLD	HTTP://WWW.MYSITES.COM/TOC	HTTP://WWW.MYSITES.COM/NEWS
CNN	HTTP://WWW.MYSITES.COM/NEWS	HTTP://WWW.MYSITES.COM/CNN
BBC	HTTP://WWW.MYSITES.COM/NEWS	HTTP://WWW.MYSITES.COM/BBC
WASHINGTON POST	HTTP://WWW.MYSITES.COM/NEWS	HTTP://WWW.MYSITES.COM/WASHINGTONPOST
▼ GAMES AND SCORES	HTTP://WWW.MYSITES.COM/TOC	HTTP://WWW.MYSITES.COM/SPORTS
FIFA HOME	HTTP://WWW.MYSITES.COM/SPORTS	HTTP://WWW.MYSITES.COM/FIFA
ESPN	HTTP://WWW.MYSITES.COM/SPORTS	HTTP://WWW.MYSITES.COM/ESPN
TORONTO MAPLE LEAFS	HTTP://WWW.MYSITES.COM/SPORTS	HTTP://WWW.MYSITES.COM/LEAFS

Figure 6-9. Tree built from template (extended form)

Using Templates for Conditional Processing

Extended templates provide the developer with conditional processing tools that aren't possible with the basic template syntax.

When we used our tree to display the "nickname" and URL in our selection, we used the simple form of the template that displayed only blanks in the URL column for the site heading's container. It is a different problem if we want to *conditionally modify* content based on the RDF properties we detect.

If, for example, we wanted to display the number of hits for a web site but display something other than a blank space for section headings, we could do so using a pair of rules. A modified XUL source file to display a tree of nicknames, URLs, and number of hits looks like this:

```
<?xml-stylesheet href="NewsSearchStyles.css" type="text/css"?>

<window
  id="treeWindow"
  title="Trees from a conditional template"
  width="800"
  height="700"
  orient="horizontal"
  xmlns:html="http://www.w3.org/1999/xhtml"
  xmlns="http://www.mozilla.org/keymaster/gatekeeper/there.is.only.xul">

<vbox flex="1" >
<tree datasources="newssites.rdf"
      ref="http://www.mySites.com/TOC"
      id="mainTree"  seltype="single" flex="1">

  <treecols>
    <treecol  primary="true" label="Nickname" flex="1"/>
    <splitter class="tree-splitter"/>
    <treecol  label="URL" flex="2"/>
    <splitter class="tree-splitter"/>
    <treecol  label="Visits" flex="2"/>
  </treecols>

 <template container="?currentContainer" member="?site" >
     <rule >
       <conditions>
         <content uri="?currentContainer"/>
         <member container="?currentContainer" child="?site"/>

         <triple subject="?site"
                 predicate="http://www.mySites.com/rdf#nickname"
                 object="?nickname"/>
         <triple subject="?site"
                 predicate="http://www.mySites.com/rdf#url"
                 object="?url"/>
```

```
        <triple subject="?site"
                predicate="http://www.mySites.com/rdf#hits"
                object="?hits"/>
      </conditions>
      <action>
        <treechildren>
          <treeitem uri="?site">
            <treerow  >
              <treecell label="?nickname"/>
              <treecell label="?url"/>
              <treecell label="?hits"/>
            </treerow>
          </treeitem>
        </treechildren>
      </action>
    </rule>

    <rule >
      <conditions>
        <content uri="?currentContainer"/>
        <member container="?currentContainer" child="?site"/>
        <triple subject="?site"
                predicate="http://www.mySites.com/rdf#nickname"
                object="?nickname"/>
      </conditions>
      <action>
        <treechildren>
          <treeitem  uri="?site">
            <treerow properties="siteHeading" >
              <treecell label="?nickname"/>
              <treecell label="-"/>
              <treecell label="-"/>
            </treerow>
          </treeitem>
        </treechildren>
      </action>
    </rule>


  </template></tree>
</vbox>
</window>
```

The first difference is the use of `container` and `member` attributes for the template tag. This is a convention we follow when a template has multiple rules—the assignments inform the template logic of the variables to be used as container and child members. Without these statements, the tree builder logic would make logic assumptions of the variables based on their use in the first rule encountered.

The first rule is matched if the three triples are asserted, indicating the presence of `nickname`, `hits`, and `url` properties. The action for that rule displays the assigned variables in the tree cells.

If the conditions of the first rule are not met, but the second rule's conditions are asserted (satisfied only with the presence of a `nickname` property), the tree cells are replaced with - rather than blanks.

IDs and URIs

One interesting feature of template generation is related to the code statement:

```
<treeitem  uri="?site">
```

This statement tells the template logic to assign an `id` attribute to the current resource being processed. We can see how that works by adding our event handler for the onselect event to the tree:

```
<?xml-stylesheet href="NewsSearchStyles.css" type="text/css"?>
<window
  id="treeWindow"
  title="Trees from a conditional template"
  width="800"
  height="700"
  orient="horizontal"
  xmlns:html="http://www.w3.org/1999/xhtml"
  xmlns="http://www.mozilla.org/keymaster/gatekeeper/there.is.only.xul">
<script>
 <![CDATA[
 function somethingSelected(event) {
   var tI = event.target.currentIndex;

    alert(event.target.contentView.getItemAtIndex(tI).getAttribute("id"));
   }

   ]]>
</script>

<vbox flex="1" >
<tree datasources="newssites.rdf"
      ref="http://www.mySites.com/TOC"
      id="mainTree"  seltype="single" flex="1"
      onselect="somethingSelected(event);"  >

  <treecols>
    <treecol  primary="true" label="Nickname" flex="1"/>
    <splitter class="tree-splitter"/>
    <treecol  label="URL" flex="2"/>
    <splitter class="tree-splitter"/>
    <treecol  label="Visits" flex="2"/>
  </treecols>
  .
  .
  .
```

Now selecting any tree item will give us a dialog that displays the resource (subject) associated with the tree item.

In our case, we are more likely to use the actual URL to send to a browser window. Rather than taking up space in the GUI to display the URL, we will use our rules to assign the url property value to the treeitem's myURL attribute. For the rule associated with headings, we will assign an empty string. We'll also change the columns and headings to provide a tree interface to display the nickname and number of site hits:

```
<?xml-stylesheet href="NewsSearchStyles.css" type="text/css"?>

<window
  id="treeWindow"
  title="Trees from a conditional template"
  width="800"
  height="700"
  orient="horizontal"
  xmlns:html="http://www.w3.org/1999/xhtml"
  xmlns="http://www.mozilla.org/keymaster/gatekeeper/there.is.only.xul">
<script>
 <![CDATA[
 function somethingSelected(event) {
   var tI = event.target.currentIndex;
   var theURL = event.target.contentView.getItemAtIndex(tI).getAttribute("myURL");
   if (theURL != "") alert("Site URL is " + theURL);
   }
   ]]>
</script>

<vbox flex="1" >
<tree datasources="newssites.rdf"
      ref="http://www.mySites.com/TOC"
      id="mainTree"  seltype="single" flex="1"
      onselect="somethingSelected(event);"  >

  <treecols>
    <treecol  primary="true" label="Nickname" flex="1"/>
    <splitter class="tree-splitter"/>
    <treecol  label="Visits" flex="2"/>
  </treecols>

<template container="?currentContainer" member="?site">
    <rule  >
      <conditions>
        <content uri="?currentContainer"/>
        <member container="?currentContainer" child="?site"/>

        <triple subject="?site"
                predicate="http://www.mySites.com/rdf#nickname"
                object="?nickname"/>
        <triple subject="?site"
                predicate="http://www.mySites.com/rdf#url"
                object="?url"/>
        <triple subject="?site"
                predicate="http://www.mySites.com/rdf#hits"
                object="?hits"/>
```

```
      </conditions>
      <action>
        <treechildren>
          <treeitem uri="?site" myURL="?url">
            <treerow  >
              <treecell label="?nickname"/>
              <treecell label="?hits"/>
            </treerow>
          </treeitem>
        </treechildren>
      </action>
    </rule>
    <rule >
      <conditions>
        <content uri="?currentContainer"/>
        <member container="?currentContainer" child="?site"/>
        <triple subject="?site"
                predicate="http://www.mySites.com/rdf#nickname"
                object="?nickname"/>
      </conditions>
      <action>
        <treechildren>
          <treeitem  uri="?site" myURL="">
            <treerow properties="siteHeading" >
              <treecell label="?nickname"/>
              <treecell label="-"/>
            </treerow>
          </treeitem>
        </treechildren>
      </action>
    </rule>
  </template></tree>
</vbox>
</window>
```

The resulting source now allows us to obtain the URL from a tree created from a template driven by our *newssites.rdf* source, as shown in Figure 6-10.

We can paste the tree example file into our *newssearch.xul* file to provide the application with a useful interface to organize pages that we will be annotating.

We copy the tree code into the vertical box that we will use to organize our marked pages:

```
<!-- a container for some kind of list -->
 <vbox flex="1" ondblclick="getTreeURL(event);">


<tree datasources="" ref="" id="mainTree"  seltype="single" flex="1">
  <treecols>
    <treecol  primary="true" label="Nickname" flex="1"/>
    <splitter class="tree-splitter"/>
    <treecol  label="Visits" flex="2"/>
  </treecols>
```

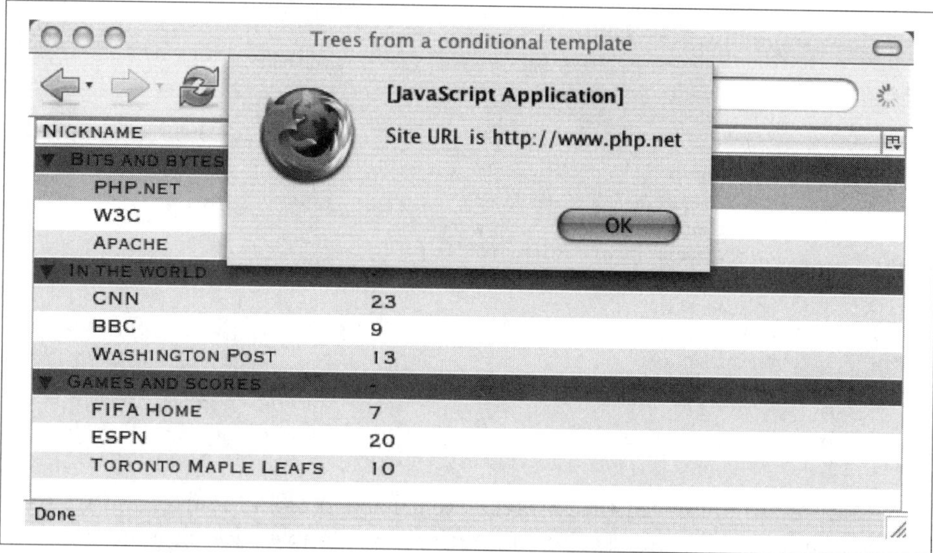

Figure 6-10. Passing RDF properties to tree attributes

```
<template container="?currentContainer" member="?site">
    <rule  >
      <conditions>
        <content uri="?currentContainer"/>
        <member container="?currentContainer" child="?site"/>

        <triple subject="?site"
                predicate="http://www.mySites.com/rdf#nickname"
                object="?nickname"/>
        <triple subject="?site"
                predicate="http://www.mySites.com/rdf#url"
                object="?url"/>
        <triple subject="?site"
                predicate="http://www.mySites.com/rdf#hits"
                object="?hits"/>

      </conditions>
      <action>
        <treechildren>
          <treeitem uri="?site" myURL="?url">
            <treerow  >
              <treecell label="?nickname"/>
              <treecell label="?hits"/>
            </treerow>
          </treeitem>
        </treechildren>
      </action>
    </rule>
    <rule >
      <conditions>
        <content uri="?currentContainer"/>
```

```
        <member container="?currentContainer" child="?site"/>
        <triple subject="?site"
                predicate="http://www.mySites.com/rdf#nickname"
                object="?nickname"/>
      </conditions>
      <action>
        <treechildren>
          <treeitem  uri="?site" myURL="">
            <treerow properties="siteHeading" >
              <treecell label="?nickname"/>
              <treecell label="-"/>
            </treerow>
          </treeitem>
        </treechildren>
      </action>
    </rule>
  </template></tree>
</vbox>
```

Note that we have removed the onselect event handler from the tree, and we have attached an ondblclick handler to the tree's vbox. Double-clicking is more useful than the simple select event for the user to indicate when some action is to accompany a mouse selection. Trees, however, do not support the dblclick event; instead, we attach the handler to the enclosing box. We will handle the dblclick event in a JavaScript function that will pass the selected URL to the display frame:

```
function getTreeURL(event) {
  var theTree = document.getElementById("mainTree");
   var tI = document.getElementById("mainTree").currentIndex;
   var theURL = theTree.contentView.
       getItemAtIndex(theTree.currentIndex).
            getAttribute("myURL");

   if (theURL != "")  {
      document.getElementById("theURL").value = theURL;
      loadURL();
      }
   }
```

This function works because of the tree template statement that assigns the RDF triple's #url property to the treeitem's attribute:

```
<treechildren>
  <treeitem uri="?site" myURL="?url">
    <treerow  >
      <treecell label="?nickname"/>
      <treecell label="?hits"/>
     </treerow>
    </treeitem>
  </treechildren>
```

The preceding fragment results in the id attribute of the tree item being set to the subject of the RDF triple, and the url value being assigned to the myURL attribute. (We will be using the id attribute shortly when we start to access and modify RDF content.) The getTreeURL function gets the index of the treeitem selected, passes the myURL attribute to the displayed text area, and calls the function to load the selected site.

We have also replaced the datasources and ref attributes on the tree with empty strings. This allows us to populate the tree only after a user has logged in by dynamically assigning these attributes after discovering its ID. The tree building logic rebuilds widgets only when an existing datasources or ref attribute is changed—the tree building logic does not work if scripts modify datasources and ref attributes if the attributes were not declared in the XUL source file.

We now change the function that manages the application's state machine to set the tree's datasources and ref attributes only when the user has logged in:

```
case (K_STARTUP): { // startup
  // enable only the new button
  document.getElementById("newButton").disabled=false;
  document.getElementById("contentIFrame").
      setAttribute("src","http://www.mozillazine.org");
  var theTree = document.getElementById("mainTree");
  theTree.setAttribute("datasources","newssites.rdf");
  theTree.setAttribute("ref","http://www.mySites.com/TOC");
  break;
  } // startup
```

The application now displays the tree selector and selected URLs only after the user logs in, as shown in Figure 6-11.

Template forms: Summary

The simple form of a template generally does a good job dealing with content organized as simple hierarchies. This is particularly true when the interface is not affected by widgets that have blanks assigned to display attributes in the event that a property is not found.

The advanced template rules are more appropriate for conditional generation of interface widgets based on the presence or absence of RDF properties. Our *newssites.rdf* file, for example, wrapped all the sites as children of site topics. If the site headings included a property such as topic_name rather than sharing the nickname property with nonheadings, we could use a template rule to assign the property to a template variable that would be used as a tree cell label; nonheading topics would be handled by rules similar to what we used in this example.

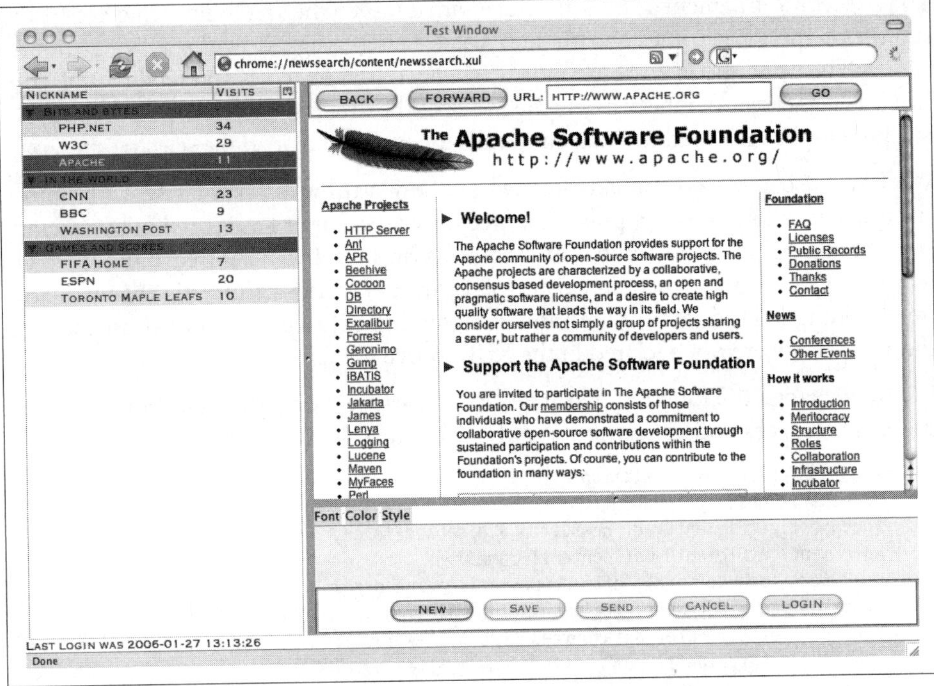

Figure 6-11. NewsSearch with tree selector

Modifying Datasources

Our interface is now useful for selecting URLs from a prebuilt RDF file. For the interface to be useful, we need to include the logic to add and remove URLs as well as section headings. That requires the addition of logic to prompt the user for new nicknames and section names, and the logic to change the underlying RDF datasource.

We now consider a limited set of functions to access and modify our list of popular sites:

- Add a URL to an existing section heading.
- Remove a URL from a section heading.
- Add a new section heading.
- Remove an empty section heading.

To accomplish these tasks, we need to take a closer look at RDF datasources and the tools used to access them.

RDF Statements: A Closer Look

Earlier, we considered an entry in an RDF file:

```
<RDF:Description RDF:about="http://www.mySites.com/apache" >
 <nssrch:nickname>Apache</nssrch:nickname>
 <nssrch:hits>117</nssrch:hits>
 <nssrch:url>http://www.apache.org</nssrch:url>
</RDF:Description>
```

This RDF statement consists of a subject, identified by the URI *http://www.mySites.com/apache*, and the properties of `nickname`, `hits`, and `url`.

Each RDF statement is referenced through its subject URI as list (`RDF:li`) elements in separate sections that are containers for the list items. The `technology` section, for example, contains a sequence of list items referencing the pages within its section. The section headings, in turn, are list items contained by the top table of contents (TOC) container:

```
<RDF:Seq RDF:about="http://www.mySites.com/TOC" >
<RDF:li>
<RDF:Seq RDF:about="http://www.mySites.com/technology">
 <RDF:li RDF:resource="http://www.mySites.com/php"/>
 <RDF:li RDF:resource="http://www.mySites.com/w3c"/>
 <RDF:li RDF:resource="http://www.mySites.com/apache"/>
</RDF:Seq>
</RDF:li>
.
.
```

To create simple RDF statements to add to an RDF datasource, we need to create a resource for each subject and property of the statement. Using the RDF terminology covered earlier, to create the `apache` statement and insert it into the proper section, we do the following in pseudocode:

1. Create a resource with the subject URI of *http://www.mySites.com/apache*.
2. Create a resource for a predicate that asserts a `nickname` property of `Apache`.
3. Create a resource for a predicate that asserts a `hits` property of `117`.
4. Create a resource for a predicate that asserts a `url` property of `http://www.apache.org`.
5. Append the completed statement to the `technology` container.

The process of creating and appending statements to RDF datasources is facilitated by a specialized collection of *interfaces* and *services*.

RDF Interfaces and Services

The Firefox framework bundles a collection of related functions and properties into interfaces. Interfaces do not represent objects per se, but they provide a logical reference with methods and properties that resemble an object from a programmatic perspective.

The interfaces themselves are not objects, but a collection of methods and properties that relate to common characteristics, even though the implementations may be very different.

Firefox also provides *services*, a special type of singleton component (meaning only one instance can exist at a time within the scope of an application running the Firefox framework).

The interfaces and services that relate to RDF manipulation include:

`nsIRDFService`
: This service provides the developer with all the tools necessary to access the RDF datasources associated with a XUL widget. All attempts to extract datasources, and to create new resources for use in a datasource, are carried out through method calls to the RDF service.

`nsIRDFDataSource`
: This interface provides the core functions through which RDF graphs are modified. This interface provides the functions to add and remove RDF statements to the RDF graph of nodes.

`nsIRDFRemoteDataSource`
: This specialized interface provides methods that allow an RDF graph to be written to a file. We can use this interface only for files on the local filesystem; chrome URLs do not support this interface.

`nsIRDFContainer`
: This interface provides the functions to query and update a datasource's container statements.

`nsIRDFContainerUtils`
: This specialized interface provides the methods that query a datasource for the presence or absence of container statements, as well as obtain information about the condition of a container. For example, JavaScript code can use a method of the `nsIRDFContainerUtils` interface to see whether a particular subject exists as a container before calling `nsIRDFContainer` methods that manipulate the subject in question.

To obtain an interface from Firefox, we start by creating a component representing the general class of interest through the `createInstance` method. We then use that component's `QueryInterface` method to obtain a specific interface. A `getService` method is called to obtain a reference to a service.

To use our noncomputer example from earlier in the book, we would use `createInstance` to obtain an object reference for a "sports car"; `QueryInterface` allows us to ask, "Does this sports car object implement a `passenger_cabin` interface?"

To obtain a file interface in JavaScript, we would use this code:

```
var aFile = Components.classes["@mozilla.org/file/local;1"].createInstance( );
if (aFile) aFile = aFile.QueryInterface(Components.interfaces.nsILocalFile);
```

The first statement obtains a `file` component by asking the `class` object to create an instance described by the Mozilla file URI (`mozilla.org/file/local;1`). The second statement inquires whether the component implements an `nsILocalFile` interface. If the component supports the interface, the object reference is cast to that interface. If not, an exception is thrown. We could, of course, combine the two statements into one.

Accessing a service is a matter of creating a service rather than an instance. To create one of the Firefox framework's bookmark services, we would use this code:

```
var myBookmarks = Components.classes
    ["@mozilla.org/browser/bookmarks-service;1"].getService( );
myBookmarks =
 myBookmarks.QueryInterface(Components.interfaces.nsIBookmarksService);
```

RDF Datasource Details

The sample code we developed assigned a `datasources` attribute to a XUL widget for use in template logic. As the plural nature of the attribute name implies, one could assign more than one datasource URI, or even create datasources in memory for use with an interface widget. Once the XUL framework detects a `datasources` attribute attached to a widget, a `database` property is created for that element. Through the `database` property, we access an RDF datasource created from the `datasources` URIs specified in the attribute.

Take careful note of the difference in the term *RDF datasource* (which refers to an `nsIRDFDatasource` interface) and the attribute `datasources`, which refers to URIs used to create a datasource. We use the term *datasource* in JavaScript to manipulate the `nsIRDFDatasource` Cross-Platform Component Model (XPCOM) (software) interface. The `datasources` attribute is set to a XUL element as the URI to provide data to the interface.

Accessing datasources

A XUL element's `database` property is actually a composite datasource—an object that aggregates multiple datasources. The `database` property holds references not only to the datasource for a specific widget, but for the entire application (this includes a "local-store" datasource used to keep track of window position and other application state). As a result, software that is looking for a specific datasource must iterate through the database property until it finds the right one.

Once the RDF datasource is obtained, we need to obtain the specific interface that provides the methods we require. The nsIRDFDataSource interface provides all the methods necessary to create and modify the underlying RDF graph. But writing the resulting modifications back to a file requires the nsIRDFRemoteDataSource interface.

Here is a function to parse our XUL tree's datasources, looking for the datasource created by our *newssites.rdf* file:

```
function fetchFileDatasource( ) {
 var retVal = null;
 var theTree = document.getElementById("mainTree");

 var dSources = theTree.database.GetDataSources( );

 while (dSources.hasMoreElements( ) && (retVal == null)) {
   var dS = dSources.getNext( );
   dS = dS.QueryInterface(Components.interfaces.nsIRDFDataSource );
   if (dS.URI.indexOf("newssites") != -1) retVal = dS;
   }
  return retVal;
  }
```

Note the use of the ds.QueryInterface function. The getNext( ) method of a simple enumerator returns a basic component (object) that was part of the enumerator's collection. Stepping through the datasources, we keep looking for the one with the URI that matches the filename of interest. We must use the QueryInterface method to obtain (cast the component to) the interface that provides the methods for access and modification.

Once modifications have been made to a datasource, we need to obtain the interface to an nsIRemoteDataSource interface. This interface is specially designed to modify files on the local filesystem.

Note that this interface works only for file URLs; chrome URLs are not supported.

The code to write a modified datasource back to a file looks like this:

```
dataSource = dataSource.
     QueryInterface(Components.interfaces.nsIRDFRemoteDataSource);
dataSource.Flush( );
```

The Flush() function results in the RDF graph being serialized and written back to the file, but not necessarily in the same format that the file was read. Upon reopening a saved RDF file, expect the appearance and order of the file elements to be significantly changed from what was originally created.

Modifying datasources: Creating and removing RDF statements

The methods for creating and accessing RDF statements use a terminology that is slightly more verbose than the straightforward parent-child relationship of XML files.

For example, the RDF file entry:

```
<RDF:Description RDF:about="http://www.mySites.com/apache" >
 <nssrch:nickname>Apache</nssrch:nickname>
 <nssrch:hits>117</nssrch:hits>
 <nssrch:url>http://www.apache.org</nssrch:url>
</RDF:Description
```

actually represents three separate RDF statements. Each statement asserts the existence of a nickname, hits, and url property. We represent the tag on a property such as nickname in the RDF graph as a resource with an identifier derived from the <nssrch> namespace—in this case, http://www.mySites.com/#nickname. To create a predicate for a valid RDF statement, we need to create an RDF resource with the appropriate URI by calling the GetResource method from a component implementing an nsIRDFService interface:

```
var rdfService = Components.classes["@mozilla.org/rdf/rdf-service;1"].
   getService(Components.interfaces.nsIRDFService);
var thePredicateNickname = rdfService.GetResource
   ("http://www.mySites.com/rdf#nickname");
```

The first statement obtains a component implementing the nsIRDFService interface; the second creates an RDF resource that we will use as a predicate for a statement.

To create a reference for the Apache property, the RDF service interface uses a GetLiteral function to bind the string value of a property to an RDF reference:

```
var theNickName = rdfService.GetLiteral("Apache");
```

Finally, we need to create a resource to represent the subject of our statement:

```
var theSubject = rdfService.GetResource("http://www.mySites.com/"
    + "someNewNickName");
```

With resource references for a statement's subject, predicate, and target, we can use the dataSource Assert method to create a new statement:

```
dataSource.Assert(theSubject,
   thePredicateURL,
     theURL,
      true);
```

The first three parameters of the method specify the subject, predicate, and target of the new statement. The final parameter is referred to as the "truth value." This field is useful when testing the return value for the absence or presence of a preexisting statement. For our example code, we should set the value to `true`. We now must add our newly created RDF statement to a container representing a section heading.

Modifying containers

We manipulate RDF containers through methods on the `nsIRDFContainer` interface. Because the Firefox framework throws exceptions if a method is called on an object that doesn't really support the interface, an additional set of tools is necessary to check whether an RDF resource is (or is not) a container before calling container functions. Utility functions provided by the `nsIRDFContainerUtils` (utilities) interface give us the services needed to inquire about an RDF statement before calling the container functions.

The simplest case of adding a newly created statement to a statement representing a container (a section heading in terms of our application) requires us to initialize a container object with the resource we know to be a container, and then append the newly created statement:

```
var theSectionHeading = rdfService.GetResource(sectionURI);
var theSectionContainer = Components.classes["@mozilla.org/rdf/container;1"].
                createInstance(Components.interfaces.nsIRDFContainer);

theSectionContainer.Init(dataSource,theSectionHeading);
theSectionContainer.AppendElement(theSubject);
```

In this case, we assume that the `sectionURI` parameter is a URI of a section heading that we obtained from our tree widget. The first statement obtains the RDF resource with that URI as the statement's subject. The resource itself has no methods to add new content; we need to create an instance of an `nsIRDFContainer` interface, and initialize it with the resource that is a container. Once the container object is initialized, it is simply a matter of calling an `AppendElement` function.

Removing resources and containers

We implement the functions for removing resources from an RDF graph via a straightforward `Unassert` method:

```
dataSource.Unassert(theSubject,
  thePredicateNickname,
     theTarget,true);
```

You may ask, how did we know what the target is for a removal?

When a user has requested to remove a page reference, we must completely build the statements to reference all the properties (`url`, `hits`, `nickname`).

For such a case, the RDF service provides a GetTarget function. Given that we can create RDF resources for the subject and predicate, GetTarget returns the resource reference for the property value (target) of the statement.

A complete sequence now looks like this:

```
var thePredicateNickname =
 rdfService.GetResource("http://www.mySites.com/rdf#nickname");
var thePredicateURL =
 rdfService.GetResource("http://www.mySites.com/rdf#url");
var thePredicateHits =
 rdfService.GetResource("http://www.mySites.com/rdf#hits");

// Fetch the RDF statements for each property to remove that resource
  var theTarget = dataSource.
   GetTarget(theSubject,thePredicateNickname,true);
  dataSource.
    Unassert(theSubject,thePredicateNickname,theTarget,true);
  theTarget = dataSource.
    GetTarget(theSubject,thePredicateURL,true);
  dataSource.
   Unassert(theSubject,thePredicateURL,theTarget,true);
  theTarget = dataSource.
   GetTarget(theSubject,thePredicateHits,true);
  dataSource.
    Unassert(theSubject,thePredicateHits,theTarget,true);
```

Removing elements from a container is equally direct:

```
theSectionContainer.RemoveElement(theSubject,true);
```

We also must consider the possibility that the user may want to remove a section heading, in which case we would want the program to make certain that all the contents have been removed first. If, for example, we had a resource (theSubject) that we suspect is a section heading, the proper code would use the container utilities to verify that the resource is indeed a container, and then verify that the container is empty before proceeding:

```
if (containerTools.
        IsContainer(dataSource,theSubject)) { // remove section heading?
   // Bail out if the section isn't empty
   if (!(containerTools.
              IsEmpty(dataSource,theSubject))) { // not empty
                alert("All content pages must be removed first.");
    return;
   } // not empty
  } // removing section heading
```

This code snippet uses the IsContainer method to verify that the resource is a container, and if so, exits the logic if it is not yet empty of all other RDF statements as flagged by the IsEmpty function.

Moving to Code

With these tools in hand, we can consider what we want the interface to look like and do, such as:

- Provide buttons to allow the user to add/remove pages as well as section headings.
- Add some type of selector to allow the user to pick the section to which a new page reference will be added.
- Add a confirmation dialog (always a good thing when deleting objects!).

Adding dialogs

A simple confirm dialog consists of little more than a XUL window with a description that is used for a message, and two buttons: OK and Cancel. As we discussed earlier, we will need to add an argument to give the dialog a callback function to modify flags or values accessible by the calling program.

The JavaScript to call such a dialog would look like this:

```
Var message = "Are you sure?";
window.openDialog("chrome://newssearch/content/confirmDialog.xul","?",
      "chrome,modal",message,OkCancelCallback);

 if (OkCancelDialogRetVal == "CANCEL") return;
 removeResource(theSectionSubjectURI,thePageSubjectURI);
```

Here is the callback function to modify variables accessible within the calling script:

```
var OkCancelDialogRetVal = -1;
function OkCancelCallback (retVal) {
 OkCancelDialogRetVal = retVal;
}
```

The XUL file for our confirm dialog includes the functions to set the description field to a message (the first window argument) and to invoke a callback (the second argument). (Note that both OK and Cancel callbacks return `true` as a requirement to signal the framework to dismiss the dialog.)

The complete *confirmDialog.xul* file follows:

```
<?xml version="1.0"?>
<?xml-stylesheet href=
   "chrome://global/skin/global.css" type="text/css"?>
<dialog id="confirm" title="Are you sure?"
        xmlns=
      "http://www.mozilla.org/keymaster/gatekeeper/there.is.only.xul"
        buttons="accept,cancel"
        onload = "setMessage();"
        ondialogaccept="return doOK();"
        ondialogcancel="return doCancel();">

<script>
<![CDATA[
```

```
function setMessage( ) {
 if (window.arguments[0])
    document.getElementById("promptMessage").
     value = window.arguments[0];
}
// Use callback to set return code
//
function doOK( ) {
window.arguments[1]("OK");
return true;
}

function doCancel( ) {
window.arguments[1]("CANCEL");
return true;
}

]]>
</script>

<description id="promptMessage" value="Positive?"/>

</dialog>
```

When we later add the dialog to our program, it will render the window shown in Figure 6-12.

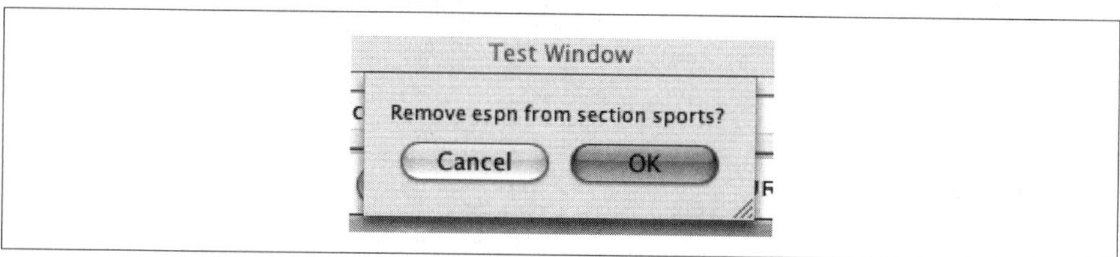

Figure 6-12. Simple OK/Cancel dialog

The next dialog we need is one that allows the user to select a section for a newly created page reference; it also makes sense for the dialog to allow some type of checkbox that tells the application that the user wants to create a brand-new section.

We can easily build a window that uses a simple template to create a list of all the section headings, and add a text field and XUL checkbox to indicate the user's intention to create a new section.

As with our simple OK/Cancel dialog, we will need to set up a callback accessible from the main script to allow the dialog to set values:

```
function openSectionSelection( ) {
 var lWindow =
   window.openDialog("chrome://newssearch/content/headingSel.xul",
      "SECTIONS","chrome,modal",setSection);
}
```

```
var sectionResource;
var nickName;
var makeNewSection;

function setSection(res,name,createSection) {
 sectionResource = res;
 nickName = name;
 makeNewSection = createSection;
}
```

The XUL file for the dialog uses a simple tree template to display only the section headings. We want the dialog to return the selected section, the typed entry for either a new section or a page reference, and an indicator if the user is requesting a new section:

```
<?xml version="1.0"?>
<?xml-stylesheet href="NewsSearchStyles.css" type="text/css"?>
<dialog
  id="headingWindow"
  title="SECTION"
  orient="vertical"
  ondialogaccept="return doOK( );"
  ondialogcancel="return doCancel( );"
  xmlns=
  "http://www.mozilla.org/keymaster/gatekeeper/there.is.only.xul">

 <script >
 <![CDATA[

  function doOK( ) {
  try { // try block
  if (!fieldsFilledIn( )) { // ask for fields to be entered
    var eMsg;
    if (document.getElementById("createSectionBox").checked )
      eMsg = "Please enter name for new section."
    else
      eMsg = "Select section and enter page name.";

     document.getElementById("promptMessage").value = eMsg;
     return false;
    } // ask for fields to be filled in

   // All fields filled in...
   //
   // If a new section is being created, no heading was selected, and
   // we programmatically set it to the "TOC"
   //
   var sectionName =
   (document.getElementById("headings").selectedItem == null) ?
             "http://www.mySites.com/TOC" :
              document.getElementById("headings").selectedItem.id;
```

```
 window.arguments[0](sectionName,
      document.getElementById("nickname").value,
      document.getElementById("createSectionBox").checked);

 } // try block

catch(e) {
 alert("doOK exception " + e);
}
 return true;
};

 //
 // Cancel passes null values to username and password; they are
 //  used as switches that will turn off a login attempt
 //
function doCancel( ) {
 window.arguments[0](null,null,false);
 return true;
};

function fieldsFilledIn( ) {

 if (document.getElementById("createSectionBox").checked) {
  return (document.getElementById("nickname").value != "");
 }
 else {
 return  ((document.getElementById("headings").selectedItem != "")
          && (document.getElementById("nickname").value != ""));
 }
};

]]>
</script>

 <vbox  flex="1" >
   <spacer flex="1"/>
     <description id="promptMessage">
      Please select heading for selected page.
     </description>
     <label value="Current Sections:" />
     <listbox datasources="newssites.rdf"
        ref="http://www.mySites.com/TOC"
       seltype="single" id="headings">
     <template>
       <listitem uri="rdf:*" >
          <label value="rdf:http://www.mySites.com/rdf#nickname"/>
       </listitem>
      </template>
     </listbox>
     <spacer flex="1"/>
     <label value="Short name:" control="nickname"/>
     <textbox id="nickname" maxlength="16"/>
```

```
      <checkbox
        id="createSectionBox"
         label="Create new heading" checked="false"/>
      <spacer flex="1"/>
    </vbox>
  </dialog>
```

Of special note is how the dialog responds if no section is selected. In this case, the script synthesizes a subject URI as the topmost container reference, and *http://www.mySites.com/TOC* if no other section heading was selected. The `fieldsFilledIn` function makes certain that either a section heading and data is entered in the dialog, or a name and the "new section" box is checked.

The interface itself introduces the `listbox` widget with a reference to the RDF file used to populate the list. Also added is a `checkbox` widget, whose `checked` property returns a Boolean indicator of its checked state. When we add this dialog to the interface, it will result in the window shown in Figure 6-13.

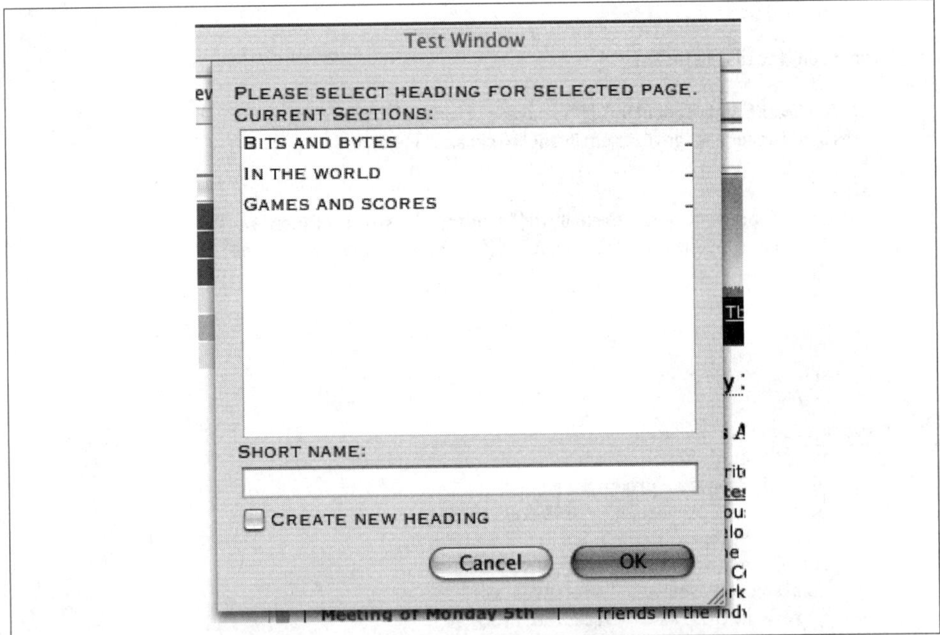

Figure 6-13. Section selection dialog

Tying Everything Together

To complete this version of the application file, we add some necessary supporting features (the numeric indexes refer to segments in the source code comments):

- We insert buttons to add/remove parts of the RDF file (1). The program will infer the details of the operation (e.g., what section, what page) based on what is selected and how the user enters data in the prompt dialog.
- We will need to merge the buttons into all the event handlers and initialization functions. We will connect these buttons to the functions `addNewLink( )` and `removeLink( )` (2).
- The application will dynamically add the `datasources` attribute to our selection tree by specifying a full pathname as the attribute (3). We use this form because the Firefox framework needs to see the *File://* location specifier in the URI to properly build the template and to provide the required `nsIRDFRemoteDatasource` interface to its datasources.

Take special note that the file pathnames are operating-system- and installation-specific. You will need to make changes to reflect your installation and target operating system.

- We add a utility function to `fetchFileDataSource` (4).
- We add a `findParentSubjectURI` (5) utility to find a selected page's parent section.
- We move the `disableEverything( )` call to the login state, allowing the browser control buttons to function before a user logs in (6).

Our new *newssearch.xul* file looks like this:

```
<?xml-stylesheet href="NewsSearchStyles.css" type="text/css"?>

<window
  id="theMainWindow"
  title="Test Window"
  width="800"
  height="700"
  onload="initialize(event);"
  orient="horizontal"
  xmlns:html="http://www.w3.org/1999/xhtml"
  xmlns:xlink="http://www.w3.org/1999/xlink"
  xmlns=
   "http://www.mozilla.org/keymaster/gatekeeper/there.is.only.xul">

<script src="NewsSearch.js"/>
<script>
 <![CDATA[
```

```
editorLoaded = function(event) {
 dump("Ed loaded Event target,
  current target and phase are: " +
   event.target + "," + event.currentTarget + "," +
    event.eventPhase + "\n");
 };

     ]]>
</script>

 <!-- main top level container -->
<vbox flex="1" >

 <!-- horizontal container for all content (except status info) -->
 <hbox flex="1" >

 <!-- a container for some kind of list  -->
 <vbox flex="1" ondblclick="getTreeURL(event);">
<!-- buttons for changing RDF (1) -->
 <hbox pack="center">
       <button id="addLinkButton" label="Add" />
       <button id="removeLinkButton" label="Remove"/>
</hbox>

<tree datasources="" ref="" id="mainTree"
   seltype="single" flex="1">
  <treecols>
    <treecol  primary="true" label="Nickname" flex="1"/>
    <splitter class="tree-splitter"/>
    <treecol  label="Visits" flex="2"/>
  </treecols>

<template container="?currentContainer" member="?site">
    <rule  >
      <conditions>
        <content uri="?currentContainer"/>
        <member container="?currentContainer" child="?site"/>

        <triple subject="?site"
                predicate="http://www.mySites.com/rdf#nickname"
                object="?nickname"/>
        <triple subject="?site"
                predicate="http://www.mySites.com/rdf#url"
                object="?url"/>
        <triple subject="?site"
                predicate="http://www.mySites.com/rdf#hits"
                object="?hits"/>

      </conditions>
      <action>
        <treechildren>
          <treeitem uri="?site" myURL="?url">
            <treerow  >
              <treecell label="?nickname"/>
```

```
            <treecell label="?hits"/>
          </treerow>
        </treeitem>
      </treechildren>
    </action>
  </rule>
  <rule >
    <conditions>
      <content uri="?currentContainer"/>
      <member container="?currentContainer" child="?site"/>
      <triple subject="?site"
              predicate="http://www.mySites.com/rdf#nickname"
              object="?nickname"/>
    </conditions>
    <action>
      <treechildren>
        <treeitem  uri="?site" myURL="">
          <treerow properties="siteHeading" >
            <treecell label="?nickname"/>
            <treecell label="-"/>
          </treerow>
        </treeitem>
      </treechildren>
    </action>
  </rule>
</template></tree>

</vbox>

 <splitter resizebefore="closest" resizeafter="closest" state="open"/>
<!-- container for messages and tool areas -->
<vbox>

<!-- some simple controls to manage display pages -->
<hbox class="buttonArea">
 <button id="stepBackward"
  label="BACK" oncommand="stepPage(event);"/>
 <button id="stepForward"
  label="FORWARD" oncommand="stepPage(event);"/>
 <hbox >
  <vbox pack="center">
  <label control="theURL" value="URL:"/>
  </vbox>
  <textbox id="theURL" size="32" type="autocomplete"
        autocompletesearch="history"/>
  <button id="loadURL" label="GO" oncommand="loadURL( );"/>
 </hbox>

</hbox>
<!-- used to display message -->
<browser id="contentIFrame"
  type="content-primary" src="about:blank" flex="4">
</browser>
```

```
<splitter resizebefore="closest"
  resizeafter="closest" state="open"/>
<!-- used to display typing area  -->
<vbox flex="2" minheight="75" minwidth="100" >


<menubar id="editor-menubar"
  oncommand="doChangeFontStyle(event);">

  <menu id="font-menu" label="Font">
    <menupopup id="font-popup">

       <menu label="Family">
        <menupopup id="font-family-popup">
          <menuitem label="serif"/>
          <menuitem label="sans-serif"/>
          <menuitem label="monospace"/>
        </menupopup>
      </menu>

      <menu label="Size">
       <menupopup id="font-size-popup">
       <menuitem label="Bigger"/>
       <menuitem label="Smaller"/>
       </menupopup>
      </menu>

    </menupopup>
  </menu>

  <menuseparator/>
    <menu id="style-menu" label="Color">
         <menupopup id="font-color-popup">
         <menuitem label="Black"/>
         <menuitem label="Red"/>
         <menuitem label="Green"/>
         <menuitem label="Blue"/>
        </menupopup>
      </menu>

    <menuseparator/>

     <menu label="Style">

       <menupopup id="font-style-popup">

        <menu label="Face">
         <menupopup id="font-face-popup">
           <menuitem label="Normal"/>
           <menuitem label="Italic"/>
         </menupopup>
         </menu>
```

```
          <menu label="Weight">
            <menupopup id="font-weight-popup">
            <menuitem label="Normal"/>
            <menuitem label="Bold"/>
          </menupopup>
         </menu>

      </menupopup>

    </menu>

  </menubar>

  <editor id="memoEditor" flex="1"
    onclick="dump('ed clicked\n');"
     type="content" src="about:blank"
      class="typingArea">

</editor>
</vbox>

 <!-- used to display tool area-->
<hbox height="50" class="buttonArea">

 <spacer flex="1"/>

   <vbox id="vbox">
    <spacer flex="1"/>
     <hbox>
      <button id="newButton" label="New" />
      <button id="saveButton" label="Save"/>
      <button id="sendButton" label="Send"/>
      <button id="cancelButton" label="Cancel"/>
      <button id="loginButton" label="LOGIN"/>
     </hbox>
     <spacer flex="1"/>
   </vbox>

 <spacer flex="1"/>

</hbox>

</vbox>
<!-- container for messages and tool areas -->

</hbox>
<!-- horizontal container for all content (except status info) -->


 <hbox>
   <statusbar id="status-bar" >
     <statusbarpanel id="status-text" label="Waiting for login.">
```

```
      </statusbarpanel>
    </statusbar>

  </hbox>  <!-- main container -->
  </vbox>
</window>
```

Assembled, our complete source file, *newssearch.xul*, looks like this:

```
var K_XUL_NAMESPACE =
 "http://www.mozilla.org/keymaster/gatekeeper/there.is.only.xul";
//
// Some constants to help us know what
// buttons and editing areas to enable
//
var K_NOT_LOGGED_ON    = 0;  // no user, no note
var K_STARTUP          = 1;  // user, no note
var K_OPEN_NOTE        = 2;  // note ready for editing
var K_NOTE_IN_PROGRESS = 3; // note editing in progress

var G_ApplicationState = K_NOT_LOGGED_ON;
var G_TOC_Datasource;

var lastCommand = "";


function genericBtnHandler(event) {
try { // try block
var infoString = "Type = " + event.type + ",";
infoString += "Target = " + event.target + ",";
infoString += "Target.tagName = " + event.target.tagName + ",";
infoString += "Target.id = " + event.target.id + ",";
infoString += "Evt.phase = " + event.eventPhase + "."
dump(infoString + "\n");
switch(event.target.id) { // switch on target
case "newButton": {
  newNote();
  break;
 }
 case "saveButton": {
 // TBD
  break;
 }
case "sendButton": {
// TBD
  break;
 }
case "cancelButton": {
  cancelNote();
  break;
 }
case "loginButton": {
  openLoginWindow()
//  doLogin();
```

```
    break;
   }
 // 2
   case "addLinkButton": {
    addNewLink( );
    break;
   }
   case "removeLinkButton": {
    removeLink( );
    break;
   }
 } // switch on target
 } // try block
 catch (e) {
  alert("genericBtnHandler exception: " + e);
  }
 }

 function loadURL( ) {
 try{
 var newURL = document.getElementById("theURL").value;
 document.getElementById("contentIFrame").loadURI(newURL);
  }
  catch (e) {
  alert("Exception loading URL " + e);
  };
 };

 // Takes care of buttons and editing areas
 // based on global variable
 function updateInterface( ) {
 try{
 dump("In update interface with state = " + G_ApplicationState + "\n");

  switch(G_ApplicationState) { // switch on state
   case (K_NOT_LOGGED_ON): { // not logged on
   document.getElementById("loginButton").disabled=false;
 // 6
   disableEverything( );
   break;
   } // not logged on
   case (K_STARTUP): { // startup
   // enable only the new button
   document.getElementById("newButton").disabled=false;
   document.getElementById("contentIFrame").
        setAttribute("src","http://www.mozillazine.org");
   var theTree = document.getElementById("mainTree");
 // 3
   theTree.setAttribute("datasources",
      "file://localhost/Applications/Firefox.app/Contents/
        MacOS/chrome/NewsSearch/content/newssites.rdf");
   theTree.setAttribute("ref","http://www.mySites.com/TOC");
   theTree.builder.rebuild( );
```

```
 document.getElementById("addLinkButton").disabled=false;
 document.getElementById("removeLinkButton").disabled=false;

 break;
 } // startup
 case (K_OPEN_NOTE): { // note ready for editing
 // Make the memo area editable, and enable the cancel button
 // to give the user a way out
 var theEditor = document.getElementById("memoEditor");
 theEditor.makeEditable("html",false);
 theEditor.contentDocument.
   addEventListener("click",editorClicked,true);
 break;
 } // note ready for editing

 case (K_NOTE_IN_PROGRESS): { // note is/has been edited
 document.getElementById("saveButton").disabled=false;
 document.getElementById("sendButton").disabled=false;
 break;
 } // note is/has been edited

} // switch on state
}
catch(e) { //
alert("update interface exception " + e);
}//
}

// function turns off all buttons, disables
// note typing area
function disableEverything( ) {
document.getElementById("newButton").disabled=true;
document.getElementById("saveButton").disabled=true;
document.getElementById("sendButton").disabled=true;
document.getElementById("cancelButton").disabled=true;
document.getElementById("loginButton").disabled=true;
// 2
document.getElementById("addLinkButton").disabled=true;
document.getElementById("removeLinkButton").disabled=true;

}

function cancelNote( ) {
 G_ApplicationState = K_STARTUP;
 updateInterface( );
}

function newNote( ) {
G_ApplicationState = K_OPEN_NOTE;
updateInterface( );
}
```

```
function editorClicked(event) {
dump("Click event " + event.target +
  " window is " + window + " location = " +
    window.location.toString( ) +  "\n");
event.target.removeEventListener("click",editorClicked,true);
G_ApplicationState = K_NOTE_IN_PROGRESS;
updateInterface( );
};



function stepPage(event) {
 try {
  if (event.target.id == "stepBackward")
    document.getElementById("contentIFrame").goBack( );
  else
    document.getElementById("contentIFrame").goForward( );
 }
 catch (e) {
  alert("exception in stepPage " + e);
  }
}

var userName;
var password;

function openLoginWindow( ) {
 var lWindow = window.
   openDialog("chrome://newssearch/content/login.xul",
     "LOGON","chrome,modal",setUNPW);
 if ((userName != null) && (password != null))
  doLogin(userName,password);
  userName = null;
  password = null;
// doLogin('bugsbunny','wabbit');
}

function setUNPW(uN,pW) {
 userName=uN;
 password=pW;
}

function doLogin(uN,pW) {
try { // try
var theArgs = new Array;
theArgs[0] = new commandArg("un",uN);
theArgs[1] = new commandArg("pd",pW);
lastCommand = "login";
dump("Logging in with uname and pw = " + theArgs[0].value +
    "," + theArgs[1].value + "\n");
doServerRequest("login",theArgs);
 } // try
```

```
 catch (e) { //
  alert("doLogin exception: " + e);
 }//
}
//
// Dynamically assign our event handler properties
//
function initialize(event) {
try {
dump("initialize: Event target,
  current target and phase are: " +
   event.target + "," + event.currentTarget + "," +
    event.eventPhase + "\n");
if (event.target == document) { // target is the main window

 document.getElementById("newButton").addEventListener
   ("command",genericBtnHandler,true);
 document.getElementById("saveButton").addEventListener
   ("command",genericBtnHandler,true);
 document.getElementById("sendButton").addEventListener
    ("command",genericBtnHandler,true);
 document.getElementById("cancelButton").addEventListener
    ("command",genericBtnHandler,true);
 document.getElementById("loginButton").addEventListener
    ("command",genericBtnHandler,true);
// 2
 document.getElementById("addLinkButton").addEventListener
    ("command",genericBtnHandler,true);
 document.getElementById("removeLinkButton").addEventListener
    ("command",genericBtnHandler,true);
 //

G_ApplicationState = K_NOT_LOGGED_ON;
  // will change to NOT LOGGED ON LATER
updateInterface();
  }  // target is the main window
 } // try
 catch (e) {
  alert ("Exception: " + e);
   }
};


function doChangeFontStyle(event) {
try {

 var atomService =
  Components.classes["@mozilla.org/atom-service;1"].
    getService(Components.interfaces.nsIAtomService);

 var theEditor = document.getElementById("memoEditor").
     getHTMLEditor(document.getElementById("memoEditor").
        contentWindow);
```

```
  var newValue = event.target.label.toLowerCase( );

  switch(event.target.parentNode.id) { // switch on the menu

   case "font-size-popup": {
   if (event.target.label == "Bigger")
     theEditor.increaseFontSize( );
     else theEditor.decreaseFontSize( );
   break;
   }
   case "font-family-popup": {
    theEditor.
     setCSSInlineProperty(atomService.
    getAtom("span"),"style","font-family:" + newValue);
    break;
   }
    case "font-color-popup": {
    theEditor.setCSSInlineProperty(atomService.
     getAtom("span"),"style","color:" + newValue);
    break;
    }

   case "font-face-popup": {
    theEditor.
    setCSSInlineProperty(atomService.
     getAtom("span"),"style","font-style:" + newValue);
    break;
    }

    case "font-weight-popup": {
    theEditor.
    setCSSInlineProperty(atomService.
      getAtom("span"),"style","font-weight:" + newValue);
    break;
    }

  } // switch on the menu
 }
 catch (e) {
 dump("doChangeFontStyle exception " + e );
 }
}



function loginOK( ) {
 G_ApplicationState = K_STARTUP;
 updateInterface( );
}


function commandArg(argKey,argValue) {
 this.key = argKey;
 this.value = argValue;
}
```

```
function loginFail() {
 alert("Sorry, user not authenticated.");
 }

//
//  CreateServerRequest
//
var theServerRequest;
//
// commandArgs is an array of arguments, each element
// is converted into a PHP POST field
function doServerRequest(commandString,commandArgs) {
 theServerRequest = new XMLHttpRequest();
 var theString ="http://localhost/doCommand.php?" +
   "&command=" + commandString + "&";
 for (var i = 0; i < commandArgs.length; i++)
 { // build remaining parameters
   theString += commandArgs[i].key +
     "=" + commandArgs[i].value ;
  if (i != (commandArgs.length-1)) theString += "&";
 } // build remaining parameters
 theServerRequest.onreadystatechange = retrieveServerResponse;
 theServerRequest.open("GET",theString,true);
 dump("About to send " + theString + "\n");
 theServerRequest.send(null);
//  dump("Server request status ="
//     + theServerRequest.status + "\n");
//   dump("Server request response =" +
//          theServerRequest.responseText + "\n");
}


function retrieveServerResponse() {

try {

 dump("server response ready state = " +
   theServerRequest.readyState + "\n");

 if (theServerRequest.readyState == 4) { // all done

  dump("Server request status =" + theServerRequest.status + "\n");
  // Check return code
   if (theServerRequest.status == 200)
   { // request terminated OK
    dump("Received from server: " +
     theServerRequest.responseText + "\n");

    //
    var theResults =
     theServerRequest.responseText.split(",");
    //
```

```
      var rCode = (theResults[0].
        substring((theResults[0].indexOf("=")+1),
                theResults[0].length)).toLowerCase( );

      if (lastCommand == "login") { // process login command

       if (rCode == "true")
        { // everything OK, we know next parameter is
                // session info
        var lastSession = "Last login was ";
        lastSession += (theResults[1].
            substring((theResults[1].indexOf("=")+1),
              theResults[1].length)).toLowerCase( );
        loginOK( );
        setStatusText(lastSession);

       } // everthing OK
       else { // user NG
        loginFail( );
        setStatusText("No user logged in");
       } // user NG

      } // process login command


    } // request terminated OK
    else { // something is wrong
     alert("Response failed.");
    } // something is wrong
   } // all done
   } // try
   catch (e) {
   alert("Retrieve response exception: " + e);
   dump (e);
   }
}

function setStatusText(theText) {
document.getElementById("status-text").
  setAttribute("label",theText);
};

 function getTreeURL(event) {
  var theTree = document.getElementById("mainTree");
  var tI = theTree.currentIndex;

   var theURL = theTree.contentView.getItemAtIndex(tI).
      getAttribute("myURL");

   if (theURL != "")  {
      document.getElementById("theURL").value = theURL;
        loadURL( );
      }
   }
```

```
 //
 // Get the URIs for the page and its section
 // name, display to user before removing. If the selection
 // is a heading, it will be removed ONLY if there are no
 // children (contents) in the section
 //
// 2
function removeLink() {

 var theTree = document.getElementById("mainTree");
 var tI = theTree.currentIndex;
 if (tI == -1) return;

  //
 // Now look for the parent section heading.

var thePageSubjectURI =
  theTree.contentView.getItemAtIndex(tI).id;
 var theSectionSubjectURI = null;
 resultNode = null;

 findParentSubjectURI(theTree.contentView.getItemAtIndex(tI));
 if (resultNode != null) theSectionSubjectURI = resultNode.id;
  else theSectionSubjectURI = "http://www.mySites.com/TOC";

 var sectionLabel =
  theSectionSubjectURI.
   substring(theSectionSubjectURI.lastIndexOf("/")+1);
 var pageLabel =
  thePageSubjectURI.
   substring(thePageSubjectURI.lastIndexOf("/")+1);
 var message =
  "Remove " + pageLabel + " from section " + sectionLabel + "?";

 window.
  openDialog("chrome://newssearch/content/confirmDialog.xul",
   "?","chrome,modal",message,OkCancelCallback);

 if (OkCancelDialogRetVal == "CANCEL") return;
 removeResource(theSectionSubjectURI,thePageSubjectURI);

}

var resultNode;

// 5
function findParentSubjectURI(searchNode) {
if ((resultNode == null) && (searchNode.parentNode != null)) {
  if (searchNode.parentNode.id != null) {
   if (searchNode.parentNode.id.indexOf("www.mySites.com") != -1) {
     resultNode = searchNode.parentNode;
     return;
     }
```

```
    else findParentSubjectURI(searchNode.parentNode);
   }

  }
 else return;
 }


 var OkCancelDialogRetVal = -1;

 function OkCancelCallback (retVal) {
  OkCancelDialogRetVal = retVal;
 }
 // 2
 function addNewLink( ) {
  sectionResource = null;
  sectionResource = null;
  nickName = null;
  openSectionSelection( );
  if ((sectionResource != null) && (nickName != null))
      addNewResource(sectionResource,nickName);
 };

 var sectionResource;
 var nickName;
 var makeNewSection;

 function openSectionSelection( ) {
  var lWindow =
    window.
      openDialog("chrome://newssearch/content/headingSel.xul",
       "SECTIONS","chrome,modal",setSection);
 }

 function setSection(res,name,createSection) {
  sectionResource = res;
  nickName = name;
  makeNewSection = createSection;
 }

 // 4
 function fetchFileDatasource( ) {
  var retVal = null;
  var theTree = document.getElementById("mainTree");

  var dSources = theTree.database.GetDataSources( );

  while (dSources.hasMoreElements( ) && (retVal == null)) {
    var dS = dSources.getNext( );
    dS = dS.QueryInterface(Components.interfaces.nsIRDFDataSource );
    if (dS.URI.indexOf("newssites") != -1) retVal = dS;
    }
   return retVal;
   }
```

```
//
// Create the new resource and add it as a child
// to the selected container
//
function addNewResource(sectionURI,newNickName) {
try {

alert("adding " + newNickName + " to " + sectionURI);
 var theTree = document.getElementById("mainTree");
 var dataSource = fetchFileDatasource( );

 if (dataSource == null) {
  alert("No file datasource found");
  return;
  }

 // fetch services to work with RDF and manage containers
 //
 var rdfService =
  Components.classes["@mozilla.org/rdf/rdf-service;1"].
   getService(Components.interfaces.nsIRDFService);

 var theSectionContainer =
    Components.classes["@mozilla.org/rdf/container;1"].
      createInstance(Components.interfaces.nsIRDFContainer);

 var containerTools =
    Components.classes["@mozilla.org/rdf/container-utils;1"].
      getService(Components.interfaces.nsIRDFContainerUtils);

 var theSubject =
  rdfService.GetResource("http://www.mySites.com/" + newNickName);

  var thePredicateNickname =
   rdfService.GetResource("http://www.mySites.com/rdf#nickname");
  var theNickName =
    rdfService.GetLiteral(newNickName);

  var thePredicateURL =
   rdfService.GetResource("http://www.mySites.com/rdf#url");
  var theURL =
    rdfService.GetLiteral(document.getElementById("theURL").value);

  var thePredicateHits =
   rdfService.GetResource("http://www.mySites.com/rdf#hits");
  var theHits =
    rdfService.GetLiteral(0);

  // If section URI has 'TOC' in it,
  // we must be creating a new section
  // heading container
```

```
   if (sectionURI.indexOf("www.mySites.com/TOC") != -1)
    { // creating a heading (container)
      alert("Creating new container");
      containerTools.MakeSeq(dataSource,theSubject);
   } // creating a heading

   dataSource.
     Assert(theSubject,thePredicateNickname,theNickName,true);

   if (!(containerTools.
     IsContainer(dataSource,theSubject))) { // add properties
    dataSource.Assert(theSubject,thePredicateURL,theURL,true);
    dataSource.Assert(theSubject,thePredicateHits,theHits,true);
   } // add properties

// Add the newly created triple to our section heading
     var theSectionHeading = rdfService.GetResource(sectionURI);

     alert("sec heading is " + sectionURI + "," + theSectionHeading);
     theSectionContainer.Init(dataSource,theSectionHeading);
     theSectionContainer.AppendElement(theSubject);

// OK, write back to file....
//
     dataSource =
     dataSource.
       QueryInterface(Components.interfaces.nsIRDFRemoteDataSource);
     dataSource.Flush( );
     dataSource.Refresh(false);

  }
 catch (e) {
  alert("exception in addNewResource " + e);
 }

}

//
// remove the resource unless it is a heading and has
// children --- give user a message if cannot remove
//
//
function removeResource(sectionURI,resourceURI) {
try {

var theTree = document.getElementById("mainTree");
var dataSource = fetchFileDatasource( );

 if (dataSource == null) {
  alert("No file datasource found");
  return;
 }
```

```
// Get services to manage RDF and to help with container utilities
var rdfService =
   Components.classes["@mozilla.org/rdf/rdf-service;1"].
         getService(Components.interfaces.nsIRDFService);

 var theSectionContainer =
    Components.classes["@mozilla.org/rdf/container;1"].
      createInstance(Components.interfaces.nsIRDFContainer);

  var containerTools =
     Components.classes["@mozilla.org/rdf/container-utils;1"].
        getService(Components.interfaces.nsIRDFContainerUtils);

  var theSubject = rdfService.GetResource(resourceURI);
  //
  // Check to see whether the subject is a container, and if so,
  // make sure it's empty
  //
  var theSectionHeading = rdfService.GetResource(sectionURI);
  theSectionContainer.Init(dataSource,theSectionHeading);

 if (containerTools.IsContainer(dataSource,theSubject)) {
  // removing section heading
  // Bail out if the section isn't empty
  if (!(containerTools.IsEmpty(dataSource,theSubject)))
   { // not empty
   alert("All content pages must be removed first.");
   return;
  } // not empty
 } // removing section heading

 // Build resources for all the predicates that we know of
 var thePredicateNickname = rdfService.GetResource
      ("http://www.mySites.com/rdf#nickname");
 var thePredicateURL =
  rdfService.GetResource("http://www.mySites.com/rdf#url");
 var thePredicateHits =
  rdfService.GetResource("http://www.mySites.com/rdf#hits");

  // Fetch the RDF statements for each property and remove that resource
 var theTarget =
  dataSource.GetTarget(theSubject,thePredicateNickname,true);
 dataSource.
  Unassert(theSubject,thePredicateNickname,theTarget,true);

 // Remove the other properties for non-section heading resources
  if (!(containerTools.IsContainer(dataSource,theSubject)))
   { // remove page properties
   theTarget = dataSource.GetTarget(theSubject,thePredicateURL,true);
   dataSource.
     Unassert(theSubject,thePredicateURL,theTarget,true);
```

```
        theTarget =
           dataSource.GetTarget(theSubject,thePredicateHits,true);
        dataSource.
          Unassert(theSubject,thePredicateHits,theTarget,true);
      } // remove page properties

      theSectionContainer.RemoveElement(theSubject,true);
    //
    // Write back to file....
    //
        dataSource =
        dataSource.
         QueryInterface(Components.interfaces.nsIRDFRemoteDataSource);
        dataSource.Flush( );
        dataSource.Refresh(false);
      }
     catch (e) {
      alert("exception in addNewResource " + e);
      }
    }
```

Figure 6-14 shows a snapshot of what the application looks like when you add a new section heading.

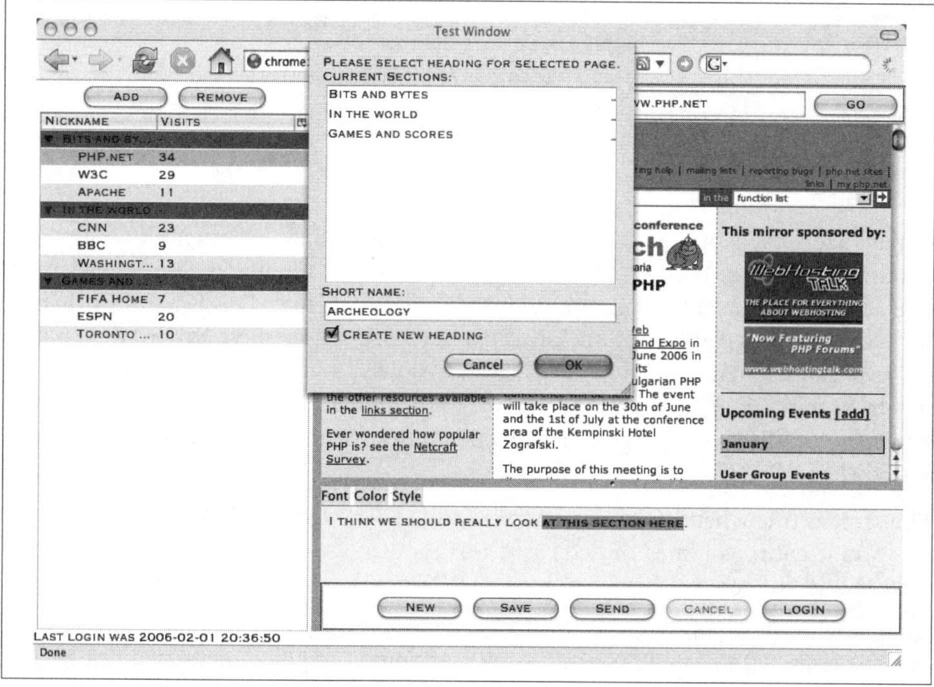

Figure 6-14. RDF content selector and editor

Summary

Table 6-4 summarizes the RDF interfaces and functions used in this exercise.

Table 6-4. Modifying RDF containers

Interface method or property	Description
`database.GetDataSources();`	Returns an enumerator of available datasources
`dataSources.getNext()`	Returns the next datasource from the enumerator
`dataSource.URI`	The URI used to create the RDF datasource
`rdfService.GetResource("someResourceURI");`	Creates and returns an RDF resource with the subject specified by the passed parameter URI
`dataSource.Assert(subjectResource, predicateResource,objectResource,true);`	Creates an RDF statement (triple) with the given subject, predicate, and object
`dataSource.GetTarget(subjectResource, predicateResource,true)`	Returns the RDF resource for the target (property) pointed to by the given subject and predicate resources
`dataSource.Unassert(subjectResource, predicateResource,targetResource,true);`	Removes an RDF statement (triple) from the datasource
`containerTools.IsContainer(dataSource, subjectResource)`	Returns `true` if the `subjectResource` is a container in the given datasource
`aContainer. Init(dataSource,subjectResource);`	Initializes (binds) a specific resource to a container interface
`aContainer.AppendElement(subjectResource);`	Adds an RDF statement to a container
`aContainer.RemoveElement(subjectResource, true);`	Removes an RDF statement from a container
`dataSource.Flush();`	Writes the RDF graph back to a file

It may take some work getting used to templates. If you are experienced with procedural software, you may find the declarative nature of templates (especially taking into account their recursive nature) to be a bit of a challenge. This is particularly true because templates can be notoriously difficult to debug. The best advice when building applications that use templates is to start slowly, gradually moving template triples from the "outer" layers of an interface to the more detailed inner layers (e.g., use a template to display the topmost container before writing triples to display heavily nested elements).

The same is true when RDF containers are added. The topic of RDF is broad enough to warrant entire volumes of dedicated text, and the seemingly laborious nature of tasks to add and remove elements from an RDF graph may discourage novice users.

Some applications simply need to display data and options that are more complex than the simple list models available in HTML. Other applications need to internally represent and manipulate complex data relationships without ready access to a "formal" database engine. For such projects, RDF's capability to create in-memory graphs and Firefox's tools to display such relationships in a GUI provide developers with a powerful tool for a concise, efficient design.

CHAPTER 7

DOM Manipulation and Input/Output

Internet applications that involve user interaction beyond simple button pushing may eventually need to capture and create portions of documents. Although XUL provides a simple `<textbox>` tag for unformatted text entry, we have seen how more advanced widgets such as the `<editor>` allow for an interface experience with richer formatting and appearance options.

This chapter puts the finishing touches on our NewsSearch note-taking application and focuses on the techniques for extracting content from web sites and either saving or forwarding references to other users. These requirements involve the following topics:

- The use of selection, range, and insertion points to move selected document content between frames
- Accessing the local filesystem
- Dynamic creation of Document Object Model (DOM) nodes to allow addition of styling information
- Using event handlers to add programmatic logic to newly created document elements
- Adding interaction with the user's email application

A Design Review

Our initial design review suggested a "copy and insert" type of application that would allow a user to select portions of a document and automatically build a citation that extracts the selected text, inserts it into the user's notebook entry, and constructs the elements of the citation that are added to the end of the notebook entry. These elements include a quote, a numeric prefix annotation to point to the footnote reference, and the electronic reference itself. Figure 7-1 summarizes the key elements of the interface.

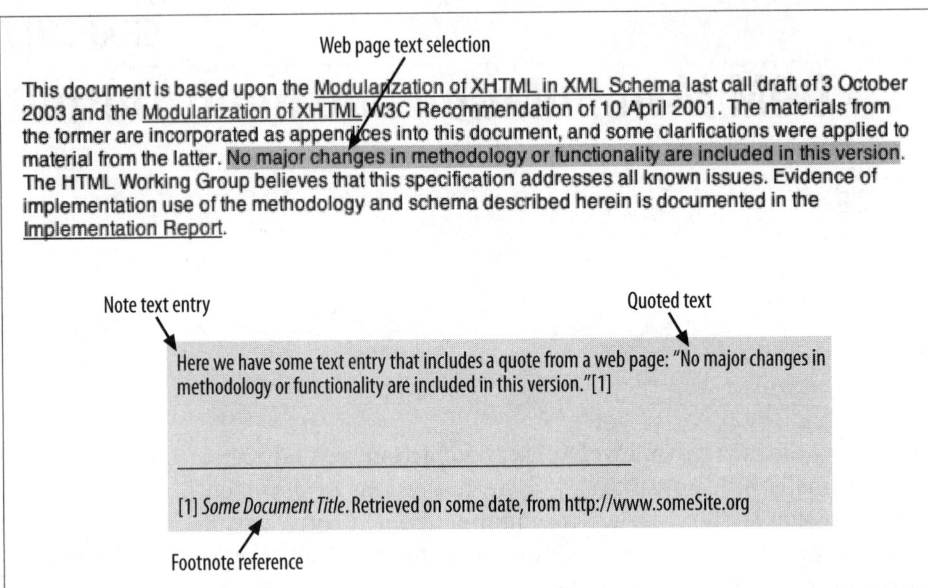

Figure 7-1. Design mockup for citations

We look at the three stages of this phase:

- The techniques used to select and extract a passage to be cited
- The techniques used to modify a document to create the appropriate reference
- The disposal of the note document, either as an external file or as part of a message

We will start by reviewing how to select content within the main browser view.

Browser Elements

We have, to this point, focused on the basic XUL widgets such as buttons, boxes, and trees. But the Firefox framework also makes available to developers a family of elements that offer much higher levels of functionality and utility. These *browser elements* wrap a programming interface around the most complex web objects: windows and documents.

Properties and Native Wrappers

Web content in XUL applications is often displayed through a `<browser>` element. As a specialized display frame, a browser can render web pages and support methods to reload recently viewed documents. The view hierarchy for our primary content is as follows:

- The <browser> is the top container for content.
- The contentWindow property references the content's top-level window.
- The contentDocument property references the object containing the DOM representation of the HTML document.

For circumstances in which a designer wants to trigger behaviors based on a browser's access to specially designed pages (pages that include scripts to communicate to top-level windows—and scripts—through window properties), the designer needs to be aware of Firefox's security restrictions.

Scripts requesting a browser's properties, such as contentWindow and contentDocument, may actually receive *wrappers* for the window and document.

If, for example, we attach an onload event handler to the browser frame:

```
<browser id="contentIFrame"
  type="content-primary" onload="browserLoaded(event);"
   src="about:blank" flex="4">
 </browser>
```

and dump the contentWindow and contentDocument properties with the following statement:

```
function browserLoaded(event) {
var theWindow = event.currentTarget.contentWindow;
var htmlDoc = event.currentTarget.contentDocument;
dump("Event received in " + event.currentTarget.tagName +
   ", doc is " + htmlDoc + " shown in window " + theWindow + "\n");
}
```

we would see the following on the console:

```
Event received in browser, doc is
[object XPCNativeWrapper [object HTMLDocument]]
shown in window  [object XPCNativeWrapper [object Window]]
```

These *native wrappers* are additional security measures that the Firefox framework adds.

Firefox considers any code to be *privileged*, or scripts to be *protected*, if such code originates from a chrome URL, or if the code or script acquires privileges through API calls to services approved by a user after some form of dialog prompt. Privileged code and protected scripts have unencumbered access to all browser resources.

Similarly, windows may be considered *trusted* or *untrusted*. Trust is implied for windows that are top-level XUL windows, windows launched from a command line with a chrome URL prefix, or windows embedded in a XUL display panel (iframe, browser) without a type of content or content-primary.

XPCNativeWrappers exist to insulate protected scripts (that have access to all browser resources) from potentially malicious properties and methods attached to untrusted windows.

Firefox creates XPCNativeWrappers to expose only object properties that are defined in that object's Cross-Platform Component Model (XPCOM) IDL (the descriptor language used to define an object's properties and methods when Firefox is built). If, for example, a script in an untrusted window attached its own property (someUntrustedWindow.aCustomProperty), that custom property would not be visible to a protected script. In this way, there is no mechanism to allow a malicious script embedded in browser content to replace or override a property that would otherwise be accessed by a script with full browser privileges.

If the designer chooses, a protected script could override the security wrapper by accessing the wrappedJSObject property someUnstrustedWindow.wrappedJSObject.aCustomProperty, but this technique is generally discouraged unless the application has strict control over the content being displayed.

In the case of our chrome application, the scripts requesting such properties are considered protected, and the wrapper can be used transparently.

Selection and Range Objects

When a user drags a mouse over window content, the Firefox framework keeps track of the selections through a collection of *range* objects.

A document that complies with the DOM organizes the display as a tree of nodes, each node being an in-memory representation of the XHTML tags present in the document text.

A window's getSelection( ) method returns the collection of ranges that identify the node, and the offsets within the node that are included in the selection. (Most applications use only the first range of a selection.)

Figure 7-2 illustrates how a simple document selection maps to range offsets.

The container for selected text will always be the document's text node. Selection objects predictably support a toString( ) method that returns only the text string of a selection.

To see how this works programmatically, we use the event handler on the browser to attach a mouseup event listener to the window, and use that listener to display information about the window's selection.

We make the following changes to the browser in *newssearch.js*:

```
function browserLoaded(event) {
var theWindow = event.currentTarget.contentWindow;
var htmlDoc = event.currentTarget.contentDocument;
theWindow.addEventListener("mouseup",doMouseUp,true);
}

function doMouseUp(event) {
 dump("mouseup event target is " + event.currentTarget + "\n");
```

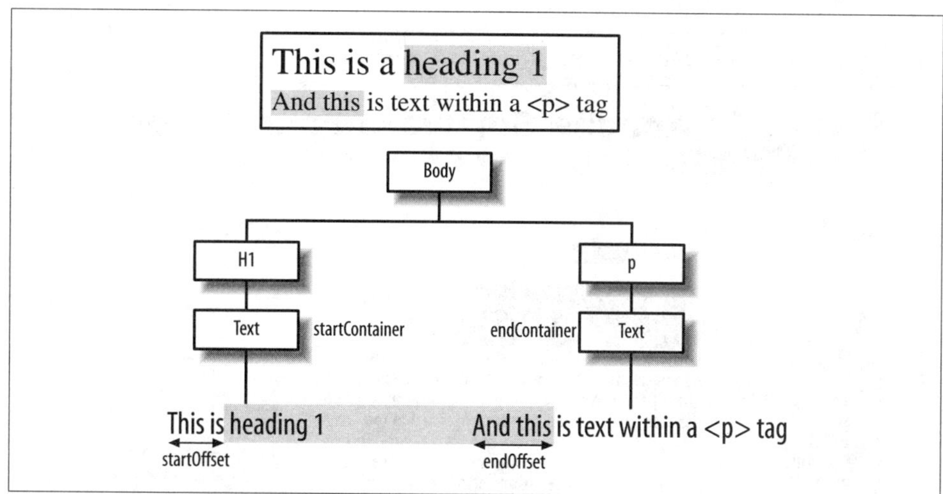

Figure 7-2. DOM selection range

```
    var theSel = event.currentTarget.getSelection( );
    var sRange = theSel.getRangeAt(0);
    dump("Start container start offset = " +
      sRange.startContainer + "," +
        sRange.startContainer.parentNode.tagName +
          "," + sRange.startOffset + "\n");
    dump("End container end offset = " +
          sRange.endContainer + "," +
             sRange.endContainer.parentNode.tagName + "," +
               sRange.endOffset + "\n");
    dump("Selection is " + theSel.toString( ) + "\n");
  }
```

The `event.currentTarget` property is presumed to reference the window to which the listener was attached. We also use the range container's `parentNode` property to display information on the tag enclosing the selected text. Figure 7-3 illustrates a selection in the application window.

After the selection has been made, the console displays the selection information:

```
mouseup event target is [object XPCNativeWrapper [object Window]]
Start container start offset = [object XPCNativeWrapper [object Text]],A,4
End container end offset = [object XPCNativeWrapper [object Text]],P,105
Selection is ome!

The Apache Software Foundation provides support for the Apache community of open-
source software projects
```

We can use the unmodified Firefox browser to view the same document. The View → Page Source menu displays the document source and allows us to compare the document tags with those reported through the range properties, verifying the `<a>` element as the tag for the starting container, and `<p>` as the selection's ending container.

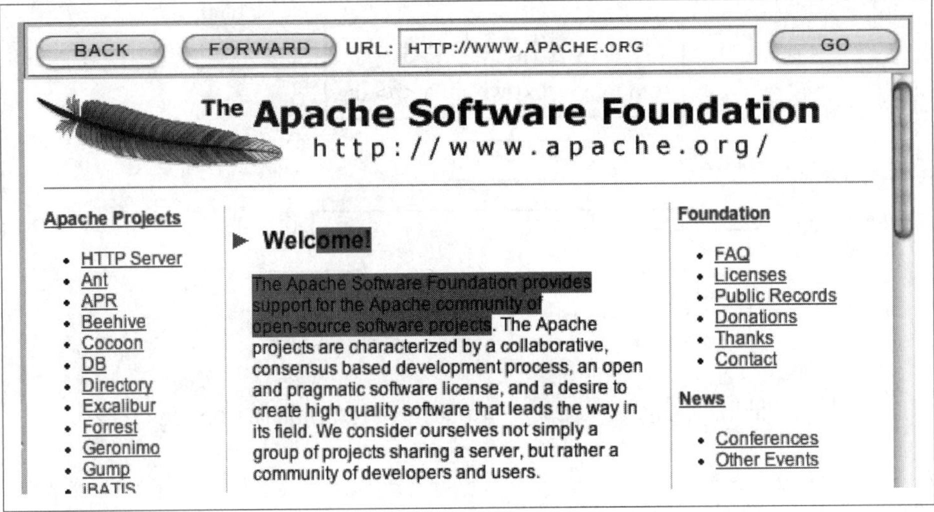

Figure 7-3. Document selection

Manipulating Selections and Ranges

Window selections allow a user to select document elements from one application "space" for use in a different portion or different operation of the application. Selection objects have a number of properties to facilitate movement of the selected text into different frames and windows, including our `<editor>` frame.

The `selection`'s `range` objects infer the presence of an *insertion point*—a position into which new (or copied) content is to be placed. The `range`'s `insertNode()` method, for example, will insert newly created document nodes at the range's insertion point defined by the range's starting boundary.

For cases when a user simply clicks the mouse within document content (without dragging across the content), the selection will return a range in which the starting point is the same as the ending point. Under these circumstances, the range is said to be collapsed; calling `insertNode()` will result in the document content being added at the point where the user clicked the mouse.

The `range` object includes methods that make document manipulation fairly straightforward.

To add simple text, text nodes are created and inserted into the range:

```
var newTextNode = document.createTextNode("someText");
someRange.insertNode(newTextNode);
```

After such an operation, it is advisable to call the *normalize* method of the text nodes' parent node; the normalize operation removes the extraneous boundaries between adjacent text nodes, merging the text into a single child text node.

Adding text to the end of the document is a matter of finding the top content node (such as the document's body node), and calling that element's `appendChild` method.

We can summarize the sequence for creating the citation in our note editor as follows:

- Develop the mechanism to track the number of citations to allow for numbering of footnotes.
- When adding the text selected in the content window, add quotation marks to the beginning of the quoted text.
- Add code to allow the user the option of inserting a simple citation or a citation with quoted text.

Now that we know what to do with text to be inserted into the editor document, we can focus on actually moving the text from the content frame into the editor frame.

Moving Text Between Frames

The simplest way to trigger the transfer of text selected in an application's content window into our note editor window is with an explicit menu command. (This allows the application to work without unnecessary interference with existing clipboard cut-and-paste logic.)

The menu items allow you to choose between inserting a citation with only a numeric annotation to a specific footnote reference, and including a complete quote of the selection with the numeric annotation.

The display of a citation will link the numeric annotation to a footer area at the bottom of the document. This area will contain a specialized <p> element that we will assign to a "footnote" class.

This footnote class will consist of the following:

- The top-level <p> element to allow for line breaks between footnotes
- A numeric link to the citation's annotation in the note's body text
- An italicized segment to highlight the title of the document
- Unformatted text to describe the date of access and URI

Following is the *newssearch.xul* segment with the menu changes to the editor frame. Take particular note of the `doInsertText` function's management of two separate selections—one for the content window and the other for the editor window:

```
<menubar id="editor-menubar" oncommand="doChangeFontStyle(event);">
  <menu id="font-menu" label="Font">
    <menupopup id="font-popup">
       <menu label="Family">
        <menupopup id="font-family-popup">
          <menuitem label="serif"/>
          <menuitem label="sans-serif"/>
```

```
            <menuitem label="monospace"/>
          </menupopup>
        </menu>
        <menu label="Size">
         <menupopup id="font-size-popup">
         <menuitem label="Bigger"/>
         <menuitem label="Smaller"/>
         </menupopup>
        </menu>
      </menupopup>
    </menu>
    <menuseparator/>
      <menu id="style-menu" label="Color">
           <menupopup id="font-color-popup">
             <menuitem label="Black"/>
             <menuitem label="Red"/>
             <menuitem label="Green"/>
             <menuitem label="Blue"/>
           </menupopup>
        </menu>
     <menuseparator/>
      <menu label="Style">
        <menupopup id="font-style-popup">
         <menu label="Face">
          <menupopup id="font-face-popup">
            <menuitem label="Normal"/>
            <menuitem label="Italic"/>
          </menupopup>
          </menu>
          <menu label="Weight">
            <menupopup id="font-weight-popup">
            <menuitem label="Normal"/>
            <menuitem label="Bold"/>
          </menupopup>
         </menu>
       </menupopup>
    </menu>
    <menuseparator/>
    <menu oncommand="doInsertText(event);" label="Cite...">
     <menupopup id="insert-type-popup">
     <menuitem label="Quote and reference"/>
     <menuitem label="Reference only"/>
     </menupopup>
    </menu>
  </menubar>
```

The source file *newssearch.js* has the doInsertText function added:

```
// --------------------------------------
// New code for citing selection
//
function doInsertText(event) {
try {
```

```
    var cF = document.getElementById("contentIFrame");

// Get some references to content elements
//
    var cW = cF.contentWindow;
    var cD = cF.contentDocument;
    var cTitle = cD.title ;
    // Let's do some groundwork and see how many 'footnotes'
    // we already have in the note (1)
    var eD = document.getElementById("memoEditor").contentDocument;
    var paragraphs = eD.getElementsByTagName("p");
    var footnoteCount = 0;

    for (var i = 0; i < paragraphs.length; i++) {
     if (paragraphs[i].hasAttribute("class"))
       if ( paragraphs[i].getAttribute("class") == "footnote") footnoteCount++;
     }
    // pop counter to this footnote entry
    footnoteCount++;

// Add full quote if requested, otherwise only the numeric
// annotation (2)
//
    var quoteString = "";
    if (event.target.label == "Quote and reference")
      quoteString += "\"" + cW.getSelection().toString( ) + "\"";
    var insertedNode = eD.createTextNode(quoteString + "[" +
        footnoteCount + "] ");

    // Remove the newly created text node by normalizing
    // parent (3)
    var editorSelection = document.getElementById("memoEditor").
        contentWindow.getSelection( );
    var selectedRange = editorSelection.getRangeAt(0);
    selectedRange.insertNode(insertedNode);

    selectedRange.startContainer.parentNode.normalize( );

    // If this is first footnote, add horizontal rule
    //
    if (footnoteCount == 1 ) { // add the HR
      var newHR = eD.createElement("hr");
      eD.body.appendChild(newHR);
    }

    // Create footnote node as a paragraph with a specialized
    // class name (4)
    var footnoteNode = eD.createElement("p");
    footnoteNode.setAttribute("class","footnote");

    // Add reference number
    footnoteNode.appendChild(eD.createTextNode("[" + footnoteCount + "]"));
    // The title will be an italicized text node
```

```
        var styledTitleNode = eD.createElement("i");
        styledTitleNode.appendChild(eD.createTextNode(cTitle + ". "));
        footnoteNode.appendChild(styledTitleNode);
        //
        // Now information on the source
        //
        var accessInfo = "Retrieved on " + Date() + " from " + cW.location.toString( );
        footnoteNode.appendChild(eD.createTextNode(accessInfo));

        // finally, attach footnote to document body
        eD.body.appendChild(footnoteNode);

        } // try
        catch (e) {
        alert("Exception: " + e);
        }
    }
```

After saving a few references to content window elements, the function looks for a specialized paragraph element that has our class attribute of `footnote`. That search allows us to keep track of the numeric annotation that will link the note text to the footnote reference (1).

The function then looks at the label attribute attached to the menu item that generated the event (the `event.target` property) to determine whether we want to build a quote, or simply keep a numeric annotation (2).

The editor's selection is obtained to determine where to insert the text from the quote, and after being added to the note text area, the normalize method is called on the parent node to merge the newly created text node with the selection (3).

Finally, the footnote reference is created, consisting of the numeric cross-reference, an italicized title string, and the information on the quote's date of retrieval and web site (4). The results of these changes show a sample citation, as in Figure 7-4.

Table 7-1 summarizes the properties and methods emphasized in this section.

Table 7-1. Properties and methods in note manipulation

Property/Method	Description
`window.getSelection( )`	Returns collection of selected node `ranges`
`selection.getRangeAt(`*`index`*`)`	Returns a specific `range` object
`range.collapsed`	Returns TRUE if starting and ending points of a range are the same
`document.createTextNode("`*`some text`*`")`	Creates a text node with the specified string as content
`range.insertNode(`*`someNewNode`*`)`	Inserts a node within a range before the point specified by the range's end `container` and end `offset` properties
`parentNode.appendChild(`*`someNewNode`*`)`	Appends a newly created node as the last child of the parent
`parentNode.normalize( )`	Normalizes a parent node to remove redundant data structures from adjacent like nodes

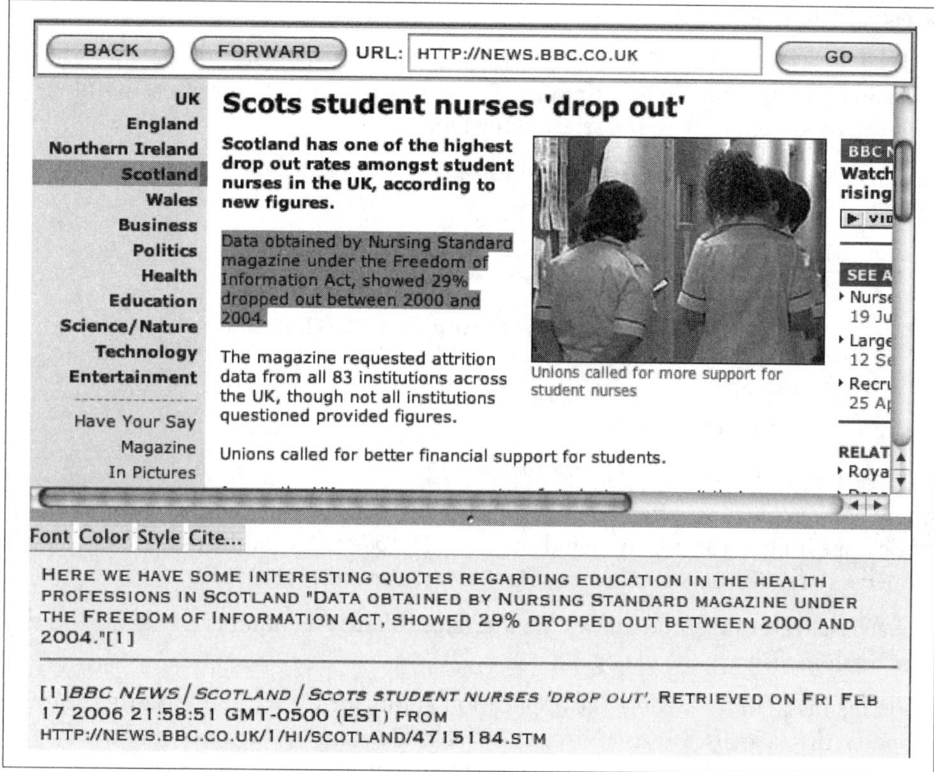

BACK
FORWARD
URL: HTTP://NEWS.BBC.CO.UK
GO
UK
England
Northern Ireland
Scotland
Wales
Business
Politics
Health
Education
Science/Nature
Technology
Entertainment
Have Your Say
Magazine
In Pictures
Scots student nurses 'drop out'
Scotland has one of the highest drop out rates amongst student nurses in the UK, according to new figures.
Data obtained by Nursing Standard magazine under the Freedom of Information Act, showed 29% dropped out between 2000 and 2004.
The magazine requested attrition data from all 83 institutions across the UK, though not all institutions questioned provided figures.
Unions called for better financial support for students.
Unions called for more support for student nurses
Font Color Style Cite...
HERE WE HAVE SOME INTERESTING QUOTES REGARDING EDUCATION IN THE HEALTH PROFESSIONS IN SCOTLAND "DATA OBTAINED BY NURSING STANDARD MAGAZINE UNDER THE FREEDOM OF INFORMATION ACT, SHOWED 29% DROPPED OUT BETWEEN 2000 AND 2004."[1]
[1]BBC NEWS | SCOTLAND | SCOTS STUDENT NURSES 'DROP OUT'. RETRIEVED ON FRI FEB 17 2006 21:58:51 GMT-0500 (EST) FROM HTTP://NEWS.BBC.CO.UK/1/HI/SCOTLAND/4715184.STM

Figure 7-4. Selection and citation

Exporting Note Document Content

Having a note with references to important content sections is not a useful feature unless the note can somehow be saved or shared with others. Next we examine the steps to save a note to an external file.

File Services

To extract the contents of a note for saving to the local filesystem, three services are relevant:

`nsIFilePicker`
: Provides a file selection dialog box

`nsILocalFile`
: Provides interface methods to the local filesystem

`nsIFileOutputStream`
: Provides simplified output services that connect application software to the file interface

Selecting a destination file

A designer uses the nsIFilePicker interface to prompt the user to select a destination directory and file creation mode. The designer can also specify a file filter to limit the filesystem view to the selected file type.

In this case, we will assume that the editor document will be HTML document types. The resulting sequence is:

```
var filePickerInterface = Components.interfaces.nsIFilePicker;
 var fileSelector = Components.classes["@mozilla.org/filepicker;1"]
        .createInstance(filePickerInterface);
 fileSelector.init(window, "Select a destination", filePickerInterface.modeSave);
 fileSelector.appendFilters(filePickerInterface.filterHTML);
 fileSelector.show( );
```

The init method is of the form:

```
init(parentView, promptText, fileMode)
```

where *parentView* most often refers to the application's parent window; *promptText* is a title appearing in the prompt window; and *fileMode* is one of the nsIFileSelector's properties of modeOpen, modeSave, modeGetFolder, or modeOpenMultiple.

The appendFilters method allows the interface to add any number of filters, and the show method displays the dialog.

Upon dismissal of the dialog, the application audits for the nsIFilePicker's returnOK property that signals the user's selection of a file, after which the interface's file property returns a reference to an nsILocalFile interface to the local filesystem:

```
if (fileSelector.show( ) == filePickerInterface.returnOK) {
   var selectedFile = fileSelector.file;
```

Finally, an instance of an nsIFileOutputStream is created to provide the utility method for writing text content to the local file:

```
var outFileStream =
  Components.classes["@mozilla.org/network/file-output-stream;1"]
    .createInstance(Components.interfaces.nsIFileOutputStream);

 outFileStream.init(someFile, 0x02 | 0x08 | 0x20, 0664, 0);
 outFileStream.write(someText,someTextLength);
```

The init method of the output stream is of the form:

```
init(localFileInterface, creationFlags, accessMode, otherUnusedFlags);
```

localFileInterface is the reference to the nsILocalFile reference obtained from the file selection dialog. The *creationFlags* field represents any combination of the following:

0x01: Read only.
0x02: Write only.
0x04: Read and write.
0x08: Create if file does not yet exist.
0x10: Set to append mode.

`0x20`: Set to truncate mode.

`0x40`: Set to synchronous mode; writing waits for file status and data to be updated before the next operation is initiated.

`0x80`: Set to exclusive mode; file is created if it does not exist, but method returns `NULL` if file exists.

`accessMode` is the conventional bit-mask setting `READ (0x4) | WRITE (0x2) | EXECUTE (0x1)` privileges for the system user, group, and all users groups. The remaining field is unused.

With the services and interfaces now available to write text to a file, we'll take a closer look at accessing the text wrapped by our note's `editor` element.

Writing document content to a file

All DOM elements have an `innerHTML` property that provides the HTML text of a node and its children. We can use this property to extract node content for serialization and writing to text files. To output the content of a complete HTML document, we need to access the `innerHTML` property of the document's topmost root node.

`Editor` and `IFrame` XUL elements have a `contentDocument` property that references the document object contained by the frame. That document object provides methods and properties to access the document through the DOM interface.

In terms of the topmost document node, the `contentDocument`'s `documentElement` property is used to access the root node of the document tree. We can see such a hierarchy by using the DOM inspector to view the structure of our editor after note entry, as shown in Figure 7-5.

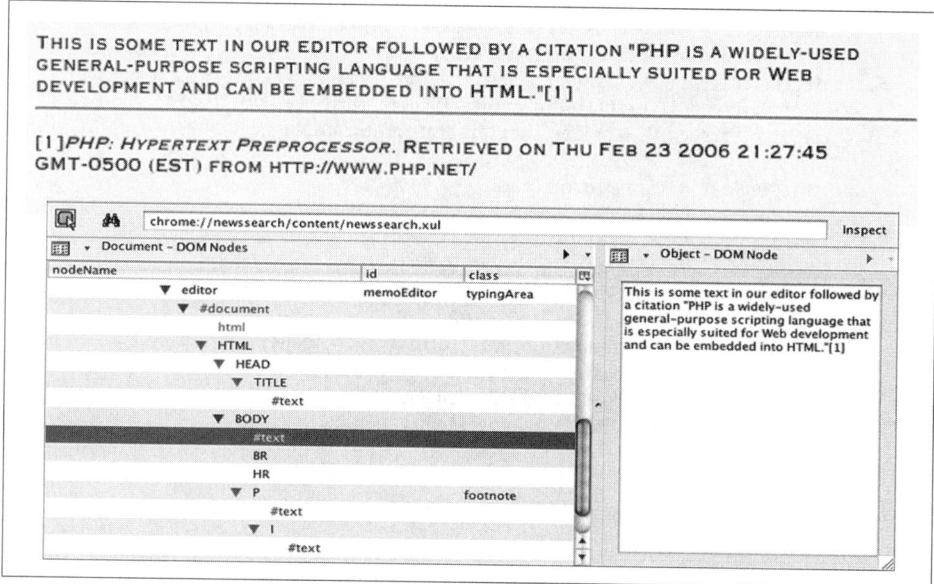

Figure 7-5. Document hierarchy for editor element

The HTML indicates that the topmost document root node is an HTML document. Other possible document types include XULDocument (the document type for this application) and XMLDocument.

The completed code to save the note text to an external HTML file in our *newssearch.js* file includes the change to the save note button handler:

```
function genericBtnHandler(event) {
try { // try block
var infoString = "Type = " + event.type + ",";
infoString += "Target = " + event.target + ",";
infoString += "Target.tagName = " + event.target.tagName + ",";
infoString += "Target.id = " + event.target.id + ",";
infoString += "Evt.phase = " + event.eventPhase + "."
dump(infoString + "\n");
switch(event.target.id) { // switch on target
case "newButton": {
  newNote();
  break;
 }
 case "saveButton": {
  saveNoteToFile();
  break;
 }
 .
 .
 .
```

The finished saveNoteToFile() function is as follows:

```
function saveNoteToFile() {
 var eD = document.getElementById("memoEditor").contentDocument;
 var filePickerInterface = Components.interfaces.nsIFilePicker;
 var fileSelector = Components.classes["@mozilla.org/filepicker;1"]
      .createInstance(filePickerInterface);
 fileSelector.init(window, "Select a destination", filePickerInterface.modeSave);
 fileSelector.appendFilters(filePickerInterface.filterHTML);
 if (fileSelector.show() == filePickerInterface.returnOK) {

   var selectedFile = fileSelector.file;

   var outFileStream =
      Components.classes["@mozilla.org/network/file-output-stream;1"]
          .createInstance(Components.interfaces.nsIFileOutputStream);

   outFileStream.init(selectedFile, 0x02 | 0x08 | 0x20, 0664, 0);
              // write, create, truncate
   outFileStream.write(eD.documentElement.innerHTML,
       eD.documentElement.innerHTML.toString().length);
   outFileStream.close();
  }
}
```

Reading document content from a file

The process to read file data is a straightforward reversal of the writing process.

Designers can access the `nsIFilePicker`'s `file.path` property to set the `src` attribute of the `editor` element. The path string requires a *file:///* prefix to make the string a valid URI. As with the cases for our other button service functions, we break the code into a main function to manage the program state based on the success indicator of the code doing the bulk of the work. The resulting code snippet (with some of the relevant changes for file reading highlighted) follows:

```
// Open note behaves just like a new note from the
// perspective of application state
function openNote( ) {
if (readNoteFromFile( ) == true) {
 G_ApplicationState = K_OPEN_NOTE;
 updateInterface( );
 }
};

function readNoteFromFile( ) {
try { // try block
 var retVal = false;
 var theEditor = document.getElementById("memoEditor");

 var filePickerInterface = Components.interfaces.nsIFilePicker;
 var fileSelector = Components.classes["@mozilla.org/filepicker;1"]
        .createInstance(filePickerInterface);
 fileSelector.init(window, "Select note file", filePickerInterface.modeOpen);
 fileSelector.appendFilters(filePickerInterface.filterHTML);
 if (fileSelector.show( ) == filePickerInterface.returnOK) {
   theEditor.setAttribute("src","file:///" + fileSelector.file.path);
  }
 } // try block
  catch (e) {
   alert("Read Note from File exception: " + e);
  }
  return retVal;
}
```

Emailing Note Document Contents

We now turn our attention to the function that sends note content to another user through the user's installed email service.

By design, we choose to send only the text of a note rather than formatted HTML. This leads to some simpler code, which not only simplifies the design of the application, but also simplifies life for users who (a) may not have interest in enabling HTML composition in their mail software, and (b) whose recipients may not be able to or interested in viewing HTML-formatted mail messages.

Although we can use the ubiquitous <a> HTML element to launch the email application, we have two things to consider:

- The <a> (<anchor>) element with an `href` (*h*ypertext *ref*erence) attribute set to a `mailto:` value meets our needs, but having an HTML link appear in the middle of the XUL interface may not be stylistically consistent with the rest of the interface, drawing undue attention.
- The application needs to respond to a request to `SEND` the node in two steps: first to obtain the text of the note and set the appropriate attributes of the <a> element, and then to fire the <a>'s response to the user request.

Mixing XUL and HTML

XUL and HTML elements can coexist in XUL files, provided the HTML elements include the `html` namespace qualifier. One solution to the need for a two-step button process is to use a XUL button to trigger code that modifies a *hidden* HTML element.

We will position the HTML element within a <div> element in the note's toolbar:

```
<button id="saveButton" label="Save"/>
    <button id="sendButton" label="Send"/>
<button id="cancelButton" label="Cancel"/>
<html:div style="visibility:hidden" >
   <html:a id="sendLink" href="mailto:">SEND</html:a>
</html:div>
    <button id="loginButton" label="LOGIN"/>
```

The handler code for the XUL Send button will manufacture the needed information for the <a> element's `href` attribute. Notice the required `html:` namespace on both the a link and the `div` elements. Without it, the Firefox framework would not know how to build their appearances and the elements would be ignored.

A closer look at the format for the `href`'s `mailto` string provides us with the background needed to pass the note body to the element:

```
mailto:recipientEmail?cc=copyToEmail&subject=subject&body=text
```

The XUL's Send button handler will extract the note's text to properly fill in the body portion of the `mailto` string.

We can easily obtain the text from the note body by creating a document `range` object, setting the range to select the entire document content, and using the range's `getSelection()` method to return all the text within the selected note. The sequence is made easier by the range's `selectNodeContents()`, a utility function that selects all the contents of a node, removing the need to manually set starting and ending container properties.

In our new code fragment, we use the `id` attribute of the link element to obtain that element's reference for its attribute setter. The `documentElement` property provides us with the topmost node of the document, and the `selectNodeContents` method places all of that node's contents into the range:

```
var tB = document.getElementById("sendLink");
 var eD = document.getElementById("memoEditor").contentDocument;
 //
 // Build a text string representation of note content
 //
  var newRange = eD.createRange( );
  newRange.selectNodeContents(eD.documentElement);
  var hrefString = "mailto:?&body=" + newRange.toString( );
  tB.setAttribute("href",hrefString);
```

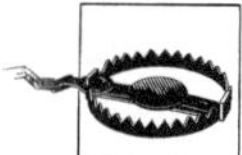

Various email programs will respond differently to the `mailto:` directive. In the event that an email package does not respond to the passing of text-only content through the body field, the user will see the mail application launch with no fields prefilled. In such cases, simple cut-and-paste operations between the note area and email body will be required.

Synthesizing DOM events

The XUL Send button handler responds to the `click` event, but we must now pass that event (or synthesize a new event) to send the `<a>` element, allowing the browser to behave as though the user clicked on the link element.

An alternative option is to directly call the `onclick` handler of the `<a>` element. The downside of that approach is that the designer must presume that the `<a>` element will support a DOM level 2 click event, and that the browser's launch of the email link is triggered by that element's `onclick` handler, which may not necessarily be the case. The more reliable approach is to send the appropriate event to the link and let whatever event handling mechanism is in place deal with triggering the response.

To synthesize a DOM event, the designer must first create an event of a particular DOM category (module) and initialize it with specific attributes.

We create an event by calling:

```
document.createEvent("eventModuleName")
```

The valid event types for event modules are as follows:

`HTMLEvents`
: Events associated with the original HTML event model (HTML 4.0). This category includes such events as `abort`, `blur`, `change`, `error`, `focus`, `load`, `reset`, `resize`, `scroll`, `select`, `submit`, and `unload`.

`UIEvents`
: This category of events adds support for user interaction with the entire document, and includes the events `DOMFocusIn`, `DOMFocusOut`, and `DOMActivate`.

`MouseEvents`
: This category includes events triggered by mouse actuations, such as `click`, `mousedown`, `mouseup`, `mouseover`, `mousemove`, and `mouseout`.

`MutationEvents`
: This category covers events associated with any alterations to the document structure, and includes the events `DOMSubtreeModified`, `DOMNodeInserted`, `DOMNodeRemoved`, `DOMNodeRemovedFromDocument`, `DOMNodeInsertedIntoDocument`, `DOMAttrModified`, and `DOMCharacterDataModified`.

Once we create an event, we need to initialize it with specific attributes. Because we will be creating a click `MouseEvent`, the form of the initialize function is:

```
event.initMouseEvent(String typeArg, boolean canBubbleArg,
                     boolean cancelableArg, AbstractView viewArg,
                     int detailArg,
                     int screenXArg, int screenYArg,
                     int clientXArg, int clientYArg,
                     boolean ctrlKeyArg, boolean altKeyArg,
                     boolean shiftKeyArg, boolean metaKeyArg,
                     short buttonArg,
                     EventTarget relatedTargetArg)
```

For the requirement to generate a "simple" click event, the coordinates and control keys are not relevant. The simplified form we need specifies the mouse event type (`click`), and allows bubbling and the ability to be canceled:

```
newEvent.initMouseEvent("click", true, true);
```

Once we have created and initialized the event, we instruct the <a> element to process the event through the element's `dispatchEvent( )` method. The complete function to launch the default mailer with the note's body text in the message area is as follows:

```
function sendNote( ) {
try {
 var tB = document.getElementById("sendLink");
 var eD = document.getElementById("memoEditor").contentDocument;
 //
 // Build a text string representation of note content
 //
  var newRange = eD.createRange( );
  newRange.selectNodeContents(eD.documentElement);
  var hrefString = "mailto:?&body=" + newRange.toString( );
  tB.setAttribute("href",hrefString);
 //
 // Now create an event to send to the <a> element
 //
 var mEvent = document.createEvent("MouseEvents");
 mEvent.initEvent("click","true","true");
 tB.dispatchEvent(mEvent);
}
catch(e) {
 alert("Send Note exception: " + e);
}
}
```

Clearing content

The only remaining task to complete the interaction of the note area buttons is creation of the Cancel button, which we will use to cancel the note creation operation. After a simple prompt to verify the user's intent, we clear the note area by removing the content from the topmost body node (we are presuming that only one body node exists in the editor document):

```
function cancelNote( ) {
if (confirm("Discard existing note?")) {
  var bodyNodes = document.getElementById("memoEditor").contentDocument.
     getElementsByTagName("body");
  while (bodyNodes[0].childNodes.length != 0)
   bodyNodes[0].removeChild(bodyNodes[0].childNodes[0]);
  G_ApplicationState = K_STARTUP;
  updateInterface( );
  }
}
```

Adding Interactivity to DOM Elements

We would enhance the value of our note citations and footnotes if the user were able to click on a footnote element to display the referenced URL in the display frame. Some appropriate graphical styling should accompany the change to give the user a cue to the hotspot's sensitivity.

The initial tendency is to restructure the footnote portion of our notes into an <a> element, but there are problems with "standard" <a> event handling when embedded in an editable document: the default behavior to display the URL does not work within a XUL-based collection of iframes.

Rather, the footnote element will be restructured as:

- A top-level <p> element to allow for line breaks
- A numeric link to the citation in the note's body text
- An italicized segment to highlight the title of the document
- Unformatted text to describe the date of access
- A <span> element to allow for styling
- An enclosed text node with the URL referenced

Our resulting footnote should look something like this:

> [numeric link] *document title*, retrieval details, URL of the access

The <span> element will also have the benefit of an event listener to send click events to a function that forwards the URL to the content frame. Because the <span> element has only one child, the text node with the URL reference, we access the URL by accessing the text node's nodeValue property. Once the URL is obtained, the event handler can call the same function used to load any manually entered URL. The function manufactures user input by copying the URL from the citation footnote into the URL field of the application, and calls the function to load the new content page.

Here is the function to insert text, along with the accompanying function to handle click events:

```
// If this is first footnote, add horizontal rule
    //
    if (footnoteCount == 1 ) { // add the HR
      var newHR = eD.createElement("hr");
      eD.body.appendChild(newHR);
    }

    // Create footnote node as a paragraph with a specialized
    // class name (4)
    var footnoteNode = eD.createElement("p");
    footnoteNode.setAttribute("class","footnote");
    // Add reference number
    footnoteNode.appendChild(eD.createTextNode("[" + footnoteCount + "]"));
    // The title will be an italicized text node (5)
    var styledTitleNode = eD.createElement("i");
    styledTitleNode.appendChild(eD.createTextNode(cTitle + ". "));
    footnoteNode.appendChild(styledTitleNode);
    //
    // Now information on the source
    //
    var accessInfo = "Retrieved on " + Date( ) + " from " ;
    footnoteNode.appendChild(eD.createTextNode(accessInfo));

    // Add a span to stylize the URI
    var accessLink = eD.createElement("span");
    accessLink.appendChild(eD.createTextNode( cW.location.toString( )));

    // Add a pointer cursor, a splash of color, and
    // an event listener
    footnoteNode.appendChild(accessLink);
    accessLink.style.cursor = "pointer";
    accessLink.style.color = "blue";
    accessLink.addEventListener("click",footnoteClicked,true);


    eD.body.appendChild(footnoteNode);

    } // try
    catch (e) {
    alert("Exception: " + e);
    }
}

function footnoteClicked( ) {
 var tD = top.document;
 tD.getElementById("theURL").value = this.childNodes[0].nodeValue;
 loadURL( );

}
```

These changes produce a footnote that looks similar to the html <a> link (blue text that changes to a pointer when the mouse passes over the element), and that provides the benefit of displaying the content page referenced in the citation's body.

The additions to manage button enabling and disabling for open, save, send, and clear, along with a removal of diagnostic test functions, now yield a useful *newssearch.js* file:

```
var K_XUL_NAMESPACE =
 "http://www.mozilla.org/keymaster/gatekeeper/there.is.only.xul";
//
// Some constants to help us know what
// buttons and editing areas to enable
//
var K_NOT_LOGGED_ON     = 0;  // no user, no note
var K_STARTUP           = 1;  // user, no note
var K_OPEN_NOTE         = 2;  // note ready for editing
var K_NOTE_IN_PROGRESS = 3; // note editing in progress

var G_ApplicationState = K_NOT_LOGGED_ON;
var G_TOC_Datasource;

var lastCommand = "";


function genericBtnHandler(event) {
try { // try block
var infoString = "Type = " + event.type + ",";
infoString += "Target = " + event.target + ",";
infoString += "Target.tagName = " + event.target.tagName + ",";
infoString += "Target.id = " + event.target.id + ",";
infoString += "Evt.phase = " + event.eventPhase + "."
dump(infoString + "\n");
switch(event.target.id) { // switch on target
case "newButton": {
  newNote();
  break;
 }

 case "openButton": {
  openNote();
  break;
 }

 case "saveButton": {
  saveNoteToFile();
  break;
 }
case "sendButton": {
  sendNote();
  break;
 }
```

```
case "cancelButton": {
  cancelNote( );
  break;
 }
case "loginButton": {
  openLoginWindow( )
//  doLogin( );
  break;
 }
 case "addLinkButton": {
  addNewLink( );
  break;
 }
 case "removeLinkButton": {
  removeLink( );
  break;
 }
} // switch on target
} // try block
catch (e) {
 alert("genericBtnHandler exception: " + e);
 }
}

function loadURL( ) {
try{
var newURL = document.getElementById("theURL").value;
document.getElementById("contentIFrame").loadURI(newURL);
 }
 catch (e) {
 alert("Exception loading URL " + e);
 };
};

// Takes care of buttons and editing areas
// based on global variable
function updateInterface( ) {
try{
dump("In update interface with state = " + G_ApplicationState +
  "\n");

 switch(G_ApplicationState) { // switch on state
  case (K_NOT_LOGGED_ON): { // not logged on
  disableEverything( );
  document.getElementById("loginButton").disabled=false;
  break;
  } // not logged on
  case (K_STARTUP): { // startup
  // enable only the new button
  document.getElementById("newButton").disabled=false;
  document.getElementById("openButton").disabled=false;
  document.getElementById("contentIFrame").
     setAttribute("src","http://www.mozillazine.org");
  var theTree = document.getElementById("mainTree");
```

```
    theTree.setAttribute("datasources",
     "file://localhost/Applications/Firefox.app/Contents/
      MacOS/chrome/NewsSearch/content/newssites.rdf");
    theTree.setAttribute("ref","http://www.mySites.com/TOC");
    theTree.builder.rebuild( );

    document.getElementById("addLinkButton").disabled=false;
    document.getElementById("removeLinkButton").disabled=false;

    break;
    } // startup
    case (K_OPEN_NOTE): { // note ready for editing
    // Make the memo area editable, and enable the cancel button
    // to give the user a way out
    var theEditor = document.getElementById("memoEditor");
    theEditor.makeEditable("html",false);
    theEditor.contentDocument.addEventListener("click",
       editorClicked,true);


    break;
    } // note ready for editing

    case (K_NOTE_IN_PROGRESS): { // note is/has been edited
    document.getElementById("saveButton").disabled=false;
    document.getElementById("sendButton").disabled=false;
    document.getElementById("cancelButton").disabled=false;
    break;
    } // note is/has been edited

  } // switch on state
  }
  catch(e) { //
  alert("update interface exception " + e);
  }//
}

// function turns off all buttons, disables
// note typing area
function disableEverything( ) {
document.getElementById("newButton").disabled=true;
document.getElementById("openButton").disabled=true;
document.getElementById("saveButton").disabled=true;
document.getElementById("sendButton").disabled=true;
document.getElementById("cancelButton").disabled=true;
document.getElementById("loginButton").disabled=true;
document.getElementById("addLinkButton").disabled=true;
document.getElementById("removeLinkButton").disabled=true;

}

function cancelNote( ) {
if (confirm("Discard existing note?")) {
  var bodyNodes = document.getElementById("memoEditor").
```

```
  contentDocument.
    getElementsByTagName("body");
 while (bodyNodes[0].childNodes.length != 0)
  bodyNodes[0].removeChild(bodyNodes[0].childNodes[0]);
 G_ApplicationState = K_STARTUP;
 updateInterface( );
 }
}

function newNote( ) {
G_ApplicationState = K_OPEN_NOTE;
updateInterface( );
}


function saveNoteToFile( ) {
 var eD = document.getElementById("memoEditor").contentDocument;
 var filePickerInterface = Components.interfaces.nsIFilePicker;
 var fileSelector = Components.classes["@mozilla.org/filepicker;1"]
        .createInstance(filePickerInterface);
 fileSelector.init(window, "Select a destination",
  filePickerInterface.modeSave);
 fileSelector.appendFilters(filePickerInterface.filterHTML);
 if (fileSelector.show( ) == filePickerInterface.returnOK) {


   var selectedFile = fileSelector.file;
   var outFileStream =
    Components.classes["@mozilla.org/network/file-output-stream;1"]
                      .createInstance(Components.interfaces.nsIFileOutputStream);

   outFileStream.init(selectedFile, 0x02 | 0x08 | 0x20, 0664, 0);
// write, create, truncate
   outFileStream.write(eD.documentElement.innerHTML,
      eD.documentElement.innerHTML.toString( ).length);
   outFileStream.close( );
  }
}

// Open note behaves just like a new note from the
// perspective of application state
function openNote( ) {
 if (readNoteFromFile( ) == true) {
 G_ApplicationState = K_OPEN_NOTE;
 updateInterface( );
 }
};

function readNoteFromFile( ) {
try { // try block
 var retVal = false;
 var theEditor = document.getElementById("memoEditor");
```

```
  var filePickerInterface = Components.interfaces.nsIFilePicker;
  var fileSelector = Components.classes["@mozilla.org/filepicker;1"]
        .createInstance(filePickerInterface);
  fileSelector.init(window, "Select node file",
     filePickerInterface.modeOpen);
  fileSelector.appendFilters(filePickerInterface.filterHTML);
  if (fileSelector.show( ) == filePickerInterface.returnOK) {
    theEditor.setAttribute("src","file:///" +
      fileSelector.file.path);
   }
  } // try block
   catch (e) {
    alert("Read Note from File exception: " + e);
   }
   return retVal;
}

function sendNote( ) {
try {
 var tB = document.getElementById("sendLink");
 var eD = document.getElementById("memoEditor").contentDocument;
 //
 // Build a text string representation of note content
 //
  var newRange = eD.createRange( );
  newRange.selectNodeContents(eD.documentElement);
  var hrefString = "mailto:?&body=" + newRange.toString( );
  tB.setAttribute("href",hrefString);
 //
 // Now create an event to send to the <a> element
 //
 var mEvent = document.createEvent("MouseEvents");
 mEvent.initEvent("click","true","true");
 tB.dispatchEvent(mEvent);
}
catch(e) {
 alert("Send Note exception: " + e);
}
}

function editorClicked(event) {
dump("Click event " + event.target + " window is " + window +
 " location = " + window.location.toString( ) +  "\n");
event.target.removeEventListener("click",editorClicked,true);
G_ApplicationState = K_NOTE_IN_PROGRESS;
updateInterface( );
};



function stepPage(event) {
 try {
```

```
 if (event.target.id == "stepBackward")
   document.getElementById("contentIFrame").goBack( );
 else
   document.getElementById("contentIFrame").goForward( );
}
catch (e) {
 alert("exception in stepPage " + e);
 }
}

var userName;
var password;

function openLoginWindow( ) {
 var lWindow = window.openDialog
 ("chrome://newssearch/content/login.xul",
    "LOGON","chrome,modal",setUNPW);
 if ((userName != null) && (password != null))
  doLogin(userName,password);
  userName = null;
  password = null;
// doLogin('bugsbunny','wabbit');
}

function setUNPW(uN,pW) {
 userName=uN;
 password=pW;
}

function doLogin(uN,pW) {
try { // try
var theArgs = new Array;
theArgs[0] = new commandArg("un",uN);
theArgs[1] = new commandArg("pd",pW);
lastCommand = "login";
dump("Logging in with uname and pw = " + theArgs[0].value +
  "," + theArgs[1].value + "\n");
doServerRequest("login",theArgs);
 } // try
 catch (e) { //
  alert("doLogin exception: " + e);
 }//
}
//
// Dynamically assign our event handler properties
//
function initialize(event) {
try {
dump("initialize: Event target, current target and phase are: "
   + event.target + "," + event.currentTarget + "," + event.eventPhase + "\n");
if (event.target == document) { // target is the main window

 document.getElementById("newButton").
 addEventListener("command",genericBtnHandler,true);
```

```
  document.getElementById("openButton").
   addEventListener("command",genericBtnHandler,true);
  document.getElementById("saveButton").
   addEventListener("command",genericBtnHandler,true);
  document.getElementById("sendButton").
   addEventListener("command",genericBtnHandler,true);
  document.getElementById("cancelButton").
   addEventListener("command",genericBtnHandler,true);
  document.getElementById("loginButton").
   addEventListener("command",genericBtnHandler,true);
  document.getElementById("addLinkButton").
   addEventListener("command",genericBtnHandler,true);
  document.getElementById("removeLinkButton").
   addEventListener("command",genericBtnHandler,true);
  //

G_ApplicationState = K_NOT_LOGGED_ON;
 // will change to NOT LOGGED ON LATER
updateInterface( );
  }  // target is the main window
 } // try
 catch (e) {
  alert ("Exception: " + e);
   }
};


function doChangeFontStyle(event) {
try {

 var atomService = Components.classes["@mozilla.org/atom-service;1"].
    getService(Components.interfaces.nsIAtomService);

 var theEditor = document.getElementById("memoEditor").
     getHTMLEditor(document.getElementById("memoEditor").
       contentWindow);


 var newValue = event.target.label.toLowerCase( );

 switch(event.target.parentNode.id) { // switch on the menu

  case "font-size-popup": {
  if (event.target.label == "Bigger")
    theEditor.increaseFontSize( );
    else theEditor.decreaseFontSize( );
  break;
  }
  case "font-family-popup": {
   theEditor.setCSSInlineProperty(atomService.getAtom("span"),
   "style","font-family:" + newValue);
   break;
  }
   case "font-color-popup": {
```

```
  theEditor.setCSSInlineProperty(atomService.getAtom("span"),
  "style","color:" + newValue);
  break;
  }

 case "font-face-popup": {
  theEditor.setCSSInlineProperty(atomService.getAtom("span"),
  "style","font-style:" + newValue);
  break;
  }

  case "font-weight-popup": {
  theEditor.setCSSInlineProperty(atomService.getAtom("span"),
   "style","font-weight:" + newValue);
  break;
  }

 }  // switch on the menu
}
catch (e) {
dump("doChangeFontStyle exception " + e );
}
}



function loginOK() {
 G_ApplicationState = K_STARTUP;
 updateInterface();
}


function commandArg(argKey,argValue) {
 this.key = argKey;
 this.value = argValue;
}

function loginFail() {
 alert("Sorry, user not authenticated.");
 }

//
//  CreateServerRequest
//
var theServerRequest;
//
// commandArgs is an array of arguments, each element
// is converted into a PHP POST field
function doServerRequest(commandString,commandArgs) {
 theServerRequest = new XMLHttpRequest();
 var theString ="http://localhost/doCommand.php?" + "&command=" +
   commandString + "&";
 for (var i = 0; i < commandArgs.length; i++)
  { // build remaining parameters
```

```
    theString += commandArgs[i].key + "=" + commandArgs[i].value ;
   if (i != (commandArgs.length-1)) theString += "&";
  } // build remaining parameters
  theServerRequest.onreadystatechange = retrieveServerResponse;
  theServerRequest.open("GET",theString,true);
  dump("About to send " + theString + "\n");
  theServerRequest.send(null);
//  dump("Server request status =" + theServerRequest.status +
   // "\n");
//   dump("Server request response =" +
// theServerRequest.responseText + "\n");
}


function retrieveServerResponse() {

try {

 dump("server response ready state = " +
   theServerRequest.readyState + "\n");

 if (theServerRequest.readyState == 4) { // all done

  dump("Server request status =" + theServerRequest.status + "\n");
  // Check return code
   if (theServerRequest.status == 200) { // request terminated OK
    dump("Received from server: " + theServerRequest.responseText +
      "\n");

    //
    var theResults = theServerRequest.responseText.split(",");
    //

    var rCode = (theResults[0].substring((theResults[0].indexOf("=")+1),
                            theResults[0].length)).toLowerCase();

    if (lastCommand == "login") { // process login command

     if (rCode == "true") { // everything OK, we know next parameter is
                            // session info
      var lastSession = "Last login was ";
      lastSession +=
       (theResults[1].substring((theResults[1].indexOf("=")+1),
                          theResults[1].length)).toLowerCase();
      loginOK();
      setStatusText(lastSession);

     } // everything OK
     else { // user NG
      loginFail();
      setStatusText("No user logged in");
     } // user NG
```

```
    } // process login command


   } // request terminated OK
   else { // something is wrong
     alert("Response failed.");
   } // something is wrong
  } // all done
  } // try
  catch (e) {
  alert("Retrieve response exception: " + e);
  dump (e);
  }
}

function setStatusText(theText) {
document.getElementById("status-text").
   setAttribute("label",theText);
};

 function getTreeURL(event) {
  var theTree = document.getElementById("mainTree");
  var tI = theTree.currentIndex;

   var theURL = theTree.contentView.getItemAtIndex(tI).
         getAttribute("myURL");

   if (theURL != "")  {
      document.getElementById("theURL").value = theURL;
      loadURL( );
      }
   }

  //
  // Get the URIs for the page and its section
  // name, display to user before removing. If the selection
  // is a heading, it will be removed ONLY if there are no
  // children (contents) in the section
  //
 function removeLink( ) {

  var theTree = document.getElementById("mainTree");
  var tI = theTree.currentIndex;
  if (tI == -1) return;

   //
  // Now look for the parent section heading.

 var thePageSubjectURI = theTree.contentView.
   getItemAtIndex(tI).id;
  var theSectionSubjectURI = null;
  resultNode = null;
```

```
  findParentSubjectURI(theTree.contentView.getItemAtIndex(tI));
  if (resultNode != null) theSectionSubjectURI = resultNode.id;
   else theSectionSubjectURI = "http://www.mySites.com/TOC";

  var sectionLabel = theSectionSubjectURI.substring(theSectionSubjectURI.
   lastIndexOf("/")+1);
  var pageLabel = thePageSubjectURI.
    substring(thePageSubjectURI.lastIndexOf("/")+1);
  var message = "Remove " + pageLabel + " from section "
    + sectionLabel + "?";

  window.openDialog("chrome://newssearch/content/
     confirmDialog.xul","?",
      "chrome,modal",message,OkCancelCallback);

  if (OkCancelDialogRetVal == "CANCEL") return;
  removeResource(theSectionSubjectURI,thePageSubjectURI);

}

var resultNode;

function findParentSubjectURI(searchNode) {
if ((resultNode == null) && (searchNode.parentNode != null)) {
  if (searchNode.parentNode.id != null) {
   if (searchNode.parentNode.id.indexOf("www.mySites.com")
     != -1) {
     resultNode = searchNode.parentNode;
     return;
     }
   else findParentSubjectURI(searchNode.parentNode);
  }

 }
else return;
}


var OkCancelDialogRetVal = -1;

function OkCancelCallback (retVal) {
 OkCancelDialogRetVal = retVal;
}

function addNewLink( ) {
 sectionResource = null;
 sectionResource = null;
 nickName = null;
 openSectionSelection( );
 if ((sectionResource != null) && (nickName != null))
     addNewResource(sectionResource,nickName);
};
```

```
var sectionResource;
var nickName;
var makeNewSection;

function openSectionSelection( ) {
 var lWindow = window.openDialog("chrome://newssearch/content/headingSel.xul",
   "SECTIONS",
     "chrome,modal",setSection);
}

function setSection(res,name,createSection) {
 sectionResource = res;
 nickName = name;
 makeNewSection = createSection;
}

//
function fetchFileDatasource( ) {
 var retVal = null;
 var theTree = document.getElementById("mainTree");

 var dSources = theTree.database.GetDataSources( );

 while (dSources.hasMoreElements( ) && (retVal == null)) {
   var dS = dSources.getNext( );
   dS = dS.QueryInterface(Components.interfaces.nsIRDFDataSource );
   if (dS.URI.indexOf("newssites") != -1) retVal = dS;
   }
  return retVal;
  }

//
// Create the new resource and add it as a child
// to the selected container
//
function addNewResource(sectionURI,newNickName) {
try {

 var theTree = document.getElementById("mainTree");
 var dataSource = fetchFileDatasource( );

 if (dataSource == null) {
  alert("No file datasource found");
  return;
  }

 // fetch services to work with RDF and manage containers
 //
 var rdfService = Components.classes["@mozilla.org/rdf/rdf-service;1"].
     getService(Components.interfaces.nsIRDFService);

 var theSectionContainer = Components.classes["@mozilla.org/rdf/container;1"].
     createInstance(Components.interfaces.nsIRDFContainer);
```

```
   var containerTools = Components.classes["@mozilla.org/rdf/container-utils;1"].
        getService(Components.interfaces.nsIRDFContainerUtils);

   var theSubject = rdfService.GetResource("http://www.mySites.com/" + newNickName);

    var thePredicateNickname =
     rdfService.GetResource("http://www.mySites.com/rdf#nickname");
    var theNickName = rdfService.GetLiteral(newNickName);
    var thePredicateURL = rdfService.GetResource
       ("http://www.mySites.com/rdf#url");
    var theURL = rdfService.GetLiteral
        (document.getElementById("theURL").value);
    var thePredicateHits = rdfService.GetResource
       ("http://www.mySites.com/rdf#hits");
    var theHits = rdfService.GetLiteral(0);

    // If section URI has 'TOC' in it, we must be
    // creating a new section
    // heading container

    if (sectionURI.indexOf("www.mySites.com/TOC") != -1)
    { // creating a heading (container)
      containerTools.MakeSeq(dataSource,theSubject);
    } // creating a heading

    dataSource.Assert(theSubject,thePredicateNickname,theNickName,
      true);

    if (!(containerTools.IsContainer(dataSource,theSubject)))
    { // add properties
     dataSource.Assert(theSubject,thePredicateURL,theURL,true);
     dataSource.Assert(theSubject,thePredicateHits,theHits,true);
    } // add properties

// Add the newly created triple to our section heading
     var theSectionHeading = rdfService.GetResource(sectionURI);

     theSectionContainer.Init(dataSource,theSectionHeading);
     theSectionContainer.AppendElement(theSubject);

// OK, write back to file....
//
     dataSource = dataSource.QueryInterface
       (Components.interfaces.nsIRDFRemoteDataSource);
     dataSource.Flush( );
     dataSource.Refresh(false);

  }
 catch (e) {
  alert("exception in addNewResource " + e);
 }

}
```

```
//
// remove the resource unless it is a heading and has
// children --- give user a message if cannot remove
//
//
function removeResource(sectionURI,resourceURI) {
try {

var theTree = document.getElementById("mainTree");
var dataSource = fetchFileDatasource( );

 if (dataSource == null) {
  alert("No file datasource found");
  return;
 }

 // Get services to manage RDF and to help with container utilities
 var rdfService = Components.classes["@mozilla.org/rdf/rdf-service;1"].
    getService(Components.interfaces.nsIRDFService);

  var theSectionContainer = Components.classes["@mozilla.org/rdf/container;1"].
     createInstance(Components.interfaces.nsIRDFContainer);

   var containerTools = Components.classes["@mozilla.org/rdf/container-utils;1"].
     getService(Components.interfaces.nsIRDFContainerUtils);

   var theSubject = rdfService.GetResource(resourceURI);
   //
   // Check to see whether the subject is a container, and if so,
   // make sure it's empty
   //
   var theSectionHeading = rdfService.GetResource(sectionURI);
   theSectionContainer.Init(dataSource,theSectionHeading);

  if (containerTools.IsContainer(dataSource,theSubject))
{ // removing section heading
   // Bail out if the section isn't empty
   if (!(containerTools.IsEmpty(dataSource,theSubject))) { // not empty
    alert("All content pages must be removed first.");
    return;
   } // not empty
  } // removing section heading

  // Build resources for all the predicates that we know of
  var thePredicateNickname =
    rdfService.GetResource("http://www.mySites.com/rdf#nickname");
  var thePredicateURL =
    rdfService.GetResource("http://www.mySites.com/rdf#url");
  var thePredicateHits =
    rdfService.GetResource("http://www.mySites.com/rdf#hits");

 // Fetch the RDF statements for each property and remove that resource
  var theTarget = dataSource.GetTarget(theSubject,thePredicateNickname,true);
  dataSource.Unassert(theSubject,thePredicateNickname,theTarget,true);
```

```
  // Remove the other properties for non-section heading resources
   if (!(containerTools.IsContainer(dataSource,theSubject)))
 { // remove page properties
    theTarget =
    dataSource.GetTarget(theSubject,thePredicateURL,true);
   dataSource.Unassert(theSubject,thePredicateURL,theTarget,true);
   theTarget =
      dataSource.GetTarget(theSubject,thePredicateHits,true);
   dataSource.Unassert(theSubject,thePredicateHits,theTarget,true);
  } // remove page properties

  theSectionContainer.RemoveElement(theSubject,true);
//
// Write back to file....
//
    dataSource =
      dataSource.
        QueryInterface(Components.interfaces.nsIRDFRemoteDataSource);
    dataSource.Flush( );
    dataSource.Refresh(false);
  }
 catch (e) {
  alert("exception in addNewResource " + e);
  }
}

// -------------------------------------
// New code for citing selection
//
function doInsertText(event) {
try {

  var cF = document.getElementById("contentIFrame");

// Get some references to content elements
//
   var cW = cF.contentWindow;
   var cD = cF.contentDocument;
   var cTitle = cD.title ;
   // Let's do some groundwork and see how many 'footnotes'
   // we already have in the note (1)
   var eD = document.getElementById("memoEditor").contentDocument;
   var paragraphs = eD.getElementsByTagName("p");
   var footnoteCount = 0;

   for (var i = 0; i < paragraphs.length; i++) {
    if (paragraphs[i].hasAttribute("class"))
      if ( paragraphs[i].getAttribute("class") == "footnote")
           footnoteCount++;
    }
   // pop counter to this footnote entry
   footnoteCount++;

// Add full quote if requested, otherwise only the numeric
```

```
// annotation (2)
//
   var quoteString = "";
   if (event.target.label == "Quote and reference")
     quoteString += "\"" + cW.getSelection().toString( ) + "\"";
   var insertedNode = eD.createTextNode(quoteString +
         "[" + footnoteCount + "] ");
   var editorSelection =
        document.getElementById("memoEditor").
            contentWindow.getSelection( );
   var selectedRange = editorSelection.getRangeAt(0);
   selectedRange.insertNode(insertedNode);

   // Remove the newly created text node by normalizing
   // parent (3)
   selectedRange.startContainer.parentNode.normalize( );

   // If this is first footnote, add horizontal rule
   //
   if (footnoteCount == 1 ) { // add the HR
     var newHR = eD.createElement("hr");
     eD.body.appendChild(newHR);
   }

   // Create footnote node as a paragraph with a specialized
   // class name (4)
   var footnoteNode = eD.createElement("p");
   footnoteNode.setAttribute("class","footnote");
   // Add reference number
   footnoteNode.appendChild(eD.
         createTextNode("[" + footnoteCount + "]"));
   // The title will be an italicized text node (5)
   var styledTitleNode = eD.createElement("i");
   styledTitleNode.appendChild(eD.createTextNode(cTitle + ". "));
   footnoteNode.appendChild(styledTitleNode);
   //
   // Now information on the source
   //
   var accessInfo = "Retrieved on " + Date( ) + " from " ;
   footnoteNode.appendChild(eD.createTextNode(accessInfo));

   // Add a span to stylize the URI
   var accessLink = eD.createElement("span");
   accessLink.
        appendChild(eD.createTextNode( cW.location.toString( )));

   // Add a pointer cursor, a splash of color, and
   // an event listener
   footnoteNode.appendChild(accessLink);
   accessLink.style.cursor = "pointer";
   accessLink.style.color = "blue";
   accessLink.addEventListener("click",footnoteClicked,true);
```

```
    eD.body.appendChild(footnoteNode);

    } // try
    catch (e) {
    alert("Exception: " + e);
    }
}

function footnoteClicked() {
 var tD = top.document;
 tD.getElementById("theURL").value = this.childNodes[0].nodeValue;
 loadURL();

}
```

The completed *newssearch.xul* file looks like this:

```
<?xml-stylesheet href="NewsSearchStyles.css" type="text/css"?>

<window
  id="theMainWindow"
  title="Test Window"
  width="800"
  height="700"
  onload="initialize(event);"
  orient="horizontal"
  xmlns:html="http://www.w3.org/1999/xhtml"
  xmlns:xlink="http://www.w3.org/1999/xlink"
  xmlns="http://www.mozilla.org/keymaster/gatekeeper/there.is.only.xul">

<script src="NewsSearch.js"/>
<script>
 <![CDATA[

editorLoaded = function(event) {
 dump("Ed loaded Event target, current target and phase are: "
  + event.target + "," +
    event.currentTarget + "," + event.eventPhase + "\n");
 };
 ]]>
</script>

 <!-- main top level container -->
<vbox flex="1" >

 <!-- horizontal container for all content (except status info) -->
 <hbox flex="1" >

 <!-- a container for some kind of list -->
 <vbox flex="1" ondblclick="getTreeURL(event);">
 <hbox pack="center">
       <button id="addLinkButton" label="Add" />
       <button id="removeLinkButton" label="Remove"/>
</hbox>
```

```
<tree datasources="" ref="" id="mainTree"  seltype="single" flex="1">
  <treecols>
    <treecol  primary="true" label="Nickname" flex="1"/>
    <splitter class="tree-splitter"/>
    <treecol  label="Visits" flex="2"/>
  </treecols>

<template container="?currentContainer" member="?site">
    <rule  >
      <conditions>
        <content uri="?currentContainer"/>
        <member container="?currentContainer" child="?site"/>

        <triple subject="?site"
                predicate="http://www.mySites.com/rdf#nickname"
                object="?nickname"/>
        <triple subject="?site"
                predicate="http://www.mySites.com/rdf#url"
                object="?url"/>
        <triple subject="?site"
                predicate="http://www.mySites.com/rdf#hits"
                object="?hits"/>

      </conditions>
      <action>
        <treechildren>
          <treeitem uri="?site" myURL="?url">
            <treerow  >
              <treecell label="?nickname"/>
              <treecell label="?hits"/>
            </treerow>
          </treeitem>
        </treechildren>
      </action>
    </rule>
    <rule >
      <conditions>
        <content uri="?currentContainer"/>
        <member container="?currentContainer" child="?site"/>
        <triple subject="?site"
                predicate="http://www.mySites.com/rdf#nickname"
                object="?nickname"/>
      </conditions>
      <action>
        <treechildren>
          <treeitem  uri="?site" myURL="">
            <treerow properties="siteHeading" >
              <treecell label="?nickname"/>
              <treecell label="-"/>
```

```
          </treerow>
        </treeitem>
      </treechildren>
    </action>
  </rule>
 </template></tree>
</vbox>

 <splitter resizebefore="closest" resizeafter="closest" state="open"/>
<!-- container for messages and tool areas -->
<vbox>

<!-- some simple controls to manage display pages -->

<hbox class="buttonArea">
 <button id="stepBackward" label="BACK" oncommand="stepPage(event);"/>
 <button id="stepForward" label="FORWARD" oncommand="stepPage(event);"/>
 <hbox >
  <vbox pack="center">
  <label control="theURL" value="URL:"/>
  </vbox>
  <textbox id="theURL" size="32" type="autocomplete" autocompletesearch="history"/>
  <button id="loadURL" label="GO" oncommand="loadURL( );"/>
 </hbox>

</hbox>
<!-- used to display message -->
<browser id="contentIFrame"  type="content-primary"  src="about:blank" flex="4">
</browser>

 <splitter resizebefore="closest" resizeafter="closest" state="open"/>
 <!-- used to display typing area  -->
 <vbox flex="2" minheight="75" minwidth="100" >


 <menubar id="editor-menubar" oncommand="doChangeFontStyle(event);">
   <menu id="font-menu" label="Font">
     <menupopup id="font-popup">
        <menu label="Family">
         <menupopup id="font-family-popup">
           <menuitem label="serif"/>
           <menuitem label="sans-serif"/>
           <menuitem label="monospace"/>
         </menupopup>
       </menu>
       <menu label="Size">
        <menupopup id="font-size-popup">
        <menuitem label="Bigger"/>
        <menuitem label="Smaller"/>
```

```
          </menupopup>
         </menu>
       </menupopup>
     </menu>
     <menuseparator/>
       <menu id="style-menu" label="Color">
             <menupopup id="font-color-popup">
             <menuitem label="Black"/>
             <menuitem label="Red"/>
             <menuitem label="Green"/>
             <menuitem label="Blue"/>
            </menupopup>
          </menu>
      <menuseparator/>
       <menu label="Style">
        <menupopup id="font-style-popup">
         <menu label="Face">
          <menupopup id="font-face-popup">
            <menuitem label="Normal"/>
            <menuitem label="Italic"/>
          </menupopup>
          </menu>
          <menu label="Weight">
            <menupopup id="font-weight-popup">
            <menuitem label="Normal"/>
            <menuitem label="Bold"/>
          </menupopup>
         </menu>
       </menupopup>
     </menu>
     <menuseparator/>
     <menu oncommand="doInsertText(event);" label="Cite...">
      <menupopup id="insert-type-popup">
      <menuitem label="Quote and reference"/>
      <menuitem label="Reference only"/>
      </menupopup>
     </menu>
   </menubar>

   <editor  id="memoEditor" flex="1"
     type="content" src="about:blank" class="typingArea">

  </editor>
  </vbox>

   <!-- used to display tool area-->
  <hbox height="50" class="buttonArea">
```

```
  <spacer flex="1"/>

    <vbox id="vbox">
     <spacer flex="1"/>
      <hbox>
       <button id="newButton" label="New" />
       <button id="openButton" label="Open" />
       <button id="saveButton" label="Save"/>
       <button id="sendButton" label="Send"/>
       <button id="cancelButton" label="Cancel"/>
        <html:div style="visibility:hidden" >
    <html:a id="sendLink" href="mailto:">SEND</html:a></html:div>
       <button id="loginButton" label="LOGIN"/>

      </hbox>
      <spacer flex="1"/>

    </vbox>

  <spacer flex="1"/>

 </hbox>

 </vbox>
 <!-- container for messages and tool areas -->

 </hbox>


 <hbox>
  <statusbar id="status-bar" >
   <statusbarpanel id="status-text" label="Waiting for login.">

    </statusbarpanel>
   </statusbar>

 </hbox>  <!-- main container -->
 </vbox>
</window>
```

Figure 7-6 illustrates the sequence the application follows to launch the user's email application.

Table 7-2 summarizes the properties and methods used in this section to save document content to a file.

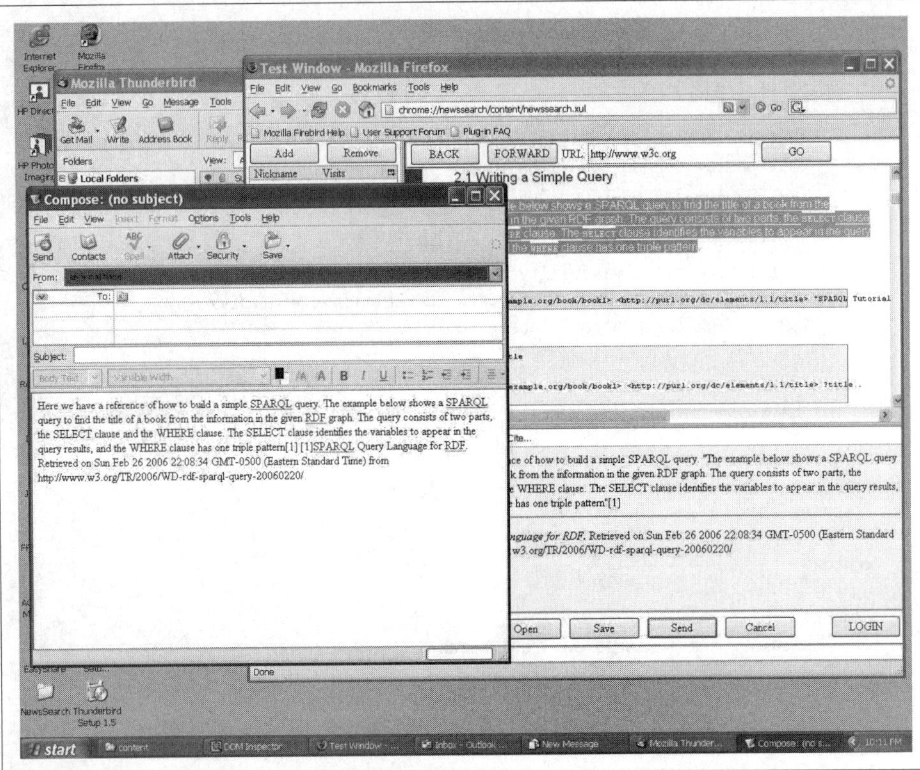

Figure 7-6. Inserting note text into email application

Table 7-2. Properties and methods for file I/O

Property/Method	Description
`nsIFilePicker.init(window, "title", mode)`	Initializes a file selector dialog to a parent window, a title that appears in the window frame, and a mode to identify whether the dialog is reading or writing files
`nsIFilePicker.appendFilters(`*`someFilter`*`)`	Adds a filter to limit the view of the filesystem
`nsIFilePicker.show( )`	Displays the file selection dialog
`nsIFilePicker.file`	The `nsILocalFile` interface to the local filesystem
`nsILocalFile.path`	The pathname of a local file
`nsIFileOutputStream.init(`*`fileReference, creationFlags, accessMode, unused`*`)`	Initializes a file output stream to bind I/O services to a specified file; creation flags that specify how to create the file; and a filesystem access mode to set the user, group, and system read, write, and execute modes
`element.innerHTML`	Property that returns the HTML markup of an element and its children
`Editor.contentDocument.documentElement`	Returns the topmost document element node that is the document root

Table 7-2. Properties and methods for file I/O (continued)

Property/Method	Description
`range.selectNodeContents(someNode)`	Sets the range's starting and ending container properties to enclose all the contents of the selected node
`document.createEvent(EventModuleName)`	Creates a new event to be dispatched
`event.initMouseEvent(initializeParameters)`	Initializes the event to a specific type
`element.dispatchEvent(someEvent)`	Dispatches an event to an element

Summary

This chapter focused on some of the techniques associated with moving and manipulating content that is structured according to the DOM. We covered the nuts and bolts of utilizing window selections and ranges, as well as moving DOM text into local files.

This chapter illustrated that although the DOM provides a powerful tool for document creation and manipulation, practical applications will always have to take into account the implications caused by multiple frame displays. This is particularly true in terms of understanding limitations caused by security models and interacting with outside applications that may or may not perform as expected.

It is now time to take leave of the NewsSearch application and turn our attention to some of the other features the Firefox framework supports, particularly in light of evolving standards for graphical representation and display: Scalable Vector Graphics (SVG).

CHAPTER 8
Graphics

Not all Firefox innovations involve the XUL descriptor format we covered in previous chapters.

Firefox's capability to render documents in XHTML that include both conventional HTML as well as other standardized XML dialects makes possible a new generation of features that focus on user interaction. One such dialect that focuses on graphics enhancement involves the use of Scalable Vector Graphics (SVG). Although numerous implementations of SVG plug-ins are available, plug-ins can rarely interact with a web document that consists mainly of traditional HTML elements.

This chapter discusses an XHTML document that combines HTML with graphics technologies designed for very different models of data flow and interaction.

We'll discuss the use of SVG in the context of a data transformation technique that adds graphics content to a data display without using proprietary authoring tools. I'll also cover the HTML canvas object and describe it in terms of its capacity to add richness to the interactive experience. This chapter will use a suggested project that involves rendering tabular data into several types of data graphs to enhance interpretation of (and add interest to) what would otherwise be an ordinary data table.

This chapter's topics include:

- A review of XHTML and namespaces
- An overview of SVG
- A discussion of the role of XSL Transformations (XSLT) to build SVG data
- The addition of Document Object Model (DOM) event processing to communicate between SVG and HTML document elements
- An overview of the HTML canvas object
- The use of JavaScript to dynamically modify the interface using the canvas object

A Sample Graphing Project

We will set the context of this discussion on graphics by proposing a project to supplement a simple collection of tabular data consisting of sample quantities with a bar graph (to show a progression of consumption), and a pie chart (to "explode" a given selection of data). We will also require interaction between the different display models. When the user moves the mouse over a quantity value, we will trigger highlighting of the companion entry in either a table of data or the graphed area. We will also design the pie chart to dynamically reflect the content of either a row of HTML data or the value represented in an SVG bar element. Such a display is appropriate for a number of billing reports, utility usage data, or other reports involving categories of usage. Figure 8-1 shows a rough mockup of how we want to apply our graphics capabilities.

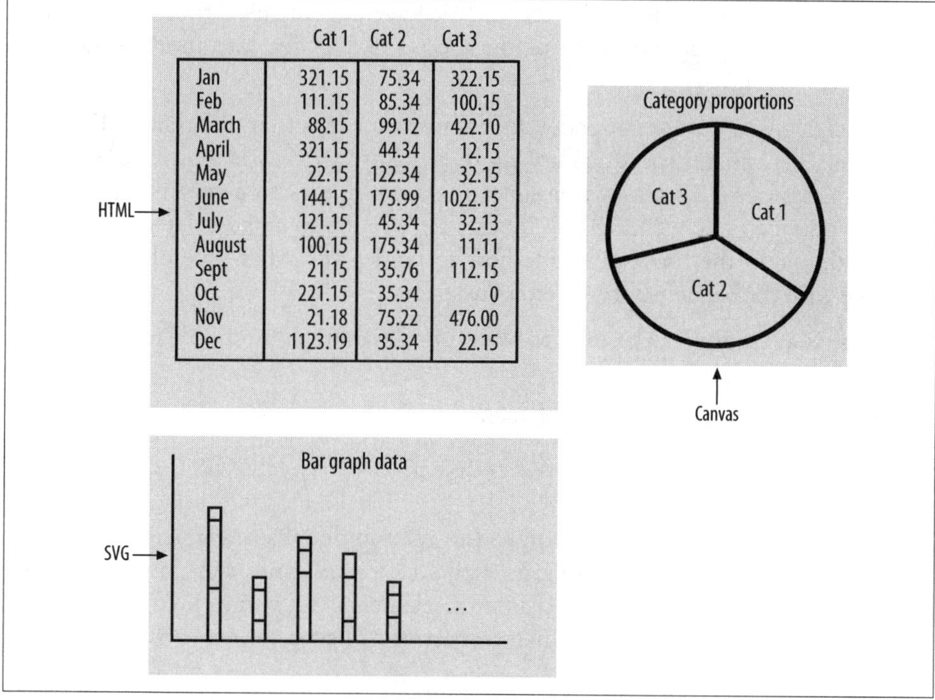

	Cat 1	Cat 2	Cat 3
Jan	321.15	75.34	322.15
Feb	111.15	85.34	100.15
March	88.15	99.12	422.10
April	321.15	44.34	12.15
May	22.15	122.34	32.15
June	144.15	175.99	1022.15
July	121.15	45.34	32.13
August	100.15	175.34	11.11
Sept	21.15	35.76	112.15
Oct	221.15	35.34	0
Nov	21.18	75.22	476.00
Dec	1123.19	35.34	22.15

Figure 8-1. HTML table and SVG graphics (mockup)

We will render the tabular data itself as a conventional `<table>` document element. We will generate the graphics representations for the bar graph from transformed source data, and dynamically create the pie chart in response to user interaction. This design solution requires a variety of XML tags.

XHTML Review

XHTML is most often associated with the requirement to structure HTML documents into an XML-compliant form (e.g., all element tags are complete). Because XHTML also provides the ability to merge different XML dialects into a single document, we must author XHTML documents with a number of additional considerations:

- How to distinguish tags that different XML dialects may share
- How to instruct browsers to read (and servers to identify) documents that contain specialized content
- How to validate an XML document that combines different XML dialects

Combining XHTML and SVG Namespaces

The topic of namespaces is not new to us. We have liberally used the `xul` namespace in our NewsSearch application to define the context of the tags used to build the interface document.

Namespaces give a browser's rendering a context for tags that different XML implementations may share; the `<iframe>` tag, for example, exists in both the XUL and HTML namespaces. To allow a designer to associate tags to a specific namespace, XHTML provides a convention that binds a tag's prefix to an associated namespace. This binding tells the browser's code how to render and what type of behaviors to associate with the elements of a given namespace.

Following is a required declaration to allow our design to combine HTML, SVG, and XUL namespaces:

```
<html xmlns:svg="http://www.w3.org/2000/svg"
  xmlns:xul=
    "http://www.mozilla.org/keymaster/gatekeeper/there.is.only.xul"
  xmlns="http://www.w3.org/1999/xhtml">
```

The `xmlns` namespace declaration applied to the top document element informs the Firefox parser that any document tags without a prefix, or not enclosed by an element with a prefix, are to be parsed as `xhtml` elements; tag names prefixed by `svg` or `xul` are to be interpreted as tags in their respective namespaces.

The URI portions of a namespace declaration do not need to point to actual web sites or locations. The URI portion merely serves as an opaque ID that the Firefox framework uses to assign prefixes to a category of rendering and behavior management.

File type and content type

Before the Firefox framework begins to decode namespaces and make rendering decisions, the framework logic needs to infer what will be required of it as the document is being read from a web server or from the local filesystem. (Otherwise, the browser logic would not even know whether namespace attributes are valid for a given document.)

For files read directly from the filesystem (e.g., using the File → Open File menu item from the browser), the extension *.xhtml* provides Firefox with the necessary hints to expect an XML-formatted document, and to expect HTML and possibly additional namespaces.

Browsers accessing files from a web server will decode the HTTP header information from the `Content-Type` field. XML files can instruct some content servers on how to construct this field with the following attributes in the document's `meta` tag:

```
<meta http-equiv="Content-Type" content="application/svg+xml;
    charset=UTF-8" />
```

The `application` portion of the `content` attribute informs the browser that rather than presuming simple text content, it should attempt to decode the document content by reading the first few source lines. The `svg` portion tells the browser that an SVG rendering engine will be required (non-Firefox browsers may use this field to trigger a prompt to download a third-party SVG plug-in).

DOCTYPE and validation

Conventional use of `DOCTYPE` declarations gives XML validation agents the information needed to validate an XML file's schema. `DOCTYPE` declarations associate the root document element with a `SYSTEM` string (representing a browser-understood reference to an existing schema) and a `PUBLIC` string (representing an actual URL of a document data type to be used for validation).

Unfortunately, the SVG specification involves a number of (slightly) moving versions, and validation for them is currently a bit problematic. For documents including SVG content, validation should be bypassed and the `DOCTYPE` declaration omitted.

SVG Overview

An SVG document is an XML document that provides a relatively simple set of tags and attributes to draw geometric shapes. Applications that are ideal for SVG implementations have any of the following characteristics:

- There is a well-understood algorithm to translate data from one form (tables of numbers) into another (graphs).
- Data is encoded in a form that naturally lends itself to graphical representations (geographic information systems [GIS]).
- There is a need to attach interactivity to geometric shapes.

SVG Drawing

All drawing is conducted in an area defined by the top <svg> element, and is optionally scaled into a viewBox that defines the units of the drawing area's coordinate system. Shapes are specified by svg elements that include attributes for position and dimension, and styling attributes to refine the object's appearance.

The topmost <svg> element defines the area, in pixels, onto which graphics are to be drawn:

```
<svg version="1.1" height="200" width="400">
....
</svg>
```

The version attribute identifies the version of SVG rendering to apply, and the height and width set pixel dimensions for the drawing area. (Positioning on the web page is most often accomplished by enclosing the svg element within a table or div html element.)

The coordinate system for SVG drawing presumes an origin at the top left of the drawing area. We can further refine the coordinate space by optionally setting a viewBox attribute, such as:

```
    viewBox = "0 0 400 800"
```

This attribute defines a coordinate system's minimum *x*, minimum *y*, width, and height dimensions. This allows a designer to shift and scale a coordinate system in the application's region onto the physical drawing region. For cases where such a transposition is not required, the viewBox attribute may be omitted.

Appearance Properties

SVG elements have many of the same graphics characteristics of HTML elements. We can set characteristics such as fill color, stroke width, stroke color, and font size on SVG elements using any of three forms:

- An attribute such as fill="blue"
- An inline style property such as style="fill:blue;"
- A Cascading Style Sheet (CSS) declaration such as { fill:blue; }

Some SVG enthusiasts prefer using the attribute assignment to specify the appearance of SVG elements, particularly for attributes that involve a dimension of length. This preference is due to a mismatch between the SVG specification and the CSS specification.

CSS requires that style properties include a reference to units in length properties, such as stroke-width, font-size, etc. For example, we should express a font size as:

```
{ font-size:10px; }
```

To omit the px would constitute a CSS error.

The SVG specification, however, states that the units of length, if omitted, default to the units defined by the mapping of the SVG dimensions to the viewBox dimensions. For example, if the viewBox mapped its 100×100 area of "user units" to a 200×200 pixel region, each "user unit" would map to 2 pixels. A perfectly legal font size attribute such as:

```
<text font-size="4" />
```

would yield text glyphs with a font size of 8 pixels.

There is no consensus on which approach should take precedence; as a result, the assignment of attributes involving a length dimension is often used to remove any possible ambiguities from those perusing a document's source. The use of such attributes is a convention that we will follow here.

Graphical Elements

For an application this straightforward, we can limit ourselves to using the basic graphical elements:

<line>
: A line that is explicitly positioned with starting and ending coordinates.

<rect>
: A rectangular area positioned at the top-left corner with explicit height and width attributes.

<text>
: A string of text.

<g>
: A graphics context container that allows styling attributes to be attached to an enclosing tag and applied to all the container's children. The <g> element is also useful to assign a unique identifier or class to a collection of graphics primitives.

Transform, Translate, and Scale

The drawing model for SVG considers the top-left corner of the drawing surface as the coordinate origin; most graphs display positive displacements working upward from an origin at the bottom of a display.

The SVG element repertoire includes an attribute that makes a transposition between the drawing model and the Cartesian model a bit less tedious than calculating offsets for each drawing instruction.

The SVG <g> element supports a `transform` attribute that, in turn, includes two optional tokens to manage the required transposition:

```
<g transform="translate(someX, someY) scale(xScale,yScale)">
```

The `translate` field instructs the SVG rendering engine to take the coordinates of any child elements and add the *x* and *y* displacements specified. Most designers use this directive to position the new drawing origin to the bottom of a graph area.

When added to the directive to apply a *y* scaling factor of –1, the designer can now issue positioning and drawing instructions that, for graphics, start at the origin of the user's graph area and adhere to the rule of positive displacement following an upward direction.

The general form for a graph of some `graphHeight` dimension becomes:

```
<g transform="translate(0, graphHeight) scale(1,-1)" >
```

Figure 8-2 illustrates the net effect of these changes.

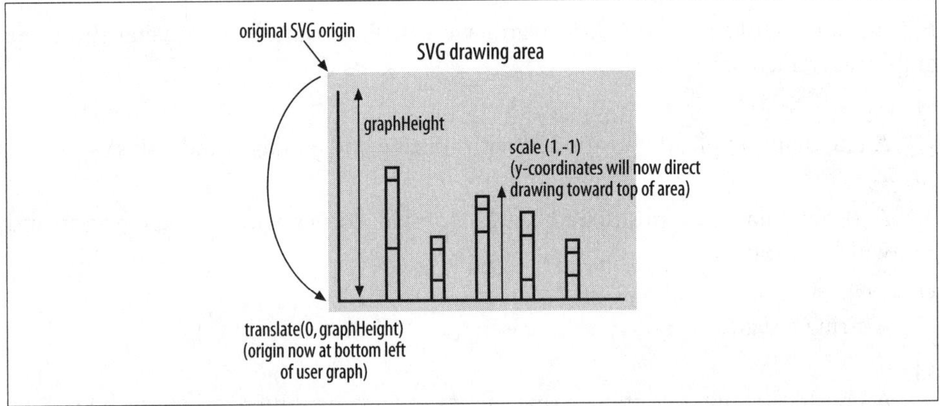

Figure 8-2. Translating SVG origin

Unfortunately, what works well for graphics requires one more adjustment for text display.

With the *y* scaling factor left at –1, text drawing would yield upside-down glyphs (the drawing logic would invert its internal drawing along the y-axis). As a result, SVG designers must make one more conversion when drawing text. This change will once again invert the *y* scale (to obtain right-side-up glyphs).

Table 8-1 summarizes the SVG elements used.

Table 8-1. SVG elements in use

Element	Attributes	Description
svg	width, height viewBox = "top left width height"	Sets drawing area of the specified width dimensions in pixels. Optional viewBox attribute maps a "user space" for scaling and mapping onto the display area. With no viewBox, "user units" map to display coordinates.
rect	x, y, width, height stroke-width	Draws a rectangle with the top-left corner at the specified coordinates, of the specified width and height. Dimensions are in scaled user units. The stroke-width dimension is often set as an attribute. Stroke-width and fill set the colors for the shape.
line	x1 y1 x2 y2 stroke-width	Draws a line between the two points. Dimensions are in scaled user units. The stroke-width dimension is often set as an attribute.
g	Style attribute transform = translate(x,y) scale (sx,sy)	Used as a container to apply a style, class, or ID to a collection of graphical objects. The transform attribute shifts the drawing origin by *x*, *y* in user units; scale allows for scaling in x and y directions.
text	x, y font-size stroke-width	Draws text of a given font size and stroke-width at the position in user coordinates.

All drawable SVG elements can have style settings applied through CSS or style attributes. Table 8-1 illustrates the use of attribute assignments for length dimensions to reduce possible confusion with CSS entries.

A snippet of SVG to draw a background for a graph area of 198×398 pixels and a stack of bars with a small label, *J*, under the bar would look like this:

```
<svg:svg version="1.1" height="198" width="398">
  <svg:rect x="0" y="0" height="198" width="398" ></svg:rect>
  <svg:g transform="translate(20,178)  scale(1,-1)">
   <svg:line x1="0" y1="0" x2="0" y2="178" ></svg:line>
   <svg:line x1="0" y1="0" x2="378" y2="0" ></svg:line>
   <svg:rect x="0" y="0" height="43" width="8" ></svg:rect>
   <svg:rect x="0" y="43" height="10" width="8"></svg:rect>
   <svg:rect x="0" y="53" height="43" width="8"></svg:rect>
     <svg:g transform="scale(1,-1)" class="axisLabel">
       <svg:text font-size="15px" stroke-width="1px"
            y="16" x="0">J</svg:text>
     </svg:g>
```

Although we could manually build an XHTML file that contains the required number of SVG bar graphs (or use a proprietary tool to build a similar graphic), the labor involved in such an exercise would be onerous.

By using source data formatted as XML, and by applying XSLT, designers can implement an automated data flow that generates the SVG rendered by the browser.

Data-to-Graphics Transformation

The unique position (and appeal) of SVG is not so much its value as a graphics language, but its combination of a graphics repertoire with its structure as an XML-compliant document.

As an XML document, SVG can be the target of an automated transformation that operates on the original data set to generate the graphical representation. The ability to create SVG without manual authoring intervention or proprietary authoring tools, and the ability to do so using standards-based open source technologies either at the server or at the browser, means that we can do such graphics transformations efficiently and cost-effectively.

Most designs involving such transformations will sketch out a number of assumptions:

- The source data will originate as an XML source.
- The transformation process will add class identifiers to allow for coloration of axes, labels, and other graphical elements.
- The transformation itself should be flexible enough to serve the transformed data to a browser, or to generate an intermediate XHTML file.

Figure 8-3 illustrates the resulting flow.

Using XSLT

A detailed explanation of XSLT is beyond the scope of this book. This section is included for completeness to illustrate one possible approach to transforming source data into an XHTML source document. Readers not versed (or interested) in XSLT are invited to skip ahead to the next section that "takes over" from the resulting XHTML file.

For more on XSLT, see *Learning XSLT* by Michael Fitzgerald (O'Reilly), or *Beginning XSLT* by Jeni Tennison (APress).

XSLT is an XML-based process that transforms one source XML document into another XML document. XSL transformations can take place on a web server by using middleware calls to conversion services, or directly within the browser as a result of a transform stylesheet declaration in the source XML document. By using XSLT rather than programmatic processes, designers can rely on a trusted standards-based process to build web documents.

The source document

In our example project, we will use a simple XML file, *billings.xml*, as the source data. For simplicity's sake, we will dispense with any Document Type Definitions (DTDs), and just present a collection of data with attributes for categories and months:

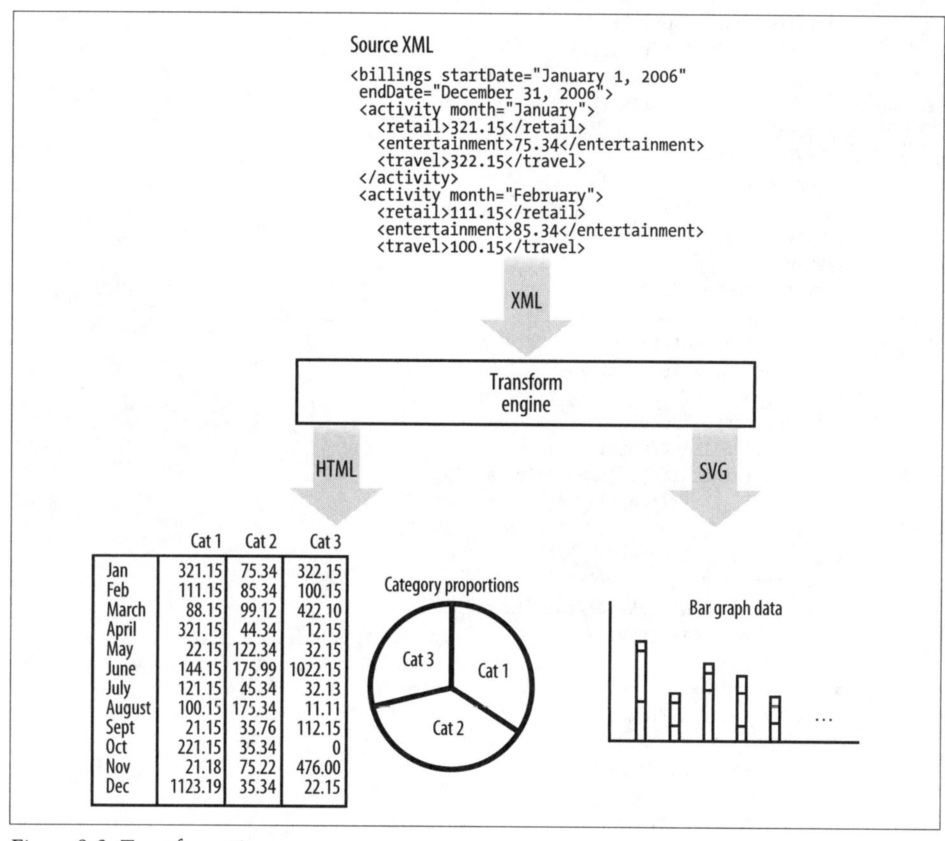

Figure 8-3. Transformation process

```
<?xml version="1.0" encoding="UTF-8"?>
<?xml-stylesheet type="text/xsl" href="billings.xsl"?>

<billings startDate="January 1, 2006" endDate="December 31, 2006">
    <activity month="January">
        <retail>321.15</retail>
        <entertainment>75.34</entertainment>
        <travel>322.15</travel>
    </activity>
    <activity month="February">
        <retail>111.15</retail>
        <entertainment>85.34</entertainment>
        <travel>100.15</travel>
    </activity>
    <activity month="March">
        <retail>88.15</retail>
        <entertainment>99.12</entertainment>
        <travel>422.10</travel>
    </activity>
```

```
    <activity month="April">
        <retail>321.15</retail>
        <entertainment>44.34</entertainment>
        <travel>12.15</travel>
    </activity>
    <activity month="May">
        <retail>22.15</retail>
        <entertainment>122.34</entertainment>
        <travel>32.15</travel>
    </activity>
    <activity month="June">
        <retail>144.15</retail>
        <entertainment>175.99</entertainment>
        <travel>1022.15</travel>
    </activity>
    <activity month="July">
        <retail>121.15</retail>
        <entertainment>45.34</entertainment>
        <travel>32.13</travel>
    </activity>
    <activity month="August">
        <retail>100.15</retail>
        <entertainment>175.34</entertainment>
        <travel>11.11</travel>
    </activity>
    <activity month="September">
        <retail>21.15</retail>
        <entertainment>35.76</entertainment>
        <travel>112.15</travel>
    </activity>
    <activity month="October">
        <retail>221.15</retail>
        <entertainment>35.34</entertainment>
        <travel>0</travel>
    </activity>
    <activity month="November">
        <retail>21.18</retail>
        <entertainment>75.22</entertainment>
        <travel>476.00</travel>
    </activity>
    <activity month="December">
        <retail>1123.19</retail>
        <entertainment>35.34</entertainment>
        <travel>22.15</travel>
    </activity>
</billings>
```

Note that the `xml-stylesheet` processing instruction allows XSLT-aware browsers to convert the XML file as delivered from the web server. Placing the source XML file on a server along with the transform file will allow the browser to open the XML file and transform the input data into the displayed document. An optional approach is to use a transformation tool such as oXygen to do the conversion and create an intermediate XHTML file to be read by the browser.

A transformation stylesheet

One suggested transform file, *billings.xslt*, includes the following directives:

```
<?xml version="1.0" encoding="UTF-8"?>

<xsl:stylesheet version="2.0"
    xmlns="http://www.w3.org/1999/xhtml"
    xmlns:xsl="http://www.w3.org/1999/XSL/Transform"
    xmlns:svg="http://www.w3.org/2000/svg">

    <xsl:output media-type="application/svg+xml" indent="yes"
        method="xhmtl"/>
```

Note that this form is designed to transform the source into an intermediate file. If we wanted to pass the source XML file directly to the browser (without generating an intermediate XHTML file), we would omit the `method` attribute. This header directs the use of a version 2.0 stylesheet and defines the namespaces to be passed to the output stream. In addition, we will place metadata in the `<head>` tag of the output document by virtue of the `xsl:output` directive.

The stylesheet next declares some variables and parameters:

```
<xsl:variable name="graphAreaWidth">400</xsl:variable>
    <xsl:variable name="graphAreaHeight">200</xsl:variable>
    <xsl:variable name="paddingValue">1</xsl:variable>
    <xsl:variable name="svgWidth"
        select="$graphAreaWidth - (2 * $paddingValue)"/>
    <xsl:variable name="svgHeight"
        select="$graphAreaHeight - (2 * $paddingValue)"/>

    <xsl:param name="margin" select="20"/>
    <xsl:param name="pointCount" select="12"/>
```

We will use these statements to set an SVG drawing area of 400 × 200 pixels. We will use a padding area of 1 pixel to help give some form of centering within an enclosing `<div>` element. Within the graph drawing area, we will use a `margin` parameter to offset the origin from the bottom left of the SVG area by 20 user units.

We now declare what, in XSL terms, is referred to as the *topmost template*:

```
<xsl:template match="/" xmlns="http://www.w3.org/1999/xhtml" >
   <xsl:processing-instruction name="xml-stylesheet">
    type="text/css" href="bargraphstyle.css"
   </xsl:processing-instruction>

<html>
   <head><title>Billing Summary</title>
     <script type="text/javascript" src="hilighter.js"></script>
   </head>
 <body onload="docLoaded( );">
```

```
    <xsl:apply-templates select="billings"></xsl:apply-templates>

   </body>
  </html>
 </xsl:template>
```

The match attribute of the xsl:template element means that the code enclosed by the template will be generated for every occurrence of the root of the document. We use an xsl:processing instruction to generate the reference to a stylesheet that will be used for colorization. HTML elements will be passed directly to the output stream, including a reference to a (to be written) JavaScript file that will manipulate the interface.

We use the statement xsl:apply-templates to apply a transformation template to all the billings nodes in the source document:

```
<xsl:template match="billings" >

        <div style="text-align:center; width:{$graphAreaWidth}px;">

            <h1>BILLING ACTIVITY</h1>
            <p>From <xsl:value-of select="@startDate"></xsl:value-of>
                 to <xsl:value-of select="@endDate"></xsl:value-of></p>
            <table border="1" id="activityTable"
               style="width:{$graphAreaWidth}px;">
                <tr>
                    <th>Month</th>
                    <th>Retail</th>
                    <th>Entertainment</th>
                    <th>Travel</th>
                </tr>
                <xsl:for-each select="./activity">
                    <tr>
                    <td><xsl:value-of
                      select="@month"></xsl:value-of></td>
                    <td><xsl:value-of
                      select="retail"></xsl:value-of></td>
                    <td><xsl:value-of
                      select="entertainment"></xsl:value-of></td>
                    <td><xsl:value-of
                      select="travel"></xsl:value-of></td>
                    </tr>
                </xsl:for-each>
            </table>
        </div>
        <div class="graphContainer"
              style="width:{$graphAreaWidth}px;
              height:{$graphAreaHeight}px;
              padding:{$paddingValue}px;">

            <xsl:call-template  name="drawSVG"/>

        </div>
    </xsl:template>
```

This "billings" template will start by sending to the output stream HTML sections for a table using the variables that set display dimensions. There are four columns for the table for the month and data categories. The `xsl:for-each` element will repeatedly generate table rows and data by selecting the `month` attribute from each activity node in the source document. The remaining table data will originate from the value of the retail, entertainment, and travel nodes for each activity node. The template then generates another `<div>` element, which will be the container for the SVG content drawn by the `drawSVG` template.

```
<xsl:template name="drawSVG" >
    <svg:svg version="1.1"
       height="{$svgHeight}" width="{$svgWidth}" >

       <svg:rect x="0" y="0" height="{$svgHeight}" width="{$svgWidth}"
            class="graphBackground"/>


     <svg:g transform="translate({$margin},{$svgHeight - $margin})
         scale(1,-1)">
      <svg:line x1="0" y1="0" x2="0" y2="{$svgHeight - $margin}"
           class="graphAxis"></svg:line>
      <svg:line x1="0" y1="0" x2="{$svgWidth -$margin}" y2="0"
           class="graphAxis"></svg:line>

        <xsl:call-template name="drawBars">

        </xsl:call-template>
      </svg:g>

    </svg:svg>

</xsl:template>
```

This template creates many of the SVG elements we discussed in the preceding section. The template uses the explicit SVG namespace for clarity. An SVG area is declared, and a rectangle is created to set some background color for the drawing (classes are added for backgrounds, axes, and labels that will be stylized using the external stylesheet). The "drawbars" template draws the bars in our graph:

```
<xsl:template name="drawBars"   >
    <xsl:param name="barInterval"
        select="$svgWidth div count(//activity)"></xsl:param>
    <xsl:param name="currentY" select="0"/>
    <xsl:param name="currentBar" select="0"/>

    <xsl:variable name="yMax">
        <xsl:call-template name="getMax" >
            <xsl:with-param name="maxValue" select="0"/>
            <xsl:with-param name="inList" select="./activity"/>
        </xsl:call-template>
    </xsl:variable>
```

```
<xsl:variable name="yScale"
          select="($svgHeight div $yMax) * 0.8"/>


<xsl:for-each select="./activity">

    <xsl:element name="svg:rect">
        <xsl:attribute name="x">
          <xsl:value-of
            select="round((position( ) - 1) * $barInterval)"/>
          </xsl:attribute>
        <xsl:attribute name="y">0</xsl:attribute>
        <xsl:attribute name="height">
          <xsl:value-of select="round(retail * $yScale)">
          </xsl:value-of></xsl:attribute>
        <xsl:attribute
            name="class">segment_retail</xsl:attribute>
        <xsl:attribute name="width">
              <xsl:value-of select="round($barInterval div 4)"/>
        </xsl:attribute>
        <xsl:attribute
             name="month"><xsl:value-of select="./@month"/>
         </xsl:attribute>
    </xsl:element>

    <xsl:element name="svg:rect">
        <xsl:attribute name="x">
            <xsl:value-of
             select="round((position( ) - 1) * $barInterval)"/>
        </xsl:attribute>
        <xsl:attribute name="y">
           <xsl:value-of select="round(retail * $yScale)">
           </xsl:value-of>
         </xsl:attribute>
        <xsl:attribute name="height">
          <xsl:value-of
            select="round(entertainment * $yScale)">
          </xsl:value-of>
         </xsl:attribute>
        <xsl:attribute
            name="class">segment_entertainment</xsl:attribute>
        <xsl:attribute name="width">
            <xsl:value-of select="round($barInterval div 4)"/>
        </xsl:attribute>
        <xsl:attribute name="month">
            <xsl:value-of select="./@month"/>
         </xsl:attribute>
    </xsl:element>

    <xsl:element name="svg:rect">
        <xsl:attribute name="x">
            <xsl:value-of
              select="round((position( ) - 1) * $barInterval)"/>
        </xsl:attribute>
```

```
            <xsl:attribute name="y">
               <xsl:value-of
                  select="round((retail + entertainment) * $yScale)">
               </xsl:value-of>
            </xsl:attribute>
            <xsl:attribute name="height">
                 <xsl:value-of
                   select="round(travel * $yScale)">
                 </xsl:value-of>
            </xsl:attribute>
            <xsl:attribute
                 name="class">segment_travel</xsl:attribute>
            <xsl:attribute name="width">
                <xsl:value-of
                  select="round($barInterval div 4)"/>
            </xsl:attribute>
            <xsl:attribute name="month">
               <xsl:value-of select="./@month"/>
            </xsl:attribute>
         </xsl:element>

         <!-- Now create a small label under the bar -->
         <xsl:element name="svg:g">
             <xsl:attribute
               name="transform">scale(1,-1)</xsl:attribute>
             <xsl:attribute
              name="class">axisLabel</xsl:attribute>
             <xsl:element name="svg:text">
                 <xsl:attribute name="font-size">
                     <xsl:value-of select="15"/>px
                 </xsl:attribute>
                 <xsl:attribute name="stroke-width">
                   <xsl:value-of select="1"/>px</xsl:attribute>
                 <xsl:attribute name="y">16</xsl:attribute>
                 <xsl:attribute name="x">
                    <xsl:value-of
                   select="round((position( ) - 1) * $barInterval)"/>
                 </xsl:attribute>
                 <xsl:value-of select="substring(./@month,1,1)"/>
             </xsl:element>
         </xsl:element>
      </xsl:for-each>
   </xsl:template>
```

The drawBars template starts by calling another template (getMax) to find the maximum value of the sum of each month's activity, and the vertical scaling factor is set so that the maximum vertical value will fill 80 percent of the vertical space. Bar spacing ($barInterval) is set by dividing the number of samples into the SVG graph width.

The remainder of this template builds a stack of three segments to form one bar of the graph. New elements and positional attributes are repeatedly created by declaring the xsl:element tag and its children. Each segment has its own class name (for styling). Coordinates are rounded to integer values to keep the data from being overly precise. The stacking of each segment's *y* coordinate is based on the vertical displacement of the previous segment, and the horizontal location is based on the position of the source node (its monthly offset from the first entry) and the bar interval.

The only remaining template is the recursive getMax template:

```
<xsl:template name="getMax" >
        <xsl:param name="maxValue" select="-9999"/>
        <xsl:param name="inList"/>

        <xsl:choose>
            <!-- still processing node -->
            <xsl:when test="$inList">
                <xsl:variable name="remainingList"
                    select="$inList[position( ) != 1]" />

                <xsl:variable name="slideNext">
                <xsl:choose>
                    <!-- use new value -->
                      <xsl:when
                         test="round(sum($inList[1]/*))
                          &gt; round($maxValue)">
                        <xsl:value-of
                            select="round(sum($inList[1]/*))"/>
                    </xsl:when>

                    <!-- keep old value -->
                    <xsl:otherwise>
                        <xsl:value-of select="round($maxValue)"/>
                    </xsl:otherwise>
                </xsl:choose>
                </xsl:variable>
                    <xsl:call-template name="getMax">
                        <xsl:with-param name="maxValue"
                            select="$slideNext">
                      </xsl:with-param>
                <xsl:with-param name="inList"
                       select="$remainingList">
                  </xsl:with-param>
              </xsl:call-template>

            </xsl:when>

            <!-- end condition has been hit -->
            <xsl:otherwise>
            <xsl:value-of select="$maxValue"/>
           </xsl:otherwise>
       </xsl:choose>

    </xsl:template>
</xsl:stylesheet>
```

This template uses a standard "recipe" as a recursive search of values through a collection of nodes. The node list is input as a string of node references—each entry is read during each iteration of the loop with the maximum value being returned to the calling template.

The resulting XHTML file

Regardless of whether the developer uses an XSLT file to directly transform a file served to a browser, or to generate an intermediate file, applying the preceding transform file results in the browser (or filesystem) receiving a stream represented by this *billings.xhtml* file, as generated by a recent edition of oXygen:

```
<?xml version="1.0" encoding="UTF-8"?>
  <?xml-stylesheet
      type="text/css"
      href="bargraphstyle.css"?><html>
       xmlns:svg="http://www.w3.org/2000/svg"
      xmlns="http://www.w3.org/1999/xhtml">
   <head>
      <meta http-equiv="Content-Type" content="application/svg+xml;
        charset=UTF-8" />
      <title>Billing Summary</title><script type="text/javascript"
         src="hilighter.js"></script></head>
   <body onload="docLoaded( );">
      <div style="text-align:center; width:400px;">
         <h1>BILLING ACTIVITY</h1>
         <p>From January 1, 2006
            to December 31, 2006
         </p>
         <table border="1" id="activityTable" style="width:400px;">
            <tr>
               <th>Month</th>
               <th>Retail</th>
               <th>Entertainment</th>
               <th>Travel</th>
            </tr>
            <tr>
               <td>January</td>
               <td>321.15</td>
               <td>75.34</td>
               <td>322.15</td>
            </tr>
            <tr>
               <td>February</td>
               <td>111.15</td>
               <td>85.34</td>
               <td>100.15</td>
            </tr>
```

```
<tr>
   <td>March</td>
   <td>88.15</td>
   <td>99.12</td>
   <td>422.10</td>
</tr>
<tr>
   <td>April</td>
   <td>321.15</td>
   <td>44.34</td>
   <td>12.15</td>
</tr>
<tr>
   <td>May</td>
   <td>22.15</td>
   <td>122.34</td>
   <td>32.15</td>
</tr>
<tr>
   <td>June</td>
   <td>144.15</td>
   <td>175.99</td>
   <td>1022.15</td>
</tr>
<tr>
   <td>July</td>
   <td>121.15</td>
   <td>45.34</td>
   <td>32.13</td>
</tr>
<tr>
   <td>August</td>
   <td>100.15</td>
   <td>175.34</td>
   <td>11.11</td>
</tr>
<tr>
   <td>September</td>
   <td>21.15</td>
   <td>35.76</td>
   <td>112.15</td>
</tr>
<tr>
   <td>October</td>
   <td>221.15</td>
   <td>35.34</td>
   <td>0</td>
</tr>
<tr>
   <td>November</td>
   <td>21.18</td>
   <td>75.22</td>
   <td>476.00</td>
</tr>
```

```
        <tr>
           <td>December</td>
           <td>1123.19</td>
           <td>35.34</td>
           <td>22.15</td>
        </tr>
     </table>
  </div>
  <div class="graphContainer"
       style="width:400px; height:200px; padding:1px;">
     <svg:svg version="1.1" height="198" width="398">
        <svg:rect x="0" y="0" height="198" width="398"
           class="graphBackground"></svg:rect>
        <svg:g transform="translate(20,178)  scale(1,-1)">
           <svg:line x1="0" y1="0" x2="0" y2="178"
             class="graphAxis"></svg:line>
           <svg:line x1="0" y1="0" x2="378" y2="0"
          class="graphAxis"></svg:line>
           <svg:rect x="0" y="0" height="38"
             class="segment_retail"
             width="8" month="January"></svg:rect>
           <svg:rect x="0" y="38" height="9"
             class="segment_entertainment"
             width="8" month="January"></svg:rect>
           <svg:rect x="0" y="47" height="38"
             class="segment_travel"
             width="8" month="January"></svg:rect>
           <svg:g transform="scale(1,-1)" class="axisLabel">
              <svg:text font-size="15px" stroke-width="1px"
                y="16" x="0">J</svg:text>
           </svg:g>
           <svg:rect x="33" y="0" height="13"
            class="segment_retail"
            width="8" month="February"></svg:rect>
           <svg:rect x="33" y="13" height="10"
            class="segment_entertainment"
            width="8"
                     month="February"></svg:rect>
           <svg:rect x="33" y="23" height="12"
             class="segment_travel"
             width="8" month="February"></svg:rect>
           <svg:g transform="scale(1,-1)" class="axisLabel">
              <svg:text font-size="15px" stroke-width="1px"
               y="16" x="33">F</svg:text>
           </svg:g>
           <svg:rect x="66" y="0" height="10"
            class="segment_retail"
            width="8" month="March"></svg:rect>
           <svg:rect x="66" y="10" height="12"
            class="segment_entertainment"
            width="8" month="March"></svg:rect>
           <svg:rect x="66" y="22" height="50"
             class="segment_travel"
             width="8" month="March"></svg:rect>
```

```
<svg:g transform="scale(1,-1)" class="axisLabel">
   <svg:text font-size="15px" stroke-width="1px"
     y="16" x="66">M</svg:text>
</svg:g>
<svg:rect x="100" y="0" height="38"
  class="segment_retail"
  width="8" month="April"></svg:rect>
<svg:rect x="100" y="38" height="5"
  class="segment_entertainment"
  width="8" month="April"></svg:rect>
<svg:rect x="100" y="43" height="1"
  class="segment_travel"
  width="8" month="April"></svg:rect>
<svg:g transform="scale(1,-1)" class="axisLabel">
   <svg:text font-size="15px" stroke-width="1px" y="16"
      x="100">A</svg:text>
</svg:g>
<svg:rect x="133" y="0" height="3"
  class="segment_retail"
 width="8" month="May"></svg:rect>
<svg:rect x="133" y="3" height="14"
  class="segment_entertainment"
  width="8" month="May"></svg:rect>
<svg:rect x="133" y="17" height="4"
 class="segment_travel"
 width="8" month="May"></svg:rect>
<svg:g transform="scale(1,-1)" class="axisLabel">
   <svg:text font-size="15px" stroke-width="1px"
     y="16" x="133">M</svg:text>
</svg:g>
<svg:rect x="166" y="0" height="17"
  class="segment_retail"
 width="8" month="June"></svg:rect>
<svg:rect x="166" y="17" height="21"
 class="segment_entertainment"
 width="8" month="June"></svg:rect>
<svg:rect x="166" y="38" height="121"
  class="segment_travel"
  width="8" month="June"></svg:rect>
<svg:g transform="scale(1,-1)" class="axisLabel">
   <svg:text font-size="15px" stroke-width="1px"
     y="16" x="166">J</svg:text>
</svg:g>
<svg:rect x="199" y="0" height="14"
  class="segment_retail"
  width="8" month="July"></svg:rect>
<svg:rect x="199" y="14" height="5"
   class="segment_entertainment"
   width="8" month="July"></svg:rect>
<svg:rect x="199" y="20" height="4" class="segment_travel"
    width="8" month="July"></svg:rect>
<svg:g transform="scale(1,-1)" class="axisLabel">
   <svg:text font-size="15px" stroke-width="1px" y="16"
     x="199">J</svg:text>
</svg:g>
```

```
<svg:rect x="232" y="0" height="12"
   class="segment_retail"
   width="8" month="August"></svg:rect>
<svg:rect x="232" y="12" height="21"
    class="segment_entertainment"
    width="8" month="August"></svg:rect>
<svg:rect x="232" y="33" height="1"
    class="segment_travel"
   width="8" month="August"></svg:rect>
<svg:g transform="scale(1,-1)" class="axisLabel">
   <svg:text font-size="15px" stroke-width="1px"
     y="16" x="232">A</svg:text>
</svg:g>
<svg:rect x="265" y="0" height="2"
     class="segment_retail"
     width="8" month="September"></svg:rect>
<svg:rect x="265" y="2" height="4"
     class="segment_entertainment"
     width="8" month="September"></svg:rect>
<svg:rect x="265" y="7" height="13"
     class="segment_travel"
     width="8" month="September"></svg:rect>
<svg:g transform="scale(1,-1)" class="axisLabel">
   <svg:text font-size="15px" stroke-width="1px"
     y="16" x="265">S</svg:text>
</svg:g>
<svg:rect x="299" y="0" height="26"
   class="segment_retail"
   width="8" month="October"></svg:rect>
<svg:rect x="299" y="26" height="4"
    class="segment_entertainment"
    width="8" month="October"></svg:rect>
<svg:rect x="299" y="30" height="0"
    class="segment_travel"
    width="8" month="October"></svg:rect>
<svg:g transform="scale(1,-1)" class="axisLabel">
   <svg:text font-size="15px" stroke-width="1px"
      y="16" x="299">O</svg:text>
</svg:g>
<svg:rect x="332" y="0" height="2"
   class="segment_retail"
   width="8" month="November"></svg:rect>
<svg:rect x="332" y="2" height="9"
    class="segment_entertainment"
    width="8" month="November"></svg:rect>
<svg:rect x="332" y="11" height="56"
   class="segment_travel"
   width="8" month="November"></svg:rect>
<svg:g transform="scale(1,-1)" class="axisLabel">
   <svg:text font-size="15px" stroke-width="1px"
     y="16" x="332">N</svg:text>
</svg:g>
```

```
                <svg:rect x="365" y="0" height="133"
                     class="segment_retail"
                     width="8" month="December"></svg:rect>
                <svg:rect x="365" y="133" height="4"
                     class="segment_entertainment"
                     width="8" month="December"></svg:rect>
                <svg:rect x="365" y="137" height="3"
                    class="segment_travel"
                    width="8" month="December"></svg:rect>
                <svg:g transform="scale(1,-1)" class="axisLabel">
                   <svg:text font-size="15px" stroke-width="1px"
                     y="16" x="365">D</svg:text>
                </svg:g>
            </svg:g>
         </svg:svg>
      </div>
   </body>
</html>
```

Style Information

Although we set SVG attributes related to length as attributes, we use CSS style properties to set the color and fill patterns for the different bar segments. Our *bargraphstyle.css* file follows:

```
svg {
fill:red;
}
.segment_retail {
fill:#0000ff;
}

.segment_travel {
fill:#00c0c0;
}

.segment_entertainment {
fill:#008080;
}

.graphLabel {
fill:black;
stroke:none;
}
.axisLabel {
fill:black;
stroke:none;
}

.graphBackground {
 fill:#e0e0e0;
}
```

```
div.graphContainer {
border-style:ridge;
border-width:2px;
border-color:#0f0f0f;
fill:red;
}

div.pieChartContainer {
border-style:ridge;
border-width:2px;
border-color:#0000f0;
}

.graphAxis {
stroke:#000080;
}
```

Adding Interactivity

To this point, nothing about the preceding transformation or intermediate XHTML file is particularly tailored to Firefox. Firefox's capability to manage elements of different namespaces (in this case, XHTML and SVG) as one coherent document provides the developer with a reasonably straightforward approach to tie all such elements together in the interface model.

Given the requirements of this application, we will code up a JavaScript file to implement these general specifications:

- When moving a mouse over one of the table rows, highlight one of the bar graphs. We will accomplish this by changing the stroke color and width of the bars.
- When moving a mouse over one of the bars, highlight the associated row. We will highlight the table data by changing the background color of the associated row.

By looking at the *billings.xhtml* file, you can get a hint about the way our code snippet will manage these tasks.

As each bar segment was created, a `month` attribute was attached to the bar matching the source table row that generated the bar's data. This attribute will serve as a hook for event handlers to connect the graph bars to the table data.

The first part of the source code, *highlighter.js*, includes global variables that we will use to save initial style values. The initialization function `docLoaded` looks for all SVG <rect> elements and all table <tr> elements to add an appropriate event listener:

```
var tableBackgroundColor;
var barColor;
var highlightTableNode;
var highlightBarNodes;

docLoaded = function( ) {
try {
```

```
var barClasses = document.getElementsByTagName("rect");
for (var i = 0; i < barClasses.length; i++) {
 var className = barClasses[i].getAttribute("class");
 if (className) { // maybe a bar
    if (className.indexOf("segment_") != -1)
     { // we have a display bar
     barClasses[i].addEventListener("mouseover",mouseInBar,true);
     barClasses[i].addEventListener("mouseout",mouseOutBar,true);
    } // we have a display bar
  } // maybe a bar
}
// Now add listener to the table data elements
//
 var theTable = document.getElementById("activityTable");
 if (theTable) {
 var theRows = theTable.getElementsByTagName("tr");
  for (var i = 0; i < theRows.length; i++) {
   theRows[i].addEventListener("mouseover",mouseInTable,true);
   theRows[i].addEventListener("mouseout",mouseOutTable,true);
  }
 }
 highlightTableNode = null;
 highlightBarNode = null;
 }
 catch (e) {
 alert("Exception: " + e );
 }
}
```

The functions managing mouse movement in and out of the SVG bars use the `month` attribute as the parameter to the function (`getTableRow`) that returns the row associated with the bar's month. (The parent node of the table data cell is the table row node containing all the cells for that month.) The original (if any) `backgroundColor` style property is saved, and a new highlight color is set to indicate the appropriate table row data:

```
// Event listeners for SVG bar graph elements
 //
 mouseInBar = function(event) {
 try {

  var segMonth = event.currentTarget.getAttribute("month");
  var tableNode = getTableRow(segMonth);
  if(tableNode) { // found our target
    highlightTableNode = tableNode;
    tableBackgroundColor = tableNode.style.backgroundColor;
    tableNode.style.backgroundColor = "#8080ff";
  } // found our target
 }
  catch (e) {
  alert("Exception: " + e );
  }
 }
```

```
mouseOutBar = function(event) {
try {
  if (highlightTableNode) {
   highlightTableNode.style.backgroundColor = tableBackgroundColor;
   highlightTableNode = null;
  }
 }
  catch (e) {
  alert("Exception: " + e );
  }
 }

 // Returns the row of the table that holds the
 // bar's category
 getTableRow = function(theMonth) {
 try {
 var retNode = null;
 var theTable = document.getElementById("activityTable");
 if (theTable) {

   var tableData = theTable.getElementsByTagName("td");
   for (var i = 0 ; i < tableData.length; i++) {
    if (tableData[i].textContent == theMonth) { // we have target row
    retNode = tableData[i].parentNode;
    break;
    // to be continued
    } // we have target row
   }
  }
 return retNode;
 }
 catch (e) {
  alert("Exception: " + e );
  }
 }
```

Finally, we use the same approach for the mousein/mouseout event handlers for the SVG table elements. When a mouse moves into the table, we use event.target to find the table row that triggered the event. We acquire its children and use the first child (presumed to be the "month" column) to obtain the month in which the user is interested. We use that month string as a parameter to fetch all the SVG bars with the matching month attribute (the function getBarsFor), and we modify the stroke color and width until the mouse moves out of the table area:

```
// Event listeners for the table elements
//
//
// Respond only if the target happens to be
// a table data element
//
// We presume the first table data entry holds the
// month of interest; that value will be used to fetch
// the data bars to highlight
//
```

```
mouseInTable = function(event) {
try {
 var rowData = event.currentTarget.getElementsByTagName("td");
 if (rowData.length > 0) {
 var targetMonth = rowData[0].textContent;
 highlightBarNodes = getBarsFor(targetMonth);
 if (highlightBarNodes) {
  for (var i = 0; i < highlightBarNodes.length; i++) {
   highlightBarNodes[i].setAttribute("stroke","red");
   highlightBarNodes[i].setAttribute("stroke-width","3px");
    }
   }
  }
 }
 catch (e) {
  alert("Exception: " + e );
  }
}
mouseOutTable = function(event) {
try {
 if (highlightBarNodes) {
  for (var i = 0; i < highlightBarNodes.length; i++) {
  dump("Clearing style for " + highlightBarNodes[i] + "\n");
    highlightBarNodes[i].setAttribute("stroke","none");
    highlightBarNodes[i].setAttribute("stroke-width","")
  }
 }
 highlightBarNodes = null;
 }
 catch (e) {
  alert("Exception: " + e );
  }
}
//
// Returns a collection of all the bars with the
// month
getBarsFor = function(targetMonth) {
try {
 var retArray = null;
 var theBars = document.getElementsByTagName("rect");
 if (theBars.length > 0) {
    retArray = new Array();
    for (var i = 0; i < theBars.length; i++) {
     if (theBars[i].getAttribute("month") == targetMonth)
        retArray.push(theBars[i]);
    }
   }
  }
  catch (e) {
  alert("Exception: " + e );
  }
  if (retArray.length == 0) return null;
  return retArray;
 }
```

The resulting application now highlights bars when the mouse moves over the associated table row, and highlights the table data when the mouse moves over the corresponding SVG area, as shown in Figure 8-4.

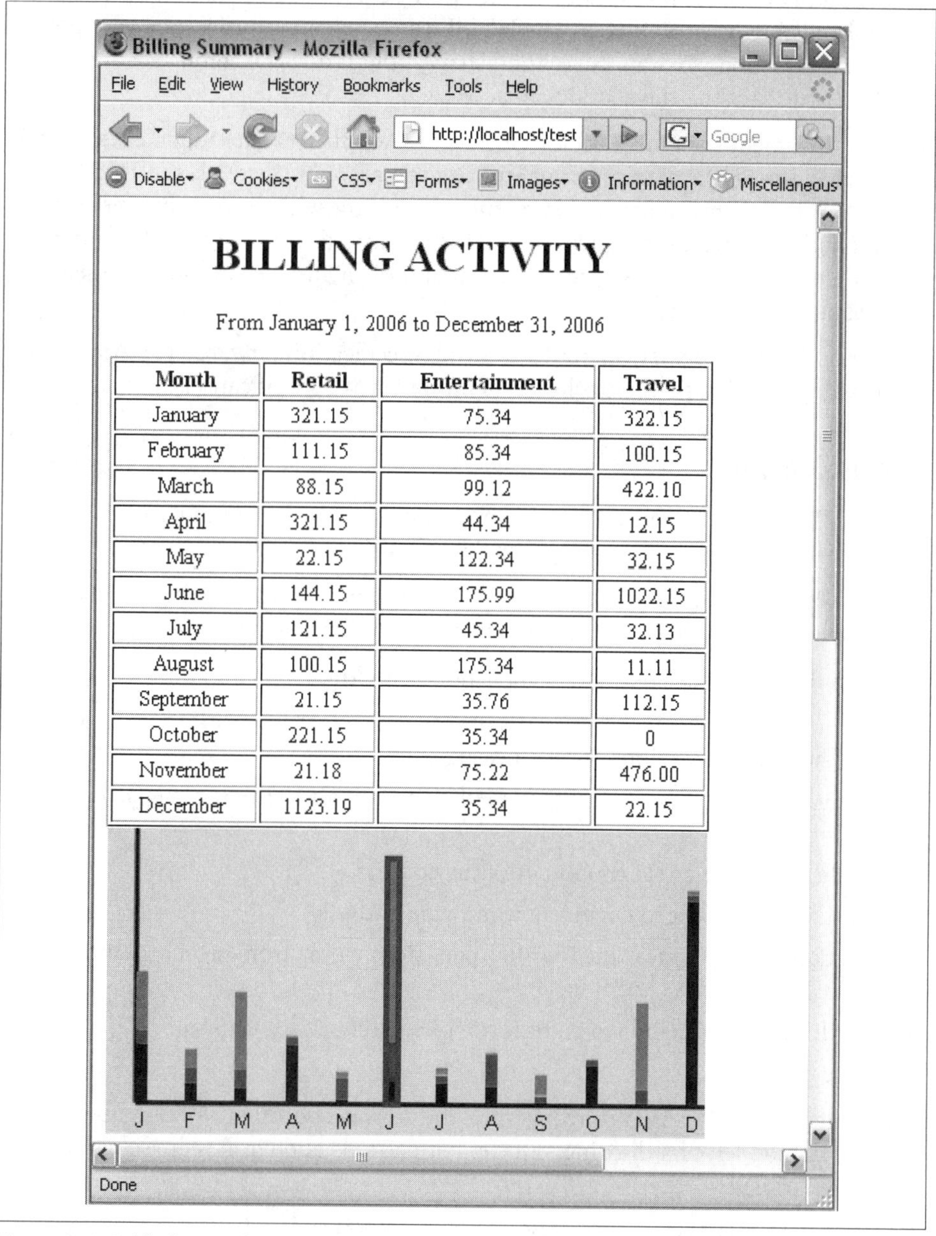

Month	Retail	Entertainment	Travel
January	321.15	75.34	322.15
February	111.15	85.34	100.15
March	88.15	99.12	422.10
April	321.15	44.34	12.15
May	22.15	122.34	32.15
June	144.15	175.99	1022.15
July	121.15	45.34	32.13
August	100.15	175.34	11.11
September	21.15	35.76	112.15
October	221.15	35.34	0
November	21.18	75.22	476.00
December	1123.19	35.34	22.15

Figure 8-4. Table data with SVG bar graph

HTML Canvas

Whereas SVG represents an XML-compliant document structure for graphics, the HTML canvas element provides a collection of JavaScript instructions to draw and manipulate geometric primitives. The HTML canvas element provides a very powerful set of instructions to draw curves and shapes, but it does not represent any persistent data structures that JavaScript can access.

An SVG document contains tags for elements to which you can attach `class` and `id` attributes, allowing JavaScript to manipulate the graphics through the DOM interface. The HTML canvas element represents an element with an API that serves more to paint and decorate an interface; canvas instructions can be triggered by manipulations of an interface, but the instructions in and of themselves do not represent any addressable object.

The canvas tag was originally part of a drawing specification forwarded by Apple, Inc., and is under consideration for inclusion in future HTML specifications.

Canvas Drawing

The HTML canvas element presents a programming interface familiar to developers who have had to program in graphics environments.

The key object behind the canvas element is a *2D context*—representing the characteristics of a virtual pen and pattern used to paint a two-dimensional surface.

The formula to draw using a canvas element is as follows:

1. Add a `<canvas>` element to the document with `width` and `height` attributes setting the pixel dimensions of the drawing area.
2. In JavaScript, use the `getContext` method to obtain the two-dimensional drawing context.
3. Set the `stroke` and `fill` properties of the context.
4. Instruct the context to begin a new drawing path.
5. Use `moveTo` to position the "virtual pen" to a point from which drawing is to begin.
6. Use drawing commands to paint rectangles, circles, arcs, or lines.
7. Close the path.

As is the case with the SVG drawing area, the canvas coordinate system uses an origin from the top left of a drawing surface. Fill patterns and strokes are set as conventional RGB triplets:

```
someContext.fillStyle = "rgb(someRed,someGreen,someBlue)";
```

where the red, green, and blue quantities represent magnitudes from 0 through 255.

Program algorithm

We will modify the XSLT file (and its resulting XHTML output) to include a canvas element with an ID to facilitate access from a JavaScript function:

```
<canvas id="pieChartCanvas" width="200px" height="150px"></canvas>
```

Initialization code will obtain a context for the pie chart to be associated with the canvas element:

```
var pieContext = theCanvas.getContext("2d");
```

The code to draw a slice of the pie chart starts by positioning the context at the center of the chart's drawing area. We will modify event handling code that responds to a mouse movement over a table row to extract the table data entries for each spending amount. The code then calculates the number of degrees (in radians) represented by each magnitude's proportionate share of the total.

Following is a snippet of pseudocode with values `a1`, `a2`, and `a3` representing the magnitudes to be plotted:

```
var r1 = ((a1 / total)  * 2 * Math.PI);
var r2 = ((a2 / total)  * 2 * Math.PI);
var r3 = ((a3 / total)  * 2 * Math.PI);

pieContext.fillStyle = "rgb(0,0,255)";
pieContext.beginPath( );
pieContext.moveTo(pieX,pieY);
pieContext.arc(pieX,pieY,pieRadius,0,r1,0);
pieContext.closePath( );
pieContext.fill( )
```

Table 8-2 summarizes the JavaScript canvas instructions for the pie chart.

Table 8-2. JavaScript canvas instructions for the pie chart

Method/Property	Attributes	Description
`canvas.getContext("2d")`	N/A	Obtains the two-dimensional drawing context for the canvas.
`context.fillStyle`	`"rgb(rVal,gVal,bVal)"`	Sets the fill color for a path.
`context.beginPath`	N/A	Resets the logic that determines the filling of a path.
`context.moveTo`	`someX, someY`	Moves the "pen" to a coordinate.
`context.arc`	`startX, startY, radius, startAngle, endAngle,sweepClockwise`	Traces a path from a starting position, with a specified radius from the starting angle through the ending angle. The last field specifies the direction of the arc's sweep.
`context.closePath`	N/A	Terminates a path.
`context.fill()`	N/A	Fills the previously traced path with the existing context's `fillStyle` property.

Text

Although the canvas tag provides a rich set of instructions to paint patterns and areas, it does not currently support text display. Therefore, to label our pie chart, we will rely on conventional HTML drawing that will position and modify the pie chart labels to be painted on top of the canvas drawing area.

We chose to place the label at half the angular displacement of a pie segment, at a radius that is three-quarters the length of the radius of the circle. Figure 8-5 shows a straightforward application of geometry to position the arc labels.

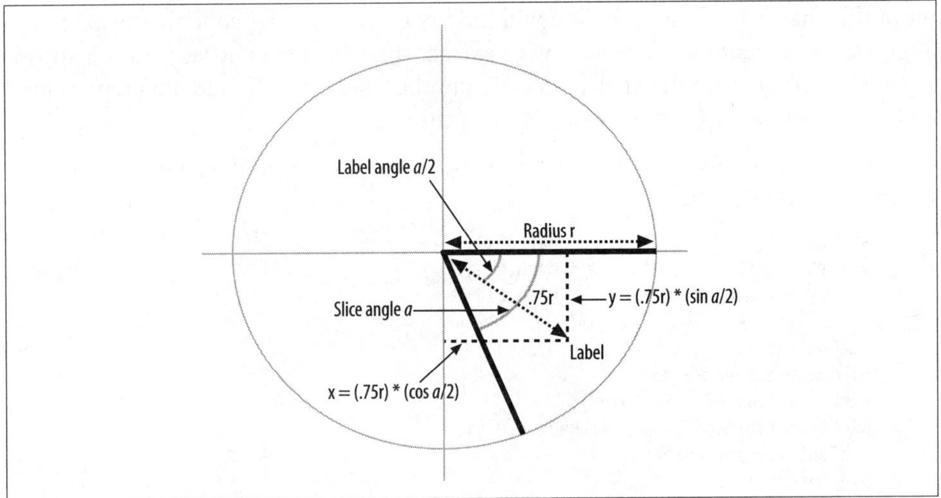

Figure 8-5. Label positioning geometry

Note that the drawing will consider "positive" to be a clockwise direction from the horizontal; this keeps the logic consistent with the canvas drawing direction of a downward positive direction and makes no conceptual difference to the viewer of the graph.

Program Code

The actual code starts with a change to the XSLT file to generate our canvas, as well as div elements to contain the labels:

```
<div class="graphContainer"
  style="width:{$graphAreaWidth}px; height:{$graphAreaHeight}px;
           padding:{$paddingValue}px;">

 <xsl:call-template  name="drawSVG"/>

    <div class="pieChartContainer"
     style="text-align:center; position:absolute;
      top:150px; left:410px;  width:200px; height:150px;">
```

```
        <canvas id="pieChartCanvas" width="200px" height="150px"/>
        <div id="entLabel" style="font-family:arial;font-size:10pt;
          font-weight:bold; position:absolute; zIndex:3; top:0px;
           left:0px; color:black; background:transparent;">
                 Ent</div>
        <div id="travelLabel" style="font-family:arial;font-size:10pt;
           font-weight:bold; position:absolute; zIndex:3; top:10px;
              left:0px; color:black; background:transparent;">
                Travel</div>
        <div id="retailLabel" style="font-family:arial;font-size:10pt;
             font-weight:bold; position:absolute; zIndex:3; top:20px;
                left:0px; color:black; background:transparent;">
                  Retail</div>
   </div>

  </div>
</xsl:template>
```

The zIndex is not absolutely necessary; as the code is written, the drawing order will result in the label being painted above the graph canvas. The zOrder does, however, provide the designer with some assurance of a proper painting sequence if the code results in a reordering of the HTML tag declarations. The background of the label text is set to transparent to allow the pie chart colors to show through as label backgrounds.

The JavaScript in the *highlighter.js* file adds global variables for the drawing context as well as the div elements for the labels. The initialization code will calculate the size of the pie chart based on the dimensions of the enclosing container. We set the size to 80 percent of the available space; we set a threshold value (K_MIN_ARC) that will be used to turn off the label of any slices that are too small to properly display a label:

```
var pieX;
var pieY;
var pieRadius;
var pieContext;
var canvasWidth;
var canvasHeight;
var retailDiv;
var travelDiv;
var entDiv;
var K_MIN_ARC = 0.1;

docLoaded = function( ) {
try {
var barClasses = document.getElementsByTagName("rect");
for (var i = 0; i < barClasses.length; i++) {
 var className = barClasses[i].getAttribute("class");
 if (className) { // maybe a bar
    if (className.indexOf("segment_") != -1) { // we have a display bar
     barClasses[i].addEventListener("mouseover",mouseInBar,true);
     barClasses[i].addEventListener("mouseout",mouseOutBar,true);
    } // we have a display bar
  } // maybe a bar
 }
```

```
// Now add listener to the table data elements
//
 var theTable = document.getElementById("activityTable");
 if (theTable) {
 var theRows = theTable.getElementsByTagName("tr");
  for (var i = 0; i < theRows.length; i++) {
   theRows[i].addEventListener("mouseover",mouseInTable,true);
   theRows[i].addEventListener("mouseout",mouseOutTable,true);
  }
 }
 highlightTableNode = null;
 highlightBarNode = null;

 // ----- added for pie chart
 // Find the center of the drawing area
 var theCanvas = document.getElementById("pieChartCanvas");
 canvasWidth = theCanvas.width;
 canvasHeight = theCanvas.height;
 pieX = Math.round(canvasWidth / 2);
 pieY = Math.round(canvasHeight / 2);
 pieRadius = Math.round((Math.min(canvasHeight,canvasWidth))
      * 0.4);
 pieContext = theCanvas.getContext("2d");

 retailDiv = document.getElementById("retailLabel");
 travelDiv = document.getElementById("travelLabel");
 entDiv = document.getElementById("entLabel");
```

We change the event handler for the table to extract the text from the table data cells and call the function to draw the pie chart. The event handler for mouse movement off the table clears the pie chart and turns off the visibility of the labels:

```
mouseInTable = function(event) {
try {
 var rowData = event.currentTarget.getElementsByTagName("td");
 if (rowData.length > 0) {
 var targetMonth = rowData[0].textContent;
 highlightBarNodes = getBarsFor(targetMonth);
 if (highlightBarNodes) {
  for (var i = 0; i < highlightBarNodes.length; i++) {
   highlightBarNodes[i].setAttribute("stroke","red");
   highlightBarNodes[i].setAttribute("stroke-width","4px");
    }
   }
   redrawPieChart(parseFloat(rowData[1].textContent),
      parseFloat(rowData[2].textContent),
       parseFloat(rowData[3].textContent));
  }
 }
 catch (e) {
  alert("Exception: " + e );
  }
}
```

```
mouseOutTable = function(event) {
try {
 if (highlightBarNodes) {
  for (var i = 0; i < highlightBarNodes.length; i++) {
  dump("Clearing style for " + highlightBarNodes[i] + "\n");
    highlightBarNodes[i].setAttribute("stroke","none");
    highlightBarNodes[i].setAttribute("stroke-width","")
  }
 }
 highlightBarNodes = null;
 pieContext.clearRect(0,0,canvasWidth,canvasHeight);
 entDiv.style.visibility="hidden";
 retailDiv.style.visibility="hidden";
 travelDiv.style.visibility="hidden";
 }
 catch (e) {
  alert("Exception: " + e );
  }
}
```

We add similar changes to the logic for the mouse movement event handlers over the displayed SVG bars:

```
mouseInBar = function(event) {
 try {

  var segMonth = event.currentTarget.getAttribute("month");
  var tableNode = getTableRow(segMonth);
  if(tableNode) { // found our target
    highlightTableNode = tableNode;
    tableBackgroundColor = tableNode.style.backgroundColor;
    tableNode.style.backgroundColor = "#8080ff";
    var theCells = tableNode.getElementsByTagName("td");
    redrawPieChart(parseFloat(theCells[1].textContent),
                   parseFloat(theCells[2].textContent),
                   parseFloat(theCells[3].textContent));


  } // found our target
 }
  catch (e) {
  alert("Exception: " + e );
  }
 }

mouseOutBar = function(event) {
try {
  if (highlightTableNode) {
   highlightTableNode.style.backgroundColor =
        tableBackgroundColor;
   highlightTableNode = null;
  }
 pieContext.clearRect(0,0,canvasWidth,canvasHeight);
 entDiv.style.visibility="hidden";
```

```
retailDiv.style.visibility="hidden";
travelDiv.style.visibility="hidden";
}
 catch (e) {
 alert("Exception: " + e );
 }
}
```

Finally, the function to draw the pie chart paints the arcs and labels. The colors for the segments are selected to match those of the SVG bars. (We can simplify these settings through stylesheet declarations.) The code does not paint labels if the slice for any given segment requires less than 6 degrees of arc sweep (approximately .1 radian):

```
// ------------------------------
// Canvas drawing added for pie chart with
// floating point numbers representing slice portions
//
// (For this application a1 = retail, a2 = entertainment,
//   a3 = travel)
//
redrawPieChart = function (a1,a2,a3) {
try {

  pieContext.fillStyle = "#e0e0e0";
  pieContext.fillRect(0.0,0.0,parseFloat(canvasWidth),
       parseFloat(canvasHeight));

  var total = a1 + a2 + a3;
  var r1 = ((a1 / total)  * 2 * Math.PI);
  var r2 = ((a2 / total)  * 2 * Math.PI);
  var r3 = ((a3 / total)  * 2 * Math.PI);

  pieContext.fillStyle = "rgb(0,0,255)";
  pieContext.beginPath( );
  pieContext.moveTo(pieX,pieY);
  pieContext.arc(pieX,pieY,pieRadius,0,r1,0);
  pieContext.closePath( );
  pieContext.fill( )

  pieContext.beginPath( );
  pieContext.fillStyle = "rgb(0,128,128)";
  pieContext.moveTo(pieX,pieY);
  pieContext.arc(pieX,pieY,pieRadius,r1,r1 + r2,0);
  pieContext.closePath( );
  pieContext.fill( );

  pieContext.beginPath( );
  pieContext.fillStyle = "rgb(0,192,192)";
  pieContext.moveTo(pieX,pieY);
  pieContext.arc(pieX,pieY,pieRadius,r1 + r2,(2 * Math.PI),0);
  pieContext.closePath( );
  pieContext.fill( );
```

```
// Take care of the labels; display only
// if there is a slice that is greater than .1 radian
// (approx 6 degrees) of sweep
//
var partRad = pieRadius * 0.75;
if (r1 > K_MIN_ARC) {
retailDiv.style.left = pieX + Math.cos(r1 * 0.5) * partRad+ "px";
retailDiv.style.top = pieY + Math.sin(r1 * 0.5 ) * partRad + "px";
retailDiv.style.visibility="visible";
}

if (r2 > K_MIN_ARC) {
entDiv.style.left = pieX + (Math.cos(r1 + (r2 * 0.5)) *
   partRad) + "px";
entDiv.style.top = pieY + (Math.sin(r1 + (r2 * 0.5)) *
   partRad) + "px";
entDiv.style.visibility="visible";
}

if (r3 > K_MIN_ARC) {
travelDiv.style.left = pieX + (Math.cos(r1 + r2 + ( r3 * 0.5) ) *
  partRad) + "px";
travelDiv.style.top = pieY + (Math.sin(r1 + r2 + ( r3 * 0.5) ) *
   partRad) + "px";
travelDiv.style.visibility="visible";
}


}
catch (e) {
  alert("redrawPieChart exception " + e);
}
}
```

The resulting code adds our pie chart to display a breakout of the individual table rows (or bars) by spending category, as shown in Figure 8-6.

Summary

Firefox designers have gone to great pains to design a rendering engine that can accommodate XHTML documents that support mixed namespace dialects as well as the most current drawing features.

Support of the SVG standard in and of itself allows designers to build applications in which textual or numeric data can readily be transformed into a document that includes SVG element representation of graphs, maps, or even data-driven illustrations such as chemical models. Such translations can take place through any number of middleware steps, including the use of XSLT, as discussed in this chapter.

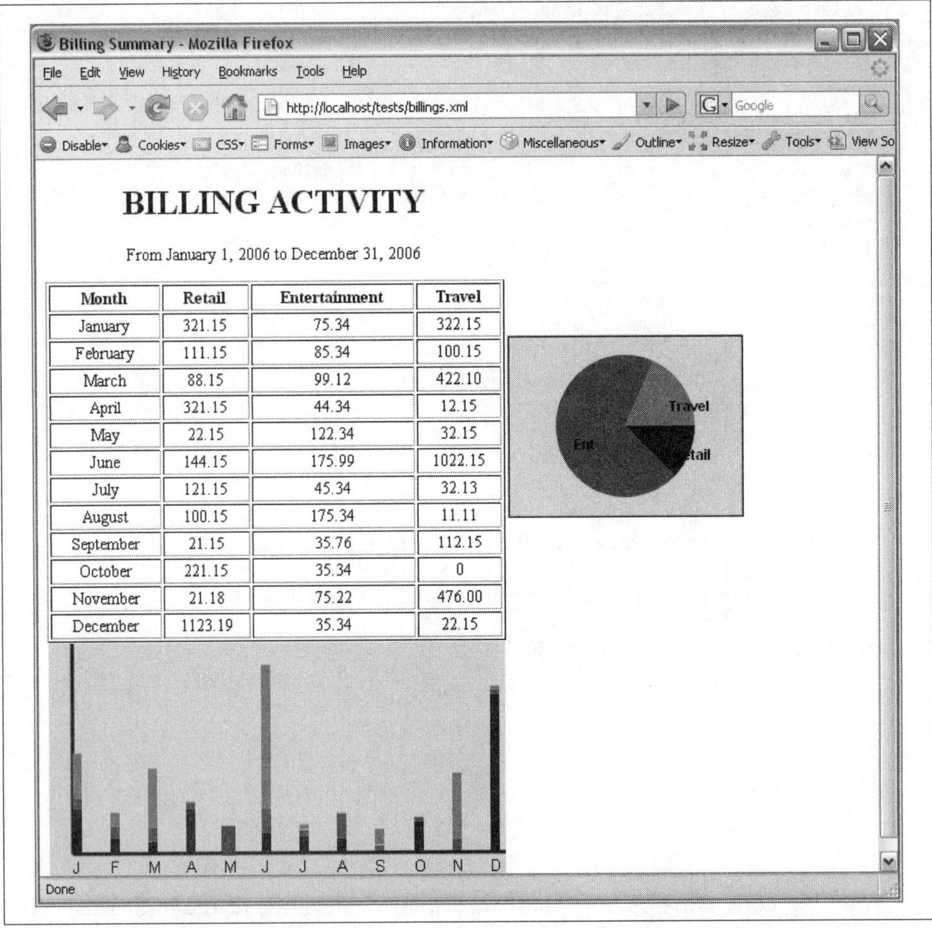

Month	Retail	Entertainment	Travel
January	321.15	75.34	322.15
February	111.15	85.34	100.15
March	88.15	99.12	422.10
April	321.15	44.34	12.15
May	22.15	122.34	32.15
June	144.15	175.99	1022.15
July	121.15	45.34	32.13
August	100.15	175.34	11.11
September	21.15	35.76	112.15
October	221.15	35.34	0
November	21.18	75.22	476.00
December	1123.19	35.34	22.15

Figure 8-6. Table data and bar chart triggering canvas drawing

The XHTML document model also allows us to freely mix SVG elements with the HTML namespace—hence, we can access the SVG documents generated through transformations, and add interactivity logic, by virtue of the standard DOM interface and JavaScript.

One more graphics feature supported by Firefox involves the use of the HTML canvas element to provide a richer graphical experience for applications.

Although the canvas cannot, by its nature, generate DOM elements that we can access from JavaScript, code can use DOM interactivity to call canvas context methods that can add significant value to an interface and are not otherwise available through simple manipulation of HTML elements.

CHAPTER 9

Extending the Interface

Up to this point, we have discussed techniques to build a standalone application based on the XUL interface. We now turn our attention to extending the existing Firefox browser interface to add functionality to the standard browser.

In this chapter, we will add elements to the browser interface by using XUL *overlay* files to add a new document styling feature. We will then use the XML Bindings Language (XBL) to add JavaScript behaviors to a custom interface widget that monitors `XMLHttpRequest` objects. Finally, I'll demonstrate the use of "hidden" widgets, known as *anonymous content*, to display return results from the asynchronous server request.

This chapter discusses:

- The background of overlay files
- Developing reusable overlays to be deployed from the chrome directory
- Attaching overlays to the browser interface
- Building processing logic into the overlay
- Implementing a custom widget described by XBL

Overlay Files

It is not uncommon for a designer to develop a collection of interface widgets that perform a common function. Dialogs that prompt users for confirmation, data entry, or file selection are examples of both interface elements and underlying logic that may be shared.

The next few pages will explore the development of a reusable interface that will change the color and size of an entire class of HTML tags for a document as part of an interactive session (a function that may be useful for web page design applications). The first step in such a development is to determine how our styling widgets will interact with the user.

One possible interaction model for our styling widgets is through a pop-up menu that the user sees when she selects text and opens some form of context menu, as illustrated in the mockup shown in Figure 9-1.

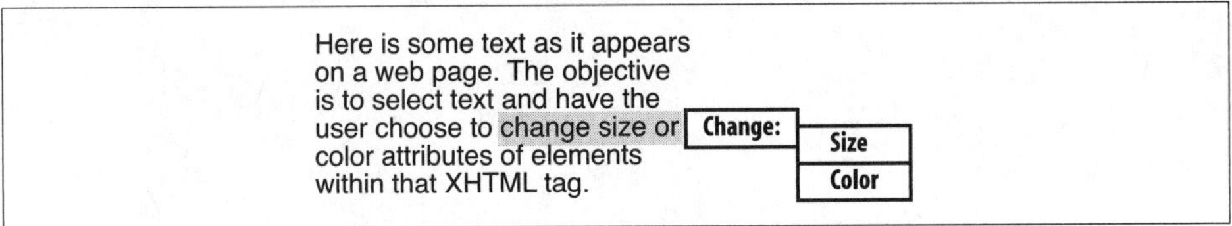

Figure 9-1. Style changer mockup

The menus and pop-up menus are items that we could easily reuse in other applications. We will collect these interface elements in an overlay file with content designed to attach to predetermined anchor points within an application's main interface window.

Overlay File Structure

An overlay is a XUL file describing a topmost `<overlay>` element. (There are no `<window>` elements in an overlay.) Within the overlay file, the XUL elements include an attribute that identifies the element within a main interface file; that target element (in the main interface file) is the point where the overlay's content is merged with the main interface file being overlaid, as shown in Figure 9-2.

The `id` attribute of the overlay menu marks the merge point for the overlay in the destination interface. The `id` attribute and the element tag must match an element tag and `id` attribute within the main interface file for an overlay to be applied.

When the Firefox framework finds an overlay point, the elements and attributes of the overlay are merged with the main interface; child elements in the overlay are appended to the main interface, and attributes in the topmost overlay element override the attributes in the main interface. Attributes in the main interface that are not specified in the overlay are passed to the interface unchanged.

The following listing of a file we will call *stylermain.xul* describes a very simple application designed to accept an overlay within a menu:

```
<?xml version="1.0"?>
<window id="stylerMain"
  xmlns="http://www.mozilla.org/keymaster/gatekeeper/there.is.only.xul">

<?xul-overlay href="styler.xul"?>

<menubar>
 <menu  label="Options" id="style-menu">
   <menupopup id="optionsPopup">
    <menu label="Menu 1">
     <menupopup>
      <menuitem label="Menu 1 item 1"/>
      <menuitem label="Menu 1 item 2"/>
```

```
      </menupopup>
     </menu>
     <menu label="Menu 2">
      <menupopup>
       <menuitem label="Menu 2 item 1"/>
       <menuitem label="Menu 2 item 2"/>
      </menupopup>
     </menu>

   <menuseparator/>

   <menu  id="menu3" Label="Menu 3">

   </menu>
   <menuseparator id="theSeparator"/>
  </menupopup>
 </menu>
</menubar>

<vbox flex="1" style="background-color:blue;">
</vbox>
</window>
```

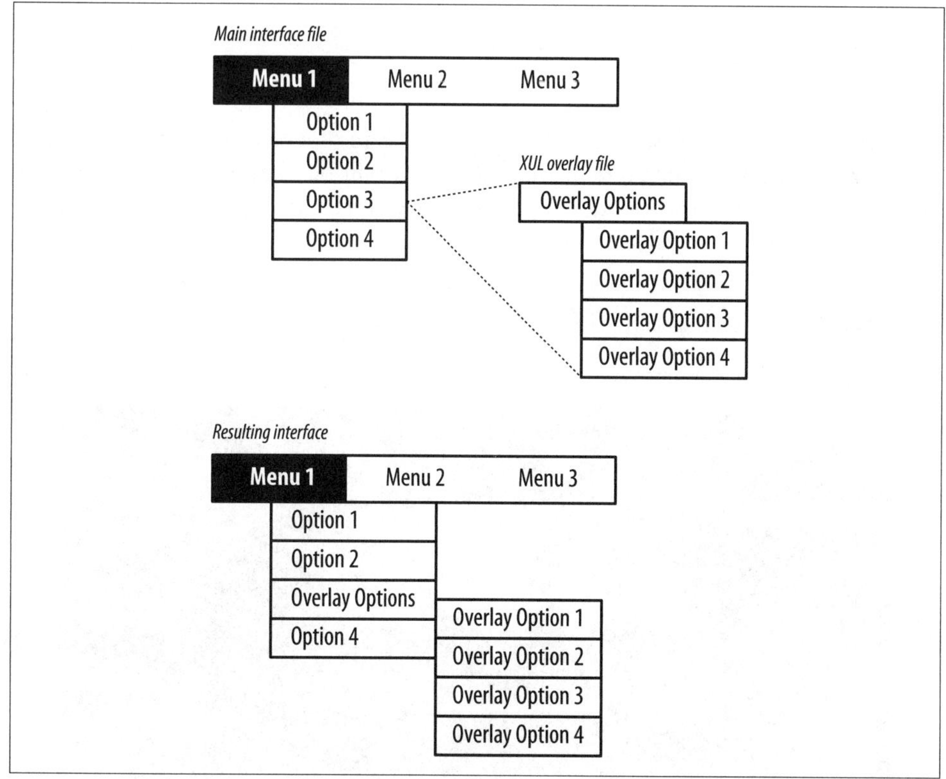

Figure 9-2. Merging overlay content into an interface

The listing includes a directive to the overlay file to be applied to the interface file. This technique is referred to as an *explicit* loading of an overlay. The `menu3` element has no content, and is designed to be the merge point for the overlay.

The overlay file *styler.xul* follows:

```
<?xml version="1.0"?>
<overlay id="styler"
  xmlns="http://www.mozilla.org/keymaster/gatekeeper/there.is.only.xul">

<menu id="menu3" label="Change..." >
 <menupopup>
  <menu label="Size">
   <menupopup>
    <menuitem label="Bigger"/>
    <menuitem label="Smaller"/>
   </menupopup>
  </menu>
  <menu label="Color">
  <menupopup>
   <colorpicker />
  </menupopup>
 </menu>
 </menupopup>
</menu>

</overlay>
```

The overlay includes a `menu` element with the same `id` of a `menu` element in the main interface file, meaning the content from *styler.xul* will be merged with the `menu` element of the main file, as shown in Figure 9-3. The overlay includes a `colorpicker` element that we will use to select a new color for text.

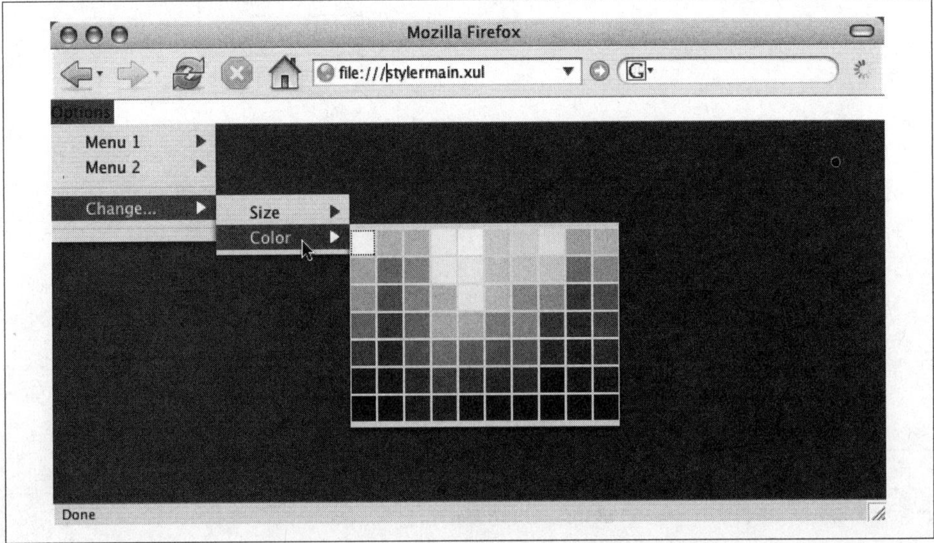

Figure 9-3. Main interface with overlay

This example uses a main interface file that has an empty element used as the merge point. In more practical implementations, overlays are used to add functionality to interfaces that need to be extended without disturbing the appearance of existing widgets. A designer can use the Document Object Model (DOM) Inspector tool to see the DOM tree of the interface that includes the results of the applied overlay. (The View → Source menu tool displays only the source document.)

Element positioning

This example of the main interface file included an empty widget used as the merge point (`menu3`). But in many settings, it is more practical to use an overlay to add completely new content to the interface without modifying the originally designed widgets. This technique requires a designer to position newly merged elements *relative to an existing element* without modifying the original widget.

Elements that are children of an overlay element have three attributes that allow the overlay designer to position the elements being merged into the interface:

`insertbefore`
: The ID matches the ID of an element in the main interface file to follow the overlay content.

`insertafter`
: The ID matches the ID of an element in the main interface file to precede the overlay content.

`position`
: The integer position (1-based) index of the overlay elements within the parent widget's list of children.

With an understanding of the destination interface structure, an overlay designer may precisely position the destination elements in the interface. He will often place the new content adjacent to existing elements that may be in the same family of functionality as the newly inserted elements. Alternatively, he may use the identifier of an existing separator to append the overlay as a completely new family of interface widgets. (In the case of our simple application, a separator with an `id` of `theSeparator` is a good candidate to anchor and delimit the newly added content.)

Dynamic loading

In addition to identifying where in a target interface to merge overlay elements, the Firefox framework must understand when to apply an overlay to a specific file. In the preceding example, we demonstrated one method to associate a main interface with an overlay. Here we use *explicit loading* of the overlay with the processing instruction:

```
<?xul-overlay href="styler.xul"?>
```

Overlay developers can also develop for existing applications by using the chrome registry for *dynamic loading* of the overlay.

We previously discussed the use of a manifest file to register applications in the chrome directory to make them eligible for enhanced security considerations. That method used the manifest file to register applications as content to be rendered. Manifest files also support references to overlays.

By moving the source files (*stylermain.xul*, *styler.xul*) into a chrome subdirectory such as *chrome/mystyler/content/*, we could remove the processing instruction from the main interface and add two entries to any manifest file (e.g., *localApps.manifest*) as follows:

```
content mystyler mystyler/content/stylermain.xul
overlay chrome://mystyler/content/stylermain.xul chrome://mystyler/content/styler.xul
```

The first line registers the main application with the chrome directory. The second line is of the form:

```
overlay targetURI overlayURI
```

With those changes in place, we can now launch the application either from the command line or by entering the chrome URL in the browser location line:

```
chrome://mystyler/content/stylermain.xul
```

Using dynamic loading allows a developer to design overlays to be appended to existing applications without modifying original distribution source files. The use of a manifest file allows us to add overlays to any appropriate interface (one with the attribute `ids`) or application. (Chapter 11 discusses distribution options in greater detail.)

Now that the basic mechanism for our overlay is in place as a chrome installation, we can consider how to attach our styling widgets to the browser interface.

Overlays and the Browser

To add our menu objects to the browser interface, we need to explore the browser's XUL interface file to find the proper location to merge the newly created interface widgets.

We can find the interface XUL file by opening the contents of the jar file containing the browser. By copying the *browser.jar* file to a temporary directory, we extract the contents:

```
jar -xvf browser.jar
```

The contents directory holds all the *.xul* and JavaScript source files that provide the core functionality of the Firefox browser; the file *browser.xul* contains the browser's main interface widgets. In our case, the `menupopup` element with the `id` of `contentAreaContextMenu` contains a number of menu items dealing with the disposition of selected text—likely candidates to serve as the merge point for our overlay:

```
<menuitem id="context-cut"
                label="&cutCmd.label;"
                accesskey="&cutCmd.accesskey;"
                command="cmd_cut"/>
      <menuitem id="context-copy"
                label="&copyCmd.label;"
                accesskey="&copyCmd.accesskey;"
                command="cmd_copy"/>
      <menuitem id="context-paste"
                label="&pasteCmd.label;"
                accesskey="&pasteCmd.accesskey;"
                command="cmd_paste"/>
      <menuitem id="context-delete"
                label="&deleteCmd.label;"
                accesskey="&deleteCmd.accesskey;"
                command="cmd_delete"/>
      <menuseparator id="context-sep-paste"/>
      <menuitem id="context-selectall"
                label="&selectAllCmd.label;"
                accesskey="&selectAllCmd.accesskey;"
                command="cmd_selectAll"/>
      <menuseparator id="context-sep-selectall"/>
```

To attach our menu to the existing interface, we will change our *styler.xul* file to merge with the browser interface after the menu with the `id` attribute `"context-sep-selectall"`. We will also use simple `buttons` rather than `menuitems` to trigger the change in button size without dismissing the pop-up menu upon actuation:

```
<?xml version="1.0"?>
<!DOCTYPE overlay>
<overlay id="someID"
  xmlns="http://www.mozilla.org/keymaster/gatekeeper/there.is.only.xul">

<popup id="contentAreaContextMenu">
<menu  insertbefore="context-sep-selectall" label="Change..." >
 <menupopup>
  <menu label="Size">
   <menupopup>
    <vbox flex="1">
     <button label="+" oncommand="biggerText( );"/>
     <button label="-" oncommand="smallerText( );"/>
    </vbox>
   </menupopup>
  </menu>
  <menu label="Color">
   <menupopup>
    <colorpicker />
   </menupopup>
  </menu>
 </menupopup>
</menu>
</popup>
</overlay>
```

To instruct the Firefox framework to apply our overlay file to the browser, we add the following line to the *browser.manifest* line in the chrome directory:

```
overlay chrome://browser/content/browser.xul          chrome://mystyler/content/
styler.xul
```

When we restart the browser, we can now select some text, open the context menu (right mouse-click), and see the applied overlay, as shown in Figure 9-4.

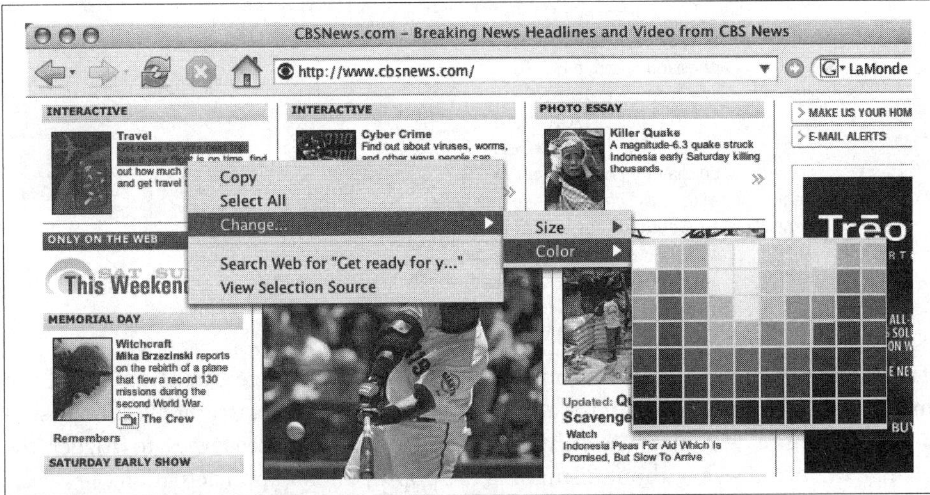

Figure 9-4. Overlay attached to browser interface

Adding Logic

The logic behind the styler function is relatively straightforward:

- The user selects text on a web page.
- The context menu includes our options to change font size and color.
- Upon pressing one of the buttons, code uses the window's selection to find the starting node of the selection.
- The style for the document's elements that match the selection will be changed to modify the document's appearance.

We will add our script directly to the *.xul* file of the overlay. Whereas the button elements will use the inline assignment of an event handler, we will programmatically add an event listener to the colorpicker. We will trigger the initialization by the popupshown event. The source file now looks like this:

```
<?xml version="1.0"?>
<?xml-stylesheet href="chrome://mystyler/content/styler.css" type="text/css"?>
<!DOCTYPE overlay>
<overlay id="someID"
  xmlns="http://www.mozilla.org/keymaster/gatekeeper/there.is.only.xul">
```

```
<script type="text/javascript">
<![CDATA[

biggerText = function( ) {
  changeFontSize(true);
 };

smallerText = function( ) {
 changeFontSize(false);
};

initStyler = function( ) {
document.getElementById("__cP").addEventListener("select",newColor,true);
};
//
// Increase/decrease font size by 20%
//
changeFontSize = function (increase) {

try {
// (1)
var cDoc = document.getElementById("content").contentDocument;
var theSel = document.getElementById("content").contentWindow.getSelection( );
if (theSel != "") { // something selected
 var theR = theSel.getRangeAt(0);
//
// (2)
 var tProp = document.getElementById("content").contentWindow.
    getComputedStyle (theR.startContainer.parentNode,"");
 var fSizeString = tProp.getPropertyValue("font-size");

// (3)
 var fSize = parseFloat(fSizeString.
    substr(0,fSizeString.indexOf("p")));

 var newSize = fSize;
 if (increase) newSize += (fSize * 0.2);
 else newSize -= (fSize * 0.2);


 var targetTag = theR.startContainer.parentNode.tagName;
 dump("Originial font size is " + fSize + " for tags " + targetTag + "\n");
 var theTags = cDoc.getElementsByTagName(targetTag);
 for (var i = 0; i < theTags.length; i++) {
   theTags[i].style.fontSize = newSize + "px";
  }
 } // something selected
}
catch (e) {
dump("Exception is " + e + "\n");
 }
};
```

```
newColor = function(event) {
try {
// (4)
var newColor = event.currentTarget.color;
var cDoc = document.getElementById("content").contentDocument;
var theSel = document.getElementById("content").contentWindow.getSelection( );
if (theSel != "") { // something selected
 var theR = theSel.getRangeAt(0);
 var targetTag = theR.startContainer.parentNode.tagName;
 var theTags = cDoc.getElementsByTagName(targetTag);
 for (var i = 0; i < theTags.length; i++) {
    theTags[i].style.color = newColor;
  }
 } // something selected
}
catch (e) {
dump("Exception is " + e + "\n");
}
};

]]>
</script>

<popup id="contentAreaContextMenu">
 <menu insertbefore="context-sep-selectall"  label="Change..." >
  <menupopup onpopupshown="initStyler( );">
    <menu label="Size">
      <menupopup>
        <vbox flex="1">
         <button label="+" oncommand="biggerText( );"/>
         <button label="-" oncommand="smallerText( );"/>
        </vbox>
       </menupopup>
      </menu>
      <menu label="Color">
       <menupopup>
        <colorpicker id="__cP" />
       </menupopup>
     </menu>
    </menupopup>
    </menu>
  </popup>
 </overlay>
```

The essential steps of the script are in place for all the functions that modify the appearance.

The script modifies the font size by first obtaining a reference to the window displaying browser content (1). The tabbed browser xul includes the main window with an id of content (this is discovered by exploring the *browser.xul* file).

To obtain the existing font size for the selected text, we obtain a reference to the parent node of the selection's starting container (usually the selection's text node). To obtain the existing font size, we use the window's `getComputedStyle` method (2). We use `GetComputedStyle` to obtain a `ComputedCSSStyleDeclaration` reference that represents an element's existing style or Cascading Style Sheet (CSS) assignment. To obtain the actual font size, we reference the style property by name:

```
var tProp = document.getElementById("content").contentWindow.
    getComputedStyle (theR.startContainer.parentNode,""); // (2)
 var fSizeString = tProp.getPropertyValue("font-size");
```

The final font size manipulation starts by removing the `px` suffix and calculating a 20 percent increment or decrement (3).

The color manipulation does not rely on any past value. The script *newcolor* is attached as an event handler to the `colorpicker`'s `select` event; the event's `currentTarget` property points to the `colorpicker` whose color property is used to obtain a reference to the newly selected color (4). Then, using the same technique we used to change font size, we change the color of all the document tags matching the tag of the selected text.

These changes result in the menu actuations modifying either the color or the text after actuation, as shown in Figure 9-5.

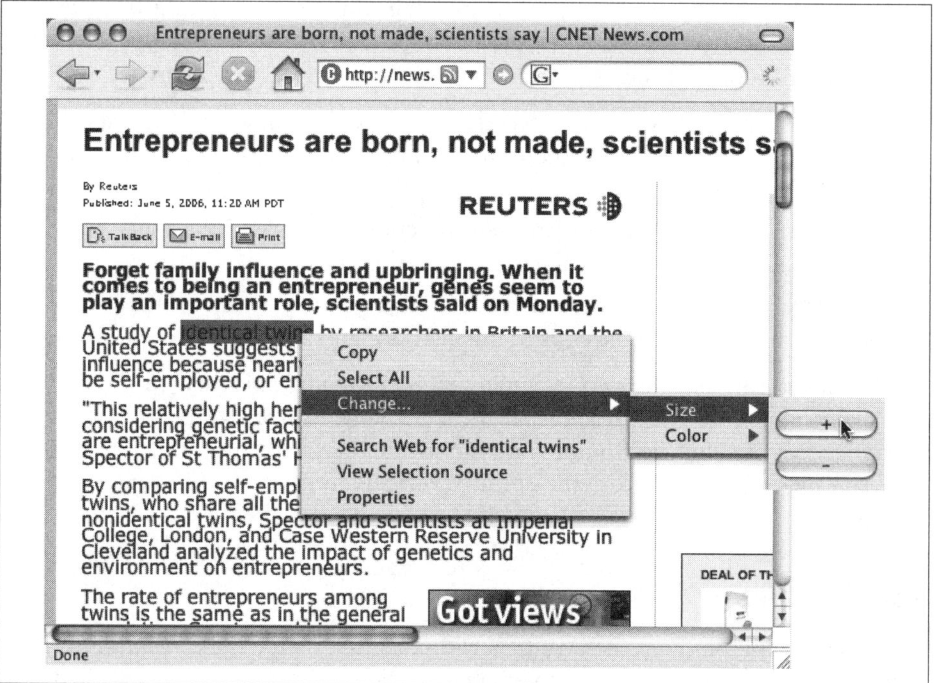

Figure 9-5. Styler overlay to change font size

Table 9-1 summarizes the relevant properties and attributes.

Table 9-1. Key methods, attributes, and properties for styler

Element/Object	Attribute/Property/Method	Description
Any overlay element	`insertAfter=(someID)` `insertBefore=(someID)` `position=(someID)`	Places merged overlay content relative to an existing interface element, or at a 1-based index as a child element
`window`	`getComputedStyle (nodeRef,null)`	Obtains a computed `CSSStyleDeclaration` object used to obtain style for an element
`CSSStyleDeclaration`	`getPropertyValue ("propertyName")`	Returns the value of an element's style property
`Colorpicker`	`color`	Color string of the last selected color

XBL

Overlay technologies provide the hooks to attach reusable segments of XUL code to applications for which developers wish to extend functionality. XUL overlays alone, however, provide only the protocol to attach existing XUL widgets (and associated functions) to an interface.

XBL provides the ability to create new elements that extend an existing XUL element (which we can call the *bound* element) by merging additional XUL widgets, fields, and properties to add new behaviors to the interface. Although this description sounds similar to the overlay feature, XBL technology features several key differences:

- Overlays associate *XUL* source code to an existing interface of a specific `id` attribute; XBL elements are added/merged based on types of tags or classes and are not dependent on the `id` attribute.
- XBL is designed to encapsulate new functionality in widgets that "hide" the details behind public methods, fields, and properties.
- Only the topmost XBL element is accessible to scripts using DOM methods; nodes that the binding file adds to the interface are not visible in the DOM tree.

That is not to say that the two technologies aren't complementary. In the previous overlay example, the `colorpicker` element is actually an XBL widget that combines special classes of color tiles to function as one interface element; the overlay file that was developed specified where the `colorpicker` was to be attached to the browser's interface.

XBL Structure

We describe XBL bindings in XML files with tags that define the *content*, *implementation*, and *event handlers* of a newly created widget. XUL elements attached to a content node define the structure and appearance of the new widget. Scripts and variable declarations attached to the `implementation` node provide the functionality of the new element. Children of the `handlers` element define methods to handle events applied to the entire widget.

XBL files are divided into any number of bindings, each binding identified by a unique `id` attribute. This `id`, in turn, is referenced by a CSS declaration with a distinctive `-moz-binding` key that binds the XBL widget to a tag or class name in the main source file. Figure 9-6 summarizes this relationship.

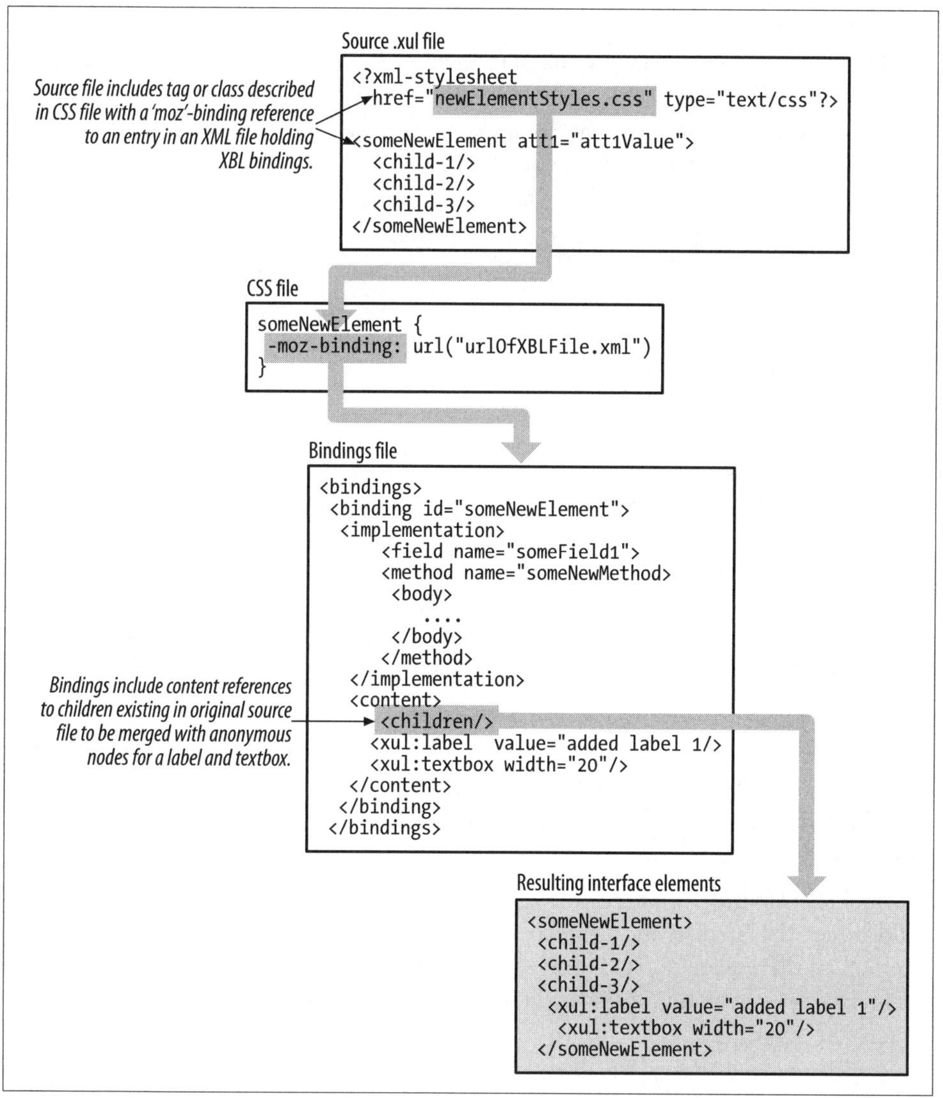

Figure 9-6. XBL bindings

XBL Content

A simple XBL example to add a gray horizontal box to a special xbltest class of boxes would start off with the following CSS declaration:

```
.xbltest {

  -moz-binding: url("chrome://someDirectory/xblTest.xml#xblsample");
  background-color:gray;

}
```

The file *xblText.xml* would include the following:

```
<?xml version="1.0"?>
<bindings xmlns="http://www.mozilla.org/xbl"
   xmlns:xul="http://www.mozilla.org/keymaster/
       gatekeeper/there.is.only.xul">

<binding id="xblsample">
 <content>
  <children/>
  <xul:hbox flex="1">
   <xul:vbox>
    <xul:label value="Left box"/>
    <xul:button label="Left button"/>
   </xul:vbox>
    <xul:vbox>
    <xul:label value="Center box"/>
    <xul:button label="Center button"/>
   </xul:vbox>
    <xul:vbox>
    <xul:label value="Right box"/>
    <xul:button label="Right button"/>
   </xul:vbox>
  </xul:hbox>
 </content>
 </binding>
</bindings>
```

Notice that because the default namespace for the XBL file is declared for the <bindings> tag, the XUL elements must include the xul: namespace to be properly processed.

The inclusion of the <children> tag instructs the Firefox framework to include all the child nodes declared in the original source file (the *explicit content*) in the output interface. If there were no <children> tag, no original elements would be displayed in the interface. If the main interface file included the following declaration:

```
<vbox class="xbltest">
  <label value="Original child"/>
</vbox>
```

the resulting interface would include the `<vbox>` declared in the main interface and its label child node, along with the `<hbox>` and children declared in the *.xbl* file, as shown in Figure 9-7.

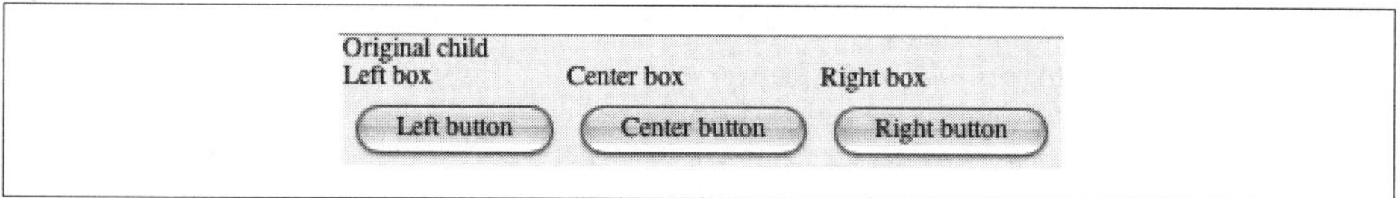

Figure 9-7. vbox with XBL content

The designer can specify which type of elements in the original interface are included in the resulting interface by using the `includes` attribute of the `<children>` element. The statement:

```
<children includes="label|button"/>
```

will add only `label` and `button` elements to the resulting interface; other child elements will be discarded. All original child elements are included in the final interface if no `includes` attribute is provided. Designers are free to add any number of child elements that merge various classes of existing widgets to different areas of the resulting interface.

Passing attributes to XBL content

XBL encapsulates appearance and function within a tag that defines the rules of access through properties, methods, and fields.

Attributes attached to the original bound widget may also be selectively moved down to XBL children through the use of the `inherits` keyword.

The general form of the `inherits` attribute is:

```
xbl:inherits="boundAttributeName"
```

or alternatively:

```
xbl:inherits="xblChildAttributeName=boundAttributeName"
```

(The `inherits` attribute may include any number of comma-delimited assignment statements.)

The first form is appropriate when the attribute name assigned to the bound element matches the name of the attribute for the XBL widgets (e.g., `pack`, `align`). The second form is more appropriate when child widgets share attribute names (e.g., XBL widgets that include a textbox and a label, both of which use a `value` attribute) or an attribute whose value needs to be reassigned from the bound attribute to an attribute name for an XBL widget. If an attribute assignment exists as well as an `inherits` attribute, the former provides a default value in the event that the bound element's attribute name is not present.

Consider our xblsample binding where the left and right sides may want different label values.

We would change the bindings element to include the xbl namespace along with the addition of the appropriate inherits attributes:

```
<bindings xmlns="http://www.mozilla.org/xbl"
        xmlns:xbl="http://www.mozilla.org/xbl"
xmlns:xul="http://www.mozilla.org/keymaster/gatekeeper/there.is.only.xul">

<binding id="xblsample">
 <content>
  <children/>
  <xul:hbox flex="1">
   <xul:vbox>
    <xul:label  value="Left box" xbl:inherits="value=llabel" />
    <xul:button label="Left button"/>
   </xul:vbox>
    <xul:vbox>
    <xul:label value="Center box"/>
    <xul:button label="Center button"/>
   </xul:vbox>
    <xul:vbox>
    <xul:label value="Right box" xbl:inherits="value=rlabel" />
    <xul:button label="Right button"/>
   </xul:vbox>
  </xul:hbox>
 </content>
</bindings>
</binding>
```

The bound element statement makes the appropriate label assignments:

```
<vbox id="xblbox" llabel="LEFT SIDE"
       rlabel="RIGHT SIDE" class="xbltest">
<label value="Original child"/>
</vbox>
```

The changes are reflected in the new appearance of the widget, as shown in Figure 9-8.

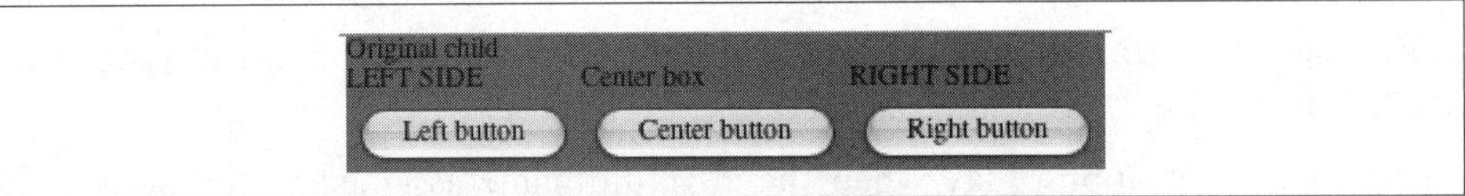

Figure 9-8. Inherited attributes

Implementation

The logic underneath the XBL element is wrapped in an implementation tag that parents fields, methods, and properties. The implementation section of an XBL widget is of the form:

```
<implementation>
 <field name="field1name">field 1 value </field>
 <field name="field2name">field 2 value </field>
 <property name="property1name">
 </property>
 <property name="property2name">
   <getter>
     Getter script
   </getter>
   <setter>
     Setter script
   </setter>
 </property>
 <method name="method1name">
  <parameter name="firstParameterName"/>
  <parameter name="secondParameterName"/>
   <body>
     Script
   </body>
  </method>
  <constructor>
    Script
  </constructor>
  <destructor>
    Script
  </destructor>
</implementation>
```

Field names are accessible from scripts using a `.fieldName` notation. Fields can hold any variable in support of the widget's logic.

Properties do not have a value in the binding declaration. Properties differ from attributes in that access is managed through the `getter` and `setter` scripts, or alternatively, through short scripts attached to a property's `onset` and `onget` attributes.

All forms of the `setter` scripts have access to a special `val` variable, which references the value passed by a script calling the property's setter. Property setters and getters are often used in place of fields when the logic needs to conduct some type of auditing or carry out some logic in response to a change in the property's value.

Methods are declared for any scripts required to carry out the logic necessary for the widget to function. All methods and scripts have access to the `this` variable that references the `anchor` element. Method parameters are declared through `<parameter>` elements with the `name` attribute providing the string used for script access. All methods are referenced as a property of that widget:

```
anchorWidgetName.someMethodName(parameter1,parameter2,...)
```

Constructor and *destructor* elements also provide access to scripts that can conduct initialization when a window displaying the XBL content is displayed (constructor), or conduct some cleanup when the displaying window is destroyed (destructor).

Anonymous content

All widgets provided by the XBL binding are referred to as *anonymous content*—their nodes are not visible within the DOM tree as is the case with all other XUL elements.

Scripts may, however, access anonymous content through the method:

```
document.getAnonymousNodes(parentNode)
```

The first use of the function usually accesses a known node, such as that provided by the `this` reference to a method. The result is an array of nodes that corresponds to the array of child nodes created by the binding. The nodes obtained from this array respond to any of the conventional DOM methods.

If the XBL finding includes nested anonymous widgets, the method `getAnonymousNodes` must be called on the topmost anonymous parent before any of the descendant nodes can be accessed.

Although using `getAnonymousNodes` works well for collections of children that don't require specialized code, the technique falls short when designers wish to reach a specific child without having knowledge of the structure of all collections within a binding.

For such situations, designers may use the following special method:

```
getAnonymousElementByAttribute(parentOfAnonymousNode,
          attributeName,attributeValue)
```

This technique is often employed by designers who use an attribute with a name such as `anonid` to provide a hook for scripts to access a specific anonymous element as part of some function. For example, if a widget includes several labels, one of which is used to display changing status information, the following XBL source could be:

```
<xul:vbox>
 <children />
 <xul:label anonid="_commandStatus" value="waiting"/>
 <xul:label value="Please press button"/>
</vbox>
```

A script within the binding could use the method:

```
getAnonymousElementByAttribute(this,"anonid","_commandStatus")
```

to obtain the reference to the appropriate label.

Event Handlers

Although any XBL element (both explicit and anonymous content) may have an event handler attached, there are circumstances when a designer will want to attach an event to the entire widget created by the XBL binding.

We can assign an event handler to an entire XBL widget through the <handlers> tag that parents individual <handler> children. Two forms of event handler script declarations are supported—an inline assignment as the object of an action attribute, and a second form in which the script is coded as the value of the <handler>:

```
<handlers>
 <handler event="someEvent">
   Handler script
 </handler>
 <handler event="someOtherEvent" action="someOtherScript"/>
</handlers>
```

An Expanded Example

An extension of the preceding example illustrates the use of fields, methods, and event handlers. We will modify the XBL source *xbltest.xml* with fields and properties, as shown in the following interface:

```
<?xml version="1.0"?>
<bindings xmlns="http://www.mozilla.org/xbl"
          xmlns:xbl="http://www.mozilla.org/xbl"
          xmlns:xul="http://www.mozilla.org/keymaster/gatekeeper/
               there.is.only.xul">

<binding id="xblsample">
 <handlers>
<!- 1 -->
  <handler event="mouseover">
   this.style.borderStyle="solid;"
   this.style.borderWidth = "2px";
   this.style.borderColor = "black;"
  </handler>
  <handler event="mouseout">

  this.style.borderStyle="none;"

  </handler>
 </handlers>
 <content>
  <children/>
  <xul:hbox flex="1">
   <xul:vbox>
    <xul:label  value="Left box" xbl:inherits="value=llabel"/>
    <xul:button label="Left button"/>
   </xul:vbox>
    <xul:vbox>
    <xul:label value="Center box"/>
    <xul:button label="Center button"/>
   </xul:vbox>
    <xul:vbox>
    <xul:label value="Right box" xbl:inherits="value=rlabel"/>
    <xul:button label="Right button"/>
   </xul:vbox>
```

```
    </xul:hbox>
   </content>
   <implementation>
  <!-- 2 -->
    <field name="field_1" >"Initial value 1"</field>
    <field name ="field_2" >"Initial value 2"</field>
    <property name="backgroundColor">
  <!-- 3 -->
     <setter>
      this.style.backgroundColor=val;
     </setter>
     </property>
  <!-- 4 -->
    <method name="showInfo">
     <body>
      alert("Field 1 = " + this.field_1 + ",  Field 2 = " + this.field_2 );
     </body>
    </method>
   </implementation>
  </binding>
```

We modified the XBL binding to include an event handler that will display a black border upon mouse movement over the widget (1); added fields with default values (2); added a property to manage changes of the background color (3); and used a public method to display the current values of the field values (4).

We modified the source code for the interface to use the new methods and field values:

```
<vbox flex="1" align="center">

<vbox id="xblbox" llabel="LEFT SIDE"
     rlabel="RIGHT SIDE" class="xbltest">
<label value="Original child"/>
</vbox>
<!--  1 -->
<button label="showInfo"
 oncommand="document.getElementById('xblbox').showInfo( );"/>
<!--  2 -->
<button label="changeRed"
 oncommand="document.getElementById('xblbox').backgroundColor =
  'red';"/>
<!--  3 -->
<button label="changeFields"
  oncommand=" { document.getElementById('xblbox').field_1 = 'v1';
  document.getElementById('xblbox').field_2 = 'v2';}"/>
```

The source interface file now includes buttons to call the XBL function showInfo (1). We have added a button to change the backgroundColor property (2), and a button to assign new values to the XBL fields (3).

The resulting application will change the border as the mouse moves over the widget, change the background color when the changeRed button is pressed, and display the modified fields with the showInfo button actuation, as shown in Figure 9-9.

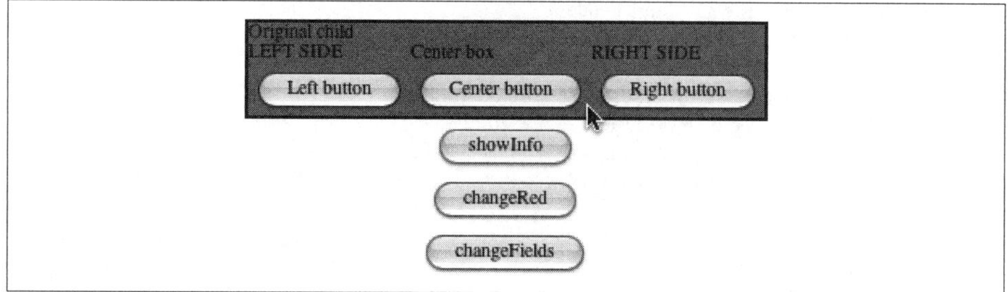

Figure 9-9. Sample XBL with event handlers

HTTP Request Widget

To illustrate the use of XBL in a more practical example, we'll develop a widget that we can use while debugging applications that use the `XMLHttpRequest` object. The newly created widget is designed to be "dropped into" applications that use asynchronous requests to a server; the widget will display return codes in a XUL grid element.

We will design the widget to pass values from a series of text boxes declared in an anchor widget to a script, with the protocol and results displayed by elements specified in the XBL binding. The widget will presume a comma-delimited sequence of return values consisting of *`key=value`* pairs:

```
retcode=true|false,retKey1=retVal1,
    retKey2=retVal2,...retKeyn=retValn
```

We will design the widget to take a series of command fields manually entered by the user and pass them to the server's PHP script.

The PHP script, *doDelayEcho.php*, that we will use for this test is a simple command to delay for an interval set by the client script, and echo a message sent by the client:

```
<?php
$cmd   = trim($_GET['command']);
$delay = trim($_GET['delay']);
$message = trim($_GET['message']);

sleep($delay);
$retString = 'retcode=true,message=server received: '."$message";
echo $retString;
exit(0);
?>
```

We will code the XBL binding for an `httprequestor` widget in a file called *httprequestor.xml*, and include the widgets and methods to pack the HTTP request string and return the results in the interface:

```
<binding id="httprequestor">
<content>
    <xul:vbox id="_hr_topBox" align="center">
     <children/>
```

```
      <xul:button  label="Send Request"
          oncommand="this.parentNode.parentNode.sendRequest();"/>
<!-- 1 -->
      <xul:textbox  anonid="_resultField"
                   readonly="true" size="20"
                   value="Waiting to send request."/>
      <xul:listbox anonid="_resultList">
       <xul:listhead>
        <xul:listheader label="KEY"/>
        <xul:listheader label="VALUE"/>
       </xul:listhead>
       <xul:listcols>
        <xul:listcol/>
        <xul:splitter/>
        <xul:listcol flex="1"/>
       </xul:listcols>
        <xul:listitem>
         <xul:listcell label = "x"/>
         <xul:listcell label = "y"/>
        </xul:listitem>
      </xul:listbox>
     </xul:vbox>
   </content>
   <implementation>
<!-- 2 -->
    <field name="myServerRequest"/>
<!-- 3 -->
     <method name="sendRequest">
     <body>
      <![CDATA[
       dump("Sending request to" + this.getAttribute("src") + "\n");
       var textArgs = this.getElementsByTagName("textbox");
       var cString = this.getAttribute("src") + "?&command=" +
         document.getElementById("theCommand").value ;
       for (var i = 0; i < textArgs.length; i++) {
         if (textArgs[i].value != "")
             cString += "&" + textArgs[i].getAttribute("id") + "=" +
               textArgs[i].value;
         }
 // 4
       this.myServerRequest = new XMLHttpRequest();
       this.myServerRequest.onreadystatechange =
          function() {document.getElementById("theRequestor").retrieveResponse() };
       this.myServerRequest.open("GET",cString,true);
       this.myServerRequest.send(null);
       this.showResults("Waiting....");
      ]]>
     </body>
     </method>
```

```
    <!-- retrieve the response and populate response field -->
     <method name="retrieveResponse">
    <body>
     <![CDATA[
      try {
       if (this.myServerRequest.readyState == 4)
         { // all done

            // Check return code
            if (this.myServerRequest.status == 200) { // request terminated OK
// 5
                   this.showResults("Response
                   received.",this.myServerRequest.responseText);
                } // request terminated OK

            else { // something is wrong
                alert("Response failed.");
            } // something is wrong
        } // all done
    } // try
     catch (e) {
      alert("Retrieve response exception: " + e);
      dump (e);
    }

     ]]>
    </body>
    </method>

<!-- move the string into our results box and parse
        results for display -->
<!-- 6 -->
   <method name="showResults">
   <parameter name="widgetStatus"/>
   <parameter name="resString"/>
    <body>
    <![CDATA[
      var theT = document.getAnonymousElementByAttribute
                (this,"anonid","_resultField");
      theT.value=widgetStatus;
      //
      // Clear list and reload
// 7
      var theL = document.getAnonymousElementByAttribute
               (this,"anonid","_resultList");
      var oldItems = theL.getElementsByTagName("listitem");
      for (var i = 0; i < oldItems.length; i++)
        theL.removeChild(oldItems[i]);

      if (resString != "") { // repopulate with new results
```

```
        var rArray = resString.split(",");
        // built new list items
        for (var j = 0; j < rArray.length; j++) { // for all new items

          var newKeyString = rArray[j].substring(0,rArray[j].
               indexOf("="));
          var newValueString = rArray[j].substring(rArray[j].
              indexOf("=")+1,rArray[j].length);


          var newItem = document.createElement("listitem");

          var newKey = document.createElement("listcell");
          newKey.setAttribute("label",newKeyString);
          newItem.appendChild(newKey);

          var newValue = document.createElement("listcell");
          newValue.setAttribute("label",newValueString);
          newItem.appendChild(newValue);

          theL.appendChild(newItem);

        } // for all new items

      } // repopulate with new results

    ]]>
    </body>
  </method>

 </implementation>
</binding>
</bindings>
```

The XBL binding includes several of the features described earlier in this chapter.

The widget includes elements that use the anonid attribute to provide a method of direct access for a widget to scripts (1). We use a field to hold a reference to the server object that the main interface must set (2); the server object provides the method to create the xml request object to be constructed (3, 4). The script to be called is passed through the widget's src attribute.

We use an XBL-defined method to process the request in the form of the asynchronous callback function (5). The showResults method (6) uses two parameter values to set a status string and display the optional result string. That method uses the getAnonymousElementByAttribute function to obtain a reference to the list containing the list cells displaying the parsed result string (7).

The source file, *requestor.xul*, creates a <vbox> with text boxes and labels that will provide the data to be sent to the script:

```
<?xml version="1.0"?>
<?xml-stylesheet
  href="chrome://requestor/content/httprequestor.css" type="text/css"?>
```

```
<window id="theWindow"
  xmlns="http://www.mozilla.org/keymaster/gatekeeper/there.is.only.xul">
<script src="requestTest.js"/>

<vbox flex="1" align="center">

<vbox  style="width:300px;" id="theRequestor"
 src="http://localhost/doDelayEcho.php" class="httprequestor">
 <grid >
 <columns>
  <column />
  <column />
 </columns>
  <rows>
  <row>
    <label value="Command:"/>
    <textbox id="theCommand" value="the command"/>
   </row>
   <row>
    <label value="Message:"/>
    <textbox id="message"  value="message"/>
   </row>
   <row>
    <label value="Delay:"/>
    <textbox id="delay" value="0"/>
   </row>
   </rows>
 </grid>
 </vbox>
</vbox>
</window>
```

Finally, the glue that connects the httprequestor class with the XBL entry, as well as some distinctive colorizing and styling, is in the file *httprequestor.css*:

```
.httprequestor {
  -moz-binding: url("chrome://requestor/content/
         httprequestor.xml#httprequestor");

    background-color:blue;
    border-width:medium;
    border-style:ridge;
    font-size:small;
}
```

After we make an appropriate entry in a manifest file in the chrome directory:

```
content requestor requestor/content/requestor.xul
```

the resulting application will display a window that will use the value entered in the time delay field to set a delayed response with the server; any text entered in the message area will be echoed by the server and displayed in the table of results, as shown in Figure 9-10.

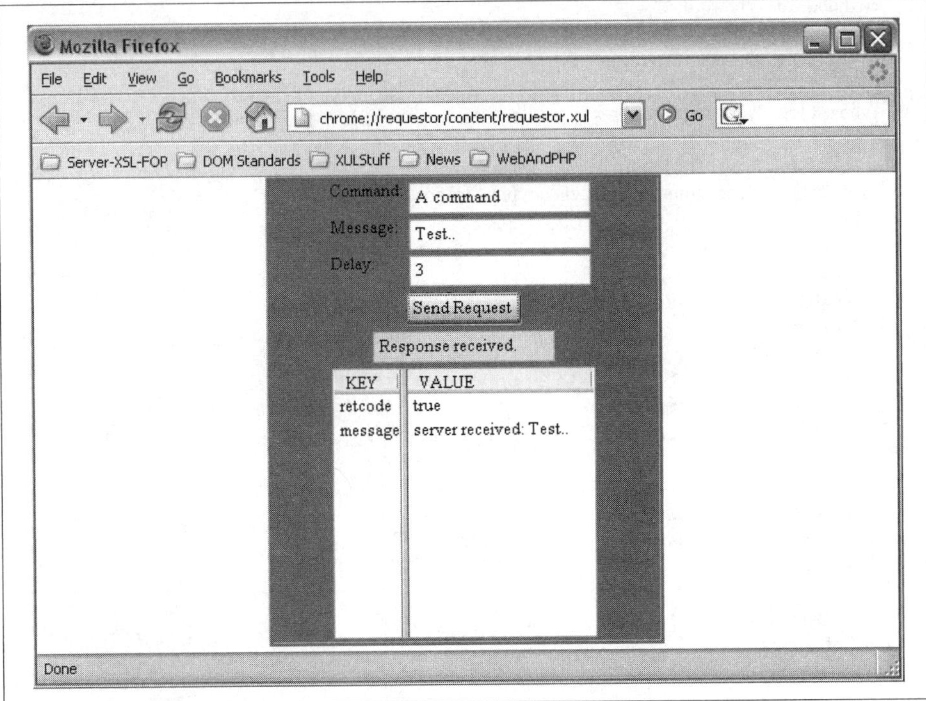

Figure 9-10. XBL httprequestor widget

Extending Bindings

Designers are free to *extend* bindings by creating new ones that reference a root binding.

The use of the `extends` attribute in a `<binding>` element allows the designer to add `<implementation>` and `<handler>` elements to an existing binding. Note that `content` elements do not participate in such an extension. A `<children>` element will move only the explicit content from the bound widget into the last extension of a binding; content of intermediate bindings is discarded.

Suppose we want to extend our requestor widget to display the HTTP header information in the display area.

We can use the `XMLHttpRequest` `getAllResponseHeaders()` method, which returns a string of CR/LF-delimited, colon-separated `label:value` pairs of the header returned by the server. We will use an extended binding to append the header information to our existing list of response values.

We will refer to the extended binding as the `httpheaderview`, and code it in the same *httprequestor.xml* file as the root binding. The code will use constructors to initialize a field that will point to an extension-specific display function:

```
<binding id="httprequestor">
<content>
    <xul:vbox id="_hr_topBox"  align="center" >
     <children/>
     <xul:button  label="Send Request"
      oncommand="this.parentNode.parentNode.sendRequest();"/>
     <xul:textbox  anonid="_resultField" readonly="true" size="20"
                  value="Waiting to send request."/>
     <xul:listbox anonid="_resultList" >
      <xul:listhead>
       <xul:listheader label="KEY"/>
       <xul:listheader label="VALUE"/>
      </xul:listhead>
      <xul:listcols>
       <xul:listcol/>
       <xul:splitter/>
       <xul:listcol flex="1"/>
      </xul:listcols>
       <xul:listitem>
        <xul:listcell label = "x"/>
        <xul:listcell label = "y"/>
       </xul:listitem>
     </xul:listbox>
    </xul:vbox>
  </content>
  <implementation>
   <field name="myServerRequest"/>
   <field name="showResultsFunction"/>

    <method name="sendRequest">
    <body>
     <![CDATA[
       dump("Sending request to" + this.getAttribute("src") + "\n");
       var textArgs = this.getElementsByTagName("textbox");
       var cString = this.getAttribute("src") + "?&command=" +
         document.getElementById("theCommand").value ;
       for (var i = 0; i < textArgs.length; i++) {
         if (textArgs[i].value != "")
             cString += "&" + textArgs[i].getAttribute("id") + "=" +
            textArgs[i].value;
        }

       this.myServerRequest = new XMLHttpRequest();
       this.myServerRequest.onreadystatechange =
          function() {document.getElementById("theRequestor").
            retrieveResponse() };
       this.myServerRequest.open("GET",cString,true);
       this.myServerRequest.send(null);
       this.showResults("Waiting....");
       ]]>
    </body>
    </method>
```

```
<!-- retrieve the response and populate response field -->
 <method name="retrieveResponse">
<body>
 <![CDATA[
  try {
    dump("Retrieving response in object " + this + "\n");
    if (this.myServerRequest.readyState == 4) { // all done
    // Check return code
        if (this.myServerRequest.status == 200) { // request terminated OK

           // (1)
            this.showResultsFunction( );

            } // request terminated OK

        else { // something is wrong
            alert("Response failed.");
        } // something is wrong
    } // all done
} // try
 catch (e) {
  alert("Retrieve response exception: " + e);
  dump (e);
}
]]>
 </body>
 </method>

<!-- move the string into our results box and parse
     results for display -->
   <method name="showResults">
   <parameter name="widgetStatus"/>
   <parameter name="resString"/>
    <body>
     <![CDATA[
      var theT =
      document.getAnonymousElementByAttribute(this,"anonid",
          "_resultField");
      theT.value=widgetStatus;
      //
      // Clear list and reload
      var theL =
      document.getAnonymousElementByAttribute
         (this,"anonid","_resultList");
      var oldItems = theL.getElementsByTagName("listitem");
      for (var i = 0; i < oldItems.length; i++)
        theL.removeChild(oldItems[i]);

      if (resString != "") { // repopulate with new results

        var rArray = resString.split(",");
        // build new list items
        for (var j = 0; j < rArray.length; j++) { // for all new items
         dump("Processing results " + rArray[j] + "\n");
```

```
          var newKeyString = rArray[j].substring(0,rArray[j].indexOf("="));
          var newValueString =
          rArray[j].substring(rArray[j].
              indexOf("=")+1,rArray[j].length);

          var newItem = document.createElement("listitem");

          var newKey = document.createElement("listcell");
          newKey.setAttribute("label",newKeyString);
          newItem.appendChild(newKey);

          var newValue = document.createElement("listcell");
          newValue.setAttribute("label",newValueString);
          newItem.appendChild(newValue);

          theL.appendChild(newItem);

        } // for all new items

      } // repopulate with new results
      ]]>
    </body>
  </method>


<!--(2) -->
  <constructor>
   <![CDATA[
    this.showResultsFunction =
     function( )
      { this.showResults("Response received."
           ,this.myServerRequest.responseText)};
    ]]>
  </constructor>

  </implementation>
 </binding>


 <!-- 3 -->
 <binding id="httpheaderview"
   extends="chrome://requestor/content/httprequestor.xml#httprequestor">

  <implementation>
  <method name="showResultsAndHeaders">
   <parameter name="widgetStatus"/>
   <parameter name="resString"/>
   <parameter name="headersString"/>
    <body>
    <![CDATA[
      var theL =
       document.getAnonymousElementByAttribute(this,
         "anonid","_resultList");
     // (4)
```

```
        this.showResults(widgetStatus,resString);

        if (headersString != "") { // repopulate with new results

          var rArray = headersString.split("\n");
          // build new list items
          for (var j = 0; j < rArray.length; j++)
           { // for all new items

           var newKeyString = rArray[j].substring(0,rArray[j].
             indexOf(":"));
           var newValueString =
             rArray[j].substring(rArray[j].
              indexOf(":")+1,rArray[j].length);

           var newItem = document.createElement("listitem");

           var newKey = document.createElement("listcell");
           newKey.setAttribute("label",newKeyString);
           newItem.appendChild(newKey);

           var newValue = document.createElement("listcell");
           newValue.setAttribute("label",newValueString);
           newItem.appendChild(newValue);

           theL.appendChild(newItem);

          } // for all new items

        } // repopulate with new results
       ]]>
      </body>
     </method>


    <constructor>
     <![CDATA[

   // (5)
      this.showResultsFunction = function( )
        { this.showResultsAndHeaders("Response received.",
            this.myServerRequest.responseText,
              this.myServerRequest.getAllResponseHeaders( ))}; // 6
      var theL =
       document.getAnonymousElementByAttribute
        (this,"anonid","_resultList");
      theL.style.width="500px"; // 7
      ]]>
    </constructor>

    </implementation>
   </binding>

  </bindings>
```

We change the initial binding (httprequestor) to call a display function (1) that was obtained from a field set during a newly added constructor (2).

The code illustrates the form of the extends attribute, which points to the id of the root binding (3). The method showResultsAndHeaders calls the existing showResults method in the intermediate binding, and appends the HTTP headers to the result list (4).

The specialized showResultsAndHeaders function was called by virtue of the extension's <constructor> element, which set up the pointer to the display function (5). That function uses the getAllResponseHeaders (6) call to obtain all the HTTP response fields for display. The constructor also changed the width of the display list to better accommodate the longer fields of the HTTP headers (7).

We declare the binding in the *httprequestor.css* file and add some distinctive color:

```
.httpheaderview {
 -moz-binding: url("chrome://requestor/content/
       httprequestor.xml#httpheaderview");

    background-color:green;
    border-width:medium;
    border-style:ridge;
    font-size:small;
}
```

The source file now references the extended binding:

```
<vbox flex="1" align="center">

<vbox  style="width:300px;" id="theRequestor"
   src="http://localhost/doDelayEcho.php"
     class="httpheaderview" >
 <grid >
 <columns>
  <column />
  <column />
 </columns>
  <rows>
  <row>
.
.
.
```

The result is rendered as an interface illustrated in Figure 9-11.

Because we changed the class reference of the text container, the resulting code now supports the use of a simple httprequestor binding or a more thorough httpheaderview.

Table 9-2 summarizes the key elements, attributes, and methods discussed in this section.

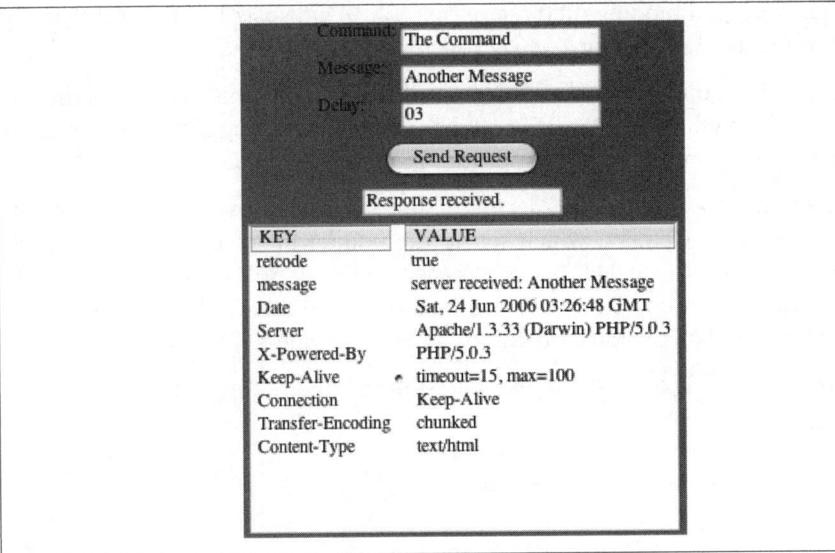

Figure 9-11. HTTPHeaderView binding

Table 9-2. New terms relating to XBL elements

Element/Object	Attribute/Property/Method	Description
`<bindings>`	`id=`*`bindingID`*	Topmost node for a binding tied to an identifier referenced in a CSS declaration.
`<content>`	N/A	Topmost container for anonymous content to be attached to the bound element.
`<constructor>` `<destructor>`	N/A	Defines scripts to be called when the widget is first displayed (`constructor`), or when the displaying window is destroyed (`destructor`).
`<children>`	`includes="`*`tag1|tag2...`*`"`	Defines the tags for elements that are to be included in the resulting output widget of an XBL binding.
Any XBL content element	`xbl:inherits="`*`anonAttrib=explicitAttrib`*`"`	Forwards an attribute for anonymous content from an attribute assigned to explicit content in the bound widget.
`<implementation>`	N/A	Topmost element containing methods, fields, and properties that define an XBL widget's functionality.
`<field name="fieldName">`	Accessible by dot (.) reference as `this.fieldName = newVal;`	Fields add variables accessible from scripts that exist outside the XBL binding.
`<property name="propName">`	Accessible through assignment, XBL getter/setter functions are invoked using the dot ('.') notation as: `this.propName = newVal;`	Properties provide the ability for XBL methods to be triggered by a script's access.

Table 9-2. New terms relating to XBL elements (continued)

Element/Object	Attribute/Property/Method	Description
<handlers>	N/A	Topmost node containing event handlers for the entire XBL widget.
<handler>	`event="`*`someDOMEvent`*`"`	Identifies the event to trigger the child handler script.
`document`	`getAnonymousNodes (parentNode)`	Returns an array of all anonymous nodes that are attached to the parent node.
`document`	`getAnonymousElementByAttribute (`*`parent, attributeName, attributeValue`*`)`	Provides a mechanism for obtaining a reference to a specific anonymous node by virtue of a known attribute name and value pair.
`XMLHttpRequest`	`getAllResponseHeaders`	Returns a string of server response headers as a collection of CR/LF-separated `field: value` pairs.

Summary

Developers can take advantage of two families of resources to extend the functionality of an existing browser or the widgets that comprise a browser's interface.

Attaching new functions and interface elements to a browser involves the use of overlay technology. Overlays provide the ability to attach existing XUL elements to known locations of a pre-existing interface structure. Such an attachment often requires the designer to have a good understanding of the existing interface as well as the context that triggers specific menus, pop ups, or other interface widgets.

Designers wishing to combine interface elements into new widgets that have distinctive behavior are likely to use the XBL.

XBL can be applied to any XUL, XHTML, or SVG element; it is a powerful tool with which a designer can assemble a reusable component for any application. Designers also can combine XBL widgets with overlay technology to add a completely new set of behaviors to an existing application, or to serve as the foundation for newly developed applications.

CHAPTER 10
XForms

Most of the technologies we have discussed to this point involve a good deal of "client-side" scripting—code to manipulate interface controls or document content. This chapter focuses on a technology designed to minimize the need for validation scripting while maximizing the portability of interface elements among different display modalities.

This chapter discusses the Firefox implementation of XForms, a World Wide Web Consortium (W3C) standard presented as an alternative technique to move structured (form-like) user entry data into served applications. The goal of an XForms implementation is to reduce the linkage between data and interface structure, reduce the amount of scripting (either at the server or at the client) required to validate entry, and expand the portability of a data model through a replaceable instance of an interface that may be customized for a specific implementation.

This chapter:

- Covers the basic structure of an XForms design
- Illustrates how an input form is transferred directly into XML at the server
- Explores the conditional styling and validation features of XForms
- Covers how we can use XML events and actions to modify interface structure

The examples will use XHTML files for the source pages served from a localhost web server such as Apache. We will code the server scripting in Personal Hypertext Processor (PHP) language.

Although Firefox supports the XForms model, you must manually install the XForms extension from the Mozilla.org development site.

Basic XForms Structure

The XForms form traces its genealogy to the conventional HTML form element—a container of input fields such as text entry boxes, checkboxes, and radio buttons, corresponding to a button that submits the collected data to a server application. The server script extracts the variables associated with an array of values keyed to the name of the input element on the page.

XForms provide application developers with an extra series of services based on the presumption that the data returned from the client will be structured as an XML tree of nodes. The XForms form on the web page defines the Document Object Model (DOM) structure through an XML instance element that provides a template defining the node names of the result tree that will be submitted to the server. This instance element is wrapped by the XForms model tag most often declared within the XHTML document's head element, as shown here (note the use of the XForms namespace):

```
<html xmlns="http://www.w3.org/1999/xhtml"
      xmlns:xf="http://www.w3.org/2002/xforms"">

<link href="nameAndAddress.css" rel="style-sheet" type="text/css" />
<head>
<title>XFORM Test Page</title>
<xf:model>
  <xf:instance>
  <!-- this is what will be sent to the server -->
  <person xmlns="">
    <name>
     <fname />
     <lname />
    </name>
    <address>
     <street/>
     <city/>
     <state/>
     <code/>
    </address>
    <phone/>
    <birthdate/>
  </person>
<!—- end of what will be sent to the server -->
 </xf:instance>
 </xf:model>
<!-- remainder of page    -->
```

This sample shows that the result will be sent as an XML tree with a topmost person node consisting of name, address, phone, and birthdate children, the name and address elements having children expressing more detailed information. The instance element defines only the structure of the data to be submitted—no styling or presentation information is included in the instance element.

To specify what to do with the XForms data, the XForms `submission` element includes the attributes that tell the XForms processor (code within Firefox) how to transfer the data. A simple `submission` that sends the form data to a PHP script is included within the `instance` element:

```
<xf:submission id="xformrequest" method="post"
  action="http://localhost/xformrequest.php"/>
</xf:model>
```

The interface elements are declared in the *interface markup*—the body of the XHTML document with XForms `input` elements. Each element includes a `ref` attribute that binds an input field to a node in the model's XML tree using an XPath address. The following fragment binds the value obtained from an `input` element to the `fname` child node of the `name` node in the `person` result tree:

```
<xf:input ref="name/fname">
<xf:label>First Name</xf:label>
</xf:input>
```

The XForms `input` element is one of several XForms *controls*, and includes a required label child element, and a `ref` attribute that binds the entered value to the `name/fname` node.

The following list summarizes the different families of XForms markup elements:

Controls
: Elements that provide the interface that interacts with the user

Bindings
: Associations between the information model and the markup interface

User interface
: Helper elements that provide programmatic support for controls

An Example Transfer to the Server

A complete illustration of a working XForms implementation includes an XHTML page with an XForms group, a Cascading Style Sheet (CSS) that provides additional formatting for the form entry, and a server script to receive the submitted data.

The Stylesheet

The stylesheet for this example, *nameAndAddress.css*, includes some new notations:

```
@namespace xf url(http://www.w3.org/2002/xforms);

/* Display a red asterisk after all required form controls */
*:required::before  { content: "* ";}
```

```
body {
background:#c0c0c0;
}

xf|group {
position:relative;
left:20%;
width:60%;
text-align:right;
border-style: solid;
border-width:thick;
border-color:#000080;
}

xf|input { display: block; }
xf|input > xf|label { color: blue; }
```

We will explore this file in more detail later in this chapter. At this point, we can see that the CSS file organizes input elements in block style layout, with the main group container being centered on the page within a dark blue frame.

The Server Script

The server script we will use to receive the XML data is a straightforward sequence that uses the standard DOM functions available as of PHP 5:

```
<?php

try {
// 1
header( 'Content-type: application/xhtml+xml' );

// 2
$inForm = $HTTP_RAW_POST_DATA;

$domDocument = new DOMDocument( );

// 3
if (!($domDocument->loadXML($inForm) )) {
    echo("input cannot be parsed");
    exit( );
}

// 4
echo $domDocument->saveXML( );

exit( );
}
 catch (Exception $exc) {
     echo("Processing exception: ".$exc->getMessage( ));
     exit( );
 }
?>
```

The script includes the PHP statement to return a header that sets the content type for an XML document to be echoed to the client (1). The XML data from the XForms form is received as serialized XML available in the `$HTTP_RAW_POST_DATA` (2). A DOM document is created, and parses the input variable with the `loadXML` statement (3). For this illustration, the example then reserializes the result and echoes the XML back to the browser (4).

An Overview of an XForms Document

A completed example XHTML file that includes the XForms form is illustrated in our *XFormRequestPage.xhtml*, which is placed at the document root served by a web server running on localhost:

```
<?xml version="1.0" encoding="iso-8859-1"?>
<!DOCTYPE html PUBLIC "-//W3C//DTD XHTML 1.0 Transitional//EN"
          "http://www.w3.org/TR/xhtml1/DTD/xhtml1-transitional.dtd">

<html xmlns="http://www.w3.org/1999/xhtml"
      xmlns:xf="http://www.w3.org/2002/xforms"
      xmlns:ev="http://www.w3.org/2001/xml-events"
      xmlns:xsd="http://www.w3.org/2001/XMLSchema"
      xmlns:xsi="http://www.w3.org/2001/XMLSchema-instance">

<link href="nameAndAdress.css" rel="style-sheet" type="text/css" />
<head>
<title>XFORM Test Page</title>
<xf:model>
  <xf:instance>
  <!-- this is what will be sent to the server -->
  <person xmlns="">
    <name>
     <fname />
     <lname />
    </name>
    <address>
     <street/>
     <city/>
     <state/>
     <code/>
    </address>
    <phone/>
    <birthdate/>
  </person>
  <!-- this is what will be sent to the server -->
 </xf:instance>


 <xf:submission id="xformrequest" method="post"
  action="http://localhost/xformrequest.php"/>
</xf:model>

</head>
```

```
<body>

<xf:group>

<xf:input ref="name/fname">
<xf:label>First Name</xf:label>
</xf:input>

<xf:input ref="name/lname">
<xf:label>Last Name</xf:label>
</xf:input>

<xf:input ref="address/street">
<xf:label>Street</xf:label>
</xf:input>

<xf:input ref="address/city">
<xf:label>City</xf:label>
</xf:input>

<xf:input ref="address/state">
<xf:label>State</xf:label>
</xf:input>

<xf:input width="32" ref="address/code">
<xf:label>Zip code</xf:label>
</xf:input>

<xf:input ref="phone">
<xf:label>Phone number</xf:label>
</xf:input>

<xf:input ref="birthdate">
<xf:label>Date of Birth "mm/dd/yyyy"</xf:label>
</xf:input>

</xf:group>
<hr/>
<div style="text-align: center;">

<xf:submit submission="xformrequest">
<xf:label>Submit</xf:label>
</xf:submit>
</div>

</body>
</html>
```

Aside from some styling information to center our submit button, the file represents simple examples that illustrate the basic XForms form. Figure 10-1 shows the resulting page.

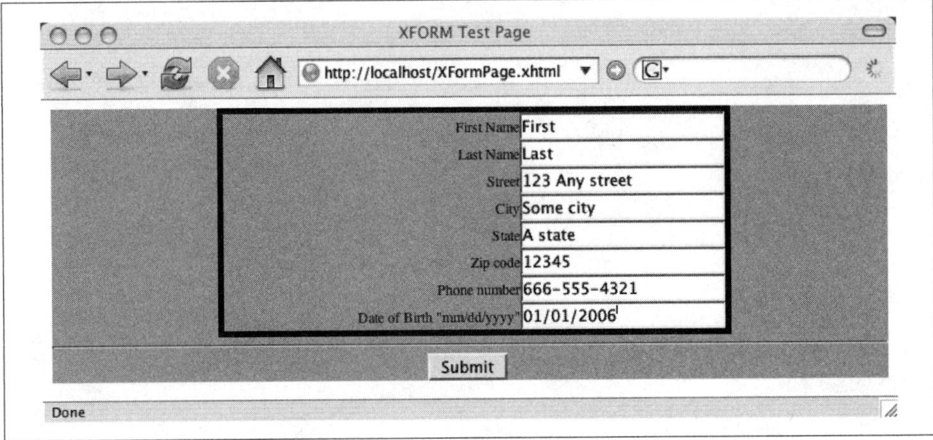

Figure 10-1. Simple XForms interface

Upon entering the data and submitting the form to the server, the XML data is echoed back to the browser. The default configuration for the browser formats XML as a simple tree, as shown in Figure 10-2.

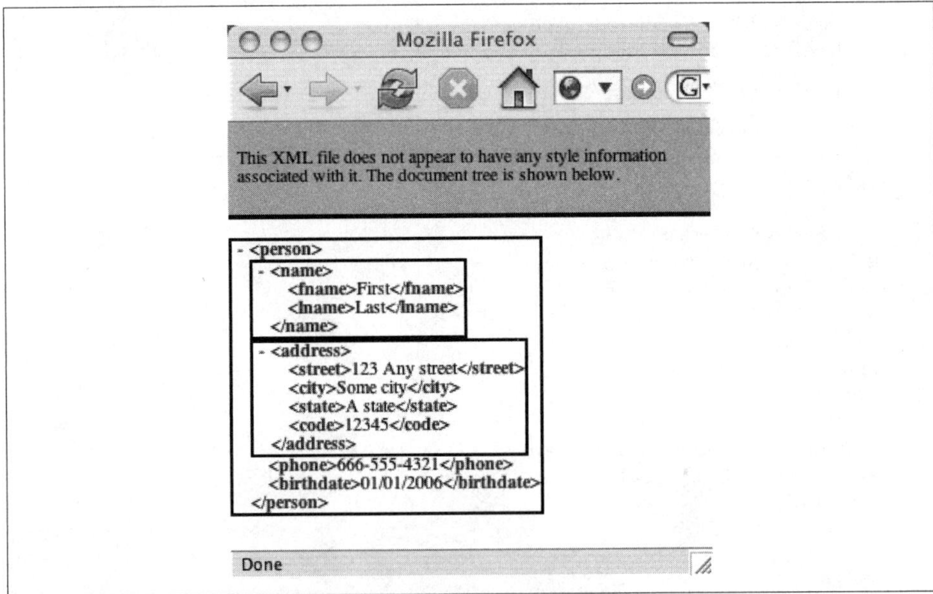

Figure 10-2. Echoed XML from XForms

The server simply returns the XForms data as initially received from the browser, illustrating how the original XForms form structured the submitted data.

XForms Controls

At the core of an XForms document are the control elements used to collect user input. All XForms control elements include labels and values. The values may be obtained from any number of different interface widgets that Firefox's XForms processor renders. The Firefox XForms processor supports the following form controls:

`input`
: An area for single-line text entry

`secret`
: A text entry area with the input characters hidden

`textarea`
: An input area allowing for multiple lines of text input

`upload`
: A file selection element

`range`
: Allows selection of an interval that exists between a range of numeric values

`select`
: Allows selection of multiple items from a list of candidate selections

`select1`
: Allows selection of one item from a list of candidate selections

XForms Validation Features

The XForms specification includes a number of features that verify that required input was provided, and that input data is properly formatted. These features include conditional formatting tools to add distinctive styling to required elements, the ability to add interactive hints to input forms, and a built-in validation process that inhibits submission if input fields do not meet certain criteria.

The association between the data model and the interface markup that controls the conditional styling—and, in some cases, value manipulation of the interface elements—is managed by a *binding* of model item properties. A binding element references nodes in the data model, and manipulates the interface rendering the node values based on a calculated expression. The calculated expression reflects the structure of data entered in other node elements. Figure 10-3 illustrates this relationship.

Pseudoclasses and Conditional Styling

One mechanism that encourages proper data entry is conditional styling. XForms allow the designer to use supporting stylesheet statements to add styling attributes and content elements to XForms elements that meet certain rules. Before we explore those features, we'll discuss some of the stylesheet's statements.

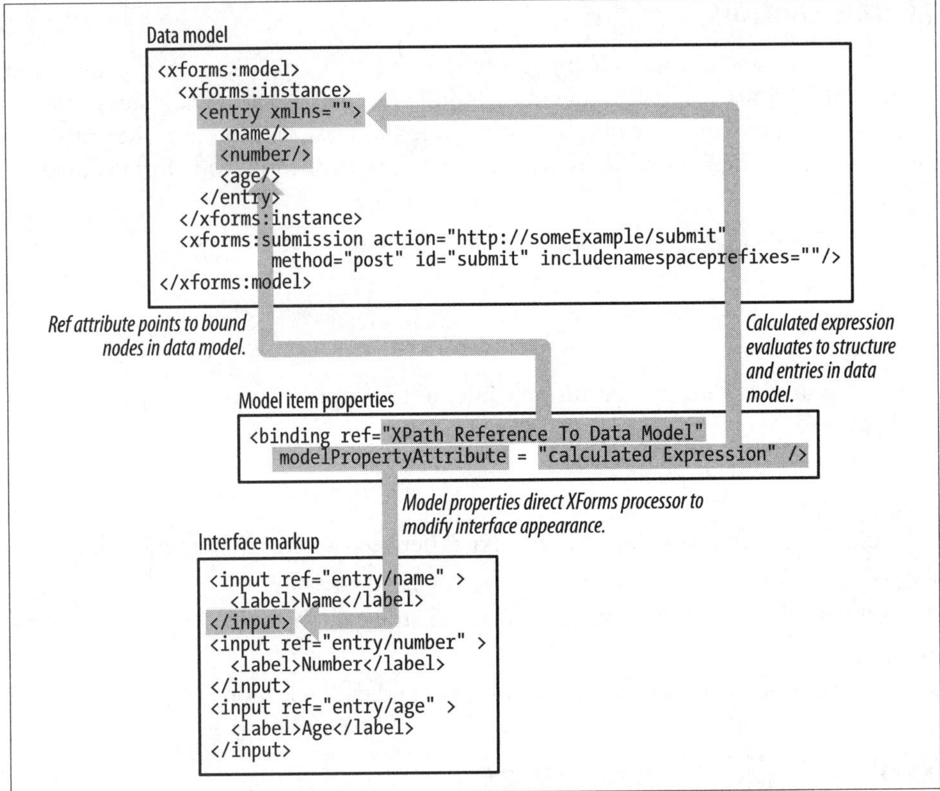

Figure 10-3. Data model–binding–interface markup

The stylesheet starts with a *namespace rule*, a statement that binds a token to a URI:

```
@namespace xf url(http://www.w3.org/2002/xforms);
```

Namespace rules allow a stylesheet designer to bind CSS selectors to a namespace-qualified element or attribute. (Because a CSS designer has no idea what namespace prefix a document may use, the CSS rule allows him to implement style rules by using a URI prefix.) The preceding namespace rule binds the `xf` prefix to the XForms namespace URI.

Within the stylesheet, the namespace prefix is bound to CSS selectors with the `|` delimiter:

```
xf|group {
position:relative;
left:20%;
width:60%;
...
```

The preceding CSS snippet selects all group elements that are bound to the xf prefix (the XForms namespace) and centers the box, which spans 60 percent of the page width.

Pseudoclasses

The CSS specification supports the notion of *pseudoclasses*, a form of notation that applies styling properties to DOM elements based on information about the element that is not captured through explicit DOM node classes or attribute values.

The Firefox framework supports a number of XForms pseudoclasses, as shown in Table 10-1.

Table 10-1. Firefox-supported XForms pseudoclasses

CSS selector	Description
::in-range/::out-of-range	Class selector for any form element that is in/out of the range of valid values
::valid/::invalid	Class selector for any valid/invalid entry
::optional/::required	Class selector for any form element that is optional/required

The CSS specification includes pseudoclasses for read-only and read-write access. As of this writing, those expressions are not supported. Designers must use :moz-read-only and :moz-read-write pseudoclasses.

These selectors become associated with individual XForms elements through the creation of a *model item*. We declare a model item with an xform:bind element that associates a nodeset attribute (which points to nodes in the data model) with a set of model item properties:

```
<xform:bind nodeset="xpath expression" properties />
```

The properties portion of the bind element consists of any number of attributes that are assigned a computed expression. For example, the attribute assignment:

```
<xf:bind nodeset="name/lname" required="true( )"  />
```

results in the lname nodes being assigned a Boolean value of true to the node's required property. We can then reference this property in the CSS to make the font bold for required elements:

```
*:required  { font-weight: bold;}
```

Be certain to remember that model property assignment takes a *computed expression* such as required="true( )", not a literal assignment as in required="true".

Table 10-2 lists the model item properties that Firefox supports.

Table 10-2. Firefox-supported model item properties

Property	Description
`calculate`	The value of the node is calculated by the computed expression.
`constraint`	The value is constrained to a relationship defined by the computed expression.
`readonly`	The value is prevented from changing.
`relevant`	The value is relevant to this instance of the form (if `FALSE`, the value will not be submitted with form data).
`required`	The value must be submitted before the form will be submitted.

At first glance, there may be some confusion between the different roles of pseudoclasses and the model item properties.

The model item properties are the attributes used in bindings; the pseudoclasses are the declarations used in stylesheets. Although in the case of the `required` model item property there is also a `::required` pseudoclass, this is not always the case. The `calculate` model item property, for example, affects the `::in-range`/`::out-of-range` pseudoclass setting, the `constraint` property affects the `::valid` pseudoclass, etc.

Required entries

By combining the features of pseudoclasses, conditional styling, and model item properties, we can provide the user with clues for appropriate values in a form without the need for a server-based verification process.

An example of conditional styling is shown in this entry in the CSS file:

```
*:required::before  { content: "* ";}
```

This statement uses the `required` pseudoclass, along with the standard `before` CSS pseudoelement selector, to select the node that precedes any required XForms nodes in the DOM tree. The statement uses the `content` specifier to create an asterisk and insert it before the required node element. The XForms document is modified to include a `bind` element that associates a `nodeset` with a `required` property:

```
<xf:bind nodeset="name/lname" required="true( )"  />
<xf:bind nodeset="name/fname" required="true( )"  />
<xf:bind nodeset="phone" required="true( )"  />
<xf:bind nodeset="birthdate" required="true( )"/>
```

The resulting interface will now include asterisks before the fields bound to the nodes for `lname`, `fname`, phone number, and `birthdate`, as shown in Figure 10-4.

Data validation

We can deliver feedback through a pop-up window to provide a hint for proper data entry. An alert dialog may be issued when an entry is invalid, or conditional styling may be used to provide a visual cue about an entry problem. These techniques will involve adding elements to the interface model of the XForms form as child nodes of the parent `input` element.

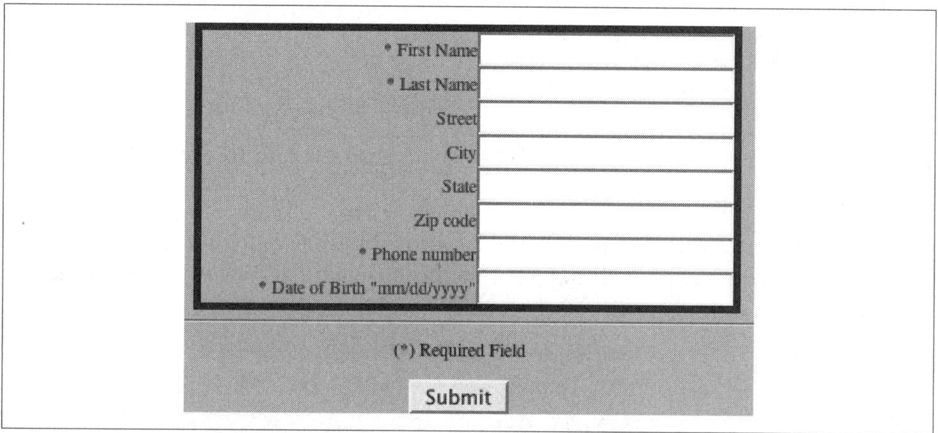

Figure 10-4. Conditional styling with pseudoclasses

We use the XForms `hint` element to provide a message to the user when the mouse moves over the input area. An `alert` element is added to provide a pop-up modal dialog to prompt the user to correct a validation error. The conditional styling technique builds upon the CSS `invalid` pseudoclass described in the preceding section.

Data is considered invalid when the user entry violates a constraint attribute assigned as a model item property. Once data falls outside the constraint range, conditional styling and/or the alert message directs the user to the source of the problem. A `testField` element, which includes the techniques to make certain the user enters a number greater than 0 into a field, can be added onto the end of the instance model:

```
<person xmlns="">
    <name>
     <fname />
     <lname />
    </name>
    <address>
     <street/>
     <city/>
     <state/>
     <code/>
    </address>
    <phone/>
    <birthdate>1900-01-01</birthdate>
    <testField>1</testField>
  </person>
```

The interface model includes a `bind` element that attaches a `constraint` attribute. This attribute uses XPath syntax to specify that the value of the current node must be greater than 0:

```
<xf:bind nodeset="testField"  constraint=". &gt; 0" />
```

The interface model includes a hint and alert to be issued if the input constraint is violated:

```
<xf:input ref="testField">
<xf:label>Test number</xf:label>
<xf:alert>Must be greater than 0</xf:alert>
<xf:hint>Enter a number</xf:hint>
</xf:input>
```

Finally, a stylesheet entry is added to set the background color for invalid entries:

```
*:invalid {background-color:red;}
```

If any of the constraints declared in the XForms' binding elements are not met, the Firefox XForms processor will not submit the form but will instead set the node's invalid property and trigger the alert, as shown in Figure 10-5.

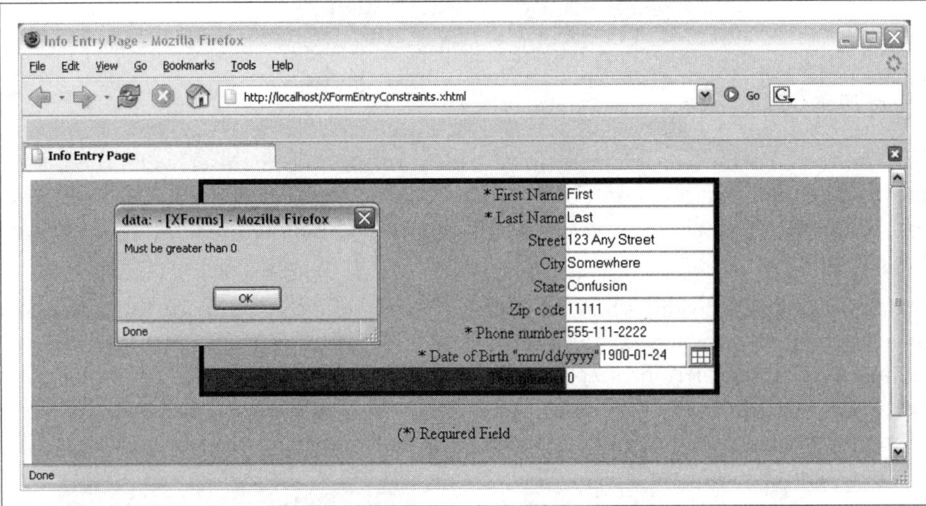

Figure 10-5. Alert triggered with invalid entry

Note that the highlighted area for the failing field is over the label of the input test number. The stylesheet declaration sets the background color for the entire `input` element when the field receives an invalid entry. To change the interface to highlight only the incorrect data portion, designers must use CSS to apply the style to a Firefox-specific `.xf-value` class. This is shown in the following change to the CSS file:

```
xf|input:invalid .xf-value { background-color:red; }
```

This statement sets the background color red for any `value` element (regardless of the specific widget used to obtain the value from the user) that is a child of an invalid XForms form, resulting in the altered appearance shown in Figure 10-6.

This is one point where the W3C specification varies from Firefox's XForms implementation. The recommended specification includes a reference to the `value` pseudoclass that Firefox does not support—the `xf-value` class is used as a replacement.

Figure 10-6. Styling Firefox's .xf-value class

Styling XForms elements can be a bit problematic. XForms elements are actually composite widgets consisting of labels, input areas, text areas, buttons, and other interface elements bundled into a single XForms element. It is not easy to predict how a style applied to an XForms element (especially declarations involving positioning and layout) will be reflected in the interface. The previous example showed how the `background-color` of an input element gives the appearance that only the label has been styled. The designer may experiment with different borders, padding, and margin settings to obtain the desired outcome on a case-by-case basis.

A closer look at a sample form that combines a number of different controls, along with the bindings that illustrate the model item properties discussed, is illustrated in this mockup of an automobile inquiry form named *XFormSamples.xhtml*:

```
<?xml version="1.0" encoding="iso-8859-1"?>
<!DOCTYPE html PUBLIC "-//W3C//DTD XHTML 1.0 Transitional//EN"
         "http://www.w3.org/TR/xhtml1/DTD/xhtml1-transitional.dtd">

<html xmlns="http://www.w3.org/1999/xhtml"
 xmlns:xf="http://www.w3.org/2002/xforms"
 xmlns:ev="http://www.w3.org/2001/xml-events"
 xmlns:xsd="http://www.w3.org/2001/XMLSchema"
 xmlns:xsi="http://www.w3.org/2001/XMLSchema-instance" >

<link href="xformSamples.css" rel="stylesheet" type="text/css" />
<head>
<title>Info Entry Page</title>
<xf:model>
  <xf:instance>
  <!-- this is what will be sent to the server -->
 <person xmlns="">
    <name>
     <fname />
     <lname />
    </name>
    <phone/>
    <birthdate>1900-01-01</birthdate>

    <password/>
    <message>
      <messageBody/>
      <attachment />
    </message>
    <dealerRange/>
```

```
    <vehicleSelection>
     <manufacturer>Ford</manufacturer>
     <types />
     <features />
    </vehicleSelection>
  </person>

  <!-- this is what will be sent to the server -->
 </xf:instance>

 <xf:bind nodeset="name/lname"  required="true( )" type="xsd:string" />
 <xf:bind nodeset="name/fname" required="true( )"  type="xsd:string"/>
 <xf:bind nodeset="phone" required="true( )"  />
 <xf:bind nodeset="birthdate" required="true( )" type="xsd:date" />
 <xf:bind nodeset="password" required="true( )"  />


 <xf:bind nodeset="message/attachment" type="xsd:anyURI"  />



<xf:submission id="xformrequest" method="post"
  action="http://localhost/chap10/xformrequest-simple.php"/>
</xf:model>

</head>

<body>

<div style="width:700px">

<xf:group >

<xf:input ref="name/fname">
<xf:label>First Name</xf:label>
<xf:alert>Invalid entry</xf:alert>
</xf:input>

<xf:input ref="name/lname">
<xf:label>Last Name</xf:label>
<xf:alert>Required</xf:alert>
</xf:input>


<xf:input ref="phone">
<xf:label>Phone number</xf:label>
<xf:hint> xxx-yyy-zzzz</xf:hint>
</xf:input>

<xf:input ref="birthdate">
<xf:label>Date of Birth "mm/dd/yyyy"</xf:label>
<xf:alert>Invalid date</xf:alert>
</xf:input>
```

```
<hr/>
<xf:secret ref="password">
<xf:label>Password:</xf:label>
</xf:secret>

<hr/>
<xf:textarea ref="message/messageBody">
<xf:label>Note text:</xf:label>
<xf:value>None</xf:value>
</xf:textarea>
<hr/>

<xf:upload ref="message/attachment">
 <xf:label>Select file:</xf:label>
</xf:upload>


<hr/>
<xf:range ref="dealerRange" start="10" end="100" step="20">
 <xf:label>Maximum distance to dealer:</xf:label>
</xf:range>

<hr/>
<xf:select1  ref="vehicleSelection/manufacturer">
<xf:label>Select Manufacturer:</xf:label>

<xf:item>
 <xf:label>Ford</xf:label>
 <xf:value>Ford</xf:value>
</xf:item>
<xf:item>
 <xf:label>General Motors</xf:label>
 <xf:value>GM</xf:value>
</xf:item>
<xf:item>
 <xf:label>Toyota</xf:label>
 <xf:value>Toyota</xf:value>
</xf:item>

</xf:select1>


<hr/>
<xf:select ref="vehicleSelection/types">
<xf:label>Vehicle types:</xf:label>
<xf:item>
 <xf:label>Trucks</xf:label>
 <xf:value>trucks</xf:value>
</xf:item>
<xf:item>
 <xf:label>Economy</xf:label>
 <xf:value>economy</xf:value>
</xf:item>
<xf:item>
```

```
 <xf:label>Hybrid</xf:label>
 <xf:value>hybrid</xf:value>
</xf:item>
<xf:item>
 <xf:label>SUV</xf:label>
 <xf:value>suv</xf:value>
</xf:item>

</xf:select>



</xf:group>
</div>

<hr/>
<div style="text-align: center;">
<p>(*) Required Field</p>
<xf:submit submission="xformrequest">
<xf:label>Submit</xf:label>
</xf:submit>
</div>
</body>
</html>
```

An accompanying stylesheet, *xformSamples.css*, uses some of the constructs described earlier:

```
@namespace xf url(http://www.w3.org/2002/xforms);

/* Display a red asterisk after all required form controls */
*:required::before  { content: "* ";}


xf|input:invalid .xf-value { background-color:red; }


body {
background:#a0a0a0;
}


 xf|* {
 margin:2px;
}

xf|input { display: block;  }


xf|label {
 font-family:arial;
 font-size:small;
 color: #000080;
 }
```

```
/* default data entry area has a thin gray border */
.xf-value {
border-style:solid;
 border-color:gray;
 border-width:thin;
}


xf|group {
position:relative;
left:20%;
width:60%;
text-align:right;
border-style: solid;
border-width:thick;
border-color:#000080;
}


xf|upload {
display:block;
}

xf|upload .xf-value {
 width:200px;
}


xf|textarea {
 width:90%;
 left:5%;
 display:block;
 position:relative;
 color:white;
 border-color:white;
 border-style:solid;
 border-width:1px;
 padding:3px;
}

xf|textarea  > .xf-value {
border-style:solid;
border-color:gray;
border-width:3px;
width:60%;
}

/* selection elements */
xf|select1  {
 border-style:groove;
 border-color:gray;
 border-width:3px;
 width:200px;
```

```
}

xf|select1 .xf-value{
 width:100px;
}

 xf|select .xf-value {
  border-style:groove;
  border-color:gray;
  border-width:3px;
  }

xf|range .xf-value {
   border-style:groove;
  border-color:gray;
  border-width:3px;
 width:150px;
}
```

Figure 10-7 shows the resulting input.

Submitting the form to a server that echoes only the XML structure of the received form shows the appropriate mapping from the interface to the form's instance model, as illustrated in Figure 10-8.

Beyond Styling: Manipulating Content and Structure

The preceding section discussed conditional styling as a tool to enhance the interface by altering an element's appearance in the event of an invalid or required entry. The same model item properties used for conditional styling can also be used for *conditional presentation*, as well as for the *dynamic calculation* of XForms fields based on the content of other form elements.

Calculating field values

Earlier we discussed the constraint model item property as a simple rule used to verify that manual data entry of a value was greater than 0. We can also use that property to set any type of rule that can be expressed as an XPath expression.

Suppose we have a form with entries for different quantities of items to be ordered. The business rule may require that the total quantity must exceed 10, regardless of the minimum entry for any individual item.

The source would include the three entry fields for the entry and one for the total in the instance model:

```
.
.
.
<vehicleSelection>
```

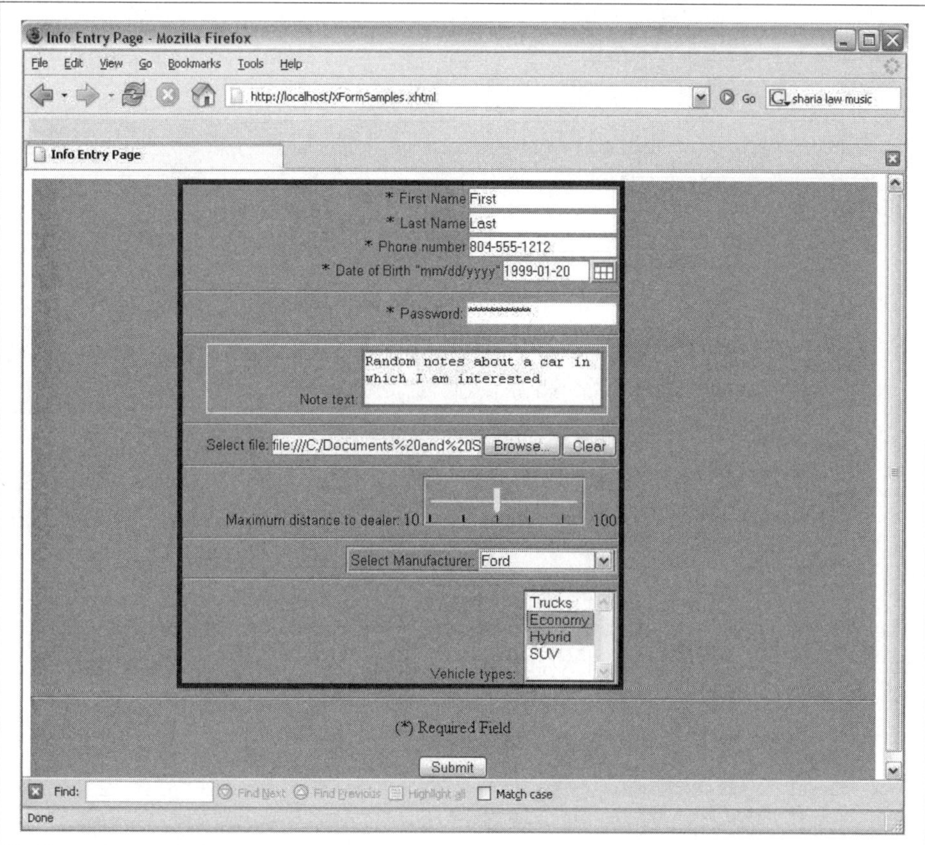

Figure 10-7. Auto interest XForms

```
<manufacturer>Ford</manufacturer>
<types />
<features />
</vehicleSelection>
<field1/>
<field2/>
<field3/>
<fieldTotal/>
</person>
```

The interface elements include the required fields:

```
<xf:input ref="field1">
<xf:label>Qty 1:</xf:label>
</xf:input>
<xf:input ref="field2">
<xf:label>Qty 2:</xf:label>
</xf:input>
<xf:input ref="field3">
<xf:label>Qty 3:</xf:label>
```

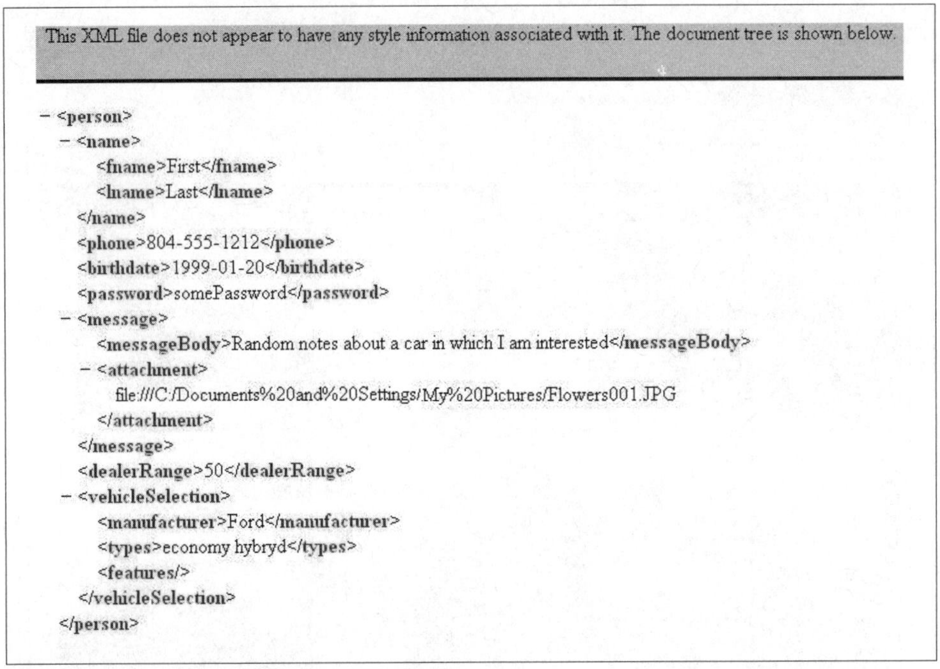

This XML file does not appear to have any style information associated with it. The document tree is shown below.

```
- <person>
  - <name>
      <fname>First</fname>
      <lname>Last</lname>
    </name>
    <phone>804-555-1212</phone>
    <birthdate>1999-01-20</birthdate>
    <password>somePassword</password>
  - <message>
      <messageBody>Random notes about a car in which I am interested</messageBody>
    - <attachment>
        file:///C:/Documents%20and%20Settings/My%20Pictures/Flowers001.JPG
      </attachment>
    </message>
    <dealerRange>50</dealerRange>
  - <vehicleSelection>
      <manufacturer>Ford</manufacturer>
      <types>economy hybryd</types>
      <features/>
    </vehicleSelection>
  </person>
```

Figure 10-8. Auto interest XML data

```
</xf:input>
<xf:input ref="fieldTotal">
<xf:label>Total:</xf:label>
<xf:alert>Value must be greater than 10</xf:alert>
</xf:input>
```

The bindings include the model item properties to assign the sum of the fields to the node value, and to set the field as a read-only element:

```
<xf:bind nodeset="fieldTotal"
        readonly="true()"
        calculate="../field1 + ../field2 + ../field3"
        constraint=". &gt; 10" />
```

The XPath reference adds the node values obtained from the parent node's reference to the elements of interest; the result is displayed in the `fieldTotal` element.

Relevant and conditional appearance

The *relevant* model item property controls the appearance of the entire XForms element based on the evaluation of the XPath expression.

As the user enters values in an XForms form, the designer is free to remove from the interface selections and items that are not relevant based on the user entry.

If, for example, we wanted to add a single choice selection that asks a user whether he wants to limit a dealer search to only local dealers, we would first have to add an element in the data model to capture flag information, as well as the interface element to prompt the user for such a selection:

```
<message>
<messageBody/>
     <attachment />
  </message>
  <dealerRange/>
  <vehicleSelection>
    <localDealerFlag />
    <manufacturer>Ford</manufacturer>
  <types>
   <type>Sedan</type>
   <type>Hybrid</type>
       <type>SUV</type>
   <type>Truck</type>
   <type>Performance</type>
.
.
.
<xf:select1 ref="vehicleSelection/localDealerFlag" appearance="full">
 <xf:label>Dealer location</xf:label>
 <xf:choices>
    <xf:item>
      <xf:label>Local Only</xf:label>
      <xf:value>local</xf:value>
    </xf:item>
    <xf:item>
      <xf:label>Short Drive</xf:label>
      <xf:value>area</xf:value>
    </xf:item>
    </xf:choices>
</xf:select1>
```

We change the model item properties for the vehicle selection node to set the `relevant` attribute based on whether the user entered **`local`** for the `localDealerFlag` entry; we set the statement such that the value is considered `relevant` if the `localDealerFlag` is not equal to `local`:

```
<xf:bind nodeset="dealerRange"
     relevant="../vehicleSelection/localDealerFlag != 'local'" />
```

As a result of these changes, the range element for dealer range will be removed from the interface if the user selects "local" from the selection bound to the `localDealerFlag` element.

User Interface Elements

We have, to this point, discussed mechanisms that manage the appearance of XForms controls based on changes of values in the interface model. XForms also provide extensive support to change how the user creates and manipulates markup items during interaction.

XForms *user interface elements* provide runtime support for the manipulation of the interface. Table 10-3 lists those elements that Firefox supports.

Table 10-3. XForms user interface elements

XForms user interface element	Description
`group`	A container for controls and elements; groups that are set as not relevant result in all enclosed items being set to not relevant.
`switch`	A container for a number of case elements that support the conditional rendering of controls.
`case`	An element representing a single instance of control rendering.
`toggle`	An action that selects one specific case in a `switch` statement.
`repeat`	An element that defines markup to be repeated with multiple instances of specific model item elements. Repeat elements generate repeated instances of any document element.
`itemset`	An element that defines markup to be repeated with multiple instances of specific model item properties. `Itemsets` are used to build entries into XForms `select` and `select1` controls.
`copy`	Moves a deep copy of a node (a copy of the node and all its children) within the instance model.
`insert`	Inserts a new node into the model.
`delete`	Removes a node from the model.
`setindex`	Sets the index that identifies a selected item within a select control or a repeat item.

User interface elements are found in an XForms form either as part of interface markup, or as children of XForms action elements (we discuss actions in the section "XForms Actions," later in this chapter).

Repeating Interface Markup

The previous auto information request model includes a single element to capture selections for the desired manufacturer and vehicle type. The optional choices are coded up in the interface markup that adds items to selection elements.

The design may be more economical if we include the possible choices in the data model and reuse references to those choices in multiple locations within the form's markup. The interface may include a selection list as well as an icon-based menu, both of which could obtain data from the same data set of vehicle types.

XForms include `repeat` and `itemset` elements that allow a designer to attach a template of interface markup to a node in the data model. These elements generate repeated instances of interface markup for each replicated node type present in the data model.

If we change the data model of the affected section to include a list of all possible vehicle types along with an element used to hold the selected item:

```
<vehicleSelection>
 <manufacturer>Ford</manufacturer>
  <types>
   <type>Sedan</type>
   <type>Hybrid</type>
   <type>SUV</type>
   <type>Truck</type>
   <type>Performance</type>
   </types>
  <selectedType/> <!-- holds user selection -->
  <features />
 </vehicleSelection>
```

the markup of the interface for the select element would also be changed:

```
<xf:select ref="vehicleSelection/selectedType">
<xf:label>Vehicle types:</xf:label>
<xf:itemset
   nodeset="/person/vehicleSelection/types/type">
  <xf:label ref="."/>
  <xf:copy ref="."/>
</xf:itemset>
</xf:select>
```

The `ref` attribute of the `select` element results in the assignment of the user's selection to the `selectedType` node. The `itemset` instructs the Firefox XForms processor to replicate interface markup for each instance of a `type` node present in the data model. The replication results in a `label` and `copy` element being displayed as selection options. The `copy` element has the effect of copying the selected node as a child node of the result node—in this case, copying an entire `type` node as a child of the `selectedType` node when a particular option is selected. Figure 10-9 illustrates the operation.

Visually, this interface looks no different from the previous implementation. But when the XForms form is submitted, the user will see a slightly different result tree that reflects the result of a multiple selection ("SUV" and "Truck") for the desired value. The XML structure submitted to the server would reflect the selection as children of the added `selectedType` element:

```
<person>
    <name>
<fname>First</fname>
<lname>Last</lname>
</name>
<phone>555-111-2345</phone>
<birthdate>2006-01-26</birthdate>
<password>somePassword</password>
<message>
 <messageBody>Some note text</messageBody>
 <attachment>
  file:///C:/Documents%20and%20Settings/My%20Pictures/Flowers001.JPG
 </attachment>
</message>
<dealerRange>50</dealerRange>
```

```
<vehicleSelection>
 <manufacturer>GM</manufacturer>
 <types>
  <type>Sedan</type>
  <type>Hybrid</type>
  <type>SUV</type>
  <type>Truck</type>
  <type>Performance</type>
 </types>
 <selectedType>
  <type>SUV</type>
  <type>Truck</type>
  </selectedType>
<features/>
</vehicleSelection>
</person>
```

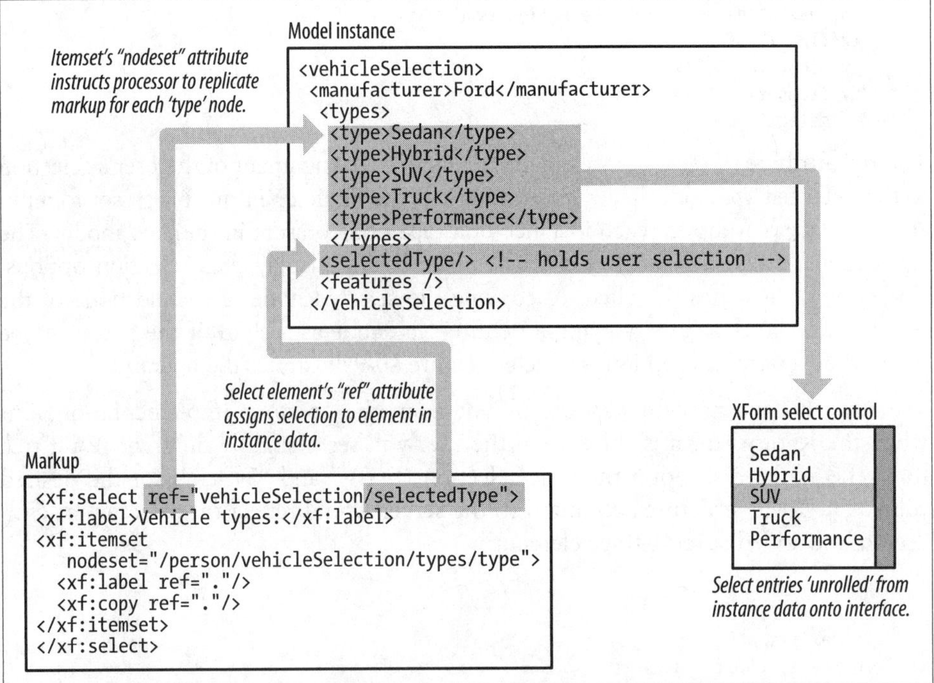

Figure 10-9. Itemset and markup replication

We use the `itemset` element for single and multiple selection elements; the `repeat` element uses the same syntax to create replicated input elements that are not part of a selection list.

By using repeated markup, a designer is free to reuse optional selections in the data model at multiple locations in the XForms document (or in multiple instances of relevant interface elements) without generating verbose interface markup to explicitly describe all possible selections.

XForms Events and Actions

The XForms standard includes support for an event handling mechanism that can handle much of the interface manipulation previously reserved to JavaScript (on the client) or server-based authentication code.

The most straightforward way to begin a discussion of the XForms event model is to consider a simple button actuation.

In HTML, a `<BUTTON>` element can fire a web page's event handling logic. The XForms standard relies on a `<trigger>` element with child nodes used to describe a label and the accompanying action:

```
xmlns:ev=http://www.w3.org/2001/xml-events
.
.
.

<xf:trigger>
 <xf:label>Press/xf:label>
 <xf:message level="modal"
        ev:event="DOMActivate">Click!</xf:message>
</xf:trigger>
```

The `<trigger>` is rendered as a simple button with a label of "Press." The `message` element is rendered as a modal dialog launched by a `DOMActivate` event.

The `message` element has an attribute that includes the XML event namespace prefix—illustrating what the W3C standard refers to as attaching XML events as an attribute of an observer element.

XML Events

The XML events W3C standard defines an event-processing model that is consistent with the DOM event model discussed earlier in this book. Any number of XML events can be assigned to a page element—the element to which the event is assigned becomes a *listener* for that event. (We will cover how the element responds to that event in the next section.)

The W3C standard defines a number of techniques to assign event handlers to an XML document. This overview focuses its discussion on the attribute assignment technique.

The XML event standard describes in detail how events are captured, bubble through the DOM hierarchy, and interact with an event target. The XForms event model builds on the same standard (for capturing and bubbling), but adds events specific to XForms.

Table 10-4 describes the XForms-specific XML events that Firefox supports.

Table 10-4. Firefox-supported XForms XML elements

XML XForms event	Targets	Description
`xforms-model-construct`	Model	Construction of model initiated.
`xforms-model-construct-done`	Model	Construction of model completed.
`xforms-ready`	Model	Dispatched as part of the model-construct-done event.
`xforms-model-destruct`	Model	Imminent shutdown of the XForms processor.
`xforms-next/xforms-previous`	Control	Dispatched as user navigates to next or previous form control.
`xforms-focus`	Control	Control received focus.
`xforms-help/xforms-hint`	Control	User request for help or hint.
`xforms-refresh`	Model	Request to update all XForms controls in the model.
`xforms-revalidate`	Model	Request to revalidate all XForms controls in the model.
`xforms-recalculate`	Model	Request to recalculate all node elements.
`xforms-rebuild`	Model	Request to rebuild internal structures.
`xforms-reset`	Model	Request to reset the model to initial values.
`xforms-submit`	Submission elements	Request to submit form data.
`DOMActivate`	Control	A control has been activated.
`xforms-value-changed`	Control	The instance data bound to a control has changed.
`xforms-select/xforms-deselect`	Item or itemset	A selection has been made or a control item has been deselected.
`xforms-scroll-first/xforms-scroll-last`	Repeat	An action has been initiated to select an item outside the range of a repeat set.
`xforms-insert/xforms-delete`	Instance	An action has successfully inserted or deleted an item.
`xforms-valid`	Control	Instance data node either while remaining valid, or has become valid.
`xforms-invalid`	Control	Instance data node either while remaining invalid, or has become invalid.
`DOMFocusIn`	Control	Control has received user focus.
`DOMFocusOut`	Control	Control has lost user focus.
`xforms-readonly`	Control	Instance data node either while remaining read-only, or has become read-only.
`xforms-readwrite`	Control	Instance data node either while remaining read-write, or has become read-write.
`xforms-required`	Control	Instance data node either while remaining required, or has become required.

Table 10-4. Firefox-supported XForms XML elements (continued)

XML XForms event	Targets	Description
xforms-optional	Control	Instance data node either while remaining optional, or has become optional.
xforms-enabled	Control	Instance data node either while remaining enabled, or has become enabled.
xforms-in-range	Control	The value of the data node has changed such that it may now be displayed by the control.
xforms-out-of-range	Control	The value of the data node has changed such that it cannot be displayed by the control.
xforms-submit-error	Submission element	Failure of the submit process.
xforms-binding-exception	Any element	The binding expression failed.
xforms-link-exception	Model	An external link to some `targetURI` failed.
xforms-compute-exception	Model	An XPath evaluation failed.

To see how XML events occur, we attach an event to a `message` element that is a child of that event's target, such as this example from our auto information XForms form:

```
<hr/>
<xf:select ref="vehicleSelection/selectedType">
<xf:label>Vehicle types:</xf:label>
<xf:itemset  nodeset="/person/vehicleSelection/types/type">
  <xf:label ref="."/>
  <xf:copy ref="."/>

</xf:itemset>
  <xf:message level="modal"
      ev:event="xforms-select">Select!</xf:message>
 </xf:select>
```

XForms events allow us to sensitize an XForms element to user interaction; we manage the response to this action through XForms actions.

XForms Actions

Several of the previous XForms examples use a `message` element as a child of a control that displays a message to the user based on some condition.

A `message` is one of several XML *actions*—elements that direct the XForms processor to conduct some operation in response to its `event` attribute.

One example of an XForms action is the `reset` element, which issues a reset event to a specific model. The following code illustrates a `trigger` element that adds a Clear button to our auto information form that resets all XForms controls to their initialized state:

```
<xf:trigger>
 <xf:label>Clear</xf:label>
 <xf:reset model="infoRequest" ev:event="DOMActivate"/>
</xf:trigger>
```

Some actions require additional information or pointers to other elements in the instance model in order to conduct the required function. Examples of such actions are a *single node binding* attribute or a *node-set binding* that includes a reference to a node or nodes providing some information required of the action (e.g., target node to manipulate). Single node or node-set bindings are encoded by any of the following attributes:

`model`
: A reference to a model identifier

`bind`
: A reference to another binding element in the model

`nodeset`
: An XPath reference to a node-set within the model

If both a `bind` and a `nodeset` attribute exist, the `bind` attribute takes precedence and the `nodeset` attribute is ignored.

Table 10-5 lists the XForms actions that Firefox currently supports.

Table 10-5. Firefox-supported XForms actions

XForms action	Specialized attributes	Description

`dispatch`	`name="eventName"`
	`target="`*`targetControl`*`"`
	`bubbles="true|false"`
	`cancelable="true|false"`
		Dispatches an XML event to the target control.

`rebuild`	`model="`*`modelID`*`"`	Forces a rebuild of the specified model.
`recalculate`	`model="`*`modelID`*`"`	Forces a recalculation.
`revalidate`	`model="`*`modelID`*`"`	Forces revalidation.
`refresh`	`model="`*`modelID`*`"`	Forces a refresh.
`setfocus`	`control="`*`controlID`*`"`	Sets user focus to the specified control.

`load`	`resource="`*`anyURI`*`"`
	`show="new|replace"`
	`optional single-node binding`
		Loads new content. If `replace` is set as a value for the `show` attribute, the current form content is replaced. `New` results in an implementation-specific manner (e.g., new window).

`setvalue`	Single node binding `value="XPath expression of value to set"`	Sets the value of a node identified by the single node binding to the value of the context node, or alternatively, the expression set by the `value` attribute.
`send`	`submission`	Initiates `SUBMIT` processing by sending an `xf-submit` event to the element identified by the `submission` attribute.
`reset`	`model`	Initiates a reset of the form to initial values.
`message`	`level = "ephemeral" | "modal" | "modeless"` `optional single node binding`	Displays a message. Ephemeral messages are displayed in a hint-like manner, and modal and modeless dialogs are rendered in an operating-system-specific fashion.

Table 10-5. Firefox-supported XForms actions (continued)

XForms action	Specialized attributes	Description
insert	Node-set binding at="*Xpath expression pointing to insertion point*" position = "before"|"after"	Inserts a new node specified by the node-set binding into the instance data model at the position identified by the at attribute.
delete	at = "*XPath expression of node to remove*"	Removes a node from the instance data.
setindex	repeat="*Reference to specific repeat item*" index="*XPath expression resolving to integer index to be selected*"	Sets the selection to an element with a control's repeat item list.

We can use an action element to collect individual actions, providing an almost programmatic method to control a sequence of actions based on an event:

```
<xf:action ef:event="someEvent">
 <xf:someAction>...
 <xf:someOtherAction...
 .
 .
</xf:action>
```

We next discuss how we can collect actions to execute a sequence of operations modifying user entries on a form.

User Interaction and Dynamic Presentation

The structure of a paper form never changes, regardless of what entry areas are appropriate to a user's session. A conventional HTML form-based application often relies on pauses in processing as the server checks the validity of entered data.

An XForms changes its interface through browser-based code that responds to the basic form entry operations before any transfer to the server. Two types of interface structure modifications are made possible within the XForms standard: changes that reflect addition or removal of entries, and changes that reflect the adaptation of the form structure based on current entries.

Dynamic Insertion and Removal of Entries

Forms are often used to collect sequences of items that may be added or removed from a list being created by a user.

Lists in XForms are often constructed with the repeat element, which is very similar to the previously described itemset element—a specially designed element that assigns one generic set of interface markup to a collection of elements present in the instance model.

Once the interface has been conducted with the repeat element, the XForms processor maintains an index pointing to the last selected item in the list. XForms actions use this index to determine where to insert or delete entries.

The next example modifies the auto interest form and builds an XForms form that is used to enter information about a trip itinerary.

Users enter some basic information (name, address, etc.) and add visit elements to an itinerary element. Each visit will have elements to capture the name of the attraction, number of persons in the party, and maximum price per person the visitors will pay:

```
<?xml version="1.0" encoding="iso-8859-1"?>
<!DOCTYPE html PUBLIC "-//W3C//DTD XHTML 1.0 Transitional//EN"
          "http://www.w3.org/TR/xhtml1/DTD/xhtml1-transitional.dtd">

<html xmlns="http://www.w3.org/1999/xhtml"
      xmlns:xf="http://www.w3.org/2002/xforms"
 xmlns:ev="http://www.w3.org/2001/xml-events"
 xmlns:xsd="http://www.w3.org/2001/XMLSchema"
 xmlns:xul="http://www.mozilla.org/keymaster/gatekeeper/there.is.only.xul"
 xmlns:xsi="http://www.w3.org/2001/XMLSchema-instance" >

<link href="nameAndAdress.css" rel="stylesheet" type="text/css" />
<head>
<title>Tour Info Page</title>
<xf:model id="infoRequest">
  <xf:instance>
  <!-- this is what will be sent to the server -->
 <person xmlns="">
    <name>
     <fname />
     <lname />
    </name>
    <phone/>
    <password/>
    <messageBody/>
<!-- 1 -->
    <itinerary startDate="2007-01-01" endDate="2007-01-01">
      <visit>
       <site>Gettysburg</site>
       <numberinparty>3</numberinparty>
       <maxpriceperperson>10.00</maxpriceperperson>
      </visit>

      <visit>
       <site>Manassas</site>
       <numberinparty>5</numberinparty>
       <maxpriceperperson>10.00</maxpriceperperson>
      </visit>

      <visit>
       <site>Smithsonian</site>
       <numberinparty>4</numberinparty>
```

```
        <maxpriceperperson>40.00</maxpriceperperson>
       </visit>

    </itinerary>

<!-- 2  -->
    <newVisit>
     <site/>
     <numberinparty/>
     <maxpriceperperson/>
    </newVisit>
  </person>

 </xf:instance>


 <xf:bind nodeset="name/lname"  required="true( )" type="xsd:string" />
 <xf:bind nodeset="name/fname" required="true( )"  type="xsd:string"/>
 <xf:bind nodeset="phone" required="true( )"/>
 <xf:bind nodeset="password"  required="true( )" />
 <xf:bind nodeset="itinerary/@startDate" required="true( )" type="xsd:date"/>
 <xf:bind nodeset="itinerary/@endDate" required="true( )" type="xsd:date"/>


<xf:submission id="xformrequest" method="post"
  action="http://localhost/chap10/xformrequest-simple.php"/>
</xf:model>

</head>


<body>

<div style="width:700px">

<xf:group >

<xf:input ref="name/fname">
<xf:label>First Name</xf:label>
<xf:alert>Invalid entry</xf:alert>
</xf:input>

<xf:input ref="name/lname">
<xf:label>Last Name</xf:label>
<xf:alert>Required</xf:alert>
</xf:input>

<xf:input ref="phone">
<xf:label>Phone number</xf:label>
<xf:hint> xxx-yyy-zzzz</xf:hint>
</xf:input>

<hr/>
<xf:secret ref="password">
```

```
<xf:label>Password:</xf:label>
</xf:secret>

<hr/>
<xf:textarea ref="messageBody">
<xf:label>Note text:</xf:label>
<xf:value>None</xf:value>
</xf:textarea>
<hr/>

<xf:input ref="itinerary/@startDate" >
<xf:label>Start date</xf:label>
</xf:input>
<xf:input ref="itinerary/@endDate">
<xf:label>End date</xf:label>
</xf:input>
<hr/>
<!-- 3 -->
<xul:hbox class="formHeading" >
 <xul:spacer flex="1"/>
 <xul:label value="Site"/>
 <xul:spacer flex="1"/>
 <xul:label value="# in party"/>
 <xul:spacer flex="1"/>
 <xul:label value="Max Price"/>
 <xul:spacer flex="1"/>
</xul:hbox>

<-- 4 -->
<div class="repeatContainer">
<xf:repeat class="someList" id="tourSites" nodeset="itinerary/visit">
<div class="formRow">
  <xf:input ref="site"/>
  <xf:input ref="numberinparty"/>
  <xf:input ref="maxpriceperperson"/>
  </div>
</xf:repeat>
</div>

<div style="text-align:center">
<!-- 5 -->
<xf:trigger>
  <xf:label>Remove</xf:label>
  <xf:delete ev:event="DOMActivate" nodeset="itinerary/visit"
   at="index('tourSites')"/>
</xf:trigger>
</div>

<hr/>
```

```
<xf:input ref="newVisit/site">
 <xf:label>Site:</xf:label>
</xf:input>
<xf:input ref="newVisit/numberinparty">
 <xf:label># in Party:</xf:label>
</xf:input>
<xf:input ref="newVisit/maxpriceperperson">
 <xf:label>Max $:</xf:label>
</xf:input>

<!-- 6 -->
<xf:trigger>
  <xf:label>Add</xf:label>
  <xf:action ev:event="DOMActivate">
  <xf:insert nodeset="itinerary/visit"
   at="index('tourSites')" position="after"/>
   <xf:setvalue ref="/person/itinerary/
          visit[index('tourSites')]/site"
       value="/person/newVisit/site"/>
   <xf:setvalue ref="/person/itinerary/
        visit[index('tourSites')]/numberinparty"
       value="/person/newVisit/numberinparty"/>
   <xf:setvalue ref="/person/itinerary/
         visit[index('tourSites')]/maxpriceperperson"
       value="/person/newVisit/maxpriceperperson"/>
   </xf:action>
</xf:trigger>

</xf:group>
</div>

<hr/>
<div style="text-align: center;">
<p>(*) Required Field</p>
<xf:submit submission="xformrequest">
<xf:label>Submit</xf:label>
</xf:submit>
</div>

</body>
</html>
```

The new source file will also initialize some instance data with three initial sites of interest (1). An entry also exists for a new item that the user will add (2).

Much of the source code resembles the fields in the auto inquiry form (3), where a familiar XUL element is used to synthesize what will approximate a heading row for the entries in the list of visits.

The `repeat` element (4) is assigned to the list of `visit` elements. As a result, a row of input elements will be created for each visit found in the information model.

Two triggers (buttons) exist for the XForms form: one to remove entries (4), and another to add new entries (5).

The code removing the entries is relatively straightforward:

```
<xf:trigger>
  <xf:label>Remove</xf:label>
  <xf:delete ev:event="DOMActivate" nodeset="itinerary/visit"
   at="index('tourSites')"/>
</xf:trigger>
```

The DOMActivate event (a button press) triggers the delete action. The nodeset attribute defines the node-set binding required to tell the delete element where in the information model an element is to be removed. The at attribute identifies which element in the list of visits is to be removed. The user interacts with the XForms form through interface markup (the elements generated by the repeat element). Any time one of the elements is selected, the index of the repeat list points to the selected item; that value is returned with the index( ) function that takes the identifier of the repeat element as its argument. The resulting action removes the element pointed to by the user.

The action to insert a new element requires a two-step process—first to insert a "slot" into the list, and then to set the newly added values:

```
<xf:trigger>
  <xf:label>Add</xf:label>
  <xf:action ev:event="DOMActivate">

  <!-- 1 -->
  <xf:insert nodeset="itinerary/visit"
   at="index('tourSites')" position="after"/>

  <!-- 2 -->
   <xf:setvalue ref="/person/itinerary/
          visit[index('tourSites')]/site"
       value="/person/newVisit/site"/>
   <xf:setvalue ref="/person/itinerary/
       visit[index('tourSites')]/numberinparty"
       value="/person/newVisit/numberinparty"/>
   <xf:setvalue ref="/person/itinerary/
         visit[index('tourSites')]/maxpriceperperson"
       value="/person/newVisit/maxpriceperperson"/>
   </xf:action>
</xf:trigger>
```

The trigger element includes the four actions required to carry out the operation.

The first insert element (1) will insert a new visit element in the information model at an index after the selection point made by the user. The default behavior of the insert is to copy the last node that exists in the collection into the newly created element, which becomes the currently selected item.

The next three actions (2) are all setvalue actions that copy the values from the user's new entry into the newly created element.

We also make a number of cosmetic changes to the stylesheet to give the XForms form a table appearance:

```
.
.
*:focus { background-color: yellow; }
.
.
div.formRow {
  position:relative;
  width:90%;
  left:5%;
  display:block;
  text-align:center;
  border-style:solid;
  border-width:1px;
  border-color:black;
}
div.formRow > xf|input {
display:inline;
}

.formHeading {
 border-width:1px;
 width:90%;
 position:relative;
 left:5%;
 background-color:black;
 color:white;
}
```

These changes help the selected item stand out with a background color, and the list takes on an appearance that looks more like a traditional form, as shown in Figure 10-10.

The Remove button will now remove whichever row the user last selected in the list of visits. The user can make new entries in the new site field with actuation of the Add button.

Changes in Form Structure

Earlier in this chapter, we discussed the use of the `relevant` model item property to remove XForms controls.

Using only one flag to control all possible configurations of interface elements is insufficient. The `relevant` property reflects the state of the model, but it is also useful to be able to change the appearance of the interface based on navigational selections that do not require persistence through a data model element. To support any number of possible interface configurations, the standard employs three related elements: `case`, `switch`, and `toggle`.

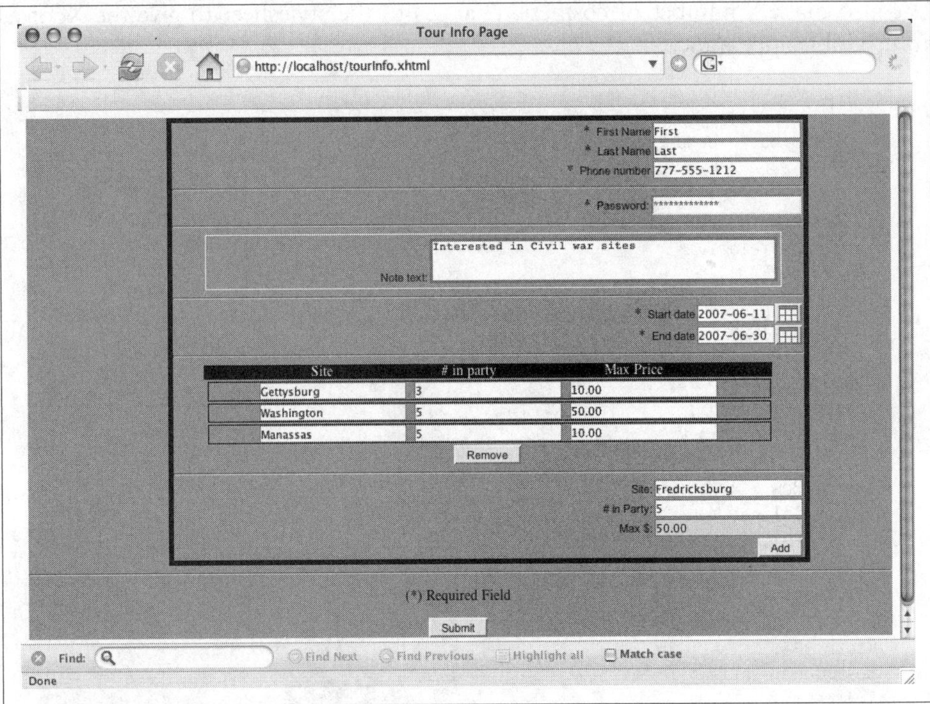

Figure 10-10. XForms form with insert and delete controls

The generic structure of an XForms `switch` statement is:

```
<xf:switch>
<xf:case id="caseID">
 <Some markup/>
</xf:case>
<xf:case id="anotherCaseID">
 <Some other markup />
</xf:case>
.
.
</xf:switch>
```

Individual "paths" of markup are constructed as a result of a `toggle` element of the form:

```
<xf:toggle ev:event="some event" case="case identifier"/>
```

The processing of the event will result in the `switch` statement being executed with only the markup of the matching case being constructed.

Changing our travel itinerary to include a toggle button to show and hide the details of a specific visit results in the following:

```
.
.
.
```

```
<xf:input ref="itinerary/@startDate" >
<xf:label>Start date</xf:label>
</xf:input>
<xf:input ref="itinerary/@endDate">
<xf:label>End date</xf:label>
</xf:input>
<hr/>

<!-- 1 -->
<xf:switch>
<!-- case for dest only -->
 <xf:case id="destOnly">
 <div style="text-align:center">

<!-- 2 -->
 <xf:trigger>
  <xf:label>Show Details</xf:label>
  <xf:toggle ev:event="DOMActivate" case="allDetails"/>
 </xf:trigger>
 </div>

 <xul:hbox class="formHeading" >
 <xul:spacer flex="1"/>
 <xul:label value="Site"/>
 <xul:spacer flex="1"/>
 </xul:hbox>

<div class="repeatContainer">
<xf:repeat class="someList" id="tourSites"
     nodeset="itinerary/visit">
<div class="formRow">
  <xf:input ref="site"/>
</div>
</xf:repeat>
</div>
</xf:case>
 <!-- case for dest only -->



<!-- case for all details -->
<!-- 3 -->
<xf:case id="allDetails">
<div style="text-align:center">
 <xf:trigger>
  <xf:label>Destination only</xf:label>
  <xf:toggle ev:event="DOMActivate" case="destOnly"/>
 </xf:trigger>
</div>

<xul:hbox class="formHeading" >
 <xul:spacer flex="1"/>
 <xul:label value="Site"/>
 <xul:spacer flex="1"/>
```

```
 <xul:label value="# in party"/>
 <xul:spacer flex="1"/>
 <xul:label value="Max Price"/>
 <xul:spacer flex="1"/>
</xul:hbox>

<div class="repeatContainer">
<xf:repeat class="someList" id="tourSites" nodeset="itinerary/visit">
<div class="formRow">
  <xf:input ref="site"/>
  <xf:input ref="numberinparty"/>
  <xf:input ref="maxpriceperperson"/>
  </div>
</xf:repeat>
</div>
 </xf:case>
<!-- case for all details -->

</xf:switch>


<div style="text-align:center">
<xf:trigger>
  <xf:label>Remove</xf:label>
  <xf:delete ev:event="DOMActivate" nodeset="itinerary/visit"
   at="index('tourSites')"/>
</xf:trigger>
</div>
.
.
```

The new version includes a switch statement (1) that includes two cases: one that displays only the selected site (2) and a toggle element to select the second case (3), which constructs the markup to show all details. We use an accompanying toggle event to resort to the "simple" display. Figure 10-11 shows the XForms form in the "simple" toggle state.

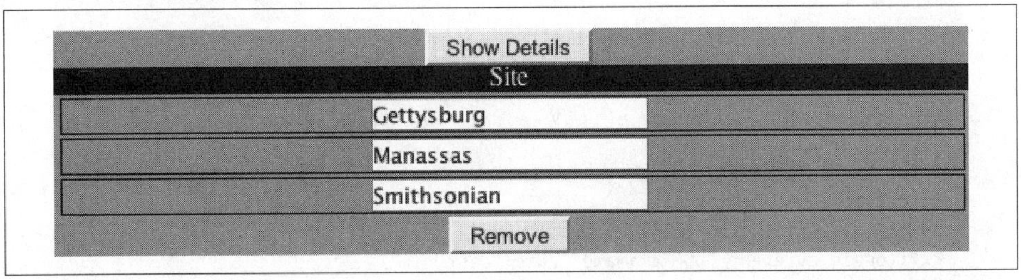

Figure 10-11. Adding toggle, switch, and case elements

What to Do When Things Go Wrong

Debugging an XForms implementation can be a bit of a challenge. Without use of tools such as the Venkman debugger and an interactive console, it can be difficult to quickly identify the source of a problem. Debugging and testing techniques generally fall into three categories:

DOM Inspector
: Once an XForms application is launched, the DOM Inspector can shed light on the objects and classes the XForms processor creates. When developers are confused about what is being painted on the screen, the DOM Inspector often provides them with the first tool to identify what is being created in the interface.

PHP echo document → `SaveXML()`
: When problems occur in variable assignment or in understanding what is happening at the server, the PHP directive to simply echo the result tree back to the browser sometimes informs the developer of the web server's WYSIWIG (What You See Is What *I Got*) status.

`xform:output`
: In the early stages of debugging the logic behind an XForms form, the output element can be used to send information to the browser about the current node or results of XPath expressions, often providing some valuable information regarding the state of the XForms processor engine.

Summary

Conventional HTML form elements suffer from the drawbacks associated with validation and with interface manipulation that must rely on scripting at the client or server validation, requiring a round trip to the web server.

The XForms standard pushes the tedium of validation and predictable interface manipulation onto the client. The use of an XML package to transfer data between the client and the server also allows designers to map more complex data structures in an instance model to any number of possible interface configurations.

The XForms standard is replete with a rich repertoire of events and actions that tempt developers to use its declarative model to completely replace procedural scripts.

Developers should be cautious in building highly complex XForms interactions. Debugging an XForms implementation can be a bit of a test. For most relatively straightforward applications, however, the XForms features provide a workable solution that could significantly improve the user experience while simplifying the design of the interface and data models.

CHAPTER 11

Installation and Deployment

The most common way to implement a Firefox-related solution is through an *extension* to the Firefox browser. An extension is designed to run within the browser while attaching its interface elements to the browser's existing window and menu hierarchy.

A second option for applications designed to run outside a browser is to run them as a XULRunner application.

XULRunner is a deployment method that uses the standalone Gecko runtime engine (also known as XULRunner) to launch XUL applications. The XULRunner executable must be downloaded onto the client's computer. The newly developed XUL application must then be downloaded to the target client and installed through a `xulrunner.exe --install-app "myApplicationName"` command.

Developers can also distribute *plug-ins*—snippets of code that augment functionality for the browser but may not have an interface with the user.

Although plug-in deployment is a process that is generally similar to that of extensions, we do not cover plug-in development in this text.

Finally, developers are free to download new themes and *skins*, files that can provide a completely customized look to Firefox or other XUL-based applications.

This chapter covers the basics of deploying applications, extensions, and skins, including:

- The basic file structure for applications, extensions, and skins
- Packaging the files for distribution
- Deploying standalone applications for XULRunner
- Developing and installing skins
- Developing and installing extensions

Deploying Standalone Applications

Standalone applications are XUL programs that don't require full browser functionality or that implement some type of interaction that the standard browser model doesn't cover. Applications that involve a great deal of graphics, feature high-performance interactivity, or have special security considerations are good candidates for standalone programs.

The developer has two choices for deploying an application: using the XULRunner runtime to execute the XUL application without the Firefox browser, or using the Firefox browser to run the executable (as we illustrated in a number of the previous examples in this book).

XULRunner applications are also of value when the user can download the XULRunner engine but would prefer not to install any code that touches the existing browser.

Chrome Registry Revisited

Recall in earlier chapters that the Firefox browser structure includes a chrome directory with subdirectories that contain the executables for XUL contributors to the browser, or applications that run within a browser window. For commercial deployment, these directories are most often wrapped up as JAR files for deployment.

Before we can use JAR files (or directory structures), we must register them through a manifest file that will play an important role in the distribution of our content applications, skins, and locales. Manifest files for browser and XULRunner applications can have any name but must end in a *.manifest* extension.

The role of the manifest file is summarized for a sample `hiworld` application; that program is packaged as a directory hierarchy of files, as illustrated in Figure 11-1. Note that the "package" can be of either content, locale, or skin.

As we build an application with a locale and skin, and redeploy it as a JAR file, we will make the appropriate changes to add new entries to the manifest, as well as change the filesystem entries that map package parts to a location in the JAR file.

XULRunner Applications

Building a XULRunner application looks and feels a great deal like building an extension. There is the familiar chrome structure and its file hierarchy, and the interface is built on the XUL widget set discussed earlier.

The differences lie primarily in the tasks that provide meta-information about the application being deployed. While Firefox extensions use the browser's registry, manifest file settings, and chrome directory to provide required installation and runtime information, these details must now be specified to the standalone XULRunner engine.

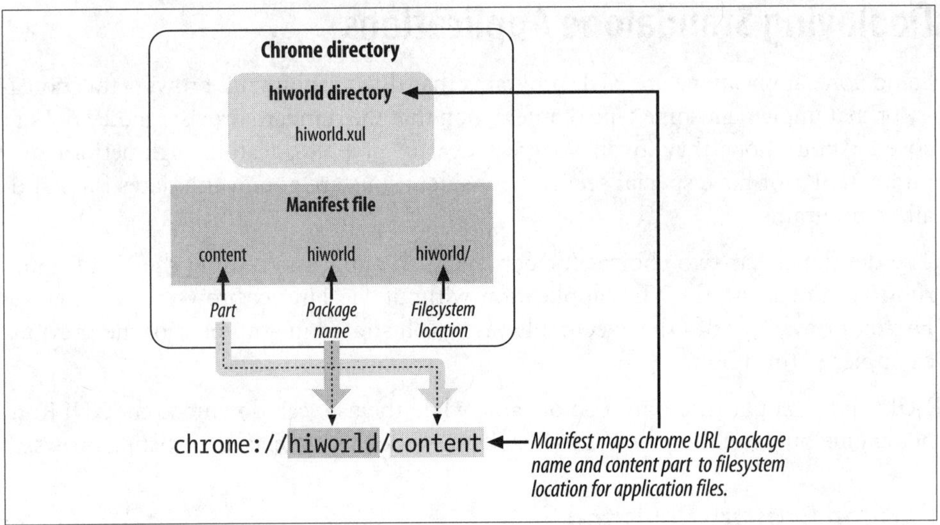

Figure 11-1. Manifest revisited: mapping of chrome URL

Directory structure

All forms of deployable XUL applications, extensions, and skins share (somewhat) the directory structure of the conventional Firefox distribution. Figure 11-2 shows a review of an installed XULRunner application and the conventional directory structure.

The hierarchy of files differs a bit for OS X and Linux installations. For OS X, the `installDir` is the *Resources* folder for the installation. In Linux applications, the executable file need not have the *.exe* extension.

This hierarchy represents the directory structure *after* installation; the developer builds a subset of these files into an install package while the installation operation takes care of the operating-system-specific structure and the XULRunner executable.

Downloading XULRunner

We must download the XULRunner runtime engine onto the client's computer for any XULRunner application to function.

The XULRunner engine includes the core Gecko rendering engine (the code that does all the drawing), along with several key technologies:

- The Cross-Platform Component Model (XPCOM)
- Networking support
- Document Object Model (DOM) editing
- Cryptography
- The XML Bindings Language (XBL)

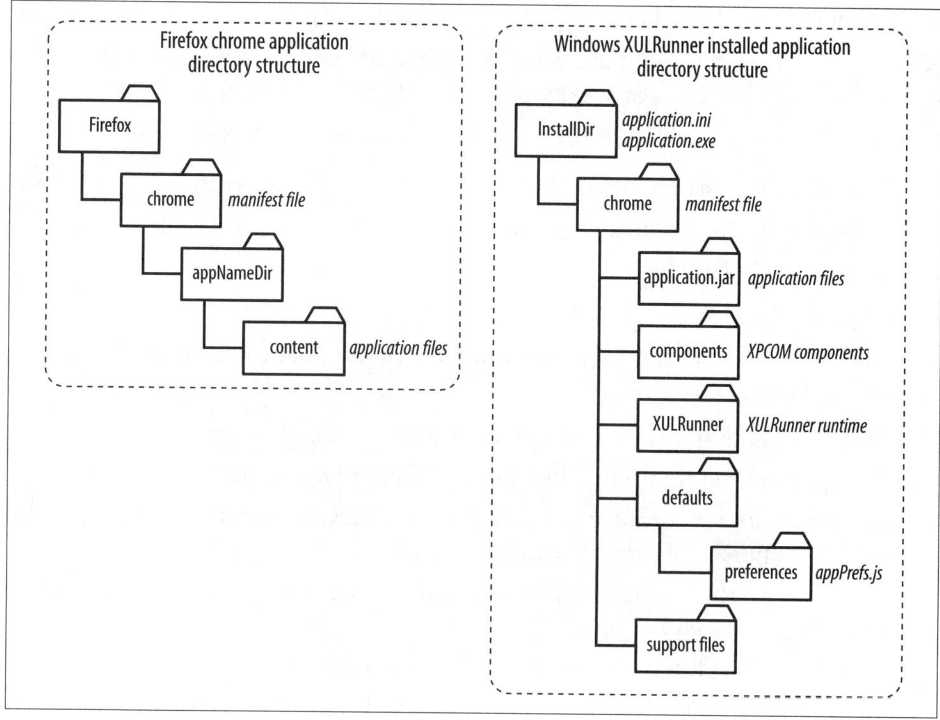

Figure 11-2. Browser versus XULRunner application directory structure

- XUL
- Scalable Vector Graphics (SVG)
- XSLT
- XML supporting technologies (DOM Inspector, `XMLHttpRequest`, etc.)
- SOAP services
- Toolbar find-ahead
- Accessibility
- History implementation

Downloading XULRunner is straightforward. Simply download the operating-system-specific version from the Mozilla developer web site.

As of this writing, significant changes are being made to the XUL installation utilities. Although the specifics of the installation are likely to change, much of the process of building and distributing the application is likely to remain unchanged.

XULRunner deployment package

XUL deployments are distributed in two forms: as zipped folders with a *.xulapp* extension for applications, or as *.xpi* (pronounced "zippy") for extensions.

In its simplest form, the *.xulapp* file is a ZIP file that contains the following:

- A chrome directory and its application's *.jar* file (or file structure)
- A *defaults* directory with a *preferences* subdirectory and a *prefs.js* file
- A *chrome.manifest* file
- An *application.ini* file

We will follow this general sequence when developing the standalone XULRunner `hiworld` application:

1. We will test the application as a XUL file in a directory hierarchy.
2. We will place the application files in a JAR file and rerun the test.
3. We will create supporting files to inform the XULRunner installation program of runtime requirements and startup locations.
4. We will wrap the application JAR and XULRunner supporting files together in a *.xulapp* compressed ZIP file.
5. We will use XULRunner to install the compressed ZIP file.
6. We will run the application as a standalone XULRunner program.

Hiworld in a directory

This illustration will use the simplest of all possible applications to draw a single window with a standard greeting. The source file, *hiworld.xul*, is unremarkable:

```
<?xml version="1.0"?>
<?xml-stylesheet href="chrome://global/skin/" type="text/css"?>

<window
    id="gwindow"
    width="100"
    height="100"
    title="InstallTest"
    orient="horizontal"
    xmlns="http://www.mozilla.org/keymaster/gatekeeper/there.is.only.xul">

    <vbox style="background-color:blue;
     color:white;"><label value="Hi World!"/></vbox>
</window>
```

Because the first implementation will use a directory structure, we will place the source file in a *hiworld* folder within the Firefox chrome directory. We create a *localApps.manifest* file in Firefox's chrome directory to map a content chrome URL to the directory with our source:

```
content hiworld hiworld/
```

Our simple window is now displayed when the chrome URL refers to the `hiworld` package and content part:

```
chrome://hiworld/content/
```

Firefox will look in the specified directory for a *hiworld.xul* file and open the window.

Moving from directory to JAR file

The next step in migrating to a deployable application is to create a JAR file that contains the executable code. Although not necessary, using JAR files is a simpler way to distribute applications.

From the topmost directory of the *hiworld* directory, we create a JAR file which, on OS X, looks like this:

```
$ jar -cvf hiworld.jar *
```

Looking at the JAR file contents, we see the application file:

```
$ jar -tvf hiworld.jar
     0 Thu Sep 07 20:35:16 EDT 2006 META-INF/
    70 Thu Sep 07 20:35:16 EDT 2006 META-INF/MANIFEST.MF
   359 Wed Sep 06 23:57:02 EDT 2006 hiworld.xul
```

We move the JAR file into Firefox's chrome directory, and the application manifest file that we changed to map the content part of the `hiworld` package to the top-level directory within the JAR file. The destination reference in the manifest entry uses this special form to declare a JAR file rather than a filesystem destination:

```
content hiworld jar:hiworld.jar!/
```

Launching the application either from the command line or as a chrome URL in the Firefox location launches the application as before.

Building necessary startup files

Figure 11-2 illustrated the resulting file structure that the XULRunner installation process will build. The ZIP file to be distributed includes only the files the application needs. The ZIP file's contents are overlaid from the distribution's chrome directory under the installation directory into the newly constructed hierarchy for the XULRunner application. (The deployment installation directory is sometimes referred to as the *root* of the application or extension.)

In this minimal application, the ZIP file will include:

- An *application.ini* file that describes the application to the XULRunner engine (e.g., version information, vendor, etc.)
- A *defaults/preferences/prefs.js* file to set JavaScript preferences such as those described by typing **`about:config`** in the Firefox location bar
- A *chrome/chrome.manifest* file to allow XULRunner to register the application's content package to the distributed file
- The *chrome/packageName.jar* file containing the application files

We may include any number of other directories for icons or other application resources for more complex applications. For this exercise, we create a separate directory into which the test files will be built.

application.ini. The *application.ini* file contains Windows-style field value pairs providing basic information about the application. The basic configuration includes `[App]` and `[Gecko]` sections. Fields for the `[APP]` section include:

`Name`
: Required application name.

`Version`
: Required version identifier with recommended four-part, dot-separated segments.

`BuildID`
: Build identifier, most often involving a coded date of release.

`Vendor`
: A string identifying the company.

`ID`
: Required ID for commercial applications (not for demonstration or test installs). Most likely a UUID or an email identifier.

Fields for the `[Gecko]` section include:

`MinVersion`
: Minimum version for the Gecko runtime engine; required for this application.

`MaxVersion`
: Optional maximum version of the runtime engine. Applications that may have different versions for various Gecko releases would use this field.

The sample *application.ini* file will have the basics filled in:

```
[App]
Vendor=MyMozCo.inc
Name=hiworld
Version=0.1
BuildID=20070606

[Gecko]
MinVersion=1.8
MaxVersion=1.8.0.*
```

prefs.js. In the working folder for our distribution files, a *defaults* folder must be built; that folder in turn contains a *preferences* folder and a *prefs.js* file. The *prefs.js* file provides the information XULRunner needs to start the application:

```
pref("toolkit.defaultChromeURI", "chrome://hiworld/content/hiworld.xul");
```

This line instructs XULRunner that the startup page will be the *hiworld.xul* file found in the content part of the `hiworld` package.

chrome.manifest. In the working file for the distribution, create a chrome directory. That directory must also hold the JAR file for the executable, and the *chrome.manifest* file that tells XULRunner to find the content part of the `hiworld` package at the top of the JAR file hierarchy:

```
content hiworld jar:hiworld.jar!/
```

A review of the directories that exist before we build the ZIP file on OS X looks like this:

```
$ ls -R
application.ini chrome          defaults

./chrome:
chrome.manifest hiworld.jar

./defaults:
preferences

./defaults/preferences:
prefs.js
```

We can use the Unix `zip` command or WinZip utility to create our ZIP file with the *.xulapp* extension common among applications:

```
$ zip -r hiworld.xulapp *
```

We can view the resulting ZIP file with any application that can read compressed archives, including the JAR utility:

```
$ jar -tvf hiworld.xulapp
```

The resulting ZIP file is distributed to the end user. Once on the client system, it can be installed with XULRunner. On an OS X system with the `$PATH` variable set properly to include the location of the XULRunner executable, the command is:

```
$ xulrunner-bin -install-app hiworld.xulapp
```

XULRunner constructs the required directories that include one named after the `vendorID` specified in the *application.ini* file, and moves the user-provided files into the required locations. Windows users may run the application from the command line (pointing to the desired *application.ini* file):

```
$ xulrunner-bin --app application.ini
```

while OS X users will click on the package directory to launch the application, as seen in Figure 11-3.

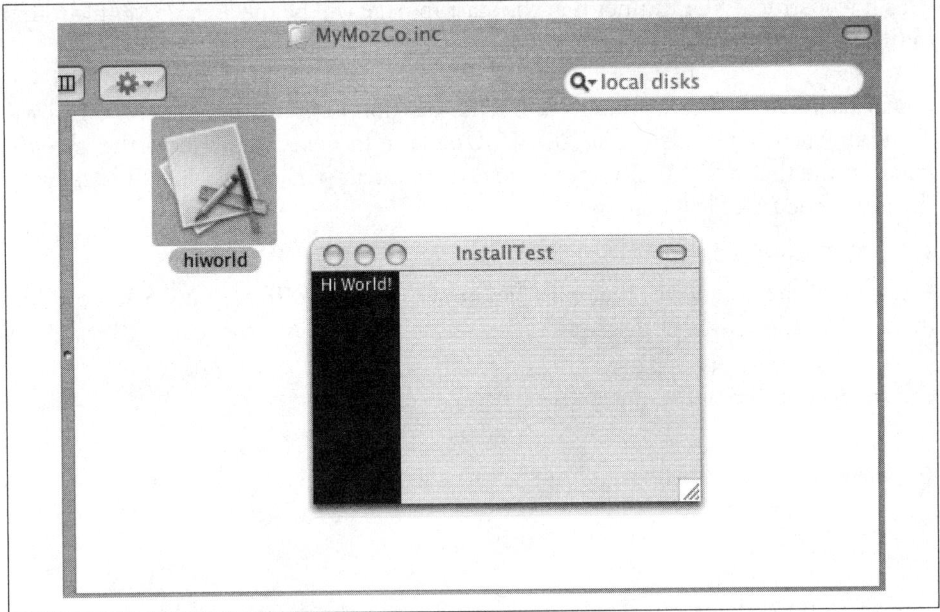

Figure 11-3. Hiworld as XULRunner application on OS X

Deploying Themes and Skins

Certain types of applications may need to deploy a look and style that differ from the conventional appearance of a browser. We can completely customize the appearance of an application through a combination of conventional stylesheets (declared in the XUL interface source file), defined in Cascading Style Sheet (CSS) files and registered through a chrome manifest reference. A collection of images—CSS files (or *skins*) that implement a distinctive style—is referred to as a *theme*.

File Structure

By now, the structure of a delivered package is familiar.

Within the root of a distribution (including the distribution of the Firefox application) exists a chrome directory. That chrome directory includes a collection of JAR files that hold all supporting interfaces, JavaScript source, and stylesheets. Accompanying each JAR file is a manifest file instructing Firefox how to map chrome URLs to directories in the chrome folder. Skins are no different.

The Firefox browser's chrome directory includes all stylesheets in the *classic.jar* file. Opening the accompanying manifest file, *classic.manifest*, illustrates the mapping between the chrome registry and the JAR contents for the browser's standard distribution:

```
skin communicator classic/1.0 jar:classic.jar!/skin/classic/communicator/
skin global classic/1.0 jar:classic.jar!/skin/classic/global/
skin mozapps classic/1.0 jar:classic.jar!/skin/classic/mozapps/
skin help classic/1.0 jar:classic.jar!/skin/classic/help/
skin browser classic/1.0 jar:classic.jar!/skin/classic/browser/
```

The entries are of a form similar to those for content entries. The first field indicates that the chrome will be registering the `skin` part of various packages. The last field is the pointer to the actual location of the files to be registered.

A new entry is the third field—in these cases, `classic/1.0`. That field is referred to as the *skinname* and is used as an identifier for a given skin. If multiple skins exist for a given package, we can use JavaScript preferences to define selection roles to determine which files should be used. For current standalone applications and extensions, the skinname `classic/1.0` should be used.

The directories and contents within the *classic.jar* file represent all the skins associated with the classic theme. If we opened the JAR file, we would see a number of directories whose contents are used for various Firefox applications:

Skin
: The topmost container for all the skins of a given theme

Classic
: The topmost container for all files composing the classic theme

Browser
: Icons and appearance of the browser toolbars

Global
: The stylesheets and supporting files for most Firefox applications

mozapps
: Container for files supporting applications such as the extensions manager

help
: Supporting files for help dialogs

You may find a *communicator* folder in the JAR file, but it is no longer used.

Developers who want to create an entirely new theme would most likely start by making copies of these folders and their contents, and editing the files to change the appearance. One technique starts with creating a special application-specific stylesheet assigned to a XUL file used to test the new appearance. The developer would then move individual styles (e.g., for buttons) into the preexisting stylesheets, resulting in the widgets for all applications taking on the new appearance.

For our application, all we need to do is to create the specialized stylesheet and install it as a skin within the application's chrome distribution.

Creating the Stylesheet

To test the next phase of this example, we move the source file back to a directory structure in which the source file resides in a *hiworld* folder in Firefox's chrome directory.

For this new skin, we copy the file *global.css* from the original classic directory and copy it as *hiworld.css*, which will hold new styles for background boxes, labels, and buttons. We paste portions of other stylesheets within the classic folder used for buttons (e.g., from *classic/globalbutton.css*) into the newly created file and modify them. Following is a snippet of the new *hiworld.css* file highlighting the changes:

```
vbox {
 background-color:#0f0f0f;
}

label {
 background-color:#0f0f0f;
 color:#fcfcfc;
}

/* ------- copied from global button.css ------------ */

/* :::::::::: button :::::::::: */

button {
  -moz-appearance: button;
  margin: 6px;
  min-width: 6.3em;
  -moz-appearance: button;
  padding: 0px 4px;
  color:black;
}

.button-text {
  margin: 0 !important;
  text-align: center;
  color:blue;
  background-color:white;
}
```

We place the file in a *skin* subdirectory of our *hiworld* folder.

We change the source file for the XUL file to add a button and refer to the new stylesheet:

```
<?xml version="1.0"?>
<?xml-stylesheet href="chrome://hiworld/skin/hiworld.css"
  type="text/css"?>
```

```
<window
    id="gwindow"
    width="200"
    height="100"
    title="InstallTest"
    orient="horizontal"
    xmlns="http://www.mozilla.org/keymaster/gatekeeper/there.is.only.xul">

    <vbox flex="1" pack="center" align="center">
    <label value="Hi World!" />
    <button label="CLICK ME"/>
    </vbox>
</window>
```

Registering the Skin

For a chrome application to access styles while adhering to the security model posed on Firefox applications, we must register the stylesheet referenced in the XUL source file through the *localApps.manifest* file:

```
content hiworld hiworld/
skin hiworld classic/1.0 hiworld/skin/
```

Note that we have changed the content referenced to refer to the local filesystem. The skin reference will associate the skin "part" of the `hiworld` package with the *hiworld/skin* directory. Launching the application now reflects the changes, as shown in Figure 11-4.

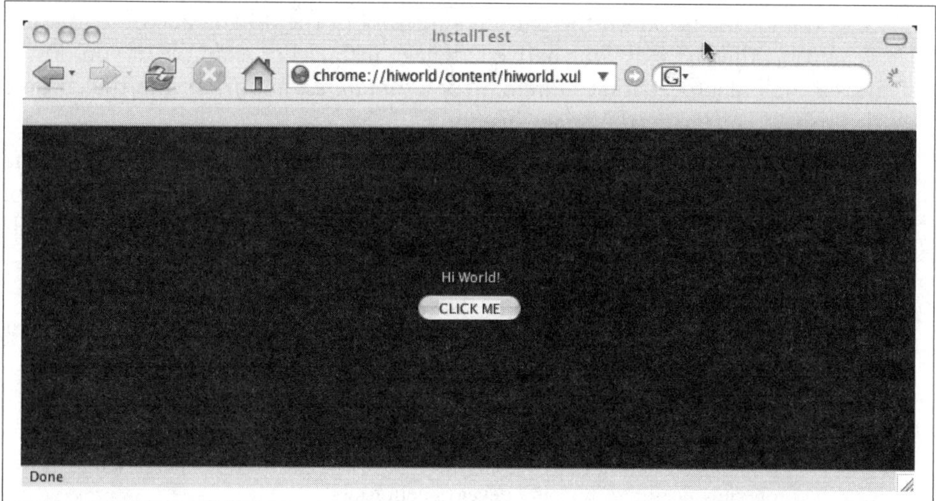

Figure 11-4. Adding new skins

Adding Locales

The Firefox framework is well suited to developing applications you can easily configure for multiple languages. Adding a *locale* to our application begins by looking at how the Firefox browser manages the feature.

As with Firefox content and skin packages, locales are stored as a package (folder) and accompanying manifest named after a particular language. The files containing strings in U.S. English are contained in the *en-US.jar* file and are registered with Firefox chrome through the *en-US.manifest* file. A French interface has strings enclosed in *fr.jar* and registered with *fr.manifest*. Other languages are organized in an identical manner.

Setting Up for Locale Development

To test out different locales, Firefox must have different languages installed and an easy way to switch among languages.

Downloading multiple languages for Firefox is a matter of visiting the Firefox web site, which has links to all the language downloads for a specific version:

1. Visit the download site for a language of interest.
2. Select a Firefox version that is the same version of your native language install. Download the desired language version of Firefox *into a folder or destination that does not override your native language installation*.
3. Copy the locale files from the chrome directory of the downloaded Firefox into the chrome directory of your native language install. For example, if you downloaded the French version of Firefox, copy *fr.manifest* and *fr.jar* into the chrome directory of your native language install.
4. Download any Firefox extension that allows you to easily switch languages. (The Firefox add-on Quick Locale Switcher is one such tool.) After the installation of that extension, the user can switch among languages using the Firefox → Tools menu, as shown in Figure 11-5.

We now have the setting to test a new locale for our `hiworld` application.

Testing and deploying multilingual applications requires a number of operating-system- and application-specific changes that are not covered here. If you want additional information on the use of text editors that support alternative character sets, consult the documentation of your specific system and development tools.

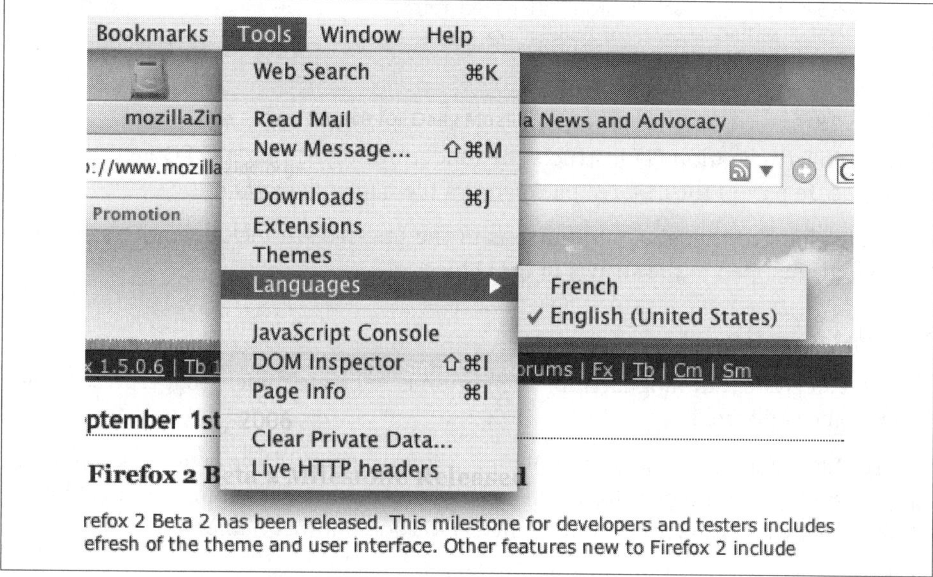

Figure 11-5. Language selection extension

Text String Mapping

Most multilingual applications implement an interface through the use of proxies or placeholders that map codes in the interface source file to language-specific strings.

The Firefox framework uses that technique by encoding *entity references* in the XUL source file. The entity references are mapped within a Document Type Definition (DTD) file; the DTD file in turn is stored on the local filesystem and referenced as a chrome URL resource.

DTD and entity mapping

The mapping begins by changing the XUL source file to add an XML definition that (a) points to a DTD that will represent localized entities, and (b) replaces the literal string references with entity references:

```
<?xml version="1.0"?>
<!-- (1) -->
<!DOCTYPE window SYSTEM "chrome://hiworld/locale/hiworld.dtd">
<?xml-stylesheet href="chrome://hiworld/skin/hiworld.css"
type="text/css"?>
<window
    id="gwindow"
    width="200"
    height="100"
    title="InstallTest"
    orient="horizontal"
    xmlns="http://www.mozilla.org/keymaster/gatekeeper/there.is.only.xul">
```

```
    <vbox flex="1" pack="center" align="center">
    <label value="&mainlabel.label;" />
    <button label="&button.label;"/>
    </vbox>
</window>
```

The DOCTYPE declaration (1) instructs the rendering engine that a DTD is to be found at the locale part of the hiworld package at a file named *hiworld.dtd*.

We have changed the label and buttons in the interface to include entity references that will be mapped to the strings in DTD files.

Creating the entities

The first step of a multilingual implementation is to create folders that represent each locale to be supported.

For our filesystem implementation of a multilingual hiworld, we create one folder for English and one for French. In the *hiworld* folder (that exists within a Firefox chrome folder), create two directories, one named *en-us* and another named *fr*.

In the *fr* folder, create a file named *hiworld.dtd*:

```
<!ENTITY mainlabel.label "Salut monde!">
<!ENTITY button.label "CLIQUEZ-MOI">
```

In the *en-us* folder, create a file named *hiworld.dtd*:

```
<!ENTITY mainlabel.label "Hi World!">
<!ENTITY button.label "PRESS ME">
```

The final step is to change the manifest file to add the statements that bind the filesystem locales to a chrome URI.

The form of a manifest statement for locales is:

```
locale packageName localeName filesystemLocation
```

The *localeName* must be one of the supported locales (e.g., en, fr, etc.).

For our filesystem example, we change the *localApps.manifest* file to register the new locales:

```
locale hiworld fr hiworld/fr/
locale hiworld en-us hiworld/en-us/
```

We can see the results of our localization by changing Firefox's language to French (using the locale switcher or any other extension that supports multiple languages). Figure 11-6 shows the results.

Moving to JAR files

The final step for developing a deployable application with its own skins and localization involves "cutting over" from our filesystem to a deployable JAR file.

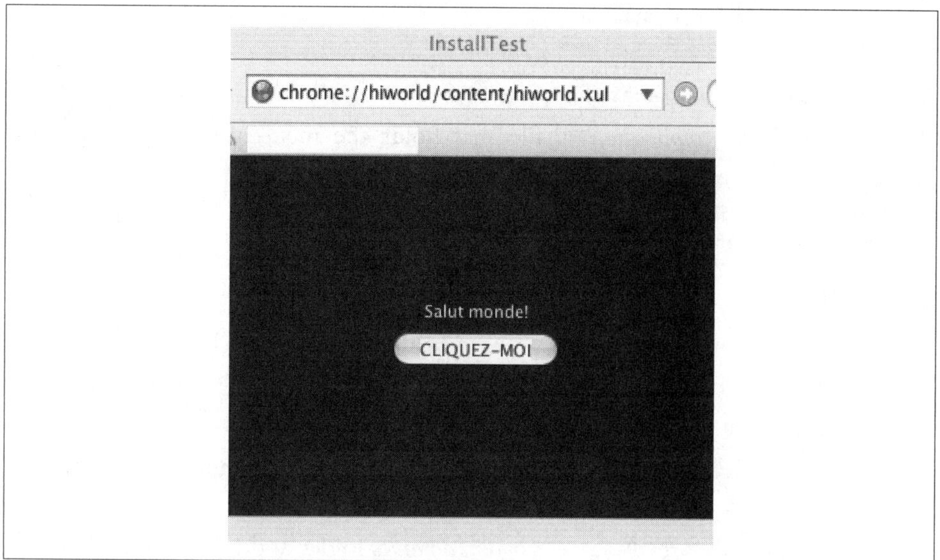

Figure 11-6. Hiworld with French localization

Following coding and testing, our filesystem view of the package is illustrated in Figure 11-7.

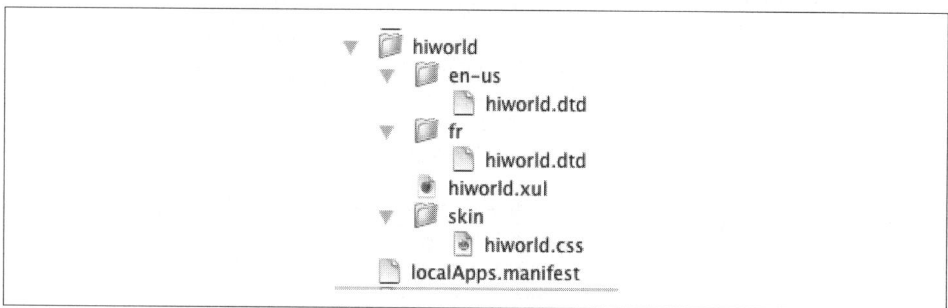

Figure 11-7. Hiworld filesystem view from Firefox chrome

We now re-create the steps discussed earlier.

We create the JAR file holding the executable, and all the folders containing the required stylesheets and DTDs, from the directory containing the *hiworld.xul* file and directories:

```
$jar -cf hiworld.jar .
```

To keep the installation cleaner, we create an install directory that will hold all the contents to be wrapped in our deployable ZIP file. In that install directory, we create a manifest file that we will call *hiworld.manifest,* and include references to all content, skin, and locale parts of the package:

```
content hiworld jar:hiworld.jar!/
skin hiworld classic/1.0 jar:hiworld.jar/skin/
locale hiworld fr jar:hiworld.jar/fr/
locale hiworld en-us jar:hiworld.jar/en-us/
```

We now create an *application.ini* file that holds the meta-information about the application:

```
[App]
Vendor=MyNewCo.inc
Name=hiworld
Version=0.1
BuildID=20070606

[Gecko]
MinVersion=1.8
MaxVersion=1.8.0.*
```

In that same install directory, we create a chrome directory that holds our *hiworld.xul* file.

Finally, in the install directory, we create a *defaults* folder and a *preferences* folder to hold the *preferences* file, which we will name *prefs.js*:

```
pref("toolkit.defaultChromeURI", "chrome://hiworld/content/hiworld.xul");
```

The resulting directory structure for the installation, as shown in Figure 11-8, now looks like the standard installation described earlier in the chapter.

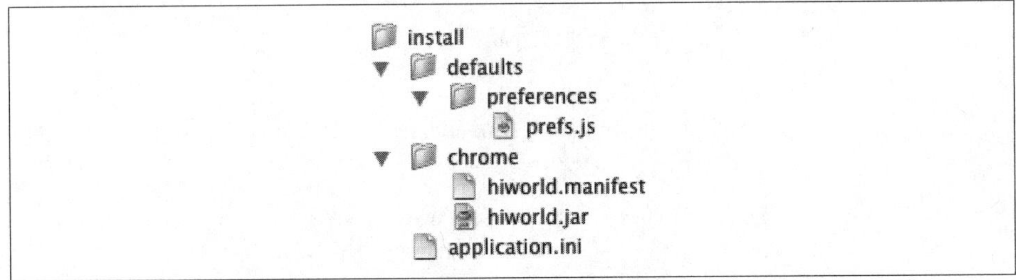

Figure 11-8. Hiworld files prior to zipping

We create the deployable ZIP file within the install directory:

```
zip -r hiworld.xulapp *
```

And we use XULRunner to install the newly created application:

```
xulrunner-bin --install-app hiworld.xulapp
```

We create the directories, and the multilingual skinned version of `hiworld` is installed.

Deploying Extensions

Extensions are combinations of interface elements and logic that extend the functionality of Firefox. Whereas standalone XUL applications require the XULRunner runtime to execute the underlying component framework, extensions run within the browser.

Extension and application development share several characteristics: they are packaged in a similar fashion, require proper registration with the chrome registry, and rely heavily on XUL interface widgets.

Extensions, on the other hand, require their interface elements to be "bolted onto" the Firefox interface. XULRunner obtains information about an application from the *application.ini* file—the Firefox extensions manager requires an *install.rdf* file to obtain information about the extension. Finally, although XULRunner automatically creates application folders and subdirectories based on the information in the *application.ini* file, the extensions packages are installed in a user's Firefox *profile* directory.

To illustrate the process, we will (again) repackage our `hiworld` application into an extension to display an alert message when a menu item button is pressed.

Extension Interfaces: Overlays Revisited

Extensions often attach their interface to the existing Firefox browser. They do this through the overlay technique discussed in Chapter 9.

Overlay interfaces are coded almost the same way as XUL windows. The special nature of overlays requires the attachment of the extension widget to a widget that exists in the interface to be extended. Overlay files include a XUL widget with an ID that must match the ID of the file being overlaid. Once the Firefox framework finds the match, the widgets in the overlay (that are children of the widget with the matching ID) are appended to the widget in the overlaid file.

We will attach our menu button to the bottom of the Firefox context menu.

As mentioned previously, developers can explore the interface structure of the Firefox browser by opening the *browser.jar* file. Within the *browser.jar* file are a *content* directory and the *browser.xul* file that will be overlaid with the `hiworld` widgets.

Scanning through *browser.xul*, we find a segment that is a likely candidate for an attachment with an ID that the overlay will use:

```
<popup id="contentAreaContextMenu"
       onpopupshowing="if (event.target != this)
            return true;
            gContextMenu = new nsContextMenu( this );
                return gContextMenu.shouldDisplay;"
```

```
            onpopuphiding="if (event.target == this) gContextMenu = null;">
        <menuitem id="context-openlink"
                  label="&openLinkCmd.label;"
                  accesskey="&openLinkCmd.accesskey;"
                  oncommand="gContextMenu.openLink( );"/>
```

The source code for our overlay, named *hiworldext.xul*, includes the reference to a newly created menu item to be appended to the context menu:

```
<?xml version="1.0"?>
<!DOCTYPE overlay SYSTEM "chrome://hiworldext/locale/hiworldext.dtd">
<?xml-stylesheet
    href="chrome://hiworldext/skin/hiworld.css" type="text/css"?>
<overlay id="hiworldext"
   xmlns="http://www.mozilla.org/keymaster/gatekeeper/there.is.only.xul">
   <popup id ="contentAreaContextMenu">
    <menuitem
          label="&button.label;"
          oncommand="alert('Hi world!')"/>
      </popup>
</overlay>
```

The code illustrates the replacement of the window root element found in applications with an overlay document type and root node. We set the popup ID to insert the menu item wherever the Firefox framework finds a pop up with an ID of contentAreaContextMenu.

Filesystem implementation

To begin testing, we can copy the filesystem structure used by our hiworld application, rename all the source files, stylesheets, and DTD files accordingly, and place the files in Firefox's chrome directory.

We also create a manifest file, *hiworldext.manifest*, and place it in Firefox's chrome directory:

```
content hiworldext hiworldext/
skin hiworldext classic/1.0 hiworldext/skin/
locale hiworldext fr hiworldext/fr/
locale hiworldext en-us hiworldext/en-us/
overlay chrome://browser/content/browser.xul
          chrome://hiworldext/content/hiworldext.xul
```

We have replicated the manifest entries from our hiworld example (with proper name substitutions). The overlay entry indicates that the *browser.xul* file in the content part of the browser package will be overlaid by the XUL file from the hiworldext package.

Launching the browser illustrates the successful attachment of the overlay, as shown in Figure 11-9.

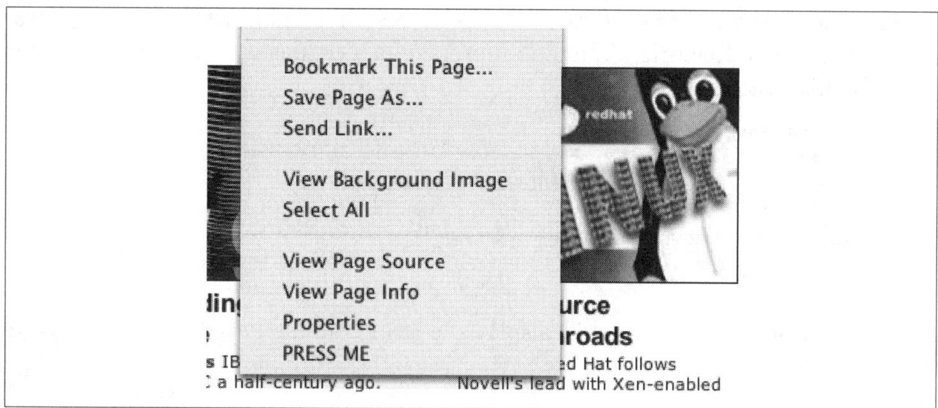

Figure 11-9. Overlay with PRESS ME applied to browser.xul

Locales and Scripting Variables

The implementation of our application as an extension points out the problem of using a script to display text in a multilingual setting.

Although entity references work well for XML attributes, strings used in scripts must employ a technique involving *properties* files to map strings to locales.

String bundles

The XUL framework supports multiple locales for scripting through the use of a `<stringbundle>` element, which provides access services to a properties file:

```
<stringbundle id="someID" src="chromeURIToPropertiesFile" />
```

The properties file itself is a simple collection of *key=value* pairs. The value of a string is obtained through the `somebundle`'s `getString` method:

```
var someString = someBundle.getString("theKey");
```

We place the properties files within the `locale` part of a package; any change in the locale results in a different set of strings being assigned within the JavaScript code.

To create a locale that supports our alert message in different languages, we create a *hiworldext.properties* file in the *us-en* directory of the *locale* folder:

```
myMessage=Hello World
```

A companion *hiworldext.properties* file exists in the *fr* directory with the French translation:

```
myMessage=Salut monde!
```

Moving the code for the alert function to an external *hiworld.js* file (in the same location as the source XUL file), a function to open an alert message illustrates how the string bundle is accessed:

```
sayHi = function() {
var myMessage = "not found";
var theBundle = document.getElementById("hiWorldBundle");
if (theBundle != null)
    myMessage=theBundle.getString("myMessage");
 alert(myMessage);
}
```

The straightforward function will display the string bundle keyed by the `myMessage` keyword.

String bundles in overlays

To work properly in an overlay, we must merge the `stringbundle` (and any overlay content, for that matter) with the browser interface. Scanning the *browser.xul* file illustrates how `stringbundles` are organized:

```
<stringbundleset id="stringbundleset">
  <stringbundle id="bundle_brand"
       src="chrome://branding/locale/brand.properties"/>
  <stringbundle id="bundle_shell"
       src="chrome://browser/locale/shellservice.properties"/>
  <stringbundle id="bundle_findBar"
        src="chrome://global/locale/findbar.properties"/>
  <stringbundle id="bundle_preferences"
       src="chrome://browser/locale/preferences/preferences.properties"/>
</stringbundleset>
```

We use the `<stringbundleset>` element as a convenience container for the `stringbundles` in an application.

The overlay must also include the reference to the `stringbundle` to be added. We must parent the code we want to merge with an element of the same `id` and type as that of the element being overlaid. The overlay XUL file now reflects the reference to the string along with the inclusion of the reference to the JavaScript file:

```
<?xml version="1.0"?>
<!DOCTYPE overlay SYSTEM
   "chrome://hiworldext/locale/hiworldext.dtd">
<?xml-stylesheet href="chrome://hiworldext/skin/hiworld.css"
     type="text/css"?>
<overlay id="hiworldext"
   xmlns="http://www.mozilla.org/keymaster/gatekeeper/there.is.only.xul">
```

```
<script type="application/x-javascript" src="hiworldext.js"/>
<stringbundleset id="stringbundleset">
  <stringbundle id="hiWorldBundle"
          src="chrome://hiworldext/locale/hiworldext.properties"/>
  </stringbundleset>

   <popup id ="contentAreaContextMenu">

   <menuitem
        label="&button.label;"
        oncommand="sayHi( );"/>
    </popup>
</overlay>
```

These changes will result in the stringbundle in the overlay file being merged with the browser's main stringbundleset.

Enabling Firefox to display French and launching the browser with our extension now provides the alert message in the correct language, as shown in Figure 11-10.

Figure 11-10. Multilocale scripts and stringbundles

Deploying the Extension

The Firefox extensions manager requires information about the application, as well as details on where to place files distributed in the *.xpi* file.

Installation Manifest: install.rdf

The *install.rdf* file provides information that the Firefox extensions manager uses to obtain installation requirements (in terms of target application) and display information about the application to the user. It is a Resource Description Framework (RDF) file with several required entries:

`id`
: An identifier for the extension formatted as *myExtension@myCompany.com*.

`version`
: A string with a version identifier.

`targetApplication`
: A complex RDF entry (meaning it is a parent of child description elements) that identifies the application the deployed file extends. Child elements include:

  `id`
  : The GUID of the target application being extended. You can find the current ID for Firefox at the Firefox Add-ons site, *http://addons.mozilla.org*.

  `minVersion`, `maxVersion`
  : These identifiers are for the minimum and maximum versions of the application that this extension supports. The target minimum version in our case will be 1.0, with the maximum version specified as 1.5.0.*.

`name`
: The display name of the extension.

There are a number of optional entries that we will add to provide additional information about the extension:

`description`
: A textual description of the extension.

`creator`
: The name of either a group of persons or an organization releasing the extension.

`developer`
: Identifies the lead developer(s).

`contributor`
: Lists other contributors to the project.

`homepageURL`
: A link to the extension vendor URL.

`updateURL`
: A link to a special URL that provides updates to the Firefox extensions manager. The Firefox update manager occasionally connects to this URL for updates. This URL must be an RDF file with fields that the add-on manager will embed:

  `%REQ_VERSION%`
  : The version of the request

  `%ITEM_ID%`
  : The ID of the add-on being updated

  `%ITEM_VERSION%`
  : The version of the add-on being updated

  `%ITEM_MAXAPPVERSION%`
  : The maximum version of the application hosting the add-on

%APP_OS%
: The identifier of the operating system targeted by the add-on

%APP_ABI%
: The value of the compiler and architecture targeted by the current add-on

There is a complete list of the fields you can include in the *install.rdf* file at the Mozilla Developer Center (*http://developer.mozilla.org*).

Our completed *install.rdf* file now has the information needed for the Firefox installation engine to work:

```
<?xml version="1.0"?>

<RDF xmlns="http://www.w3.org/1999/02/22-rdf-syntax-ns#"
     xmlns:em="http://www.mozilla.org/2004/em-rdf#">
  <Description about="urn:mozilla:install-manifest">
    <!-- properties -->

        <em:id>hiWorldExt@myNewCo.com</em:id>
        <em:version>2.0.0</em:version>
        <em:description>Multi-locale extension test.</em:description>
        <em:creator>I.M. Cool</em:creator>
        <em:contributor>Curly</em:contributor>
        <em:contributor>Larry</em:contributor>
        <em:contributor>Moe</em:contributor>

   <em:targetApplication>
    <Description>
      <em:id>{ec8030f7-c20a-464f-9b0e-13a3a9e97384}</em:id>
      <em:minVersion>1.0</em:minVersion>
     <em:maxVersion>1.5.0.*</em:maxVersion>
    </Description>
   </em:targetApplication>

   <em:name>Hi world extension</em:name>


  </Description>
</RDF>
```

Extensions and the Manifest File

There is a subtle difference that we must note when moving from a testing and debugging environment (where files are manually placed into Firefox's chrome directory) to the deployment of extensions.

The installation package for XULRunner places the manifest file in the same directory as the installed *.jar* file. The installation structure for *extensions* places the manifest file in the directory *above* the chrome directory that holds the content files. Extensions also generally name the manifest file *chrome.manifest*.

Both the *install.rdf* and the *chrome.manifest* files must be at the top of the installation root. Figure 11-11 shows our directory structure prior to creating the *.xpi* file.

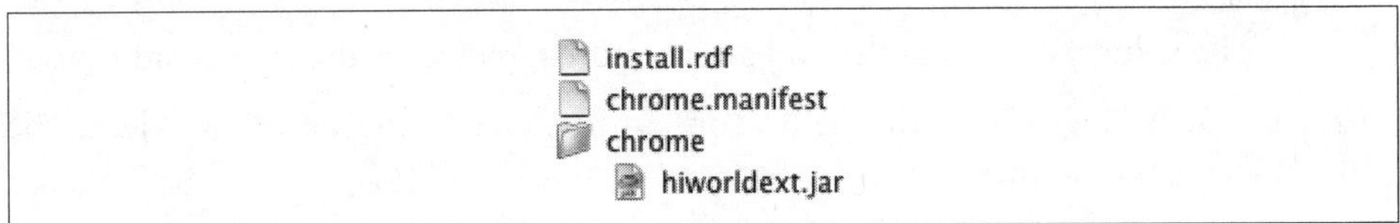

Figure 11-11. Installation hierarchy for hiworld extension

The *chrome.manifest* file is a version of the original *hiworldext.manifest* file, with the change reflecting the additional directory between the manifest and the content files:

```
content hiworldext jar:chrome/hiworldext.jar!/
skin hiworldext classic/1.0 jar:chrome/hiworldext.jar!/skin/
locale hiworldext fr jar:chrome/hiworldext.jar!/fr/
locale hiworldext en-us jar:chrome/hiworldext.jar!/en-us/
overlay chrome://browser/content/browser.xul
   chrome://hiworldext/content/hiworldext.xul
```

With our filesystem in place, we create the *.xpi* file (from the top of the installation root directory shown earlier) to provide us with our installable zippy file:

```
zip -r hiworldext.xpi *
```

Installing and Testing

The extension is most likely to be installed from a web server, but we can perform the initial test by opening Firefox's extensions window (Tools → Extensions) and dropping the *hiworldext.xpi* file onto the extensions window. We are then prompted to continue the installation, as in Figure 11-12.

Once the installation takes place and we restart Firefox, we see that our extension is properly installed and provides us with our multilocale `hiworld`. Opening the extensions manager, selecting our extension, and clicking the About menu (right-mouse or Option-Click) presents the information entered in our *install.rdf* file, as shown in Figure 11-13.

With the integrity of the deployable *.xpi* file verified, we can place the file on a web server for download by users.

The last step in enabling web download is to verify that the web server properly tags the *.xpi* files for its clients. In the case of Apache, we must modify the *httpd.conf* file to add the appropriate file type:

```
AddType application/x-xpinstall .xpi
```

Figure 11-12. Extension installation prompt

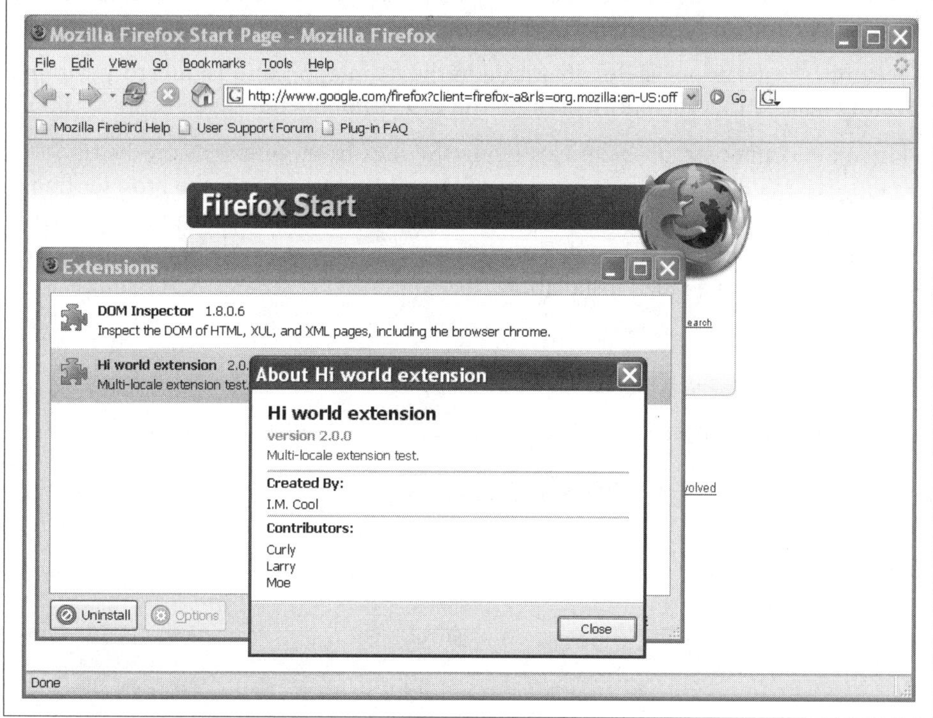

Figure 11-13. Extension information

What to Do When Things Go Wrong

The deployment of applications, extensions, themes, and locales is not a particularly difficult task, but it is an intricate task that involves the creation of a number of different files in different locations. Problems with deployments can also be very difficult to track, because few tools are available that give a good deal of information about the sources of a failure.

In general (aside from the developed application working as designed), there are a few key questions to ask about a deployment that is encountering problems:

- Were the files installed?
- Is the deployment being successfully registered with Firefox chrome?
- Is the deployment being integrated into the Firefox/XULRunner runtime?
- Is the deployment being properly loaded by the Firefox extensions manager?

Were the Files Installed?

Both XULRunner and the Firefox extensions manager must move files out of the zippy file (*xulapp* for XULRunner, *xpi* for extensions) and onto the local filesystem.

XULRunner installations are easily found in the main applications directory within a directory named after the information in the *application.ini* file.

If Firefox encounters a problem extracting the files from an extension distribution, you may see the Firefox startup window with an error area under the browser frame, indicating some form of serious problem during the browser's startup, as shown in Figure 11-14. (Note that although there is no error message in the panel, its appearance at least hints at a failed installation.)

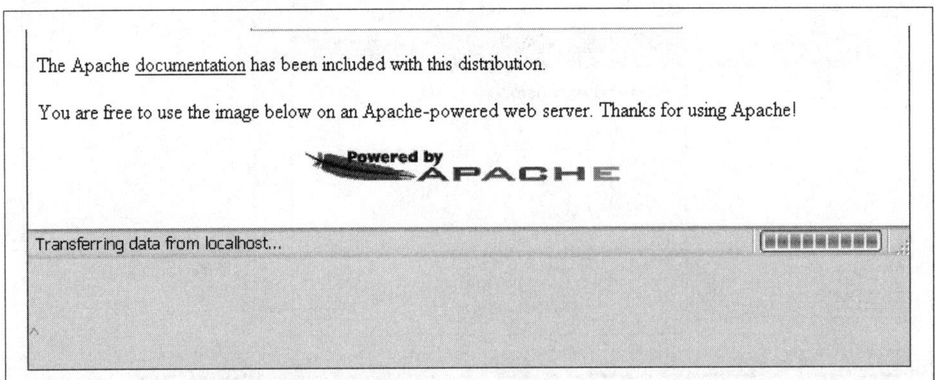

Figure 11-14. Error panel for failed extension load

To verify that the files were properly extracted during the extension's installation, we must find the user's default profile folder. For OS X, this is located in *Library/ApplicationSupport/Firefox/Profiles/someCodedFolderName/extensions*. For Windows, the user's extensions are in *Documents and Settings\userName\Mozilla\Firefox\profiles\someFoldedFolderName\extensions*.

Within the user's extensions directory will be a folder with the name extracted from the `id` field in the *install.rdf* file. Figure 11-15 shows a successful install from the *.xpi* file.

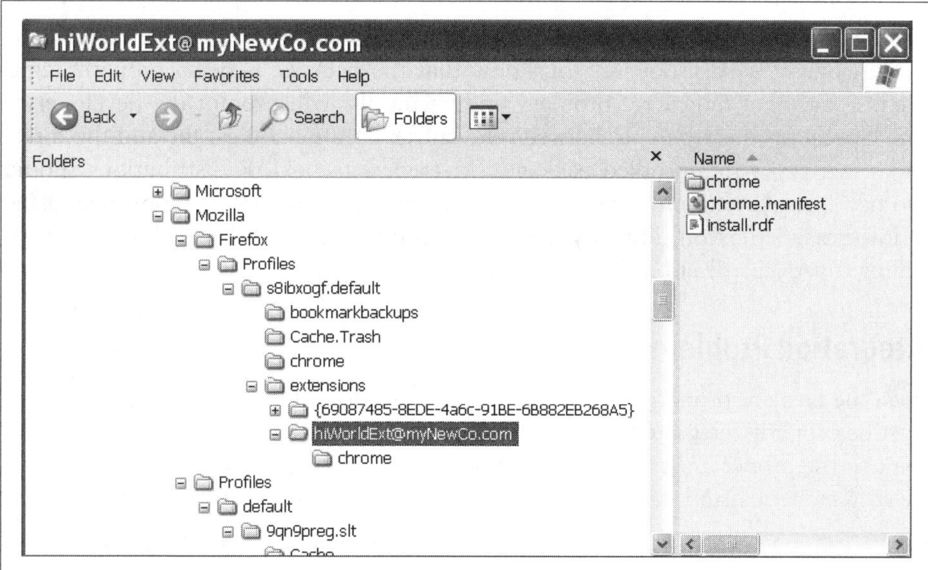

Figure 11-15. Successfully installed extensions hierarchy

Chrome Problems

It is important to remember that when Firefox launches a chrome application or extension, the framework provides those applications with access to files and resources only within the chrome URL. Entries in manifest files are the only way the Firefox framework (Firefox browser and XULRunner runtime) can register a chrome URL (which is used to reference resources) with a location on the local filesystem. By convention, the filesystem location for browser-based chrome and XULRunner applications is often the same chrome directory where the manifest is found.

Manifest files, in turn, must be placed in the chrome directory of the Firefox runtime or in the chrome directory of the application to be launched by XULRunner. There is no real requirement for the name of a manifest file, only that its extension is *.manifest*. If the manifest file is not in the chrome directory, or if there is a syntax error in the manifest file, the entries will not register parts of the package with the local filesystem.

Extensions, on the other hand, must have the manifest file named *chrome.manifest*, and the placement of that file above the chrome folder holding the distribution JAR means that the manifest used for filesystem testing must be changed to include the additional directory.

The easiest way to determine whether a chrome package is being properly registered is to type a reference to a package file in the Firefox URL bar. (It doesn't matter what the file is, and it can even be a simple text file such as *foo.txt* placed in the same folder as your package.)

If the file contents are displayed in the browser, or if you can see the file contents by selecting View → Page Source, you know that the package is being properly registered. Errors that indicate a problem finding the file will prompt the developer to look closely for discrepancies between the entries in the manifest file and the directory structure of the installed package. Developers using JAR distributions should also pay special attention to the fact that JAR references are not case-sensitive; using all lowercase letters on directory names is a good practice and will simplify transitioning to JAR distributions.

Integration Problems

Once the files are properly registered with the Firefox chrome, the deployment files must be properly integrated with the framework. Application initialization files must point to the proper XUL file for XULRunner applications, overlays must connect to the correct menus, and extensions must have the scripts properly executed.

For XULRunner applications, precious few tools are available to help debug a problematic installation. Using the system console during a XULRunner install yields only one error message (hinting at a failed *application.ini* file)—a message can be triggered by error conditions.

Fortunately, problems with the XUL interface file itself are reported with a distinctive error message in the browser window (e.g., if the startup XUL file cannot be found). With that in mind, if a XULRunner application simply doesn't launch, debugging becomes a matter of verifying the chrome installation (described earlier), or focusing on the *application.ini* file and the JavaScript startup preferences statement.

One final technique to isolate the cause of an install problem of a XUL application is to make certain the JAR implementation runs successfully before the creation of the deployable ZIP file. Once the JAR implementation is proven, problems must reside within the startup or *application.ini* files. Pay close attention to "silly" mistakes such as typographical errors or the accidental inclusion of a package in multiple manifest files (a not uncommon mistake to make during debugging).

Iterative Deployment

The best advice for developers considering deployment of an application or extension is to first decide how the deployment will be delivered:

Determine whether you're developing for multiple locales
: One of the most difficult transitions to make for an application is to modify existing code for multilanguage support *after* the functional development is completed. If multiple languages are desired, the interface code and locale files will be developed from the start.

Decide whether an application or extension is to be installed
: Standalone applications can have free reign over look and feel, and can be installed at sites where multiple browser installs are not desirable. Extensions fit nicely into requirements that point to enhanced functionality to a known Firefox user.

Start development with a skeleton deployment scenario
: A simple "hello world" application or extension skeleton can be developed from the start. Team members can then be made aware of any special requirements for custom installers, language settings, or GUI design from the beginning, resulting in a development that has fewer surprises as the delivery date approaches.

Summary

The deployment of a XUL-based application or extension can involve some of the most frustrating tasks related to Firefox development.

Developers must remember to take into account subtle changes in directory structure as they move from a develop-and-test environment to a packaging suitable for deployment. The variables related to the various types of developments (XULRunner, browser applications, extensions), coupled with the developer's individual choice of how to lay out content distributions, will often lead to some tedious debugging as developments take shape. And although the Firefox framework provides many tools to assist in code development, the error reporting and debugging services related to installation could use some embellishment.

Regardless of the shortcomings of deployment support tools, the overall Firefox design boasts features to help develop standalone applications or extensions on an international scale:

- Locale development is straightforward thanks to the use of locale-specific entity references to support substitution in the XUL source, and `stringbundles` used for string substitution in runtime scripts.
- Extensions management provides a robust deployment scheme that can accommodate physical distribution of files either on the filesystem or through a web server.
- The XULRunner engine provides a reliable option for developers wanting to use the Gecko engine and most of the Firefox framework without requiring the client to install multiple browser packages.

CHAPTER 12

XUL Widget Reference

Complex open source software such as the Firefox framework can be an intimidating read when you're trying to make sense of its nuances and structure. But a basic understanding of how XUL widgets are defined and implemented is essential if developers are to take full advantage of the rich features of such a framework.

This chapter provides a basic overview of how to define and implement XUL widgets, including a discussion of:

- The organization of file families that define XUL widgets
- How and where core classes are defined
- How to read the XML Bindings Language (XBL) bindings to determine a widget's properties and methods
- A reference list of the XUL widgets that comprise interface elements

Browser Package Files

In this book we have discussed a large number of XUL elements—XML tags that the Firefox framework reads as instructions for painting an interface and providing services to an application. This section discusses a subset of XUL elements: the widgets that provide the appearance and interaction tools for an application's interface.

All XUL widgets have attributes whose values are obtained and modified by the `get/setAttribute("someAttributeName")` method, properties whose values are obtained by a dot (`.`) reference such as *`someElement.someProperty`*, and methods.

Methods that access attributes by way of `getAttribute( )` return the string assigned to the attribute in the XUL source file, and property references return the value of an expression (e.g., Boolean `TRUE` versus `"true"`, `1` versus `"1"`).

Element attributes are specified by the XUL element's Cross-Platform Component Model (XPCOM) interfaces—such as `nsIDOMXULElement`—as described in the file *nsIDOMXULElement.idl*, which you can explore using Mozilla's LXR tool. A simplified file listing for all the XUL component interface files is available at *http://lxr.mozilla.org/seamonkey/source/dom/public/idl/xul*. These XPCOM interfaces are the starting point for all XUL elements. We build XUL widgets by wrapping or extending the core `nsIDOMXULElement` programmatic interface into graphical interface widgets.

> In a limited number of XUL elements—notably `iframe`, `browser`, and `editor`—attributes that specify the source and type of web content are coded into the C++ files. No IDL references to such attributes exist.

We reference the XPCOM interfaces in XBL binding classes that wrap some attributes by property references, and implement new properties and methods to provide the XUL widget's distinctive behavior.

This relationship summarizes the "plumbing" under a XUL interface: all widgets start with an XPCOM XUL element *interface*; we implement specialized widgets and make methods public to scripts by defining XBL *bindings* between the XPCOM interfaces and XUL widget *tags*. In some cases, XUL tags are bound to combinations of XPCOM interfaces, and sometimes they are bound to other XUL primitives to form the library of elements for the XUL interface.

Figure 12-1 shows a generalized view of this relationship among interfaces, bindings, and widget tags.

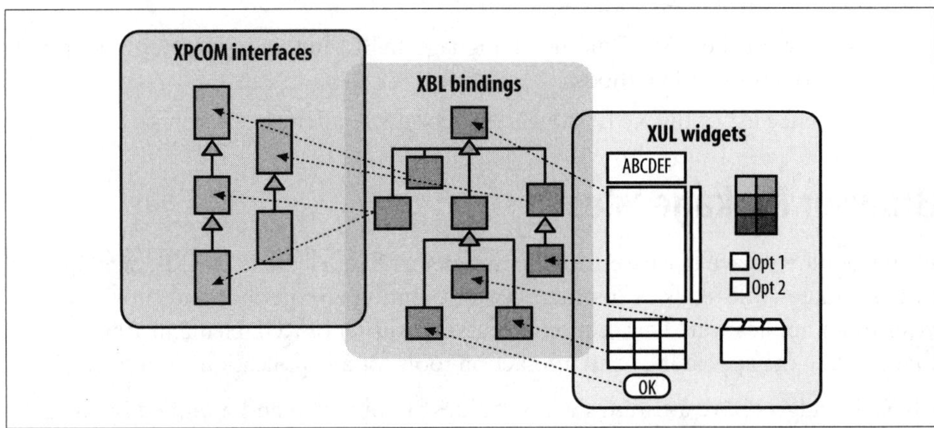

Figure 12-1. Interfaces, bindings, and XUL widgets

Following the Files

A designer may view the relationship among XPCOM, XUL, and XBL by unpacking the browser JAR with any Firefox distribution. Most of the files discussed in this section are located within the */content/global* directory of *toolkit.jar*.

Many developers will never need to explore the source files for the XUL widgets and their bindings. But as web applications built on Firefox become more ambitious, it is likely that some designers will want to look "under the hood." It should also be noted that although the filenames are likely to remain unchanged, the JARs in which the files are packed are sometimes changed between releases. Developers may have to explore different JARs to find the files being discussed.

The files that define a XUL widget include:

someInterface.idl
: These interface files define the attributes and methods of the underlying interface(s) that provide much of the logic behind a XUL widget. The interface (*.idl*) files are not included in a distribution package, but they may be explored through the Mozilla LXR cross-reference, and they provide a good quick reference when designers aren't interested in opening distribution packages.

chrome/content/global/xul.css
: This file holds the Cascading Style Sheet (CSS) reference that associates a XUL class with its entry in an XML binding file.

chrome/content/global/bindings/someWidget.xml
: This file holds the bindings for a widget. The bindings may point to other XML binding files or to other entries in the same file.

For example, we can take apart the components behind XUL's `button` widget by looking at its hierarchy of stylesheets and JavaScript files.

At the very "bottom" of a binding hierarchy, the file *xul.css* includes the following entry:

```
button {
 -moz-binding:
    url("chrome://global/content/bindings/button.xml#button");
}
```

This declaration points to the following `binding` tag in the *button.xml* file:

```
<binding id="button" display="xul:button"
   extends="chrome://global/content/bindings/button.xml#button-base">
 <content>
.
.
.
```

Note the statement indicating that a `button` binding will be drawn as a XUL button, and that the binding extends the `button-base` binding. The `button-base` binding includes the following:

```
<binding id="button-base"
 extends=
  "chrome://global/content/bindings/general.xml#basetext">
 <implementation implements="nsIDOMXULButtonElement,
                             nsIAccessibleProvider">
```

```
<property name="accessible">
.
.
<property name="dlgType"
      onget="return this.getAttribute('dlgType');"
        onset="this.setAttribute('dlgType', val); return val;"/>

<property name="group"
     onget="return this.getAttribute('group');"
       onset="this.setAttribute('group', val); return val;"/>
.
.
```

This binding shows that button-base extends the binding basetext and implements the nsIDOMXULButtonElement and nsIAccessibleProvider XPCOM interfaces. The binding also includes the property declarations that map attributes (dlgType, group) to property getters and setters.

The entries in the file *general.xml* show bindings for basetext and its super class, basecontrol (note the reference to nsIDOMXULControlElement as an implements attribute):

```
<binding id="basecontrol">
    <implementation implements="nsIDOMXULControlElement">
      <!-- public implementation -->
      <property name="disabled"
          onset="if (val)
            this.setAttribute('disabled', 'true');
                    else this.removeAttribute('disabled');
                      return val;"
          onget="return this.getAttribute('disabled')
                == 'true';"/>

      <property name="tabIndex"
       onget="return parseInt(this.getAttribute('tabindex'));"
            onset="if (val) this.setAttribute('tabindex', val);
             else this.removeAttribute('tabindex'); return val;"/>
    </implementation>
  </binding>

  <binding id="basetext" extends=
       "chrome://global/content/bindings/general.xml#basecontrol">
    <implementation>
      <!-- public implementation -->
      <property name="label"
                onset="return this.setAttribute('label',val);"
                onget="return this.getAttribute('label');"/>
      <property name="crop"
              onset="return this.setAttribute('crop',val);"
              onget="return this.getAttribute('crop');"/>
      <property name="image"
              onset="return this.setAttribute('image',val);"
              onget="return this.getAttribute('image');"/>
.
.
.
```

For thoroughness, we can use the Mozilla cross-reference LXR tool to look up the `nsIDOMXULControlElement` and find the following declaration in the IDL file:

```
[scriptable, uuid(007b8358-1dd2-11b2-8924-d209efc3f124)]
 interface nsIDOMXULControlElement : nsIDOMXULElement {
   attribute boolean disabled;
   attribute long tabIndex;
```

The XPCOM interface for a control element (`nsIDOMXULControlElement`) defines the attributes `disabled` and `tabIndex`, attributes that are made public (accessible to JavaScript) by the `basecontrol` binding through property declarations that include the `getAttribute('disabled')` and `getAttribute('tabIndex')` methods.

A button's base class binding (`button-base`) implements the `nsIDOMXULButtonElement`; attributes defined in the IDL file are implemented through the properties declared in the binding.

Figure 12-2 illustrates these relationships and shows the various classes of XBL bindings, XPCOM interfaces, and related associations.

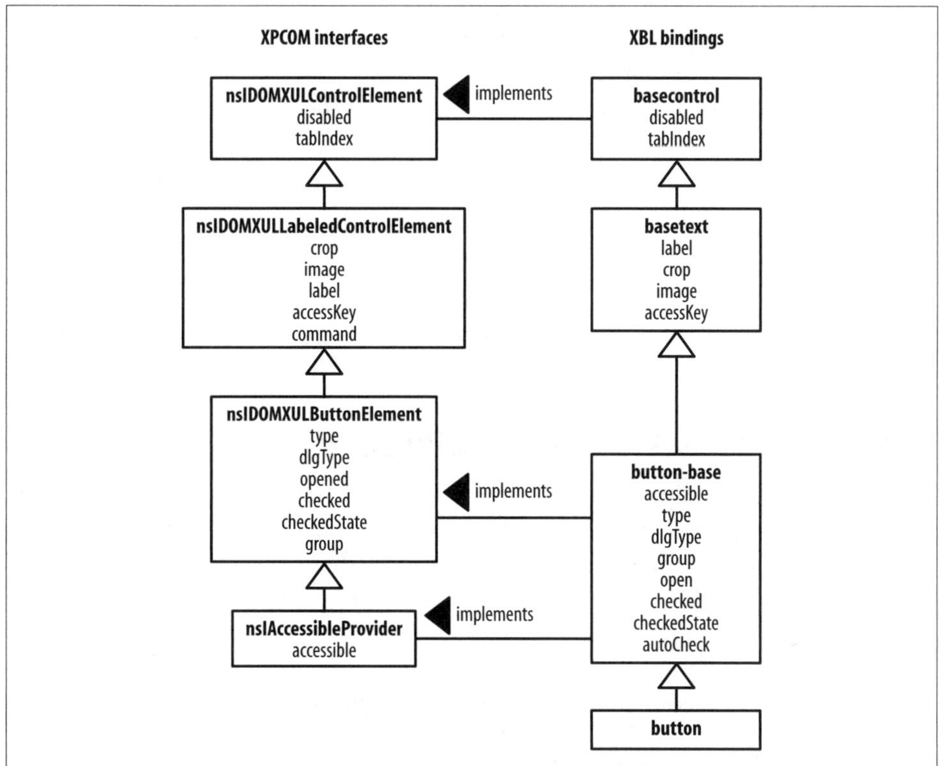

Figure 12-2. Sample widget implementation diagram

The framework does not imply a one-to-one relationship between IDL files and XUL widgets. IDL files describe core components that provide a library of tools for applications that include interface elements and services. XUL widgets are for interface design and may implement any number of IDL components. The XBL to implement an interface may, due to different operating and windowing systems, map properties from one IDL file to multiple classes of bindings. Other XML binding files may include the bindings to any number of related XUL widgets.

Web developers using JavaScript will manipulate widgets with the attributes and properties described by XBL bindings, but the attributes described through the entire hierarchy of XBL bindings *and* XUL XPCOM are also available for more extensive applications.

Developer Reference

The Firefox framework provides developers with three tiers of development approaches:

- Most often, accessing XUL elements as Document Object Model (DOM) elements, attributes, properties, and methods through JavaScript will suffice.
- Sometimes developers may need to use additional functionality provided by the XUL XPCOM interfaces, by using property references supported by the IDL (IDL properties often support a level of logic detail that is not available through node attributes and properties).
- Building additional functionality for application-specific tasks is accomplished by extending the XBL hierarchy.

The remainder of this chapter summarizes the resources available for all three approaches.

JavaScript Widgets, Attributes, and Properties

Most methods and attributes described in IDL references are accessible as JavaScript properties and methods. Mozilla's *XPConnect* technology glues IDL attributes to JavaScript properties. Additional properties and methods are included in the XBL bindings (`colorpicker`, for example, is a compound widget built completely from other widgets).

Developers must take care in noting the contextual distinctions for the terms *attributes* and *properties*. *IDL attributes* refer to the generic attributes listed in IDL files. These attributes are mapped to *JavaScript properties* that are inherited by XUL widgets. XPConnect also maps many of these IDL attributes to *DOMNode attributes* (accessible with `getAttribute`), and *node properties*.

There are several aspects to figuring out the attributes and properties associated with a widget:

- The lineage of XUL components indicates the inherited properties and methods described by the base IDL files (e.g., `nsIDOMXULControlElement`, etc.).
- The specific widget references list attributes, properties, and methods supported by that widget.
- Additional properties and methods added through XBL are listed in the XBL bindings section.

Some specialized elements (e.g., `browser`, `editor`) may not have conventional bindings, but properties and methods are listed here for completeness.

The Glossary includes a description of attribute and property values.

Component Interfaces

This section lists the properties and methods declared by XUL component IDL declarations and made accessible to JavaScript by way of XPConnect.

All XUL widgets inherit from the following interfaces:

`nsIDOMXULElement`
: Properties and methods related to XUL widget appearance and position

`nsIDOMEventTarget`
: Properties and methods related to event handling (`addEventListener`, etc.) and described in *nsIDOMEventTarget.idl*

`nsIDOMElement`
: Describes the World Wide Web Consortium (W3C) standard implementation for DOM elements (e.g., `getAttribute( )`, `setAttribute( )`, etc.) and described in *nsIDOMElement.idl*

`nsIDOMNode`
: Provides attributes and methods for node manipulation (e.g., `getChildNodes( )`, `appendChild( )`, etc.) and described in *nsIDOMNode.idl*

Following is a list of the interface descriptions.

nsISomeInterfaceName

The interface being described.

Interface file
: The interface file declaring most of the attributes and methods that are mapped to JavaScript

Inherits from
: The XPCOM interface classes that describe this interface's inheritance chain (only inheritances that extend the basic XUL element interface are described)

IDL attributes
: IDL attributes that are mapped to JavaScript properties

Methods
: List of methods

nsIDOMXULButtonElement

The base interface for XUL buttons.

Interface file
: *nsIDOMXULButtonElement.idl*

Inherits from
: `nsIDOMXULLabeledControlElement`, `nsIDOMXULControlElement`, `nsIDOMXULElement`

IDL attributes
: `boolean autoCheck`, `boolean checked`, `long checkState`, `DOMString dlgType`, `DOMString group`, `boolean open`, `DOMString type`

nsIDOMXULCheckBoxElement

Interface for checkboxes.

Interface file
: *nsIDOMXULCheckboxElement.idl*

Inherits from
: `nsIDOMXULLabledControlElement`, `nsIDOMXULControlElement`, `nsIDOMXULElement`

IDL attributes
: `boolean autoCheck`, `boolean checked`, `long checkState`

nsIDOMXULControlElement

An element that responds to user input.

Interface file
: *nsIDOMXULControlElement.idl*

Inherits from
: `nsIDOMXULElement`

IDL attributes
: `boolean disabled`, `long tabIndex`

nsIDOMXULDescriptionElement

Elements to display noneditable text, possibly in a multiline form.

Interface file
: *nsIDOMXULDescriptionElement.idl*

Inherits from
: `nsIDOMXULElement`

IDL attributes
: `boolean crop, boolean disabled, DOMString value`

nsIDOMXULElement

The topmost interface used to implement XUL elements. These attributes are accessible from scripts for all XUL elements.

Interface file
: *nsIDOMXULElement.idl*

Inherits from
: `nsIDOMElement`

IDL attributes

`DOMString align`	`DOMString flexGroup`	`DOMString ordinal`
`DOMString allowEvents`	`DOMString height`	`DOMString orient`
`nsIBoxObject boxObject`	`Boolean hidden`	`DOMString pack`
`nsIXULTemplateBuilder builder`	`DOMString id`	`DOMString persist`
`DOMString className`	`DOMString left`	`DOMString ref`
`boolean collapsed`	`DOMString maxHeight`	`nsIRDFResource resource`
`nsIController controllers`	`DOMString MaxWidth`	`DOMString statusText`
`DOMString contextmenu`	`DOMString menu`	`DOMString tooltip`
`DOMString datasources`	`DOMString minHeight`	`DOMString tooltiptext`
`DOMString dir`	`DOMString minWidth`	`DOMString top`
`DOMString flex`	`DOMString observes`	`DOMString width`

Methods

```
blur( )
focus( )
click( )
doCommand( )
nsIDOMNodeList getElementsByAttribute(in DOMString name, in DOMString value)
nsIDOMNodeList getElementsByAttributeNS(in DOMString namespaceURI, in DOMString
name, in DOMString value)
```

nsIDOMXULImageElement

Widget to display image.

Interface file
: *nsIDOMXULImageElement.idl*

Inherits from
: `nsIDOMXULElement`

IDL attributes
: `DOMString src`

nsIDOMXULLabelElement

Bottommost XUL widget for noneditable text.

Interface file
: *nsIDOMXULLabelElement.idl*

Inherits from
: `nsIDOMXULDescriptionElement`, `nsIDOMXULElement`

IDL attributes
: `DOMString accessKey`, `DOMString control`

nsIDOMXULLabeledControlElement

This provides the interface for a control element with a physical appearance.

Interface file
: *nsIDOMXULLabeledCntrlEl.idl*

Inherits from
: `nsIDOMXULControlElement`, `nsIDOMXULElement`

IDL attributes
: `DOMString accessKey`, `DOMString command`, `DOMString crop`, `DOMString image`, `DOMString label`

nsIDOMXULMenuListElement

Element used to contain lists of input items, as in a menu.

Interface file
: *nsIDOMXULMenuListElement.idl*

Inherits from
: `nsIDOMXULSelectControlElement`, `nsIDOMXULControlElement`, `nsIDOMXULElement`

IDL attributes
: `DOMString crop`, `boolean editable`, `DOMString image`, `DOMString label`, `Boolean open`, `nsIDOMNode inputField`

nsIDOMXULMultiSelectControlElement

A control element capable of a state reflecting multiple selections.

Interface file

nsIDOMXULMultiSelectCntrlEl.idl

Inherits from

`nsIDOMXULSelectControlElement`, `nsIDOMXULControlElement`, `nsIDOMXULElement`

IDL attributes

`long currentIndex`, `nsIDOMXULSelectControlItemElement currentItem`, `long selectedCount`, `nsIDOMNodeList selectedItems`, `DOMString selType`

Methods

`void addItemToSelection(in nsIDOMXULSelectControlItemElement item)`
Adds the item to the selection

`void removeItemFromSelection(in nsIDOMXULSelectControlItemElement item)`
Removes the item from the selection

`void toggleItemSelection(in nsIDOMXULSelectControlItemElement item)`
Toggles the state of an item within the list

`void selectAll( );`
Selects all items

`void invertSelection( )`
Inverts the selection of all items

`void clearSelection( )`
Clears all selections

`nsIDOMXULSelectControlItemElement getSelectedItem(in long index)`
Gets the item from a list of selected items using the 1-based index from the collection of selected items

nsIDOMXULPopupElement

Element for pop-up buttons and menus.

Interface file

nsIDOMXULPopupElement.idl

Inherits from

`nsIDOMXULElement`

IDL attributes

`DOMString position`

Methods

`void showPopup(in unsigned short alignment, in nsIDOMElement target, in nsIDOMElement anchor)`
Displays the popup element

`void hidePopup( )`
Hides the popup element

nsIDOMXULSelectControlElement

A control capable of managing multiple items that the user may select.

Interface file
: *nsIDOMXULSelectCntrlEl.idl*

Inherits from
: `nsIDOMXULControlElement`, `nsIDOMXULElement`

IDL attributes
: `long selectedIndex`, `nsIDOMSelectControlItemElement selectedItem`, `DOMString value`

Methods

`nsIDOMXULSelectControlItemElement appendItem(in DOMString label, in DOMString value)`
: Adds the string to the control

`nsIDOMXULSelectControlItemElement insertItemAt(in long index, in DOMString label, in DOMString value)`
: Inserts the string into the control

`nsIDOMXULSelectControlItemElement removeItemAt(in long index)`
: Removes the string from the control

nsIDOMXULSelectControlItemElement

An element that responds to user input and is able to retain a selected state.

Interface file
: *nsIDOMXULSelectCntrlItemEl.idl*

Inherits from
: `nsIDOMXULElement`

IDL attributes
: `DOMString accessKey`, `nsIDOMXULSelectControlElement control`, `DOMString command`, `DOMString crop`, `boolean disabled`, `DOMString image`, `DOMString label`, `boolean selected`, `DOMString value`

nsIDOMXULTextboxElement

Elements containing editable text.

Interface file
: *nsIDOMXULTextboxElement.idl*

Inherits from
: `nsIDOMXULControlElement`, `nsIDOMXULElement`

IDL attributes
: `nsIDOMNode inputField`, `long maxLength`, `long selectionEnd`, `long selectionStart`, `long size`, `long textLength`, `DOMString type`, `DOMString value`

Methods

`void select()`
: Selects the text within the control

`void setSelectionRange(in long selectionStart, in long selectionEnd)`
: Sets a selection within the text box control at the given beginning and end points

nsIDOMXULTreeElement

Base element to display hierarchical trees.

Interface file
: *nsIDOMXULTreeElement.idl*

Inherits from
: `nsIDOMXULElement`

IDL attributes
: `nsIDOMElement body, nsITreeColumns columns, boolean editable, nsIDOMXULTextBoxElement inputField, nsITreeView view`

Widget-Specific Attributes, Properties, and Methods

At the bottom of the XUL widget hierarchy are the XBL and CSS files that represent the actual interface widgets. At the widget level, the Firefox framework often adds attributes and properties (beyond those mapped from IDL declarations). The XBL bindings further extend the XPCOM library by providing additional JavaScript properties and methods. Some widget binding files also contain a number of compound widgets consisting of several primitive interface elements, as well as the functions necessary to manage user interaction.

The following list provides details for the XUL widgets and their attributes. Each entry includes the following information.

widget_element (the XUL tag used for an interface element)

Binding file
: The filename that maps XUL elements to XBL base classes and component interfaces

Extends
: The XBL base bindings upon which the widget's binding is built

Component hierarchy
: The XUL element's inheritance of component interfaces (in addition to the base inheritance of all XUL elements). Widgets with an interface hierarchy implement properties and methods defined in the inherited component's IDL. Widgets without a component hierarchy inherit methods, attributes, and properties through XBL bindings that extend other widgets.

Attributes
List of supported attributes

XBL properties
List of supported properties

Methods
List of supported methods

Common attributes, properties, and methods

The following attributes, properties, and methods are common to all XUL widgets. Attributes marked with a (✓) use the same identifier for both attributes and properties. (When parentheses are used, the property uses the altered naming form.) Some attributes are relevant only when used with templates (annotated with a *T*) or overlays (annotated with an *O*).

Attributes

`align` (✓)	`hidden` (✓)	`position`
`allowevents` (✓– `allowEvents`)	`id` (✓)	`preference-editable`
`allownegativeassertions`	`insertafter` (O)	`ref` (✓)
`class`	`insertbefore` (O)	`removeelement` (O)
`coalesceduplicatearcs` (T)	`left` (✓)	`resource` (✓, T)
`collapsed` (✓)	`menu` (✓)	`sortDirection`
`container`	`maxheight` (✓)	`sortResource` (T)
`containment` (T)	`maxwidth` (✓)	`sortResource2` (T)
`context`	`minheight` (✓)	`statustext` (✓–'`statusText`')
`contextmenu` (✓–'`contextMenu`')	`minwidth` (✓)	`style` (✓)
`datasources` (✓, T)	`mousethrough`	`template`
`dir` (✓)	`observes` (✓)	`tooltip`
`empty`	`ordinal` (✓)	`tooltiptext` (✓–'`tooltipText`')
`equalsize`	`orient` (✓)	`top` (✓)
`flags`	`pack` (✓)	`uri`
`flex` (✓)	`persist` (✓)	`wait-cursor`
`height` (✓)	`popup`	`width` (✓)

XBL properties not sharing identifier used as attributes
`boxObject`, `builder`, `className`, `controllers`, `database`, `listBoxObject`, `resource`, `value`

Methods

`focus( )`

`click( )`

`doCommand( )`

`nsIDOMNodeList getElementsByAttribute(in DOMString name, in DOMString value)`

`nsIDOMNodeList getElementsByAttributeNS(in DOMString namespaceURI, in DOMString name, in DOMString value)`

arrowscrollbox

We use an `arrowscrollbox` (see Figure 12-3) to display large numbers of items in a limited area. The user may scroll through the items by placing the mouse over either the up or down arrow at the top and bottom of the box.

Binding file

scrollbox.xml

Extends

`scrollbox-base`

Attributes

`disabled`, `disableKeyNavigation`, `preference`, `rows`, `seltype`, `suppressonselect`, `tabindex`, `value`

XBL properties

`accessible`, `disabled`, `disableKeyNavigation`, `selectedCount`, `selectedIndex`, `selectedItem`, `selectedItems`, `selType`, `tabIndex`

Methods

`scrollByIndex(lineCount)`

Scrolls the list by the specified number of lines. Positive `lineCount` values scroll forward, and negative values scroll backward.

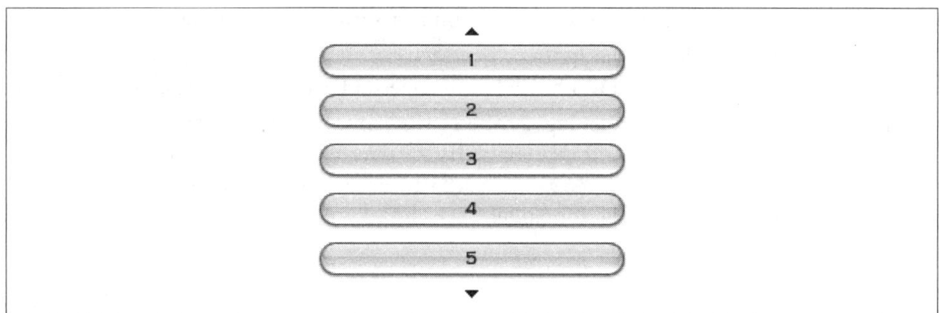

Figure 12-3. Arrowscrollbox

browser

A browser serves to display web pages while retaining history references to previous pages and providing the ability to step through the page history. Although browser elements are part of the XUL framework, they are not primitive XUL elements.

Binding file
: *browser.xml*

Extends
: `xul:browser`

Component hierarchy
: `nsIAccessibleProvider`, `nsIObserver`

Attributes
: `autocompleteenabled`, `autocompletepopup`, `autoscroll`, `disablehistory`, `disablesecurity`, `homepage`, `src`, `type`

XBL properties
: `accessible`, `canGoBack`, `canGoForward`, `contentDocument`, `contentTitle`, `contentViewerEdit`, `contentViewerFile`, `contentWindow`, `currentURI`, `docShell`, `documentCharsetInfo`, `homePage`, `markupDocumentViewer`, `preferences`, `securityUI`, `sessionHistory`, `webBrowserFind`, `webNavigation`, `webProgress`

Methods

`addProgressListener(theListener)`
: Adds `theListener` of a type `nsIWebProgressListener` interface as a progress listener.

`goBack()`
: Displays the web page previously displayed.

`goForward()`
: Advances through the session history of visited web pages.

`goHome()`
: Goes to the home page.

`goToIndex(theIndex)`
: Goes to the URL specified by the session history at the given index.

`loadURI(theURI, refURI, theCharset)`
: Loads `theURI` using the given `refURI` as the referrer URI, and `theCharset` character set.

`loadURIWithFlags(theURI, theFlags, refURI, theCharset, thePostData)`
: Loads the URI with the specified flags, referrer URI, and character set. An `nsIInputStream` may be used as `thePostData` parameter to append data to the HTTP request header. Valid flags include:

`LOAD_FLAGS_NONE`
: No flags set

`LOAD_FLAGS_BYPASS_CACHE`
: Reloads any content in the cache

`LOAD_FLAGS_BYPASS_PROXY`
: Ignores proxy server while reloading page (e.g., use origin server)

`LOAD_FLAGS_CHARSET_CHANGE`
: Repaints page content due to a change in character set

`LOAD_FLAG_IS_REFRESH`
: Used to indicate that the load is caused by a redirect or refresh

`LOAD_FLAGS_IS_LINK`
: Load caused by following a link

`LOAD_FLAGS_BYPASS_HISTORY`
: URL is not logged in session history

`LOAD_FLAGS_REPLACE_HISTORY`
: The current URL in the session history is replaced with the new URL

`reload()`
: Reloads the current web page.

`reloadWithFlags(theFlags)`
: Reloads the current web page with conditional flags:

`LOAD_FLAGS_NONE`
: No flags set

`LOAD_FLAGS_BYPASS_CACHE`
: Reloads any content in the cache

`LOAD_FLAGS_BYPASS_PROXY`
: Ignores proxy server while reloading page (e.g., use origin server)

`LOAD_FLAGS_CHARSET_CHANGE`
: Repaints page content due to a change in character set

`removeProgressListener(theListener)`
: Removes `theListener` interface as a progress listener.

`stop`
: Stops the current loading process.

button

We use a button to trigger interaction after it is pressed. Its content includes an optional image (for iconic display) and label. Figure 12-4 illustrates a collection of buttons with various `type` properties. Figure 12-5 shows the effect of different combinations of `orient` and `dir` properties. The button widget serves as a container for anonymous child nodes created as a result of various attributes that provide the physical characteristics and appearance of the button, while most behavior properties are defined in its base class bindings (see the `button-base` class for a list of properties and attributes).

Binding file
: *button.xml*

Extends
: `button-base`

Component hierarchy
: `nsIDOMXULButtonElement`, `nsIAccessibleProvider`

`nsIDOMXULLabeledControlElement`

`nsIDOMXULControlElement`

Attributes

accesskey, autoCheck, checkState, checked, command, crop, dir, disabled, dlgType, group, icon, image, label, open, orient, tabindex, type

XBL properties

accessKey, accessible, autoCheck, checkState, checked, command, crop, dir, disabled, dlgType, group, image, label, open, orient, tabIndex, type

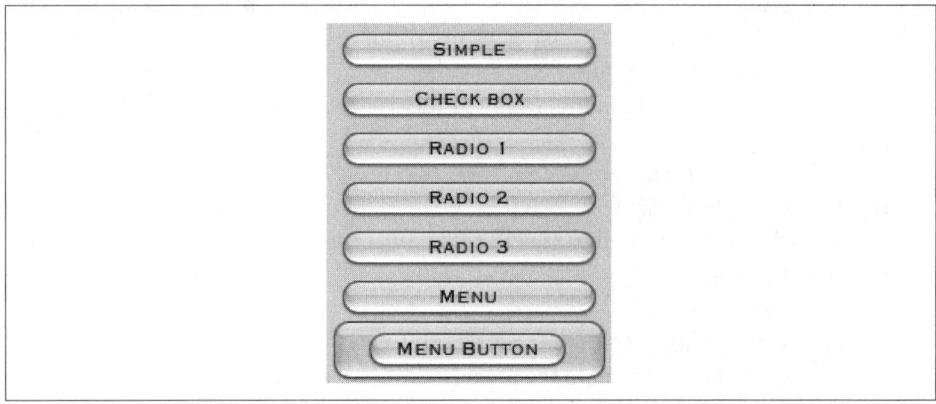

Figure 12-4. Button types

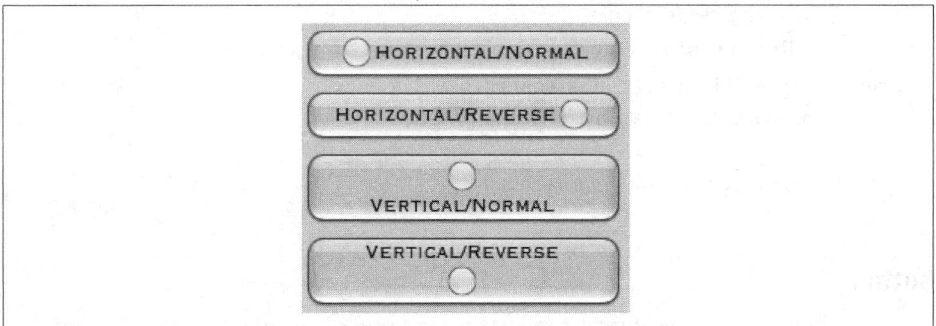

Figure 12-5. Buttons with various orient and dir attributes

caption

A caption provides a mechanism to display a line of text and an optional image. Adding a caption to a radiogroup or groupbox displays the caption along with a border around the enclosed controls. See the radiogroup widget for an example.

Binding file

groupbox.xml

Extends

basetext

Component hierarchy

`nsIDOMXULControlElement`

`nsIDOMXULElement`

Attributes

`accesskey`, `crop`, `image`, `label`, `tabindex`

XBL properties

`accessKey`, `crop`, `image`, `label`, `tabIndex`

checkbox

A type of button that includes the graphical representation of a common checkbox (see Figure 12-6).

Binding file

checkbox.xml

Extends

`basetext`

Component hierarchy

`nsIDOMXULCheckBoxElement`, `nsIAccessibleProvider`

`nsIDOMXULLabeledControlElement`

`nsIDOMXULControlElement`

Attributes

`accesskey`, `checked`, `command`, `crop`, `disabled`, `image`, `label`, `preference`, `tabindex`

XBL properties

`accessKey`, `accessible`, `checked`, `command`, `crop`, `disabled`, `image`, `label`, `tabIndex`, `value`

Methods

`setChecked(newCheckedValue)`

Sets the checked state of the button

Figure 12-6. Checkbox

colorpicker

`Colorpickers` allow a user to select a color for use in scripts (see Figure 12-7). As color cells are selected, tiles are "raised" to show the currently selected tile. Tiles are also outlined as the user's mouse passes (hovers) above them. Row and cell indexes are 0-based. Color cells are specialized `spacers` with preset background colors.

Binding file

colorpicker.xml

Extends

`basecontrol`

Component hierarchy

`nsIDOMXULControlElement`

Attributes

`disabled`, `color`, `onchange`, `preference`, `tabindex`, `type`

XBL properties

`color`, `disabled`, `tabIndex`, `value`

Methods

`initColor("colorString")`
: Initializes the color picker to the specified color without requiring user selection

`getColIndex(aCell)`
: Returns the column index of the cell

`isColorCell(aCell)`
: Returns `true` if the input cell is a color cell

`hoverLeft( )`
: Moves the hover point one cell to the left

`hoverRight( )`
: Moves the hover point one cell to the right

`hoverUp( )`
: Moves the hover point one cell up

`hoverDown( )`
: Moves the hover point one cell down

`hoverTo(aRow, aCol)`
: Moves the hover point to the row, column coordinate

`hoverCell(aCell)`
: Moves the hover point to the specified cell

`selectHoverCell( )`
: Selects the color value associated with the current hover tile

`selectCell(aCell)`
: Selects the color value associated with the specified cell

`addKeyListener( )`
: Adds a keyboard listener with a behavior that moves the hover point in response to arrow keys

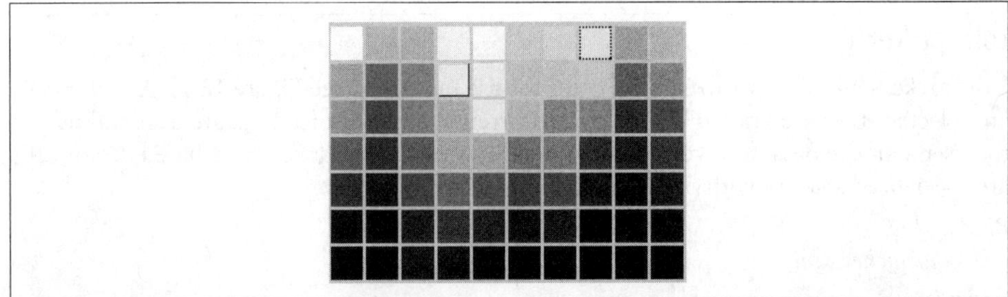

Figure 12-7. Colorpicker

deck

A container for other elements. Only the child element at the selectedIndex is displayed.

Binding file

general.xml

Attributes

selectedIndex

XBL properties

selectedIndex, selectedPanel

description

A description is a container for a multiline text area. The description tag is bound to the text-base binding in *xul.css* (see the text-base base class for attributes and properties). When description tags are used to wrap text, the resulting box supports multiline text displays that may be styled.

Attributes

accesskey, control, crop, disabled, value

XBL properties

acccessKey, accessible, control, crop, disabled, value

dialog

Dialogs are pop-up windows (most often launched within an application's chrome URL) used to prompt the user for a course of action. Dialogs take on appearances that are dependent on the platform-specific windowing environment.

Binding file

dialog.xml

Extends

dialog-base

Attributes

buttonaccesskeyaccept, buttonaccesskeycancel, buttonaccesskeydisclosure, buttonaccesskeyextra1, buttonaccesskeyextra2, buttonaccesskeyhelp, buttonalign, buttondir, buttonlabelaccept, buttonlabelcancel, buttonlabeldisclosure, buttonlabelextra1, buttonlabelextra2, buttonlabelhelp, buttonorient, buttonpack, buttons, defaultButton, ondialogaccept, ondialogcancel, ondialogdisclosure, ondialoghelp, title

XBL properties

buttons, defaultButton, ondialogaccept, ondialogcancel, ondialogdisclosure

Methods

acceptDialog( )

Closes the dialog as though the accept button was pressed

cancelDialog( )

Closes the dialog as though the cancel button was pressed

`getButton(dialogButtonType)`
: Returns the button reference with `dialogButtonType` being one of the tokens specified in the `buttons` property

`moveToAlertPosition( )`
: Moves the dialog toward the top-left quadrant of the calling window

`centerWindowOnScreen( )`
: Centers the dialog on the screen

dialogheader

The `dialogheader` is the element used to contain a dialog's title and optional description field (see Figure 12-8).

Binding file
: *dialog.xml*

Extends
: `dialog-base`

Attributes
: `crop`, `description`, `title`

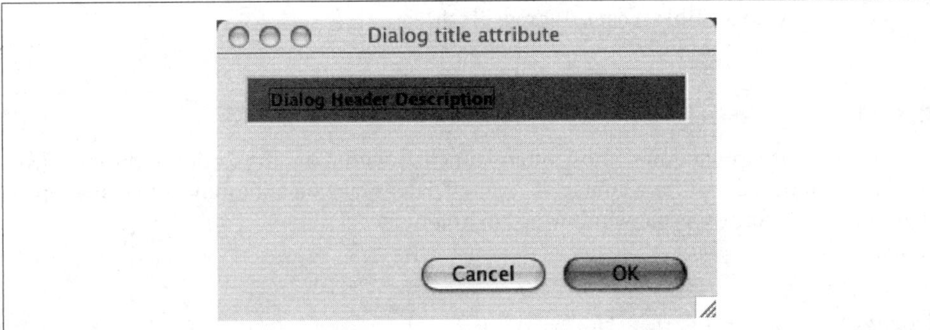

Figure 12-8. Dialog and dialogheader

editor

An editor acts as an `iframe` element with content that may be edited. For the `src` document to be editable, the `makeEditable( )` method must be called *after* the document has been loaded in the frame. Developers must add interface elements to control editing and styling through calls to the `nsIEditor` or `nsIHTMLEditor` interfaces obtained through the `getEditor( )` or `getHTMLEditor( )` method.

Binding file
: *editor.xml*

Component hierarchy
: `nsIAccessibleProvider`

Attributes
: `editortype`, `src`, `type`

XBL properties
: `accessible`, `commandManager`, `contentDocument`, `contentWindow`, `docShell`, `editingSession`, `editortype`, `webBrowserFind`, `webNavigation`

Methods

`makeEditable(editorType, waitForURILoad)`
: Makes the document editable using the `editorType` parameter (same values as `editortype` property). The `waitForURILoad` parameter, if true, creates the editor after the URI has been loaded.

`getEditor()`
: Returns a reference to the `nsIEditor` interface that provides methods for simple text editing.

`getHTMLEditor()`
: Returns a reference to the `nsIHTMLEditor` interface that provides methods for editing and text styling.

grid

A `grid` is a simple layout container that acts much like an HTML table element (see Figure 12-9). Grids contain children of `columns` (which contain `column` children), and a collection of `rows` (which contain `row` children).

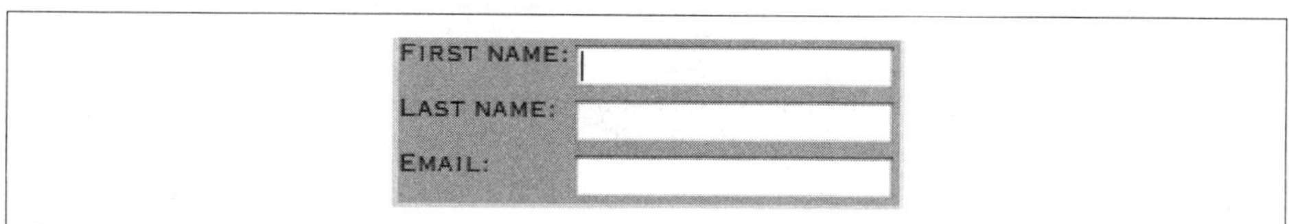

Figure 12-9. Grid

Grid elements are implemented as a styling directive in *xul.css*.

grippy

A glyph used to "snap" a splitter open or closed. Grippy elements are placed within splitters elements.

Binding file
: *splitter.xml*

groupbox

A groupbox is designed to contain other control elements. Group boxes exist to provide a visual association to a collection of interface elements (see Figure 12-10). A border is drawn around a groupbox by default, with any caption children being positioned atop the border. A groupbox inherits the attributes common for all container boxes (pack orient, align).

Figure 12-10. Groupbox

Binding file
: *groupbox.xml*

Extends
: `groupbox-base`

Component hierarchy
: `nsIAccessibleProvider`

XBL properties
: `accessible`

iframe

An iframe element provides functionality very similar to that of an html:iframe in displaying a separate web page within a portion of the interface.

Binding file
: *general.xml*

Component hierarchy
: `nsIAccessibleProvider`

Attributes
: `src`

XBL properties
: `accessible`, `contentDocument`, `contentWindow`, `docShell`, `webNavigation`

image

Displays an image.

Binding file
: *general.xml*

Component hierarchy
: nsIDOMXULImageElement, nsIAccessbileProvider

nsIDOMXULElement

Attributes
: onerror, onload, src, validate

XBL properties
: accessible, src

key

An element used to define keyboard accelerators for a window. All key elements must be enclosed by a keyset parent. The key element has no physical appearance and is not rendered as a XUL element.

Attributes
: command, disabled, key, keycode, keytext, modifiers, oncommand, phase

keyset

A keyset is a parent container for key elements. A keyset and its children are not displayed in the interface, but are used to map accelerators and key actuations to menus and buttons. The keyset element has no physical appearance and is not rendered as a XUL element.

label

A simple text display that may be associated with a control (see Figure 12-11). Labels are directly mapped to the text-base binding in *xul.css*.

A SIMPLE LABEL

Figure 12-11. Simple label

Binding file
: *text.xml*

Component hierarchy
: nsIDOMXULLabelElement, nsIAccessibleProvider

nsIDOMXULDescriptionElement

Attribute
: accesskey, control, crop, disabled, value

XBL properties
: accessKey, accessible, control, crop, disabled, value

listbox

A container for <listitem> elements.

Binding file
: *listbox.xml*

Extends
: basecontrol

Component hierarchy
: nsIDOMXULMultiSelectControlElement, nsIAccessibleProvider

  nsIDOMXULSelectControlElement

  nsIDOMXULControlElement

Attributes
: disabled, disableKeyNavigation, preference, rows, seltype, suppressonselect, tabindex, value

XBL properties
: accessible, disabled, disableKeyNavigation, selectedCount, selectedIndex, selectedItem, selectedItems, selType, tabIndex

Methods

timedSelect(item, timerValue)
: Selects the specified item after the timerValue number of milliseconds; deselects other items.

appendItem(label, value)
: Creates and returns a new listitem element and appends it to the list using the label and optional value as attributes of the newly created element.

insertItemAt(index, label, value)
: Creates and returns a new listitem element and places the item at the specified index; items previously at the index are pushed down the list. The new item's label and optional value attribute are set to the provided parameters.

removeItemAt(index)
: Removes the item at the specified index and returns the item, or null if the index was out of range.

getSelectedItem(index)
: Returns the item that is at the index of the selected item collection.

addItemToSelection(item)
: If selType is multiple and items are currently selected, the new listitem item is pushed onto the collection of selected items.

removeItemFromSelection(item)
: The listitem item is removed from the collection of selected items.

toggleItemSelection(item)
: The listitem item is added to the selected collection if it was not previously selected; the item is removed from the selected collection if it was previously selected.

`selectItem(item)`
: The `listitem item` is set as the only item selected in the list.

`selectItemRange(startItem, endItem)`
: If `selType` is `multiple`, all `listitem` items are selected from the `startItem` to the `endItem`.

`selectAll( )`
: All items in the list are selected.

`invertSelection( )`
: All previously selected items are deselected, and all previously unselected items are selected.

`clearSelection( )`
: All items in the list are deselected.

`getNextItem(startItem, delta)`
: Returns the `listitem item` offset from the `startItem` by `delta` positions (delta must be nonzero) down the list. Returns `null` if target index exceeds list length.

`getPreviousItem(startItem, delta)`
: Returns the item offset from the `startItem` by `delta` positions (delta must be nonzero) up the list. Returns `null` if target index is less than 0.

`getIndexOfItem(item)`
: Returns the index of `listitem item`.

`getItemAtIndex(index)`
: Returns the `listitem` item at the index.

`ensureIndexIsVisible(index)`
: List scrolls to make item at `index` visible (if item was not previously visible).

`ensureElementIsVisible(element)`
: List scrolls to make `listitem` element visible (if element was not previously visible).

`scrollToIndex(index)`
: List scrolls to display item at `index` as first visible item.

`getNumberOfVisibleRows( )`
: Returns number of visible rows.

`getIndexOfFirstVisibleRow( )`
: Returns index of first list element that is visible.

`getRowCount( )`
: Returns number of elements in list.

`moveByOffset(offset, isSelecting, isSelectingRange)`
: Moves the selection by `offset`. If `isSelectingRange` is `true` and `multiple` is the `selType`, new selection ends with the previously selected item and begins with the item at the new target index. Otherwise, if `isSelecting` is `true`, only one item is selected at the new target index.

`scrollOnePage(direction)`
: Scrolls one "page" (page being defined as the integral number of visible rows). If `direction` = `1`, scroll down; if `direction` = `-1`, scroll up.

listcell

A cell representing the row and column offset of a multicolumn list (see Figure 12-12). `Listcells` support a number of attributes used by labeled controls. If the `type` attribute is `checkbox`, the list cell is displayed as a checkbox. `Listcells` also implement the `image` attribute as an icon when the class attribute is `listcell-icnonic`.

Binding file
: *listbox.xml*

Extends
: `listbox-base`

Component hierarchy
: `nsIDOMXULControlElement`

Attributes (if `class` = `listcell-iconic`*)*
: `crop`, `disabled`, `image`, `label`, `type`

XBL properties
: `disabled`

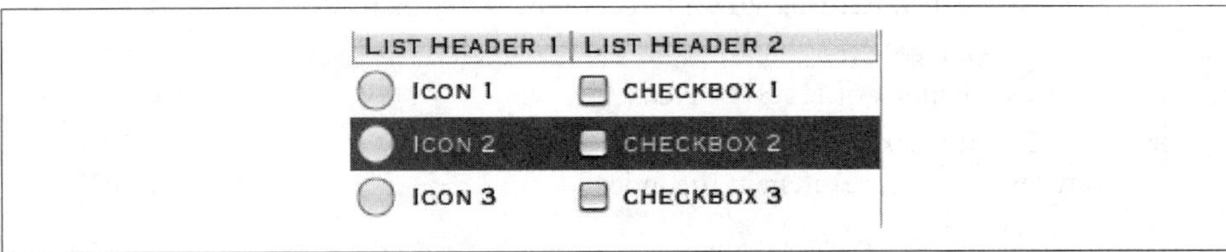

Figure 12-12. List cells as listcell-iconic and with type="checkbox"

listcol

An element used to define a column for a `listbox`.

listcols

A container for `listcol` elements in a `listbox`.

listhead

A container for `listheader` elements used to mark the headings for `listbox` columns. See Figure 12-13 for a list with header columns.

Binding file
: *listbox.xml*

Extends
: `listbox-base`

Component hierarchy

nsIDOMXULControlElement

Attributes

disabled

XBL properties

disabled

LIST HEADER 1	LIST HEADER 2
LIST CELL R1 C1	LIST CELL R1 C2
LIST CELL R2 C1	LIST CELL R2 C2
LIST CELL R3 C1	LIST CELL R3 C2

Figure 12-13. List with headers and columns

listheader

A cell used to label a column heading in a list.

Binding file

listbox.xml

Extends

listbox-base

Component hierarchy

nsIDOMXULControlElement

Attributes

disabled

listitem

A cell that is contained within a list. Attributes and properties are inherited from the basetext binding. Listitems are placed as a row within a listbox.

Binding file

listbox.xml

Extends

basetext

Component hierarchy

nsIDOMXULSelectControlItemElement, nsIAccessibleProvider

nsIDOMXULControlElement

Attributes

accesskey, checked, command, crop, current, disabled, image, label, preference, selected, tabindex, type, value

XBL properties

accessKey, accessible, checked, control, crop, current, disabled, image, label, selected, tabIndex, value

menu

A container for menu pop-up elements.

Binding file
: *menu.xml*

Extends
: `menuitem-base`

Component hierarchy
: `nsIDOMXULSelectControlItemElement`, `nsIAccessibleProvider`

  `nsIDOMXULControlElement`

Attributes
: `acceltext`, `accesskey`, `allowevents`, `crop`, `disabled`, `key`, `label`, `menuactive`, `open`, `sizetopopup`, `value`

XBL properties
: `value`

menubar

A container for menu elements.

Binding file
: *toolbar.xml*

Extends
: `toolbar-base`

Component hierarchy
: `nsIAccessibleProvider`

Attributes
: `accessible`, `statusbar`

XBL properties
: `statusbar`

menuitem

An item in a menu capable of holding pop-up children. Use of the class `menuitem-iconic` applies the `image` attribute as an icon to be added to the menu item. Use of the class `menuitem-non-iconic` removes any left-side margin from the menu items.

Binding file
: *menu.xml*

Extends
: `menuitem-base`

Component hierarchy
: `nsIDOMXULSelectControlItemElement nsIAccessibleProvider`

Attributes
: acceltext, accessible, accesskey, allowevents, autocheck, checked, command, crop, description, disabled, image, key, label, name, selected, tabindex, type, validate, value

XBL properties
: label, value

menulist

A container for a menupopup that can be used as a pull-down selection widget. Figure 12-14 shows an example of a menulist. Figure 12-15 shows an example of a menulist with editable items.

Binding file
: *menulist.xml*

Extends
: menulist-base

Component hierarchy
: nsIDOMXULMenuListElement, nsIAccessibleProvider

  nsIDOMXULSelectControlElement

  nsIDOMXULControlElement

Attributes
: accesskey, crop, disableautoselect, disabled, editable, focused, image, label, open, preference, readonly, sizetopopup, src, tabindex, value

XBL properties
: accessible, crop, description, disableautoselect, disabled, inputField, label, menuBoxObject, menupopup, open, selectedIndex, selectedItem, src, tabIndex, value

Methods

`appendItem(label, value, description)`
: Appends a new menuitem to the existing menupopup (or creates a new menupopup if none exists) with the given label, value, and optional description attributes set to the provided parameters.

`insertItemAt(index, label, value, description)`
: Creates and returns a new menuitem element and places the item at the specified index; items previously at the index are pushed down the list. The new item's label, value, and optional description attributes are set to the provided parameters.

`removeItemAt(index)`
: Removes the item at the specified index and returns the item or null if the index was out of range.

`select( )`
: Used with editable menulists to select all the text in the box.

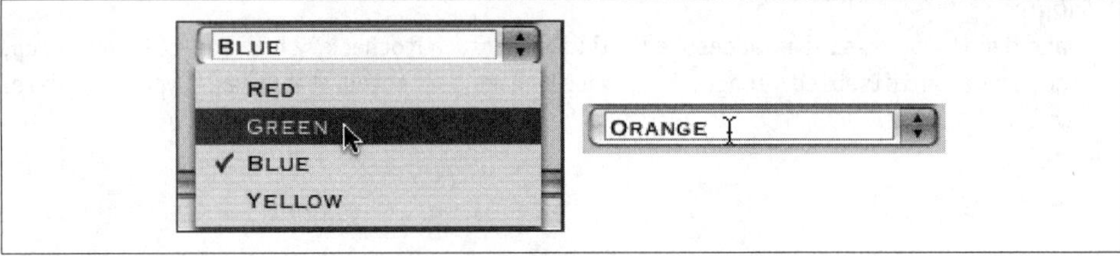

Figure 12-14. Editable menu list

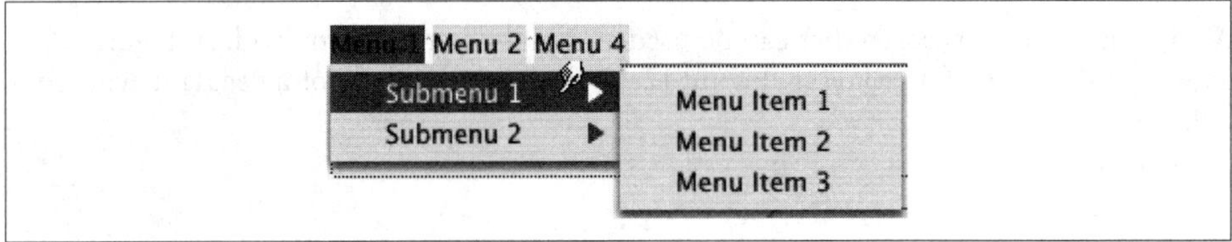

Figure 12-15. Menus, pop ups, and menu items

menupopup

A popup that can be attached to an element, mostly connected to a `menuitem`. Menu popups are mapped directly to popups in *xul.css*.

Binding file
: *popup.xml*

Extends
: `popup-base`

Component hierarchy
: `nsIDOMXULPopupElement` `nsIAccessibleProvider`

  `nsIDOMXULElement`

Attributes
: `ignorekeys`, `left`, `onpopuphidden`, `onpopuphiding`, `onpopupshowing`, `onpopupshown`, `position`, `top`

XBL properties
: `accessible`, `popupBoxObject`, `popup`

Methods
: `showPopup(element, x, y, popupType, anchor, align)`

  Opens a popup. The coordinates `x` and `y` specify a screen position in pixels. If either value is (or both values are) `-1`, the popup is opened relative to the `element` parameter. The anchor argument corresponds to the `popupanchor` attribute on the element. The `align` argument corresponds to the `popupalign` attribute on the element. The `anchor` and `align` attributes are ignored if either `x` or `y` is not `-1`. Values for `popupType` are `popup`, `context`, or `tooltip`.

  `hidePopup( )`

  Hides the popup element.

`sizeTo(width, height)`
    Sizes the popup to the dimensions expressed in pixels.

`moveTo(x, y)`
    Moves the popup to the specified screen position.

menuseparator

A separator usually drawn as a thin line.

Binding file
    menu.xml

Extends
    `menuitem-base`

Component hierarchy
    `nsIDOMXULSelectControlItemElement`, `nsIAccessibleProvider`

XBL properties
    `accessible`

popupset

A `popupset` is a container used to enclose `popup` elements.

prefpane

A preference pane is one pane of a collection contained in a `prefwindow`. Preference panes consist of `preferenceElements` (describing variables modified by the interface), and any XUL elements used to access the variables.

Binding file
    preferences.xml

Attributes
    `helpURI`, `image`, `label`, `onpaneload`, `selected`, `src`

XBL properties
    `image`, `label`, `preferenceElements`, `preferences`, `selected`, `src`

Methods

`preferenceForElement(uiElement)`
    Returns the preference value associated with a user interface element

prefwindow

A specialized window used to render a collection of preference panes.

Binding file
    preferences.xml

Extends
    `dialog`

Attributes
: buttonalign, buttondir, buttonorient, buttonpack, buttons, defaultButton, lastSelected, onbeforeaccept, ondialogaccept, ondialogcancel, ondialogdisclosure, ondialoghelp, onpanelload, title, type

XBL properties
: buttons, currentPane, defaultButton, lastSelected, preferencePanes, type

Methods

`acceptDialog()`
: Accepts the dialog and returns

`addPane(newPane)`
: Adds a new preferences pane

`cancelDialog()`
: Cancels the dialog and returns

`centerWindowOnScreen()`
: Centers the preference window

`getButton(buttonType)`
: Returns the button element from the dialog that is of the specified type

`openSubDialog(url, features, params)`
: Opens a subdialog window in a fashion similar to the `openWindow` method

`openWindow(windowtype, url, features, params)`
: Opens a child window parented by the preference window

`showPane(thePane)`
: Shows a specific preference pane

progressmeter

An operating-system-specific display of progress.

Binding file
: *progressmeter.xml*

Component hierarchy
: nsIAccessibleProvider

Attributes
: mode, value

XBL properties
: accessible, mode, value

radio

A button with a "checked" state. When a `radiogroup` element contains `radio` elements, only one `radio` element is allowed to be checked within the group (see Figure 12-16).

Binding file
: *radio.xml*

Extends
: `control-item`

Component hierarchy
: `nsIAccessibleProvider,nsIDOMXULSelectControlItemElement`
: `nsIDOMXULLabeledControlElement`
: `nsIDOMXULControlElement`

Attributes
: `accesskey, command, crop, disabled, focused, image, label, selected, tabindex, value`

XBL properties
: `accessKey, accessible, crop, disabled, image, label, radioGroup, selected, tabIndex, value`

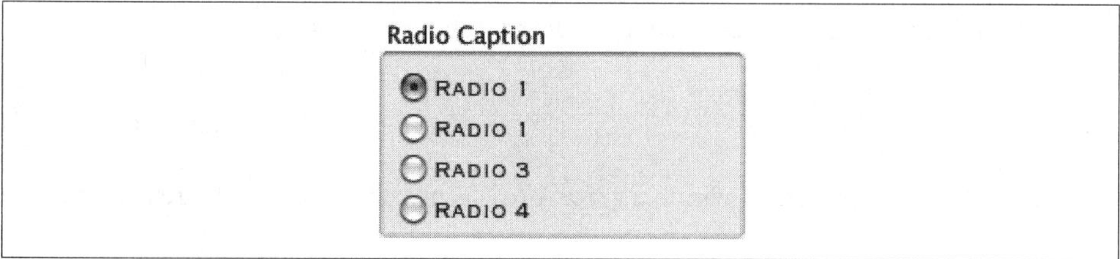

Figure 12-16. Radio group with caption

resizer

A visible handle used to resize windows.

Binding file
: *popup.xml*

Extends
: `resizer-base`

Attributes
: `dir`

richlistbox

A container used in a fashion similar to listboxes, but that can support children other than simple text content.

Binding file
: *richlistbox.xml*

Component hierarchy
: `nsIDOMXULSelectControlElement, nsIAccessibleProvider`

Attributes
: `suppressonselect`

XBL properties
: `accessible, children, scrollBoxObject, selectedIndex, selectedItem, suppressOnSelect`

richlistitem

An item contained by a `richlistbox`.

Binding file
: *richlistbox.xml*

Extends
: `basecontrol`

Component hierarchy
: `nsIDOMXULSelectControlItemElement`, `nsIAccessibleProvider`

Attributes
: `disabled`, `selected`, `tabindex`, `value`

XBL properties
: `accessible`, `control`, `disabled`, `label`, `selected`, `tabIndex`, `value`

row

A container for items presented within a `grid`. A row is placed as a child of a `rows` element.

rule

Used to define the conditions for element generation in a template.

Attributes
: `iscontainer`, `isempty`, `parent`, `parsetype`

scrollbar

A vertical or horizontal slider used to move through a container that is larger than the visible region of a box. Scrollbars may also be used standalone to allow selection of a value tied to the slider.

Binding file
: *scrollbar.xml*

Extends
: `scrollbar-base`

Attributes
: `curpos`, `increment`, `maxpos`, `pageincrement`

scrollbox

A box that can be used to scroll content. By default, the application must adjust the position of the content in the viewport. Designers who want `scrollbars` to appear should add a style declaration to the `selement: "style=overflow: auto;"`.

Binding file
: *scrollbox.xml*

Extends
: `scrollbox-base`

scrollcorner

The corner glyph where vertical and horizontal scrollbars meet.

separator

A thin separator of a fixed dimension (1.5 em). Use the styling classes `groove`, `groove-thin`, and `thin` to specify appearance (default style does not draw any line).

Attributes
: `orient`

spacer

An element used to insert flexible spaces between elements via the `flex` attribute.

splitter

A bar used to manually adjust the space allocated to visible containers. Splitters are placed within a container and between the elements whose space is to be adjusted.

Binding file
: *splitter.xml*

Attributes
: `collapse`, `resizeafter`, `resizebefore`, `state`, `substate`

stack

A container that presents child elements over one another.

statusbar

A container for `statusbarpanel` elements, spacers, and other items often used to present ongoing status and progress information to the user.

Binding file
: *general.xml*

Component hierarchy
: `nsIAccessibleProvider`

XBL properties
: `accessible`

statusbarpanel

A container for either an image or a label; `statusbarpanels` are placed within a `statusbar` with the `label` or the `image` used to provide user feedback of some status. The styling class `statusbarpanel-iconic` is used to specify use of an image in the panel. The class `statusbarpanel-menu-iconic` allows for the addition of a `menupopup` within the `statusbarpanel`.

Binding file
: *general.xml*

Attributes
: `crop`, `label`, `src`

XBL properties
: `label`, `src`

stringbundle

`Stringbundle` elements are placed within a `stringbundleset`. They are used to reference a property file containing property-key value pairs.

Binding file
: *stringbundle.xml*

Attributes
: `src`

XBL properties
: `appLocale`, `src`, `stringBundle`, `strings`

stringbundleset

A container for `stringbundle` elements.

tab

A type of button contained within a `tabs` element. Clicking on a `tab` element opens the associated tab panel enclosed within a `tabbox`.

Binding file
: *tabbox.xml*

Extends
: `tab-base`

Component hierarchy
: `nsIDOMXULSelectControlItemElement`, `nsIAcessibleProvider`

Attributes
: `accesskey`, `afterselected`, `beforeselected`, `crop`, `disabled`, `image`, `label`, `linkedpanel`, `tab`, `validate`

XBL properties
: `accessible`, `label`, `linkedPanel`, `selected`, `tabs`

tabbox

A container for a collection of tabpanel elements. Tabbox elements contain a tabs container for the tab buttons, and a tabpanels element that contains the displayed panes.

Binding file
: *tabbox.xml*

Extends
: tab-base

Component hierarchy
: nsIAccessibleProvider

Attributes
: eventnode, handleCtrlPageUpDown, handleCtrlTab

XBL properties
: accessible, eventNode, handleCtrlPageUpDown, handleCtrlTab, selectedIndex, selectedPanel, selectedTab

tabbrowser

A tabbrowser combines the functionality of multiple browsers, each browser present as a tabpanel.

Binding file
: *tabbrowser.xml*

Attributes
: autocompleteenabled, autocompletepopup, autoscroll, contentcontextmenu, contenttooltip, handleCtrlPageUpDown, onbookmarkgroup, onnewtab

XBL properties
: browsers, canGoBack, canGoForward, contentDocument, contentTitle, contentViewerEdit, contentViewerFile, contentWindow, currentURI, docShell, documentCharsetInfo, homePage, markupDocumentViewer, securityUI, selectedBrowser, selectedTab, sessionHistory, tabContainer, webBrowserFind, webNavigation, webProgress

Methods

addProgressListener(listener)
: Adds a progress listener (an object that implements the nsIWebProgressListener interface) to the browser.

addTab(URI)
: Adds a new tab loading the specified URI. The method returns the tab element.

getBrowserForTab(tabElement)
: Returns the browser element attached to the specified tab.

goBack( )
: Goes back one page in the browser history.

goForward( )
: Goes forward one page in the browser history.

`goHome()`
: Goes to the user's home page URI.

`goToIndex(theIndex)`
: Goes to the page in the browser's history that matches the index relative to the current page. Positive values are interpreted as forward indexes, negative numbers as reverse indexes.

`loadURI(uri, referrer, charset)`
: Loads a URL into the document, with the given referrer and character set.

`loadURIWithFlags(uri, flags, referrer, charset)`
: Loads a URL into the document, with the specified load flags and the given referrer and character set. The following flags are also valid:

  `LOAD_FLAGS_IS_REFRESH`
  : This flag is used when the URL is loaded because of a metatag refresh or redirect.

  `LOAD_FLAGS_IS_LINK`
  : This flag is used when the URL is loaded because a user clicked on a link. The HTTP `referrer` header is set accordingly.

  `LOAD_FLAGS_BYPASS_HISTORY`
  : Does not add the URL to the session history.

  `LOAD_FLAGS_REPLACE_HISTORY`
  : Replaces the current URL in the session history with a new one. This flag might be used for a redirect.

`reload()`
: Reloads the document in the browser.

`reloadAllTabs()`
: Reloads the browser content in all tabs.

`reloadTab(theTab)`
: Reloads the content of the specified tab.

`reloadWithFlags(theFlags)`
: Reloads the document in the browser with the given load flags. The flags may be combined using `|`.

  `LOAD_FLAGS_NONE`
  : No special flags. The document is loaded normally.

  `LOAD_FLAGS_BYPASS_CACHE`
  : Reloads the page, ignoring it if it is already in the cache. This is the flag used when the reload button is pressed while the Shift key is held down.

  `LOAD_FLAGS_BYPASS_PROXY`
  : Reloads the page, ignoring the proxy server.

  `LOAD_FLAGS_CHARSET_CHANGE`
  : This flag is used if the document needs to be reloaded because the character set changed.

`removeAllTabsBut(tabElement)`
: Removes all tabs other than the tab specified in the parameter.

`removeCurrentTab()`
: Removes the currently selected tab. This method has no effect if only one tab is being displayed.

`removeProgressListener(listener)`
: Removes the progress listener.

`removeTab(tabElement)`
: Removes the specified tab.

`stop()`
: Stops loading the current document.

tabpanel

An individual panel contained by a `tabpanels` parent element.

tabpanels

The container for `tabpanel` elements. `Tabpanels` are placed within a `tabbox`.

Binding file
: *tabbox.xml*

Extends
: `tab-base`

Component hierarchy
: `nsIAccessibleProvider`

Attributes
: `selectedIndex`

XBL properties
: `accessible`, `selectedIndex`, `selectedPanel`

tabs

Container for a row of `tab` elements.

Binding file
: *tabbox.xml*

Extends
: `tab-base`

Component hierarchy
: `nsIAccessibleProvider`, `nsIDOMXULSelectControlElement`

Attributes
: `closebutton`, `disableclose`, `first-tab`, `last-tab`, `onclosetab`, `onnewtab`, `onselect`, `setfocus`, `tooltiptextnew`

XBL properties
: `selectedIndex`, `selectedItem`

Methods

`advanceSelectedTab(dir, wrap)`
: If the `dir` is set to `1`, the currently selected tab changes to the next tab. If the argument `dir` is set to `-1`, the currently selected tab changes to the previous tab. If the `wrap` argument is `true`, the adjustment will wrap around when the first or last tab is reached.

`element appendItem(label, value)`
: Creates a new item element and adds it to the end of the existing list of items. The newly created element is returned.

`element insertItemAt(index, label, value)`
: Creates a new item element and inserts it at the specified position. The new item element is returned.

`element removeItemAt(index)`
: Removes the child item in the element at the specified index. The removed item is returned.

template

Declares a template for rules-dependent element construction.

Attributes

`container`, `memember`

textbox

An input field used to enter text that displays a line of text.

Binding file

textbox.xml

Component hierarchy

`nsIAccessibleProvider`, `nsIDOMXULTextboxElement`

`nsIDOMXULControlElement`

Attributes

`cols`, `disabled`, `maxlength`, `multiline`, `onchange`, `oninput`, `preference`, `readonly`, `rows`, `size`, `tabindex`, `timeout`, `type`, `value`, `wrap`

XBL properties

`accessible`, `disabled`, `inputField`, `maxLength`, `readonly`, `selectionEnd`, `selectionStart`, `size`, `tabIndex`, `textLength`, `timeout`, `type`, `value`

Methods

`select()`
: Selects all the text in the `textbox`.

`setSelectionRange(start, end)`
: Sets the selected portion of the `textbox`, where the `start` argument is the index of the first character to select and the `end` argument is the index of the character after the selection. Set both arguments to the same value to move the cursor to the corresponding position without selecting text.

textbox (type= "autocomplete")

This widget is a textbox with the autocomplete type attribute. It includes a popup containing a list of possible completions for the user's text entry.

Binding file
: *autocomplete.xml*

Extends
: textbox

Component hierarchy
: nsIDOMXULTextboxElement, nsIAccessibleProvider
: nsIDOMXULControlElement

Attributes
: accesskey, autocompletepopup, autocompletesearch, autocompletesearchparam, completedefaultindex, crop, disableautocomplete, disabled, disablekeynavigation, enablehistory, focused, forcecomplete, ignoreblurwhilesearching, inputtooltiptext, label, maxlength, maxrows, minresultsforpopup, nomatch, onchange, oninput, onsearchcomplete, ontextentered, ontextreverted, open, readonly, showcommentcolumn, size, tabindex, tabscrolling, timeout, type, value

XBL properties
: accessible, completeDefaultIndex, controller, crop, disableAutoComplete, disableKeyNavigation, disabled, editable, focused, forceComplete, ignoreBlurWhileSearching, inputField, label, maxLength, maxRows, minResultsForPopup, open, popup, popupOpen, searchCount, searchParam, selectionEnd, selectionStart, showCommentColumn, size, tabIndex, tabScrolling, textLength, textValue, timeout, textbox.type, value

Methods
: getSearchAt(index)
  : Returns the search component with the given index. The components are set with the autocompletesearch attribute.
: select()
  : Selects all the text in the textbox.
: setSelectionRange(start, end)
  : Sets the selected portion of the textbox, where the start argument is the index of the first character to select and the end argument is the index of the character after the selection. Set both arguments to the same value to move the cursor to the corresponding position without selecting text.

titlebar

Displays a title bar used to provide a mechanism allowing a user to move contents around the screen.

Binding file
: *popup.xml*

toolbar

A container typically holding a row of buttons.

Binding file
: *toolbar.xml*

Extends
: `toolbar-base`

Component hierarchy
: `nsIAccessibleProvider`

Attributes
: `currentset`, `customindex`, `customizable`, `defaultset`, `grippyhidden`, `grippytooltiptext`, `mode`, `toolbarname`

XBL properties
: `accesible`, `currentSet`, `firstPermanentChild`, `lastPermanentChild`, `toolbarName`

Methods
: `element insertItem(id, beforeNode, wrapper, beforePermanent)`

Adds an item with the given ID to the toolbar and returns the element reference. The new item is added just before the item given by the second argument. If the second argument is `null`, but the `beforePermanent` argument is `true`, the item is added to the beginning of the toolbar before the first permanent item. Otherwise, if the `beforePermanent` argument is `false`, the new item is added to the end of the toolbar. The third argument can be used to wrap the new item in another element. Usually, the last argument will be `null` as it is mainly for the use of the customize dialog.

The ID should match an element in the toolbar's `toolbarpalette`. Some special IDs may also be used to create special spacing items:

`"separator"`
: A separator, which is drawn as a vertical bar

`"spacer"`
: A nonflexible space

`"spring"`
: A flexible space

toolbarbutton

A button appearing on a toolbar.

Binding file
: *toolbarbutton.xml*

Extends
: `button-base`

Component hierarchy
: `nsIAccessibleProvider`, `nsIDOMXULButtonElement`
`nsIDOMXULLabeledControlElement`
`nsIDOMXULControlElement`

Attributes
: accesskey, autoCheck, checkState, checked, command, crop, dir, disabled, dlgType, group, image, label, open, orient, tabindex, type, validate

XBL properties
: accessKey, accessible, autoCheck, checkState, checked, command, crop, dir, disabled, dlgType, group, image, label, open, orient, tabIndex, type

toolbaritem

A container used within a toolbar that is the parent for all nonbutton items.

toolbarpalette

A `toolbarpalette` is a collection of available `toolbar` items. `Toolbarpalette` elements are not displayed, but they serve as the container for items that are accessible to a toolbar through its `currentset` attribute.

toolbarseparator

A separator used between groups of toolbar items. The element is mapped to the `toolbardecoration` XBL binding.

Binding file
: *toolbar.xml#toolbardecoration*

Extends
: `toolbar-base`

Component hierarchy
: `nsIAccessibleProvider`

XBL properties
: `accessible`

toolbarset

A parent container used for custom toolbars added through a custom toolbar dialog.

toolbarspacer

A spacer between toolbar items. It is mapped to the `toolbardecoration` XBL binding.

Binding file
: *toolbar.xml#toolbardecoration*

Extends
: `toolbar-base`

Component hierarchy
: `nsIAccessibleProvider`

XBL properties
: `accessible`

toolspring

A flexible space that expands to fill the area between toolbar items. It is mapped to the `toolbardecoration` XBL binding.

Binding file
: *toolbar.xml#toolbardecoration*

Extends
: `toolbar-base`

Component hierarchy
: `nsIAccessibleProvider`

XBL properties
: `accessible`

toolbox

A box that contains `toolbars`. The `orientation` is vertical by default.

Binding file
: *toolbar.xml*

Extends
: `toolbar-base`

Component hierarchy
: `nsIAccessibleProvider`

XBL properties
: `accessible`, `customToolbarCount`, `palette`, `toolbarset`

Methods

`element appendCustomToolbar(name, currentset)`
: Adds a custom toolbar to the toolbox with the given `name` and returns the toolbar element. You can supply a comma-separated list of toolbar item `ids` as the `currentset` argument to add some items by default.

tooltip

An element used for popups that provides additional information about a widget when the user's mouse hovers over an element.

Binding file
: *popup.xml*

Extends
: `popup`

Attributes

`crop`, `default`, `label`, `noautohide`, `onpopuphidden`, `onpopuphiding`, `onpopupshowing`, `onpopupshown`, `position`

XBL properties

`label`, `popupBoxObject`, `position`

Methods

`hidePopup( )`

Closes the pop up.

`moveTo(x,y)`

Moves the pop up to the new location on the screen.

`showPopup(element, x, y, popupType, anchor, align)`

Opens a `popup` element. Pop ups can appear either at a specific screen position, or relative to some element in the window. If either `x` or `y` is set to a value other than `-1`, the pop up will appear at the screen coordinate specified by the `x` and `y` parameters. If both `x` and `y` are `-1`, the pop up will be positioned relative to the element specified as the first argument. In this case, the `anchor` and `align` arguments may be used to further control where the pop up appears relative to the element. The `anchor` argument corresponds to the `popupanchor` attribute on the element. The `align` argument corresponds to the `popupalign` attribute on the element. The `anchor` and `align` arguments are ignored if either coordinate is not –1.

The `popupType` should be `"popup"`, `"context"`, or `"tooltip"`.

`sizeTo(width, height)`

Changes the size of the pop up to the specified pixel width and height.

tree

A container holding a tabular or hierarchical set of rows and elements. Each tree row may contain indented child rows. The interfaces provided by a tree and the availability of tree children as DOM nodes are dependent on the nature of the tree's construction.

Binding file

tree.xml

Extends

`tree-base`

Component hierarchy

`nsIAccessibleProvider`, `nsIDOMXULTreeElement`

`nsIDOMXULMultiSelectControlElement`

Attributes

`disableKeyNavigation`, `disabled`, `enableColumnDrag`, `flags`, `hidecolumnpicker`, `onselect`, `rows`, `seltype`, `statedatasource`, `tabindex`

XBL properties

`accessible`, `builderView`, `columns`, `contentView`, `currentIndex`, `disableKeyNavigation`, `disabled`, `enableColumnDrag`, `firstOrdinalColumn`, `selType`, `selstyle`, `tabIndex`, `treeBoxObject`, `view`

treecell

A single cell that exists within a `treerow` element. The `label` attribute specifies the text displayed in the cell. Setting the `mode` attribute allows the tree cell to be displayed as a progress meter.

Attributes

`label`, `mode`, `properties`, `ref`, `src`, `value`

treechildren

The topmost container for elements that represent the body elements of a tree's root. The `treechildren` element is mapped to the `treebody` XBL binding.

Binding file

tree.xml#treebody

Extends

`tree-base`

Attributes

`alternatingbackground`

treecol

The container of a column of a tree. `Treecol` elements should always have an `id` attribute for the column-positioning algorithm to work properly.

Binding file

tree.xml

Extends

`treecol-base`

Component hierarchy

`nsIAccessibleProvider`

Attributes

`crop`, `cycler`, `dragging`, `fixed`, `hidden`, `hideheader`, `ignoreincolumnpicker`, `label`, `primary`, `sort`, `sortActive`, `sortDirection`, `src`, `type`

XBL properties

`accessible`

treecols

A container for `treecol` elements.

Binding file

tree.xml

Extends

`tree-base`

Component hierarchy
: nsIAccessibleProvider

Attributes
: pickertooltiptext

XBL properties
: accessible

treeitem

A treeitem is a child of a treechildren element and parent of treerow elements. A treeitem contains a single row and all the children of a row's descendants.

Attributes
: container, empty, label, open, uri

treerow

A single row of content parented by a treeitem element. Treerows should contain treecell elements. (Child rows should be wrapped by treeitem elements that are parented by treerow elements.)

treeseparator

A separator row used in a tree.

triple

An element used to describe the assertion for a Resource Description Framework (RDF) graph.

Attributes
: object, predicate, subject

vbox

A container element that imposes a vertical orientation on children.

window

The top-level container of a XUL document.

Component hierarchy
: nsIDOMAbstractView, nsIDOMEventReceiver
: nsIDOMEventTarget, nsIDOMJSWindow
: nsIDOMViewCSS, nsIDOMWindow, nsIDOMWindowInternal

Attributes

height, hidechrome, id, screenX, screenY, sizemode, title, width, windowtype

XBL properties

closed, content, controllers, crypto, defaultStatus, directories, document, frameElement, frames, fullScreen, innerHeight, innerWidth, length, location, locationbar, menubar, name, navigator, opener, outerHeight, outerWidth, pageXOffset, pageYOffest, parent, pernalbar, pkcs11, prompter, screen, screenX, screenY, scrollbars, scrollMaxX, scrollMaxY, scrollX, scrollY, sel, status, statusbar, textZoom, toolbar, top, window, windowRoot

Methods

alert(String message)
: Displays specified message.

atob (String aciiString)
: Decodes a string that has been in base-64 encoding.

back( )
: Displays previous page in history.

btoa(String base64Data)
: Creates a base-64-encoded ASCII string from binary data.

clearInteral(intervalID)
: Clears the window's timer interval. Timer intervals are initially created with a call to setInterval( ).

clearTimeout(timerID)
: Clears the window's timeout value.

close( )
: Closes the window.

confirm(String message)
: Displays a confirmation dialog message.

dump(String str)
: Dumps the string to the console.

boolean find(String str, boolean caseSensitive, boolean backwards, boolean wrapAround, boolean wholeWord, boolean searchInFrames, boolean showDialog)
: N/A

focus( )
: Brings the window to the front of the visual hierarchy and gives it focus.

forward( )
: Moves window content forward one page in history.

getAttention( )
: Flashes the window frame or application icon in an operating-system-specific manner.

nsISelection getSelection( )
: Accesses the window's selection object.

home( )
: Sends the window content to the home URL.

`moveBy(int xDif, int yDif)`
: Moves the window by the specified offset in pixels.

`moveTo(int xPos, int yPos)`
: Moves the window to the specified screen position.

`open(String URL, String name, string options)`

`openDialog(String URL, String name, string options)`
: Opens the window at the specified URL with the given `name` and `options`. The `options` string contains a comma-delimited sequence of *`someOption`*`=yes` fragments. The loading is executed asynchronously (the window loading will complete sometime after the `open` command has returned). If any options are present, all other parameters of a window are assumed to be omitted from the window (except for `close` and `titlebar`, which are included by default). The following are example fragments to enable specific options area (parameters with a (✓) require `UniversalBrowserWrite` privileges, unless the program is running as a privileged chrome application):

  `alwaysRaised=yes` (✓)
  : The window is always raised (in front of other browser windows).

  `alwaysLowered=yes` (✓)
  : The window is displayed under (in terms of z-order) the parent window.

  `chrome=yes` (✓)
  : Only the chrome frame is displayed.

  `close=yes` (✓)
  : If this is set to `no`, the system close icon is removed from the frame. This feature works only for dialog windows.

  `dialog=yes`
  : The window removes all restore, minimize, and maximize frame icons from the window.

  `dependent=yes`
  : The window is dependent on the parent window, meaning that if the window closes its parent window closes, and is minimized if its parent window is minimized.

  `directories=yes`
  : The bookmarks toolbar is rendered.

  `location=yes`
  : The window displays the location bar.

  `menubar=yes`
  : A menu bar is displayed.

  `minimizable=yes`
  : The minimize icon is included. This setting is useful only for dialog windows, as other windows ignore this parameter.

  `modal=yes` (✓)
  : The window must be dismissed to allow focus to return on the parent window.

`personalbar=yes`
Same as directories.

`resizable=yes`
Resizer (grippy) elements will be made available within the window status bar, as well as adjustable window frames (the Mozilla Developer Center site recommends this feature always be set to yes). Setting this value to no removes the flexibility of the window frames, but the statusbar grippy remains.

`scrollbars=yes`
Scrollbars are displayed if the document does not fit in the window.

`status=yes`
Status bar is displayed.

`titlebar=yes` (✓)
Title bar is displayed.

`toobar=yes`
Navigation toolbar containing and browser control buttons are displayed.

`print()`
Opens the operating-system-specific print dialog.

`prompt(string someText)`
Opens a prompt dialog displaying the text message.

`resizeBy(int xDelta, int yDelta)`
The window's size is changed by the specified values.

`resizeTo(int newWidth, int newHeight)`
The window is resized to the specified dimensions.

`scroll(int xCoord, int yCoord)`
The window is scrolled so that the coordinates of the document are displayed in the top left of the window.

`scrollBy(int xScroll, int yScroll)`
The window is scrolled by the specified number of pixels along the *x* and *y* directions.

`scrollByLines(int lineCount)`
The window is scrolled by the number of text lines in the document.

`scrollByPages(int pageCount)`
The window is scrolled by the number of pages as inferred by the document design.

`scrollTo(int xCoord, int yCoord)`
The window is scrolled so that the specified document coordinates are located in the top left of the window.

`setInterval(someFunction, int delay, [additionalArguments])`
A function `someFunction` is called every `delay` milliseconds. The function returns an `intervalID` that can be used with the `clearInterval` function to terminate the timer. The `additionalArguments` are passed as an `arguments` array to the function whose elements are extracted by the index.

`setTimeout(someFunction, int delay, [additionalArguments])`
: A function is called after the passage of `delay` milliseconds. The function returns a `timeoutID` that can be used with the `clearTimeout` function to terminate the timer. The `additionalArguments` are passed as an `arguments` array to the function whose elements are extracted by the index.

`sizeToContent( )`
: Window is sized to fit the content document.

`stop( )`
: Window stops loading the document.

`unescape(string escapedString)`
: Returns a regular string given an `escapedString`.

`updateCommands(string someCommandString)`
: Enables or disables items by setting or clearing the `disabled` attribute on the command node specified by `someCommandString`.

wizard

An element containing navigation buttons and a collection of `wizardpage` elements. Figure 12-17 shows an example of a wizard page on OS X.

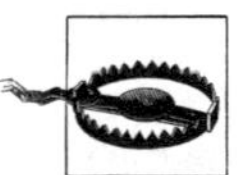

Wizard panes must be launched from applications running in a chrome URL.

Binding file
: *wizard.xml*

Extends
: `wizard-base`

Attributes
: `firstpage`, `lastpage`, `onwizardback`, `onwizardcancel`, `onwizardfinish`, `onwizardnext`, `pagestep`, `title`

XBL properties
: `canAdvance`, `canRewind`, `currentPage`, `onFirstPage`, `onLastPage`, `pageCount`, `pageIndex`, `pageStep`, `title`, `wizardPages`

Methods

`advance(pageID)`
: Advances to the next `wizardpage` of the specified `ID`. Execution is dependent on the `canAdvance` or `canRewind` property.

`cancel( )`
: Cancels and closes the wizard.

`getButton(string type)`
: Returns the button in the dialog specified by the button type.

`getPageById(pageID)`
: Returns the element reference to the `wizardpage` of the specified `ID`.

`goTo(pageID)`
: Advances to the page of the specified `ID`. This function is executed regardless of the `canAdvance` or `canRewind` property.

`rewind( )`
: Wizard goes back one page.

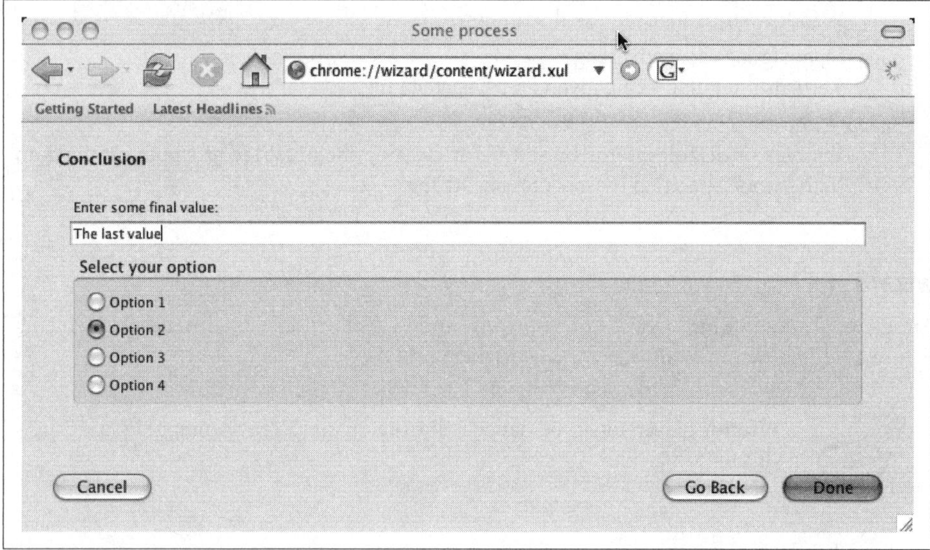

Figure 12-17. Last page of a wizard

wizardpage

A container for interface elements that gather information as part of a sequence of user-controlled operations. `Wizardpage` elements are enclosed by a wizard.

Binding file
: *wizard.xml*

Extends
: `wizard-base`

Attributes
: `description`, `label`, `next`, `onpageadvanced`, `onpagehide`, `onpagerewound`, `onpageshow`, `pageid`

XBL properties
: `next`, `pageid`

Base XBL Bindings

The following base XBL binding section is most relevant for developers who are interested in extending widget functions by developing their own extended bindings. This section provides a background for existing bindings and serves as a good jumping-off point to build additional functionality.

basecontrol

The base class for controls that implements the `nsIDOMXULControl` interface.

Binding file
: *general.xml*

Component hierarchy
: `nsIDOMXULControlElement`
: `nsIDOMXULElement`

XBL properties
: `disabled`, `tabIndex (tabindex)`

basetext

The `basetext` base class encapsulates the behavior of many of the physical characteristics of a control that includes a text label.

Binding file
: *general.xml*

Extends
: `basecontrol`

XBL properties
: `accessKey(accesskey)`, `crop`, `image`, `label`

button-base

The button-base is the base binding for various types of buttons.

Binding file
: *button.xml*

Extends
: `basetext`

Component hierarchy
: `nsIDOMXULButtonElement`, `nsIAccessibleProvider`
: `nsIDOMXULLabeledControlElement`
: `nsIDOMXULControlElement`
: `nsIDOMXULElement`

The nsAccessibleProvider interface provides properties and methods in support of software accessibility guidelines such as those defined by the Microsoft Active Accessibility (MSAA) architecture and the Accessibility Toolkit (ATK).

XBL properties
: accessible, autoCheck, checked, checkState, dlgType, group, open, type

listbox-base

The base binding for listboxes and child elements.

Binding file
: *listbox.xml*

Extends
: basecontrol

menu-button-base

The base class for menu buttons that implement methods to manage mouse movement over and on top of menu buttons.

Binding file
: *button.xml*

Extends
: button-base

XBL properties
: buttondown
: Returns true if the button is being pressed.
: buttonover
: Returns true if the mouse is over the button.

menuitem-base

The base class binding for menu items.

Binding file
: *menu.xml*

Component hierarchy
: nsIAccessibleProvider, nsIDOMXULSelectControlItemElement
: nsIDOMXULElement

XBL properties
: accessible
: Reference to nsIAccessibility interface

scrollbox-base

The `scrollbox-base` class is a generic box container used by bindings that add scrolling behavior.

Binding file
: *scrollbox.xml*

tab-base

The `tab-base` finding is the base binding for tab elements.

Binding file
: *tabbox.xml*

text-base

The `text-base` finding is the base binding for simple text fields.

Binding file
: *text.xml*

Extends
: `basecontrol`

Component hierarchy
: `nsIDOMXULDescriptionElement`, `nsIAccessibleProvider`
: `nsIDOMXULElement`

XBL properties
: `accessible`, `crop`, `value`

text-label

The `text-label` binding is used for text that may be associated with a control element.

Binding file
: *text.xml*

Extends
: `text-base`

XBL properties
: `accessKey`, `control`

toolbar-base

Base binding for toolbars and menu bars.

Binding file
: *toolbar.xml*

Implements
  `nsIAccessibleProvider`

XBL properties
  `accessible`

tree-base

The `tree-base` binding describes the visible elements of a tree.

Binding file
  tree.xml

Extends
  `basecontrol`

wizard-base

The `wizard-base` binding is the base binding for wizard elements.

Binding file
  wizard.xml

GLOSSARY

XUL Widgets: Attributes, Properties, and Methods

The following list describes the inventory of attributes, properties, and methods used by the XUL elements that are accessible from JavaScript code.

Although all JavaScript-managed attributes are accessed as strings, this glossary adds data types to provide guidance if the string value should represent a specific type. Examples of these types include Boolean, integer, and the name of a required interface. Properties without such qualifiers are presumed to be strings whose context is set by the application or by a specific interface design (e.g., the "ID" of widget). For ease of reference and to distinguish them from their data types, attribute, property, and method names are set in boldface font.

`nsIAccessible` **`accessible`**
: The `accessible` property is available on all elements that inherit from the `nsIAccessible` interface. The interface provides assistive technology services similar to those of the Accessibility Toolkit (ATK) and Microsoft Active Accessibility (MSAA).

`char` **`accessKey`**
: The character used as a keyboard accelerator; when coupled with an operating-system-specific keyboard combination, it triggers the control actuation.

`boolean` **`afterselected`**
: When assigned to a tab, returns `true` if the tab is immediately after the currently selected tab.

`align`
: Sets the alignment characteristics of the button in a manner consistent with all box containers. Interpretation of the `align` attribute is subject to the `dir` attribute:

  `"start"`
  : Elements are positioned along the top or left edge of the button.

  `"end"`
  : Elements are positioned along the right or bottom of the button.

  `"center"`
  : Elements are centered.

  `"baseline"`
  : Elements are such that all text elements are in line.

  `"stretch"`
  : The image element grows to fit the size of the box.

boolean **allowevents**
: If true, event is passed to children of the element. Otherwise, event passing stops at the element.

boolean **alternatingbackground**
: For tree elements, causes the tree rows to be displayed in alternating colors.

nsILocale **appLocale**
: The Cross-Platform Component Model (XPCOM) element containing information about the user's locale.

boolean **autoCheck**
: If true or if omitted, a checkbox button toggles states upon actuation; if false, checkbox state must be set programmatically.

autocompletepopup
: ID of the popup element to hold the browser's autocomplete results.

boolean **autoscroll**
: Enables or disables autoscrolling for the browser.

beforeselected
: When assigned to a tab, returns true if the tab is immediately before the currently selected tab.

nsIDOMElement **body**
: For trees rendering Document Object Model (DOM) content, the topmost body node of the tree.

nsIBoxObject **boxObject**
: The base box container for an element.

nodelist **browsers**
: A list of the browser elements inside a tabbrowser.

nsIXULTemplateBuilder **builder**
: The tree builder object used to manage rendering of tree elements.

nsIXULTreeBuilder **builderView**
: A synonym for a tree element's view property.

buttonalign, buttondir, buttonorient, buttonpack
: For preference windows, sets the align, dir, orient, and pack attributes of the box containing the buttons.

buttons
: A string of comma-delimited tokens that specify which buttons are to be included on a dialog. Supported tokens include accept, cancel, disclosure, help, extra1, and extra2. (The labels for the "extra" buttons are set with the dialog's buttonlabelextra1 and buttonlabelextra2 attributes.) An example string of "accept, cancel, help" would create a dialog with accept, cancel, and help buttons.

boolean **canAdvance**
: For wizards, determines whether the user can press the Next button to advance. This property affects the appearance of the wizard's Next button (and Finish button if the wizard is displaying the last page).

boolean **canGoBack**
: Read-only property that returns true if the session history includes a web page that was previously displayed.

boolean **canGoForward**
: Read-only property that returns true if forward movement through the history is possible.

boolean **canRewind**
: For wizards, determines whether the user can press the Back button to navigate to the preceding page. This property affects the appearance of the wizard's Back button.

boolean **checked**
: If true, the checkbox button is checked.

long **checkState**
: The state of a button:

  0
  : Unchecked; actuation transitions to state 1.

  1
  : Checked; actuation transitions to state 0.

  2
  : Mixed; actuation transitions to state 0 (see autoCheck attribute).

`element[]` **`children`**
Returns an array of elements that are children of a `richlistbox` element.

`className`
The class name of the element.

`boolean` **`closebutton`**
If `true` on a `tabs` element, the tabs row will have a "new tab" button and a "close" button on the ends. This feature is used by the tabbrowser to provide the facilities for adding and closing tabs.

`collapse`
When used on a splitter, determines how the splitter "snaps" when the `grippy` is pressed:

`none`
No collapsing takes place.

`before`
The content before the `grippy` is collapsed.

`after`
The content after the `grippy` is collapsed.

`both`
Either the element immediately before the splitter or the element immediately after the splitter is collapsed depending on the minimum size of the content.

`boolean` **`collapsed`**
True if element is collapsed (hidden with a splitter element).

`string` **`color`**
An RGB triplet representing the selected color (`#RRGGBB`).

`nsITreeColumns` **`columns`**
Returns the interface that manages a `tree` element's columns.

`Window` **`content`**
The content window of a XUL window.

`nsITreeContentView` **`contentView`**
For trees without the "don't-build-content" value in the `flags` attribute, returns the interface that provides DOM access based on a row access. This property is not available for trees with the "don't-build-content" value.

`command`
The element ID of the `command` attribute.

`commandManager`
Returns a read-only reference to `nsICommandManager` interface that provides much of the command-handling logic for the editor.

`boolean` **`completeDefaultIndex`**
If set to `true` on an `autocomplete` text box, the best match value will be filled in as the user types. If `false` or omitted, autofilled value must be selected from list.

`container`
If attached to tree columns, `true` if tree column is to be used as a container (e.g., a folder). If set as an attribute of a template element, set to the variable to use as the container or reference variable.

`containment`
Set to the URI of a Resource Description Framework (RDF) resource on elements with attributes defining `datasources` and `ref` attributes. This attribute indicates which elements are allowed to contain children.

`document` **`contentDocument`**
Read-only document object.

`contentTitle`
Read-only string containing the title of the element's document object.

`contenttooltip`
An `id` reference to the `tooltip` element to be used for the content area in the `tabbrowser`.

`nsIContentViewerFile` **`contentViewerFile`**
Reference to the `nsIContentViewerFile` interface for the document.

`window` **`contentWindow`**
Returns read-only document window property as a reference to `nsIDOMWindow` interface.

`context`
See `contextmenu`.

contextmenu
The element ID of a pop up to be used when the user context-clicks on an element.

control
The `id` attribute of a control associated with a label.

`nsIAutoCompleteController` **controller**
For text boxes of type `autocomplete`, returns the controller for the text element.

`XULControllers` **controllers**
The XUL controllers associated with a XUL window.

crop
Identifies how the control's label is to be cropped if the enclosing box is too small. Cropped characters are replaced by an ellipsis. Values include:

`start`
Beginning of control label is truncated with an ellipsis.

`end`
End of control label is replaced with an ellipsis.

`center`
Both ends of the control are replaced with an ellipsis.

`none`
Text is truncated.

`nsIDOMCrypto` **crypto**
The DOM `crypto` property of a XUL window.

curpos
When used with a slider, the current position of the scroller.

`int` **currentIndex**
The index of a selected item. This value is `-1` if no item is selected.

`nsIDOMXULSelectControlItemElement`
currentItem
The control item currently selected.

`wizardpage` **currentPage**
For `wizards`, returns the `wizardpage` currently being displayed.

currentSet
Gets the list of names for elements within the toolbar.

currentURI
The currently loaded URL.

`boolean` **customindex**
Used to specify that toolbars can be customized and causes the set of buttons to persist across sessions.

`integer` **customToolbarCount**
The number of custom `toolbar` elements within a `toolbox` element.

`boolean` **cycler**
When `true` and attached to a `treecol` element, the cell state will alternate state after actuation between on and off.

`nsIRDFCompositeDataSource` **database**
The database used to access resources associated with RDF content generation.

datasources
Space-delimited list of URIs or RDF files to be used as the `datasources` for content generation.

defaultButton
The default button actuated with the Enter key.

defaultSet
A comma-delimited set of items displayed on a `toolbar`. The `ids` should match `ids` from a `toolbarpalette`.

`string` **description**
A descriptive line of text that appears along with a dialog title.

dir
For `resizer` elements, dictates the direction of growth when a `resizer` is dragged:

`left`
Resized to the left

`right`
Resized to the right

`top`
Resized top

`bottom`
Resized down

`bottomleft`
: Resized down and to the left

`bottomright`
: Resized down and to the right

`topleft`
: Resized up and to the left

`topright`
: Resized up and to the right

`string` **`dir`**
: The ordering of children placed within a parent container:

  `normal`
  : Children are placed as presented in the source file.

  `reverse`
  : Children are placed in reverse order as presented in the source file.

`BarProp` **`directories`**
: Manages the visibility of a `window`'s directories.

`boolean` **`disableAutoComplete`**
: Gets and sets the value of the `disableautocomplete` attribute.

`boolean` **`disableautoselect`**
: Used with editable `menulists`. If `true` or omitted, selected menu item is updated to match entered text.

`boolean` **`disableclose`**
: If `true`, the `close` button on a `tabs` element is disabled.

`boolean` **`disabled`**
: If `true`, element does not respond to user interaction.

`disableKeyNavigation`
: If `true`, `keyNavigation` is disabled. If property is `false`, using the keyboard selects the list item beginning with the pressed key.

`dlgType`
: Used for buttons on dialogs when the designer wants to replace the standard dialog buttons with buttons of a distinctive appearance:

  `accept`
  : Button replaces OK dialog button.

  `cancel`
  : Button replaces Cancel dialog button.

  `help`
  : Button replaces Help dialog button.

`disclosure`
: Button used to disclose additional information such as a drop-down hint or explanation.

`nsIDocShell` **`docShell`**
: Returns read-only reference to the document shell.

`documentCharsetInfo`
: Read-only reference to the `nsIDocumentCharsetInfo` interface to provide character set information.

`boolean` **`dragging`**
: An attribute set by the Firefox framework on `treecol` elements to indicate the user is dragging a column to change its position.

`boolean` **`editable`**
: The input control responds to user text entry.

`editingSession`
: Returns read-only reference to the `nsIEditingSession` interface that provides details on the editor capabilities and status.

`editortype`
: Gets/sets the field specifying the type of editor:

  `html`
  : If `html` type, the `getHTMLEditor` method will return a reference to an interface capable of adding style information to text.

  `text`
  : Only unformatted text entry is supported.

`boolean` **`enableColumnDrag`**
: For tree elements, set to `true` to enable the user to change the order of column headers by dragging individual columns to different positions.

DOMNode **eventNode**
For tabbox elements, the node to which listeners for keyboard navigation events are attached.

treecol **firstOrdinalColumn**
For tree elements, a reference to the first treecol child element.

boolean **firstpage**
Used to indicate whether a wizard is displaying the first page.

firstPermanentChild
First toolbar child element that cannot be modified.

boolean **first-tab**
Set to true for the first tab.

boolean **fixed**
When assigned to a treecol element, indicates that the column cannot be resized.

flex
Integer value used by parent container to allocate available space among child containers. Excess space is allocated to child containers in proportions that match the relative values of the flex attribute. A flex attribute of 0 sets the element dimension to the minimum possible space.

boolean **forceComplete**
Gets and sets the value of the forcecomplete attribute; if true, text is filled in with the best match when it loses focus; otherwise, it is filled in only when the user makes a selection.

Element **frameElement**
The frame element of a window.

WindowCollection **frames**
The child windows of a XUL window.

boolean **fullScreen**
If true, a XUL window is displayed fullscreen.

group
Buttons with the same group string value are controlled such that only one radio button can be checked within the group.

boolean **handleCtrlPageUpDown**
When attached to tabbox elements, if set to true or omitted, the Ctrl and Page Up or Page Down key actuations switch to the next or previous tab.

handleCtrlTab
When attached to tabbox elements, if set to true or omitted, the tabbox Ctrl and Tab key actuations will switch to the next tab. If the Shift key is also held down, the previous tab will be displayed.

integer **height**
The height of the element in pixels.

helpURI
The URI of a help page that will be displayed when the help button of a preference pane is pressed.

boolean **hidden**
If true, element is hidden.

boolean **hidechrome**
If true as a window attribute, the chrome (including title bar) is hidden.

boolean **hidecolumnpicker**
For tree elements, if set to true, the drop-down control that allows the user to hide columns is omitted.

boolean **hideheader**
When assigned to a treecol element, the tree heading is hidden.

homePage
The home page.

id
The id attribute of an element.

boolean **ignoreBlurWhileSearching**
Gets and sets the value of the ignoreblurwhilesearching attribute; if true, blur events are ignored while searching (autocomplete pop up remains visible).

boolean **ignorecolumnpicker**
When set to true on treecol elements, the column does not appear in the column picker drop-down menu.

boolean **ignorekeys**
If true, keyboard navigation across popup elements is disabled.

image
URL of an image file.

increment
When used with a scrollbar, the amount of cursor movement when the scrollbar arrows are clicked.

integer **innerHeight**
The inner height (in pixels) of a XUL window.

integer **innerWidth**
The inner width (in pixels) of a XUL window.

DOMNode **inputField**
For menu lists and text entry fields, the node of the input field.

boolean **iscontainer**
When used as an attribute with template elements, set to true if the rule matches only nodes marked as containers. If false, matches nodes that are not marked as containers.

boolean **isempty**
When used as an attribute with template elements, set to true to have the rule match only nodes that have no children. If false, rule will match only nodes with one or more child elements.

char **key**
The displayable character from the key to be used as the accelerator.

keycode
Used as an alternative to the key attribute to specify a nondisplayable keyboard actuation (e.g., Enter) as the accelerator.

keytext
An optional label displayed next to menu items with a matching key attribute.

label
The text label of a control.

boolean **lastpage**
Indicates whether wizard is displaying last wizardpage.

lastPermanentChild
Last permanent child of a toolbar that cannot be modified.

lastSelected
For preference windows, the id of the last selected pane.

boolean **lastTab**
Set to true for the last tab.

integer **left**
The position in pixels of popup and stack elements. For popups, the attribute represents screen coordinates. For children of stack elements, the attribute represents position relative to parent container.

integer **length**
The number of child frames contained by a XUL window element.

linkedpanel
The id of the linked tabpanel element that will be displayed when the tab is selected. If this attribute is not used, the tab is connected to the panel at the corresponding index within the tabpanels element.

Location **location**
The location of a XUL window element.

BarProp **locationBar**
Determines the visibility of a XUL window's location bar.

markupDocumentViewer
Read-only property to the nsIMarkupDocumentViewer that manages drawing of the document content.

integer **maxHeight**
Maximum height of element in pixels.

long **maxLength**
For text boxes, the maximum number of characters allowed.

integer **maxpos**
When used with a scrollbar, sets/gets the value assigned to the maximum slider displacement.

integer **maxWidth**
Maximum width of element in pixels.

member
When used as an attribute for `template` elements, optionally set to the variable to use as the member variable. If not specified on a `template`, the variable specified in the `uri` attribute in the action body of the template's first rule is used.

DOMString **menu**
The ID of an accompanying `popup` element.

boolean **menuactive**
An attribute set by the framework to `true` indicates that the user interface is hovering over an item in the menu.

BarProp **menubar**
Determines the visibility of a XUL window's menu bar.

nsIMenuBoxObject **menuBoxObject**
Returns menu box object that contains a menu.

boolean **menuopen**
An attribute set by the framework to `true` when the menu's children are visible.

integer **minHeight**
Minimum height of element in pixels.

integer **minWidth**
Minimum width of element in pixels.

integer **minResultsForPopup**
When used on an `autocomplete textbox`, the minimum number of results that must be returned for the pop up to be displayed.

mode
When used with progress meters, sets the appearance of the meter to be either a "busy" state or a percentage completion:

`determined`
The value attribute represents a number from 0 to 100 that is reflected in the meter.

`undetermined`
The meter is set to a busy state.

When used with toolbars, specifies how toolbar buttons are displayed:

`icons`
Shows only icons

`text`
Shows only text

`both`
Shows icons and text

When used with `treecell` elements, determines whether a progress meter is displayed:

`none`
No progress meter is displayed.

`normal`
The cell uses the integer in the `value` attribute to determine the degree of completion.

`undetermined`
The progress meter is set to the undetermined state.

modifiers
Specified optional modifiers to be coupled with the key or keycode. May be one of the following:

`shift`
Shift key

`alt`
Alt key or option key for Macintosh technology

`meta`
Meta key or command key for Macintosh technology

`control`
Ctrl key

`accel`
The operating system default accelerator key

name
The name of a XUL `window` element.

Navigator **navigator**
The navigator associated with a XUL window. Navigators provide general information regarding the browser's security policy, cookies, platform, etc.

`next`
For `wizardpage` elements, set to the `pageid` of the next page to be displayed (used for situations in which the sequence of pages may not relate to the sequencing of `wizardpages` in the program source).

`script` **`onclosetab`**
Script to be called when the Close Tab button is clicked.

`script` **`ondialogaccept`**, **`ondialogcancel`**, **`ondialogdisclosure`**...
Scripts to handle the pressing of the Accept button or to respond to the `acceptDialog()` method. Handlers may also be set as properties to respond to any of the other button types, such as `ondialogcancel`, `ondialogdisclosure`, `ondialoghelp`, etc.

`script` **`onerror, onload`**
Scripts to handle loading of image elements.

`boolean` **`onFirstPage`**
For `wizards`, indicates whether the user is on the first page.

`boolean` **`onLastPage`**
For `wizards`, indicates whether the user is on the last page.

`script` **`onpageadvanced`**
Script executed when a user presses the Next button while on the current `wizardpage`. Returns `true` to allow the next page to be displayed.

`script` **`onpagehid`**
Script called when a `wizardpage` is hidden. Returns `true` to accept the page change and `false` to prevent hiding.

`script` **`onpagerewound`**
Script on a `wizardpage` when the user presses the Back button. Returns `true` to allow the previous page to display, `false` to inhibit navigation.

`script` **`onpageshow`**
Script on a `wizardpage` called when it is shown.

`script` **`onpaneload`**
Script executed when a preference pane loads.

`script` **`onpopuphidden`**
Script responding to event triggered after a pop up is hidden.

`script` **`onpopuphiding`**
Script responding to event triggered just before pop up is hidden.

`script` **`onpopupshowing`**
Script responding to event triggered just before pop up is shown.

`script` **`onpopupshown`**
Script responding to event triggered just after pop up is shown.

`script` **`onselect`**
Script executed with a XUL element is selected.

`script` **`onwizardback`**
Script executed when a user presses the Back button on a `wizard`. Returns `true` to allow the wizard to navigate backward and `false` to disable wizard navigation.

`script` **`onwizardcancel`**
Script executed when user presses the Cancel key on a `wizard`.

`script` **`onwizardfinish`**
Script executed when the user presses a Finish button on a `wizard`. Returns `true` to allow wizard to be closed, `false` to prevent closure.

`script` **`onwizardnext`**
Script executed when user presses the Next button on a `wizard`. Returns `true` to allow navigation forward and `false` to inhibit navigation.

`boolean` **`open`**
An attribute used by menu buttons to indicate that the menu is open. The attribute exists only if the menu is open.

`nsIDOMWindowInternal` **`opener`**
The window that opened a XUL `window` element.

integer **ordinal**
: The integer position of a child widget within its parent.

orient
: String to determine the direction of layout for child elements:

  vertical
  : Children are laid out along the y-axis.

  horizontal
  : Children are laid out along the x-axis.

integer **outerHeight**
: The outer height (in pixels) of a XUL window.

integer **outerWidth**
: The outer width (in pixels) of a XUL window.

pack
: Describes how child elements are positioned along their orientation:

  start
  : Elements are placed closest to the top edge of vertically oriented containers or adjacent to the left edge of horizontally oriented containers.

  center
  : Elements are placed such that they appear to be centered along their axis of orientation.

  end
  : Elements are placed closest to the bottom edge of vertically oriented containers or adjacent to the right edge of horizontally oriented containers.

integer **pageCount**
: The number of pages in a `wizard`.

string **pageid**
: Sets a `wizardpage`'s ID for use by the wizard to support navigation functions.

integer **pageincrement**
: When used with a scrollbar, defines the displacement when the slider tray is moved.

integer **pageIndex**
: The index of a `wizard`'s currently displayed page.

integer **pagestep**
: Integer of a `wizard`'s currently displayed page.

integer **pageXOffset**
: The X page offset (in pixels) of a XUL `window` element.

integer **pageYOffset**
: The Y page offset (in pixels) of a XUL `window` element.

element **palette**
: Returns the `toolbarpalette` element within a `toolbox`.

tagName **parent**
: If set as an attribute to a `template` element, forces the rule to match only nodes of the corresponding `tagName`.

Window **parent**
: The parent window of a XUL `window` element.

parsetype
: When used as an attribute of a template, specifies that the rule matches only RDF nodes of the specified type.

persist
: A comma-delimited string of attributes whose values persist when the parent window is closed.

BarProp **personalbar**
: Sets the visibility properties of a XUL `window`'s `personalbar` element.

phase
: Specifies the event bubbling phase when the command handler is invoked. May be `target` or `capturing`. If omitted, the handler is invoked during bubbling phase.

nsIDOMPkcs11 **pkcs11**
: The `pkcs11` element of a XUL `window`.

popup
: The element `id` of the pop up associated with an element.

nsIPopupBoxObject **popupBoxObject**
: The `popup` box object that implements a `popup` element.

`boolean` **popupOpen**
Returns `true` if the pop up associated with an element is open.

`position`
Used for `popup` elements to define the position of an element relative to its parent:

`after_start`
The pop up appears underneath the element with the `popup`'s upper-left corner aligned with the lower-left corner of the element. The left edges of the element and the pop up are aligned.

`after_end`
The pop up appears underneath the element with the `popup`'s upper-right corner aligned with the lower-right corner of the element. The right edges of the element and the pop up are aligned.

`before_start`
The pop up appears above the element with the `popup`'s lower-left corner aligned with the upper-left corner of the element. The left edges of the element and the pop up are aligned.

`before_end`
The pop up appears above the element with the `popup`'s lower-right corner aligned with the upper-right corner of the element. The right edges of the element and the pop up are aligned.

`end_after`
The pop up appears to the right of the element with the `popup`'s lower-left corner aligned with the lower-right corner of the element. The bottom edges of the element and the pop up are aligned.

`end_before`
The pop up appears to the right of the element with the `popup`'s upper-left corner aligned with the upper-right corner of the element. The top edges of the element and the pop up are aligned.

`start_after`
The pop up appears to the left of the element with the `popup`'s lower-right corner aligned with the lower-left corner of the element. The bottom edges of the element and the pop up are aligned.

`start_before`
The pop up appears to the left of the element with the `popup`'s upper-right corner aligned with the upper-left corner of the element. The top edges of the element and the pop up are aligned.

`overlap`
The pop up appears over the top of the element with the upper-left corners aligned.

`at_pointer`
The pop up appears at the same position as the mouse pointer.

`after_pointer`
The pop up appears at the same horizontal position as the mouse pointer, but vertically, it is placed just below the element.

`nodeList` **`preferenceElements`**
List of elements that compose the interface for preference pane.

`boolean` **`primary`**
When set to `true` on `treecol` elements, the column will have indentation and "twisties" to indicate row hierarchies.

`nsIPrompt` **`prompter`**
The prompter object for a XUL `window` responsible for dialog prompt display and management.

`element` **`radioGroup`**
The `radiogroup` object that encloses a radio-style button.

`ref`
The root RDF resource used for content generation for the element.

resizeafter
When used with a splitter, determines how space is reallocated among children:

`closest`
The element closest to the splitter to the right or closest below the splitter is resized.

`farthest`
The element farthest from the splitter to the right or farthest below the splitter is resized.

`grow`
The entire container changes size (if the contained items are not flexible).

resizebefore
When used with a splitter, determines how space is reallocated among children:

`closest`
The element closest to the splitter to the left or closest above the splitter is resized.

`farthest`
The element farthest from the splitter to the left or farthest above the splitter is resized.

`nsIRDFResource` **resource**
For elements generated by RDF datasources, this is the RDF resource used for content.

`integer` **rows**
The number of rows to display in a `tree` element.

`Screen` **screen**
A XUL `window`'s screen property that provides information about the screen dimensions and pixel depth.

`integer` **screenX, screenY**
Horizontal and vertical position in pixels of a `window`'s top-left corner.

`BarProp` **scrollbars**
Determines the visibility of a XUL `window`'s scrollbars.

`integer` **scrollMaxX**
The maximum X-scroll value of a XUL `window`.

`integer` **scrollMaxY**
The maximum Y-scroll value of a XUL `window`.

`integer` **scrollX**
The current X-scroll value of a XUL `window`.

`integer` **searchCount**
Returns the number of search components used for autocomplete text boxes.

searchParam
The value of the `autocompletesearchparam` attribute passed to the search component of an autocomplete text box.

`nsISecureBrowserUI` **securityUI**
Read-only object reference to an `nsISecureBrowserUI` interface that may be used to determine the security state of a document.

`boolean` **selected**
If `true`, control item is selected.

`long` **selectedCount**
Number of items selected.

selectedIndex
The index of the currently selected item; setting this property or attribute changes the displayed item.

`integer` **selectedIndex**
Index of first selected item; `-1` if no items selected.

`nsIDOMSelectControlItemElement` **selectedItem**
Sets the initially selected item for the interface.

`DOMNodeList` **selectedItems**
Array of selected nodes.

`element` **selectedPanel**
Holds a reference to the currently selected panel within a `tabbox` or `deck` element. Assign a value to this property to modify the selected panel.

`element` **selectedTab**
Holds a reference to the currently selected tab within a `tabbox` element. Assign a value to this property to modify the currently selected tab.

long **selectionEnd**
For text boxes, the beginning index of selected text.

long **selectionStart**
For text boxes, the ending index of selected text.

nsIDOMWindowInternal **self**
A XUL window's reference to itself.

selstyle
For tree elements, if this property is primary, only the label of the primary column is highlighted when a row is selected.

selType
The type of selection supported by the control:

single
Only one item may be selected.

multiple
Multiple items may be selected.

sessionHistory
Read-only session history interface.

boolean **setfocus**
If true or omitted in a tabs element, the focus will be given to the first element in the corresponding tabpanel when tabs are navigated through the keyboard.

boolean **showCommentColumn**
For autocomplete text boxes, the showcommentcolumn attribute that displays a comment column above the pop up. Used for URL history to display page titles with each URL.

long **size**
For text boxes, the number of characters to be displayed.

sizemode
Specifies the state of a window element:

maximized
Window occupies the full size of a screen.

minimized
Window is minimized or hidden.

normal
Window is a normal state.

sizetopopup
Defines the rules of how menus accommodate the width of menupopup children:

none
Width is unaffected by width of children menupopups.

always
Width will by the size required of the children menupopups.

sort
Set to the RDF property on which treecol content is to be sorted.

sortDirection
Set on a treecol element to specify how the column is to be sorted:

ascending
Data is sorted in ascending order.

descending
Data is sorted in descending order.

natural
Data is presented in the order in which it is stored.

src
The source URI for images or documents.

state
When used with a splitter, indicates the state of the splitter, based on the value of the splitter's collapse attribute:

open
The content before or after the splitter (depending on collapse attribute) is displayed.

collapsed
The content before or after the splitter (depending on collapse attribute) is hidden.

dragging
The user is dragging the splitter.

URI **statedatasource**
For tree elements, the optional datasource used to store tree state information between chrome-based XUL sessions. Without this property, tree state information is maintained in the local store `rdf:local-store`.

status
The status of a XUL `window`.

statusbar
For most XUL elements, gets/sets the ID of the status bar. Setting this value will result in values of `statustext` attributes being passed to the status bar. For XUL `window` elements, this property returns a `BarProp` indication of whether the status bar is visible.

statusText
For `menuitems` on a menu bar, this text is placed in any existing status bar text as a hint regarding the nature of the menu command.

nsIStringBundle **stringBundle**
The XPCOM string bundle object which implements `nsIStringBundle`.

nsISimpleEnumerator **strings**
An enumeration of all of the strings in the string bundle. The enumeration contains `nsIPropertyElement` objects.

substate
For splitters that have `state="collapsed"` and `collapse="both"`, determines the direction of the splitter's closure.

suppressOnSelect
If `true`, rich list items do not fire events when selected.

element **tabContainer**
Returns the `tabs` element containing `tab` children.

integer **tabIndex**
The integer representing the relative sequencing of control items receiving focus as a result of Tab key actuation.

boolean **tabScrolling**
For autocomplete textboxes, if `true`, user is able to cycle through results by pressing the Tab key. If `false`, the Tab key moves focus to the next element.

integer **textLength**
For text areas, the length of the text entered in the box (read-only).

textValue
For text boxes, returns the content of the text box.

flat **textZoom**
The current document scaling factor for a XUL window expressed as a multiplier of the window's default font size.

integer **timeout**
For timed text boxes, the number of milliseconds before the timer fires a command event. The timer starts after the user types a character. If the user types another character, the timer resets.

title
The title of a dialog or window.

BarProp **toolbar**
Determines the visibility for the XUL window's toolbars.

toolbarName
Gets/sets the name of a toolbar.

element **toolbarset**
The `toolbarset` element within a `toolbox`.

integer **top**
The position in pixels of `popup` and `stack` elements. For `popups`, the attribute represents screen coordinates. For children of `stack` elements, the attribute represents the position relative to the parent container.

Window **top**
Accessor for the root window of an application.

nsITreeBoxObject **treeBoxObject**
For tree elements, the `nsIBoxObject` that renders the tree to a window. The `treeBoxObject` provides functions for retrieving cells at given coordinates and for managing scrolling and redrawing.

type

For text boxes, indicates a specialized type of text box:

`autocomplete`
: A text box supporting autocomplete features.

`password`
: A field with the text characters hidden.

`timed`
: Timed text boxes fire the `command` event a specified period of time after the user stops typing in a text box. The duration is specified as milliseconds in an accompanying `timeout` attribute value.

For buttons, indicates the type of button:

`checkbox`
: A button that retains either a true or false "checked" property. Note that a button with a type of `checkbox` looks the same as a simple button.

`radio`
: A button that is a member of a group in which only one button may have a "checked" property if `true`. Note that a button with type of `radio` looks the same as a simple button.

`menu`
: A button that supports a `popup` menu child. When a `menupopup` is placed as a child of this type of button, the submenu pops up when the parent button is pressed.

`menu-button`
: Similar to a menu button but allows the parent button of the pop up to be pressed separately from the actuation of the pop up. (These types of buttons may demonstrate subtly different appearances based on the operating system.)

For content windows, describes the type of content displayed:

`content-primary`
: Window holds browser content. Additional security restrictions are placed on content windows. Main window's `content` property will reference this frame's window.

`content`
: Window holds browser content. Additional security restrictions are placed on the window.

`string` **validate**

If `never`, image elements are loaded from cache. If `always`, image is checked to determine whether it should be loaded from cache.

value

A widget-specific attribute. Many XUL elements allow a programmatic setting of an arbitrary value attribute. For `progressmeter` elements, the value is an integer from 1 to 100 representing a percentage completion. For `textbox` elements, the value `attribute` is a default string initially displayed in the box. The value `property` is the current value in the text box.

`nsITreeView` **view**

For trees, the view object that is responsible for generating the data to be displayed. This property is created by the Firefox framework for trees that build from an RDF datasource. Other forms of trees can have this property assigned under program control. The interfaces provided by the `view` property depend on how a tree was constructed:

`Custom tree view`
: Built when the developer builds the `nsITreeView` and attaches it to the tree. The `view` property supports the `nsITreeView` interface.

`Content tree`
: Built when the tree has tree item elements placed within `treechildren` elements. Trees of this type have children accessible as DOM nodes, and the `view` property implements the `nsITreeView` and `nsITreeContentView` interfaces.

RDF tree
Built when a tree is created from an RDF datasource, and has a flags value of dont-build-content. DOM treeitems are not created. The view property implements the nsITreeView and nsIXULTreeBuilder interfaces.

RDF content tree
Built when a tree is created from an RDF datasource, but is without a flags attribute. DOM tree items are created and the view property implements the nsITreeView, nsIXULTreeBuilder, and nsITreeContentView interfaces.

nsIWebBrowserFind **webBrowserFind**
Returns read-only reference to an nsIWebBrowserFind interface that provides methods for searching through a document's text.

nsIWebNavigation **webNavigation**
Returns a read-only reference to an nsIWebNavigation interface that provides methods to navigate through a history of displayed web pages.

nsIWebProgress **webProgress**
The nsIWebProgress object used to monitor progress of a document being loaded.

integer **width**
Width of element in pixels.

nsIDOMWindowInternal **window**
Reference to a XUL window's internal window interface.

EventTarget **windowRoot**
The window root for a XUL window.

windowtype
An application-specific string that may optionally be used to identify different types of windows.

nodeList **wizardPages**
Returns list of wizardpage elements in a wizard.

string **wrap**
When used as an attribute for a textbox, set to off to disable word wrapping.

Index

Tags

A

We'd like to hear your suggestions for improving our indexes. Send email to *index@oreilly.com*.

B

C

F

G

H

I

J

K

L

M

N

O

P

R

S

T

U

V

W

X

About the Author

Kenneth Feldt develops XUL-based solutions for Cholabris Workgroup Solutions, otherwise known as the Electric Book Company. Ken's work experience involves electronic document production and distribution, electronic imaging, digital video workflow, and technical communications. Currently, Ken is turning his attention to the merger of publishing and messaging technologies, where he hopes XUL can deliver high-quality technologies to students of mathematics and science.

Colophon

The animal on the cover of *Programming Firefox* is a red fox (*Vulpes vulpes*, *Vulpes fulva*). Found throughout Canada, Alaska, most of the contiguous United States, Europe, Asia, and parts of northern Africa, the red fox is the most widely distributed wild carnivore in the world. Its habitat includes forests, tundras, prairies, farmlands, and increasingly, suburban areas. Red foxes are identified by their reddish-brown coats, white-tipped tails, and black ears and legs. Although American red foxes are typically smaller than their European counterparts, the average size of the red fox is 36–42 inches long (including its 15-inch tail) and 16 inches tall, weighing approximately 15 pounds.

Red foxes are solitary and do not form packs like wolves. For most of the year, they sleep concealed in high grasses or thickets. The exception is breeding season, during which a fox pair establishes a den, often taking over one created by rabbits or marmots. Foxes may dig larger dens in the winter, or during birth and rearing of their pups. The same den is often used over a number of generations. With tunnels connecting the main den to other nesting sites, the animals generally remain in the same home range for life.

Red foxes feed on insects, earthworms, small birds and mammals, eggs, carrion, and vegetable matter. Although they have a reputation for raiding chicken coops, they're often beneficial to farmers because they keep the rodent population low. They have a distinctive method for catching mice: they stand perfectly still, listening and watching intently, then leap high, bringing their forelimbs straight down to pin the mouse to the ground. However, because of their small size, red foxes are not only predator, but also prey: they're hunted by larger mammals such as wolves and bobcats, and pups are often killed by birds of prey. Humans, who kill red foxes for their fur and for sport, are the red fox's biggest predators. In 2005, foxhunting—a popular sport in Europe since the 14th century—was banned in Great Britain, and most fox species continue to flourish.

The cover image is from the Dover Pictorial Archive. The cover font is Adobe ITC Garamond. The text font is Linotype Birka; the heading font is Adobe Myriad Condensed; and the code font is LucasFont's TheSans Mono Condensed.